Daniel Dumitran, Valer Moga (Eds.)

Economy and Society in Central and Eastern Europe

Economy and Society in Central and Eastern Europe

Territory, Population, Consumption

Papers of the International Conference
Held in Alba Iulia, April 25th – 27th, 2013

edited by

Daniel Dumitran, Valer Moga

LIT

Cover image:
The city of Alba Iulia: image from the early twentieth century
(Collection of "National Museum of Union," Alba Iulia).

This book is printed on acid-free paper.

Bibliographic information published by the Deutsche Nationalbibliothek
The Deutsche Nationalbibliothek lists this publication in the Deutsche Nationalbibliografie; detailed bibliographic data are available in the Internet at http://dnb.d-nb.de.

ISBN 978-3-643-90445-4

A catalogue record for this book is available from the British Library

Klosbachstr. 107
CH-8032 Zürich
Tel. +41 (0) 44-251 75 05
Fax +41 (0) 44-251 75 06
E-Mail: zuerich@lit-verlag.ch
http://www.lit-verlag.ch

LIT VERLAG Dr. W. Hopf
Berlin 2013
Fresnostr. 2
D-48159 Münster
Tel. +49 (0) 2 51-62 03 20
Fax +49 (0) 2 51-23 19 72
E-Mail: lit@lit-verlag.de
http://www.lit-verlag.de

Distribution:
In Germany: LIT Verlag Fresnostr. 2, D-48159 Münster
Tel. +49 (0) 2 51-620 32 22, Fax +49 (0) 2 51-922 60 99, E-mail: vertrieb@lit-verlag.de
In Austria: Medienlogistik Pichler-ÖBZ, e-mail: mlo@medien-logistik.at
In the UK: Global Book Marketing, e-mail: mo@centralbooks.com
In North America: International Specialized Book Services, e-mail: orders@isbs.com
e-books are available at www.litwebshop.de

Contents

Donation as a Sign of Change in Religious Sensibility

Population Mobility and Social Integration

Economy, Trade and Human Capital During the Twentieth Century

Über Wirtschaft und Gesellschaft in Mittel- und Osteuropa der Neuzeit – Der Fall Siebenbürgens. Ein Plädoyer für die Erneuerung der Forschung

Es war nicht die Wirtschaftsgeschichte in ihrer traditionellen Auffassung, die vorrangig im Zentrum der Aufmerksamkeit der im Frühjahr dieses Jahres, vom 25. bis zum 27. April, in Karlsburg zum Kolloquium „Economy and Society in Central and Eastern Europe" versammelten Forscher stand, sondern der Versuch der sozialen und kulturellen Untersuchung der Wirtschaft, mit vornehmlichem Bezug zur Neuzeit. Chronologisch gesehen war die Option der Initiatoren des Kolloquiums stark von der Geschichte der Gegenwart her motiviert. Für die Länder Zentral- und Osteuropas stellen die letzten zwei Jahrzehnte eine Übergangszeit von der Planwirtschaft zur Marktwirtschaft dar, wobei ihre verschiedenartige historische Erfahrung eine entscheidende Rolle spielte. Andererseits können die Verhandlungen aus derselben Zeit betreffend die Reformkriterien des Staatsorganismus' in seiner Gesamtheit einen Vergleichspunkt *à rebours* in den Projekten des Staatsaufbaus finden, die in der Vormoderne sowie in der Spätmoderne entworfen wurden. Das „soziale Problem" aber, worauf sich Pierre Manent,[1] in einem neueren Werk bezieht und seinen „Angelpunkt" für den Westen in die Zeitspanne 1848-1968 legt, hat in Zentral-Osteuropa sicherlich eine andere Chronologie mit einem auf die gleiche neuere Geschichte bezogenen Terminus *ad quem*.

Vom methodischen Standpunkt her besteht weiterhin eine gewisse historiographische Ungleichheit zwischen den beiden erwähnten europäischen Zonen. Ein anschauliches Beispiel dafür bietet der kürzlich unter der Ägide des Internationalen Institutes für Wirtschaftsgeschichte erschienene Band „F. Datini",[2] mit einem einzigen thematischen Beitrag zu einem Staat aus dem ehemaligen kommunistischen Block (Polen). Ohne eine, auch noch so kurze, bibliographische Revue bieten zu wollen, ist zu beobachten, dass die grundlegenden methodischen Verhandlungen betreffend die Notwendigkeit der Modernisierung des Instrumentariums der interdisziplinären Forschung dringend sind. Die politisch-ideologischen Umwandlungen der letzten Jahrzehnte haben ein Überdenken der allgemein anerkannten Theorien begünstigt, wie z.B. durch den Versuch der Annäherung der Sozialgeschichte an die Kulturgeschichte. Ein Beispiel dafür bietet jene „sozial- und kulturgeschichtlich erneuerte Wissenschaftsgeschichte der Historie", auf die sich Josef Mooser[3]

---

[1] *La raison des nations. Réflections sur la démocratie en Europe* (Paris: Éditions Gallimard, 2006; București: Nemira, 2007, für die rumänische Version).

[2] *Dove va la storia economica? Metodi e prospettive. Secc. XIII-XVIII / Where is Economic History Going? Methods and Prospects from the 13th to the 18th Centuries.* Atti della "Qurantaduesima Settimana di Studi," 18-22 aprile 2010, a cura di Francesco Ammannati (Firenze: Firenze University Press, 2011).

[3] Kap. „Sozial- und Wirtschaftsgeschichte, Historische Sozialwissenschaft, Gesellschafts-geschichte", in Hans-Jürgen Goertz (Hg.), *Geschichte. Ein Grundkurs*, 3. revidierte und erweiterte Auflage (Reinbeck bei Hamburg: Rowohlt Taschenbuch Verlag, 2007), 585-588, mit Hinweis zu Christian Simon, *Historiographie. Eine Einführung* (Stuttgart, 1996). Siehe auch das Kap. „Ideen-, Geistes-, Kulturgeschichte", von Luise Schorn-Schütte, ebenda, im besonderen 563-564.

beruft, oder das Verhältnis zwischen wirtschaftlicher und anthropologischer, religiöser, politischer und wissenschaftlicher Problematik, worauf Paolo Prodi[4] aufmerksam macht. Die Divergenzen zu den Vertretern der Sozialwissenschaften bleiben aber bedeutend,[5] so dass es notwendig ist, die Vorgaben der Forschung möglichst genau zu definieren.

Das Konzept einer regionalen Wirtschaftsgeschichte (in der oben detaillierten Auffassung),[6] ausgerichtet an den vielfältigen Wertigkeiten des Territoriums, war der Grundgedanke des Kolloquiums. Das Verständnis des Territoriums in Beziehung zu den Menschen und Gemeinschaften, aber auch zu dem komplexen Prozeß des sozialen Wandels, also der Modernisierung der Gesellschaft, veranschaulicht von Giovanna Motta,[7] war auch in unserem Fall hilfreich. Eine erschöpfende Verhandlung war allerdings nicht möglich dank der Vielfalt der Aspekte, die im Blick behalten werden mußten und der Verschiedenheit der Zentral-Osteuropäischen Regionen, welche Themen für Fallstudien liefern konnten. Die getroffene thematische Auswahl enthält folglich bloß einige Vorschläge zur Entwicklung einiger Forschungsrichtungen, die in Zukunft noch aufgefächert werden können.

So geplant, kann sich die Forschung nicht auf eine einheitliche Methodik beschränken. Die Vorteile des Vergleichens sind am besten ersichtlich beim Thema des Warenumlaufs zwischen dem Südosten und dem Zentrum Europas.[8] Wir haben es in diesem Fall nicht nur mit einer Geschichte des Bergbaues und Handels zu tun, sondern auch mit einer der Handelspolitik und auch schon mit der Geschichte einer Bevölkerungspolitik – eine vorrangige Sorge der Staaten in der vorindustriellen Zeit (Marius Diaconescu, Mária Pakucs, David Do Paço).[9] Die Handelswege waren zugleich auch Besiedlungswege und die Kaufleute, das heißt, die Menschen, hatten ihre eigene Geschichte, jeweils gebunden an die Gemeinschaften, in denen sie sich entschlossen, sich niederzulassen und sich zu integrieren. Letztlich stellt sich auch das Problem ihrer Annahme,[10] vor allem der „Grie-

---

[4] In *Introduzione allo studio della storia moderna*, con la collaborazione di Giancarlo Angelozzi e Carla Penuti (Bologna: Il Mulino, 1999), 86.

[5] Siehe, z.B., das Kap. „Rationality versus Relativism", mit einer für unsere Nachforschung fruchtbaren Definierung des Kulturkonzeptes, in Peter Burke, *History and Social Theory*, 2. Auflage (Cambridge, UK; Malden, MA: Polity Press, 2009), 116-122.

[6] Siehe auch das Kap. „Landes- und Regionalgeschichte", von Ernst Hinrichs, in Goertz (Hg.), *Geschichte*, 611-627.

[7] *Paesaggio, territorio, ambiente. Storie di uomini e di terre*, ed. Giovanna Motta (Milano: Franco Angeli, 2004), 216-235.

[8] Vgl. Gelina Harlaftis, „International Business of Southeastern Europe and the Eastern Mediterranean, 18th Century: Sources, Methods, and Interpretive Issues", in *Dove va la storia economica?*, 389-415; Olga Katsiardi-Hering, Maria A. Stassinopoulou, „The Long 18th Century of Greek Commerce in the Habsburg Empire. Social Careers", in *Social Change in the Habsburg Monarchy. Les transformations de la société dans la monarchie des Habsbourg : l'époque des Lumières*, Hg. Harald Heppner, Peter Urbanitsch, Renate Zedinger (Bochum: Verlag Dr. Dieter Winkler, 2011) [*Das Achtzehnte Jahrhundert und Österreich.* Internationale Beihefte 3], 191-213; Olga Katsiardi-Hering, „Greek Merchant Colonies in Central and South-Eastern Europe in the Eighteenth and Early Nineteenth Centuries", in *Merchant Colonies in the Early Modern Period*, Hg. Viktor N. Zakharov, Gelina Harlaftis und Olga Katsiardi-Hering (London, Vermont: Pickering & Chatto, 2012), 127-139.

[9] Die Hinweise in Klammer beziehen sich auf die Autoren der Studien aus dem vorliegenden Band.

[10] Siehe, z.B., David Do Paço, "Institutionnaliser la coexistence religieuse? « Turcs et sujet turcs de Vienne »,

chen" (ein Ausdruck, der bis heute historiographische Dispute auslöst), aber auch der Armenier, Juden u.a. Betreffend Siebenbürgen, selbst wenn beachtliche Beiträge nicht fehlen,[11] bietet das Thema noch umfassende Möglichkeiten zur Vertiefung, vor allem im Bezug auf die Forschungen zum selben Thema in den benachbarten Territorien.[12]

Eine Strukturanalyse bezüglich des Modernisierungsprozesses ist unvermeidlich, trotz aller erbrachten Kritik.[13] Im Übrigen wurde die Nützlichkeit der Methodenvielfalt bei der Untersuchung des sozialen Wandels, wie sie unsere Perspektive vorsieht, neulich von Harald Heppner unterstrichen in Beziehung zum Territorium der Habsburger in der Zeit der Aufklärung.[14] Im Falle des Fürstentums Siebenbürgen (beziehungsweise dessen Territorium, das nach dem Ausgleich von 1867 Ungarn einverleibt wurde), benötigen wesentliche Fragen wie die betreffend die Neueinteilung des Territoriums, die administrativen Strukturen, die Sozialkontrolle des Staates, das Beamtenwesen (Auswahlkriterien und Rolle), die Fiskalität, die Agrarwirtschaft u.a. (Daniel Dumitran, Kálmán Árpád Kovács) noch eingehende und aufmerksame Forschungen bei der Komplexität dieser Themen.[15] Sie werden die Umwandlungen über einen längeren Zeitraum hinaus verfolgen müssen im Einklang mit der Regionalgeschichte, ohne der Versuchung einer Synthese zu erliegen. Die vergleichende Erforschung auf der Ebene der Regionen verschiedener Provinzen/Staaten, doch ähnlich unter sozio-ökonomischem Aspekt, erhält auch hier äußerste Wichtigkeit, indem sie den Schlußfolgerungen eine gesteigerte Relevanz verleiht (Eva Ondrušová). Sicherlich waren die Folgen der sozialen Veränderungen

---

dans la seconde moitié du XVIIIe siècle", in *Des religions dans la ville. Ressorts et stratégies de coexistence dans l'Europe des XVIe-XVIIIe siècles*, Hg. David Do Paço, Mathilde Monge und Laurent Tatarenko (Rennes: Presses Universitaires de Rennes, 2010), 143-162; Ikaros Madouvalos, „*Conscriptiones Graecorum* in Eighteenth-Century Central Europe. Crossing Borders: The Sociocultural Identifications of Migrants from the Balkans to Hungarian Territories", in *Encounters in Europe's Southeast. The Habsburg Empire and the Orthodox World in the Eighteenth and Nineteenth Centuries*, Hg. Harald Heppner, Eva Posch (Bochum: Verlag Dr. Dieter Winkler, 2012) [*Das Achtzehnte Jahrhundert und Österreich.* Internationale Beihefte 5], 121-133.

[11] Vgl. Olga Cicanci, *Companiile greceşti din Transilvania şi comerţul european în anii 1636-1746* [Griechische Handelsgesellschaft in Siebenbürgen und europäischen Handel in den Jahren 1636-1746] (Bucureşti: Editura Academiei, 1981); Mária Pakucs-Willcocks, *Sibiu-Hermannstadt: oriental trade in sixteenth century Transylvania* (Köln, Weimar, Wien: Böhlau Verlag, 2007); Ruxandra Moaşa Nazare, *Sub semnul lui Hermes şi al lui Pallas. Educaţie şi societate la negustorii ortodocşi din Braşov şi Sibiu la sfârşitul secolului al XVIII-lea şi începutul secolului al XIX-lea* [Unter dem Zeichen des Hermes und Pallas. Bildung und Gesellschaft in den Orthodoxen Kaufleute von Braşov und Sibiu in den späten 18. Jahrhundert und frühen 19. Jahrhunderts] (Bucureşti: Editura Academiei, 2010).

[12] Ein gutes Beispiel ist Vera Bácskai, *Towns and Urban Society in Early Nineteenth-Century Hungary* (Budapest: Akadémiai Kiadó, 1989).

[13] Siehe Mooser, „Sozial- und Wirtschaftsgeschichte", 587.

[14] Siehe Introduction, in *Social Change in the Habsburg Monarchy*, 18-19.

[15] Siehe einige gute Beispiele bei P. G. M. Dickson, *Finance and Government under Maria Theresia 1740-1780*, Bd. I. *Society and Government*; Bd. II. *Finance and Credit* (Oxford: Clarendon Press, 1987) und Idem, „Monarchy and Bureaucracy in Late Eighteenth-Century Austria", *The English Historical Review* 110, 436 (Apr. 1995): 323-367; für Fürstentum Siebenbürgen im besonderen, siehe Ioan Bolovan, Rudolf Gräf, Harald Heppner, Ioan Lumperdean (Hg.), *Demographic Changes in the Time of Industrialization (1750-1918). The Example of the Habsburg Monarchy*, International Conference (Cluj-Napoca, 16th-20th October 2008), *Transylvanian Review* XVIII, Supplement No. 1 (2009).

komplex und konnten für die spätmoderne (Cornel Sigmirean, Alexandru Onojescu, Valer Moga), oder die zeitgenössische Periode (Vlad Paşca) anhand der Untersuchung der Universitätsbildung, der politischen Optionen und der sozialen Mobilität veranschaulicht werden.

Die Geschichte der kulturellen Formung der ethnischen und konfessionellen Gemeinschaften erbringt die einer Strukturanalyse nötigen Nuancierungen und Ergänzungen. Sie ist an den Werten und Haltungen interessiert, die in das soziale Verhalten Eingang gefunden haben, am Verhältnis zwischen mündlicher und schriftlicher Kultur, an dem, was die Eliten lesen und was das Volk liest (Greta-Monica Miron, Attila Verók), am Vorgang des Schenkens (Oana Valentina Sorescu) usw.[16] Bezeichnend sind auch die Untersuchungen betreffend den erstaunlichen Güterkonsum und die Schenkungen zugunsten der Gemeinschaft:[17] der erste Aspekt widerspiegelt eine Strategie der Unterscheidung sozialer Gruppen oder der Individuen (Roxana Marin), der zweite eine Art der Kundgabe gemeinschaftlicher Identität (Márta Nagy, Ion Cârja). Aufs Ganze gesehen sind die Themen besonders in städtischen Umfeldern relevant, die einen Hang zu territorialer Ausbreitung und Entwicklung im Kontext demographischer Veränderungen und Industrialisierung haben und wo die kleinen Unternehmer eine große Rolle spielen (Felicia Waldman). Doch auch die dörflichen Umfelder befinden sich nicht außerhalb dieser Entwicklungen, wenn wir zum Beispiel die Veränderungen innerhalb der geschlossenen szeklerischen Gemeinschaften in der Spätmoderne betrachten (Levente Pakot), oder die religiösen Gewaltausbrüche in der rumänischen Gemeinschaften der Vormoderne: hier brachte die Tendenz zur Identitätsbekundung der „Nichtunierten" (Orthodoxen) Rumänen Vertreter weltlicher Kategorien in den Vordergrund, wobei ihre Handlung als Anfang der Äußerung einer öffentlichen Meinung interpretiert wurde (Radu Nedici, Monika Imregh). Die Weiterführung der Forschung in dieser Richtung durch Vermehrung der untersuchten Fälle kann zu äußerst interessanten Ergebnissen führen.

Die geschichtliche Bildkunde bietet noch Neuland durch die Auswertung der Bedeutung ikonographischer Quellen und ihrer ikonologischen Interpretation.[18] Die neueren Forschungen betreffend die Übernahme und Anpassung barocker Elemente in Kulturgebieten, die durch das nachbyzantinische Erbe geprägt wurden, sind ein aufschlußreiches Beispiel.[19] Die komplexe Welt der religiösen Ikonographie und ihre Rolle in

[16] Siehe Burke, *History and Social Theory*, 120, und Hinrichs, „Landes- und Regionalgeschichte", 615-616.
[17] Burke, *History and Social Theory*, das Kap. „Consumption and Exchange", 68-69.
[18] Siehe Heike Talkenberger, „Historische Erkenntnis durch Bilder. Zur Methode und Praxis der Historischen Bildkunde", in Goertz (Hg.), *Geschichte*, 88-103.
[19] Siehe, z.B., Nagy Márta, *Ortodox ikonosztázionok Magyarországon* [Orthodoxe Ikonostasen aus Ungarn] (Debrecen: Fábián Bt. Nyomda, 1994) und Eadem, *A Bizánci ikontól a nyugati barokkig. Tanulmániok a magyarországi görög diaszpóra egyházművészetéről* [Die byzantinischen Ikonen des abendländischen Barocks. Studien zur kirchlichen Kunst der griechischen Diaspora] (Debrecen: Debreceni Egyetem Kossuth Egyetemi Kiadója, 2008); Olga Katsiardi-Hering, „Southeastern European Migrant Groups between the Ottoman and the Habsburg Empires. Multilateral Social and Cultural Transfers from the Eighteenth to the Early Nineteenth Centuries", in *Encounters in Europe's Southeast*, 135-162.

plurikonfessionellen Gebieten (Anna Tüskés, Cristina Bogdan, Silvia Marin Barutcieff, Waldemar Deluga), die Äußerungsformen der „Gedächtniskultur" und der oralen Kultur in mittelalterlichem oder vormodernem Kontext[20] (Marco Bogade, Cristina Bogdan), die Rolle der Gemeinschaften und der individuellen Kommanditäre in Patronatsfragen (Ana Dumitran, Waldemar Deluga), die allmähliche Durchsetzung der Künstler bei Darstellungen (Silvia Marin Barutcieff, Ana Dumitran), oder der Anfang der Verweltlichung der Tematik (Cristina Bogdan), die Bedeutung der Wandlung einiger ikonographischer Typen zum Gebrauchsgut (Ana Dumitran) sind bloß einige Beispiele für die Relevanz solcher Forschungen. Sie beleuchten hauptsächlich die Veränderung der Empfindlichkeit und der religiösen Praxis im Zuge der gesellschaftlichen Umwandlungen.

Es sind somit Probleme des Wechsels, des Territoriums, der Konsums, der Bevölkerung als Gegenstand der Regierung, oder der Menschen als Subjekte der Geschichte. Die Wiederherstellung, die wir vorschlagen, jetzt schon vielfältig, befindet sich vorläufig im Stadium von Arbeitshypothesen und kann in viele Richtungen ausgebaut werden. Wichtig ist die Erarbeitung von eingehenden Untersuchungen, die methodisch konvergent und kohärent sein müssen und der Neugier der Historiker sowie den gegenwärtigen Fragestellungen möglichst nuancierte Antworten bieten.

Abschließend drücken wir dem Kreisrat Alba unsere ganze Dankbarkeit für die Unterstützung dieses Symposiums aus. Denen, die hier nicht erwähnt worden sind, deren Hilfe uns aber genauso wichtig war, sprechen wir in gleicher Weise unsere Anerkennung aus.

ALBA IULIA, AUGUST 2013
DANIEL DUMITRAN

[20] Vgl. Hans-Werner Goetz, „Moderne Mediävistik – Methoden und Inhalte heutiger Mittelalterforschung", in Goertz (Hg.), *Geschichte*, 334-335.

A Forerunner of Capitalism in Central Europe in the Mid-Sixteenth Century: Peter Deák Szentgyörgyi of Baia Mare

Marius Diaconescu

The sixteenth century is usually considered to be the boundary between the long Middle Ages and the dawn of modernity. The Renaissance, the Reformation, the geographical discoveries, and the development of urban society germinated the seeds of modernity for the following centuries. The first capitalists emerged in this century of radical transformations for European societies and, according to the theories advocated by Max Weber and his supporters, there was a causal link relationship between religious reform and the seeds of capitalism. Discrepancies between Western and Eastern Europe existed even then, while Central Europe, including Hungary and Transylvania, was a border region. Sixteenth-century Transylvania offered some of the same requisites for the emergence of capitalists as could be found in Western Europe, and the Reformation found fertile ground for its ideas in Transylvania at least. But besides the freedom of thought required by any entrepreneur, other key economic preconditions were essential in allowing the formation of capitalist enterprisers.

When Peter Deák Szentgyörgyi, a bureaucrat from the mining region of Baia Mare, was accused of corruption by the Habsburg authorities in 1553, an inventory of his mobile property and real estate was drawn up.[1] This register and a number of subsequent lists catch our attention because of the rarity of such information; they itemise jewellery, luxurious items of clothing and bedding, stone houses in the town centre, mines, smelters, mills, etc. Nor is it just the glitter of Peter Deák's wealth that makes his an interesting case worthy of deeper study, but particularly his very close relationship with one of the leaders of the Transylvanian Reformation, Gáspár Heltai.

The career

Peter Deák was a Transylvanian nobleman who had settled in the town of Baia Mare sometime before the mid-sixteenth century. Bishop Martinuzzi, effectively the governor of Transylvania, appointed him to the position of chamber count for the mines at Baia Mare.[2]

Immediately after he heard of Martinuzzi's murder by the Austrians, Peter Deák switched to the side of the new authority. Before Habsburg troops reached Baia Mare, he had already removed his old master's appointed castellan from the mint castle and desig-

[1] About the history of the mines and mint in Baia Mare at the middle of the sixteenth century see Gustav Gündisch, "Geschichte der Munzstätte Nagybánya in habsburgischer Zeit (1530-1828)," *Numismatische Zeitschrift* 25 (Wien, Neue Folge, 1932): 69-71.

[2] Maria Holban, M. M. Alexandrescu-Dersca Bulgaru and Paul Cernovodeanu, eds., *Călători străini despre Țările Române* [Foreign Travellers about the Romanian Countries], vol. II (București: Editura Științifică, 1970), 85.

nated one of the town's jurors to that office.[3] In order to win the confidence of his new masters, Peter Deák surrendered to General Castaldo a considerable amount of gold and silver, a part of which was in coins, from the revenues of the mines and mint: 163,498 kg of silver and 4,536 gold florins.[4] Despite his opportunism, he was accused by the new Austrian authorities of appropriating part of Martinuzzi's fortune and of the chamber's revenues. He was also charged with destroying the Franciscan monastery. General Castaldo imprisoned him in Cluj early in 1552, but he was freed after a number of guarantors bailed him out.[5]

To rescue his position, Peter Deák offered his services to restore the finances of the mining operation and the mint, which needed an urgent capital infusion. He was willing to finance a loan from his own funds to reopen the royal mines and cover all other expenses required for the Treasury to operate the mines and mint as normal, only asking for an assurance that he would be able to recover the loan from the chamber's revenues.

In a report of 1552, the royal commissioners expressed their reservations about maintaining Peter Deák in the position of chamber count, but did not dispute his abilities as a manager: "it seems he has some sort of knowledge in running the business of the chamber." The commissioners had doubts because Peter Deák's mines neighboured those of the Treasury, and he extracted more gold and silver than all other private mine owners put together. He was "more powerful than the others not only as a chamber count, but even as a townsman." The commissioners suggested that he could keep his office if there was no alternative, on condition that he was to be seconded by a well prepared and reliable controller.[6]

On 1st December 1552, instructions to the imperial commissioners ordered his arrest and the seizure of all his mobile and real estate assets. A new chamber count was appointed, and the wealth of Deák's stepsons was to be administered by the town's judges and jurors.[7] General Castaldo informed King Ferdinand that a conspiracy had been discovered between Deák and a supporter of the Szapolyai party, Peter Petrovics. Castaldo alleged that according to rumours Deák had sent Peter Petrovics 1,000 shields and as many lances, together with the promise of future assistance.[8] Peter Deák was arrested in the summer of 1553. In a letter of 16th July 1553, King Ferdinand instructed the royal commissioners to explain to the judges, jurors, and townsmen of Baia Mare why it had been necessary remove Deák from office and confiscate his property.[9] Such an instruction indicates the important position that he had previously held in the town community.

---

[3] Ibid., 65.
[4] Ibid., 66.
[5] Ibid.
[6] Ibid., 85.
[7] Johann Christian Engel, *Geschichte des ungrischen Reiches und seiner Nebenländer*, III (Halle, 1801), 105.
[8] B(arabás) S(amu), "Erdély történetére vonatkozó regeszták 1551-1553" [Abstracts Regarding to the History of Transylvania 1551-1553], VI, *Történelmi Tár* 15 (1892): 671, no. 409.
[9] Eudoxiu de Hurmuzaki, ed., *Documente privitore la istoria Românilor* [Records Regarding to the History of Romanians], II/5 (Bucuresci, 1897), 85.

On 9th September 1553 the judges and jurors of Baia Mare made an inventory of his mobile and real estate assets, proving that by that time Peter Deák had already been arrested.[10] A few months later, the royal commissioners received the confiscated goods.[11]

Meanwhile, the case came to be discussed by the Transylvanian Diet. At the Târgu-Mureş Diet of 25th January 1554, the Transylvanian estates interceded with King Ferdinand on behalf of Peter Deák, requesting that he be judged before the Transylvanian voivodes and bishop according to the laws of the realm (*judicium justiciaque [...] vigore juris hujus regni administretur*).[12] There is only one plausible explanation for this intervention by the estates. Baia Mare did not form part of the voivodate of Transylvania, so that the Diet and voivodes had no administrative and judicial competence there. Only if Deák was a native member of the Transylvanian nobility, would the Diet have any right to intercede and demand that the judgement be carried according to the laws of the realm and before its voivodes.

On 17th April the king answered the Transylvanian Diet's requests, approving them all, with one single exception: the application in favour of Peter Deák. The king responded to the Transylvanian estates that the latter had not awaited royal mercy, but had tried to escape (*qui licet non expectata regia gratia fuga sibi consulere proposuerat*). He was to be brought before the royal court of justice, where the king promised to gracefully acknowledge the request made by the estates.[13]

We do not know whether Peter Deák was ever brought before the royal court for a fair trial. What is known for sure is that his confiscated assets were once again inventoried, together with those of the mint, on 10th January 1556, when the Habsburg authorities installed a new chamber count in Baia Mare.[14] In the spring of the same year Queen Isabella and her son, John Sigismund Szapolyai, were re-enthroned under Ottoman patronage and the Austrian army had to withdraw from Transylvania.

During the following decade, the Transylvanians and the Habsburgs fought over Baia Mare and the neighbouring region. It seems that in the intervals when John Sigismund Szapolyai ruled over the region, Peter Deák was in his prince's service.

In 1559 a register of the mint mentions that Deák had passed certain sums of money to Szapolyai in Alba Iulia.[15] It is very likely that when Melchior Balassa, commander in Baia Mare, betrayed the Transylvanian prince and surrendered the town to the

---

[10] David Prodan and Samuel Goldenberg, "Inventarele din 1553 şi 1556 ale minelor şi monetăriei din Baia Mare" [The Inventories from 1553 and 1556 of the Mines and Mint in Baia Mare], *Anuarul Institutului de Istorie din Cluj* VII (1964): 128-131.

[11] Magyar Országos Levéltár [Hungarian National Archives], Budapest, Hungary (henceforth abbreviated MOL), Fund *Urbaria et Conscriptiones*, fasc. 99, no. 29.

[12] Sándor Szilagyi, ed., *Monumenta comitialia regni Transylvaniae*, I (Budapest, 1875), 503.

[13] Ibid., 516.

[14] Prodan and Goldenberg, "Inventarele," 131-144.

[15] Samuel Goldenberg, "Contribuţie la o istorie a cămării şi monetăriei din Baia Mare" [A Contribution at the History of the Chamber and Mint from Baia Mare], *Anuarul Institutului de Istorie din Cluj* I-II (1958-1959): 161.

Habsburgs, Deák lost his fortune again. According to the extant sources, at least in 1563 one of his mines was in Melchior Balassa's possession, which, by extension, could indicate that his assets had been seized.[16]

In the short period of time when the prince of Transylvania ruled the region once more, in February 1565 he granted a privilege to the miners in Baia Sprie; this document mentions Peter Deák as prefect of the chamber in Baia Mare.[17] A short while afterwards the Habsburgs reconquered the region and Peter Deák's name appeared on the list of exiled townsmen in the census made in 1566.[18] Following Szapolyai's successful siege of Baia Mare in 1567 it is possible that Deák returned to the town. In January 1569 the prince interceded with the town magistrate in favour of his protégé.[19]

After the Austrians had retaken Baia Mare once more, they inventoried all assets of the Treasury assigned to the castle of Sătmar. On this occasion yet another list was drawn up of the confiscated assets – for the umpteenth time (?!) – of Peter Deák, of whom the document noted that he had recently died (*iam demortui*).[20] Thus ended the life and career of a gold tycoon of Baia Mare, whose fate was so unfortunately marked by the political instability of his time.

Peter Deák's wealth

Peter Deák's wealth was registered in a number of records: the inventories of the assets seized for the Treasury in September 1553[21] and the following winter,[22] the inventories of the fiscal assets at the chamber of Baia Mare (1556)[23] or of Sătmar castle (1569).[24] There are also lists in various documents preserved in the protocols of the town of Baia Mare, especially concerning the complicated issue of inheritance.

Deák made his fortune investing in particular in the gold mines of Baia Mare. The majority of mine owners operated the mines themselves, using ancient techniques, and sold the ore on to the owners of the stamp mills and smelters. Peter Deák was among the few who operated mines a using paid workforce and modern techniques. His mines employed one or two ore extraction machines, and hence were large scale operations, on a

---

[16] Serviciul Judeţean Maramureş al Arhivelor Naţionale [The Maramureş County Branch of the National Archives of Romania], Baia Mare, Romania (henceforth abbreviated SJMAN), Fund *Primăria oraşului Baia Mare*, seria *Registre*, no. 1: 24.

[17] Serviciul Judeţean Cluj al Arhivelor Naţionale [The Cluj County Branch of the National Archives of Romania], Fund *Arhiva oraşului Baia Sprie*, no. 2 (8): *egregiis nobilibus Petro Literato Zentgyeorgy prefecto camere nostre Nagybaniensis*.

[18] Ferenc Maksay, ed., *Urbáriumok XVI-XVII. század* [Inventories from the 16th-17th Centuries] (Budapest: Akadémiai Kiadó, 1959), 619.

[19] SJMAN, *Primăria oraşului Baia Mare*, *Registre*, no. 1: 34-36.

[20] Marius Diaconescu, *Izvoare de antroponimie şi demografie istorică. Conscripţiile cetăţii Sătmar din 1569-1570* [Sources of Historical Antroponymy and Demography. The Census of Sătmar Castle's Estate in 1569-1570] (Cluj-Napoca: Editura Mega, 2012), 157-158.

[21] Prodan and Goldenberg, "Inventarele," 128-131.

[22] MOL, *Urbaria et Conscriptiones*, fasc. 99, no. 29.

[23] Prodan and Goldenberg, "Inventarele," 138-144.

[24] Diaconescu, *Conscripţiile Sătmar*, 157-158.

par with the royal mine. He also had his own stamp mills and smelters, and could thus control the whole production process.

He possessed three mines on the Săsar Mountain, where he had extraction machineries with one or two ropes. He explored new deposits, setting up new mines in the Băiţa valley in Tăuţi Mountains, thus becoming a pioneer of mining in the region.[25] In the period when he returned to Baia Mare after 1556, he invested in at least one mine in Baia Sprie.[26] He sometimes invested in association with other entrepreneurs. His competence in the mining industry was acknowledged even by the royal commissioners, although they disliked him.

A list of 1556 allows us to compare the potential of the royal mine in Săsar Mountain and some of Peter Deák's mines. Next to the royal mine there were about 2,000 mine carts, including the ore extracted in the last ten days. Next to Peter Deák's *Gewzwad* mine there were 1,000 mine carts, including the ore extracted in the last few days. Therefore one of Deák's mines produced on its own half of what the royal mine was capable of producing. The other mine, *Gepel Schacht*, possessed 1,850 mine carts of ore, almost the same as the royal mine.[27] A simple comparison of these numbers confirms the royal commissioners' assessment in 1552 that "he alone gathers more gold and silver from these mines than all other mine owners."[28]

The political crisis that followed, lasting about two decades, destroyed his investments, the final blow being given by the Transylvanian and Ottoman soldiers in 1567-1568. In the census of 1569, only the memory of Peter Deák's once famous mines survived.[29] The extracted ore was crushed and refined by washing in the stamp mills, which were machines equivalent in function to the modern flotation equipment. Deák possessed his own stamp mills, as well as those of his stepsons, and also operated other stamp mills that he leased. He thus possessed six stamp mills with a total of 66 hammers.

Of interest is also the evaluation of the extracted and processed ore. Four of the listed locations held ore extracted from Peter Deák's mines at his own expense, valued at over 3,000 florins, which was processed in the stamp mills from the autumn until the onset of the first frost. The inspector was not able to evaluate the amount of gold and silver that could be refined from that ore, but in duration of two weeks, a stamp mill of 24 hammers gave four marks in golden globes of 13 carats.[30] In 1569 a single stamp mill that had belonged to Peter Deák was still in existence, with an unknown number of hammers, but it too was destroyed by the Transylvanian army.[31]

---

[25] MOL, *Urbaria et Conscriptiones*, fasc. 99, no. 29: 2. Today Băiţa is a part of the town Tăuţii-Măgherăuş, county Maramureş, Romania.
[26] SJMAN, *Primăria oraşului Baia Mare*, *Registre*, no. 1: 24.
[27] Prodan and Goldenberg, "Inventarele," 138-139.
[28] Holban, Alexandrescu-Dersca Bulgaru and Cernovodeanu, *Călători străini*, II, 85.
[29] Diaconescu, *Conscripţiile Sătmar*, 157-158.
[30] MOL, *Urbaria et Conscriptiones*, fasc. 99, no. 29: 1.
[31] Diaconescu, *Conscripţiile Sătmar*, 157.

For a comparison of the processing capacity of Peter Deák's stamp mills and those of the Treasury, let us return to the inventory of 1556.[32] The stamp mill near the *Naghwerem* royal mine had 24 hammers and 534 mine carts waiting to be processed. Peter Deák's stamp mill near the *Gewzewd* mine also had 24 hammers, but 742 mine carts with ore ready to be processed. The stamp mill near the *Gepel Schacht* mine on the Ferneziu valley had 21 hammers and only 24 mine carts waiting to be processed. From 40 mine carts of ore, Peter Deák's stamp mill obtained one mark and 26 pisetas of silver, one mark having 7 pisetas of gold, that is the same profitability rates as the royal mine.

The ore processed in the stamp mills was then taken to the smelter for the extraction of gold and silver. In 1553 the existence of a smelter is attested that Deák shared with Emeric Kamanczy's orphans.[33]

In 1556 Deák owned two smelter furnaces. By them stood 623 mining carts with gold concentrate (*Slak*) that belonged to the assets of Peter Deák, together with other 996 mining carts (*par*) that had been accumulated by his son-in-law.

In 1569 the smelting facilities comprised four furnaces, one of which belonged to his stepson.[34] For a proper evaluation of the significance of Deák's ore processing equipment and capacity, let us mention that in the same year, 1569, the Treasury's smelter, which at the time lay abandoned, also had four furnaces, two of which belonged to private individuals.

In 1554 Deák's houses contained articles and devices required for mining and processing the ore, lead, cloth and tools, estimated at a total value of 1970 florins.[35] Peter Deák never put his money into buying estates, as some wealthy burghers did in the fifteenth and sixteenth centuries. He possessed only the village of Baţa in the county of Inner Szolnok, which he had received from Prince John Sigismund Szapolyai, probably after the prince returned to power in 1556 and Peter Deák was freed from the prison in Hust. This donation seems to have been devised as compensation for the loss of assets in Baia Mare, at a time when the town was still in the hands of the Habsburgs. At Deák's death, the village returned to the possession of the prince, who donated it in 1570 to one of his councillors.[36]

Peter Deák was interested instead in investments in farming activities, with a rapid rate of return: vineyards, mills, and livestock. The region of Baia Mare was well suited to wine-growing. The inventories mention a number of vineyards that belonged to Peter Deák, some that he had bought, others that he had leased. In 1553 he possessed a total of eight vineyards, three of which had been bought; two belonged to the orphans of

[32] Prodan and Goldenberg, "Inventarele," 138-139.
[33] Ibid., 130.
[34] Diaconescu, *Conscripţiile Sătmar*, 157.
[35] MOL, *Urbaria et Conscriptiones*, fasc. 99, no. 29: 1.
[36] Fejér Tamás, Rácz Etelka, Szász Ankó, eds., *Az erdélyi fejedelmek királyi könyvei*, I. *János Zsigmond királyi könyve 1569-1570* [The King Book of the Transylvanian Principality, I. The King Book of the Prince John Sigismund 1569-1570] (Kolozsvár: Az Erdélyi Múzeum-Egyesület Kiadása, 2003), 80, no. 243.

his wife, while the remaining three were leased from other orphans.[37] In the autumn of 1553 his cellars still held 63 wine barrels, before the new harvest.[38] In 1569 the three vineyards seized were said to require the work of 300 men in a day, in an era when vineyard size was calculated based on the number of men needed to complete the work in a full day.[39]

Peter Deák had a small farm outside town, producing some milk but mainly cheese. The first item on the inventory is 75 bellows of fresh cheese (*formule sew formadia cum cascis*).[40] The quantity indicates systematic production oriented to the market. There were also four crocks or amphorae for butter, and at the time the farm had a livestock of 25 cattle, which Deák grazed in 1553 on a very large pasture (*pratum [...] amplissimum*) which he had bought. In 1569 his estate seized by the Treasury included two large hayfields, requiring the workforce of 200 men in a day.[41]

Another area of investment was milling. In 1553 Peter Deák owned two mills in Baia Mare: one on the river Săsar near the little gate of the town, the other near the gate called *Zathmar*, towards Sătmar. The latter was administered by John Nagy's orphans, the stepsons of Peter Deák.[42] These two mills practically meant a monopoly on milling in Baia Mare in the mid-sixteenth century, since only one river, the Săsar, crossed the town and the possibilities of establishing mills were therefore limited. In 1569 only one mill is recorded in the possession of the Treasury, seized from Deák, which had five waterwheels and two millstones.[43] It was probably the mill at the town's little gate of 1553, which he further expanded in the short period of time when he returned to Baia Mare about 1565. Meanwhile the other mill, which belonged to his stepsons, had entered in their actual possession.

The mills, vineyards and farm were investments that, besides providing necessities for one's own consumption, were also sources of safe profit. Practically, Deák invested in various fields in mining and agriculture, which were able to provide him with rapid rates of return and little risk in the long run.

Spiritual life: Peter Deák, fervent promoter of the Reformation

The cognomen *litteratus* (Deák) indicates intellectual training; in the Middle Ages only those who knew to read and write and used this knowledge in any capacity were given this epithet, which offered them a certain social prestige.

We might never know the place of Peter Deák's studies and the level that he reached, because of the absence of written records providing such information. Except for those universities that have kept lists of medieval students in their archives, there are no

---

[37] Prodan and Goldenberg, "Inventarele," 130.
[38] Ibid.
[39] Diaconescu, *Conscripţiile Sătmar*, 157.
[40] Prodan and Goldenberg, "Inventarele," 130.
[41] Diaconescu, *Conscripţiile Sătmar*, 157.
[42] Prodan and Goldenberg, "Inventarele," 130.
[43] Diaconescu, *Conscripţiile Sătmar*, 157.

other similar sources on educational life histories. At least at this stage of the research, we have not been able to identify Peter Deák among the Hungarian students at European universities.

For all that, his intellectual training was above the average level of a local school. This is proven not only by his career in administration, but also by the number of his books. In 1553 he possessed a library of 35 books.[44] Unfortunately, whoever drew up the inventory of goods in Peter Deák's house did not take the time also to record the titles. This comes as no surprise, for he belonged to the ranks of the Baia Mare magistrate's office, whose members shared an intellectual training well below that of Peter Deák.

The inventory of 1556 was more detailed, listing the assets of the mint and Treasury in Baia Mare together. This time, the maker or makers of this inventory were officials of the Treasury and had a superior intellectual training. The book titles again went unrecorded, but their number had meanwhile risen to 38. Either they were sloppily counted at the first inventory, books being considered assets of minor importance, or three books were indeed added in the meantime. The list only tells us that they were small and large volumes.[45] There was also a bag with various documents, labelled as insignifi-cant by the maker of the inventory in 1556.[46] All these goods, together with many others of different character, were stored in the attic of the old house.

What could have been the titles or subjects of the 38 books in Peter Deák's library, which was quite a large one for the era?

It is possible that at least some volumes were related to his main activity of mining and gold extraction. In 1556 there was a book in the house of the mint's prefect comprising tables for calculating carats, needed to evaluate gold entering the mint.[47] We cannot rule out that at least some of Deák's books dealt with similar subjects, especially since 37 calculation tools were also found in his house in 1553![48] Such a quantity of tools, stored together with the 35 books, suggests that his intellectual preoccupations lay in the field of the mining industry and gold processing. Also in the house of the mint's prefect, the inventory mentions a "ciphered" table with a black panel, probably left over from the time when Deák had served as chamber count.[49] There was also a painting on parchment depicting the castle, the administrative seat of the mint in Baia Mare.[50]

Presumably some of the books in Peter Deák's own library belonged to the field of theology. Gáspár Heltai dedicated the 1553 edition of the Lutheran catechism in Hungarian: "*Ajánla Szentgyörgyi Péter deáknak, N. Bányán lakozónak.*"[51] This dedication

---

[44] Prodan and Goldenberg, "Inventarele," 129: "Libri numero 35."
[45] Ibid.: "Libri maiores et minores simul 38."
[46] Ibid., 141: "In vno saccula litere diuerse et carte inutiles."
[47] Ibid., 137: "Liber continens tabellas gradum marcarum 1."
[48] Ibid., 129: "Calculi computatorij 37."
[49] Ibid., 136: "Mensa cifrata cum tabula nigra Petri literati."
[50] Ibid.: "Tabula pergamenum in qua depictus situs castelli." We do not necessarily link this painting with Peter Deák, but we would like to draw the attention to this local object of art.
[51] Károly Szabó, *Régi Magyar Könyvtár. Az 1531-1711. megjelent magyar nyomtatványok könyvészeti*

was written on 21st May 1553, before Deák's arrest.[52]

In order to correctly understand Gáspár Heltai's gesture in dedicating an edition of his catechism to Peter Deák, we should look back at the other figures to whom he dedicated his books. The first volumes which Heltai printed in the years 1550-1552 carried no dedication.[53] The first dedication is dated 1552, when a book of theological dialogues was dedicated to Antál Kendi, the grandfather of Francis Kendi, a magnate in mid sixteenth-century Transylvania.[54] This was followed by the 1553 catechism dedicated to Peter Deák of Baia Mare. The same year, Heltai dedicated another book of Christian learning to Anna Báthory, George Báthory's wife.[55] The following two volumes in 1559 and 1560 he dedicated to John Sigismund Szapolyai, the prince of Transylvania.[56] In 1562 he dedicated an edition of the New Testament to Anna Nádasdi, Stephen Mailath's widow.[57]

Behind all these dedications stood the financing of the printing work. The New Testament dedicated to Anna Nádasdi was printed in 1561, but the title page and the dedication were ready only in 1562, suggesting that the recipient of the dedication had sponsored the printing. The New Testament of 1565 carries no dedication, indicating that the investment was Heltai's alone.[58]

Peter Deák thus appears as one of the patrons of Gáspár Heltai's books, together with leading figures of the era: Antál Kendi, grandfather of the magnate Francis Kendi; Anna Báthory and Anna Nadásdi, and, not least, John Sigismund Szapolyai, the prince of Transylvania. It should be noted that Deák was the only burgher and enterpriser on the very short list of patrons, in the company of great landowners, a patron just like some of the most illustrious noble and princely families of Transylvania!

The Reformation was adopted by the townspeople of Baia Mare in 1547. The Habsburgs accused Peter Deák of having destroyed the Franciscan monastery in Baia Mare, which suggests the part he played in promoting the Reformation from the very beginning. His relationship with Gáspár Heltai further indicates the true dimension of his involvement in supporting the Reformation in the north of Transylvania. We should also mention in this context that around 1574 his brother, Thomas Kapliani, was the rector of the Unitarian school in Alba Iulia.[59]

---

kézikönyve [The Old Hungarian Library. The Bibliography of the Hungarian Printed Materials Between 1531-1711] (Budapest, 1879), 15, no. 31: „Catechismvs mellybe à menyei tvdomannac Sommáia, à derec szent irásbol, es sok keresztyén Tanitóknac irásokból röuideden egybe szerzetettöt es befoglaltattot: HELTAI GASPARTOL à Colosuari Plebanostól. Az együgyü, keresztyéneknec épitésére: Colosvarba 1553."

52 http://www.arcanum.hu/oszk/lpext.dll/eRMK/1f0f/2167/2206?f=templates&fn=document-frame. htm&2.0, accessed on 23.12.2011.

53 Szabó, *Régi Magyar Könyvtár*, 11, no. 22; 12-13, no. 25-26; 13-14, no. 28.

54 Ibid., 14, no. 29.

55 Ibid., 15, no. 32.

56 Ibid., 17-18, no. 37; 20, no. 41.

57 Ibid., 25, no. 51.

58 Ibid., 29-30, no. 57.

59 Marius Diaconescu, "Noi date despre învăţământul din Transilvania: şcoala din Alba Iulia şi rectorul ei în 1574, Toma Kapliani" [New Data Concerning the Education in Transylvania: The School of Alba Iulia and its Rector in 1574, Toma Kapliani], *Annales Universitatis Apulensis*, Series *Historica* 16, 1 (2012): 309-317.

Privat life

Peter Deák owned three stone houses in the town centre, one belonging to his wife and stepsons, near the house of the town judge, another that he had recently built himself near the town hall, both of these being two-storey buildings with ground floor and upper level, and another that was older and smaller but also of stone. According to a detailed description of Baia Mare in the year 1697, most houses built of stone were found in the town centre, a situation that can be extrapolated for the middle of the sixteenth century as well.[60]

The inventory of 1553 describes the first house thusly: the ground floor consisted of a small room with windows opening to the square, a large room with two old tables, a kitchen and annex.[61] Upstairs was one large room with four wardrobes and four beds or sofas. The inner courtyard featured a wooden extension where the carriage was kept, above which was Deák's private cabinet, and also housed a small stable.

The house interior was distinguished by the four wall rugs, one icon (*Imago charitatis affixa parieti*), the copper chandelier or the gilded copper clock.[62] The room on the first floor served as the bedroom. In addition to the ever-present blankets and large pillows, the description of the bedclothes is intriguing. One quilt was made of red fabric woven with wool and gold thread, with an azure green seam around the edges. Of another piece the maker of the inventory felt compelled to record that, although small in size, it was nonetheless elegant (*stragulum lecti exiguum, sed elegans*).

The document records only Deák's wife's wardrobe, firstly a luxurious women's dress, called *peplum*, with rich pleats and decorated with gold thread and precious stones. The adornments on the blouses were also picked out with gold thread. There was a plural number of chest ornaments, not further specified. The hems used to embellish the chest of the blouses were made of gold leaf; there were also two gold hems used to adorn blouse sleeves. The wardrobes contained a number of veils or kerchiefs: seven painted veils of silk with gold thread and a red Turkish veil (*faciletum rubrum turcicum*). A kerchief of fine tissue, probably muslin, of rectangular shape, was also embellished with gold thread (*faciletum inauratum ex molli sindone retiforme*) and recorded with the Hungarian word *fátyol* (*wlgo faatyol*).

By comparison, the jewels were more modest, suggesting that for Peter Deák the commercial value of gold was more important than its symbolic value as wealth. His wife had two decorated gold necklaces, another two gilded necklaces, and a further three simpler gold necklaces adorned with precious stones. A pouch of black fabric with gold thread decorations (*marsupium de veluto nigro intextum auro*) was recorded in the same category.

Finally we should mention the weaponry in the household: a stiletto in its scabbard was kept in the main room upstairs. In the attic of the courtyard extension, which

---

[60] MOL, *Urbaria et Conscriptiones*, fasc. 27, no. 45: 1-54.

[61] Prodan and Goldenberg, "Inventarele," 128-131.

[62] Presence of icon in the home of a supporter of the Reformation may seem strange, but it is explained in just a few years after the adoption of Lutheranism.

probably used to be Peter Deák's private cabinet, were two long daggers. There were also pistols, a silvered crest, and two pieces of armour.

The extant sources, though brief, have allowed us to investigate this interesting character in mid-sixteenth century history. We have only grasped fragments of his career, his fortune, and his lifestyle. We note in the first instance his entrepreneurship, in the mining and processing industries as in farming and milling for the urban market. We have seen how Peter Deák's free spirit manifested itself in his support for the Reformation, not just in the destruction of a Catholic monastery, which must have been a "normal" way of acting in the heat of religious disputes, but in particular through his patronage for the printing of Gáspár Heltai's catechism. We cannot deny his political opportunism or the use of public administrative positions as levers for social ascension. It is of interest in this context that, after his death, a burgher from Baia Mare complained to the town magistrate that when Peter Deák married, he had lent him 50 florins for the expenditures of that event, and that the money was never returned.[63] Although he seems not to have had enough money for the wedding ceremony, Peter Deák managed to amass a fortune in a matter of years.

All of the above elements indicate Peter Deák's close connection to the emergent social category of capitalists in Europe of the day. To be sure, one might speculate widely about what exactly a capitalist is. We have not undertaken here to establish exactly how far Max Weber's criteria, or those of other scholars, are applicable in the present case. It is highly significant though that the royal commissioners, who loathed Deák, could not help but notice his entrepreneurial ability in 1553. All the more, I believe, it is our responsibility as historians to rescue such figures from the oblivion of documents and restore an image as close to reality as possible of the society of earlier times.

---

[63] SJMAN, *Primăria oraşului Baia Mare, Registre*, no. 1: 36.

The Transit of Oriental Goods Through the Customs of Sibiu/Hermannstadt in the Sixteenth and Seventeenth Centuries: An Overview

Mária Pakucs-Willcocks

This paper examines the overall trends of the trade with Oriental goods in early modern Transylvania. The primary sources are the extant customs accounts of Sibiu (Hermannstadt, Nagyszeben), a major trading town of the Transylvania principality, and the capital of the Transylvanian Germans (Saxons). The results presented here comprise the findings of my doctoral research on the sixteenth century customs journals and those of the subsequent investigation of the seventeenth century registers.[1]

Why oriental goods and oriental trade? Approaching only one segment of the international trade connecting Western and Central Europe to the Levante and the East was decided by the nature of the Sibiu customs accounts: many of them are restricted to the detail recording of the goods coming into Transylvania from the Ottoman Empire. The *res turcales* or the "Türkische Waren" were much sought after products for local consumption and further distribution into Transylvania or Poland and Hungary.

Connected since the fourteenth century, to the network of roads that linked East and West,[2] Sibiu was never a crucial player in international trade, and had not evolved into a large exchange market, but it was a steadfast destination for products coming from the Ottoman Empire via the Balkans. The supply of oriental products was shipped either on land or on water; it is difficult to discern which routes prevailed in the Balkan trade. Especially for the seventeenth century, recent research has shown that the Black Sea, the Danube and land routes played their role in the international distribution of goods into Central Europe.[3]

---

[1] The Ph.D. was published as a monograph, Mária Pakucs-Willcocks, *Sibiu-Hermannstadt: oriental trade in sixteenth century Transylvania* (Cologne: Boehlau, 2007); the research on seventeenth century customs journals was funded through a postdoctoral grant of the Romanian Academy, financed through the European Social Fund, contract no. POSDRU 89/1.5/S/61104.

[2] Mihail Dan and Samuel Goldenberg, "Le commerce balkano-levantin de la Transylvanie au cours de la second moitié du XVIe siècle et au début du XVII siècle," *Revue des études sud-est européenes* V, 1-2 (1967): 102-3.

[3] Cristian Luca, "Greek-Levantines Merchants in the Black Sea Harbors in the Early Eighteenth Century. New Sources," *Transylvanian Review* XIX, 4 (2010): 112-120; Idem, "The rise of the Greek 'conquering merchant' in the trade between the Eastern Mediterranean and the Romanian principalities in the sixteenth and seventeenth centuries," *Journal of Mediterranean Studies* 19 2 (2010): 311-334; Anca Popescu, "Portul Constanţa în comerţul Mării Negre în secolul al XVI-lea" [The Port of Constanţa in the Black Sea Trade in the Sixteenth Century], in *Izvoare istorice, artă, cultură şi societate. În memoria lui Constantin Bălan* [Historical Sources, Art, Culture and Society. In Memory of Constantin Balan], ed. Constantin Rezachevici (Bucureşti: Fundaţia culturală Gheorghe Marin Speteanu, 2010), 199-209; Marco Moroni, "I rapporti commerciali delle regioni de Basso Danubio con le città dell'Adriatico tra cinque e seicento," in *La storia di un riconoscimento: i rapporti tra l'Europa Centro-Orientale e la Penisola italiana dal Rinascimento all'Età dei Lumi*, ed. Cristian Luca and Gianluca Masi (Brăila: Istros, 2012), 169-193.

Having customs registers covering such a large timespan is exceptional for this region, thus the enormous potential of these sources is evident. The customs accounts of the sixteenth century I have already described to great length.[4] From the seventeenth century twelve customs registers are available, covering 11 complete and 8 incomplete years,[5] with one group of five registers from 1614-1623 and a second group from 1672 to 1692.

These customs accounts bear witness to the continuity and longevity of trade connections in South-Eastern and Central Europe. Agents of this trade were mainly merchants of the Ottoman Empire, of various ethnic, social and religious backgrounds.[6] The scope of this paper restricts the threads of argument to general trends of commerce; therefore I shall discuss the merchants only cursorily. I shall discuss also the changes in the composition of trade, according to main categories of products.

All figures provided in this paper are expressed in gold (Hungarian) florins. Values are deflated from the money of account, following exchange rates found in various sources and in the customs accounts themselves.[7] This method enables an accurate assessment of the values of trade over the two centuries.

There are some variations in the manner of record keeping at the customs of Sibiu. Customs registers record the following set of data: the date of the merchant's passing through the customs, the merchant's name and place of departure/origin, the quantities of merchandise, the quantities of goods (when paying in kind) or cash levied as customs duties. The registers from the sixteenth century and 1614-1623 more often than not do not offer information about the merchant's entire consignment, except for the amount they gave as customs duties.[8]

In Figure 1 I have illustrated the values of recorded trade in oriental goods.

Figure 1 and 2 sum up the core information in the customs registers. The finds regarding the secular trends of trade values and those of recorded numbers of merchants and transports are consistent with the overall trends in international trade. For the six-

---

[4] Pakucs-Willcocks, *Sibiu-Hermannstadt*, 34-41.

[5] Arhivele Naţionale ale României. Direcţia Judeţeană Sibiu [The Sibiu County Branch of National Archives], Fund *Primăria şi magistratul oraşului Sibiu, Socoteli vamal*e, Inventory 197: no. 43 (1614-1615), no. 44 (1616-1617), no. 45 (1615-1616), no. 46 (1618-1619), no. 47 (1622), no. 52 (1672), no. 53 (1673), no. 59 (1682-1686), no. 63 (1686), no. 64 (1687-1688), no. 66 (1687-1689), no. 67 (1689-1692).

[6] An excellent overview of available literature, sources and interpretations of international and regional trade in South-Eastern and Central Europe at Gelina Harlaftis, "International Business of Southeastern Europe and the Eastern Mediterranean, 18th century: Sources, Methods, and Interpretive Issues," in *Dove va la storia economica? Metodi e prospettive. Secc. XIII-XVIII - Where is Economic History Going? Methods and Prospects from the 13th to the 18th centuries. Atti della "Quarantaduesima Settimana di Studi," 18-22 aprile 2010*, ed. Francesco Ammannati (Florence: Firenze University Press, 2011), 389-415.

[7] For the sixteenth century exchange rates can be found in my *Sibiu-Hermannstadt*, 50. For the entire period the most reliable data by Tibor Antal Horváth, "A magyar aranyforint értékváltozása, 1490-1700" [The Change in Value of the Gold Florin, 1490-1700], *Numizmatikai Közlöny* LVIII-LIX (1959-1960): 33-42. For 1614-1623: Lajos Huszár, *Bethlen Gábor pénzei* [The Coins of Gabriel Bethlen] (Cluj: Erdélyi Magyar Tudományos Intézet, 1945), 12, note 25.

[8] Discrepancies between the recorded goods and actual stock of the merchant were obvious in the case of a certain Hartha of Târgovişte in 1597. See Pakucs-Willcocks, *Sibiu-Hermannstadt*, 135, table 31.

teenth century, the "revival of Levantine trade"[9] is clearly shown in the increased levels of traffic in oriental goods until 1559. The second half of the century bears witness to the effects of warfare on trade: in 1595, at the height of military conflict on the Danube at Giurgiu, during the Long War, goods could not reach Transylvania to the average annual levels.[10] While there are yearly variation, medium-term trends can be assessed based on the data: during the first half of the sixteenth century, the annual value of imported oriental goods through the customs of Sibiu averaged around 15,000 gold florins, while in the second half of that century it dropped to under 10,000. The end of the sixteenth century and the second decade of the seventeenth century see the average value of the oriental trade rise again to around 15,000 gold florins, anticipating the increase in values to nearly 20,000 in the 1690s.

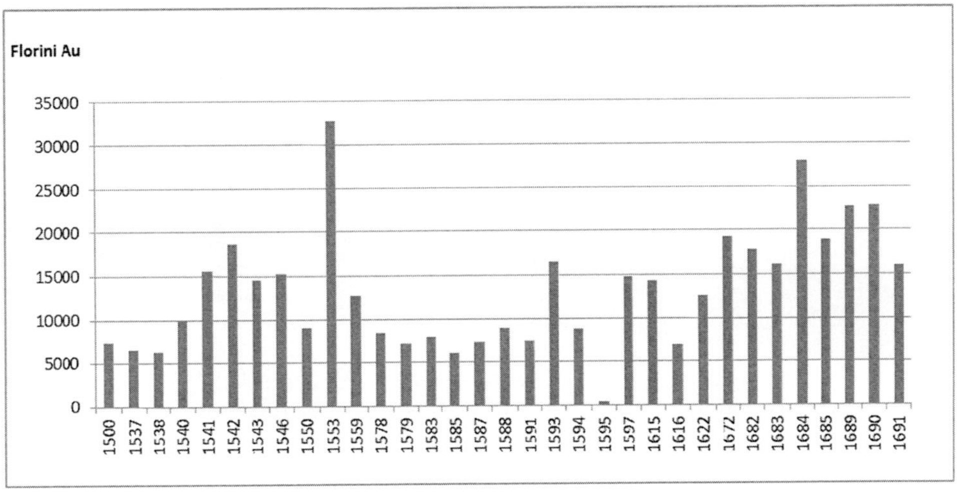

Fig. 1: Oriental trade through the customs of Sibiu, 1500-1691

The trends outlined briefly here follow the patterns of commercial exchange between Europe and the Ottoman Empire. The most salient change throughout these two centuries concerns the number of merchants and transports, introduced in figure 2. In 1672 there is a doubling of merchants involved in trade, while the number of transports

[9] Frederic Lane, "The Mediterranean Spice Trade: Further Evidence for its Revival in the Sixteenth century," repr. in *Spices in the Indian Ocean*, ed. M. N. Pearson (Aldershot: Variorum, 1996), 116.

[10] At the beginning of the sixteenth century, Giurgiu (Yörgügü) was not the most important crossing point on the Danube. See János Hóvári, "Az oszmán gazdasági struktúra az al-Dunánál 1496-1517" [The Ottoman Economic Structure on the Lower Danube] (Ph.D. diss, Hungarian Academy of Sciences, 1996-97), 41. It is clear however that disruption of the trade routes and fighting around it had a serious impact on trade. For the warfare during the Thirteen Years War and the role of Michael the Brave see most recently: Ovidiu Cristea, "A Second Front: Wallachia and the Long War against the Turks," in *Europe and the 'Ottoman World'. Exchanges and Conflicts (sixteenth to seventeenth centuries)*, ed. Gábor Kármán and Radu Păun (Istanbul: The Isis Press, 2013), 12-26.

has increased more than twofold. It is a significant change, pointing towards a "popularisation" of trade with Transylvania. While it is clear that the double selection on data (once through survival in the archives and then through my own, albeit random, choice) prompts us to avoid any strong conclusion, I can assert that over the two centuries there was a shift towards more numerous but more inexpensive transports. This would indicate a change in the typology of merchants as well, which cannot be studied in-depth for lack of primary sources concerning them.

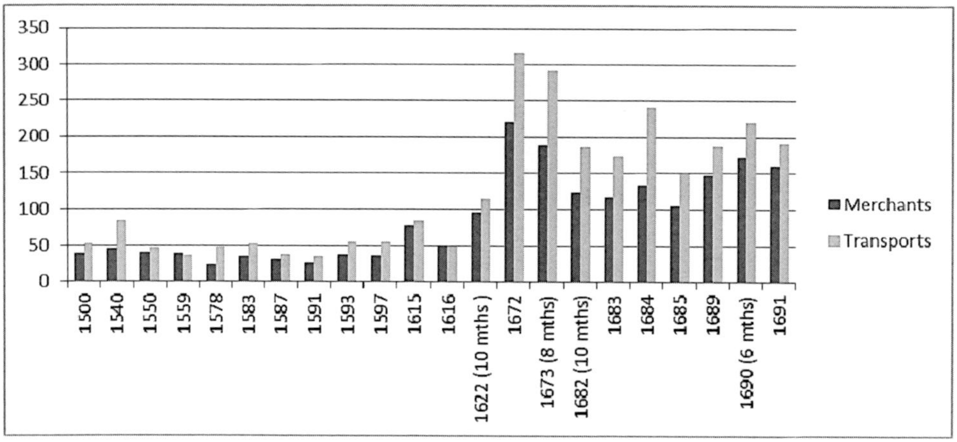

Fig. 2: Number of transports and merchants recorded at the customs of Sibiu, 1500-1691

The average and maximum values of transports better illustrate this development. I did not include the minimum values of transports because they are of no relevance to my argument. They vary usually between 1 and 2 gold florins.

Year	Average	Maximum
1500	147	3455
1550	197	1143
1585	155	1017
1597	268	1188
1615	166	1623
1672	58	729
1682	98	563
1691	85	730

Table 1: The average and maximum values of oriental trade, in gold florins

A breakdown of the figures on categories of goods might enable us to understand better the great shift that took place in the second half of the seventeenth century. A good place to start is to define the "oriental goods." The "Turkish wares" comprises certain products of the Ottoman workshops in Anatolia and the Balkans, such as textiles and leather goods, but also spices that were in transit through the Ottoman Empire. These oriental goods can be identified invariably in historical sources of Southeastern and Cen-tral Europe from the fifteenth century onward: in the consignments of the Ottoman ships calling at Caffa, various accounts of transports of merchandise in Poland and Lithuania, Ottoman customs accounts of Tulcea, Giurgiu, and the Hungarian Plain in the sixteenth century, or Transylvanian customs accounts from the seventeenth century.[11]

In the following section of this paper I shall present the dynamic of trade in oriental products. When talking about Orient and the Levante, the first word that springs to mind is "spices." By the sixteenth century, from a transit region between East and West, Central Europe had become a consumer of aromatic products, especially of pepper.[12]

Spices and spice trade through Transylvania have been at the heart of a debate regarding the Central European supply. At the beginning of the sixteenth century, extraordinarily high amounts of pepper (worth over 32,000 gold florins)[13] reached Transylvania via Braşov, its main trading centre.[14] The data from the 1503 customs register of this town have been employed to prove the role of the Transylvanian towns in the spice trade and, implicitly, that of the land routes, in provisioning Central Europe with the much-sought after products.[15] For Sibiu data from 1500 is available. Here the spice trade was les impressive, although made up the largest share of the recorded oriental trade.[16] Zsigmond Pál Pach calculated that at the beginning of the sixteenth century, the traffic of spices for both Transylvanian towns represented 8% of the Venetian imports.[17]

---

[11] For the Caffa registers: Halil Inalcik, *Sources and Studies on the Ottoman Black Sea. I. The Customs Register of Caffa, 1487-1490* (Cambridge: Harvard University Press, 1995), 189-190. For Poland-Lithuania and trade in Ottoman goods: Gilles Veinstein, "Marchands ottomans en Pologne-Lithuanie et en Moscovie sous le règne de Soliman le Magnifique," *Cahiers du monde russe* 35, 4 (1994): 729-30. For Tulcea see János Hóvári, "Customs registers of Tulça (Tulcea)," *Acta Orientalia Academiae Scientiarum Hungaricae* XXXVIII, 1-2 (1984): 115-41; For Giurgiu and the Lower Danube: Hóvári, "Az oszmán," 120-1, 125-30, 192-195 and Anca Popescu, "Circulaţia mărfurilor la Dunărea de Jos reflectată în *kanunname*-le (a doua jumătate a secolului al XVI-lea)" [The Merchandise Circulation at the Lower Danube Reflected in the *Kannuname* of the Second Half of the Sixteenth Century], *Revista istorică* VI, 3-4 (1995): 273. For the Hungarian Plain see Zsigmond Pál Pach, "Aba, kebe, igriz. Posztófajták a hódoltság török vámnaplókban a 16. század derekán" [Cloth Types in the Turkish Customs Accounts from the Middle of the Sixteenth Century], *Történelmi Szemle* 37, 2 (1995): 1-19. For Transylvania see Ferenc Pap, *Kolozsvári harmincadjegyzékek, 1599-1637* [Customs Accounts from Cluj, 1599-1637] (Bucureşti: Kriterion, 2000). A similar list of oriental goods in the Glossary to Nikolai Todorov's *The Balkan City, 1400-1900* (Seattle: University of Washington Press, 1983).

[12] Andrzej Wyczanski, *La consommation alimentaire en Pologne aux XVI-XVII siècles* (Paris: Institut d'etudes slaves, 1981).

[13] My own calculations based on the 1503 customs register, published in *Quellen zur Geschichte der Stadt Kronstadt in Siebenbürgen*, vol. 1 (Braşov: Zeidner, 1876), 1-81.

[14] Radu Manolescu, *Comerţul Ţării Româneşti şi Moldovei cu Braşovul, secolele XIV-XVI* [The Trade of Wallachia and Moldavia with Braşov, Fourteenth-Sixteenth Centuries] (Bucureşti: Editura Ştiinţifică, 1965).

[15] Pach, "The Transylvanian Route of Levantine Trade at the Turn of the Fifteenth and Sixteenth Century," *Etudes Historiques Hongroises* 1 (1980): 113-66 with further debates.

[16] See Pakucs-Willcocks, *Sibiu-Hermannstadt*, 151, table AI.1.

[17] Pach, "The Transylvanian Route of Levantine Trade," 165.

In the course of the sixteenth century, however, the spice distribution through southern Transylvania lost it share in the overall imports of goods from the Ottoman Empire. The analysis of the sixteenth century customs registers showed clearly that textiles and not spices dominated trade. In the sixth decade of the century, the increase in the overall incomes at the custom of Sibiu saw the doubling of pepper imports compared to 1500, but they could no longer overtake the textile trade.[18] European imports of Asia textiles have grown generally in the sixteenth century: even Portuguese ships started carrying fabrics alongside the traditional cargo of spices.[19]

The main focus of the following analysis shall be therefore placed on the textile trade as reflected in the Sibiu customs accounts of the sixteenth and seventeenth centuries. Throughout this period, the balance between textiles and spices altered radically. Before discussing textiles into more details, a few figures shall illustrate the dynamic of oriental trade in randomly selected years.

YEAR MERCHANDISE	**1500 %**	**1541 %**	**1553 %**	**1597 %**	**1615 %**	**1672 %**	**1682 %**	**1690 %**
Textiles	21	59	47.8	56	56.2	46	62.5	71
Spices	63	28	27	14	2.4	0.5	3	0
Cotton, cotton yarns	0	1.8	4.2	9.2	2.2	2.7	12.5	10.8
Silk	3	0.6	0.9	0.2	5.5	17	6.3	3
Textile products	8	7.6	14.3	6.9	6.3	4.1	0.5	2
Leather products	1	1.3	2	4.8	6.8	19	4	12
Foodstuffs	3	1.3	2	0	1.6	0.7	0	0
Other	1	0.4	1.8	8.9	19	10	11.1	1.2
	100	100	100	100	100	100	100	100

Table 2: Structure of oriental trade of Sibiu, in percentages

The categories of goods in Table 2 reflect the main composition of the oriental trade while being also too large to reveal the finer nuances. Cotton and cotton yarns were not included with the textiles because of their separate history in fashion and consumption in Central Europe: the "red yarn" was such a fashionable commodity, that Viennese workshops were set up to produce threads to the model of the Ottoman yarns.[20] Unspun cotton lost its appeal during the seventeenth century, while it had been more popular in the pre-

[18] Ibid.

[19] Sanjay Subrahmanyam and Luís Filipe F. R. Thomas, "Evolution of empire: The Portuguese in the Indian Ocean during the sixteenth century," in *The Political Economy of Merchant Empires: State Power and World Trade 1350-1750*, ed. James D. Tracy (Cambridge: Cambridge University Press, 1994), 308-9.

[20] Olga Katsiardi-Hering, "The Allure of the Red Cotton Yarn, and how it Came to Vienna: Associations of Greek artisans and merchants operating between the Ottoman and Habsburg Empires," in *Merchants in the Ottoman Empire*, ed. Suraiya Faroqhi and Gilles Veinstein (Leuven: Peeters, 2008), 97-132.

vious one.[21] Further, under the generic category of "other" are included: various dyestuffs and tannings (alum, indigo), wool, and the tobacco, which is consistently recorded in the customs accounts of Sibiu beginning with 1672.[22]

Returning to the previous discussion on spices, the disappearance of the spices from the Balkan trade routes is definitive by the end of the seventeenth century: the last consignment of pepper at the customs of Sibiu was recorded in 1684.

Oriental carpets, woven in Anatolia or in workshops in the Balkans, were prized items in the trade, as the collections preserved in the Saxon churches of Transylvania show. Although they had no great impact in the overall value of trade, the prestige these carpets enjoyed in the region is demonstrated by the fact that the largest extant collection of historic Anatolian rugs is still to be found in Transylvania.[23] Other textile objects recorded at the customs offices of southern Transylvania are blankets and various towels. Clothing and footwear are also found all over the region and known to be of Anatolian or Balkan production: many leather or woollen and silk belts, girdles, headscarves, mantles and trousers, as well as slippers and saffian boots.[24]

A list of prices dating to the end of the seventeenth and the beginning of the eighteenth century and containing goods sold by the Greek trading companies in Sibiu and Braşov, itemizes mostly cotton and silk textiles,[25] again underlining the significance of textiles as the most prominent trading item in early modern times, locally and globally. This preference for Ottoman cotton textiles is even more striking if we take into account Suraiya Faroqui's recent argument that the cotton and cotton textile output of Ottoman workshops was not export-oriented but primarily intended for local consumption.[26] For the sixteenth century, information about trade with textile produces or carried through the Ottoman Empire I have provided elsewhere.[27] For the late seventeenth century, the increase in imports of Ottoman textiles is clear, although it is more difficult to discern the exact amounts and values of each type of fabric. Customs registers record generic names: "Brusa merchandise," "Istanbul merchandise," "Adrianopol merchandise" or "Rumeli mer-

---

[21] See the figures in Pakucs-Willcocks, *Sibiu-Hermannstadt*, 83, table 11.

[22] There is little research on smoking and tobacco in Transylvania. Most recently Ana-Maria Gruia has approached the topic: "Pipe smoking on horseback. New sources on the history of tobacco smoking in early modern Transylvania," *Brukenthal. Acta Musei* VII, 1 (2012): 135-41. The wool from the Balkan peninsula had better quality and was appreciated in Transylvania for the local cloth production: Samuel Goldenberg, "Italieni şi raguzani în viaţa economică a Transilvaniei în secolul al XVI-lea" [Italians and Ragusans in Transylvanian Economy in the Sixteenth Century], *Studii* 16, 3 (1963): 612-4; Idem, "Comerţul, producţia şi consumul de postavuri de lână în Ţările Române" [Trade, Production and Consumption of Woolen Cloth in the Romanian Principalities], *Studii* 24, 5 (1971): 890.

[23] See, most recently, *Antique Ottoman Rugs in Transylvania*, ed. Stefano Ionescu (Rome: Esselibri, 2007).

[24] Todorov, *The Balkan City*, 103.

[25] Olga Cicanci, *Companiile greceşti din Transilvania şi comerţul european în anii 1636-1746* [The Greek Companies in Transylvania and European Trade in the Years 1636-1746] (Bucureşti: Editura Academiei, 1981), 139-140, table 1.

[26] Suraiya Faroqui, "Ottoman Cotton Textiles: The Story of a Success that did not Last, 1500-1800," in *The Spinning World: A Global History of Cotton Textiles 1200-1850*, ed. Giorgio Riello and Prasannan Parthasarati (Oxford: Oxford University Press, 2009), 89-93.

[27] Pakucs-Willcocks, *Sibiu-Hermannstadt*, 77-82.

chandise." Such consignments consisted of various goods, such as cotton twill textiles (the well known bogasia), cotton yarns, silk and carpets. Their composition was not consistent; therefore the name indicates the source of the goods. Lidia Demény offers a useful glimpse into the composition of oriental trade in 1685 in her study of the Sibiu customs journal of that year.[28]

The late seventeenth century customs accounts also record the further destination of the merchants that is whether they were taking their goods into Poland or Hungary.

The final section of this paper presents briefly the merchants engaged in Sibiu's oriental trade. Figure 2 has shown a doubling in the number of recorded traders in the second half of the seventeenth century. One reason for this could lie within the more favourable trading conditions for the Ottoman merchants in Transylvania and particularly in Sibiu.

The town enjoyed the benefits of the staple and depositing right granted in the late fourteenth century by the Hungarian kings: this offered them the advantage of halting any foreign merchants at the depositing place outside the city and buying the much sought-after goods in wholesale.[29] Thus, local merchants controlled the distribution of the oriental textiles, leather products and spices on the Transylvanian markets and carried them further into the continent. Things changed rapidly however with the stronger presence of the "Greek" merchants (Greeks from Epirus and Thessaloniki, Vlachs from the Balkans, but also Armenians, Turks and Jews were sometimes included in this category) around the middle of the sixteenth century.[30]

Destination YEAR	**Poland %**	**Hungary %**
1682	32.77	
1683	44.24	0.4
1684	24.18	
1685	48.28	
1681 (Jan-Oct)	10.29	10.14
1689	3.08	17
1690	16.12	16.5
1691	10.81	41.4
1692 (Jan-May)	24.54	16.15

Table 3: Destination of oriental products from Sibiu, 1682-1692

[28] Lidia Demény, "Le commerce de la Transylvanie avec les régions du sud du Danube effectué par la douane de Turnu Roşu en 1685," *Revue Roumaine d'Histoire* 7, 5 (1968), 764-9.

[29] Mária Pakucs-Willcocks, "Dreptul de etapă al Sibiului în secolele XIV-XVII. Parcursul secular al unei instituții medievale" [The Staple Right of Sibiu in the Fourteenth-Seventeenth Centuries. The Historical Evolution of a Medieval Institution], in *Viam inveniam aut faciam. In honorem Ştefan Andreescu*, ed. Ovidiu Cristea, Gheorghe Lazăr and Petronel Zahariuc (Iaşi: Editura Universităţii, 2012), 143-172.

[30] Dan and Goldenberg, "Le commerce," 99. Also from the same authors "Marchands balkaniques et levantins dans le commerce de la Transylvanie aux XVIe et XVIIe siècles," in *Actes du Premier Congrès des études sud-est européennes*, vol. III (Sofia: AIESEE, 1969), 646.

These Balkan-Levantine merchants, subjects of the Sultan, took advantage of the Ottoman supremacy over the Balkans and suzerainty over Wallachia, Moldavia and, beginning with 1541, Transylvania. "Turks" as merchants are recorded in diplomatic sources as merchants trading in Wallachia in the fifteenth century;[31] the "Greeks" started to play a significant role in the oriental trade with Transylvania by the middle of the sixteenth century.[32] Previous scholarship has established that these terms were used in European sources chiefly to denote Levantine, Greek-Orthodox and other merchants subject to the Ottoman Empire; Transylvanian and Wallachian documents conform to the same usage.[33] In Transylvanian sources, the "Greek" merchants are more easily identifiable by the oriental goods they were trading in.[34]

The Sibiu customs accounts capture the expansion of the geographical "catchment area" for traders interested in the Transylvanian market. In the sixteenth century, towns of origin or departure declared by merchants at the customs were mostly towns in Wallachia: Râmnic, Argeş or Piteşti.[35] The end of the sixteenth and the second decade of the seventeenth century attracted increasing numbers of merchants from towns south of Danube, in nowadays Bulgaria: Nikopol, Târnovo, and Ruse. In the second half of the seven-teenth century, in a trend consistent with the records of the Greek company of Sibiu, even more remote localities become listed as places of origin, places in historical Epirus, such as: Ioannina, Melnik, Kosturi, Kozan, Kopilotz, and Dipalitsa.[36]

There was undeniable pressure from these foreign merchants to enter unhindered onto the Transylvanian market. Otto Fritz Jickeli mentions that in 1577, a Greek merchant obtained the first princely privilege to sell salted fish, blankets, and sheep.[37] Sibiu and Braşov succeeded in having the Transylvanian Diet on their side throughout the sixteenth century, but the general mood and consequently the legislation gradually shifted in favour of the Greek merchants.

In the course of the seventeenth century, Greek and other Ottoman merchants ob-

---

[31] Inalcik, *The customs register of Caffa*, 121 found that Muslim Turkish merchants were the most active participants in the Black Sea trade at the turn of the sixteenth century.

[32] The strong presence of Greek merchants in Wallachia is better documented from the end of the sixteenth century: Gheorghe Lazăr, "« De la boutique à la terre » : Les marchands grecs et leurs stratégies d'insertion sociale (Valachie, XVIIe siècle," *Studii şi materiale de istorie medie* 26 (2008): 57.

[33] On the Hungarian situation, see the excellent study by Lajos Gecsényi, ""Turkish Goods" and "Greek Merchants" in the Kingdom of Hungary in the 16th and 17th Centuries," *Acta Orientalia Academiae Scientiarum Hungariae* 60, 1 (2007): 55-71.

[34] Mária Pakucs-Willcocks, "Negustori şi practici comerciale în relaţiile de schimb dintre Sibiu şi Ţara Românească, secolele XIV-XVI: între istoria economică şi cea socială" [Merchants and Commercial Practices in the Commercial Exchange Between Sibiu and Wallachia, 14th-16th Centuries: Between Economic and Social History], *Revista de istorie socială* 8-9 (2003-2004): 67. This equation of "Greek" with 'merchant of oriental goods' was known in Wallachia as well; see Gheorghe Lazăr, *Les Marchands en Valachie, XVIIe-XVIIIe siècles* (Bucureşti: Institutul Cultural Român, 2006), 107.

[35] Pakucs-Willcocks, *Sibiu-Hermannstadt*, 136.

[36] Cicanci, *Companiile greceşti*, 145-55.

[37] Otto Fritz Jickeli, „Der Handel der Siebenbürger Sachsen in seiner geschichtlichen Entwicklung," *Archiv des Vereins für siebenbürgische Landeskunde* 39 (1913): 88, quoting the work of Alexis von Bethlen, "Grundlinien zur Kulturgeschichte Siebenbürgens," *Blätter für Geist, Gemüth und Vaterlandskunde* II (1839): 246.

tained, albeit limited, privileges for trading and living in Transylvania. During this time, a divide between "settled" (i.e. tax-paying) and non-settled Greeks came about.[38] The most significant privilege obtained by Transylvanian Greeks was the grant by Prince George Rákóczi I, whereby they could administer justice between local and foreign Greeks, collect the annual tax and have limited freedom to sell oriental goods.[39]

In 1627, Jews obtained the right to settle in the princely capital Alba Iulia provided that they supplied plenty oriental goods from Constantinopol.[40] Armenians received the official grant to settle into Transylvania in 1672. Obviously, oriental trade was not carried out exclusively by Greeks and Greek speaking Vlachs or Romanians, while we can assert that they were the most visible actors in this trade.

The population of Greeks in Transylvania in the seventeenth century was still quite mobile:[41] visiting homes and families, undertaking business trips or fleeing uncomfortable situations in Transylvania were strong reasons for the mobility of Greeks and other Balkan merchants.

The frictions between the settled and non-settled Greeks in Transylvania reveal how dynamic their diaspora was and how the communities were constantly replenished with new members. Late seventeenth century data from the account books of Siguli Stratu show how a Greek trading house operated: based in Sibiu, the merchant had family members acting as his agents at fairs and in other trading centers, buying and selling, borrowing and settling debts, exchanging money.[42] Armenian long-distance trade relied on similar family based networks.[43]

The studies of Márta Búr have shown the situation of the Greeks in Hungary, where the first official associations were founded in Tokaj, Gyöngyös and Miskolc and so

---

[38] In a grant to the settled Greeks in 1627, Prince Gabriel Bethlen names them "my faithful subjects of the Greek nation." M. Pakucs-Willcocks, "Negustori din Imperiul otoman în comerţul Sibiului, 1614-1623" [Merchants from the Ottoman Empire in the Trade of Sibiu, 1614-1623], *Studii si materiale de istorie medie* XXX (2012): 193.

[39] The text was published by T. Bodogae, "Le privilège commercial accordé en 1636 par G. Rákócz aux marchands grecs de Sibiu," *Revue Roumaine d'Histoire* XI, 4 (1972): 651-653, with minor typos. A critical edition of a copy of the charter, as recorded in the protocols of the Greek Company in Sibiu at Despoina-Eirini Tsourka-Papastathi, *I Elliniki emporiki kompania tou sympiou Transylvanias 1636-1848* [The Greek Trading Company in Transylvania 1636-1848] (Thessaloniki: Institute for Balkan Studies, 1994), 375-378. A digitized version of the copy in the princely protocols, *Librii regii*, available on the DVD *Az erdélyi fejedelmek oklevelei. Erdélyi Királyi Könyvek* [The Transylvanian Princes Charters. Transylvanian Royal Books] (Budapest: Arcanum, 2004).

[40] *Monumenta comitialia regni Transilvaniae*, ed. Sándor Szilágyi, VIII (Budapest: 1882), 143-5.

[41] For mobility in early modern Europe excellent studies by Leo Lucassen, "Towards a Comparative History of Migration and Membership in Southeast Europe (1500-1900)," *Ethnologia Balkanica* 13 (2009): 20-21, 31.

[42] *Catalogul documentelor referitoare la viaţa economică a ţărilor române în sec. XVII-XIX. Documente din arhivele statului Sibiu* [The Catalogue of Documents Concerning the Economy of the Romanian Principalities in the Seventeenth-Nineteenth Centuries. Documents from the Sibiu County Archives], vol. I, ed. D. Limona (Bucureşti: 1966), 19-29.

[43] Michel Aghassian and Kéram Kévonian, "The Armenian merchant network: overall autonomy and local integration," in *Merchants, Companies and Trade: Europa and Asia in the Early Modern Era*, ed. Sushil Chaudhury and Michel Morineau (Cambridge: Cambridge University Press, Paris: Maison des Sciences de l'Homme, 1999), 82-83.

on in the second half of the seventeenth century. Local authorities, similarly to Transylvania, had assigned Hungarian Greeks the role of providers of Ottoman products, but Búr noticed that they chose to settle in market towns where they could have good access to natural products and livestock. Greeks buying and selling grains, cattle and sheep organised themselves in these trading companies to protect themselves and their business, whereas Greeks dealing in Turkish goods remained individual traders with no guild-like bonds between them. Greeks in Hungary, at least in the early stages of their settlement, also constantly returned to their hometowns in the Balkans.[44]

Vassiliki Seirinidou argued that there were two of the Greek diaspora in Central Europe, an early one in the sixteenth-seventeenth centuries, carrying out retail trade in Turkish products but also keeping shops and monopolising retail distribution of local goods in towns and villages. The second diaspora was formed around the middle of the eighteenth century, doing wholesale trade between the Ottoman and Habsburg Empires. She further argued that while the second diaspora was born out of the first one, it had a different status, outlined in the peace treaties of Karlowitz (Sremski Karlovci, 1699) and Passarowitz (Požarevac, 1718).[45] I agree with Seirinidou that the statute of the Greek merchants changed drastically after the Ottomans lost their authority over Hungary and Transylvania, but I cannot second her opinion that the second diasporas was formed by new merchants, who had to have the capital to undertake the wholesale trade. The Greeks and the other merchants, subjects of the Ottoman sultans, were very diverse in their origin, financial capability, interests and status. What is the most drastic change that the eighteenth century brings is the fact that most Greeks stop being "nomadic," settling with their families in the countries where they conducted their business. In a privilege granted to the Sibiu trading company by Empress Maria Theresia in 1741, this was one prerequisite for the membership.[46] Also, when the Greek merchant Pater Janos obtained his nobility title, he was requested that he bring his wife and children into Transylvania.[47]

Understanding the mechanisms that underlie the creation of a Greek diaspora in early modern Central Europe needs to take into account a variety of factors. In the sixteenth and seventeenth centuries, the migration of the Greek merchants was still marked by a constant return to their homeland: the absence of the close family and the reliance of the extended male kinship for conducting business is, in my opinion, a better indicator of the status of the Greeks. While some of them acquired either a membership of a trading company or paid their share of the common tax, until the eighteenth century when the ex-

---

[44] Márta Búr, "Handelsgesellschaften-organisationen der Kaufleute der Balkanländer in Ungarn im 17.-18. Jh," *Balkan Studies* 25, 2 (1984): 289-291.

[45] Vassiliki Seirinidou,"Grocers and wholesalers. Ottomans and Habsburgs, foreigners and 'our own': the Greek trade diasporas in Central Europe, seventeenth to nineteenth centuries," in *Merchants in the Ottoman Empire*, 81-95.

[46] Cicanci, *Companiile grecești*, 83.

[47] Lidia Demény, "Le régime des douanes et des commerçants grecs en Transylvanie au cours de la période de la principauté autonome (1541-1691)," *Makedonika* (1975): 105.

tended privileges were granted by the Habsburg authorities, they could be considered part of the "migratory labour"[48] force. They had a highly-specialized profession, which relied on decades of shared experience, knowledge about the target markets, capitals and so on. In Transylvania, the Greeks, Jews and Armenians were assigned specific tasks: their role was to provide goods from the Ottoman Empire. This is not an uncommon feature of the institutional organization of foreign trade: Sheilagh Ogilvie has noted that "a ruler [...] granted it [a merchant guild] an exclusive privilege for its members to trade in particular wares, transaction types, routes or destinations."[49]

Apart from paying taxes and the services agreed upon with the Transylvanian Prince (such as postal services), these foreign merchants were put to good use by central authorities, more often than not to the traders' detriment. For instance, in 1670 Greek and Armenian traders were obliged by the Diet to exchange two thirds of the copper and other small coins collected as tax for good coins.[50]

Of the several types of Balkan merchants categorised by Traian Stoianovich, the Greeks coming to Transylvania were "Greek, Vlach and Macedo-Slav muleteer and forwarding agent of Epirus, Thessaly and Macedonia."[51] The customs registers of Sibiu also show this geographic area as the origin of many oriental trade merchants. Recent research has revealed the strong business connections that bonded merchants across the Balkan Peninsula and Central Europe.[52]

In this paper I have not mentioned the traffic of Western goods into the Ottoman Empire, which was naturally part of the commercial exchanges. The style of the primary sources utilized here, the customs journals of Sibiu, favour exclusively the trade with oriental products. This commerce made the fortune of the Greek and other Balkan-Levantine merchants, becoming their trademark and offering them a specific role in the Central European societies where they eventually settled.

---

48 According to the typology suggested by Lucassen, "Towards a Comparative History," 17.

49 Sheilagh Ogilvie, *Institutions and European Trade. Merchant guilds, 1000-1800* (Cambridge: Cambridge University Press, 2011), 162.

50 *Monumenta Comitialia* XV (Budapest: 1892), 149.

51 Traian Stoianovich, "The Conquering Balkan Orthodox Merchant," *Journal of Economic History* XX, 3 (1960): 234.

52 Cristian Luca, "Greek and Aromanian merchants, protagonists of the trade relations between Transylvania, Wallachia, Moldavia, and the Northern Italian Peninsula," *Transylvanian Review* XIX, suppl. 5 (2010), *Recent Studies on Past and Present. IV. Tradition and Invention*: 313-36.

Eighteenth Century Central Europe in Transcontinental Trade: The Trading Company of Molla Mustafa and the Viennese *Conscription* of 1767

David Do Paço

From December 1766, the Board of Trade of the Austrian *Hofkammer* implemented the *Conscription deren allhier in Wien sich befindenden Türken und türkischen Unterthanen*, gathering the legal statements of 268 Ottoman merchants living in Vienna during the first half of 1767.[1] Molla Mustafa is one of them.

> Molla Mustafa *wohnhaft im Kohlmasserischen Haus und dem Salzgries, 26. Jahr alt; zu Alaja in Asien gebürtig, ledigen Stands, derzeit zu Constantinopel ansässig.*
>
> *Sagt: Er seÿe von 3½ Jahren zum erst-und leztenmal beÿ der Semliner Gräniz in die Kaiserl: Konigl: Erbland herein gekommen, und habe damalen auch eine* Contumaefoede *samt behörigen Paßbrief mitgebracht; es wäre ihm aber nicht mehr wissend, ob er selbst solche noch zu Haus, oder aber der dama-len mit ihme hieher gekommen Hagi Ahmed mitgenommen hätte. Wehrend diese Zeit habe er sich beständig hier ausgehalten, künftigen Montag aber denke er wie-derum in die Türkey nach Macedonien zurük zu reise. Er hätte zwar in ihr Leo-poldstadt beÿ der goldenen Kron ein Baumwoll-Niederlag gehabt, nunmehro aber kein. Er habe auch 4. Handlungs* Compagnons, *wovon einer zu Constantinopel Namens* Hagi Ibrahim Aga*; einer zu* Alaja *Namens* Hagi Ahmed*; einer* Mehmed Aga*; und einer zu* Mehadia *mit Namen Molla Hassan, befindlich seÿe, welch lez-terer auch anstatt seiner demnächstens hieher kommen werde. In den Kaiser: Königl: Erblanden handle er mit Baumwoll, und führe entgegen in die Türkeÿ Kaiserl: Königl:* Specie *Thaller.*[2]

The *Conscription* is very well-known among historians of Ottoman merchants in Early Modern Central Europe but has been considered as a meta-source, i.e. a kind of catalogue offering instances with which to write a history of a national colony or, nowadays, of an ethnoreligious trading Diaspora.[3] According to the four parts of the document,

---

[1] Österreichische Staatsarchiv (henceforth abbreviated ÖStA), Haus-, Hof- und Staatsarchiv (henceforth abbreviated HHStA), Finanz- und Kommerz, Neue Hofkammer (henceforth abbreviated NHK), Kommerz Ober- und Niederösterreich (henceforth abbreviated KONÖ), 130, fol. 227-309 (henceforth abbreviated *Conscription*) and its copy: ÖStA, HHStA, Staatenabteilung, Türkei IV, 27. A partial edition: Polychrones K. Enepekides, *Griechische handelsgesellschaften und kaufleute in Wien aus dem jahre 1766: (ein konskriptionsbuch) Aus den Beständen des Wiener Haus-, Hof-, und Staatsarchivs* (Thessalonica: Hetaireia Makedonikōn Spoudōn, 1959).

[2] *Conscription*, p. 7-9.

[3] Olga Katsiardi-Hering, "Greek Merchant Colonies in Central and South-Eastern Europe in the Eighteenth and Early Nineteenth Centuries," in *Merchant Colonies in the Early Modern Period*, ed. Victor N. Zakharov, Gelina Harlaftis and Olga Katsiardi-Hering (London: Pickering & Chatto Publishers, 2012), 127-139; Ina Badgdiantz McCabe, Gelina Harlaftis and Ioanna Pepelasis Minoglou, *Diaspora Entrepreunarial Networks. Fore Centuries of History* (New York, Oxford: Berg, 2005); Vassiliki Seirinidou, "The "Old" Diaspora, the "New" Diaspora, and the Greek Diaspora in the Eighteenth through Nineteenth Centuries Vienna," in *Homelands and Diasporas. Greeks, Jews and Their Migrations*, ed. Minna Rozen (London, New York: Tauris, 2008), 155-159; Francesca Trivellato, *The Familiarity of Strangers. The Sephardic Diaspora, Livorno and Cross-Cultural Trade in the Early Modern Period* (New Haven: Yale University Press, 2009). On the use of the concept of "trading Diaspora" Guillaume Calafat and Sonia Goldblum, "Diaspora(s) : liens, historicité,

Ottoman history in Austria is divided into Greek, Sephardic, Armenian or Muslim strands.[4] Studying the specific case of only one merchant is a way to achieve distance from the Austrian administrative patterns which organized the *Conscription*, and from the premises of Diasporas studies which prevent us from apprehending the whole document. Naturally, choosing a Muslim merchant is no innocent choice. If it contributes to the new history of Muslims in early modern Europe, it also revaluates the importance of Muslim merchants as well as writing a global Ottoman history of trade in Central Europe.[5] The practices of Molla Mustafa and of the members of his trading company will be compared to other Ottoman subjects running their business in Vienna at the same time, whatever their nation or religion.

The case study starts by considering a legal fact: if Greeks, Turkish Jews, Armenians or Muslims from the Ottoman Empire were allowed to trade in Austria, it is only because they were subjects of the Sultan in Istanbul. Of course, "the world is under no obligation to correspond to the categories by which it is thought," meaning that a legal status, or any other political or cultural identity, does not necessarily involve specific trading practices and that there is no reason to maintain the division of the economic history of Ottoman merchants into ethno-religious groups. At least, the perspectives of global history tempt us to consider the local integration of a merchant abroad and the relevance of this process for the urban history of Vienna.

Legal dialog and the identification of Ottoman merchants

Molla Mustafa's legal statement contributes to a dialogue that developed between Ottoman merchants and the Austrian administration since the late seventeenth century, beginning in the 1680s when Emperor Leopold I invited Christian merchants from Turkey to maintain their trade within Austria in spite of the war.[6] In 1699, the Treaty of Karlowitz (Sremski Karlovci) put them legally under his protection, but they were the only such merchants officially allowed in Imperial lands. The treaties of Passarowitz (Požarevac) and

échelles," *Tracés. Revue de sciences humaines* 23 (2012): 7-18; Stéphane Dufoix, *La dispersion : une histoire des usages du mot diaspora* (Paris: Éditions Amsterdam, 2011) and Robin Cohen, *Global Diasporas: An Introduction* (Seattle: Routledge, 1997).

4 David Do Paço, "Identité politique et grand commerce des marchands ottomans à Vienne, 1739-1792," *Mélanges de l'École Française de Rome – Histoire Moderne* (at press) and "Invisibles dans la banalité et le mépris. Les Musulmans à Vienne des années 1660 à la fin du XVIIIe siècle," in *Les Musulmans en Europe occidentale au Moyen-Âge et à l'époque moderne*, vol. 1. *Une intégration invisible*, ed. Jocelyne Dakhlia and Bernard Vincent (Paris: Albin Michel, 2011), 56-80; Vassiliki Seirinidou, "Griechen in Wien im 18. Jahrhundert. Soziale Identitäten im Alltag," *Das achtzehnte Jahrhundert und Öesterreich. Jahrbuch der österreichischen Gesellschaft zur Erforschung des achtzehnten Jahrhunderts* 12 (1997): 7-18; Karl Teply, "Die erste armenische Kolonie in Wien," *Wiener Geschichtsblätter* 28 (1973): 105-118; Natan M. Gelber, "The Sephardic Community in Vienna," *Jewish Social Studies* 10 4 (1948): 359-396.

5 *Les musulmans dans l'histoire de l'Europe*, vol. 2. *Passages et contacts en Méditerranée*, ed. Jocelyne Dakhlia and Wolfgang Kaiser (Paris: Albin Michel, 2013) and *Les Musulmans en Europe occidentale*, vol. 1. See also Markus Friedrich, "Türken im Alten Reich. Zur Aufnahme und Konversion von Muslimen im deutschen Sprachraum (16.-18. Jahrhundert)," *Historische Zeitschrift* 294, 2 (2012): 329-360.

6 Karl Teply, *Die Einführung des Kaffees in Wien: Georg Frank Koltschitzky, Johannes Diodato, Isaak de Luca* (Vienna: Verein für Geschichte der Stadt Wien, 1980).

Belgrade, in 1718 and 1739, enlarged this freedom of trade to all Ottoman merchants. However, in 1748, Maria Theresa unilaterally decided to make a legal distinction between Catholic and "a-Catholic" Ottoman merchants.[7] The first were permitted trade wholesale as well as retail all year long, while the second were allowed to trade wholesale all the time but retail only at fairs. In consequence, during the 1750s and 1760s, the Board of Trade was swamped with petitions from Ottoman merchants protesting against these measures and finally begging for dispensations and privileges to trade as and when they wished.[8]

The *Hofkammer*'s decision in 1766 to take a census of the Turkish subjects in Vienna falls within a wider plan to estimate the importance of Ottoman trade, to shape it and to reorganise it administratively. It is also very significant evidence of the dialogue between Ottoman merchants and the Austrian administration. While Molla Mustafa was interviewed on 1st January 1767, the *Conscription* is based in all on eleven enquiries from January to June. The interviews present no visible religious, ethnic or national logic. They seem to have been conducted in the street or in specific trading spaces such as the Hoher Markt in the old city, in the semi-private courts where merchants rented warehouses or shops, near the Fleischmarkt or the Danubian docks of the Leopoldstadt. Moreover, the *Conscription* does not respect the chronology of the interviews but goes back over them. It reshapes the group and equips the Board of Trade with a tool to manage Ottoman trade in the Imperial Residence.

Indeed, all data in the *Conscription* have been chosen to be useful to the administration. The questioning preceding the legal statements is made up of a set list of fifty questions, in three categories. The first relates to police matters (private address in Vienna, age, place of birth, place of installation, matrimonial status...). The second concerns evidence that the merchant is a subject of the Ottoman Empire (proof of payment of the capitation, health attestation from the lazaretto at the border, passport...). Last but not least, the main part of the data is related to professional activity (when the merchant came to the Empire first and most recently, the nature of the goods, trading methods and capital...). Each statement is thus composed of two parts. A brief description of the merchant precedes a declaration rewritten in free indirect discourse.[9]

Such administrative reshaping of the Ottoman community makes the *Conscription* unsuitable as material for studying a merchant's private identity, but not for the process of his identification. The words of the merchant disappear so completely under the formatting of the document that all the legal statements are entirely similar. Thus the *Con-*

---

[7] Snežka K. Panova, "Zum Handel der Länder Südeuropas mit dem Übrigen Europa im 17. und 18. Jahrhundert," in *Das Osmanische Reich und Europa 1683 bis 1789: Konflikt, Entspannung und Austausch*, ed. Gernot Heiss and Grete Klingenstein (Munich: Oldenbourg, 1983), 153-166.

[8] David Do Paço, "Institutionnaliser la coexistence religieuse ? Turcs et sujets turcs de Vienne dans la seconde moitié du XVIIIe siècle," in *Des religions dans la ville. Ressorts et stratégies de coexistence dans l'Europe des XVIe-XVIIIe siècle*, ed. David Do Paço, Mathilde Monge and Laurent Tatarenko (Rennes: Presses Universitaires de Rennes, 2010), 141-161.

[9] Ibid.

scription is important proof of the Imperial administration's early use of statistics in trade management.[10] In fact the petitions that the Ottoman merchants sent to the administration do not help to access to their words. The bulk of the materials retained in the *Hofkammer* archives are final decisions of the Board of Trade, in which merchants' claims are merely reported.[11] Original letters are enclosed only in some few cases.

Nevertheless, most petitions were written in fluent German, which can be explained by the merchants' familiarity with the Austrian state and the length of time they spent settled there. When not written in German, petitions were sent in Greek or Armenian and immediately translated by interpreters of the Board at the borders of Semlin, Mehadia or Agram, or perhaps in Vienna.[12] Some were involved in the Ottoman trade. It should be noted that the Muslim merchants used to write petitions in Italian or in a kind of *lingua franca* close to Italian, the language of maritime commercial law in the Mediterranean.[13] The fact that all statements reported in the *Conscription* are in German – unlike the petitions – is simply further proof that the document is a source (as well as an obstacle) for understanding the socio-economic condition of Ottomans in Vienna.

The identification of merchants

Molla Mustafa is singled out from the *Conscription* only because he is a Muslim. However, according to Maria Theresa, no legal distinction can be made except between Catholics and non-Catholics. Molla Mustafa and other Muslim merchants enjoy the same commercial rights as the Greeks and the Turkish Jews. The difference between religious, legal and social identities must be developed.

An Ottoman...

Born in Alaja on the South coast of Anatolia, Molla Mustafa came from one of the three Ottoman areas represented in Vienna (Fig. 1). Mainly Muslim and secondly Armenian, the merchants were from Anatolia and the Muslims particularly from the port of Alaja. Some had settled in Istanbul and the rest remained citizens of their birth-city. They traded in a company, and seem to have been organized in open Diasporas which sometimes included merchants from other religions. In Istanbul they sold cotton and Mediterranean merchandise landed in Alaja, and then invested the proceeds in Macedonian cotton supplied to the Viennese textile manufacturies. Like some Armenians, Molla Mustafa handled a transcontinental trade. Nevertheless, most Ottomans trading in Vienna were Greeks from the Balkans, in particularly from such hubs of the Pindus as Kastoriá, Siátitsa or Voscopoli. They contributed to the economic integration of European Turkey into Central Europe.

---

[10] Christine Lebeau, *Aristocrates et grands commis à la Cour de Vienne, 1748-1791 : le modèle français* (Paris: CNRS éditions, 1996).

[11] KONÖ, 130-131 et ÖStA, NHK, Kommerz Litorale Akte (henceforth abbreviated KLA), 1035-1047.

[12] David Do Paço, "Vienne, place politique orientale de l'Europe du XVIIIe siècle," *Austriaca, Cahiers universitaires d'information sur l'Autriche* 74 (2013): 59-78.

[13] Jocelyne Dakhlia, *Lingua Franca. Histoire d'une langue métisse en Méditerranée* (Arles: Actes Sud, 2008).

Greek and Muslim companies are wholly similar.[14] Divided into three groups, they offer the same forms of organisation. The first group is composed from associates from one locality; most are equal even if sometimes one may be called the *Prinzipal*. They do not necessary belong to the same family, even if this is often the case since trust is essential in such far-flung trade.[15] Merchants from the hinterland of the city where the company is based compose a second group of associates. The family and local base explain why these companies usually present significant religious homogeneity, rather than ethnic patterns. The last group brings together merchants potentially from all over the Ottoman Empire since they have the skills to manage trade in a very specific place.

However, Greek companies are sometimes the go-betweens for Muslim traders, used to develop internal Ottoman trade. Indeed, if the case of Molla Mustafa's company is significant compared with the great Ottoman companies, it has a very specific place in Muslim trade. Muslim traders essentially connected Istanbul to Anatolia, Syria and Egypt, while Greek and also a few Sephardic companies enjoy a quasi-monopoly in European Turkey. Hence, there are more similarities between transcontinental companies than between companies sharing the same religion.

... Muslim ...

Under the terms of the *Conscription*, a second group must be closely considered as an administrative creation. "Nations and religions" enable the Board of Trade to distinguish and preserve particular privileges related to religious practice. It is a late but very basic confessionalisation.[16]

Legally, Islam cannot be professed or observed in the Habsburg Monarchy. But the *Conscription* records that a certain Imam Emir Ahmet Effendi had frequented the Imperial and Royal lands since 1752 and did not leave after 1759 until, in 1767, he declared that he was settled in Belgrade.[17] That legal trick allows him to spend time and to trade in the Monarchy easily. Such ordinary practise is corroborated by recent studies on Islam in early modern Europe. Moreover, in 1786 Peter Herbert, Imperial ambassador in Turkey, presented a project to accept *de jure* what was tolerated *de facto*: legal status for Muslims in the Imperial and royal lands.[18]

---

[14] Ioanna Pepelasis Minoglou, "Toward a Typology of Greek-diaspora Entrepreneurship," in Baghdiantz McCabe, Harlaftis and Minoglou, *Diaspora*, 173-189.

[15] Trivellato, *The Familiarity of Strangers*, and Guillaume Calafat, "Familles, réseaux et confiance dans l'économie de l'époque moderne. Diasporas marchandes et commerce interculturel," *Annales. Histoires, Sciences sociale* 66 (2011): 513-531.

[16] Willibald Plöchl, *Die Wiener orthodoxen Griechen. Eine Studie zur Rechts- und Kulturgeschichte der Kirchengemeinden zum hl. Georg und zur hl. Dreifaltigkeit und zur Errichtung der Metropolis von Austria* (Vienna: Verlag des Verbandes der Wissenschaftlichen Gesellschaften Österreichs, 1983).

[17] *Conscription*, p. 6-7.

[18] Peter Herbert to Philipp Cobenzl, from Bujucdéré the 16th June 1786 in Türkei V, 19, fol. 784r-786r.

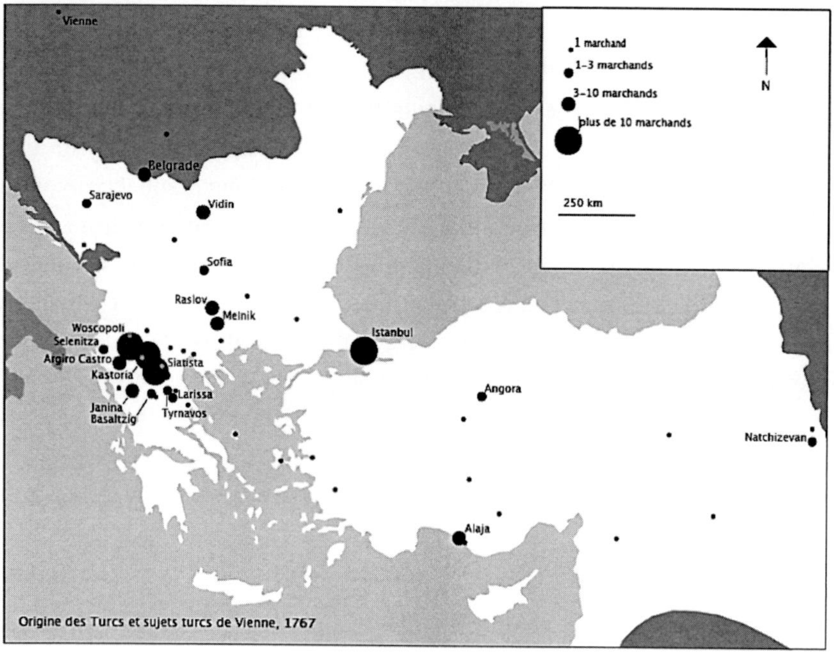

Fig. 1

In 1767, Greeks already enjoyed some privileges related to their religion, primarily because they were subjects of the Sultan.[19] In 1723, Charles VI allowed them to settle in the little Steyrerhof, between the Fleischmarkt and the Rotenturmstrasse. Unlike the Emperor's Orthodox subjects, they also had use of the little Chapel of Saint George where they could pray in privacy. In 1776 the chapel became a church and official toleration was established; confessionalisation of the group had been achieved. Moreover, from 1778 Turkish Jews enjoyed the same privilege, since Maria Theresa allowed them to build a Sephardic synagogue, while it remained illegal for Imperial Jews to pray in the city.[20] Both Greek and Jewish Ottomans in Vienna formed one of the test beds of Joseph II's global toleration.

Hence, the four national groups formally recognised in the *Conscription* were, in the final analysis, the result of religious claims from Ottoman merchants as well as of the administrative desire to differentiate legal and political categories within a religious

[19] Snežka K. Panova, "Zu Fragen über die Rolle Österreich-Ungarns im wirtschaftlichen Prozeß der Heranreifens der Balkanvölker (17.-18. Jahrhundert)," in *Österreich im Europa der Aufklärung. Kontinuität und Zäsur in Europa zur Zeit Maria Theresias un Josephs II*, ed. Richard Georg Plaschka and Grete Klingenstein (Vienna: Österreichischen Akademie der Wissenschaften, 1985), 167-172; Seirinidou, "Griechen in Wien" and Plöchl, *Die Wiener orthodoxen Griechen.*
[20] Gelber, "The Sephardic Community."

group. According to the Imperial administration, this was totally unrelated to trading issues except for encouraging Ottoman merchants to move to Vienna. Thus developments in the legal status of the Muslim Ottomans in Vienna simply complied with the Greek and Turkish Jew experiences.

...Merchant

Molla Mustafa was an Ottoman and he was a Muslim too. He also had a third social identity: he was a merchant. Twenty-six years old, although still young, he was no longer at the beginning of its career. According to his statement, he came to the Monarchy for the first time in 1762, when he was 22 – approximately the average age at which an apprentice could be in charge and associated, for the first time, to an official company. Previously, he may have spent a long time in apprenticeship. By 1767, some Ottoman merchants had been trading in Vienna for a very long time; Emir Ibrahim Pasha first came to Vienna as a seven-year-old boy.[21] Nevertheless, Vienna seems to have been reserved for experienced apprentices and merchants who had earned their spurs.

The presence of apprentices is very difficult to detect in the *Conscription* since they were not legally in charge and did not interest the Board of Trade. Noting them would be superfluous, and it is only possible to detect their presence from the merchants' statements. Alongside the associates and apprentices, we should also note the presence of factors, who unlike apprentices were in charge but who were not associated, meaning that they were paid for faring but took no share of the revenue even if a part of the legal authority of the merchant they represented was vested in them. Molla Hassan, settled in Mehadia at the Austro-Ottoman border, was factor for Molla Mustafa's company,[22] regularly delivering cotton to Molla Mustafa and also handling the transport of merchandise between Macedonia and Vienna too.

Further, not all Ottoman subjects in Vienna were merchants, or not only. The imam Emir Ahmet Effendi has already been mentioned. Among the Muslims, we may mention some soldiers, janissaries for the most part, who were merchants as well. Considering the Ottoman groups as a whole, we discern an Ottoman *micropolis*. The *Conscription* is dotted with barbers, dressmakers, interpreters, cooks or coffeemakers. Taken together, they attest to the permanence and the longevity of the Ottoman presence in Vienna and the different social scales of Viennese cosmopolitanism. Last but not least, analysis of the *Conscription* reveals the great social importance of the family. Almost 78 wives, 147 children and 5 other parents had followed merchants to Vienna by 1767, and overall there were more children than merchants. As an unmarried man, Molla Mustafa was in the minority among Muslims.

The *Conscription* represents an administrative vanishing point that turns our eyes away from the complexity of the group. Ottomans are painted in shades of grey according

---

[21] *Conscription*, p. 10-13.
[22] Ibid., p. 8.

to their legal importance and their utility to the Board of Trade. A number of them remain in the darkness.

The scales of trade

The *Conscription* conceals, the *Conscription* reveals. In fact such a document constitutes a major source for a spatial analysis, enabling researchers to position Vienna within the Ottoman trade as well as to position Ottomans within Viennese economic and social urban areas, offering new outlooks on the Viennese urban history.

The Viennese situation within the Ottoman trade

Studying mercantilism defines the Viennese market in the framework of the Holy Roman Empire.[23]

Firstly, Molla Mustafa used Vienna as a warehouse. He received the cotton that Molla Hassan sent him from Macedonia through the border at Mehadia and sold it exclusively to Austrian State manufactories, some of which were privileges granted to Ottoman merchants.[24] This is characteristic of all Ottoman companies, whatever the religion of the merchants or their geographic origin. Textiles such as cotton, red yarn or camel yarn were the most traded, but some very specific foodstuffs are also notable, such as sugar, coffee or dried fruits. The oldest function of foreign trade was to supply the city, while the trade of the Vienna merchants was protected by the ban on foreigners selling retail. In the sixteenth century, Ferdinand I invited the so-called *Niederläger* from Innsbruck to set up in Vienna, foreigners exempt from security deposit. During the seventeenth century, supported by the Habsburgs, they became more and more numerous and challenged the monopoly of the Vienna merchants. The treaties of Passarowitz and Belgrade treated Ottoman merchants as *Niederläger*, except the Armenians, until 1774 and the patent of Maria Theresa that created a new legal category: the "Oriental merchant."[25]

Vienna is a warehousing point but not a terminus for trade. Though Molla Mustafa declared that he had never left Vienna after 1762, 30% of Ottoman companies carried on their trade to several places in the Austrian monarchy or the Holy Roman Empire. Leipzig must be mentioned especially, and Brno, Prague, Breslau (Wrocław), Nuremberg, Graz, Trieste, Hamburg and even Amsterdam are also named in the Ottoman statements. The Ottoman Merchants were based in Vienna and left the city for a couple of months during the fairs. Bohemian studies show that some merchants went to the very famous glass manufactories to buy and export Bohemian confections. To enable as well as to control this trade, warehouses of Bohemian glass were opened in the Leopoldstadt

---

[23] Guillaume Garner, *État, économie, territoire en Allemagne. L'espace dans le caméralisme et l'économie politique, 1740-1820* (Paris: éditions ÉHÉSS, 2005).

[24] Olga Katsiardi-Hering, "The Allure of red Cotton Yarn, and how it came to Vienna: Associations of Greek Artisans and Merchants operating between the Ottoman and Habsburg Empires," in *Merchants in the Ottoman Empire*, ed. Suraiya Faroqhi and Gilles Veinstein (Paris: Peeters, 2008), 97-131.

[25] Ignaz De Luca, *Wiens gegenwärtiger Zustand und Josephs Regierung* (Vienna: Verlag Georg Philipp Wucherer, 1787), 101, 166, 218, 380 and 446.

for Ottoman merchants.[26] This activity differed from Ottoman trade at the border or in the cities they crossed to return to Vienna, such as Pest or Bratislava.

There is no evidence that Molla Mustafa pursued any second activity in Vienna, and all that he exported to Turkey were some thalers. It is nowadays well known that the Oriental trade was a real problem for the Austrian mercantilist model, which was based on the export of locally manufactured goods. The capital flight was so significant that the Maria Theresa thaler remains a very important currency in the Eastern Mediterranean until the late nineteenth century.[27] A process of capital market integration is to be supposed between Central European and Ottoman market places.[28] To be viable, the Austrian State had to earn more money exporting goods made from its own raw materials than it lost to Ottoman capital flight. In 1766, Count Rudolph Chotek, President of the *Hofkammer*, testified that Oriental trade was profitable despite capital flight and counterfeiting.[29]

Ottoman settlement in the city

Currently, it is conventional to talk of a Greek "quarter" in Vienna in the neighbourhood of the chapel of Saint George. If we consider that there is no reason to make distinctions within the Ottoman trading group, and that religion and geographical origins are not effective terms for an economic or even a social analysis of Ottoman presence in Vienna, this convention must be tested.

The Ottoman statements of 1767 distinguish between places for trade and private places, and Molla Mustafa's statement is actually very simple in this regard. Mustafa lived in Salzgries, a street close to the Hoher Markt, and traded on the opposite side of the Donaukanal in the suburbs of the Leopoldstadt. Some other Ottomans also lived and/or traded in the surroundings of the Steyrerhof and on the Fleischmarkt, actually a street and its related courtyards. Each of these places is associated with a specific period of Vienna's urban development.[30] The Hoher Markt is the oldest mediaeval square, where the city hall stands. The Fleischmarkt is the heart of the first mediaeval suburb that arose after foreign merchants were invited to trade in the city, the classical cosmopolitan space in Vienna, integrated into the town during the thirteenth century. Lastly the Leopoldstadt, in

---

[26] "Es wird dem *Publico* bekannt gemacht, daß auf ein von Ihro Kaiserl. Königl. Majestät der nacher Orient mit Böhmischen Glaß-Waaren Handlung triebenden *Compagnie* allergnädigst ertheiltes *Privilegium* alhier in der Kaiserl. Königl. Residenz-stadt Wien eine offene Niederlag in der Leopold-stadt in dem Schindelbergischen Haus nahe bey dem Wirt-haus zum goldenen Hirschen auf gerichtet worden, worinnen man Böhmische Gläser von allerhand Gattungen, feine, geschlissene, vergoldete, wie auch Hang-leuchter, Flaschenkeller, und dergleichen bekommen kann, jedoch wird aus dieser Niederlag nichts *alla minuta*, sondern nur al *ingrosso* verkauffet." *Wienerisches Diarium* of the 5th and 8th July 1752.

[27] Snežka K. Panova, "Der Münzhandel zwischen Österreich und dem Osmanischen Reich (den Ländern Südosteuropas) im 18. Jahrhundert," *Mitteilungen des Österreichischen Staatsarchivs* 43 (1993): 317-341.

[28] David Chilosi and Oliver Volckart, "Money, states and Empire: Financial integration and institutional change in Central Europe, 1400-1520," *Journal of Economic History* 71, 3 (2011): 762-791.

[29] KLA, 1035, fol. 868v-869r.

[30] Peter Eigner, "Mechanismen urbaner Expension: am Beispiel der Wiener Stadtentwicklung, 1740-1938," in *Wien. Wirtschaftsgeschichte, 1740-1938*, vol. 2. *Dienst-leistungen*, ed. Günther Chaloupek, Peter Eigner and Michael Wagner (Vienna: Jugend und Volk, 1991), 625-756 and Elisabeth Lichtenberger, *Die Wiener Altstadt: von der mittelalterlichen Bürgerstadt zur City* (Vienna: Deuticke, 1977).

front of both the Hoher Markt and the Fleischmarkt, was the first and biggest suburb of Vienna, separated from the Innere Stadt by Danube canal but connected to it via the Schalgbruck. Fishing and trading port was set up on its bank.[31]

The trading activities of Ottoman merchants connected and embraced the three areas in a single network. Molla Mustafa received cotton on the docks of the Leopoldstadt port before putting it in his own warehouse, not far from the bank. Thereafter he sold it directly from the warehouse, or in the market of Saint Margaret – also in the Leopoldstadt – or even in the Hoher Markt where he lived, the site of the greatest Vienna yearly fairs. His coreligionist and fellow citizen from Alaja, Molla Hassan, also lived in a street off the Hoher Markt, Judengasse, i.e. the ancient ghetto, renting warehouses in the Leopoldstadt and one in the Rotenturmstrasse at a right angle to the Fleischmarkt. He kept his imported merchandise in his warehouse in the Leopoldstadt and used the warehouse in the Rotenstrumstrasse to store the "inländische Waaren" that he bought on the Hoher Markt for export.[32] Indeed, although the Greek merchants were more numerous than the other Ottomans near the Fleischmarkt, we can no longer consider this area as Greek, if only because Ottoman subjects lived there in the same buildings as Imperial merchants and shared their warehouses too.[33]

The *Conscription* and secondary documents make it possible to describe the Ottoman merchants' neighbourhood. According to the *Conscription*, Molla Mustafa lived in the same building as three other subjects of the Sultan, two Muslims and one Armenian.[34] However, in 1768 a report from the Municipality names gardens and buildings, especially in Salzgries, shared by Viennese citizens and foreigners.[35] The cases of Imperial and Ottoman Jews are mentioned particularly. Some places, such as Baron Wöber's building, are even more revealing. The *Conscription* and some previous reports mention Ottoman merchants renting rooms and warehouses in a house with Imperials, where Baron Wöber also lived. Moreover, the building housed an inn open to locals and foreigners and named *Zum Weißen Wolfen*.[36] According to the German traveller Johan Caspar von Riesbeck, such a place in Vienna was devoted to "die unmäßig grosse Anzahl der reich besoldeten Hofbedienten, der zahlreiche Adel, und die vielen Fremden".[37] Baron Wöber and the well-known Baron Penckler were among the administrators who protected the Ottoman merchants and contributed to the cosmopolitan Viennese surrounding.[38]

---

[31] *Im Reiche des Goldenen Apfels. Des türkischen Weltenbummlers Evliyâ Çelebi denkwürdige Reise in das Giaurenland und in die Stadt und Festung Wien, anno 1665*, trans. Richard F. Kreutel (Graz, Vienna, Cologne: Verlag Styria, 1987), 139.
[32] *Conscription*, p. 4-7.
[33] On the contrary to Seirinidou, "Griechen in Wien."
[34] *Conscription*, p. 2, 7, 9 and 72.
[35] Stadt- und Landesarchiv Wien, Bericht, No. 373/1768.
[36] KONÖ, fol. 225r-v; *Conscription*, p. 24, 27, 94, 96, 98, 104, 204, 225, 226.
[37] Johann Caspar Baron von Riesbeck, *Briefe eines reisenden Franzosen über Deutschland an seinen Bruder zu Paris* (1783), 269.
[38] Renate Zedinger, "Vom „Sprachknaben" zum Internuntius Freiherr Heinrich Christoph von Penckler (1700–1774) im diplomatischen Dienst an der Hohen Pforte," in *Kuppeln - Korn - Kanonen. Unerkannte und*

Toward a new urban history of Vienna

Studying the settlement of Ottomans in Vienna opens new historic perspectives. Until its historiographical turn a few years ago, the urban history of Vienna had remained compartmentalised.[39] Nowadays, we must question the separate histories of Court and city, of the history of the city and the history of its suburbs and, finally, of economic and social histories.

After 1526, Vienna was politically under Habsburg control and included in their estates. The *Hofkammer*, created in 1527, managed the city and its economic development was aligned with the development of the Monarchy.[40] The interests of the archduke prevailed over the interests of the municipality, which explains why the Ottoman merchants were so warmly welcomed by the Imperial administration. Their trade contributed to the economic growth of Austria and in the second half of the century, on the pretext of protecting Ottoman privileges, the *Hofkammer* chipped away at the rights of the Viennese municipality. Yet international trade must be considered as an economic lever for enlightened absolutism.

Further, the merchants' commercial activities delineated an integrated urban area crossing the walls of the old city and structured by the Donaukanal, an area not specific to the Ottomans but to merchants as such. Ottoman subjects merely used and reinforced the economic structures of the city, flowing through the arteries of the commercial heart of Vienna and attesting a high level of adaptation. It would be excessive to talk here about "transcultural trade." Socially, Ottoman merchants were just merchants, trading with others in a common commercial area. If we assume a social focus, the urban integration of the Ottoman merchants into Vienna becomes obvious and we may consider Ottomans only as members of what Italian historians call the *repubblica internazionale del denaro*.[41]

Last but not least, that integration was only possible thanks to the protection offered by Viennese administrators. In 1767, Barons Wöber and Penckler were long-standing members of the *Hofkriegsrat*, which between 1706 and 1747 handled both economic and political Turkish affairs. Baron Wöber's father was second in command after Prince Eugene of Savoy, and Baron Penckler served as interpreter and diplomat in its dealings with the Ottoman merchants in Vienna. In 1747, when commercial Turkish affairs were integrated into the global economic management of the *Hofkammer*, the social position of members of the *Hofkriegsrat* was strongly challenged. Wöber inherited his father's Otto-

---

unbekannte Spuren in Südosteuropa von der Aufklärung bis in die Gegenwart, ed. Ulrike Tischler-Hofer and Renate Zedinger (Innsbruck: Studienverlag, 2010), 215-242; David Do Paço, "Extranéité et lien social : l'intégration des marchands ottomans à Vienne au XVIIIe siècle," *Revue d'histoire moderne et contemporaine* (at press).

[39] Susanne Claudine Pils and Jan Paul Niederkorn, *Ein Zweigeteilter Ort? Hof und Stadt in der Frühen Neuzeit* (Innsbruck, Vienna: Studien Verlag, 2005).

[40] Andreas Weigl, "Die Bedeutung des Wiener Hofes für die städtische Ökonomie in der zweiten Hälfte des 17. Jahrhunderts," in Pils and Niederkorn, *Ein Zweigeteilter Ort?*, 55-80.

[41] Paolo Prodi, *Settimo non rubare. Furto e mercato nella storia dell'Occidente* (Bologna: Il Mulino, 2009), 169-201.

man clients and Penckler remained in charge, and safe in his career, thanks his ties to Ottoman merchants – and diplomats – whom he personally protected. In 1755, he took an oath of allegiance to Count Kaunitz in order to stay in office. Thus studying the Ottoman merchants reveals a social history of Vienna beyond the multitude of notaries.

Conclusion

The Viennese *Conscription* of 1767 allows historians to understand the integration of Central Europe into eighteenth-century transcontinental trade via the activities of Ottoman merchants. Travelling alone or gathered in a private trading company, they were present in great numbers in the Habsburg monarchy and challenged the privileges of the legal *bourgeoisie*, thanks to support from the Imperial administration. The settlement of Ottoman merchants in Vienna forced the *Hofkammer* to soften its policy and make significant legal concessions. Ottoman presence in the city benefitted the Emperor and the economic development of his lands. Last but not least, the legal identification of Ottoman merchants means that the papers of the *Hofkammer* are unsuitable for studying the so-called ethno-religious trading Diasporas. The Board of Trade produces the only identities singled out in the documentation, and these yield no reason to study the several religious groups from the Ottoman Empire one at a time. Quite the opposite, economically speaking them all took part together in the integration of Central Europe into transcontinental trade.

Die Landesbeschreibungen als Reformierungs-Instrument: Fürstentum Siebenbürgens im letzten Jahrzehnt Maria Theresia's

Daniel Dumitran

„[...] kein Land wesentlichere Verbesserungen bedürfe,
als das vor Alters noch unter denen Römern
so berühmte Fürstenthum Siebenbürgen."
Leopold von Clary-Aldringen[1]

Die Statistik, jene „neue Wissenschaft" – der es möglich ist, die unerlässlichen Daten in einem System zusammenzufassen und dieses in den Dienst der Regierung zu stellen –, hat im Laufe des 18. Jahrhunderts eine der treffendsten Formulierungen ihrer Charakteristika in dem deutschen Ausdruck „Staatenkunde" gefunden, wie im Jahre 1804 August Ludwig Schlözer bemerkt.[2] Etwa zwei Jahrzehnte später bezeichnete Karl August Malchus die Hauptaufgaben dieser Wissenschaft: die Darstellung der Fragen betreffend die Quellen der Staatsmacht, die Umstände, die die Entwicklung des Staates begünstigen oder behindern können, das Verhalten dazu und die möglichen Folgen für die Entwicklung des Staates selber, als auch der Untertanen, sowie betreffend die Verfassung und die Verwaltung.[3] Die Beiträge der Theoretiker des Kameralismus,[4] (die deutsche Variante des Merkantilismus), aus dem vorhergehenden Jahrhundert, Johann Heinrich Gottlob von Justi oder Joseph von Sonnenfels, waren sicher ausschlaggebend für das Zustandekommen dieser Auffassung. Die Haltung der Wiener Hofämter aus der Zeit des Theresianischen und Josephinischen Reformismus zeugt von einem solchen Einfluß. Die vorliegende Darstellung versucht auf die Frage zu antworten, ob dieser Einfluß auch für die östlichen Territorien des Habsburgerreiches, im besonderen für das Fürstentum Siebenbürgen, gilt.

Es hat in Siebenbürgen beachtenswerte Bemühungen zur Darstellung des Staates in moderner wissenschaftlicher Manier gegeben. Diese waren von den Ideen Schlözers beeinflußt, und ihre Autoren haben die Beiträge des vorherigen Jahrhunderts zu dieser Fragestellung kritisch bewertet. Es ist in erster Reihe die Rede von Lucas Joseph Marienburg (1770-1821), Rektor des Evangelischen Gymnasiums von Kronstadt, danach evangelischer Pfarrer von Rothbach (gehört heute zur Gemeinde Marienburg / Feldioara, Kreis Kronstadt), Weidenbach (Ghimbav) und Marienburg (Feldioara), Mitglied und

---

[1] Ileana Bozac, Teodor Pavel (Hg.), *Călătoria împăratului Iosif al II-lea în Transilvania la 1773/ Die Reise Kaiser Josephs II. durch Siebenbürgen im Jahre 1773* (im weiteren Bozac, Pavel (Hg.), *Die Reise*), Bd. I (Cluj-Napoca: Institutul Cultural Român. Centrul de Studii Transilvane, 2006), 331.

[2] In *Theorie der Statistik. Nebst Ideen über das Studium der Politik überhaupt*. Erstes Heft. Einleitung (Göttingen, 1804), 1-3.

[3] In *Statistik und Staatenkunde. Ein Beitrag zur Staatenkunde von Europa* (Stuttgart und Tübingen, 1826), 1.

[4] Dazu siehe Michel Foucault, *Securitate, teritoriu, populaţie. Cursuri ţinute la Collège de France (1977-1978)* [Sicherheit, Landschaft, Bevölkerung. Vorlesungen am Collège de France (1977-1978)] (Cluj: Idea Design & Print, 2009, für die rumänische Version), 23.

auswärtiger Assessor, von 1805 an, der Mineralogischen Gesell-schaft von Jena, der Stadt, wo er seine Hochschulstudien beendet hatte.[5] Sein Werk, *Geographie des Großfürstenthums Siebenbürgen* in zwei Bänden, im Jahr 1813 veröffent-licht, umfasst die Statistik oder allgemeine Geographie Siebenbürgens, beziehungsweise die Chorographie und Topographie Siebenbürgens, und die von ihm angewandte Untersuchungsmethode zeigt seine Vertrautheit mit den europäischen Auseinandersetzungen auf dem Gebiet.[6] Ein anderes Beispiel ist das des Militärbeamten, Historiographen und Ethnographen Josef Heinrich Benigni von Mildenberg (1782-1849), Autor eines *Handbuchs der Statistik und Geographie des Großfürstenthums Siebenbürgen* (3 Bde, Hermannstadt, 1837).[7]

Ich beabsichtige hier keine historiographische Untersuchung, ähnlich der von dem Historiker Mathias Bernath empfohlenen, der sich auf die „genealogische" Reihenfolge der Quellen aus der Blüte- und Spätzeit des Josephinismus bezog.[8] Eine solche Analyse setzt vor allem die Klärung der Bedeutung der wichtigsten Quellen aus dem 18. Jahrhundert voraus, die auch von den Autoren des nachfolgenden Jahrhunderts benutzt wurden.[9] In ihrem Fall handelt es sich nicht, wie meistens, um ein wissenschaftliches Vorgehen, sondern um Fragen der Regierung. Die Beschreibungen des Landes konnten somit die Reformprojekte begründen, von denen einige später Gesetzeskraft erhielten. Es wurde somit eine Umgestaltung der siebenbürgischen Gesellschaft (oder Gesellschaften) im Einklang mit den Wiener Reformprinzipien bezweckt.

a. Die Beschreibungen des Fürstentums Siebenbürgen

> „Ein Land, was [...] alle Vortheile der Natur hat, [...] kann billig ein Land genennet werden, von welchem dem höchsten Landes Fürsten, dem Staat, und denen selbst eigenen Inwohnern die wessentlichste Vortheile zugehen sollen; vornehmlichst in einem Jahrhundert, wo Künste, Wissenschaft, Erfahrniss und Fleiss so hoch gestiegen, und [...] bis zu dem Geringsten der Unterthannen sich preisswürdigst herablassenden Regierung angeeiferet, und erhoben werden [...]. Wenn aber aller dieser natürlichen Segnungen ungeachtet, in einem solchen Lande Betrübniss, und Armuth, Noth und Elend, keine wahre Pflege der Gerechtigkeit, Zerüttung- und Missverstand in denen wessentlichsten Stücken herrschet; wenn der grösste Theil der Menschen, der Reiche und Arme, der Gelehrte und Ungelehrte, der Adliche und Unadliche, der Ingebohrne, und Ausländer, alle, oder doch

---

[5] Ernst Wagner, Einführung, in Lucas Joseph Marienburg, *Geographie des Großfürstenthums Siebenbürgen*, Hg. Ernst Wagner (Köln, Wien: Böhlau Verlag, 1987), VII-VIII.

[6] Siehe, in der oben zitierten Ausgabe, die Einleitung zum ersten Band, insbesondere den Kommentar zu den Quellen und die Darstellung der Einteilung des Werkes (ebenda, 4-15).

[7] Er definierte hier die Statistik als ein „Gemälde des gegenwärtigen Zustandes eines Landes" das „bietet von Jahr zu Jahr nothwendig Veränderungen dar, weil auch der abgeschilderte Gegenstand fortwährend Veränderungen leidet". J. H. Benigni von Mildenberg, *Handbuch der Statistik und Geographie des Großfürstenthums Siebenbürgen*, II. Heft. *Statistik*, Vorwort, III. Über ihn, siehe *Österreichsches Biographisches Lexikon 1815-1950*, Bd. 1 (Lfg. 1, 1954), 69.

[8] Mathias Bernath, *Habsburgii şi începuturile formării naţiunii române* [Habsburg und die Anfänge der rumänischen Nationsbildung] (Cluj: Dacia, 1994, für die rumänische Version), 211.

[9] L. J. Marienburg bezieht sich somit auf drei anonyme geographische Beschreibungen Siebenbürgens, unter denen eine militärische, die er in Handschrift eingesehen hat und die ihm „von nicht geringem Nutzen" gewesen sind (*Geographie*, 11); die Auskunft stammt von Bernath (*Habsburgii*, a.a.O., Fußnote 111).

> die meiste Stände der Menschen, deren Religionen, Nationen und Absichten so sehr verschieden sind [...] über Anwendung und Verwirrung in einem Lande Klagen, wenn sie selbe ohne einem daraus siehenden ungerechten Nutzen erweisen können [...]; so lässt sich die Quelle des Unheils und Verderbens niergends, als in seinem inneren Umfang, oder in solchen Benehmungen suchen und finden, die Dienstwidrig und gemein schädlich sind."[10]

Der Befund Grafs Leopold von Clary-Aldringen, ehemaliger Verwalter des Thesaurariats (Schatzamtes) Siebenbürgens in der Zeit von 1770 bis 1772,[11] war das Ergebnis einer aufmerksamen Untersuchung, vielleicht die gründlichste Arbeit, die dem Fürstentum aus Sicht der Kameralwissenschaft gewidmet war.[12] Bezeichnenderweise leitete er den Bericht *Alleruntertänigst und gründlich zusammengestellte Bemerkungen über die gegenwärtige Lage des Großfürstenthums Siebenbürgen*,[13] verfasst am 23. Mai 1772, nach Ablauf seiner Amtszeit, zur Information des Kaisers Joseph II. weiter. Ein umfassenderer Bericht, eigentlich eine richtige Beschreibung des Landes, ist seiner ersten Berührung mit den siebenbürgischen Gegebenheiten aus dem Jahr 1768 zu verdanken. Als damaliger Burggraf von Eger war er nicht zufällig mit der Schilderung der wirtschaftlichen Lage des Landes beauftragt worden, da er doch nach dem Tod des Barons Ignaz Josef Bornemisza, ohne Vermittlung des Landstages, zur Leitung des Thesaurariats eingesetzt wurde.[14] Sein Bericht, *Siebenbürgen. Verbesserung des Landes*, der vom Staatsrat günstig eingeschätzt wurde und sich der Zustimmung der Kaiserin erfreute, wurde dem neuen Generalkommandeur und Präsidenten des Guberniums Siebenbürgen Carol O'Donell zugesandt.[15]

Der Bericht widerspiegelt eine kamerale Sicht mit deutlichen Hinweisen auf die

---

[10] Bozac, Pavel (Hg.), *Die Reise*, 322. Die Klagen der Untertanen, als Rechtfertigung des korrektiven Eingreifens der Zentralmacht aufgrund des Prinzips der guten und wohltätigen Regierung, wurden auch in der Präambel der für Ungarn und Siebenbürgen bestimmten Texte des Toleranzpatentes des Kaisers Joseph II. vom 25. Oktober, bzw. 8. November 1781 angeführt. Siehe Mályusz Elemér (Hg.), *Iratok a türelmi rendelet történetéhez* [Quellen zur Geschichte des Toleranzediktes] (Budapest, 1940), Nr. 17a, S. 272; Nr. 23, S. 285-286.

[11] Georg Adolf Schuller, *Samuel von Brukenthal*, Bd. I (München: Verlag R. Oldenbourg, 1967), 224, 270. Die Aufzeichnung der mit ihm in Temeswar geführten Gespräche zeigen eine eher herablassende Haltung von seiten Josephs II. Bozac, Pavel (Hg.), *Die Reise*, Nr. 60, S. 559-560, „Jurnalul de călătorie [...]" [Reisejournal ...]. Im Tagebuch wiedergegebene indirekte positive Charakterisierungen stammen von General Gyulai, dem Gubernialrat Grafen Nemes, und insbesondere vom Rat des Schatzamtes Baló. Ebenda, 607, 685, 686.

[12] Allgemeine Erwägungen zur *Kameralwissenschaft*, bei Karl Vocelka, *Glanz und Untergang der höfischen Welt. Repräsentation, Reform und Reaktion im Habsburgischen Vielvölkerstaat* [*Österreichische Geschichte 1699-1815*, hg. von Herwig Wolfram] (Wien: Ueberreuter, 2001), 281-284.

[13] *Allerunterthänigst und gründlich gefasste Bemerkungen der den itzigen Zustand des Gross-Fürstenthum Siebenbürgen, und die Laage dasiger Geschäften mit denen zur selbst allerläuchtest dereinstens ermessenden näheren Behebung angeführt-dermaligen Umständen, woraus die Nothwendigkeit gereichtestschleünig- und ergiebigster Abhülfe erhellet*, bei Bozac, Pavel (Hg.), *Die Reise*, Nr. 28, S. 322-356. Siehe auch Schuller, *Samuel von Brukenthal*, 283-285; Bernath, *Habsburgii*, 219f. Eine Kopie gibt es in Österreichisches Staatsarchiv, Haus- Hof- und Staatsarchiv (im weiteren ÖstA, HHStA), *Ungarische Akten. Transylvanica Separata*, fasz. 362, fol. 110-184.

[14] Schuller, *Samuel von Brukenthal*, 218-219, bezieht sich auf die Einwände Samuel von Brukenthals, der praktisch die Hofkammer Siebenbürgens leitete, gegen die Ernennung Clarys zum Schatzmeister, die er als schädlich für die Verfassung des Fürstentums betrachtete.

[15] Ebenda, 209, 218. Neuere Bezugnahmen auf diesen Bericht zu finden bei Bozac, Pavel (Hg.), *Die Reise*, 45 und 316; es ist möglich, dass die Beschreibung Siebenbürgens, auf welche dieselben Autoren S. 368 hinweisen, den gesamten besagten Bericht im Blick hatte.

Ideen Justi's, dessen Werke[16] ihn beeinflusst haben könnten. Die Prinzipien der Bevölkerungspolitik, gestützt auf den Ideen der Aufklärung (eine gute Regierung, wirtschaftliche, persönliche und religiöse Freiheit, Ermutigung der Industrie und der Manufakturen, Anziehung der begüterten, fleißigen und ausgebildeten Ausländer, Erteilung von Privilegien und Freiheiten an Einwanderer, Sorge für die Verbesserung der Medizin, der Hygiene u.a.)[17] durchsetzen seinen Text. Dieser ist in sieben Teile gegliedert, bezüglich Wirtschaft (mit gesonderten Behandlung der Agrarwirtschaft), militärische Fragen, Bevölkerung, Nationen und Religionen, Polizei[18] und Kameralangelegenheiten, Handel.[19] Die behandelten Themen entsprechen dem Interesse der Kameralistik jener Zeit und dem Kompetenzbereich des Guberniums Siebenbürgen.[20] Eine deutlichere Definierung der letzteren durch die Hofinstruktionen konnte die zahlreichen Mängel dennoch nicht beseitigen, auf die die Vertreter der kaiserlichen Autorität aufmerksam gemacht hatten. Dieses wird vor allem durch die kritischen *Bemerkungen* Clarys aus dem Jahr 1772 veranschaulicht.

Die Durchsicht der *Bemerkungen* hinterlässt einen fast gänzlich deprimierenden Eindruck: obwohl einsichtig, war im Falle Siebenbürgens kein einziger der oben aufgezählten Grundsätze der Bevölkerungspolitik zufriedenstellend in die Tat umgesetzt worden. Die Resourcen des Fürstentums wurden nicht verwertet, vor allem was den Bergbau betraf, der die reichste und sicherste Einnahmequelle Siebenbürgens darstellte; die Förderung dieser Reichtümer war allerdings abhängig von einer Erneuerung der Einrichtungen und der Ansiedlung von weiteren deutschen Bergleuten und Köhlern.[21] Durch die Erteilung des Bürgerrechtes an die ausländischen Handwerker (so wie das in gewissen Komitaten in Böhmen und vor allem in Ungarn möglich war, nicht aber in den sächsischen Städten Siebenbürgens), konnten sich die Manufakturen entwickeln, während die Zusicherung der Privilegien an die armenische Nation („durchwegs katholisch") und die Handelskompanien der Griechen in Hermannstadt und Kronstadt (die zwar „Schismatiker"

---

[16] Die Wiener Hofkreisen schätzten seine Werke; siehe Albion W. Small, *The Cameralists. The Pioneers of German Social Polity* (Chicago: Chicago University Press, 1909), 310, die Anmerkung Justi's betreffend die Verbreitung seiner Abhandlung, *Kurzer systematischer Grundriss aller Oeconomischen und Cameralwissenschaften* (1755), unter den Mitgliedern des *General Directoriums*, durch den Grafen Friedrich Wilhelm von Haugwitz, der in den Kameralforen bezüglich das Fürstentum Siebenbürgen bedeutende Befugnisse inne hatte, darunter auch die des Vizepräsidenten des Hofdeputation *in Transsilvanicis, Banaticis et Illyricis* und des Präsidenten des Direktoriums *in Publicis et Cameralibus*. Siehe Constant von Wurzbach, *Biographisches Lexikon des Kaiserthums Oesterreichs* (im weiteren Wurzbach, *Lexikon*), achter Theil (Wien: 1862), 68; Schuller, *Samuel von Brukenthal*, 108.

[17] Adam Wandruszka, *Theorie und Praxis der österreichischen Populationistik. Siedlungs- und Bevölkerungsgeschichte Österreichs* (Wien, 1974), 121, zitiert in Vocelka, *Glanz und Untergang*, 297.

[18] Zu einer kurzen Erläuterung der Bedeutungen des Begriffes siehe Vocelka, *Glanz und Untergang*, 283-284, und ausführlicher bei Foucault, *Securitate*, 261-287. Die erste Erwähnung des Begriffes in rumänischer Sprache weist auf das selbe Wirkungsfeld der „Polizei" hin wie auf europäischer Ebene, nämlich das urbane: *politia = városi mód, városi rend*. Siehe Ioan Bobb, *Dictionariu rumanesc, lateinesc si unguresc* [Rumänisches, Lateinisches und Magyarisches Wörterbuch], Bd. II (Cluj, 1823), 207-208.

[19] ÖstA, HHStA, fasz. 362, fol. 249-372.

[20] Siehe im Einzelnen Rolf Kutschera, *Landtag und Gubernium in Siebenbürgen. 1688-1869* (Köln, Wien: Böhlau Verlag, 1985), 150-152 und Fußnote 36, zu den benutzten Quellen.

[21] Bozac, Pavel (Hg.), *Die Reise*, 323, 347.

waren, gleichzeitig aber auch kaiserliche Untertanen) eine ertragreichere Handelstätigkeit begünstigt hätte.[22]

Der offenbare bisherige Kameralismus kennzeichnet auch die übrigen Beobachtungen im Rahmen einer unmittelbar auf die Fragestellung der Bevölkerung gerichteten Gesamtschau. Die Vermehrung derselben und implizite die Beschränkung der Einwanderung waren aus Clarys Sicht gebunden an die Lösung der angezeigten Hauptmängel: die unbefriedigende Regelung im Beitragssystem, in der Ausübung der Justiz und der Abgrenzung der Eigentumsrechte, die oft zu Mißbrauch führte;[23] das Fehlen von Polizeinormen in Hermannstadt und anderen Städten, wie auch im ganzen Fürstentum;[24] die Rivalität zwischen den Provinzialbehörden, den militärischen und den Kameralbehörden Siebenbürgens (Gubernium, Thesaurariat, General-Kommandantur).[25] Hinsichtlich der Re-gelungen ist eine unbestreitbare Erklärung *die ungenügende Kenntnis des Fürstentums*: es fehlte eine genaue Erforschung der Lage der Ortschaften, der Qualität der Böden, der Kommunikationsmittel, der Möglichkeiten der Verwertung, wie auch der Pflichten der Steuerzahler.[26]

Die Lage konnte gebessert werden durch eine Landvermessung und eine gründliche Aufzeichnung mit Hilfe der Offiziere, die mit der Erstellung einer Landkarte beauftragt waren, während die Abgaben der Untertanen durch die Einführung des neuen Urbariums nach ungarischem Vorbild mit Berücksichtigung des siebenbürgischen Adelsstandes geregelt werden konnte.[27]

Ein Teil dieser Aufgaben waren schon in Angriff genommen worden. Unter der Leitung des Oberst und späteren Generals Dominik de Fabris, Graf von Casano, wurde von 1769 bis 1773, im Zuge einer umfassenden Vermessung des gesamten Reichsterritoriums, die erste topographische Karte des Fürstentums Siebenbürgen angefertigt; bis dahin waren nur die Karten Schlesiens, Tschechiens, Mährens, der Maramuresch und des Zipser Komitates, Oberungarns, Oberösterreichs und des Banates erarbeitet worden.[28]

---

[22] Ebenda, 332-333, 353.

[23] Ebenda, 323-348 (*Allerunterthänigst und gründlich gefasste Bemerkungen*, Teile I-III).

[24] Ebenda, 331.

[25] Ebenda, 354-356 (*Allerunterthänigst und gründlich gefasste Bemerkungen*, Teil V). Betreffend die konfessionellen Aspekte, im IV. Teil der „Bemerkungen" erörtert (ebenda, 348-354), siehe Daniel Dumitran, „Hin zu einer Gemeinschaft der Rechte in Siebenbürgen? Grundgedanken der Toleranzpolitik im siebenbürgischen Fürstentum zur Zeit des Kaisers Joseph II.", *Transylvanian Review* XXI, Supplement No. 1 (2012), *One Hundred Years Since the Birth of Emil Turdeanu*, ed. Ioan-Aurel Pop, Ana Dumitran, Jan Nicolae (im weiteren Dumitran, „Grundgedanken"): 295-296.

[26] Bozac, Pavel (Hg.), *Die Reise*, 325, 328.

[27] Ebenda, 328, 329.

[28] Ernst Hofstätter, *Beiträge zur Geschichte der Österreichischen Landesaufnahmen. Ein Überblick der topographischen Aufnahmeverfahren, deren Ursprünge, ihrer Entwicklungen und Organisationsformen der vier österreichischen Landesaufnahmen*, I. Teil (Wien, 1989), Anhang, XXIV; Andor Borbély, Julia Nagy, „Magyarország I. katonai felvétele II. József korában" [Die erste militärische Aufnahme Ungarns zur Zeit Josephs II.], in *Az első katonai felmérés Erdély és a Temesi Bánság* [Die erste militärische Vermessung Siebenbürgens und des Banats von Temes] (DVD, Budapest, 2005). Die Karte wird auch von L. J. Marienburg erwähnt, der sie aber nicht hat einsehen können; er wußte bloß, dass sie angefertigt war, etwa 300 Blätter umfasste und vermutete, dass sie an Ausführlichkeit nicht ihresgleichen hatte (*Geographie*, 9).

Der Vorrang der beiden Provinzen an der Ostgrenze der Reiches ist im Zusammenhang der militärischen Lage der Zeit durchaus erklärbar; es war aber beabsichtigt, auch eine „Wirtschaftstopographie", also ein Grundbuch anzulegen, gemäß den Instruktionen des Marschalls Franz Lacy, Präsident des Hofkriegsrates, an den Generalkommandeur des Fürstentums Carl O'Donell.[29] Die geforderte doppelte Vermessung war nur im Banat teilweise erfolgreich,[30] doch auch die Karte Siebenbürgens (mit der Darstellung der Ortschaften, der Bauwerke, einschließlich derer mit wirtschaftlichem Zweck, der Bodenarten, der Bodenschätze und der Kommunikationswege)[31] war eine bedeutende Leistung (Abb. 1-2).

Andererseits kann die Karte als eine Vorankündigung der Absichten zur Vereinheitlichung des Kaisers Joseph II.,[32] wie auch einiger Repräsentanten des Hofes betrachtet werden, die durch die Verwaltungsreform aus dem Jahr 1784 verwirklicht werden sollte (Abb. 3-4). In die selbe Richtung deutet auch die Tatsache, dass die mit der Aufsicht beauftragten Offiziere Ähnliches auch in den Erbprovinzen des Reiches getan hatten: Philipp Baron von Elmpt (der die Anfertigung der Karte des Banats koordinierte), in Böhmen, Mähren, Oberösterreich und Ungarn, und de Fabris in Schlesien, Böhmen und Mähren.[33]

Die zeitgenössische Beschreibung des Banates und Siebenbürgens durch Ignaz Edler von Born in den *Briefen* an seinen Freund Johann Jakob Ferber widerspiegelt eine praktische Beschäftigung mit dem Bergwerkswesen im Fürstentum. Gebürtig aus Karlsburg, gemäß der eigenen Bezeugung, war Born 1770, als er die Reise durch Ungarn, das Banat und Siebenbürgen unternahm, Assesor des Münz- und Bergbaudirektoriums in Prag, und 1779 sollte er Rat der Hofkammer im Münz- und Bergwesen werden.[34] Ohne

---

[29] Hofstätter, *Beiträge*, 37; Madalina-Valeria Veres, „Putting Transylvania on the Map: Cartography and Enlightened Absolutism in the Habsburg Monarchy", *Austrian History Yearbook* 43 (April 2012): 147.

[30] Es ist die Rede von *Original Aufnahmskarte des Temesvarer Banats ausgeführt in den Jahren 1769-1772, unter der Direktion des Obersten Elmpst des Generalquartirmeisterstabes*, die die Anzahl der Familien enthielt, der Ortschaften nach Distrikten und deren Grenzen, erwähnt in Aurel Răduțiu, Ladislau Gyémánt, *Repertoriul izvoarelor statistice privind Transilvania, 1690-1847* [Verzeichnis der statistischen Quellen Siebenbürgens, 1690-1847] (București: Univers Enciclopedic, o.J.), 218, Nr. 1581. Auf die fertige Landkarte bezieht sich Joseph II. in seiner Aufzeichnung vom 11. Mai 1773 im *Reisebericht*; das Grundbuch hingegen war weniger gelungen, da, obwohl beide es als das „Hauptwerk" bezeichneten, Elmpt behauptete, es sei völlig falsch angelegt, während Clary von einer zukünftigen „gänzlichen Berichtigung" sprach. Bozac, Pavel (Hg.), *Die Reise*, 558, 560. Siehe auch Benjamin Landais, „Savoir et production des ingénieurs-cartographes locaux en Hongrie méridionale : des enjeux centraux dans l'évolution de la société paysanne 1767-1805", in *Images en capitale : Vienne, fin XVIIᵉ – début XIXᵉ siècles*, Hg. Christine Lebeau, Wolfgang Schmale (Bochum: Verlag Dr. Dieter Winkler, 2011) [*Jahrbuch der Österreichischen Gesellschaft zur Erforschung des 18. Jahrhunderts* 25 (2010)], 140-141.

[31] Siehe Veres, „Putting Transylvania on the Map", 155-156. Siehe auch Paldus, „Die militärischen Aufnahmen im Bereiche der Habsburgischen Länder aus der Zeit Kaiser Josephs II.", zur Liste der Wirtschaftsobjekte, die beschrieben werden sollten, gesendet von Marschall Lacy im Jahr 1769, in *Az első katonai felmérés* (DVD, gem. Veres, Fußnote 64).

[32] Dazu siehe auch Veres, „Putting Transylvania on the Map", 150-151.

[33] Hofstätter, *Beiträge*, 51. Zu Philipp Elmpt, siehe auch Bozac, Pavel (Hg.), *Die Reise*, Nr. 39, S. 419-423 („Geographische und oeconomische Beschreibung von Temesvarer District [...]", vom 12 Mai 1773).

[34] Wurzbach, *Lexikon*, zweiter Theil (Wien, 1857), 71-72.

dass zweifelsfrei der Einfluß nachgewiesen werden könnte, den seine Bemerkungen auf die Beschreibung Siebenbürgens aus den Jahren 1769-1773 gehabt haben, waren sie eher wissenschaftlich begründet dank seines Interesses für Mineralogie und Bergbau.[35]

Aus dieser Sicht äußert sich der Autor in einem Brief aus Zlatna (Kleinschlatten / Goldmarkt), datiert vom 15. Juli 1770, über die Reichtümer Siebenbürgens, und bezieht sich dabei kritisch auf die einzigen Autoren, die sich bis dahin mit dem Thema beschäftigt hatten: Samuel Köleséri (in *Auraria Romano-Dacica*) und der Jesuit János Fridvalszky (in *Mineralogia Transilvaniae*).[36] Die Beschreibung der Goldförderung von Săcărâmb (Gross-Astdorf), Zlatna, Abrud (Großschlatten / Altenburg), Roşia Montană (Rotseifen / Goldbach), der Salzbergwerke von Thorenburg, oder der entwickelten Städte der Region (Kleinschlatten, Karlsburg, Thorenburg, Klausenburg), ist häufig begleitet von Kritik an Fridvalszky. Sein Werk erschien ihm unwürdig, für den Dienst den eine solche Nachforschung dem Staat und der Wissenschaft zu bringen habe.[37]

Der Beitrag Ignaz von Borns ist an sich wertvoll und verdient es, beachtet zu werden auch wegen der impliziten Werbung für eine bessere Verwertung der natürlichen Resourcen des siebenbürgischen Fürstentums; sie konnte dem Staat Nutzen bringen, aber auch zur Hebung des Wohlstandes der Menschen dienen. Die aufklärerischen Überzeugungen des Verfassers rundeten so seine pragmatische Vision auf, wie es von einem Repräsentanten der höfischen Kameralämter zu erwarten war.[38]

---

[35] *Briefe über mineralogische Gegenstände, auf seiner Reise durch das Temeswarer Bannat, Siebenbürgen, Ober- und Nieder-Hungarn, an der Herausgeber derselben* (Frankfurt und Leipzig, 1774), wurden von J. J. Ferber herausgegeben, später ins Englische übersetzt (1777), ins Italienische (1778) und ins Französische (1780). Wurzbach, *Lexikon*, zw. Theil, 71. Dafür findet sich in der zur Information des Kaisers Joseph II. vor seiner Reise in das Fürstentum zusammengestellten Akte ein kürzerer und technischer Bericht mit ähnlichem Inhalt, verfasst am 4. Mai 1768 von Franz von Gerstorff (*Nachricht von denen Berg-Wercken des Gross-Fürstenthum Siebenbürgen verfasset anno 1768*, in Bozac, Pavel (Hg.), *Die Reise*, Nr. 38, S. 408-419). Zu einem direkten Einfluß von Borns Schrift auf die Reise des Kaisers durch das Banat und Siebenbürgen äußert sich Veres aufgrund eines neueren bibliografischen Hinweises. Siehe „Putting Transylvania on the Map", 158, mit Hinweis auf Alex Drace-Francis, „A Provincial Imperialist and a Curious Account of Wallachia: Ignaz von Born", *European History Quarterly* 36, 1 (1 January 2006): 65-67.

[36] „Siebenbürgen verdiente gewiß von einem Naturforscher, der aber zugleich einen guten Theil bergmännischer Kenntnisse hätte, in Absicht auf die Naturgeschichte genau untersucht zu werden. In allen Gebürgen dieses schönen Landes trifft man Spuren von Metallen an, die daselbst noch unaufgeschlossen liegen. Wäre mir die Zeit nicht festgesetzet worden, in welcher ich wiederum in Schemnitz zurück sein muss, so würde ich nicht so bald ein Land verlassen, das nicht nur darum, weil ich hier gebohren wurde, sondern auch wegen seiner natürlichen Schätze, in meinen Augen einen vorzüglichen Werth hat, und vielleicht mir meine Mühe, die ich auf die Durchforschung derselben verwenden würde, reichlich ersetzet haben könnte." *Briefe über mineralogische Gegenstände*, 104.

[37] Ebenda, 145.

[38] Zur Interpretation seiner Beschreibung, berichtet am Reisetagebuch Josephs II., siehe Veres, „Putting Transylvania on the Map", 158-161; eine Analyse mit Betonung auf seinen Ideen betreffend die Bevölkerung des Banates und Siebenbürgens stammt von Ovidiu Marinel Koch-Tufiş, „Populaţia Banatului şi Transilvaniei oglindită în scrisorile pe care Ignaz von Born le-a scris în anul 1770 în timpul călătoriei sale prin cele două provincii" [Die Bevölkerung von Banat und Siebenbürgen erläutert in Briefen, die Ignaz von Born im Jahr 1770 auf seiner Reise durch die oben genannten Gebiete geschrieben hat], *Banatica* 19 (2009): 117-158; deutsche Fassung in *Codrul Cosminului* XVII, 2 (2011): 7-35. Siehe auch Marianne Klemun, „Reisen, Aufzeichnen, Beschreiben. Visualisierung erdwissenschaftlichen Wissens und „Mineralogische Reisen" innerhalb habsburgischer Territorien", in *Images en capitale : Vienne, fin XVIIᵉ – début XIXᵉ siècles*, 101-103.

Die militärischen Schriften, angefertigt auf Anforderung des Hofkriegsrates, ergänzen das Informationsmaterial betreffend das Fürstentum. Eine historisch-politische Beschreibung Siebenbürgens (*Historisch-Politische Beschreibung des Gross-Fürstentums Siebenbürgen*) wurde in den Jahren 1771-1775 angefertigt; sie wurde dem kommandierenden General Johann Franz Freiherr von Preiss schon am Anfang seiner Amtszeit im Fürstentum aufgetragen: durch die Order vom 18. Mai 1771 gab ihm der Hofkriegsrat Anweisungen sowohl was den Aufbau der Arbeit als auch die hinzuziehenden Mitarbeiter betraf.[39] Eine andere, vornehmlich das militärische Grenzterritorium betreffende, stammt aus dem Jahr 1773.[40] Obwohl der Hinweis nur im zweiten Fall ausdrücklich ist, können beide mit der Vorbereitung des ersten kaiserlichen Besuchs im Fürstentum in Verbindung gebracht werden. Beiden gemeinsam ist das Interesse für eine ähnliche Problematik: die Verwaltungsstruktur des Staates, beziehungsweise die Anzahl und die soziale wie konfessionelle Struktur der Bevölkerung. Sicherlich beeinhaltete die erste eine vollständigere Beschreibung des Landes, die in einer umfangreicheren Version im Jahre 1781 wieder aufgenommen wurde. Damals wurde mit einer neuen Beschreibung begonnen, von einem Militärbeamten, der die wirtschaftlichen, kulturellen, religiösen, politischen und administrativen Zustände der Provinz detaillierte, mit besonderem Augenmerk auf die Lage in den Territorien der drei politischen Nationen.[41] Die Betrachtung der rumänischen Problematik in diesen Quellen, auf die der Historiker Mathias Bernath[42] eingeht, stellt bestimmt nur einen Teilaspekt ihres Inhaltes dar. Das Unternehmen scheint uns bereits konvergent zu sein mit den vorher besprochenen Quellen, da wir durchaus ähnliche Formulierungen mit jenen aus dem Bericht des Grafen Clary finden. Letztlich widerspiegeln diese Beschreibungen die Rolle, die der Militärstruktur der Provinz bei der Vorbereitung der Reformtätigkeit zugeteilt wurde.

b. Reformprojekte

Die Untersuchung der Akte mit den direkten Bemerkungen des Kaisers Joseph II., die er während seines Besuches in Siebenbürgen im Jahr 1773 gemacht hat, kann den Einfluß der Beschreibungen des Fürstentums über die Reformprojekte betreffend dieses Territorium bestätigen oder widerlegen. Wie zu erwarten war, widerspiegeln die Fragebogen betreffend die wesentlichen Probleme des Fürstentums, die auf Anordnung des Koregenten vor seinem Besuch angefertigt wurden, schon diese Beeinflussung. Sie wurden den

---

39 Bernath, *Habsburgii*, 209-210. Unter den Mitarbeitern erwähnt Bernath den Hofsekretär Lichtensteiner, auch er ein Unterzeichner, neben Preiss, des offiziellen Exemplars der Beschreibung.

40 Ebenda, 218-219, wo der Titel des Werkes angeführt wird (*Kurz gefasste Auszüge zur Kanntnuss verschiedener Gegenständen in dem Grossfürstenthum Siebenbürgen die zum Theil auf das Provinciale, dann den Militar Stand, besonders aber, und umständlicher auf die Gränitz-Regimenter ihre Beziehung haben, nebst dem dabey befindlichen Plan von der fürseyenden für dieses Land hochbeglükten Reise Euer Majestät*) und sein Inhalt.

41 Datiert am 31. Oktober 1781, hat diese Beschreibung (*Beschreibung von Siebenbürgen*) zum Autor einen gewissen Thoman, *Feldkriegs-Concipist*. Mathias Bernath, der auch dieses vermerkt (ebenda, 210-211), zeigt die Tatsache an, dass Thoman ganze Abschnitte aus der vorhergehenden Beschreibung übernommen hat.

42 Ebenda, 212-217.

politischen, den kameralischen, den administrativen und den militärischen Behörden Siebenbürgens in den Monaten März bis April 1773 zugeleitet. Die Fragen beziehen sich vornehmlich auf die Bevölkerung und die wesentlichen Tätigkeitsbereiche – institutionell, fiskalisch, wirtschaftlich, kommerziell, administrativ und kulturell.[43]

Im Sinne der Populationistik richtete sich die Aufmerksamkeit des Kaisers in erster Reihe auf die Mittel zur Eindämmung der Emigration und der Erledigung der Klagen betreffend Abgaben und Dienstleistungen, ohne die Lage der „Transmigranten" aus Oberösterreich zu vergessen. Institutionell beschäftigte ihn die Verbesserung der Arbeit des Guberniums und des Thesaurariat, der Beziehungen zwischen ihnen und den untergeordneten Behörden, der juristischen Verfahren, der urbanen Polizei und nicht zuletzt die Durchsetzung des Verdienstkriteriums bei der Ämterbesetzung.[44] Kameralprobleme sowie wirtschaftliche und kommerzielle sind Gegenstand der Fragen bezüglich die Verbesserung der Einhebung der Beiträge und die Beseitigung der Hinterziehungen, der Hebung der wirtschaftlichen Produktivität durch Hinzuziehen ausländischer Fachleute, Einführung einer höheren Nutzungstechnik oder die Erschließung neuer Bergwerke. Andererseits waren die Begünstigung der Handelstätigkeit der armenischen und griechischen Handelskompanien mit den Fürstentümern außerhalb der Karpathen angebracht, aber auch deren Anwesenheit auf den Märkten der Erbterritorien, oder die Förderung einiger Handwerke, die die örtlichen Resourcen verwerten konnten.[45] Die Förderung der Schulbildung wurde als ein Mittel angesehen, den beklagenswerten Zustand der Bevölkerung, insbesondere der rumänischen, zu ändern, aber auch zur Lösung der Zwistigkeiten zwischen den verschiedenen Nationen und Religionen, die einer dem Gemeinwohl des Vaterlandes dienenden Zusammenarbeit hinderlich waren.[46]

Ohne so umfassend zu sein, betonen die an den Staatsrat gerichteten Fragen ebenfalls Aspekte der Beiträge, der Militärgrenze, Kameralangelegenheiten und den Bergbau, die öffentlichen und die Provinz betreffenden Probleme (bezüglich Gesetzgebung, Institutionen, Bevölkerung, konfessionelle, kulturelle und polizeiliche Aspekte), militärische, kamerale, kommerzielle. Der Rat Stepan gibt auch eine Beschreibung der konfessionell-religiösen Lage des Fürstentums und schildert die Zwistigkeiten zwischen den verschiedenen Nationen und Religionen, die nur durch das gemeinsame Interesse geeint seien, eine bevorzugtere Stellung der Katholiken zu verhindern. Der Rat Gebler, etwas

[43] Bozac, Pavel (Hg.), *Die Reise*, Nr. 42-45, S. 428-449. Unter den vier Fragebogen, die hier abgedruckt sind, wendet sich der umfangreichste an die Gubernialräte mit 25 Punkten (Nr. 42); in einer kürzeren Form findet sich der Inhalt wieder in den 15 Fragen des Bogens, der an die Verwaltungsbehörden und den Präsidenten der königlichen Tafel gesandt wurde (Nr. 44). Ohne gänzlich verschieden zu sein, verfolgen die an die Räte des Schatzamtes und die Militärbehörden gesandten Fragebogen (Nr. 43 und 45) dennoch die spezifischen Belange der Tätigkeitsbereiche derselben.

[44] Siehe auch Bozac, Pavel (Hg.), *Die Reise*, Bd. II (Cluj-Napoca: Academia Română. Centrul de Studii Transilvane, 2011), Nr. 71, S. 134-139. Unter anderem empfielt der Kaiser hier die Aufstockung der Hofkanzlei Siebenbürgens mit jüngeren Kennern der Probleme des Fürstentums.

[45] Siehe auch ebenda, Nr. 68, S. 115-116; Nr. 72, S. 143.

[46] Ebenda, Bd. I, Nr. 42, S. 432, Punkte 23-25, und Nr. 42a, S. 440, zu dem letzten Aspekt.

systematischer, schlägt nicht weniger als 37 Fragen vor.[47]

Die Auffindung der auf diese Fragebogen gegebenen Antworten ist eine noch zu erfüllende Aufgabe. Wie aufschlußreich sie sein können, beweist die umfassende Antwort, die am 2. Juli 1773 vom Hermannstädter Bürgermeister Johann Georg von Honnamonn[48] eingereicht worden war. Seine kurze Charakterisierung auf der „geheimen Liste", die der Kaiser nach seinem Besuch im Fürstentum zusammenstellte, drückte eher Mißtrauen in die Fähigkeiten aus, die ihm zugeschrieben wurden.[49] Katholisch und Nichtsiebenbürger, ehemaliges Mitglied der Seeberg-Kommission, ursprünglich ein Gegner der Sachsen und Samuel von Brukenthals, doch nach und nach den siebenbürgischen Umständen angepasst, des Mißbrauchs beschuldigt, für den er zu Schadensersatz verurteilt werden sollte,[50] ist Honnamonn folglich ein wertvoller Zeuge. Das Lob der günstigeren sozialen Bedingungen in den sächsischen Stühlen und die gehobene Organisation der Städte, insbesondere Hermannstadts, im Vergleich zu der Lage in den Komitaten, das Übersehen der negativen Aspekte, könnte seine Objektivität schon in Frage stellen; dennoch nähern sich seine Ansichten in mehrfacher Hinsicht den anderen Informationsquellen, die dem Kaiser zur Verfügung gestellt wurden. So sind die Töne, in denen er die Leibeigenschaft verurteilt und sie dem abgesicherten Wohlstand der freien sächsischen Bauern gegenüberstellt, nicht sehr verschieden von denen des Grafen Clary oder der Militärbeschreibungen des Fürstentums;[51] für die Eindämmung der Auswanderung und die Entwicklung des Landes schlug er als Maßnahmen die Befreiung der Leibeigenen vor, die Beschränkung des Frondienstes auf drei Tage pro Woche und die Reduzierung der zu

[47] Ebenda, Nr. 49, S. 481-490; Schuller, *Samuel von Brukenthal*, S. 282. Das Dokument ist mit dem 21. April 1773 datiert (das Datum der Ergänzungen durch den Grafen Hatzfeld, den Präsidenten des Staatsrates, und der Übergabe an den Kaiser); außer den erwähnten haben darauf noch geantwortet die Räte Löhr (viel bündiger) und Kressel (der keine Frage formulierte). Allerdings konnten sie zu den Fragebogen, die an die Gubernialräte und die des Schatzamtes von Siebenbürgen gesandt wurden, fast keine Ergänzungen mehr vorschlagen (ebenda, Nr. 50, S. 490-492, vom 2. Mai 1773; sehr kurze Ergänzungen machten bloß Gebler und Hatzfeld). Ein anderer Fragebogen enthält Fragen bezüglich die religiösen Aspekte (zu Katholiken, Unierten und Armeniern), die mit dem Gubernator besprochen werden sollten, mit den Bischöfen und den katholischen Räten (ebenda, Nr. 51, S. 492-493).

[48] Bozac, Pavel (Hg.), *Die Reise*, Nr. 48, S. 453-481; einen Bezug zu dieser Antwort macht auch Schuller (*Samuel von Brukenthal*, 294-295). Es muß angemerkt werden, dass diese im Hermannstädter Brukenthal-Fond aufbewahrt wird, während die bisher behandelten Quellen sich in Wiener Archiven befinden.

[49] Bozac, Pavel (Hg.), *Die Reise*, Nr. 63, S. 769. Die mit ihm besprochenen Probleme bei ihrer Begegnung in Hermannstadt am 8. Juli 1773 sind vom Kaiser in seinem Reisetagebuch verzeichnet (ebenda, 699-700).

[50] Mehrere detailliert Auskünfte über Honnamonn bietet Schuller, *Samuel von Brukenthal*, Bd. I, 96-97, 149-150, 180-181, 226-227, 255-257, 359-361; Bd. II (München: Verlag R. Oldenbourg, 1969), 26-27, 36; eine neuere Anmerkung findet sich bei Angelika Schaser, *Reformele iosefine în Transilvania şi urmările lor în viaţa socială. Importanţa Edictului de concivilitate pentru oraşul Sibiu* [Josephinische Reformen und sozialer Wandel in Siebenburgen: Die Bedeutung des Konzivilitatsreskriptes fur Hermannstadt] (Sibiu: Editura hora, 2000, für die rumänische Version), 57. Zur Kommission Seeberg, siehe Kutschera, *Landtag und Gubernium*, 254-255.

[51] Dazu siehe Bernath, *Habsburgii*, 216, wo die zitierten Bemerkungen sich allerdings nicht bloß auf die schwere Lage der Leibeigenen beziehen, sondern auch auf ihre Ausbeutung durch die ungarischen und szeklerischen Landbesitzer und auf die Opposition der sächsischen Stuhlbehörden, sie auf Königsboden anzusiedeln.

zahlreichen Feiertage der Rumänen.[52] Er kritisiert auch die beklagenswerte Unwissenheit der Rumänen, deren Priester (uniert und nichtuniert) kaum die Messe lesen konnten und allzu wenige, vielleicht gar keiner, besaß die Kenntnis jener Dinge, die den Menschen an Gott und das Gemeinschaftsleben binden. Schuld daran war die Leibeigenschaft, aber auch die Faulheit, wozu diese veranlaßte.[53] Die Lösung sah er in dem sächsischen Modell, dass nämlich jede Gemeinschaft ihren eigenen Lehrer habe, der auch der Priester sein konnte, der die Kinder zumindest zur Winterzeit die Stücke des Glaubens, und die aufgeweckteren unter ihnen auch lesen und schreiben lehren sollte. Ebenfalls er schlug auch die Gründung von Normalschulen vor, wie in den deutschen Territorien, aber auch die Bekanntgabe der Schulpflicht auf dem Dorf, um lesen und schreiben zu lernen, für alle, die Priester, Beamten oder Militärs (der Fall jener aus dem Grenzgebiet) werden wollten.[54]

Einen kritischen Blick hatte Honnamonn auch für die den Untertanen abverlangten Beiträge und das System der Einhebung der Abgaben.[55] Dafür war er aber geneigter, den Standpunkt der Sachsen zu rechtfertigen, was die Besetzung der Ämter betraf (er befürwortete das System der „geometrischen Proportion”, beklagte aber das Fehlen der ausgebildeten Kandidaten unter den Katholiken, was an den bescheidenen Schulungsmöglichkeiten lag),[56] die Polizeiordnungen der Stadt Hermannstadt[57] und die der griechischen Handelskompanie auferlegten Einschränkungen zum Schutz der sächsischen Kaufleute.[58]

Die unmittelbare Kenntnis der siebenbürgischen Verhältnisse, die grundlegend war für eine gute Regierung und Verwaltung,[59] war das wesentliche Ziel der Reise des Kaisers Joseph II. durch das Fürstentum. Zur Orientierung dienten ihm auch die *Anmerkungen zur siebenbürgischen Reise* Samuel von Brukenthals, von wo er auch die Beschreibungen der Ortschaften in sein Tagebuch übernahm.[60] Wahrscheinlich nicht mehr als diese,[61] da der zukünftige Guvernator andere Meinungen vertrat als die übrigen kaiserlichen Würdenträger, die den Herrscher beraten hatten; das muss allerdings noch über-

[52] Bozac, Pavel (Hg.), *Die Reise*, 460-461.
[53] Ebenda, 470-471 und 473, wo er den Gedanken wieder aufnimmt, und die Unwissenheit der Rumänen an ihre Neigung zu Lastern knüpft.
[54] Ebenda, 471-472.
[55] Ebenda, 475-477.
[56] Ebenda, 463-464.
[57] Ebenda, 473-475.
[58] Ebenda, 479-481. Honnamonn moniert in diesem Fall, die Einrichtung des Sanitär-Gürtels habe den Handel der Sachsen wesentlich beeinträchtigt zu gunsten der „Griechen” aus der Walachei, von denen einige in Siebenbürgen ansäßig geworden waren, ihre Verbindungen zu jenen jenseits der Berge aber beibehalten hatten; noch schwerwiegender war, dass sie zu unlauteren Handelspraktiken gegriffen hatten, die zum Bankrott der sächsischen Kaufleute geführt hätten, wenn man ihnen nicht den Vertrieb der deutschen Waren (aus Leipzig) untersagt und sie auf die „türkischen” beschränkt hätte.
[59] Diesen Gedanken äußert der Herrscher selbst am Schluß seiner Zuschrift vom 10. Juli 1773, durch die er Maria Theresia seinen Schlußbericht über die Reise durch Siebenbürgen vorlegt (ebenda, Nr. 61, S. 716); siehe auch Veres, „Putting Transylvania on the Map“, 141.
[60] Bozac, Pavel (Hg.), *Die Reise*, 377-394, der Auszug gedruckt unter Nr. 32 (der Gesamttext der „Anmerkungen” ist noch nicht gefunden worden); Schuller, *Samuel von Brukenthal*, Bd. I, 288-290.
[61] Schuller äußert sich mit Bestimmtheit in dieser Richtung, nicht ohne eine reichlich subjektive Note (*Samuel von Brukenthal*, 314).

prüft werden, nachdem der Gesamttext der *Anmerkungen* erschlossen ist. Die Divergenz ist ersichtlicher in der Schrift Brukenthals betreffend die siebenbürgischen Institutionen aus den Territorien der drei politischen Nationen, die er dem Kaiser im Jahr 1773 übersandte (*Die ältere Verfassung Siebenbürgens des Kaisers Majestät vor seiner Reise dahin, von Br. Bruckenthal im J. 1773 zu Füssen gelegt*).[62] Dennoch hat Joseph ihn geschätzt, indem er ihm neben den Baronen Buccow und Seeberg die bedeutendste Rolle zuwies unter denen, die auf das Land aufmerksam gemacht und begonnen hatten, ihm eine dem Staat nützliche Organisation zu verleihen, ähnlich deren anderer zivilisierter Länder („anderen wohl policirten Ländern").[63] Mit Rücksicht auf all diese Umstände, scheint die Interpretation G. A. Schullers offensichtlich vereinfachend, da sie die Debatte über die Einflußquellen des Konzeptes Josephs II. hauptsächlich auf die Berichte Clarys und Auerspergs beschränkt.[64] Es ist wohl wahr, dass die Nähe zwischen den *Verbesserungen*, für die der ehemalige Schatzmeister Clary plädiert hatte und der Ansicht der Sinnlosigkeit von Notbehelfen, die der Kaiser wiederholt in seinem Schlußbericht geäußert hat,[65] offensichtlich sind. Die Darlegung Josephs II. ist aber mehr als die Summe von unkritisch übernommenen Einflüssen, sie ist eine radikale Kritik des Standes der Dinge im Fürstentum, beruhend auf direkter Erkundung.

Ausgerichtet auf die sechs Hauptsachen (die Militärische, die Wirtschaftliche und Kommerzielle, die Kamerale, die Politische und Administrative, die Konfessionelle und Kulturelle, die Sanitäre) ist der Schlußbericht des Kaisers Joseph II.[66] vor allem durch die Prinzipien der Populationistik und des Kameralismus charakterisiert und dazu ein kohärentes Projekt für eine moderne politische und administrative Neuorganisierung des Territoriums. Als Beilage hat er eine interessante sogenannte „geheime Liste" der bedeutenden Persönlichkeiten des Fürstentums,[67] eigentlich eine Bewertung der Inhaber der wichtigsten politischen und administrativen Ämter (des Guberniums, des Thesaura-

---

[62] Johann Georg Schaser, *Denkwürdigkeiten aus dem Leben des Freiherrn Samuel v. Brukenthal, Gubernators von Siebenbürgen* (Hermannstadt, 1848), Anhang VIII, 22-38; Schuller, *Samuel von Brukenthal*, 290-291. Bei anderer Gelegenheit habe ich die Übernahme einiger Aussagen von hier in die Militärbeschreibungen des Fürstentums angedeutet (Dumitran, „Grundgedanken", 310, Fußnote 40).

[63] Eine Bemerkung aus der Zuschrift vom 10. Juli, zitiert auch oben (Bozac, Pavel (Hg.), *Die Reise*, 715). Sehr wahrscheinlich hatte Joseph II. ebenfalls in erster Reihe Brukenthal im Blick, als er einige Mitglieder der Hofkammer Siebenbürgens hervorhob unter den andern Hofräten und -referenten, die sich durch eine „gänzliche Unkenntnis" der siebenbürgischen Gegebenheiten auszeichneten (ebenda, 716); er vermerkte auch Brukenthals Bestreben, seine eigene Nation zu heben, die bis dahin von den Ungarn unterdrückt war (ebenda, 715).

[64] Schuller, *Samuel von Brukenthal*, 313.

[65] Bozac, Pavel (Hg.), *Die Reise*, Nr. 62, S. 730, 737, 762; mit Hinweis auch auf andere Quellen findet sich die Überlegung auch bei Bernath, *Habsburgii*, 238, 246-247. Für ein Beispiel des Einflusses der *Bemerkungen*, siehe Bozac, Pavel (Hg.), *Die Reise*, Bd. II, Nr. 72, S. 139-144.

[66] Bozac, Pavel (Hg.), *Die Reise*, Bd. I, Nr. 62, S. 716-762; eine Darstellung des Inhaltes des Berichtes auch bei Schuller, *Samuel von Brukenthal*, 307-312, und eine Analyse seiner Herausgeber bei Bozac, Pavel (Hg.), *Die Reise*, 77-101.

[67] Bozac, Pavel (Hg.), *Die Reise*, Nr. 63, S. 762-769. Der Versuch einer Analyse ebenda, Bd. II, 46-52. Für die Liste, siehe auch P. G. M. Dickson, in *Finance and Government under Maria Theresia 1740-1780*, vol. I. *Society and Government* (Oxford: Clarendon Press, 1987), 377-380.

riats, der Leitung der Komitate und der Stühle), von denen er die Umsetzung in die Praxis des Reformprogrammes erwartete. Besonders anschaulich sind die Abschnitte drei, vier und fünf des Berichtes durch die Art der behandelten Aspekte. Die Aufmerksamkeit, die er der Bevölkerung aus sozial-wirtschaftlicher und konfessionell-kultureller Perspektive widmet, ist aber aus dem zweiten Abschnitt ersichtlich, wo es um die Lage der Grenzregimenter geht, beziehungsweise aus den Abschnitten sechs und sieben, betreffend die Lage der Konfessionen und das Sanitäts Wesen.[68]

Der dritte Abschnitt ist den wirtschaftlichen Aspekten gewidmet: die Beschreibung des Landes mit seinen Reichtümern, die ihm Wohlstand sichern konnten, zumindest in Jahren mit reichen Ernten; der Zustand der Bevölkerung und die Gründe der Emigration, die bedeutendsten vorhandenen Rohstoffe, mit denen gehandelt werden konnte, hauptsächlich nach Ungarn auf Wasserstraßen, und die den Bedarf deckten, so dass nur noch Luxusartikel importiert werden mußten; die Schwierigkeiten in den Handelsbeziehungen zur Moldau und der Walachei angesichts des tobenden russisch-türkischen Krieges; die bescheidenen Früchte der wenigen Industriezweige; die Lage des Handels, insbesondere die Rolle der armenischen Kaufleute und die Spezialisierung der Händler, die von den Sachsen durchzusetzen versucht wurde „wie in grossen polizirten Städten", die aber völlig kontraproduktiv war in einem Land, wo es kaum Handel gab; die Mängel des Aufteilungssystems der öffentlichen Beiträge und die Lasten, die die Privatleuten zu tragen hatten, insbesondere die Leibeigenen, die in diesem Land wie in keinem anderen nach einer Urbarialregelung verlangten.[69]

Die Ressourcen und das Steuerwesen sind das Thema des vierten Abschnittes, wobei die ersteren, wie der Koregent bemerkt, in Siebenbürgen die beachtlichsten seien, die eine Provinz des Reiches zu bieten habe. Den Eisengruben und vor allem den Salzgruben schenkte er besondere Aufmerksamkeit und machte Vorschläge zu einer besseren Verwertung der Salzvorräte, die große Gewinne bringen konnten. Im Steuerwesen bemerkte der Kaiser das Ungleichgewicht in den bisherigen Verhandlungen, die sich auf die sächsische Nation konzentriert und den ungarischen Adel vernachlässigt hatten; eine äußerst kritische Haltung hatte er gegenüber der Organisation und Funktion des Thesaurariats, die er unmittelbar kennengelernt hatte, als er an einer von dessen Sitzungen teilgenommen hatte.[70]

Politisch-administrative Angelegenheiten werden im fünften Abschnitt behandelt, wo der Einfluß des Berichtes des Grafen Clary bemerkbar ist.[71] Joseph II. spürte hier den Wettkampf der beiden Alleinansprüche: des Adels (ein betonterer *fanatismus constitutionum* als beim magyarischen Adel in Ungarn) und der Sachsen (eigentlich des Patriziates, seiner Meinung nach bestehend aus 60-70 Personen), die mit Verbissenheit ihre „absurde"

---

[68] Bozac, Pavel (Hg.), *Die Reise*, Bd. I, 725-737, 758-761.
[69] Ebenda, 737-742.
[70] Ebenda, 742-746; die Verhandlungen der betreffenden Sitzung des Schatzamtes vom 5. Juli sind aufgezeichnet in einem selbst geschriebenen Fragment im Reisetagebuch (ebenda, 687-690).
[71] Ebenda, 746-757.

„Reinheit der Nation" zu bewahren trachteten, indem sie den ungarischen Adligen verboten, Immobilien oder Eigentum auf ihrem Territorium zu kaufen und die Handwerker dieser Ethnie in ihre Städte und Körperschaften aufzunehmen. Dieser Wettstreit hatte für den Staat negative Folgen wegen der Art der Beförderung in öffentliche Ämter (gemäß der Regel der „geometrischen Proportion"), durch die nicht Ehrlichkeit oder Fähigkeit der Personen den Vorrang hatten, sondern ihre konfessionelle Zugehörigkeit; diese Tatsache, die der Gleichberechtigung der vier Konfessionen widersprach, die durch die Gesetze des Fürstentums anerkannt war, führte zur opportunistischen Konversion der Protestanten, beziehungsweise zur Besetzung der Ämter mit Katholiken, die hierfür nicht die nötigen Qualitäten und Ausbildung besaßen.[72]

Die vorgeschlagene radikale Lösung, im Zusammenspiel mit dem Projekt der administrativen Neuordnung Siebenbürgens (Einteilung in Komitate und Vereinigung mit dem nicht militarisierten Territorium des Banates und mit den östlichen Komitaten Ungarns) bestand in der Gewährung der adligen Rechte für die Sachsen (*jus possedendi perennaliter* und den Adel) wie auch der Konzivilität für die Adligen (das Recht mobiles und immobiles Eigentum in den Städten der sächsischen Stühle zu erwerben). Auf diesem Wege sollten die Unterschiede zwischen den „Nationen" Siebenbürgens, von Joseph „Anstände" (der Begriff hatte die Bedeutung von verfehlten gesellschaftlichen Regeln) genannt, abgeschafft werden, und alle sollten so zu Siebenbürgern werden („dass alle Nationen Siebenbürger wären und heisseten").[73] Die mangelhafte Leitung der Institutionen (unter ihnen das Gubernium, die königliche Tafel und die Polizeiregeln, zusammen mit den politischen Nationen, den Bauern – „diese arme wallachische Unterthanen" – und den Verwaltungsstrukturen[74]) konnte auch auf einem längeren Weg geordnet werden: durch ein neues Steuergesetz, eine Neuordnung der Justiz, die Beseitigung der konfessionellen Zwistigkeiten, die Ernennung von fähigeren Beamten, die Verbesserung im Bereich des Militärs, der Kameralia, der Wirtschaft, der Polizei u.a.[75] Beide Lösungen bildeten eigentlich den Grundriß des Reformprogramms, das Kaiser Joseph II. beginnend mit dem Jahr 1781 durchsetzen sollte.[76]

c. Höfische Debatten über den kaiserlichen Reformprojekten

Für die stufenweise Ausarbeitung dieses Programms hatten eine entscheidende Rolle die Verhandlungen im Staatsrat über den Bericht, die der Koregent zur Verfügung stellte.[77] Die umfangreiche Notiz vom 12. September 1773, die dem Präsidenten des Hofkriegsrates, Graf Franz Moritz Lacy, zugeschrieben wird, enthält, obwohl auf militärische An-

---

[72] Ebenda, 748-751.

[73] Ebenda, 756-757.

[74] Ebenda, 751-756. Die Verhandlungen der Gubernialsession vom 6. Juli sind in einem ähnlichen Fragment des Reisetagebuches wie vorhin erwähnt, aufgezeichnet (ebenda, 691-695).

[75] Ebenda, 757.

[76] Aus einer anderen Perspektive sind einige der hier verhandelten wirtschaftlichen und politischen Aspekte bei Dumitran, „Grundgedanken", 291-294.

[77] Eine bündige Problemstellung bei Schuller, *Samuel von Brukenthal*, 314-317.

gelegenheiten ausgerichtet, kurze Einschätzungen betreffend das Projekt der administrativen Neuordnung des Fürstentums, die Konfessionen, die Schulbildung und die Bevölkerung.[78] Die wichtigsten Verhandlungen fanden allerdings im Frühling des darauf folgenden Jahres im Staatsrat statt.

Gemäß den erhalten gebliebenen Quellen setzte sich damals die Ansicht des Präsidenten des Staatsrates, Graf Karl Fr. Anton von Hatzfeld (1718-1793) durch. Seine Vorsicht beeinflußte die angenommenen Vorschläge für die wesentlichen verhandelten Fragen, die er in einem Schlußbericht Maria Theresia vorlegte: die Neuorganisierung der Grenzregimenter, die beabsichtigte „Union der Nationen" des Fürstentums, das Abgabenwesen und die Urbarialregelung.[79] Die Verhandlungen betrafen aber alle vom Kaiser Joseph II. in seinem Schlußbericht angezeigten Probleme, sowie auch die Ansichten dazu, die in den *Anmerkungen* des Gubernators Auersperg und der Barons Brukenthal abgefasst waren.[80] Anschaulich sind die Standpunkte, die zum Unterschied zwischen den Nationen geäußert wurden, zur Regierungsform, zur Polizei und zum Rechtswesen.

So war die Beseitigung des Unterschiedes zwischen den siebenbürgischen Nationen als Abhilfe gegen Aufruhr und Neid im Fürstentum grundsätzlich akzeptiert worden. Die Art der Umsetzung glich aber im besten Fall der „palliativen" Lösung, die der Kaiser vorgeschlagen hatte. In diesem Sinne wurde der Gedanke der administrativen Neuorganisierung des Fürstentums (durch die Integration des Banates und der westlichen Komitate) als die Ausweitung des sozio-juridischen Systems eines der in Frage kommenden Gebiete (Ungarn, Siebenbürgen oder das Banat) und nicht als eine tiefgreifende Reform verstanden. In ihrer Eigenschaft als Repräsentanten der Zentralmacht hätten die Räte der Durchsetzung des Banater Systems zugestimmt (wo die Autorität des Herrschers nicht durch Privilegien der Stände begrenzt war), oder sogar der Verallgemeinerung der Organisation der Erbländer; das Prinzip der Erhaltung der gegebenen Zustände war dennoch überwiegend.[81] Andererseits veranlassten Überlegungen konfessioneller Art den Vorschlag zum Festhalten am Grundsatz der „geometrischen Proportion" für die Besetzung der Ämter in den sächsischen Stühlen, den Hatzfeld für ein „notwendiges Übel" hielt.[82]

Dafür schlugen sowohl der Kaiser als auch die Mitglieder des Staatsrates Baron Brukenthal als den augenblicklich geeignetesten Nachfolger für den Gubernator Auersperg vor. Als Evangelischer wurde er bloß königlicher Kommissar und Präsident des Guberniums (1777 erhielt er dennoch den Titel des Gubernators). Als Hauptaufgaben hatte er den Abschluß der Urbarialregelung und des Finanzsystems sowie die sogenannte „Union der Nationen".[83] Letzteres hieß praktisch die Einführung der Konzivilität in den

[78] Bozac, Pavel (Hg.), *Die Reise*, Bd. II, Nr. 74, insbesondere S. 187-193. Die selben Herausgeber schlagen auch eine einleitende Untersuchung vor (ebenda, Bd. I, 103-110).
[79] Ebenda, Bd. II, Nr. 76, S. 273.
[80] Ebenda, Nr. 75, S. 211-272.
[81] Ebenda, 235-236.
[82] Ebenda, 241-243, 252.
[83] Ebenda, Nr. 76, S. 275-276; Schuller, *Samuel von Brukenthal*, 316-321.

sächsischen Städten und Stühlen, ein Projekt, das in den folgenden Jahren an Bedeutung immer mehr zunehmen sollte.[84]

Die Wahl scheint die richtige gewesen zu sein, wenn man das Lob betrachtet, das Brukenthal schon wenige Monate nach seiner Ernennung zum Gubernator erntete.[85] Tatsächlich widerspiegelt sich sein Einsatz zur Lösung der wesentlichen Probleme des Fürstentums (Fiskalität, Wahl der Beamten, Wirtschaft, Handel, Schulbildung, konfessionelle Angelegenheiten u.a.) in den Berichten, die er dem Wiener Hof zusandte.[86] Aufträge von höchster Wichtigkeit, die ihm bei seiner Ernennung erteilt wurden, wie die Verbesserung der Gesetze, die Gleichbehandlung aller Untertanen, die Beschleunigung der Umsetzung der Urbarialregelung und der Einberufung zum Militär,[87] waren Ende 1780 noch bloße Wünsche. Es ist wahr, das Fehlen einer eingehenden Forschung aufgrund von Urquellen,[88] macht es recht schwer, die reale Bedeutung der Zeitspanne zwischen 1774 und 1780 einzuschätzen, als der Tod Maria Theresias dem Kaiser Joseph II. die Möglichkeit gab, sein Reformprogramm in die Tat umzusetzen.

Schlußfolgerungen

Es kann bemerkt werden, am Ende dieser vorläufigen Untersuchung, dass wesentliche Maßnahmen vom neunten Jahrzehnt, wie die Edikte der Konzivilität und der Toleranz, die Verwaltungsreform[89] und der Versuch, die Struktur der Kirchenverwaltung neu zu ordnen, andererseits die Volkszählung im Fürstentum besser verstanden werden können, wenn man sie in Beziehung setzt zu den Vorgängen aus dem vorhergehenden Jahrzehnt, die hier verhandelt wurden. Selbst der Versuch der Durchführung einer Aufzeichnung der Grundstücke muss, obwohl gescheitert, in Verbindung gebracht werden mit der Schlußfolgerung des Koregenten betreffend die Dringlichkeit einer Urbarialregelung, hinsichtlich deren schon Graf Clary die Anwendung des ungarischen Modells vorgeschlagen hatte.[90] Später immer wieder aufgegriffen (die Schwierigkeit der Durchführung

[84] Schuller, *Samuel von Brukenthal*, 361-371. Die Forderung der Katholiken nach Gleichheit mit den Lutheranern in den sächsischen Stühlen und das Problem der Höhe der Einbürgerungstaxe erscheinen noch in Quellen des Jahres 1774. Siehe Bozac, Pavel (Hg.), *Die Reise*, Nr. 84, S. 299-302; Nr. 87-89, S. 306-309.

[85] Siehe den Brief des Sekretärs der Kabinetts und des Staatsrates Karl Josef Püchler, vom 27. Februar 1778, zitiert bei Schuller, *Samuel von Brukenthal*, Band II, 13.

[86] Ebenda, 9-10, der Bericht von Anfang 1778, nach zwei Monaten Tätigkeit als Gubernator und 22-30, die Ansichten vorgelegt 1779-1780, während der acht in Wien verbrachten Monaten. Eine Darlegung der wiederholten Revisionsvorschläge des Fiskalsystems, die damit endeten, dass der Staatsrat den Plan Brukenthals im Januar 1777 annahm, zu finden bei Dickson, *Finance and Government*, Bd. II. *Finance and Credit* (Oxford: Clarendon Press, 1987), 260-265.

[87] Kutschera, *Landtag und Gubernium*, 262.

[88] Das Werk G. A. Schullers, der die Dokumente aus dem Archiv des Staatsrates einsehen konnte, ehe diese vernichtet wurden, stellt bloß den Anfang einer derartigen Forschung dar, aus der methodischen Sicht des Endes des 19. Jahrhunderts. Das Schwerwiegende des Verlustes dieses Archivs wurde von Dickson unterstrichen in *Finance and Government*, Bd. I, 12.

[89] Eine anschauliche Untersuchung des Problems, brauchbar auch als Forschungsmodell, bringt P. G. M. Dickson, in „Monarchy and Bureaucracy in Late Eighteenth-Century Austria", *The English Historical Review* Vol. 110, No. 436 (Apr., 1995): 323-367.

[90] Für eine detaillierte Darstellung, beginnend mit der Verhandlung des Sache im Staatsrat, zusammen mit den anderen Aspekten, dargelegt im Schlußbericht des Kaisers, fortfahrend mit den Regelungen für die

war im Übrigen nicht eine Besonderheit Siebenbürgens),[91] hat die Urbarialangelegenheit die Schwierigkeit der Durchsetzung einer radikalen Reform im Fürstentum bewiesen,[92] die kurze Zeit nach anderen Reformen derselben Art kam und zeitlich zusammenfiel mit der umfassenden Volkszählung. Dies alles sind genügend Argumente für die Relevanz einer vertieften Untersuchung, deren wesentliche Linien in der vorliegenden Mitteilung nur angedeutet werden konnten.

Bergbaugebiete von Goldmarkt und Offenburg (Baia de Arieş) und das Banat mit den Eintragungen begonnen 1785 und dann die Vorgänge der nachfolgenden Jahrzehnte, siehe David Prodan, *Problema iobăgiei în Transilvania, 1700-1848* [Das Problem der Leibeigenschaft in Siebenbürgen, 1700-1848] (Bucureşti: Editura Ştiinţifică şi Enciclopedică, 1989), 114-146, 186-289, 335-349. Das Problem wurde erneut zur Sprache gebracht in Beziehung zum josephinischen Reformismus bezogen vor allem auf Ungarn von P. G. M. Dickson, „Josephs II's Hungarian Land Survey", *English Historical Review* Vol. 106, No. 420 (Jul. 1991): 611-634.

[91] Der Rahmen einer interessanten Analyse auf Reichsebene wurde umrissen von Christine Lebeau, in der Studie „Reconfigurer les « échecs » du joséphisme. L'exemple de la réforme fiscale", in *Josephinismus – eine Bilanz / Échecs et réussites du Joséphisme*, Hg. Wolfgang Schmale, Renate Zedinger, Jean Mondot (Bochum: Dieter Winkler, 2008) [*Jahrbuch der Österreichischen Gesellschaft zur Erforschung des 18. Jahrhunderts* 22 (2007)], 245-255. Hinweise und die wichtigsten Quellen sind zu finden bei Răduţiu, Gyémánt, *Repertoriul izvoarelor statistice*, 240, Nr. 1747, und 299, Nr. 2214 (für Ungarn); 461, Nr. 3604 (für Siebenbürgen).

[92] Siehe auch Prodan, *Problema iobăgiei*, 199, 215-216.

ABBILDUNGEN

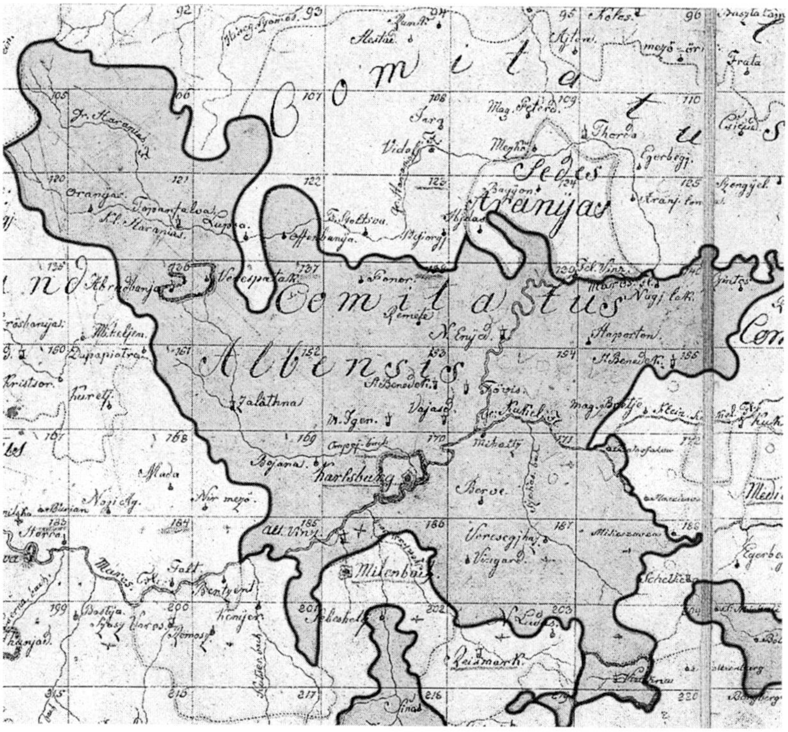

Abb. 1: Aufnahmskarte des Grossfürstentums Siebenbürgen: *Comitatus Albensis*.

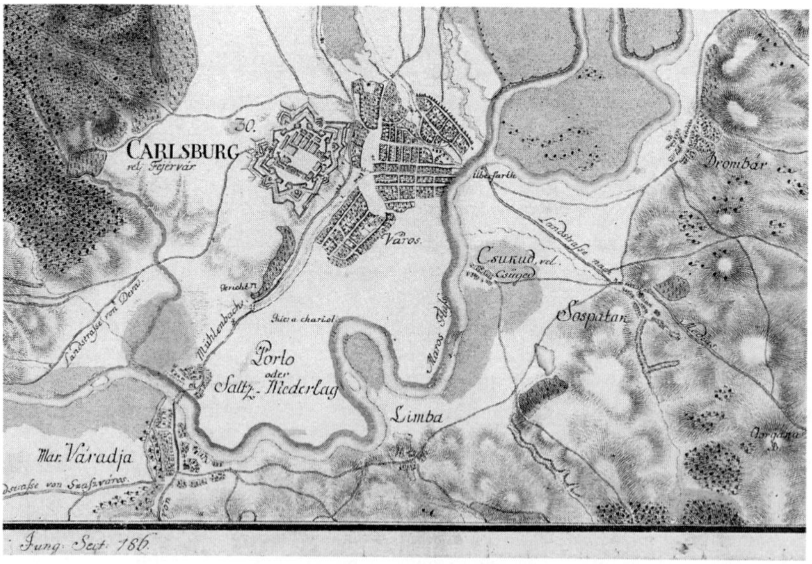

Abb. 2: Aufnahmskarte des Grossfürstentums Siebenbürgen: *Carlsburg vel Fejérvár*.

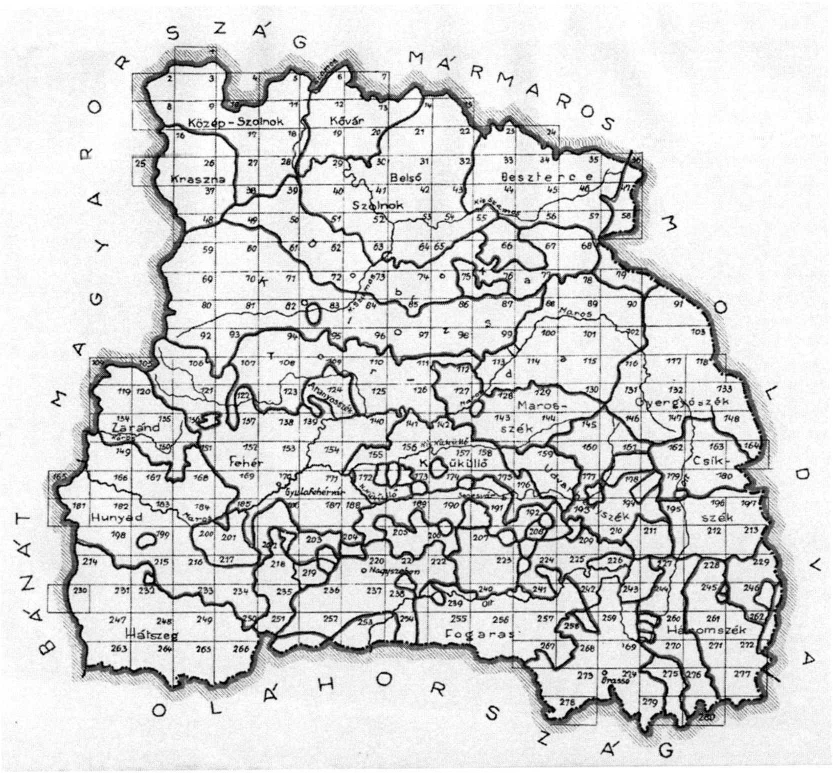

Abb. 3: Aufnahmskarte des Grossfürstentums Siebenbürgen, mit den 280 Sektionen.

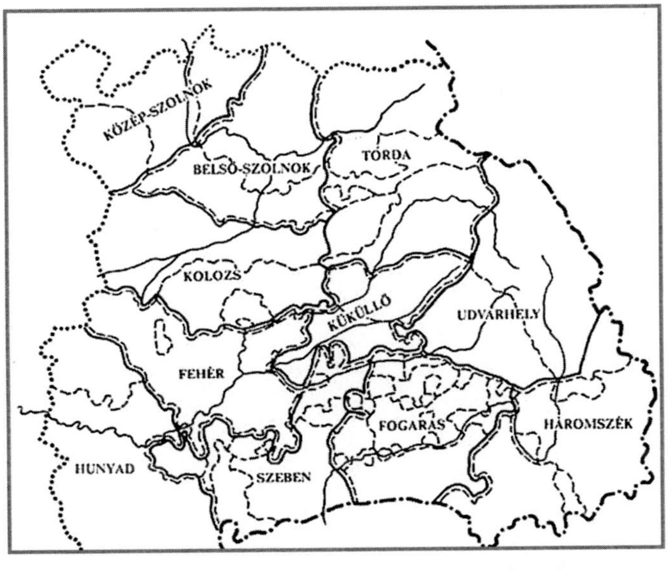

Abb. 4: Karte des Grossfürstentums Siebenbürgen, mit der ersten Komitatseinteilung Josephs II. von 1784.

Staatswirtschaftslehre des Kameralismus: Theorie und Praxis am Beispiel von den Kameralherrschaften im mittelslowakischen Bergbaugebiet. Einführung in das Thema

Eva Ondrušová

Obwohl Ungarn im Vergleich zu anderen Ländern in Westeuropa ein deutlich rückständigeres Agrarland war, ist es im späten 18. Jahrhundert schon auf dem Weg der Modernisierung angekommen. Die Geschichte der Neuzeit beginnt in der Habsburgermonarchie ungefähr um das Jahr 1740, als Kaiserin Maria Theresia den Thron bestieg. Die Maßnahmen, die die Kaiserin in den kommenden Jahrzehnten allmählich in die Praxis umsetzte, waren nicht nur bemerkenswert innovativ und hatten eine tiefgreifende Wirkung, sondern leiteten auch die allgemeine Konsolidierung und Modernisierung der Monarchie ein. Das Gebiet der heutigen Slowakei war damals nicht eine separate administrativ-territoriale Einheit und konnte sich auch nicht als eine wirtschaftliche Einheit entwickeln. Es war zwar ein Bestandteil des ungarischen Wirtschaftsraums, aber gleichzeitig war es auch in wirtschaftliche Aktivitäten innerhalb des Habsburger Reich einbezogen, wobei sich diese wirtschaftlichen Beziehungen in der folgenden Zeit noch mehr intensivierten.

Die Wirtschaft der Frühen Neuzeit in der Habsburger Monarchie war im ungarischen Teil fast ausschließlich agrarisch orientiert. Der überwiegende Teil der Bevölkerung waren Bauern, die den wichtigsten Platz in der Wirtschaft der Zeit einnahmen, vor allem in der Primärproduktion. Das Handwerk der Städte war auf den individuellen Kunden ausgerichtet, für dessen Bedarf man produzierte. Einzige Ausnahmen bestanden im Fernhandel und in der Montanindustrie. Besonders im Bereich des Buntmetallbergbaus (d.h. Gold, Silber, Kupfer) wurden sehr früh kapitalistische Produktionsweisen entwickelt. Später aber begann sich ein anderer Wirtschaftszweig auszubilden, der große Veränderungen mit sich brachte, und das war die Produktion von Gütern, die in der Verbindung zu den Wirtschaftstheorien der Zeit, die als Merkantilismus (im deutschsprachigen Gebiet Kameralismus) bezeichnet wurden, standen und dies war ein Neuansatz.[1] Die merkantilistische Theorie entwickelte sich in Frankreich und der eigentliche Name Merkantilismus wurde von deutschsprachigen Autoren in der zweiten Hälfte des 19. Jahrhunderts verwendet. Eine besondere Art der deutschen merkantilistischen Lehre war der Kameralismus. Kameralismus war eine mitteleuropäische „Variante" des Merkantilismus[2] mit dem er vor allem, die Lehre der Handelsbilanz und der Idee eines starken Staates teilte. In einer relativ kurzen Zeit wurde aus dem Kameralismus eine wirtschaftliche und administrative Richtung, die durch staatliche Eingriffe in alle Bereiche des gesellschaftlichen und wirtschaftlichen Lebens hineinwirkte.

---

[1] Karl Vocelka, *Geschichte Österreichs – Kultur-Gesellschaft-Politik* (München: Wilhelm Heyne Verlag, 2011), 150.

[2] Oder eine typische Wiener Angelegenheit/des Wiener Hofes.

In dem vorliegenden Beitrag behandle ich die Meinungen und Haltungen der Theoretiker der Staatswirtschaftslehre des Kameralismus, die unter dem Einfluss der zeitgenössischen staatswissenschaftlichen und volkswirtschaftlichen Lehren in der frühen Neuzeit standen. Das Wesen der Ideen war, eine neue, bessere Verwaltung der öffentlichen Angelegenheiten und die Hebung des materiellen Status der Bewohner zu verbessern. Die Ideen der kameralistischen Lehre bieten nicht nur eine hervorragende theoretische Grundlage für die Untersuchung der Wirtschaftgeschichte, sondern rufen auch nach ihrer allgemeinen Anwendung in der Praxis. Nur wenig Aufmerksamkeit wurde bisher der Geschichte der kameralistischen Lehre in der slowakischen Geschichtsschreibung gewidmet, wobei im Ausland, vor allem im deutschsprachigen Raum dieses Thema, nicht im Vordergrund stand und bis heute steht, wobei es gerade die Möglichkeit bietet, das Gesamtbild des Zustandes der öffentlichen Angelegenheiten und Regieren des Landes in der Neuzeit zu verstehen. Damit sind die königlichen Domänen, die von der Krone unzertrennbar und unveräußerlich waren eng verbunden. Es gibt uns die Möglichkeit die eigentlichen Prozesse, welcher die Staatswohlfahrt beeinflussten, verstehen.

Die politische Ökonomie

Unter dem Begriff „politische Ökonomie" verstehen wir die Geisteswissenschaft, die die entstehenden Beziehungen zwischen wirtschaftlichen Einheiten untersucht und Prognosen und ökonomische Gesetze formuliert. Die politische Ökonomie war im 19. Jahrhundert die gebräuchlichste Bezeichnung sowohl für Wirtschaftswissenschaft, Nationalökonomie als auch Volkswirtschaftslehre. Zu Beginn des 19. Jahrhunderts waren jedoch in verschiedenen Ländern auch andere Ausdrücke für derlei Betrachtungen des Wirtschaftslebens im Umlauf und je nach Autor werden auch mit „politischer Ökonomie" unterschiedliche Begriffsinhalte verknüpft, etwa solche, die späterhin „reine Ökonomie" oder „ökonomische Theorie" genannt wurden. Seit der zweiten Hälfte des 20. Jahrhundert wird der Begriff entweder als Synonym für Wirtschaft, normativen Ökonomie, oder als eine Art von der Kombination der ökonomischen Theorie und Politik eingesetzt.[3] Die Grundlagen der modernen öffentlichen Verwaltung stehen mit dem Ende des Dreißigjährigen Krieges (in der ersten Hälfte des 17. Jahrhunderts) im Zusammenhang, als die Umwandlung der sozialen Struktur der mittelalterlichen Gesellschaft eintrat. Der Wohlfahrtsgedanke nahm im Verlauf der Entwicklung des Territorialstaats stetig zu und die Friedenserhaltung nahm einen immer größeren Platz ein. Die neue Form des Staates, die aus den Reformationskämpfen und den neuen gesellschaftlichen Bedingungen entstanden war, war nicht Resultat einer bewussten Verwirklichung eines sozio-politischen Programmes, sondern das Ergebnis einzelner Maßnahmen und Beschränkungen, die sich zwangsläufig aus den politischen, wirtschaftlichen, sozialen und kulturellen Gegebenheiten entwickelten.[4] Nach

---

[3] Joseph A. Schumpeter and Elizabeth B. Schumpeter (Hg.), *Geschichte der ökonomischen Analyse*, Erster Teilband (Göttingen: Vandenhoeck Ruprecht, 1965), 53.

[4] Jutta Brückner, *Staatswissenschaften, Kameralismus und Naturrecht* (München: C.H. Beck Verlag, 1977), 4.

dem Dreißigjährigen Krieg entstand eine Situation, die die Notwendigkeit zeigte, in Zukunft auf bestimmte Systeme und Theorien zurückzugreifen, um ein organisiertes System der Verwaltung zu schaffen. Die Antwort auf diese Situation stellt in Westeuropa das merkantilistische ökonomische Denken dar, dessen Ursprünge bis ins 16. Jahrhundert zurückreichen.

Merkantilismus

Der Begriff „Merkantilismus" ist wegen seiner häufigen Verwendung durch verschiedene Autoren der unterschiedlichsten Denktraditionen kein sehr präziser Begriff. Es existierte im Merkantilismus keine allgemein akzeptierte Übereinkunft, die die Thesen in ein geschlossenes Theoriegebäude einbettete.[5] Der eigentliche Name Merkantilismus war in seinen verschiedenen nationalen Ausprägungen wie viele andere Denkschulen auch nicht in einem Jahr oder Jahrzehnt entstanden. Es handelte sich vielmehr um eine allmähliche Entwicklung, begleitet von vorbereitenden Debatten und einer sich verändernden wirtschaftlichen und politischen Realität und deren Wahrnehmung. Der Merkantilismus besaß starke nationale Ausprägungen und Eigenheiten, die neben allgemeinen Übereinstimmungen oft auch zu stark voneinander abweichenden Meinungen einzelner Autoren führten. Problematisch ist auch ein Fehlen einer gemeinsamen Terminologie, was einen Vergleich zwischen den verschiedenen Autoren schwierig macht. Leitbild war aber bei allen als merkantilistisch bezeichneten Autoren das Streben nach „politischer und militärischer Macht durch die Entwicklung der Wirtschaftskraft des eigenes Landes auf Kosten des wirtschaftlichen Wachstum in allen anderen Ländern".[6] Zu berücksichtigen ist dabei auch noch, dass die wirtschaftliche Entwicklung in den europäischen Ländern unterschiedlich war. Das Hauptinteresse des absolutistischen Staates war die Stärkung des Staates durch Bevölkerungswachstum und durch Akkumulation von Geld, die Vergrößerung des Staatshaushaltes, was durch eine aktive Handelsbilanz erreicht werden sollte. Ziel des Merkantilismus war hauptsächlich die Erhöhung der inländischen Produktion (Eigenproduktion), um den zuvor notwendigen Import zu minimalisieren.[7]

Kameralismus

Eine besondere Art („die österreichische Art") der deutschen merkantilistischen Lehre war der Kameralismus. Kameralismus ist eine theoretische Lehre, in der verschiedene Konzepte der Wirtschaftswissenschaften miteinander ineinander aufgehen.[8] „Kameralismus ist die politische Ökonomie."[9] Der eigentliche Begriff Kameralismus oder Kameralwis-

---

[5] Hans-Werner Holub, *Eine Einführung in die Geschichte des ökonomischen Denkens*, Band II, (Wien: LIT Verlag, 2005), 10.

[6] Fritz Blaich, *Staatliche Umverteilungspolitik in historischer Perspektive: Beitrage zur Entwicklung des Staatsinterventionismus in Deutschland und Österreich* (Berlin: Duncker & Humblot, 1980), 250.

[7] Jürgen Georg Backhaus, ed., *Handbook of the History of Economic Thought: Insights on the Founders of Modern Economics* (The European Heritage in Economics and the Social Sciences) (New York: Springer, 2012), 95.

[8] Johann H. G. Justi, *Staatswirtschaft oder systematische Abhandlung aller ökonomischen und Cameralwissenschaft* (Leipzig, 1755), 7.

[9] Ebenda, 20.

senschaft kommt aus dem Griechischen und Lateinischen *camera*, die ursprünglich den Sitz des Herrschers oder später die Schatzkammer bezeichnete.[10] Später überwog ein Begriff, der aus dem französischen Milieu (*science de police - Polizeiwissenschaft*) abgeleitet worden war und sich auch unter preußischen, österreichischen und sonstigen deutschen Bedingungen als *Polizeiwissenschaft* oder *Policeywisenschaft* durchsetzte.[11]

Der Kameralismus beinhaltete neben einer dominanten Staats- und Verwaltungslehre vor allem fiskalische, juristische und soziale Ziele und blieb letztlich auf die deutschsprachigen Länder beschränkt. Bei der Habsburger Monarchie kann man überblicksartig zwei Phasen unterscheiden: Erstens die Leopoldinische Ära, mit Kameralisten wie Becher, Hörnigk und Schröder, und die Theresianische Ära mit dem Ziel der Schaffung eines Gesamtstaates, mit Kameralisten wie Justi und Sonnenfels. Wegen des stark gestiegenen Finanzbedarfes wurde sowohl versucht, die Anzahl der besteuerbaren Menschen zu erhöhen, als auch Steuerprivilegien aufzuheben und eine Erhöhung der einzelnen Steuerleistungen vorzunehmen. Die Finanzbehörden waren deshalb auch die Behörden, denen das vorrangige Interesse galt und denen die vorrangige Zuweisung neuer Machtbefugnisse zufiel.

Die meisten Kameralisten wirkten im 17. Jahrhundert, aber die Ideen der Kameralismus wurden in der Donaumonarchie größtenteils erst im 18. Jahrhundert in die Tat umgesetzt. Zu den frühen Kameralisten, die in Österreich wirkten, gehörten Theoretiker wie Johann Joachim Becher, Wilhelm von Schröder oder Philipp Wilhelm von Hörnigh. P. W. Hörnigk legte mit *Oesterreich über alles wann es nur will* die Programmschrift des österreichischen Kameralismus vor.[12] Die Kameralistische Lehre war die politische Ökonomie, welche das theoretische Wissen in die Wirtschaftspraxis der Staatspolitik umsetzte. Wie J. J. Becher schrieb, die reine Theorie kann nicht auf die Praxis verzichten:

> „Denn alles Werk ohne die Theoria ist ungewiß, und die Theoria ohne Praxi liegt eben an diesem Fieber. Doch muss die Theoria vor der Übung und Praxi hergehen."[13]

Die kameralistische Theorie schuf verschiedene öffentliche Bereiche des täglichen Lebens, wie z.B. die Gründung und Entwicklung von staatlichen Banken, der Ausbau der Infrastruktur (d.h. Bau von Kanälen, Brücken, Häfen und Straßen), das Baugewerbe, die Landwirtschaft, der Handel und das Handwerk, um auf diese Weise die Modernisierung des Landes voranzutreiben. Viele Maßnahmen, wie die Einführung von Schutzzöllen oder die Unterstützung der Industrie und die Importsubstitution waren mit den Ideen des

---

[10] Kurz D. Heinz and Tribe Keith and Nishizawa Tamotsu, *The Dissemination of Economic Ideas* (Cheltenham: Edward Elgar Publishing Limited, 2011), 68.

[11] Siehe auch Dušan Hendryk, *Správní věda: Teorie veřejné správy* [Die Verwaltungslehre: Theorie der Verwaltungslehre] (Praha: ASPI Publishing, 2003) oder Reiner Schulze, *Policey und Gesetzgebungslehre im 18. Jahrhundert* (Berlin: Duncker & Humblot, 1982).

[12] Roman Sandgruber and Wolfram Herwig (Hg.), *Österreichische Geschichte: österreichische Wirtschaftsgeschichte vom Mittelalter bis zur Gegenwart. Ökonomie und Politik*, Band 12 (Wien: Ueberreuter, 2005), 139-141.

[13] Johann J. Becher, *Chymisches Laboratorium oder unterirdische naturkündigung* (Frankfurt, 1680), 262.

Merkantilismus identisch und dienten als Mittel, Reichtum und Wohlstand im Land zu erhöhen. Die kameralistische Lehre legte im Vergleich zum „reinen" Merkantilismus weit größeren Wert auf das Bevölkerungswachstum. Die Gründe dafür waren generell sehr prosaisch. Mehr Bevölkerung zu haben, bedeutete eine größere Armee, mehr Steuerzahler zu haben, dabei setzten mehr Bewohner auch einen größeren Markt und eine größere Produktion voraus.

Kameralismus als Staatswirtschaftslehre

Das erste Institut *Cameralia oeconomica und Policey-Sachen* wurde in Halle 1727 gegründet. Der Leiter des Instituts war Simon Gasser, der den Kameralismus nicht nur von den politischen, sondern auch von den Wirtschaftswissenschaften unterschied. Interessant ist dabei die königliche Begründung für die Errichtung des Instituts:

> „[...] damit die studierende Jugend, die sich im Dienst erhalten könnte eine gute Grundlage in der obigen Wissenschaften bekommen könnte (Das bedeutet: Kameralistik, Wirtschaft und Polizeiwesen) [...]."[14]

Ein ähnliches Institut wurde von demselben auch in Frankfurt an der Oder errichtet. Weil die Ideen des Kameralismus in der Donaumonarchie größtenteils erst im 18. Jahrhundert verbreitet wurden, war der Kameralismus bis 1749 formell in der Donaumonarchie nicht institutionalisiert. Der Impuls dafür kam von Kaiserin Maria Theresia, die dann das kameralistiche Institut am Theresianischen Kollegium gründete. Deshalb könnte sich in der Habsburger Monarchie die kameralistische Lehre entwickeln. Es muss jedoch gesagt werden, dass der Kameralismus besonders in Ländern, in denen die Amtssprache Deutsch war, eine signifikante Anwendung gefunden hat.[15] Viele Arbeiten preußischer, deutscher oder österreichischer Kameralisten waren populär und wurden mehrmals publiziert, aber nur ein paar von diesen Veröffentlichungen wurden damals in eine andere Sprache übersetzt. Bei Philipp Wilhelm von Hörnigks *Oesterreich über alles wann es nur will* kam es zwar zu sechzehn deutsche Auflagen, aber zu keiner einzigen Übersetzung. Ein anderes Beispiel dieser Art ist Wilhelm von Schröders *Fürstliche Schatz- und Rent-Kammer*, wobei acht Auflagen erschienen, aber keine Übersetzungen zur Verfügung gestanden ist.[16]

Die wichtigsten Träger der kameralistischen Lehre waren zwei Theoretiker und zwar Johann von Justi und Joseph von Sonnenfels, die die wichtigsten Ideen des österreichischen Kameralismus besonders in ihren Werken *Grundsätze der Polizeywissenschaft*, *Der Grundriss einer guten Regierung* und *Staatswirthschaft oder Systematische*

---

[14] Dušan Hendrych, *Základy správný vědy* [Grundlagen der Verwaltungswissenschaft] (Praha: Aleko, 1992), 41.

[15] Siehe auch Aladár Madarász, „Kameralizmus, történelmi iskola, osztrák gazdaságtan: Három vázlat a német és osztrák közgazdasági diskurzus történetéből" [Kameralizmus, Geschichte der Schule und der österreichischen Wirtschaft: Drei Skizzen aus der Geschichte von deutschen und österreichischen ökonomischen Diskurs], *Közgazdasági Szemle* 49 (2002): 838-857.

[16] „The Economic Bestsellers before 1850", accessed April 28, 2013, http://www.othercanon. org/uploads/ AJALUGU%20THE%20ECONOMIC%20BESTSELLERS%20BEFORE1850.pdf.

Abhandlung aller Oeconomischen und Cameralwissenschaften darlegten.[17] Justis Hauptleistung lag wohl in der Systematisierung des damals bekannten Wissens, ein Vorhaben, das er ganz bewusst und erfolgreich umsetzte. Deshalb wurden seine *Grundsätze der Polizeywissenschaft* auch für die Lehre an den Universitäten – was Justi durchaus beabsichtigt hatte („zum Gebrauch Academischer Vorlesungen abgefasset") – für die Ausbildung der Beamtenschaft wegweisend. Eine gute Ausbildung der Beamtenschaft war ihm wichtig, denn der Staat sollte Organisator der Wirtschaft zum Wohle der Untertanen sein, wofür gut ausgebildete Beamte eine unabdingbare Voraussetzung waren. Justi wollte „Universalcameralisten" ausbilden, die in mehreren Disziplinen ausgebildet wurden und auch eine „Einsicht in das Ganze" haben sollten. Er unterstützte auch eine Exportförderung nach kameralisticher Manier: Ausfuhrverbot für Rohrstoffe, Einführverbot für Waren, die im Inland auch produziert wurden, Zölle auf ausländische Waren und staatliche Preisbildung für Exportartikel. Justis Thesen waren sehr breit und umfassten verschiedene Bereiche des Lebens. Die Modernisierung beruhte nach Justi auf der Kultivierung allen verfügbaren Landes; den Landwirten sollten neue Techniken gelehrt werden oder die Erfindungen sollten – wie Justi betonte – durch den Staat belohnt und durch Patente geschützt werden. Er trat für religiöse Toleranz, Rechtssicherheit, den Ausbau individueller Freiheiten und eine Beendigung der Frondienste der Bauern zugunsten eines „Dienstgeldes" ein. Justi etablierte die Wirtschaftspolitik und die Verwaltungswissenschaft als „Polizeiwissenschaft", wobei es ihm letztlich (modern gesagt) um eine Art *welfare economics* ging. Dabei war es ein Ziel der Polizeiwissenschaft, im Lande eine gute Gesellschaftsordnung herzustellen, die die entscheidende Voraussetzung für den Wohlstand sei. Er strebte, was auch seinen *Grundsätzen der Polizeywissenschaft* entnommen werden kann, eine Art „Modernisierung von oben" an.[18]

In dieser Zeit dominierte aber in der Habsburger Monarchie ein anderer Kameralist und zwar Joseph von Sonnenfels. Seine Rolle als Initiator wichtiger politischer Reformen im aufgeklärten Absolutismus kann nicht bestritten werden (Rechtsreformer, insbesondere Strafvollzug, Didaktiker, Herausgeber sozialkritischer Zeitschriften). Er war gleichzeitig ein Vertreter der österreichischen Variante der Aufklärung, besser eines aufgeklärten Absolutismus. Wie Justi sah auch Sonnenfels in der Vermehrung der Bevölkerung ein wesentliches Ziel staatlichen Handels. Oberster Grundsatz des ganzen kameralistischen Lehrgebäudes war der *Bevölkerungssatz.* Aus der Zunahme der Bevölkerung als wichtigstem Verwaltungsziel ergeben sich alle Grundsätze für die einzelnen Verwaltungszweige: je größer die Bevölkerung, je größer die Sicherheit nach außen (Politik) und innen (Polizei), je größer die Bequemlichkeit (Handlung) und je kleiner der Steueranteil

[17] Johann H. G. Justi, *Grundsätze der Polizeywissenschaft*, I-II. Bände (Wien: Rehm, 1816); Ders., *Der Grundriss einer guten Regierung* (Frankfurt und Leipzig: Verlag Johann Gottlieb Garbe, 1759); Ders., *Staatswirtschaft oder systematische Abhandlung aller ökonomischen und Cameralwissenschaft*, I-II. Bände (Leipzig: 1755); Joseph Sonnenfels, *Grundsätze der Policey, Handlung, und Finanzwissenschaft* (München: Johann Baptist Strobel Verlag, 1787).

[18] Holub, *Eine Einführung in die Geschichte des ökonomischen Denkens*, 230.

eines jeden (Finanz). Sonnenfels hat damit versucht, die kameralistische Populationstheorie wissenschaftlich zu fundieren.[19] Der von den Kameralisten, vor allem Justi und Sonnenfels vorgetragene Gedanke einer Ablösung der Fron durch Geldabgaben und der Verwandlung der adeligen Güter in bäuerliche Kleinbetriebe war in der Habsburger Monarchie schon um 1760 lebhaft erörtert worden. Ende 1770 wurde dieses neue System probeweise auf zwei Meierhöfen[20] der böhmischen Kameralherrschaft Pardubitz eingeführt.[21] Im Jahre 1773 schrieb Sonnenfels eine Arbeit unter dem Titel *Von der Verwandlung der Domänen in Bauerngüter*, wo er seine Thesen noch einmal ausführlich präsentierte.[22]

Kameralherrschaften

Unter dem Begriff *Kameralherrschaften* verstehen wir solche feudale Herrschaften, die entweder durch das Aussterben einer Familie oder am häufigsten durch Beschlagnahmung unter die Verwaltung der Wiener Hofkammer gekommen sind. Ursprünglich waren die Domänen in Ungarn, wie in allen europäischen Reichen, die erste und sicherste Quelle der königlichen Einkünfte, denn mit den Regalien, das waren die gar nicht unbeträchtlichen Gerichts- und Kanzleieinnahmen, die Fiscalitäten, das Recht die Münze zu abzuwerten und so weiter, war nicht immer zu rechnen. Dahingegen war der König von Anfang an der größte Grundbesitzer, er und seine Familie lebten von der Landwirtschaft, Erhaltung und Glanz der Krone hingen von landwirtschaftlichen Einnahmen ab und was heute bei Schwartner Verbesserung der Finanzen heißt, hieß damals, als Staatsbedürfnisse gering waren, Verbesserung der Landwirtschaft. Es waren aber die Krongüter (königliche Domänen), die von der Krone nicht zu trennen, also unveräußerlich (*bona coronae sunt abalienabilia*) waren oder dem Fiskus (Fiscus) von Zeit zu Zeit anheimgefallene Besitzungen (Kameralherschaften oder Kameralgüter), welche der König an verdiente Männer nach seiner Willkür wieder vergeben konnte und dem Gesetz folgend auch wirklich häufig vergab. Im Jahr 1810 betrug nach Martin von Schwartners *Statistik des Königreichs Ungarn* die Zahl der Kameraldomänen in Ungarn etliche 20, ohne die banatischen und ohne die Kronherrschaften Altofen, Diosgyör, Vissegrad, Huszt (Chust).[23] In der ersten Ausgabe der Statistik des Königreichs Ungarn lag der jährliche Brutto Ertrag der Kameralgüter bei 4 Millionen Gulden, nach einer späteren, aber sehr tief angesetzten handschriftlichen Angabe sollte der (wahrscheinlich Netto) Ertrag von neun Jahren im Durchschnitt jährlich 1.200.000 Gulden ausmachen. Die Privatherrschaften des Königs Holitsch und Sassin, welche der Römische deutsche Kaiser Franz I. für sein Geld gekauft

---

[19] Sonnenfels, *Grundsätze der Policey*, 23 (§ 24).

[20] Meierhof (*praedium*) ist eine historische Bezeichnung für das Herrengut (herrschaftlicher Gutshof) oder für den Hof, zu dem Dominikalland gehörte. Unter Dominikalland verstand man im Mittelalter Herrschaftsland, also Land, das direkt durch die Herrschaft bewirtschaftet wurde. Josef Kulischer, *Allgemeine Wirtschaftsgeschichte des Mittelalters und der Neuzeit*, Band 1 (Oldenbourg: Wissenschaftsverlag, 1988), 51.

[21] Karl Heinz Osterloh, „Joseph von Sonnenfels und die österreichische Reformbewegung im Zeitalter des aufgeklärten Absolutismus", *Historische Studien* 409 (1970): 84.

[22] Joseph Sonnenfels, *Von der Verwandlung der Domänen in Bauerngüter, Nebst angehängten Lehrsätzen aus der Polizey, Handlung und Finanz...* (Wien: Kurzböck, 1769), 83.

[23] Martin von Schwartner, *Statistik des Königreichs Ungarn*, Teil Drei (Pest, 1798), 485.

hat, waren darin nicht enthalten.[24] Die Kameralherrschaften waren also dem Herrscher anvertraut, beziehungsweise in unserem Fall diente als Administrator das Oberst-Kammergrafenamt in Schemnitz (Banská Štiavnica/Selmecbánya). Die Herrschaften selbst gehörten nicht zu dem persönlichen Eigentum des Königs. Nach dem *Opus tripartitum* konnten Ursache für die Konfiskation dieses Vermögen entweder das Aussterben der Familie – *caducitas*, Majestätsbeleidigung – *crimen laesae majestatis* oder der Ehebruch (Verrat) – *casus notae infidelitatis* sein.[25] Zur Pflege dieses umfassenden Zweiges der ungarischen Staatswirtschaft, welcher in Ungarn teils auf Kosten der Regierung, teils gesellschaftlich von Gewerken (Waldungen), mit einem größeren und kleineren Anteil am Grubenbau besteht, das Oberst-Kammergrafenamt zu Schemnitz, welches nicht nur die weitläufige Wirtschaft, besonders das vielfältige Waldwesen ordnete, sondern auch auf die königlichen Einkünfte achtgab, den Bergbau in jeder Hinsicht belebte, und in Bergwerksstreitigkeiten das Ober-Berggericht für Niederungarn auf seiner Seite hat.[26] Dem Oberst-Kammergrafenamtes waren die Kameralherrschaften administrativ untergeordnet und das Amt mietete die ärarischen Häuser, Wälder, Grundstücke, Teiche weiter und vergab einige Privilegien wie das Jagen oder Angeln. Gebaut wurden neue Einrichtungen in den Wäldern und wie auch dem Bergbau dienenden Wasserwerke, Straßen und so weiter. Das Oberst-Kammergrafenamt kümmerte sich um die Gesundheit, Ausbildung und Geistesleben der Bevölkerung, die auf der Kameralherrschaften gelebt haben. Im ersten Drittel des 19. Jahrhundert begannen die Prozesse, in denen man begann, das Bergwesen mit der ungarischen Hofkammer zu verbinden. Großteils aber blieben die eigentlichen Bergwerksangelegenheiten administrativ unter der Hofkammer für Münz- und Bergwesen in Wien.[27] Nach der *Neueste statistisch-geographische Beschreibung des Königreichs Ungarn, Kroatien, Slawonien und der ungarischen Militär-Grenze* (1832) hing das Oberst-Kammergrafenamt in Schemnitz teils von der ungarischen und teils von der Wiener Hofkammer ab.[28] Die Hauptquellen, aus denen die eigentlichen Kammern und Administrationen die königlichen Einkünfte erhoben, waren die Kameral- (Krön- oder Fiskal-) Herrschaften (Güter, Domänen). Jene waren von der Krone untrennbar und unveräußerlich. Diese adeligen Herrschaften, welche entweder durch das Aussterben der Familie oder wegen Hochverrat an der Krone anheimgefallen waren, wurden früher oder später durch den König an verdienstvolle Männer entweder unentgeltlich oder gegen Bereitstellung einer gewissen Summe wieder verliehen.

An der Wende des 18. und 19. Jahrhundert bildeten die Kammer-herrschaften in dem Gebiet der Slowakei ein umfangreiches und weitgehend zusammenhängendes Territorium. Die Kameralherrschaften Revistye und Sachsenstein befanden sich im Komitat

---

[24] Ebenda, 484.
[25] *Tripartitum opus iuris consuetudinarii inclyti regni Hungariæ*, Pars I, Titulus 14.
[26] Schwartner, *Statistik des Königreichs Ungarn*, 495.
[27] Ebenda, 495.
[28] *Neueste statistisch-geographische Beschreibung des Königreichs Ungarn, Kroatien, Slawonien und der ungarischen Militär-Grenze* (Leipzig: Weygand´sche Buchhandlung, 1832), 144.

Barsch, im Sohler Komitat lag die Bergherrschaft Liptsch und im Liptauer Komitat waren es die Herrschaften Likava und Liptau-Hradek (veraltet auch Neuhäusel in der Liptau).[29]

Unter der Verwaltung der Wiener Hofkammer standen auch mehrere Kameralherrschaften, die sich nicht nur im Oberungarn, sondern auch in Böhmen, im Banat oder in Marmarosch (Bocskó, Rhónaszék, Dolha und Sziget) befanden. Die Kameralherrschaften dienten vor allem dazu, die Bedürfnisse des Bergbaus zu sättigen, der zu dieser Zeit eine starke wirtschaftliche Basis brauchte. Die Verwaltung des Besitzes aller Güter besorgte das Oberst-Kammergrafenamt in Schemnitz durch seine Angestellten, die dem Oberstkammergrafen untergeordnet waren. Das Oberst-Kammergrafenamt gehörte zu einer der wichtigsten wirtschaftlichen Institutionen in Ungarn. Im Jahre 1747 versuchte Kaiserin Maria Theresia das Amt zu reorganisieren. Mit einer Instruktion desselbigen Jahres restrukturalisierte die Kaiserin das Oberst-Kammergrafenamt vollständig. Die endgültige Direktive wurde fünf Jahre später erstellt und war zum Teil die gleiche wie die provisorische aus dem Jahre 1747. Alle Anweisungen und Instruktionen waren von diesem Jahre ab dem Oberst-Kammergrafenamt als Institution geschickt und nicht mehr dem Oberst-Kammergrafen persönlich.[30]

Dem Mangel an Holz suchte man im mittelslowakischen Bergbaugebiet unter anderem dadurch beizukommen, dass man den Adeligen die Verfügungsgewalt über ihre Wälder auf ihren Herrschaften nahm und diese den Bergkammern unterstellte. Da in der Schemnitzer Umgebung die Berg- und Hüttenwerke schon lange mit Holzmangel zu kämpfen hatten und die städtischen Wälder weitgehend verbraucht waren, wurde zuerst dieses neue Verfahren angewandt. Als nämlich 1640 die sogenannte Brenner-Gesellschaft aufgelöst und die Mehrzahl ihrer Gruben in Schemnitz von der Krone übernommen wurde, löste die Hofkammer den akuten Holzmangel dadurch, dass sie 1662 die Schemnitzer Bergkammer beauftragte, die Burgdomäne Revistye der Familie Dóczy zu übernehmen. Der Schemnitzer Bergkammer gelang es 14 Jahre später, von der Familie Lippay die Domäne Sachsenstein zu erwerben. Diese Unternehmenspolitik wurde fortgesetzt und im Jahre 1676 kaufte die Bergkammer zu Neusohl (Banská Bystrica) die Burgdomäne Liptsch (Lupča). Diese einzige Kamerallherrschaft war nicht direkt dem Oberst-Kammergrafenamt in Schemnitz untergeordnet sondern gehörte der Bergkammer zu Neusohl bis ins Jahr 1851. Kaiser Franz I. ordnete 1805 an, der Familie Esterhazy die Domänen Altsohl (Zvolen) und Dobrá Niva für fast 1,6 Millionen fl. abzukaufen.[31] Unter die Verwaltung

---

[29] Pavel Horváth, „Súpisy komorských panstiev na Slovensku z konca 18. a začiatku 19. storočia a ich význam pre vlastivedný výskum“ [Die Aufstellung der Kameralherrschaften in der Slowakei aus dem späten 18. und frühen 19. Jahrhundert und ihre Auswirkungen für den heimatkundliche Forschung], *Vlastivedný časopis* 1, 14, 3 (1965): 133.

[30] Franz Anton Schmidt, *Chronologisch-Systematische Sammlung der Berggesätze der Königreiche Ungarn, Kroatien, Dalmatien, Slavonien und des Großfürstenthumes Siebenbürgen*, Band VII (Wien: Hof- und Staats-Aerarial-Druckerey, 1834), 417.

[31] Jozef Vozár, „Die Versorgung der staatlichen Bergwerks- und Hüttenbetriebe in mittelslowakischen Bergbaugebiet mit Produktionsmaterialien vom 16. bis 18. Jahrhundert“, in *Bergbaureviere als Verbrauchszentren im vorindustriellen Europa: Fallstudien zu Beschaffung und Verbrauch von Lebensmitteln sowie Roh- und Hilfsstoffen (13.-18. Jahrhundert)*, Hg. Ekkehard Westermann (Stuttgart: Steiner, 1997), 308.

der Hofkammer gehörte ebenfalls eine kleinere Herrschaft Dekýš (Gyökös, Gyekés*)*. Außer dieser Herrschaften verwalteten die Bergkammern, insbesondere das Oberst-Kammergrafenamt andere Besitztümer und Herrschaften, die aus verschiedenen Gründen dem Ärar gegeben wurden. Die Bergkammer zu Neusohl gehörte die Kameralherrschaft Likava, Lietava (Ljetava) und Hrádok (Liptau-Hradek, Liptóújvár).

Die großen wie auch die kleinen Domäne erwarb die Krone vor allem deshalb, um den Berg- und Hüttenbetrieben des mittelslowakischen Bergbaugebietes zureichend mit Holz versorgen zu können. Damit gewann noch die Hofkammer Arbeitskräfte für Waldarbeiten, für Köhlerei und Holztransporte, Erz- und anderen Rohstoffen. Zur Verbreiterung der Versorgungsbasis der Berg- und Hüttenleute vor allem mit Fleisch, Getreide, Talg und von Häuten ganz zu schweigen. Besonderer Bedeutung erlangten diese staatlichen Maßnahmen im Laufe des 18. Jahrhunderts im mittelslowakischen Bergbaugebiet, als der große Aufschwung in Berg- und Hüttenwesen einsetzte und damit auch der Holzverbrauch stieg. Den Staat brachten die zu dieser Zeit dominierenden kameralistischen wirtschaftlichen Ansichten auf diesen Gedanken, der den Staat stärken und Wohlstand bringen sollte. Die Leitung der von der Bergkammer verwalteten Herrschaften lag in den Händen eines Ober-Verwalters (*praefectus bonorum* oder *Cameral-Herrschafts-Praefectus, Oberwürtschafts- und Waldungs- Inspector*), der ein Beamte des Oberst-Kammergrafenamtes war. Die gesamte Wirtschaft der Herrschaften wurde von ihm geführt, seine Aufgabe war es die Rechnungsbücher zu kontrollieren und er vertrat die Herrschaften als juristische Person. Unter der Leitung des Amtes arbeitete aber auch ein selbständiger Beamter, der für Rechtsangelegenheiten zuständig war. Das war der sogenannte *causarum regalium director*, *fiscus camerarum et dominiorum montanorum*, oder einfach *Kamerfiscal*. Nach dem Dekret von 1752 wurde er als *in cameris et dominiis montanis constitutus procurator* oder einfach *fiscalis procurator* oder *camerae procurator* genannt.[32] Seine Rolle war es die Beschwerden der Untertanen zu empfangen und zu beurteilen. Die Gerichte wurden unter seinem Vorsitz und in der Anwesenheit von Hofrichtern und Claviger jeden Monat auf jeder Kamerallherschaft in bestimmten „Amtstagen" gehalten. Zu seiner Kompetenz zugehörte auch die Rechtsumsetzung. *Camerae procurator* übernahm das Vermögen, das das Ärar *per caducitatem* bekam. Ebenso nahm er teil an den Komitatssitzungen, in deren Territorien die einzelnen Kamerallherrschaften lagen und damit repräsentierte er den Staat und vertrat seine Interessen. An der Spitze der einzelnen Herrschaften stand der Hofrichter (*Provisor*), der für die Wartung der ärarischen Gebäuden zuständig war und auch die Steuern, Abgaben und den Zehnten einforderte. Ebenso führte er die Kasse und gab die Finanzdaten der Kameralherrschaften ein. Die Daten über die Einnahmen und Ausgaben musste er jährlich zum Ober-Verwalter senden auf dem Oberst-Kammergrafenamt in Schemnitz.[33] Zu seinen Kompetenzen

[32] Franz Anton Schmidt, *Chronologisch-Systematische Sammlung der Berggesätze der Königreiche Ungarn, Kroatien, Dalmatien, Slavonien und des Großfürstenthumes Siebenbürgen*, Band X, 41.

[33] Jozef Vozár et al., *Štátny slovenský ústredný archív v Bratislave: sprievodca po archívnych fondoch / 3 / oddelenie hospodárstva v Banskej Štiavnici* [Slowakisches Staatsarchiv in Bratislava: Leitfaden für die

gehörte auch das Justizwesen der Kamerallherrschaft. In dringenden Fällen hatte er das Recht zu intervenieren und gleichzeitig konnte er auch physische und finanzielle Sanktionen setzen. Ansonsten sollte er die Sache an seinen Vorgesetzten melden. Einmal im Jahr musste er die ganze Herrschaft abgehen und kontrollieren. Die Verwaltung der Herrschaft konnte er nicht allein führen. Jede Woche fanden sogenannten *Konsultationen* statt, wo er mit anderen Beamten (Claviger und Schaffer) Beratungen über die Verwal tung der Kamerallherrschaft führen sollte. Dem Hofrichter war der Claviger („Schlüsselträger") untergeordnet. Er war für die Naturalien und für die Produkte der Untertanen verantwortlich. Unter anderen sollte gleichzeitig er auch die Buchhaltung führen und eine Bestandsaufnahme aller beweglichen Anwesen jährlich herzustellen. Nach der Instruktion aus dem Jahre 1755 (31. Dezember), die ein Jahr später genehmigt wurde,[34] wurde die vorige Aufgabentrennung, wo der Hofrichter für Finanzen (*das Pecuniale*) und Claviger für materielle (*das Materiale*) Verwaltung zuständig war, aufgehoben.[35] Beide sollten die Herrschaft zusammen zu leiten und die Finanzbuchführung und materielle Administration gemeinsam unterzeichnen. Auf den Kamerallherrschaften Likava, Revistye, Sachsenstein und Liptsch arbeitete zusätzlich ein Schaffer, ein Beamte der in der Regel für die Verwaltung eine kleinere Einheit verantwortlich war. Meistens ging es um einen Meierhof. Außer diesen Beamten arbeiteten auf den Kamerallherrschaften auch andere Angestellten wie zum Beispiel der Zehntensammler, Brauereien- und Kneipens- Verwalter und andere.

Die Zugehörigkeit der einzelnen Herrschaften zu den Bergkammern wurde auch in dem Herrschaftsnamen (Bergkameralherrschaft, k.k. Montan Domäne usw.) hervorgehoben und bis 1851 diese Benennung nicht verändert.[36] Revistye gehörte in der Vergangenheit zu dem ungarischen Herrschergeschlecht und im Jahre 1672 ist es dann unter die Verwaltung des OberstKammer-grafenamts gekommen. Seit der Jahre 1678 befand es sich administrativ unter dem Oberst-Kammergrafenamt in Schemnitz wie auch die Kameralherrschaft Sachsenstein. Beide Herrschaften dienten vor allem dem Bergbau und stellten eine starke wirtschaftliche Basis dar.[37] Zur Kameralherrschaft Revistye gehörten 18 Dorfgemeinden. Von diesen Gemeinden waren 15 Dörfer unter dem Besitz von der Bergkammer und Drei (Paulisch, Senitz, Eisenbad)[38] zur gemeinsame „Gütergemeinschaft".[39] Mitbesitzer des Dorfes Paulisch war die Herrschaft des Paulaner Kloster

---

Archivbestände / 3 / Abteilungsleitung in Banska Štiavnica] (Bratislava: Slovenská archívna správa, 1964), 208-209.

[34] Bewilligt wurde durch der Wiener Hofkammer in 18. März 1756.

[35] Schmidt, *Chronologisch-Systematische Sammlung der Berggesätze der Königreiche Ungarn, Kroatien, Dalmatien, Slavonien und des Großfürstenthumes Siebenbürgen*, Band X, 325.

[36] Nach 1851 wurde die Bezeichnung „Bergkameralherrschaft" zum Rentamt umgewandelt. Nach dem Österreichisch-Ungarischen Ausgleich benutzte man wieder eine adere Benennung und zwar das „Wirtschaftsamt" („gazdászati hivatal").

[37] Jozef Gindl, „Banskokomorské majetky na strednom Slovensku vo svetle zrovnacích štatistík k roku 1721" [Bergbau- und Kameralverwaltung in der Mittelslowakei in der Licht von der Vergleichsstatistik aus dem Jahre 1721], *Historický zborník kraja* 4 (1968): 89.

[38] Heute sind es Dörfer Píla, Bzenica, Vyhne.

[39] Unter die Gütergemeinschaft verstehe ich eine Form der Eigentumsverhältnisse in einer Gemeinschaft oder Gesellschaft und zwar in unseren Fall geht es um die Gütergemeinschaft vor allem Wälder und Wiesen, die

St. Johann in Oberelephant (Lefantovce), die zum religiösen Fond gehörte. Nach András Vályi war Paulisch ein Dorf im Komitat Bars, wo eine Drittel das Paulaner Kloster St. Johann besaß und die Bevölkerung der katholischen Religion angehörte.[40] In den Dörfern Senitz und Eisenbad besaß die Stadt Schemnitz und die Bergkammer 7/9 und 2/9 gehörten zum Eigentum der Familie Botka. Die ganze Kameralherrschaft war 29.370 ungarisches Joch groß. Die meisten Untertanen waren Slowaken, abgesehen von Dorf Paulisch, das von deutscher Bevölkerung bewohnt war. Die Kameralherrschaft Sachsenstein war 19.536 ungarisches Joch groß. Die Untertanen sprachen Slowakisch mit Ausnahme des Dorfes Blaufuss (Prochot'), wo sich Anfang des 18. Jahrhunderts Deutsche angesiedelt hatten. Im Jahre 1715 wurde in diesem Dorf auch eine Brauerei betrieben.

Die meistens genannten Gebiete waren von Wäldern bedeckt. Im Jahre 1765 reorganisierte Kaiserin Maria Theresia nicht nur die Bergkammern, sondern auch das kaiserliche Waldamt. Die Hauptkontrolle über die Waldbewirtschaftung im Rahmen der neuen Waldschutzpolitik hatte der Oberwirthschafts-und Waldinspector, der ein Mitglied des Oberst-Kammergrafenamtes in Schemnitz war. Das Forstwesen war weiterhin der Bergbau und Hüttenproduktion untergeordnet, aber die Erweiterung der Anzahl von Förstern bedeutete einen weiteren Fortschritt in der Waldwirtschaft. Ein anderer Fortschritt war die Veröffentlichung der Holz- und Waldordnung für das Königreich Ungarn. Holz war in der zweiten Hälfte des 18. Jahrhunderts sowohl für Gewerbebetriebe als auch für Privatpersonen nach wie vor der Energieträger Nummer eins. Um die Bevölkerung und Industrie mit mehr Energie zu versorgen, forderten Maria Theresia und Joseph II. einerseits eine erhöhte Holzproduktion: Baumschulen, Fichtenmonokulturen und Aufforstungen sollten den Ertrag steigern. Andererseits reglementierten zahlreiche Verbote und Ordnungen wie die theresianische Waldordnung[41] von 1767 den Holzverbrauch – beispielsweise sollten unberechtigte Holzentnahmen strenger bestraft werden. Die bäuerliche Bevölkerung betrachteten diese obrigkeitlichen Verordnungen als einen Eingriff in ihre traditionellen Nutzungsrechte.[42] Dieses Gesetz verhinderte weitere Waldzerstörung durch urtümliche Anbaumethoden und ermöglichte die Entwicklung einer modernen Forstwirtschaft. Bereits am Anfang des 18. Jahrhunderts wurden in Kammeralwaldungen regelmäßige Begehungen und Waldbestandsaufnahmen, sogenannte „Waldbereitungen“, durchgeführt.[43]

---

auf dem zeitgenössischen ungarischen feudalen Recht begründet war.

[40] Paulisch oder *PILA*. *„Német falu Bars Vármegyében, földes Ura a' Religyiói Kintstár, és a' Kir. Kamara, az előtt az Elefánti Paulinus Atyáknak birtokok vala harmad része, lakosai katolikusok, fekszik Zsarnótzhoz egy mértföldnyire, határja jól termő, vagyonnyai szépek, második osztálybéli.*“ András Válayi, *Magyar Országnak leírása*, 3. Kötet [Die Landschaftsbeschreibung der Königreich Ungarn, Band 3] (Buda: A Királyi universitásnak betüivel, 1796).

[41] Auf Slowakisch wurde es unter dem Name *„Porádek hor, aneb lesuw zachování*“ (1770) veröffentlicht.

[42] Günther Chaloupek (Hg.), *Österreichische Industriegeschichte* (*1700 bis 1848. Die vorhandene Chance*), Band 1 (Wien: Verlag GmbH, 2003), 80-86.

[43] Ľubica Miľanová and Viktória Jozsová, *Od lesov kráľovských k lesom štátnym* [Von den königlichen Wäldern zu den Staatlichen Waldungen] (Martin: Lesnícke a drevárske múzeum vo Zvolene, 2003), 26-27.

Meine Intention ist es zu zeigen, dass die Kameralherrschaften ein besonderes wirtschaftliches und soziales Phänomen darstellen, von dem der Staat nicht nur wirtschaftlich profitierte, sondern auch die soziale Entwicklung beeinflussen konnte.

Zum Besitz der Herrschaften gehörten Felder, Wiesen, Wälder, Mühlen, Wirthäusern, Ziegelbrennereien, Brauereien, Kurbäder oder Fleischereien. Die Kameralherrschaft Revistye bekam das Einkommen unter anderem aus dem Verkauf von Mühlsteinen, für die die Steinarbeiter aus dem Dorf Hlinik seit dem 14. Jahrhunderte bekannt waren. Die Untertanen arbeiteten meistens als Fuhrleute, Bauern, Brauer, Müller, Vieh Züchter, Schuster, Schneider, Schmiede, Kohlenbrennern, Bader bzw. Feltscher oder Imker. In der zweiten Hälfte des 18. Jahrhunderts begannen in den Kameralherrschaften Revistye und Sachsenstein signifikanten Veränderungen. Allein in Scharnowitz (Žarnovica), wo das Verwaltungswesen der Kameralherrschaft Revistye angesiedelt war, wurden neue Hütten geöffnet, eine Brauerei gebaut, der Erbstollen „Kaisers Joseph II." wurde geöffnet und schließlich die Leibeigenschaft abgeschafft. Zu diesem Zeitpunkt änderte dieses Gebiet seinen überwiegend landwirtschaftlichen Charakter und fing an, sich auf Bergbau, Güterproduktion und auf andere wirtschaftliche Tätigkeiten zu konzentrieren. Die Aufgabe des Oberst-Kammergrafenamtes in Schemnitz war nicht nur die Finanz- und Wirtschaftsfragen der Kameralherrschaften zu überwachen, sondern sich auch mit allgemeinen Problemen der Untertanen zu beschäftigen. Im Jahre 1785 kritisierte das Oberst-Kammergrafenamt seine Beamten, weil sie sich nicht in Schafzucht auskannten und deshalb sollten sie ihre Kenntnisse ergänzen und vertiefen.[44] Um die landwirtschaftliche Produktion zu erhöhen, haben sie in der Herrschaft Revistye auch neue landwirtschaftliche Methoden eingeführt, wie das Setzen neuer Kulturpflanzen auf Probe. Die Beamten haben auch ein Werk von Albrecht Daniel Thaer *Grundsätze der rationellen Landwirtschaft* zur Verfügung gehabt, um sich Kenntnisse aneignen zu können.[45] Albrecht Daniel Thaer gilt als Begründer der Agrarwissenschaften. Neben der Gründung der ersten landwirtschaftlichen Forschungs-und Bildungseinrichtungen durch Thaer, veröffentlichte er die erste Abhandlung über die Theorie des landwirtschaftlichen Betriebes (*Grundsätze der rationellen Landwirthschaft*).[46] Diese Grundsätze sind aus heutiger Sicht als eine Art erstes Handbuch der Landwirtschaft anzusehen. Thears hauptsächliches Ziel bestand darin, dass alles künftig durchdachter und systematischer gehandhabt wird als bisher.

Die Kameralherrschaften Revistye und Sachsenstein lagen im Heiligenkreuzer Kessel besser gesagt in dem Mittellauf des Flusses Hron (deutsch *die Gran*, ungarisch *Garam*).[47] Die ursprünglichen königlichen Herrschaften wie Revistye und Sachsenstein gehörten während der 15. und 17. Jahrhundert zu ungarischen Magnatenfamilien, aber in

---

[44] Štátny ústredný banský archív [Das Zentral Staatsarchiv für Bergbau] (ŠÚBA), Komorské panstvo Revište [Kameralherrschaft Revistye] (KPR), Inv. Nr. 175/1785.

[45] ŠÚBA, KPR, Inv. Nr. 201/1811.

[46] Albrecht Daniel Thaer, *Grundsätze der rationellen Landwirthschaft*, Band 1 (Leipzig, 1823), 1-3.

[47] Jozef Baďurík, „Z dejín Revištského panstva do polovice 17. storočia" [Aus der Geschichte der Herrschaft Revistye bis die Hälfte des 17. Jahrhundert], *Zborník Filozofickej fakulty UK – Historica* 26 (1975): 180-181.

der zweiten Hälfte des 17. Jahrhundert entwickelte der Ärar eine erhebliche Anstrengung um die Herrschaften wieder zu bekommen. Die Intention zu dieser Zeit war auf die dominierende kameralistische Wirtschaftspolitik, welche die Staatswirtschaft stärken und unterstützen sollten, zurückzuführen. Nach der Konsolidierung der Verhältnisse entstand im 18. Jahrhundert in den Kameralherrschaften ein ausgezeichneter Raum für neue Modernisierungstendenzen wie im Industriebereich so auch in der landwirtschaftlichen Produktion. Die Wiener Hofkammer führte durch die Vermittlung von dem Oberst-Kammergrafenamt in Schemnitz rationelle Wirtschaftsmethoden ein, um den Wohlstand auf den Kameralherrschaften zu erhöhen. Diese einzelnen Maßnahmen und Verordnungen hatten Einfluss auf die Organisation des Verwaltungswessen der Kameralherrschaften.

Die Kirchenpolitik als staatliche Finanzierungsfrage in Siebenbürgen der 1760er und 1770er Jahre

Kálmán Árpád Kovács

Meine Doktorarbeit von 2008 trägt den Titel „Das System der siebenbürgischen Religionspolitik in den 1760-70er Jahren". Für meine Dissertation habe ich vor allem folgende Bestände ausgewertet: Staatratsprotokolle, Siebenbürgische Hofkanzlei Acta Generalia, Acta gubernatoris Auersperg, Protokolle der Commissio in Publico-ecclesiasticis, die Koller-Akten, die ehemaligen Kabinettakten, darunter vor allem die sogenannten Blümegen-Akten. Während eines Stipendiums im Jahre 2009 besuchte ich auch das Hofkammerarchiv und das Kriegsarchiv. Diese in Wien und in Budapest aufbewahrten Materialien bieten eine breite Quellenbasis für meine erweiterte Fragestellung: „Welche wirtschafts- und sozialpolitischen Motive und Modernisierungsaspekte hatte die theresianische Religionspolitik in Siebenbürgen in den 1760-er und 1770-er Jahren?"

Theologisch gesehen ist die Abgabenfrage schon im Alten Testament in Form der Zehnt reguliert. Das Neue Testament machte die Freigiebigkeit zum Maßstab der freiwilligen Zahlungen.[1] Die Apostel hielten Spenden für ein sogenanntes Charisma, also göttliche Gnadengabe.[2] Der Gläubiger gibt unter der Wirkung der göttlichen Gnade dem Allmächtigen nur das zurück, was er sowieso aus den göttlichen Händen bekommen hatte.[3] Im ungarischen Ständetum war es eindeutig, dass der christlich göttliche Kultus aus gesellschaftlichen und staatlichen Interessen aufrecht erhalten wurde.[4] Der Zehnt wurde zum Symbol der Sesshaftigkeit und christlicher Demut.[5] Ohne näher in die Theorie, Praxis und die Tagespolitik einzugehen, kann behauptet werden, dass die staatliche Finanzierung meist mit einem Staatskirchentum verbunden ist. Die in der Türkenzeit entstandene konfessionelle, ethnische und nationale Vielfalt Siebenbürgens war weiterhin in ein entwickeltes Ständewesen eingebettet. Der wichtigste Schwerpunkt für Wien war die Restaurierung der vorprotestantischen kirchlichen Verhältnisse, teilweise durch eine neue Bevölkerung, durch Übertritt der Rumänen zur mit Rom unierten Kirche. Die karolinische und die theresianische Religionspolitik hatten das Ziel, die Vorherrschaft des Katholizismus zu schaffen, welches Bekenntnis in Siebenbürgen in keinerlei Hinsicht ein Übergewicht tragen sollte. Das galt auch in der Bevölkerung, im

---

[1] 2 Kor 8-9 (darunter siehe 8,5).

[2] Röm 12, 8.

[3] 2 Kor 8,5.

[4] Die Anordnung der Zehnt im mittelalterlichen ungarischen Rechtswesen: Das zweites Buch der Dekreten des I. (Heiligen) Stephan Kap. 52, in *Corpus Juris Hungarici. Magyar Törvénytár*, Band I, Hg. Dezső Márkus (Budapest: Franklin Társulat, 1896) (im weiteren *CJH*).

[5] Siehe z.B. in den siebenbürgischen Gesetzen *Approbatae Constitutiones* Pars III. Titulus V. articulus 2, in *CJH*, Band VII, *Az 1540-1848. évi erdélyi törvények* [Die siebenbürgischen Gesetze aus den Jahren 1540-1848], Hg. Dezső Márkus (Budapest: Franklin Társulat, 1900).

politischen Gewicht unter den Ständen und in geistigen und materiellen Kräften. Außerdem wurde der Katholizismus in sich gespalten. Die griechisch-unierte Konfession erwarb 1744 formell die Vorrechte und Privilegien der Römisch-Katholiken. Diese Gleichberechtigung veränderte aber das Szatmárer Kompromiss vom Jahre 1711 zwischen dem Hof und den Ständen nicht. Es wurde nachdrücklich festgelegt, dass die griechisch-unierten Glaubensgenossen, wenn sie bürgerlich oder adelig sind, nach Art der ständischen Nationen ihre Privilegien erhalten. Unter dem ungarischen und szeklerischen Adel und den Magnaten wirkten solche nationalen und sprachlichen Gemeinschaftsgefühle, die die Vorurteile gegen den unierten Rumänen und ihrem Klerus verstärkten. Die griechisch-unierte Religion war zweitrangige rezipierte Religion. Die Griechisch-Katholischen fühlten sich keineswegs gleichberechtigt, nicht einmal mit den Kalvinisten und den Lutheranern, die viel weitergehende Privilegien genossen als sie. Privileg heißt in diesem Sinne nicht nur einen erhöhten gesellschaftlichen Status, sondern auch die Zugang dieser Religionsgemeinschaften und ihrer Vertreter zu öffentlichen Einkünften. Diese Einkünfte waren die Zehnt- und Zehntquarten oder Viertelgaben. Der Zehnt war nach der ständischen Rechtsauffassung hoheitliche Abgaben zur Erhaltung der Kirche und des kirchlichen Kultus. Nach dem Zusammenbruch der mittelalterlichen Kirche fiel sie durch verschiedene Rechtsakten an den Staat zurück, der sie nach erwogenem Gutbefund durch öffentliche Verträge an verschiedene Grundherren, Kommunitäten, Institutionen, meist an Protestanten weiterschenkte. Diese Verträge wurden dann auch bei der Machtübernahme durch den habsburgischen Zentralstaat anerkannt und durch verschiedene Rechtsgarantien bestätigt.[6] Neben der rechtlichen Anerkennung wollte die karolinische und die theresianische Religionspolitik das Land erneut missionieren. In Siebenbürgen übten vor allem die verschiedenen Klöster und Ordenshäuser eine bedeutende seelsorgerische und Missionstätigkeit aus.[7] Unter Karl VI. kam es zu den meisten Gründungen, Neugründungen, Rückerwerbungen aus dem 18. Jahrhundert. In der ersten Hälfte des 18. Jahrhunderts war es z.B. in den franziskanischen Ordensprovinzen der Stephanskrone einfacher Klöster in einem Umkreis von 50 km zu bauen, als Pfarren mit einem Weltpriester in den einzelnen Ortschaften einzurichten. Die verschiedene kleinere Ordensanstalten, wie Residenzen und Missionen hatten eine geringere Reichweite (etwa die Hälfte wie Klöster und Kollegien). Diese Gründungen, Neugründungen und Rückerwerbungen verfügten aber meist über keinen festen finanziellen Fonds, deshalb mussten sie auch mit anderen (Ordens- oder staatlichen)

---

[6] Zum politischen Hintergrund dieser Frage siehe Zsolt Trócsányi, *Habsburg-politika és Habsburg-kormányzat Erdélyben 1690-1740* [Habsburgische Politik und habsburgische Verwaltung in Siebenbürgen 1690-1740] (Budapest: Akadémiai Kiadó, 1988), 201, 207, 211, 221-223, 242-243, 247, 249-250, 251-253.

[7] Siehe Ungarisches Staatsarchiv (im weiteren UstA), B2. Siebenbürgische Hofkanzlei. Acta generalia (im weiteren SHK), Nr. 1594/1773: *Verzeichniß der Zahl derjenigen, die von dem in Siebenbürgen befindlichen Irrlehren zur Röm.-Catholischen Religion, oder aber zur Heil. Union in denen zweyen letzt abgewichenen 1771, und 1772 Jahren herüber getretten sind, mit Anmerkung deren Missionen, oder Pfarretheyen, in welchen der Glaubensbekanntniß abgeleget worden.*

Quellen finanziert werden. Die Religionssitzung vom 15. März 1773 weist z.B. darauf hin, dass die immer neuen Bitten dieser Ordensstellen für staatliche Subventionen, ihre baufälligen Kirchen und Klöster renovieren zu können, bedeutet für die Staatskasse eine schwere Last.[8] Im Januar-Februar 1761 fanden in dem kurz vor seiner Auflösung stehenden Direktorium in Publicis et Cameralibus wichtige Religionsverhandlungen statt. Der siebenbürgische römisch-katholische Bischof Freiherr von Bajtay bezog sich auf die allerhöchsten Beschlüsse vom 5. Februar 1761 so: die Regentin will die Mission auch in Siebenbürgen urgieren.[9] Der ernster Versuch war die Rückerwerbung der Zehnteinnahmen, die während der Fürstenzeit an die Protestanten vergeben worden waren.[10] Noch im Jahre 1734 fing ein sogenanntes Produktionsverfahren (Privilegrechtfertigung) wegen des Burzenländer Zehnten an. Dieses tritt bereits 1761 in seine neuere Phase. 1758-1762 fand der Prozess des Fiscus gegen der Sächsischen Nation wegen des sogenannten Martinszinns statt. Wegen der rückzuerwerbenden ehemaligen katholischen Kirchengüter und kirchlichen Einkünfte verordnete Maria Theresia im Januar 1763 eine heimliche Untersuchung und Berichterstattung.[11] 1770, als das Urteil wegen des Burzenländer Zehnten in Kraft trat, begann die Schatzhalterei einen neuen Prozess gegen den Sachsen für die „kleineren" Zehnten. Aufgrund der Staatsratsprotokolle kann ich behaupten, dass es wegen der sächsischen Zehnten noch zwei große Aktenproduktion in der theresianischen Epoche gab, 1771-1772 und 1776. Die Aufarbeitung dieser zahlreichen Einträge lässt noch aber auf sich warten. Wegen der nichtsächsischen Zehnten wurden die meisten Maßnahmen getroffen, als 1762 der kommandierende General und Gubernialpräsident Buccow eine sogenannte Adelskonfirmation begann. In diesem Zusammenhang erbat der Bischof das Zurücklösungsrecht (also das *ius reluitionis*) auf die Zehnten der Siebenbürger „Hegyalja", wozu aber er nicht berechtigt gewesen wäre, waren diese Zehnten nicht gänzlich Fiscalitäten, also Einkünfte, die dem Herrscher zustanden.[12] Aufgrund dieser Verahandlungsergebnisse behauptete der römisch-katholische Ordinarius gegenüber dem reformierten Gubernialsekretär Halmágyi im Sommer 1765, dass es große Veränderungen im Religionswesen zu erwarten sind. Maria Theresia entschied sich für die Ausmessung

---

[8] SHK, Nr. 1591/1773, Schriftstück d, Nr. 3: *Protocollum Consessus in Religiosis Transylvanicis 15^{a} Martii 1773. celebrati in puro* (im weiteren SHK, Schriftstück d).

[9] István Miskolczy, *Bajtay J. Antal* (Budapest: 1914), 50.

[10] Z.b. für die Zehnten der Sachsen, Georg Daniel Teutsch, *Das Zehntrecht der evangelischen Landeskirche A. B. in Siebenbürgen* (Schässburg: 1858), 75-111, und für die Zehnten im Erdélyi Hegyalja (das Gebiet zwischen Karlsburg / Alba Julia und den Westkarpaten / Munţii Apuseni) Péter Bod, *Önéletírás* [Sein Lebenslauf] (siehe Magyar Elektronikus Könyvtár, http://mek.oszk.hu/00600/00616, herunterladen am 23. April 2013).

[11] Österreichisches Staatsarchiv (im weiteren ÖstA), Haus-, Hof- und Staatsarchiv (im weiteren HHStA), Staatsratsakten (im weiteren *StRA*); wegen der Verbrennung dieser Akten im April 1945, während der Belagerung Wiens, sind die erhalten gebliebenen Zitaten und Notizen von Győző Ember hier quellenmäßig), Nr. 131/1763. Győző Ember, „Egy katolikus államférfi a XVIII. században. Báró Boriè Egyed" [Ein katholischer Staatsmann des 18. Jahrhunderts. Freiherr Egyd von Borié], *Regnum. Egyháztörténeti Évkönyv* (1936): 345.

[12] Bod, *Önéletírás*.

von kanonischen Portionen,[13] aber dafür wird sie ihnen alle Zehnteinkommen entnehmen. Die so entstandene Zunahme der Zehnteinkünfte widmet die Herrscherin zu Gunsten eines allgemeinen Religionsfonds in Siebenbürgen.[14] Der siebenbürgische Bischof wies auf die Tatsache hin, dass der wichtigste Gegenstand der siebenbürgischen Religionsverhandlungen im Jahre 1765 die Lösung der Finanzierungsprobleme der siebenbürgischen Missionen war. Die Einwände des Freiherrn von Brukenthal zeigten aber in den Verhandlungen im Herbst 1765, dass die Sache viel komplizierter war. Deswegen bekam er vom Staatsrat Borié ein strenges Urteil.[15] Die Richtigkeit der Einwände Brukenthals zeigte sich auch darin, dass die Wiener Hofelite auch andere Wege offen hielt. István Halmágyi erwähnt in seinem Tagebuch den allerhöchsten Entschluss, dass jährlich 2.000 Gulden aus den ungarischen Kameraleinkünften an solche siebenbürgischen Geistlichen verliehen werden müssen, die über keine angemessenen kanonischen Portion verfügen.[16] Diese reichte aber nicht aus. Deshalb kam im Staatsrat der Gedanke auf, dass man auch aus den Einkünften der sogenannten ungarischen Pfarrerkasse (*Cassa parochorum*) Geldmittel an siebenbürgische Religionsziele widmen sollte. Der Staatskanzler Kaunitz war aber gegen den Plan. Eine solche Tatsache würde die Ansprüche der Ungarn auf Siebenbürgen verstärken, behauptete er.[17] Die Argumente von Kaunitz und Brukenthal in Kenntniss genommen entschied die Kaiserin, das sogenannte Portugiesische Kapital dem siebenbürgischen Missionswesen zu widmen. 1759 ließ der Marquis von Pombal den Jesuitenordnen auf den Gebieten der portugiesischen Krone verbieten, die Ordensmitglieder wurden vertrieben und die Fremden als Spione und Fürstenverräter eingekerkert. So geriet ein Teil des Vermögens nach Rom. Der Almirante di Castiglione legte im Oktober 1765 diese 400.000 Gulden bei dem Wiener Staatsbanco an.[18] Der *fundus lusitanicus* sollte nach dem Wunsch Maria Theresias weiterhin auch Missionszwecken dienen. In der genauen Situation fand die Wiener Hofelite darin das Mittel, katholische Priester, Schulmeister und Missionen zu

[13] Der kanonische Anteil war in diesem Sinne ein steuerfreies Grundstück, das man aus den Gemeinde absonderte, welches von den Gemeindeglieder bebaut wurde und dessen Ertrag zur Besoldung eines Geistlichen diente.

[14] *Halmágyi István naplói 1752-53. 1762-69. és iratai 1669-1785* [Die Tagebücher des István Halmágyi 1752-53. 1762-69 und seine Schriftstücke 1669-1785], Hg. Lajos Szádeczky (Budapest: Athenaeum Könyvnyomda, 1906) (im weiteren Halmágyi, *Tagebücher*), 203.

[15] *Ich umbgehe, wie [...], dieses anzusehen seyn wolle, dass mann einen Lutheraner zu der Berathung einer solchen Sache haben beyziehen, und dessen schlaue, die Sachen auf die lange Ewigkeit hinausziehende und solche in unübersteigliche Einhangungen verleithende Ratschläge gelten lassen mögen. StRA*, Nr. 2609/1765, zitiert in Ember, „Egy katolikus államférfi,“ 336 und Fußnote.

[16] Halmágyi, *Tagebücher*, 206.

[17] Ember, „Egy katolikus államférfi,“ 344 bezogen auf die ehemaligen *StRA* Nr. 1848/1765.

[18] ÖStA, HHSTA, Staatsratsprotokolle (im weiteren *StRP*), Nr. 2402/1765: *Vortrag des Fürsten von Kaunitz-Rittberg dd° 30sten Oct. circ. 31sten Oct. in Ansehen der von dem Almirante di Castiglione in dem Banco anliegenden für die Missionen bestimmten 400 m. f. betr.* Billet an Grafen von Hatzfeld; Ders., Nr. 2904/1765: *Vortrag des Grafen von Hatzfeld dd° 21sten Dec. circ. 23sten Dec. exp. 13ten Jan. in Ansehen der von dem Almirante di Castiglione in dem Banco anliegenden für die Missionen bestimmten 400 m. f. betr.*

dotieren, Kirchen-, Pfarr- und Schulgebäude zu bauen oder zu reparieren.[19] Ab 1. Januar 1767 kam es zu den ersten Auszahlungen. Im Sommer dieses Jahres behauptete der Schatzmeister Bornemissza dem Gubernialsekretär Halmágyi, dass aus dem Portugiesische Fonds den armen Neokonvertiten finanzielle Hilfe verabfolget werden wird,[20] aber dieser Plan wurde letztendlich nicht verwirklicht. Sieben Jahre später (am 2. Juli 1774) verordnete Maria Theresia die Konvertitenbeihilfe mit einem Betrag von 3.000 rheinischen Gulden aus der Kameralkasse.[21]

Also geriet der Konvertitenbeitrag und Beihilfe letztendlich nicht zu den Agenden des Religionsfond. Aber wen sollte man aus den Portugiesischen Fonds finanzieren? Wie wir feststellen konnten, wurde 1761 die Vermehrung der Missionen auch in Siebenbürgen zu einem wichtigen Grundprinzip. Am Anfang 1765 wurde die Idee im Staatsrat aufgebracht, Ordensgeistliche zu Erfüllung von seelsorgerischen Aufgaben zu verpflichten. Vor allem befürwortete Kaunitz diese Idee.[22] Schon dieser Vorschlag bedeutete einen Kurswechsel: die Ordensgeistlichen sollten vor allem nicht zu Missions-, sondern zur seelsorgerischen Tätigkeit eingesetzt werden. Ab 1771-73 kam es zur Unterordnung der Kirche unter den Staat nach dem böhmisch-österreichischen Muster. Ab 1772 wurde ein Kurswechsel bei der Verbesserung der Seelsorge in den böhmischen und österreichischen Erblanden vollzogen. Die allerhöchste Anordnung vom 20 Juni 1772 schrieb vor, dass die Bischöfe die Anzahl der Weltpriester vermehren sollten. Die Ordinarios hatten auch zu berichten, auf welcher Art und Weise die Anzahl der Ordensgeistlichen zu verringern wäre, ohne dass die Seelsorge vernachlässigt würde.[23] Auf Grund dieser Richtlinie wurden April 1773 Informationen von den siebenbürgischen Klöstern und Ordenshäusern verlangt. Der Wandel ab 1772 setzte schon die Auflösung des Jesuitenordens voraus. Nach der Auflösung des Ordens verloren die Patres ihren Ordenscharakter, wurden zu Weltpriestern. Die früheren jesuitischen Missionare verblieben meist an ihren Aufenthaltsorten und wurden als königliche Benefitiate und Pfarradministratoren eingesetzt. Das Jesuitenvermögen wurde seit 1773 zusammen mit dem Portugiesischen Kapital verwaltet. Dieses Vermögen bildete den Religionsfonds des Landes.[24]

Infolge der Zehntpolitik und der Auflösung der Gesellschaft Jesus fielen mehr geistliche Güter und Einkünfte an den Staat. Die Jesuiten waren in Siebenbürgen nach

---

[19] *StRP*, Nr. 2609/1765: *Concertatio zwischen Grafen von Hatzfeld, dem Hof-Kriegs-Rath, der Siebenbürgischen Kanzley und der Hof-Kammer die Erhebung des catholischen Pfarr- Schul- und Kirchen-Weesen in Siebenbürgen betreffend.*

[20] Halmágyi, *Tagebücher*, 313.

[21] Jakab, Elek, „A r. kath. hittéritési alap (fundus convertitarum) rendeltetése és története“ [Die Verordnung und Geschichte des Konvertitenfonds (fundus convertitarum)], *Keresztyén Magvető* 2 (1883): 99-100.

[22] *StRA*, Nr. 19/1765, zitiert in Ember, „Egy katolikus államférfi“, 345.

[23] SHK, Nr. 1631/1773: *Verzeichnus der in publico ecclesiasticis ausgegebenen Generalvorschriften*, Nr. 30.

[24] ÖstA, Hofkammerarchiv (im weiteren HKA), Nr 34, Kt. 505, Copia Nr. 162: A. 1775. 64. ex Aprili 1775. *Protocollum der untern 30. Novembris 1774. zwischen der Kai.[serlich-] Auch Kai.[serlich-Königl.[ichen] Hofkammer, und der Siebenbürgischen Hofkanzley abgehaltenen Zusammentrettung Zweyter Abschnitt Achtens Votum.*

meinen bisherigen Forschungen Grundherren in Kolozsmonostor, Neppendorf oder Nebendorf (Turnişor, Kreis Sibiu) und in Kajántó (Chinteni, Kreis Cluj). Das Gut Kolozsmonostor wurde am 18. September 1776 zu einem standhaften Fonds des Hermannstädter Theresianum-Waisenhauses. Im Vertausch dagegen mussten die kleinere Einkünfte (z.B. die Einkünfte der Lotto di Genova in Siebenbürgen, die protestantischen Ehedispensations-Gelder, die Zollgebühren der wallachischen Weine) die das Orphanotrophium vorher genoss, weiterhin in den Religionsfonds einflossen.[25] In Neppendorf gab es eine Landlergemeinde, die sich von der grundobrigkeitlichen Macht befreien und gänzlich der sächsischen Gemeinschaft angehören wollte, aber ihre Fürbitte wurde abgeschlagen.[26] 1774 wurde Freiherr von Brukenthal als königlicher Kommissar und Präsident an die Spitze des Guberniums gestellt. 1775 wollte er schon die Erfolge des neuen Präsidiums aufzeigen. In diesem seinem Vortrag vermied er auch nur ein Wort über die nationalen Gehässigkeiten zu erwähnen.[27] In einem Promemoria bat auch der siebenbürgische griechisch-katholische Bischof Major, um das Allodialgut Neppendorf, ein früheres Jesuitenvermögen für den Hermannstädter griechisch-katholischen Pfarrer, damit er ein auskömmliches Einkommen efrzielen konnte. Der Pfarrer wurde mit der Seelsorge der 180 griechisch-katholischer Familien getraut. Der Bischof wollte für das kleine Gut 800 Gulden bezahlen, nötigen falls 1000. Im Falle einer öffentlichen Lizitation hätte aber der protestantische Hermannstädter Magistrat den Preis irreal in die Höhe getrieben, um die Einführung des Pfarrers zu verhindern.[28] In Kajántó waren die Leute vorwiegend reformiert. Ihre Kirche wurde 1766 auch weggenommen und den Katholiken übergeben. Jedoch wurde dieser staatliche Entschluss 1768 damit ergänzt, dass die Jesuiten als Grundherren verpflichtet sind, das zu beachten, dass die Katholiken der nicht katholischen Gemeinde bei der Errichtung ihrer neuen Kirche Beihilfe leistet. Da aber bis Mai 1774 keine Schritte in diese Richtung gemacht wurden, suchten die reformierten Einwohner aus Kajántó die Rückerstattung ihrer Kirche an. Die endgültige Entscheidung ist in diesem Falle nicht bekannt.[29] Vor dem Staat standen zwei verschiedene Möglichkeiten wegen der katholischen kirchlichen Güter und Einkünfte: entweder ihre Weitergabe an Privatleute oder Kommunitäten durch öffentliche Verpachtungen, oder ihre eigene Bewirtschaftung. Das hieß ab 1773 die Bewirtschaftung durch Kirche unter strenger staatlichen Kontrolle oder aber immer öfter Bewirtschaftung direkt durch den

---

[25] *StRP*, Nr. 2275/1776: *b[revi] m[anu im Staatsrat vorgekommen] Nota des Sieb. Kanzlers Gr. Kornis 11. Sept. Nebst einer anonymischen Nota de dato 17. Sept. (sic!) a.c.: Die Überlassung der unbeweglichen Exjesuiten Güter in Siebenbürgen an das Hermannstädter Waisen Haus betreffend exp. 18. Sept.* Billet an die Sieb. Kanz. 4to.

[26] Siehe zum Beispiel *StRP*, Nr. 1697/1776.

[27] *[...] die noch kurze Dauer des jetzigen Praesidii [...].* UstA, Archiv der Ungarischen Hofkanzlei, A98. Ehemalige Kabinettakten Hungarica et Transylvanica (im weiteren A98), Kt. 6, 22r-v; 24r-29v, Nr. 11. Andere Daten sind auf dem Schriftstück nicht vermerkt.

[28] A98, Kt. 6, 23r-v: *Ein Promemoria des griechisch-katholischen Bischofs Major das allodial Güttlein Nebendorf betreffend.*

[29] ÖstA, HKA, Neue Hofkammer (im weiteren NHK), Nr. 34, 223 ex Mayo (sic!) 1774. Sess. De dato 25ta May 1774. Nota des Gr. Blümegen dd^{o} 17ten Maji 1774.

Staat. Als Fazit der vorhin ausgeführten Problematik kann festgestellt werden: Es muss mit weiteren Detailuntersuchungen geklärt werden, welches Vorgehen den größeren Nutzen und Gewinn für die Gesellschaft und für den Staat bedeutete. Meiner Meinung nach spielten hier nicht nur staatswirtschaftliche, sondern auch staats- und gesellschaftspolitischen Überlegungen und Interessen eine Rolle. Als die Siebenbürgische Hofkommission am 26. Oktober 1771 die Mietsverträge („*Bestandverlassung*“) des Zehnts an die Sächsische Nation vorschlug, begutachtete der damalige Hofkammer-Präsident Graf von Hatzfeld die Sache so, dass die Fiskalzehnten noch ein Jahr lang kameraliter zu administrieren wären. Maria Theresia ließ die Siebenbürgische Kanzlei nach diesem Vorschlag bescheiden. Während dieses einen Jahrs musste die Differenz zwischen dem Fiscus und der Sächsischen Nation schleunigst foro productionali geklärt werden. Nach diesem Jahr zeigte sich die Herrscherin geneigt, diese Zehnten den einzelnen Ortschaften und Kommunitäten der Nation gegen einen angemessenen Pachtschilling zu überlassen.[30] Vier wichtige Kleinigkeiten müssen hier unterstrichen werden. 1. Die kamerale Administration in einem Jahr ermöglichte eine Beurteilung, wie viel Geld der Staat selbst aus diesen Einkünften einheben könnte. Das war eine wichtige Information zur Festsetzung eines zukünftigen anständigen Pachtschillings. 2. Der im Staatsrat verfasste herrscherliche Entschluss widersetzte sich in einen wichtigen Punkt dem Brukenthal'schen Vorschlag: Die Verpachtung der Zehnteinkünften soll einzeln an Ortschaften und Kommunitäten überlassen werden und nicht der Sächsischen Nation als einer rechtlichen Ständegemeinschaft. 3. Dabei muss man erwähnen, dass die Kirchengüter in Siebenbürgen zahlen- und flächenmäßig klein waren, und im Bereich des Grundbesitzes ungarischer Adel und Siebenbürger Sachsen Privilegien besaßen, die mit großen Steuerlasten verbunden waren.[31] 4. Diese Zeit bedeutet auch der Anfang der modernen Forstwirtschaft: der Staat beobachtete die besondere Befolgung der neuen Prinzipien bei den geistlichen Beneficien oder dem Militär gehörigen Waldungen.[32]

Wie wir schon gesehen haben, bildete das Portugiesische Kapital den Kern des siebenbürgischen Religionsfonds. Aber auf welcher Art und Weise wurde der Fonds aufgebraucht? Graf Blümegen berichtete am 15. März 1773 im Namen des siebenbürgischen Religionsdepartements, dass es noch viele katholische Kirchen aufzubauen wären, vor allem in solchen Kreisen (Komitaten und Stühlen), wo zahlreiche Nichtkatholiken aufzufinden sind. Gleicherweise wären noch viele Pfarr- und Schulgebäuden zu errichten, und außerdem wären noch einige Pfarrer und Schulmeister zu bedenken, für die noch Kongrua auszumessen wäre. Es blieben noch verschiedene alte katholische Kirchen, die einstürzgefährdet sind und zu renovieren wären. Diese alle Aufgaben könnten nicht allein aus dem Portugiesischen Kapital verwirklicht werden. Die

[30] HHStA, *StRP*, Nr. 3649/1771: Vortrag der Siebenbürgischen Commission ddo 26. Oct. (den 28. Oct. in die Circulation gegeben); HHStA, *StRP*, Nr. 3913, 3915/1771: zwei Vorträge des Gr. Hatzfeld ddo 5. Nov. (den 19. Nov. in die Circulation gegeben). Resolution den 4. Dec. expediert.

[31] SHK, Schriftstück d., Nr. 1 Punkt 7.

[32] HHStA, *StRP*, Nr. 2275/1776.

Interessen des Kapitals wurden seit 1767 zu siebenbürgischen Zwecken ausgezahlt, aber es würde noch lange Jahre dauern, bis man allein mit Hilfe dieses Fonds alle seine Ziele vollziehen könnte. Das Religionsdepartement bat deswegen die Herrscherin, die bei der ersten Bestimmung angeordneten 4.000 Gulden, womit nämlich jährlich das Kapital selbst zuzunehmen war, zu beheben, und sechs Jahre lang durch direkte Auszahlung an die Beschleunigung der Sachen zu widmen. Dadurch wäre auch die Staatskasse von solchen Zahlungen befreit, die in den letzten Jahren an verschiedene Ordensgeistliche vorgenommen wurden, um ihre alte, baufällige Kirchen reparieren zu können. Aus der zeitweiligen Zunahme der staatlichen Religionsabgaben könnten auch an solche Ordensgeistliche einige Beiträge gerichtet werden, die selbst sonst über keinen anderen Fonds verfügen.[33] Der dem Religionsprotokoll beigefügten Auszug des Gubernators Grafen von Auersperg sagt wenig aus. Nämlich: das Kapital selbst wurde 1767 bei dem Wiener Stadt-Banco auf einem Zinsfuß von 4% angelegt. Im FolgeJahr wurde es zu gleichen Konditionen beim Kupferamt angelegt. Die eingesehene Anordnung über die Anlage der 4.000 Gulden bedeutete, dass der Ertrag des Kapitals von 17.492 Gulden im Jahre 1767 in fünf Jahren auf 18.132 Gulden gemehrt wurde, aber die Summe der direkt für Religionszwecke gewidmete Gelder blieb bei 13.492 und 14.132 Gulden. Im Oktober 1772 befand sich insgesamt 9.516 Gulden 5 ¾ Kreuzer nicht aufgebrauchtes Restgeld an drei Orten: 2.497 Gulden 20 Kreuzer bei der Stadt-Banco, 266 Gulden 40 Kreuzer beim Kupfer-Amt und 6.752 Gulden 5 ¾ Kreuzer im Bargeld bei dem Kameralzahlamt.[34] Das siebenbürgische Thesaurariat machte nach der Auflösung des Jesuitenordens einen Versuch, sein Kapital in Siebenbürgen zu halten. Der Bericht vom 11. April fragte nach dem Verbleib jener 2.000 Gulden, welche für Anton Demels von einer weiter nicht gekannten vormaligen Jesuiten Residenz ausgeliehen wurde. Die Frage war: wenn das Geld zurückgezahlt würde, wäre es in Siebenbürgen oder bei dem Wiener Kupferamt anzulegen? Die Hofkammer begutachtete am 13. Mai die Sache in dem Sinne, dass – nachdem in Siebenbürgen kein öffentlicher Fundus vorhanden ist, bei welcher dieses Capital Frucht bringen könnte – es bei der Staatsschuldenkasse angelegt werden sollte. Die an das Thesaurariat nach Siebenbürgen ergangene Verordnung vom 20. Mai machte diese Maßnahme auch für die anderen eingehenden Gelder geltend. Die hierüber erhaltende Schuldverschreibungen waren dann in dem Wiener Depositen-Amt aufzubewahren.[35] Aus dem Portugiesischen Fonds konnte vom 1. Januar 1767 bis Ende 1772 etwas weniger als 71.454 Gulden direkt für siebenbürgische Religionszwecke ausbezahlt werden.[36] Als Veranschaulichung über die Höhe des Betrages können wir heranziehen, dass die angemessene Kongrua eines Pfarrers in Siebenbürgen auf 150

---

[33] SHK, Schriftstück d.

[34] SHK, Nr. 1591/1773, Schriftstück b: *Conspectus Capitalium Fundi Lusitanici, obcingentiumque de iis Intersuriorum per Extractoratum (sic!) Cameralem Cibiniensem, a 1ª Januarii 1767 usque finem Octobris 1772 elaboratus* (im weiteren SHK, Schriftstück b).

[35] NHK, Nr. 34, 275, N°. 5. Sess. 19. dd° 13ten May 1774 (expediert am 20. Mai 1774).

[36] SHK, Schriftstück b.

Gulden[37] und die eines Schulmeisters auf 75 Gulden[38] von Bischof Bajtay gennannt werden. Den Aufwand spezifierte Graf von Auersperg nicht vereinzelt. Im Jahre 1770 berichtete der Bischof Bajtay über 47 notleidende katholische Pfarrer.[39] Nach meiner Schätzung wurde deswegen ein Viertel des Ertrages des Portugiesischen Kapitals für Bauarbeiten, die Hälfte auf die Besoldung römisch-katholischer Priester und ein Viertel auf die Unterstützung von Ordenshäuser und Missionen verwendet. Dieser letzte Betrag sollte mit Vollendung der Bauarbeiten im Prinzip langsam zunehmen oder zu andere Zwecke, wie z.B. für die griechisch-katholische Mission freigegeben werden. Dass der Wiener Hof selbst diese Vortstellung hatte, wissen wir von den Reaktionen der siebenbürgischen oberen Verwaltung. In einer anonymen Zusammenfassung der Unionssachen schrieb (höchst wahrscheinlich) der Hofrat van der Marck folgendes:

> *Aus dem Portugesischem Capital zum Nutzen der Union etwas zu verwenden ist der Zeit nicht wohl thunlich, da noch viele kathol. Pfarren und Schulhäuser zu errichten erübrigen. Bey Gelegenheit aber, wo der Bischoff Bajtai mit Ausgang dieses Jahrs seine Bericht über die dießfällige Verwendung erstatten wird, solle E[uer] M[ajestät] ein so anders näher vor Augen geleget werden.*[40]

Wir konnten belegen, dass die in siebenbürgischen Religionsangelegenheiten zuständigen Hofelite noch im Frühjahr 1773 es fand, dass es genügend dringende Bauarbeiten an römisch-katholischen Kirchen und Einrichtungen für die mindest folgenden sechs Jahren gäbe. Der Anspruch blieb seitens der Unierten auf diese Religionsgelder erhalten. Als der Fogarascher unierte Bischof Major 1774 einen Plan zur Errichtung eines neuen Bistum in Bistriz vorschlug, und sein Vorschlag auch vom illyrischen Deputationspräsidenten Graf von Koller übernommen wurde, wollten sie die zusätzlichen Kosten durch die Anwendung der vorläufig auf 80.000 Gulden zugenommenen Zehnteinkommen oder durch den Beisatz des Portugiesischen Fonds decken.[41] Den Vorgang begutachtete seitens der Siebenbürgischen Hofkanzlei Hofrat van der Marck. Er hielt das Projekt auch aus materiellen Gründen für nicht möglich. Von den Kosten konnte nämlich der Religionsfonds zu Beginn des Jahres 1775 nichts übernehmen, weil die zur Erhaltung der Pfarren und Trivialschulen nötigen Ausgaben so gesteigert wurden, dass der Religionsfonds gänzlich ausgeschöpft wurde. Man konnte auch mit den Kameraleinkünften nicht rechnen, weil die Staatskasse gänzlich gebunden war durch jene Verpflichtungen, die es nach der Auflösung des Jesuitenordens

---

[37] Miskolczy, *Bajtay J. Antal*, 101.
[38] *StRP*, 1503/1771: Das Protokoll der Siebenbürgischen Hofkanzlei in Religiosis vom 8. März Punkt 4 am 23. April in die Zirkulation gegeben.
[39] UstA, Materialien des königlichen Gubernium Siebenbürgens, F53. *Protokolle der Commissio in Publico-ecclesiasticis*, Band 3536, 64r, Nr. 100/1770, in der Sitzung am 27. Juni 1770.
[40] UstA, Archiv der Ungarischen Hofkanzlei, A108. Ehemalige Kabinettakten Transylvanica, Kt. 20, f. 156r-156v: anonymische Zusammenfassung des (höchst wahrscheinlich) Hofrats van der Marck über die Unionssachen und wie darüber ein zusammenhängendes Kenntnis zu gewinnen wäre, siehe f. 161r-v.
[41] UStA, A98, Kt. 7, f. 214r-216v; 233v-237v: Die Nota des Grafen Koller vom 24. November 1774, siehe f. 236v.

übernommen hatte. Ab 1773 versuchte die Staatsmacht die ehemaligen Aufgaben des Ordens einigermaßen zu ersetzen („*zu suppliren*").[42] Die wegen der Auflösung der Societas Jesu entstandene finanzielle Situation kostete mehr als der vorige Zustand. Die Differenz verbrauchte auch die Zunahmen der Zehnteinkünfte, außerdem war der Religionsfundus im höchsten Betrieb völlig ausgeschöpft. Ob es diese Sichtweise der Geschehnisse richtig ist, muss durch weitere Detailforschung erforscht werden. Im Endergebnis aber bedeutete das auch, dass die Verbesserung der materiellen Lage der unierten Geistlichen und der Aufbau ihres Schulwesens (wie bisher, so auch weiterhin) ohne höhere Geldzuwendungen gelöst werden mussten.

[42] Ders., f. 236r-v: Wohlmeinung. Betreff: über das Promemoria des Bischofs Major, dass nebst ihme noch zwei griechische Bischöfe noch zu ernennen wären, siehe f. 236v.

Religious Violence, Political Dialogue, and the Public: The Orthodox Riots in Eighteenth-Century Transylvania

Radu Nedici

For the peoples of Central Europe living under Habsburg rule, the mid-eighteenth century marked the start of a period of reforms and transformations that impacted at every level of their daily existence. The confessional absolutism that had defined the Monarchy for the past century and a half was gradually abandoned, in favour of a pragmatic attitude towards non-Catholic groups in the various provinces. In a dramatic readjustment of strategy, on 13th July 1759 Empress Maria Theresa introduced a decree that was expected to put an end to the dissent and violence that for years had swept through the Romanian villages in southern Transylvania. Under certain conditions, it guaranteed pardon for the actions and religious toleration for the consciences of the many who, in the name of Byzantine Orthodoxy, opposed the Greek Catholic Church. The moment is central to a series of historical questions, as it allows us to examine the tempo of reform, the influence common subjects could have had on those in power, and consequently the emergence of modern public opinion in a society that so little resembled that of the Atlantic World to which the birth of the public sphere has traditionally been connected.[1] Focusing on the popular disturbances of 1744-1761, this article examines the patterns of crowd violence and whether or not these were a political expression of the nascent public.

A time of conflict

The successful Habsburg military offensive in the aftermath of the Ottoman defeat under the walls of Vienna in 1683 had effects that reached further than those readily visible on the political map of East-Central Europe, as configured a decade and a half later by the peace treaty signed in Sremski Karlovci. By the time of the treaty, the Habsburg armies had conquered most of the provinces that were once part of the medieval kingdom of Hungary, reuniting them under the same crown for the first time in over 150 years.[2] In Transylvania proper, continued rounds of negotiations had led to an agreement between Emperor Leopold I and the Estates in 1691, which guaranteed all privileges and instituted a very subtle mechanism to regulate the distribution of power within the constitutional

[1] Jürgen Habermas, *The Structural Transformations of the Public Sphere: An Inquiry into a Category of Bourgeois Society* (Cambridge, Massachusetts: The MIT Press, 1989; German original edition published in 1962). Among the ever growing literature, see the critical contributions in Craig Calhoun, ed., *Habermas and the Public Sphere* (Cambridge, Massachusetts: The MIT Press, 1992) and the recent synthesis by James Van Horn Melton, *The Rise of the Public in Enlightenment Europe* (Cambridge: Cambridge University Press, 2004). The present study is part of a more extensive investigation into the making of a plebeian public sphere in the easternmost provinces of the Habsburg Monarchy.

[2] Charles W. Ingrao, *The Habsburg Monarchy, 1618-1815* (Cambridge: Cambridge University Press, 2000), 75-83.

system of three nations and four confessions.[3] Even more than in Hungary itself, these provisions, which sought to maintain the religious status quo of the Principality, impeded any serious Catholic offensive against the Protestant denominations. However, the charter of 4th December 1691 failed to make any mention of the Romanian Greek Orthodox Church, whose followers accounted for almost half of the province's population but which, despite that, did not enjoy a legal position. The political significance of this omission was soon acknowledged, as both Catholics and Calvinists embarked on trying to win the support of the Byzantine-rite hierarchy for their side. Jesuit missionaries success-fully laid the theological foundations for its full communion with Rome, while the imperial promises of social benefits eased all remaining hesitations from the bishop and the synod. Officially proclaimed in June 1701, through the re-enthronement of Bishop Athanasie Anghel in the course of a sumptuous ceremony, the ecclesiastical union strengthened the Catholic party's ranks, and helped legitimize its future claims to supremacy in Transylvanian politics.[4]

Together with Habsburg rule, a new era commenced for the Romanian Church. Looking to enhance the fidelity of this key institution for their political agenda, the Viennese authorities actively promoted the creation of rejuvenated clerical elite. Scholarships for the formation of future high-ranking priests were funded at Catholic colleges and universities in Cluj, Trnava, Vienna and Rome. By mid-century this policy resulted in a generation of leaders saturated by Latin theology, devotions, and practices, who were to dominate the Uniate Church until the early 1780s. In an accelerated bid for confessional formation, the foreign-educated hierarchy emphasised its ties to Roman Catholic dogma, canon law, and spirituality, thereby inventing a new identity for which the label Greek Catholic would be coined.[5]

Church Union with Rome had been an apparent success in the first decades of the eighteenth century. Except for a restricted number of communities linked to the Balkan trade routes, who were granted the privilege of keeping their Orthodox allegiance, the rest of the almost one thousand Romanian parishes in Transylvania had passed silently under

[3] Paul W. Roth, "Das Diploma Leopoldinum. Vorgeschichte, Bestimmungen," in *Siebenbürgen in der Habsburgermonarchie: vom Leopoldinum bis zum Ausgleich (1690-1867)*, ed. Zsolt K. Lengyel and Ulrich A. Wien (Köln, Weimar, Wien: Böhlau Verlag, 1999), 1-10.

[4] Political considerations on the imperial side were indeed dominant, so much so that the Romanian Church was described as an *instrumentum regni* in the events of those years: see Mathias Bernath, *Habsburgii și începuturile formării națiunii române* [The Habsburgs and the Beginnings of the Romanian Nation-Building] (Cluj: Dacia, 1994; German original edition published in 1972), 73-86. The religious choice at the turn of the eighteenth century remains a disputed subject in the Romanian historiography; the studies gathered by Johann Marte et al., eds., *Die Union der Rumänen Siebenbürgens mit der Kirche von Rom / Unirea românilor transilvăneni cu Biserica Romei*, vol. 1 (București: Editura Enciclopedică, 2010), attempt a rare bringing-together of the Orthodox, Greek Catholic, and secular perspectives, but their tone is at times oversaturated with an ecumenical concern.

[5] Radu Nedici, "Formarea identității confesionale greco-catolice în Transilvania în secolul al XVIII-lea" [The Formation of Greek Catholic Confessional Identity in Eighteenth-Century Transylvania] (PhD diss., University of Bucharest, 2011).

the spiritual authority of the new bishop.[6] Whether those who accomplished this mass conversion really saw any significance in it is, at this point, impossible to ascertain.[7] Whatever the answer, the Habsburgs had every reason to consider the solution to be definitive.

It was to remain this way until the spring of 1744, when a pious monk commissioned by the Serbian Orthodox metropolitan in Sremski Karlovci entered Transylvania, preaching violently against the ecclesiastical union with the Latins and urging his audiences to return to the faith of their ancestors.[8] His capture and imprisonment did little to calm the spirits of those who had heard his message in the southern counties of Transylvania and in the Saxon seats, and years were to pass before the measures devised by the imperial authorities allowed for optimist voices to proclaim the end of all religious dissent.[9] Priests who had been chased out returned to their parishes and the Uniate hierarchy in Blaj was formally recognised, signalling to interested parties that a return to the idyllic conformity of yore was still possible. Nevertheless, the truce was only temporary and unrest remained endemic throughout the 1750s.

Eager to preserve good diplomatic ties with its Russian ally, the Habsburg Monarchy had already slightly eased religious pressure on the Orthodox communities in Transylvania in the early 1750s. The government was ordered to refrain from imposing any penalties on individuals who had abandoned the Catholic faith, provided that they did not disturb the confessional peace of their community or try to gain converts.[10] In essence though, this remained a form of private tolerance, not sanctioned by any official document, and, most importantly, not calling into question the fiction that all Byzantine rite Christians in Transylvania belonged to the Uniate Church.

---

[6] Daniel Dumitran, "Formen der Identität im Siebenbürgen (XVIII. Jahrhunderts). Einleitung zur Kritik der Darstellung der Nichtunierten Rumänen in der Geschichtsschreibung," *Anuarul Institutului de Cercetări Socio-Umane «Gheorghe Şincai»* 15 (2012): 23-55.

[7] Zenovie Pâclişanu, *Istoria Bisericii Române Unite* [The History of the Romanian Uniate Church], part 1, *Perspective* 17 (1994-1995): 317-18; part 2, *Perspective* 14-16 (1991-1993): 41-42.

[8] Ibid., 1, 318-21; Dumitru Deac, "Beiträge zur Geschichte der Bewegung des Mönches Visarion Sarai in Siebenbürgen," *Studia Universitatis Babeş-Bolyai, Theologia Catholica* 47, 4 (2002): 23-35.

[9] Augustin Bunea, *Din istoria românilor. Episcopul Ioan Inocenţiu Klein (1728-1751)* [From the History of the Romanians. Bishop Ioan Inocenţiu Klein (1728-1751)] (Blaj: Tipografia Seminarului Archidiecesan Greco-Catolic, 1900), 187-203; Silviu Dragomir, *Istoria dezrobirii religioase a românilor din Ardeal în secolul XVIII* [The History of the Religious Emancipation of the Romanians in Transylvania in the Eighteenth Century], vol. 1 (Cluj-Napoca: Dacia, 2002; first published 1920), 203-237, 437-41; Pâclişanu, *Istoria*, 1, 346-57; ibid., 2, 29-30; Mihai Săsăujan, *Politica bisericească a Curţii din Viena în Transilvania (1740-1761)* [The Ecclesiastical Policy of the Viennese Court in Transylvania (1740-1761)] (Cluj-Napoca: Presa Universitară Clujeană, 2002), 151-60; Greta-Monica Miron, "Acţiune ortodoxă – acţiune catolică. Efectele mişcării lui Visarion Sarai în Hunedoara, Haţeg, Zarand şi Alba" [Orthodox Action – Catholic Action. The Aftermaths of Visarion Sarai's Movement in Hunedoara, Haţeg, Zarand, and Alba], *Studia Universitatis Babeş-Bolyai, Historia* 50, 2 (2005): 1-36.

[10] Bunea, *Episcopul Klein*, 252-55; idem, *Episcopii Petru Paul Aron şi Dionisiu Novacovici sau istoria românilor transilvăneni de la 1751 până la 1764* [Bishops Petru Paul Aron and Dionisiu Novacovici or the History of the Romanians in Transylvania from 1751 to 1764] (Blaj: Tipografia Seminarului Archidiecesan, 1902), 66-67; Săsăujan, *Politica bisericească*, 165-67.

Elsewhere swift changes were about to occur. The impressive progress of the ecclesiastical union in the district of Hălmagiu and the county of Bihor claimed by its promoters received devastating blows in the course of the decade. To put an end to the conflicting accounts reaching Vienna from the Catholic and Orthodox parties, and to avoid the escalation of the tensions of which first signs were already troubling, the Habsburg authorities resorted to a method never used before. Independent imperial commissioners were to determine the real numbers for each denomination by conducting an inquiry into the personal religious convictions of every single believer. The populace's reply was unexpected and overwhelming. Convened in May 1754, the commission in Hălmagiu established that only three priests and four laymen were from then on to form the flock of the Uniate bishop, out of a total of over fifty villages inhabited by Greek-rite Christians.[11] In Bihor, where the contention between the Catholic hierarchy and the Orthodox bishops had a longer history with its own twists and turns, the investigation carried out from 1754 to 1756 found only 255 Uniate families, against the 8667 that declared their affiliation to the Serbian eparch.[12]

It was a grim discovery as the news reached the imperial capital. This divorce between popular feeling and the high ecclesiastical dignitaries projected a shadow of doubt in the minds of Habsburg ministers, which subsequently impacted their stance on similar disputes in Transylvania. It was undoubtedly not by chance that in the later 1750s, the voices in the Vienna cabinets calling for a refashioned view of confessional realities became dominant. Nor should we assume that the controversies that surfaced during the ensuing debate had much to do with a genuine and detached endorsement of any of the opposing Romanian religious communities. These, in fact, mirrored deeper political conflicts inside Habsburg central government institutions and were more concerned with the distribution of power among the various authorities undergoing significant transformations in that same era.[13] The main proponent of religious freedom for the Orthodox in Transylvania, Johann Christoph von Bartenstein, president of the Illyrian Deputation, could not have ignored the fact that removal of the Greek Catholic monopoly would have extended the jurisdiction and influence of the department he headed at the expense of the minister-delegate for Transylvania, of the Transylvanian Chancellery, and of the Court

[11] Bunea, *Episcopii Aron şi Novacovici*, 68-93; Dragomir, *Istoria dezrobirii*, 1, 286-322.

[12] Vincze Bunyitay, *Bihárvarmegye oláhjai s a vallás-unió* [The Romanians in the County of Bihor and the Religious Union] (Budapest: Kiadja a Magyar Tudományos Akadémia, 1892), 65-74; Pâclişanu, *Istoria*, 2, 183-88; Gheorghe Gorun, *Reformismul austriac şi violenţele sociale din Europa Centrală: 1750-1800* [The Austrian Policy of Reform and the Social Violences in Central Europe: 1750-1800] (Oradea: Editura Muzeului Ţării Crişurilor, 1998), 142-48.

[13] A detailed account on the intricacies of reform is Franz A. J. Szabo, *Kaunitz and Enlightened Absolutism, 1753-1780* (Cambridge: Cambridge University Press, 1994), 73-99. The successive changes in the consultative and executive bodies entrusted with the administration of the Transylvanian affairs are discussed by Zsolt Trócsányi, "Erdélyi konferenciák, Erdélyi miniszterek (Erdélyi kormányzatának legfelsőbb irányítása 1752-1761)" [Transylvanian Conferences, Transylvanian Ministers (The Top Leadership of the Transylvanian Government 1752-1761)], *Levéltári Közlemények* 59, 2 (1988): 219-26.

Treasury, which understandably were against any change in the legislation.[14] The influential state chancellor Wenzel Anton von Kaunitz mediated between the two positions, proposing a moderate solution built around the same necessity to recognize the Orthodox community. He considered the topic of when and to what extent the Orthodox had been granted religious freedom in Transylvania to be outdated, since all contemporary evidence reported their presence in great numbers. He also argued by invoking the prospect of mass migration by discontented subjects and his conviction that Catholicism had to be spread through individual education, though these reasons were derivative of the central argument. For Kaunitz, a return to the previous uniformity was impossible not only because of the dangers it posed to the Habsburg state but also because all efforts made in more than ten years had proved unavailing against the resistance of the people.[15] One could not hope for a more direct acknowledgement of public opinion, aware of the issues at stake and critical of the government's actions.

Following consultation with her advisers, Maria Theresa approved the nomination of an Orthodox bishop for Transylvania on 13th October 1758 and rather less than a year later, on 13th July 1759, issued the edict declaring religious toleration.[16] There were a series of limitations, however. The bishop, whom the Court had yet to designate, was to be exempt from the authority of the Serbian see in order to block an undesired increase in the metropolitan's political influence and to permanently remove him from Transylvanian affairs. Toleration was also conditional on an immediate cessation of all religious violence and the return of the forcefully occupied churches to the Uniate parishes. In exchange, no precise deadline was set for the clarification of the canonical status of the Orthodox Church.

Accordingly, instead of calming tensions, the uncertain future set out in the two documents further complicated the matters, as did the rumoured appointment of a bishop who did not enjoy the support of the undisputed champion of Orthodoxy in the Monarchy, Pavle Nenadović, the metropolitan of Sremski Karlovci.[17] The new outbreak of violence, which soon converged in the uprising led from 1759 to 1761 by the monk Sofronie from Cioara, brought the Greek Catholic diocese of Făgăraş close to collapse.[18] With no

---

[14] See their respective arguments summarized in Trócsányi, "Erdélyi konferenciák," 237-75; Săsăujan, *Politica bisericească*, 174-211. Some of the documents referred were later published as Mihai Săsăujan, ed., *Habsburgii şi Biserica Ortodoxă din Imperiul Austriac (1740-1761): Documente* [The Habsburgs and the Orthodox Church in the Austrian Empire (1740-1761): Documents] (Cluj-Napoca: Presa Universitară Clujeană, 2003).

[15] Săsăujan, *Habsburgii*, 196-97, 144-45.

[16] Bunea, *Episcopii Aron şi Novacovici*, 126-33, 161-70; Dragomir, *Istoria dezrobirii*, vol. 2 (Cluj-Napoca: Dacia, 2002; first published 1930), 129-38; Săsăujan, *Politica bisericească*, 208-11.

[17] Gorun, *Reformismul austriac*, 162-65.

[18] Bunea, *Episcopii Aron şi Novacovici*, 171-224; Dragomir, *Istoria dezrobirii*, 2, 146-243; David Prodan, *Supplex Libellus Valachorum. Din istoria formării naţiunii române* [Supplex Libellus Valachorum. From the History of the Romanian Nation-Building] (Bucureşti: Editura Enciclopedică, 1998; first published 1948), 244-56; Gorun, *Reformismul austriac*, 165-79; Ovidiu Ghitta, *Naşterea unei Biserici. Biserica greco-catolică din Sătmar în primul ei secol de existenţă (1667-1761)* [The Birth of a Church. The Greek Catholic Church in Sătmar in its First Century of Existence (1667-1761)] (Cluj-Napoca: Presa Universitară Clujeană, 2001), 302-

military force capable of containing the spread of dissent, the central authorities reluctantly had to take the final steps that had until then been postponed. In the spring of 1761 the bishop of Buda, Dionisije Novaković, was also confirmed as bishop over Transylvania. Simultaneously, an imperial commission began its work of separating the faithful and the ecclesiastical properties of the two Romanian denominations now legally recognized. By the end of its investigation, almost five-sixths of the original community had made the passage to the Orthodox Church.[19]

From one decade to another

The violent uprising of the Romanian Orthodox in Transylvania and Partium is undoubtedly the best known feature of those decades of religious confrontation. The events shocked contemporaries and have induced ecclesiastical historians to consider them as paradigmatic manifestations of popular dissent. However, one should distinguish between the frenzy with which the villagers attacked the Uniate priests in the 1740s and 1750s, and the public uproar and disorder that followed from 1759 to 1761, which was the immediate result of failed political communication.

The first scenario is not that far from other forms of crowd violence in early modern European history. The pioneering study by Natalie Zemon Davis on the religious riots in sixteenth-century France offers a detailed typology against which to check the potential advances. The parallel makes clear that, two hundred years afterwards and at the other end of the continent, violence was still very much grounded in the micro-context, in the sense that it pursued no general political objectives. The crowds would gather to restore what they perceived to be the ancient order, taking the place of the authorities that had apparently failed to protect it, but without submitting any further claims to the state officials once the local conflict seemed to have been settled in their favour.[20]

That is not to say that the violence of the rioters was irrational and random, nor that their deeds were signs of pathological brutality or a return to barbarism.[21] Over the last half century, social historians mainly investigating food protests in pre-industrial Europe and early labour strikes have challenged the prevailing vision of the riots as mind-

38; Greta-Monica Miron, *Biserica Greco-Catolică din comitatul Cluj în secolul al XVIII-lea* [The Greek Catholic Church in the County of Cluj in the Eighteenth Century] (Cluj-Napoca: Presa Universitară Clujeană, 2007), 73-142.

[19] Bunea, *Episcopii Aron și Novacovici*, 208, 228-31; Dragomir, *Istoria dezrobirii*, 2, 232-39; Gorun, *Reformismul austriac*, 171-72.

[20] Natalie Zemon Davis, "The Rites of Violence: Religious Riot in Sixteenth-Century France," *Past & Present* 59 (1973): 51-91.

[21] Not surprisingly, the accounts dressed by the magistrates called to investigate on the disturbances voiced the common prejudices against the lower orders and have consequently left an image of an incomprehensible savage and ignorant rabble; see the report by Petru Dobra, one of the four "protectors of Union" invested in 1746, Magyar Országos Levéltár, Budapest, *Erdélyi Kancelláriai levéltar, Erdélyi Kancellária regisztratúrája, Acta generalia* (henceforth abbreviated MOL, *B2*), no. 92/1749, fols. 23r–34r (electronic copy in Laura Stanciu, Keith Hitchins, Daniel Dumitran, eds., *Despre Biserica românilor din Transilvania: documente externe (1744-1754)* [On the Church of the Romanians in Transylvania: External Documents (1744-1754)] (Cluj-Napoca: Mega, 2009), DVD/Latina/Lat_5/Lat_5_1/img. 120-142).

less violent mobs. Collective action or the mere threat of it functioned, in fact, as means of instituting a social dialogue in times of economic crisis, and the authorities did not neglect its relevance. Nevertheless, they belonged to an age of pre-political movements, as the participants were not bound together by any specific ideology save for their conservative and traditionalist demands. The protesters shared a distinct notion of the social hierarchy and of their own rights and, consequently, took direct action whenever they felt threatened by the inherent changes induced by nascent capitalism, seeking to redress rather than challenge the existing order. Although their organization was minimal, their violence was clearly targeted, disciplined and restrained. In a highly influential article on the subject, Edward Palmer Thompson termed the latter attributes the 'moral economy' of the crowd.[22]

A very brief look at the religious riots in Transylvania and Partium is enough to convince us that these fitted the same pattern of Early Modern popular disturbances. After the passage of Visarion Sarai in 1744, crowd violence aimed to achieve two related objectives: the repossession of the church buildings and the expulsion of the Uniate priests, thought to have violated the sacred bonds of community.[23] As the Habsburg bureaucracy initially attempted to deal with the protests by way of terror and repression, and simultaneously salvage the patrimony of the Greek Catholic Church, the documents it created abound in details on the alleged abuses perpetrated by the common people.[24]

Manifesting the rift between the spiritual leaders and the laymen, the riots were not the work of socially or otherwise distinctive groups inside the local community, but generally involved the village as a whole. In Săliște, one of the main centres of revolt throughout the 1740s and 50s, the Uniate priests testified in May 1745 that during the last Nativity Fast their parishioners convened to the sound of bells and solemnly vowed to act together and punish those who would renege. Only then did the crowd enter the church and forcefully confiscate the keys, sacred objects and books from the serving ministers.[25] The priests in the county of Bihor told their stories in almost identical fashion ten years later, reporting threats from the rebellious villagers who had casted them out of the churches. Out of fear or simply under the social pressure from the community, many of

---

[22] Eric J. Hobsbawm, *Primitive Rebels: Studies in Archaic Forms of Social Movement in the 19th and 20th Centuries* (Manchester: Manchester University Press, 1971; first published 1959), in particular 108-25; George Rudé, *The Crowd in History: A Study of Popular Disturbances in France and England, 1730-1848* (New York: John Wiley and Sons, 1964); Edward Palmer Thompson, "The Moral Economy of the English Crowd in the Eighteenth Century," *Past & Present* 50 (1971): 76-136. See also the critical discussions by Robert J. Holton, "The Crowd in History: Some Problems of Theory and Method," *Social History* 3, 2 (1978): 219-33; Mark Harrison, *Crowds and History: Mass Phenomena in English Towns, 1790-1835* (Cambridge: Cambridge University Press, 1988), 3-46.

[23] Keith Hitchins, *The Idea of Nation: the Romanians of Transylvania, 1691-1849* (Bucharest: Editura Științifică și Enciclopedică, 1985), 76.

[24] A general overview of the turbulences after 1744 is Miron, "Acțiune ortodoxă – acțiune catolică," 1-36; eadem, *Biserica din comitatul Cluj*, 94-116, offers a detailed account of the upheavals in the years 1759-1761 for one of the counties in Transylvania.

[25] Ioan Lupaș, *Două anchete oficiale în satele din scaunul Sibiului: 1744 și 1745* [Two Official Inquiries in the Villages of the Seat of Sibiu: 1744 and 1745] (Sibiu: Tiparul Tipografiei Arhidiecezane, 1938), 20-22.

them had denounced the ecclesiastical union with Rome, hoping thereby to reverse popular sentiment toward them.[26]

Summoned to justify the sums collected in fines from Orthodox parishes in southern Transylvania, Petru Dobra, chief prosecutor of the Principality, produced a lengthy report in January 1749 on the sacrilegious behaviour of the crowds. Since the account was intended to give a summary of his operations spanning three years, being specific was not a priority. However, Petru Dobra's taste for generalization and classification should also be read as indicating that a certain typology of riotous action did seem to emerge. Above all, his observations point to the fact that crowd violence was focused on a set of well-defined targets, which embodied the much hated Uniate Church. Once seized by the protesters, the places of worship had first to go through the rites of purification, which involved cleaning the sacred vessels, washing the walls and holy icons, and even digging out the ground that a Greek Catholic priest had previously stepped on. Likewise, the holy oil consecrated by the Uniate bishop was thrown out and the crucifixes and holy images donated by Catholic benefactors were broken and burned.[27] In those villages where the sanctions imposed on the commune led to the recovery of the church building and the return of the Uniate priests, it was not uncommon for the protesters to continue to boycott the sacred services and to take part in alternative ceremonies, which drifted more or less from the Christian practices.[28]

As a side note, the riots offered good reason for gender barriers to be ignored and, at times, completely overrun. In Colun, a village belonging to the Saxon seat of Sibiu in southern Transylvania and residence of a Uniate archpriest, the women not only instigated but also carried out the assault on the parish church in 1759. After the male conspirators failed to riot, their wives took charge of the action and entered the church where the protopope was celebrating Mass, asking him to leave immediately. Outnumbered, with his hair pulled and his clothes torn, he had to abandon the church to the crowd, who proceeded to install the new Orthodox priests.[29]

The narrative preserved in all official records, according to which religious dissent was sudden and violent wherever it happened, should be taken with a grain of salt. Even in the days of open confrontation in 1760-1761, when various inquisitors repeatedly questioned the same people at short intervals about their confessional affiliation, hence presumably producing a more accurate image of the process, the tempo of the revolt remained distinguishably threefold. For some of the parishes they visited, the religious census takers in the county of Cluj recorded different dates on which the faithful had aban-

---

[26] Nicolae Firu, *Biserica ortodoxă română din Bihor în luptă cu unirea: 1700-1750. Schiță istorică* [The Romanian Orthodox Church in Bihor in Its Struggle Against the Union: 1700-1750. Historical Outline] (Caransebeș: Tiparul Tipografiei și Librăriei Diecezane, 1913), 65-68.
[27] MOL, *B2*, no. 92/1749, fol. 27v.
[28] Ibid., fols. 27v-28r.
[29] Dragomir, *Istoria dezrobirii*, 2, 138-44, 329-38.

doned church union, had then occupied the church buildings, and had ultimately dislodged the priests from the benefice of the parsonage houses and glebe lands.[30]

Expelled from the churches they used to serve in, the Greek Catholic parish priests found themselves discriminated against by members of their former flock: their houses razed, their livestock banished from grazing the common pasturelands, their daughters unable to find a husband, themselves condemned to die and be buried without any assistance on the outskirts of the cemetery.[31] Where resistance was opposed, the clerics complained of enduring harsh physical punishments. In Răşinari, after the Uniate priest refused to surrender the church, the mob even threw stones at him during the celebration of the Holy Mass, while the house of worship was desecrated by bringing in the corpse of a dog.[32] In the town of Sebeş, following a heated dispute between the Uniate archpriest and the Orthodox faithful, the intervention of the local magistrate in October 1756 resulted in the return of the church to the former owner. Dissatisfied with the decision, a group of protesters attacked the protopope in the sanctuary during the Eucharistic liturgy on Sunday and ousted him from the church. After a moment of apparent truce, during which each side had the church locked with their own set of keys, the archpriest was cautioned against attempting to reclaim the edifice, and on the following Sunday the Orthodox service was finally resumed.[33]

Despite the very aggressive rhetoric employed by Visarion Sarai and some of his followers, the instances where riot turned into bloodshed were minimal.[34] In one significant incident in January 1746 in the village of Păuca a mob armed with clubs and pitchforks attacked the public clerks and liberated the Orthodox priest they had just arrested. In the ensuing fight, one of the soldiers fired his gun and killed the leader of the mob. In revenge, the villagers threatened to lynch the county officials, but the intervention of two local noblemen calmed the situation down, and allowed them to eventually get away unharmed.[35]

Gradually, as the envisaged solution for religious tensions failed to appear, popular anxiety grew stronger, and consequently acts of brutality were perhaps more prevalent towards 1760 than they had been before. The simultaneous circulation of false imperial letters promising free exercise of the Orthodox confession further exacerbated tensions, since these offered legitimacy and the sentiment of impunity for popular attitudes of disrespect to the authorities, civil or ecclesiastical.[36] In and around the communes of Deal and Jina, a certain Popa Cosma preached against the religious union for years without

[30] Miron, *Biserica din comitatul Cluj*, 88-90, 93.
[31] MOL, *B2*, no. 92/1749, fol. 28r-v.
[32] Ibid., fol. 28r.
[33] Bunea, *Episcopii Aron şi Novacovici*, 113-17.
[34] Pâclişanu, *Istoria*, 1, 319-20; Deac, "Beiträge," 27-33.
[35] Bunea, *Episcopul Klein*, 194.
[36] Idem, *Episcopii Aron şi Novacovici*, 102-3, 136-37; Dragomir, *Istoria dezrobirii*, 2, 124-28. See also in this volume the contribution by Monika Imregh.

ever being seriously troubled by the Saxon officials assigned to capture him.[37] When, at long last, the central government in Transylvania decided in March 1757 to take action against those who had abusively seized parish churches, its officials were beaten and chased away by the crowd gathered to rescue the arrested priests.[38]

The announcement of the decree of toleration in the summer of 1759 only strengthened the protesters' position, lending credit to previous rumours.[39] Sent by their bishop to pacify villages in the region of Sibiu in April of the same year, the Basilian monks Grigore Maior and Silvestru Caliani left a very vivid image of the resentments and violence with which they were greeted by the rural crowds that refused to listen to their sermons, as they had to run for their lives on a number of occasions.[40] What is absolutely striking, until the very late events, is the isolation in which every single case of popular disturbance happened. Suspicious officials, who would have not failed to denounce it had the case been otherwise, do not mention any cooperation between rioting crowds in one village and the next. Chased away by the members of one parish, Maior and Caliani could still optimistically look forward to starting all over again the next morning in the neighbouring village. There is an important implication here: in spite of sharing a common religious identity, most rioters did not extend their interests to the abstract community but rather remained localized. In their eyes, at stake was neither the institution of the Church nor the well-being of some distant coreligionists, but everyday relations in the parish.

Together, these episodes are highly revealing of the lack of radicalism in the riots until the late 1750s, for the mobs articulated no demands for social or institutional reforms beyond their immediate agenda. Almost without exception, those questioned in the course of the numerous inquiries by the local or central authorities asserted their fidelity to the sovereign and to the state, and asked only for the right to profess their ancient religion, in the name of what might be called a particular understanding of the individual freedom of conscience.[41] The concurrent threats that, if not offered satisfaction, the Orthodox would migrate en masse over the Carpathians or as far away as Russia introduced an additional element of coercion, integral to the established dialogue between the subjects and the state.[42] Confined in the boundaries of every single parish, the acts of violence were,

---

[37] Bunea, *Episcopii Aron și Novacovici*, 98-106.

[38] MOL, *B2*, no. 276/1757, 641-44, 647-50 (electronic copy in Stanciu, Hitchins, Dumitran, eds., *Documente externe*, DVD/Latina/Lat_3/img. 641-44, 647-50).

[39] Hitchins, *The Idea of Nation*, 68-69.

[40] Pâclișanu, *Istoria*, 2, 38-39; Greta-Monica Miron, "Spre disciplinarea și sporirea turmei păstorite. Vizitații episcopale în dieceza unită din Transilvania secolului al XVIII-lea" [Towards the Disciplining and Incrementing the Shepherded Flock. Pastoral Visitations in the Uniate Diocese of Eighteenth-Century Transylvania], in *Biserica Română Unită cu Roma, Greco-Catolică: istorie și spiritualitate. 150 de ani de la înființarea Mitropoliei Române Unite cu Roma, Greco-Catolică, la Blaj* [The Romanian Church United with Rome, Greek Catholic: History and Spirituality. 150 Years Since the Establishment of the Metropolitanate of the Romanian Church United with Rome, Greek Catholic, in Blaj] (Blaj: Buna Vestire, 2003), 273-75.

[41] Dragomir, *Istoria dezrobirii*, 1, 216-21.

[42] Ibid., 1, 243, 2, 106-10; Săsăujan, *Habsburgii*, 96.

for the time being, less the expression of public opinion about to arise, and to a far greater extent that of a pre-political form of resistance to change.

Sofronie's riot as political negotiation

Despite appearances, the imperial decree on tolerance of 13th July 1759 marked the failure of negotiations, as it sanctioned the Habsburg state's resolve to act alone in this matter and make no concessions to the public. Together with the subsequent explanatory proclamations issued by Empress Maria Theresa and Governor Kemény, it denied any extension of jurisdiction requested by the Serbian metropolitan and contained a number of provisions intended to prevent further defections from the Greek Catholic Church.[43] Because of this hard-line approach, the tensions were sharpened instead of mitigated.[44] As a result, Metropolitan Nenadović tried to channel popular anger into a large-scale rebellion that was to prove to the Court the following he enjoyed among the Transylvanian Orthodox.[45]

Certainly it started with the same incidents and seizures of churches that characterized dissent in the times of Visarion Sarai.[46] But there was more to it than that. The movement had finally found a unifying charismatic leader in Sofronie, a monk from the village of Cioara, who had spent a few months in Sremski Karlovci on the eve of assuming a prominent role in Transylvania. Most probably it was his personal abilities, rather than any true or invented title he carried, that promoted him to the undisputed commanding authority he held from 1759 to 1761.[47] Having established his headquarters in the mountainous region of Zarand after successfully escaping a first attempt to arrest him, Sofronie claimed to represent the whole Orthodox community in Transylvania, drafting supplications and exchanging virulent letters with all relevant instances in the Principality.[48] Threatened by the growing signs of armed resistance from the crowds mobilized by Sofronie's public speeches, the provincial administration was left with no alternative but to accept him as a partner for dialogue.[49] The safe-conduct he received in October 1760

---

[43] Their text in Bunea, *Episcopii Aron și Novacovici*, 162 footnote 1, 174 footnote 2, and 166 footnote 2. See the contemporary interpretation of the edict as being favourable to the Greek Catholic side in Bishop Aron's letter of 16 April 1760, Archivio Storico della Congregazione per l'Evangelizzazione dei Popoli o "de Propaganda Fide," Vatican, *Scritture riferite nei Congressi, Greci di Croazia, Dalmazia, Schiavonia, Transilvania, Ungheria*, vol. 1, fol. 573r-v.

[44] Gorun, *Reformismul austriac*, 162-65.

[45] The evidence for his involvement is scant, since the metropolitan seems to have been extremely careful with leaving written traces of his actions. The proclamation he issued on 26 or 27 August 1759 is a rare exception, Dragomir, *Istoria dezrobirii*, 2, 189 footnote 5; Zoltán I. Tóth, *Primul secol al naționalismului românesc ardelean, 1697-1792* [The First Century of the Transylvanian Romanian Nationalism, 1697-1792] (București: Pythagora, 2001; Hungarian original edition published in 1946), 215 footnote 1.

[46] Hitchins, *The Idea of Nation*, 70-71.

[47] In a number of proclamations he styled himself "vicar of the synod in Sremski Karlovci," Bunea, *Episcopii Aron și Novacovici*, 172; Gorun, *Reformismul austriac*, 165.

[48] Dragomir, *Istoria dezrobirii*, 2, 167-76.

[49] See the episode of his second arrest and liberation, ibid., 2, 163-66; Ioan Ranca, "Date noi privind mișcarea lui Sofronie" [New Information Concerning the Movement of Sofronie], *Apulum. Arheologie - Istorie - Etnografie* 18 (1980): 282-84.

marked the moment when local government abandoned what little control it still had over the spread of tension and propaganda. The ever-present instances of violence tended however to blend into a quite different set of measures, which targeted the institutionalization of the Orthodox confession through the implantation of a strong parochial structure and its subordination to a central authority.[50]

One of Sofronie's greatest achievements was to put in place a vast network of faithful collaborators who recognized him as their head and acted in his rather than their own name. The overwhelming success of religious unrest in a very brief space of time was due at least in part to this capacity to disseminate a convergent public discourse from multiple centres of dissent. Their proliferation is attested above all by the long list of meetings held between the summer of 1760 and the first months of 1761, which focused on dislodging entire groups of parishes from the Uniate camp, as proven by the well-documented cases in the counties of Cluj and Sătmar. Analysis of these shows that a clear plan was in place, indicating the coordinated nature of the campaign. The whole strategy rested on a step-by-step advancement from the villages already conquered by dissent to neighbouring parishes, which in turn were to become new centres of propaganda. Not everyone would attend such gatherings, for the organisers made it clear that they requested the presence only of the most influent laypersons, who were to bear the message onward and multiply the calls that they heard. Furthermore, the parishes were being bombarded with letters said to emanate from Sofronie himself, describing the freedom awaiting those who would make the right choice.[51]

It is irrelevant for the moment whether his many disciples truly kept in close contact with Sofronie or whether his name simply became synonymous with the disturbances, to the point that it was invoked by partisans and detractors alike. There is enough evidence to suggest that the monk from Cioara was genuinely interested in imposing his influence over local leaders. The priests and protopopes he instituted were to replace the informal leaders who had made their name during the earlier unrest, putting under his command a new elite, which reported and was responsible to him.[52] When the situation called for extraordinary measures, Sofronie appointed special deputies, as he did in February 1761 for the northern territories of the eparchy, whence disturbing news had arrived concerning the abuses said to have been perpetrated in his name.[53]

Sofronie's leadership peaked at the general synod over which he presided in Alba Iulia from 25th February to 1st March 1761. Prepared by a whole series of local gatherings and regional meetings of clergy in the months leading up to it,[54] the synod was conceived as a sort of a national assembly, inspired perhaps by the similar role already vested in the

[50] Bunea, *Episcopii Aron și Novacovici*, 193-94; Dragomir, *Istoria dezrobirii*, 2, 178-79.
[51] Miron, *Biserica din comitatul Cluj*, 75-92; Ghitta, *Nașterea unei Biserici*, 302-38.
[52] Miron, *Biserica din comitatul Cluj*, 78-81.
[53] Dragomir, *Istoria dezrobirii*, 2, 180.
[54] Miron, *Biserica din comitatul Cluj*, 85.

Serbian National Congress in the 1740s.[55] Hence, ignoring the objections of the provincial officials, it brought together priests and laymen, called to debate the most stringent questions of institutional organization of the revived Orthodox Church.[56] A look at the agenda of the synod is all it takes to grasp the advances religious dissent had made in little more than a decade. Its aims were no longer limited to the boundaries of single parishes, but were obviously driven by a political pursuit of the general welfare of the community. Initial indications that the synod was prepared to demand the nomination of a bishop who was to enjoy the blessing of the metropolitan in Sremski Karlovci were superseded during the proceedings, allowing an important opportunity for compromise.[57] The official account submitted to the government reported that the participants were asked in a temperate tone whether or not they supported the idea of having a bishop, and what was to be done in case of a negative answer.[58] Despite all previous connections linking Sofronie to the Serbian prelate, the name of Pavle Nenadović was not even mentioned during the public sessions, after it became clear that Vienna would oppose any negotiation involving him.[59] In an effort to further his image of responsibility, Sofronie renewed the calls to the Transylvanian Orthodox to preserve the social peace and act as loyal subjects of the Empress, whilst also condemning those who had used the circumstances to gather illicit sums of money from the faithful.[60] In a radical departure from the accustomed pattern however, this time the political topics of debate ran in parallel with an equally significant attempt to legislate the functioning of parishes and the mutual obligations between the priest and his flock. Of the decrees adopted by the assembly, most concerned not the list of claims put forward by the community but a set of disciplinary rules meant to lay the foundation for restoring the spiritual life of the Orthodox in Transylvania after years of abuse and neglect.[61] Sofronie went so far as to produce a parallel discourse for internal consumption, which proclaimed only those canons touching the renewed discipline and obliterated all others.[62]

In these terms, the synod of February 1761 can arguably be deemed a major turning point in the evolution of the public it embodied. By abandoning one of the main re-

---

[55] Johann Heinrich Schwicker, *Politische Geschichte der Serben in Ungarn* (Budapest: Ludwig Aigner, 1880), 83-85, 95-102. For the impact of the Church hierarchy on the process of building a confessional-nationality for the Orthodox in the Habsburg Monarchy, see Emanuel Turczynski, *Konfession und Nation. Zur Frühgeschichte der serbischen und rumänischen Nationsbildung* (Düsseldorf: Schwann, 1976).

[56] Ranca, "Date noi," 286; Péter Bod, *Brevis Valachorum Transylvaniam incolentium Historia*, in *Relații interconfesionale româno-maghiare în Transilvania (mijlocul secolului XVI - primele decenii ale secolului XVIII)* [Romanian-Hungarian Interconfessional Relations in Transylvania (Mid-Sixteenth Century - First Decades of the Eighteenth Century)], ed. Ana Dumitran, Botond Gudor and Nicolae Dănilă (Alba Iulia: Altip, 2000), 429.

[57] Dragomir, *Istoria dezrobirii*, 1, 572.

[58] Ibid., 1, 573.

[59] Ibid., 2, 184-85; Gorun, *Reformismul austriac*, 167.

[60] Dragomir, *Istoria dezrobirii*, 1, 572, 574.

[61] Ibid., 1, 574; Gorun, *Reformismul austriac*, 167-68.

[62] Viorica Pop, "Sinodul de la Alba Iulia din 14-18 februarie 1761" [The Alba Iulia Synod of 14-18 February 1761], *Apulum. Arheologie – Istorie - Etnografie* 8 (1970): 124-25.

quests of the last decade and a half, the demand for a Serbian bishop to be suffragan to the metropolitan in Sremski Karlovci, the Orthodox party proved its political maturity and of its choice for dialogue instead of confrontation. At the same time, the programme of reform that the synod had outlined was the unquestionable sign of the Orthodox community's readiness to reason beyond the logic of religious conflict and act toward a future where it was to hold a lawful place.

Style as a Weapon. A Fake Imperial Edict in Péter Bod's *Brevis Valachorum Transilvaniam incolentium Historia*

Monika Imregh

In the summer of 2012, I translated from Latin into Hungarian Péter Bod's *Brevis Valachorum Transilvaniam incolentium Historia* (1764), which was published in Sfântu Gheorghe - Miercurea Ciuc together with its earlier and shorter variant (1745, written in Hungarian) and the original Latin text.

In the second part of his book Bod quotes in their entirety nearly every princely and imperial edict sent out by the Hungarian princes (between 1609-1669) and later by Leopold I, Charles VI and Maria Theresa (between 1698-1760) which concerned the Romanian people and their religion in Transylvania. The issue of all these edicts is the merging of the Romanian Orthodox Church into the Catholic Church in Transylvania. Among them there is a fake edict, published and distributed in 1754 in the Romanian language in Transylvania. Péter Bod presents its Latin variant, written for the sovereign Maria Theresa (princess in Transylvania), who mentions it in her edict dated the 13th of July 1759. The content of the fake edict permits the Orthodox Romanian people who didn't join the Catholic Church to practise their religion. The aforementioned genuine edict permits the same thing (along with a lot of other orders), but with many restrictions. The conditions of the free practice of their religion are so strict that the imperial edict seems more forbidding than permitting. The earlier, fake edict obviously shows the wishes of the Romanian people in Transylvania: they can practise their orthodox religion without any restriction, and nobody can force them to join the Catholic Church. In my paper I will examine these two edicts – the differences between their content and style – and I will show how you could know that it really is fake, even though Maria Theresa's edict didn't say so.

Qualis poeta, tale carmen. – "Like poet, like poem." *Similes habent labra lactucas*[1] – "His lips are like lettuce" – writes Bod about Sofronie, the Romanian monk's letter to general Bucow. He adds that this letter "is not too polite", and "dispenses with every splendour of our age."[2]

He also criticises the composition of the fake imperial edict prepared by Romani-

[1] Bod Péter, *Az erdélyi románok egyháztörténetének két könyve, 1745 és 1764,* Latinból fordította, gondozta, és előtanulmánnyal ellátta: Imregh Monika. Szerkesztés, előtanulmány és jegyzetek: Gudor Kund Botond [History of Church of Romanian People in Transylvania, 1745 and 1764, translated from Latin by Monika Imregh. Edition, preface and notes: Kund Botond Gudor] (Sfântu Gheorghe, Miercurea Ciuc: Háromszék Vármegye kiadó és Státus Kiadó, 2012), Book II, chapter 5, § IX, signe (492), p. 356. (Signs are the manuscript pages.)

[2] *[...] ex epistola [...] incivili, phalerisque saeculi destituta.* Ibid.

ans: "The poor forger, who wanted to simulate the Court's style, did not succeed."[3] However he highlights the orthodox monk Visarion Sarai's eloquence, which he considers wise and learned:

> "His words impressed the Romanian people so much that it was as if they were listening to an angel sent from heaven who had come to call them back from limbo, and they were ready to do everything he suggested to them."[4]

While his words were simple, according to Bod's description "he was cautious in phrasing his speeches" and "he talked sense." Therefore the Romanians "attributed to him superhuman wisdom."[5]

So it is obvious how important the style of writing is for our author, and we can tell this by the way that it appears in his own Latin texts. His style is animated, enjoyable and, despite writing long baroque passages, he does not drown in countless supplements like all of the contemporary imperial, royal and governor edicts, which he quotes. The second part of his book presents the events by quoting every edict regarding the religion of the Romanian people, so Bod confines himself to a short introduction. He cites the whole text of the edict and, after a short explanation; he follows with the next one until the 5th and 6th chapters,[6] where[7] he narrates the incidents in detail in his own words.

If we compare the first Hungarian variant with the latter Latin work, we can be sure that Bod used the first one while he was writing the second, because sometimes we read the same sentences and at other times he just completes them or changes the Latin phrasing a little compared with the Hungarian. Obviously it can only be true if the chapters are in both works, since the Latin one's ethnographic descriptions (in the first part, chapter 2nd-13th) are totally new compared with the Hungarian variants, as he could not talk in the first composition (finished in 1745) about the events that happened up until 1764, as he does in the latter variant. In a few places he elaborates more on certain topics in the earlier writing: in those he gives examples that he chose to omit from the Latin.[8] For example, the case of the Protestant vicar in Corneşti (Sövényfalva), who's Tithe was taken by the Romanian archdeacon. After the (78) mark, in the Hungarian text he narrates the whole story and he cites the letter of the archdeacon to the vicar. In the Latin variant this story is missing. Before that he criticises the Catholic and Jesuit writers (without

---

[3] Ibid., book II, chapter 4, § XXXIV, s. (459), p. 350: *Infelix falsarius, qui Curiae stilum imitari voluit, non expressit.*

[4] Ibid., book II, chap. 4, § IV, s. (349), p. 327: *Valachi ita ejus sermone capiebantur ac si Angelum e Coelo missum praesentem, eos ex orci facibus revocantem audirent, promptissime ad ea, quae suadebat exequenda sese offerentes.*

[5] Ibid., book II, chap. 4, § V, s. (351), p. 327: *In miscendis sermonibus fuit cautus, cum autem ex rerum circumstantiis, vir longe rerum experientia exercitatus, multos rerum eventus acute perspiceret, ac prudenter edissereret. Valachi sapientiam ipsi humana excellentiorem tribuebant [...].*

[6] Ibid., book II, chap. 5, § I-XIV, s. (477-500), pp. 353-358: *De Strepitu Valachorum in Transilvania Sofroniano.* After the Hungarian translation I give the content prepared by myself; at the end of Bod's work you can find the list of the edicts and main events in the text.

[7] Ibid., book II, chap. 6, § I-XXIX. s. (501), p. 358: *De Commissione in negotio Valachorum Buccowiana.*

[8] Ibid., p. 84: "Melly ez historiácskából is kitettzik." etc.

naming them), pointing out their mistakes and fabrications about the history of the Romanian Church's union with the Catholic Church. On this point the phrasing in so many words is the same as the latter Latin variant; moreover in this he completes his criticism with additional information.[9] In the Hungarian he quotes three citations from the volume entitled *Nova Dacia* without mentioning the author, Francisc Fasching, and he alludes to a work without author and title, which was published in Cluj (Kolozsvár) in 1737. He quotes the same citations in the Latin as well, and there we can find in the notes Fasching's name as well as Thuróczi's with his book's title, *Hungary*. Where he recites the Catholic writers' fabrications regarding the number of Romanian people Uniate with the Catholic Church (from 80,000 to *more than* 200,000), in the Hungarian he names only Thuróczi, but in the Latin he also mentions Mátyás Bél and Jesuit Timón with their works' titles. The quotations are mostly the same, although in the Latin he adds Péterfi's mistake about the synods in Munkács, especially the synod in 1692. Bod refutes Péterfi's statements and demonstrates that it was impossible that in 1692 "more than 200 Romanian priests joined the Roman pope's Church."[10] Besides that, the order of the narration is changed, namely the citations which he began in Hungarian but continues, after the refutations, in Latin.

We can read about the adversities of Bod's Latin text in Botond Gudor's paper.[11] For the translator, apart from the mistakes of copying, the most difficult part was the language of the edicts. On the one hand because of the official terminology and on the other hand because of the flavour of the day. According to that, the edicts are cluttered with ornaments, restrictions and supplements; every now and then they add two or three synonyms, so the text seems not only redundant but sometimes meaningless – at least on the first reading. For example, the verb figures often after 15-20 lines and in Maria Theresa's edict dated the 20th of March 1760[12] we can find it on the 26th line – after a long specification. In the translation I kept this phrasing, just to keep that style, otherwise I tried to make the Hungarian text fluid.

As you can imagine, among the quoted edicts of the second part of Bod's book, his own narration was refreshing in its translation, as in the letter of Sofronie, the monk, and the fake royal edict I referred to previously. Such was the request of the Romanian people to the governors of Transylvania[13] which was criticised by Bod, just like the

[9] In the Hungarian variant between s. (73) and (83), pp. 82-85; in the Latin: book II, chap. 2. § XIX-XXI, s. (264-273), pp. 178-180.
[10] Ibid., s. (269), p. 179.
[11] Ibid., pp. 7-32: Botond Kund Gudor, "Az erdélyi románok tudományos történetírója: Bod Péter (1712-1769), a magyarigeni református lelkész" [Historian of Romanian People in Transylvania: Péter Bod (1712-1769), Vicar in Magyarigen], and pp. 33-51: Idem, "Istoriograful românilor transilvăneni, notarul general reformat (vicarul episcopal) Péter Bod (1712-1769)" [Historian of Romanian People in Transylvania: Péter Bod (1712-1769), Vicar in Magyarigen].
[12] Ibid., book II, chap. 4, § XXXVI, s. (462-477), pp. 350-353.
[13] Ibid., book II, chap. 5, § II, s. (479-482), pp. 353-354. They submitted the application to the synod in Hunyad, in 1760.

monk's writings: "Despite its style and phrasing it is very poor, I publish it here as I received it."[14] Among them, the most exciting for the researcher and philologist is the issue of the fake: based on what rules about an edict can we determine that it is not genuine? Obviously we have to check formal elements and subject-matter.

It seems that the Empress's tolerance consisted mostly in prohibitions, and the decree pronounces that only after those prohibitions can the non-Uniate people practise their religion hereafter with impunity. We can read it in the admonition of the Romanian bishop:

> "Therefore we graciously order you, our Royal Government, that you let the said orthodox people gravely know this our benevolent decree, who had declared having a different opinion from the Uniate people ere now, and make them known every single one; at the same time you will personally notify the Uniate bishop in Fogaras, that *he absolutely has to keep from persecuting the non-Uniate people in the future*, whether they are priests or *profane people, [namely] because they personally did not join the union (450), and* furthermore, in the locations where such people are living, *as to those permitted to practise their religion, he, who rejoices at tolerance, must allow them to practise it with the conditions above.*"

After that the edict admonishes the officials and landowners, because in part it is their fault that people's riots could spread so much, consequently it threatens those who will not obey the said orders with divestiture of office and punishment. Finally, it mentions a fake edict published by non-Uniate Romanians in the name of the Empress Maria Theresa which was read out at their prohibited synod in Újegyház (Nocrich, in German: Leschkirch) Saxon Seat, in the village of Glimbocha,[15] and then proclaimed village by village. She issues a warrant of arrest against the author and distributors of the fake edict and commands an investigation and interrogation of the royal magistrate of Újegyház (who supposedly wrote it) and the other officials involved in the case. The edict was written in Romanian and the Empress received a Latin translation.

The fake edict stands out from the imperial edicts by its terseness and brevity: it is only one fourth of the quoted edict's length, which can be considered of typical length.[16] The Empress's edict suggests that the fake edict was originally written in Romanian because she has its Latin translation. Where and how was it actually made? This issue needs further research, but now I will confine myself to the examination of formal elements and the subject-matter.

In many ways the fake edict misses the rules of editing edicts, which go back through several hundreds years of tradition:

1. It is not dated precisely; it is conspicuous at first sight.

---

[14] Ibid., book II, chap. 5, § II, s. (479), p. 353; ibid., (480): *Rarioris cum sit formae ac stili hic eundem exhibebo ut nactus sum.*

[15] Bod mentions it as *Glimbocha*, its German name is Hüchnerbach.

[16] 6651 characters without spaces, and the fake edict consists of only 1555 characters.

2. It mentions twice the validation by a seal (*corroboratio*), which usually comes in the last sentence of the edict, once in the correct place, but once more two-thirds of the way down the text, which I have never seen before.
3. It misses the usual title-formula at the beginning (*inscriptio*),[17] which appears at the top of almost every edict proclaimed.
4. It misses the *notificatio*,[18] which is included where it is not written in the title to which the edict is directed: *Memoriae commendamus tenore praesentium significantes quibus expedit universis* – i.e.: "With the contents of the present edict we would like to let everybody who is concerned know."
5. *Nos* – that is "We" figures only in the first of the eight Maria Theresa edicts before the name of the Empress quoted in Bod's book. It was published in 1743 for the Uniate Romanian bishop as a validation of privileges given by Leopold I and Charles VI. This formula is not typical in edicts of Charles VI, father and predecessor of Maria Theresa (in Leopold I's decrees it is still common). – The fake edict begins with: *Nos, Maria Theresa...* To sum up: if we consider only those very external characteristics, we can see at once that it is probably a fabrication.

It would be great to compare the Latin terms of the above quoted genuine edict (and other edicts published by Maria Theresa) with the expressions of this *suppositicium* – fabrication – if its original was written in Latin. However, according to the cited genuine decree, it was circulated all over Transylvania in Romanian and the Empress had its Latin translation. Who translated it and when? We do not have any information about that. At the same time there is an expression which is salient even in the translation, and probably comes from the Romanian term: union is everywhere denoted by the term *unio*, only here we find it as: *unacia*.[19] A question presents itself: how could they perpetrate that an official, namely the magistrate in Újegyház (Nocrich), published it officially. If it is true (this is not clear, according to the imperial decree), then it was possible for two reasons:
1. The said official was not erudite enough to recognise that the edict was fake;
2. He sympathised with the Orthodox people and helped their cause by closing his eyes to the facts. Further research could answer this question. Now we will examine the issue of genuineness from the angle of the subject-matter.

As I have explained, the fake edict is quite short (it consists only of four phrases not counting the signature and date). Though it tries to make rather long sentences just like the genuine edicts, from the intonation and style it is obvious that it was not written in the Empress's Court. Here it is in English:

> "We, Maria Theresa, by the grace of God Roman Empress and Queen of Hungary, Bohemia, Dalmatia, Croatia, Slavonia and Princess of Transylvania.

---

[17] Ibid., 18.
[18] Ibid., 19.
[19] Bod, *Az erdélyi románok*, right before s. (459), p. 350.

From what we hear, in our Principality of Transylvania several affrays and dissensions have arisen among Romanian nationals because of religion and faith, and, although there are many of our Catholic henchmen whose duty it is to make peace and strengthen love among people, they, as we hear from the complaints of the poor, sully (458) the orders and will of our Majesty, dissipate love, destroy common peace and law, and unfairly rob poor people because of their religion and faith. Let the Romanian nationals in Transylvania know that this evil treatment does not happen, and has never happened, according to our knowledge or will. Therefore, in order that our enemies and the malefactors will settle and calm down, and that from now on and in the future there will be peace, love and tranquillity among the people, and no more complaint or lamentation will reach our Majesty because of religion and faith, we want graciously to give them our decree, which we validate with the seal of our Majesty: let the Romanian people in Transylvania be free to keep the Greek religion, and have priests according to the Eastern church's rite, and whoever wants to, of their own free will and choice, can join the union, whoever in turn (459) does not want to, no-one will dare force to; if such transpires, then, as enemies of peace and those who perturb tranquillity, and as those who violate the orders of our Majesty, they will suffer from the grave anger of our Majesty and her punishment. For major ratification of these, we fortify this edict, i.e. decree with the seal of our Majesty. Dated in Vienna, our imperial city in 1754.

Locus Sigilli"[20]

(Bod's cited remark comes after this: "Miserable forger, who wanted to imitate the Court's style! He failed.")

From the subject-matter we recognize the author is taking sides in the first sentence, since he blames the Catholics because they have not yet made peace among the fractious Romanian people, although this is the duty of many of them. On this point, it is obvious that he alludes to the majority of Catholic noblemen in the government of the Principality of Transylvania. It can be considered as an emotional element that he says their duty is also to "strengthen love among people;" such a phrase does not exist in a genuine edict: only the Empress's love and her motherly care for her subjects occurs

---

[20] *Nos Maria Theresia, clementia Dei Imperatrix Romanorum, et Regina Regni Hungariae, Bohemiae, Dalmatiae, Croatiae, Sclavoniae, et Princeps Transylvaniae.*

Audientes varia disturbia, et dissensiones fieri in Principatu Nostro Transylvaniae inter Nationem Valacham, propter Religionem et fidem, et cum multi essent in Nostros fideles Catholicos, quorum obligatio est facere pacem, et confirmare Charitatem inter homines, illi autem, quemadmodum audimus ex querelis pauperum, inculcant /458/ Mandata, et Voluntatem Majestatis Nostrae, defruunt Charitatem, communem pacem et Constitutionem cruciant, et depraedantur pauperes, contra justitiam, propter suam Religionem et Fidem. Quae malitia notum sit Nationi Valachae ex Transylvania, quod nunquam fuerit, neque sit, cum scitu et voluntate Majestatis Nostrae. Quapropter ut conquiescant, et sedentur adversarii, et malefactores, ut sit pax a modo imposterum, charitas, et bona tranquillitas inter homines, et ne plures querelae, et lamentationes veniant coram Majestate Nostra propter religionem et fidem, voluimus clementissime eis dare Decretum, sigillo Majestatis Nostrae roboratum; liberum sit Valachis ex Transylvania servare Graecam Religionem, et habere Sacerdotes secundum ordinem Ecclesiae orientalis, et qui voluerit, ex sua bona voluntate, et suo arbitrio amplecti Unaciam sit liber, qui autem /459/ noluerit, nemo praesumat eum cogere; quia tales ubi innotuerint, tanquam refractarii pacis et tranquillitatis perturbatores, et tanquam legum, et Mandatorum Majestatis Nostrae transgressores, in gravem indignationem Majestatis Nostrae, et ultionem cadent. Quae ut majus robur habeant, has Literas, seu Decretum isthoc, sigillo Majestatis Nostrae corrobaramus. Datum in Civitate Nostra Imperiali Viennae Anno 1754.

L[ocum] S[igillii] In Bod's quoted work, book II, chap. 4, § XXXIV, s. (457-459), pp. 349-350.

sometimes in the *arengas*.[21] He takes on this emotional strand in the following text, where he refers to "the complaints of the poor," which does not occur ever: the edicts only talk about complaints and requests of Romanian subjects in general terms. And to top it all, those Catholic noblemen "trample on" (inculcant) the Empress's will and orders. At best, it occurs in other edicts that they neglect them (*negligentes*), or show contempt (*contemptores*), perhaps transgress (*transgressores*). Next he refers again to love: they "dissipate" it (*defruunt*); they "destroy" (*cruciant*) common peace – we could only read that in imperial decrees about rebel Romanians; and they "destroy" (cruciant) law and constitution – such a thing is never mentioned about Catholic noblemen. After that he talks again about poor people, whom they undeservedly "rob" (*depraedantur*) because of their religion and faith. In Maria Theresa's edicts we only read once about discouraging noblemen's cruelty: in the edict dated the 9th of September 1743:

> "But we seriously want, as these laws make possible, and without trespassing upon third party's rights, to treat Romanian people well and especially to discourage squires' cruelty against peasants, with clear and proper orders, through their perfect enforcement, and so we will safeguard those who give service and are able to sustain their charges."[22]

However, as you can see, she does not protect peasants on emotional grounds but based on utilitarian considerations. The next sentence contrasts most strikingly with the sleepy, long passages of Court phrasing – first of all by its shortness and terseness, which, even if it does not reach the eloquence of Cicero, gives strength and almost a flavor of fables to the text:

> "Let Romanian nationals in Transylvania know that this evil treatment does not happen, and has never happened, according to our knowledge or will."

The Romanian peasants could not expect more reassuring news than that, trusting the Empress's justice. Further on, hinting at the aforementioned Catholic noblemen, it calls them "our enemies" and "malefactors." Therefore the Empress publishes the edict with the aim that those who did not obey would calm down and "there will be peace, love and tranquillity among the people." Well, the Empress mentioned peace in previous edicts but mostly as an order and not as here. The other justification is, so that "no more complaint or lamentation will reach our Majesty" – with reference to that, Maria Theresa threatens with punishment only those who complain gratuitously.[23] At this point there follows the first validation (*corroboratio*) which, as I explained previously, is in the wrong place.

---

[21] *Arenga* is a short speculative justification at the beginning of the middle part (*contextus*) of the decree. See *Vocabulaire International de la Diplomatique*, ed. Mª Milagros Cárcel Ortí (València: Universitat de València, 1994), and László Solymosi, *Írásbeliség és társadalom az Árpád-korban* [Literacy and Society in the Árpád Era] (Budapest: Argumentum Kiadó, 2006), 18.

[22] See Bod, *Az erdélyi románok*, Book II, chap. 4, § II, s. (345), p 326.

[23] *[...] perperam e converso querulantibus promerita irrogetur poena*; see ibid., book II, chap. 4, § XXXI, s. (443), p. 346, edict dated on the 22th of April 1759.

The most important sentence of the fake edict is the pronouncement that the non-Uniate Romanian people had been yearning for and was now being proclaimed very clearly, which is this:

> "let the Romanian people in Transylvania be free to keep the Greek religion, and have priests according to the eastern church's rite, and whoever wants to, of their own free will and choice, can join the union, whoever in turn (459) does not want to, no-one will dare to force to."

They wanted to hear this long before, so, as the genuine decrees did not proclaim it, they phrased it like this themselves and circulated it among their devotees.

The reason why the Empress never phrased it so clearly is obvious: she did not want to support the independent Orthodox Church in Transylvania. She gave them a new Orthodox bishop from Hungary but he was only an instrument in her hands to suppress them. The final lines could even be from a genuine edict (though they are not typical for the epoch because of their simple phrasing): they tell about the punishment of those who violate the decree (*sanctio negativa*) and they contain validation (*corroboratio*) once again, and the date, though the year only, which is not correct for an edict.

As a summary, I can tell that both types of edict, the genuine as with the fake, have their strengths in their style. The genuine Habsburg-edicts with their overcomplicated, never-ending sentences, that are full of ornaments and synonyms so that you do not understand them when reading for the first time, made them very hard to imitate – their composition became a kind of cryptography, protecting their genuineness in this way. On the other hand, the fake uses simple, easily comprehensible statements with common sense as well. It tries to work upon emotions and, what is more important, it expresses clearly and explicitly what its hearers have waited for. It spread like wildfire among the Romanian people and rekindled their latent enthusiasm for keeping their original religion. Just like the two Orthodox monks, Visarion Sarai in 1744 and Sofronie between 1759-61, who, by their quiet speech and with their simple and searching words, convinced the Romanian peasants and noblemen of their truth.

JEWISH MOBILITY AND SETTLEMENT IN BUCHAREST

FELICIA WALDMAN

The first reference to a stable Jewish presence in Bucharest dates back to 1550, when a document issued by Prince Mircea Ciobanul mentioned the existence of Jews in the city who owned shops and land. A responsa of Rabbi Samuel de Medina of Salonica, issued at about the same time, as well as a responsa issued by Rabbi Josef Caro of Nicopole, in 1559, both referring to the assassination of Jewish merchants in and near Bucharest, confirm the information.[1] Additional evidence includes a document issued from the princely court of Bucharest in 1560 by the court copyist "Shain, son of Josef,"[2] as well as two firmans (royal decrees) issued by Sultan Selim II in 1568: one ordering the *kadi* (Turkish judge) of Cirmen (Cernova) to investigate the Jew Istergun, *previously employed by the late Prince Mircea Ciobanul*, who had allegedly stolen six carts of goods, and escort him to Constantinople for punishment, and another ordering Prince Alexander II to protect Ottoman subjects from the Jews, who were in the habit of lending money to the villagers at very high interest rates just before their payments to the Sublime Porte were due, ordering that such acts be prevented in the future. (A document issued by Prince Alexander Mircea in 1575 shows that, in fact, among the creditors of the time who lent money at interest, alongside the Jews, Greeks and other Orientals there were plenty of Turks as well).[3]

Groups of Jewish families are mentioned in Bucharest in the seventeenth century, despite the discriminatory stipulations against non-Christians in the laws passed under the rule of Matei Basarab (1632-1654) or in Archbishop Teofil's 1640 "Govora Bill of Rights," which anathematized those priests "who would call Jews brethren" or "eat with them."[4] A Jewish presence in Bucharest at the time is also mentioned in Dimitrie Cantemir's *Descriptio Moldaviae*.[5]

More information about the Jews of Bucharest emerges toward the end of the century. They are mentioned, for instance, in missionary Urbano Cerri's report to Pope Innocent XI of 1676-1678, which reads: "there are many Jews and Turks in Bucharest, but rich Jews from Turkey, who have come along with the other Eastern elements."[6] The

---

[1] Victor Eskenasy, ed., *Izvoare şi mărturii referitoare la evreii din România* [Sources and Testimonies on the Jews of Romania] (henceforth abbreviated Eskenasy, *IMER*), vol. I (Bucureşti: Federaţia Comunităţilor Evreieşti din Republica Socialistă România, Centrul de documentare, 1986), 30-31, 34.

[2] Constantin C. Giurescu, *Istoria Bucureştilor din cele mai vechi timpuri până în zilele noastre* [History of Bucharest, from the Earliest Times until Nowadays] (Bucureşti: Editura pentru literatură, 1966), 276.

[3] Eskenasy, *IMER*, 42, 47.

[4] Ibid., 96.

[5] Demetriu Cantemiru, *Descrierea Moldaviei* [Description of Moldavia] (Bucureşti: Tipografia Curţii, 1875), 129.

[6] Mihai Spielmann, ed., *IMER*, vol. II/1 (Bucureşti: Federaţia Comunităţilor Evreieşti din Republica Socia-

information is only partially accurate, as besides the Sephardim, who had come mainly from the Ottoman Empire, there were also Ashkenazi Jews from the Ukraine and Poland in Bucharest, who had taken refuge here after the Cossack massacres of 1648-1649 (Meyer Abraham Halevy even believed there were Ashkenazi Jews in Bucharest from in 1550).[7]

As for Jewish commercial life in Bucharest, we know for instance that in 1678, Gheorghe Grigore Cantacuzino gave "the Jew Isaac and his wife, Soria, a piece of barren land on the street of the Şerban Vodă Inn, to build shops and houses on, for a rent of 6 talers per year. Isaac and his descendants may keep the place, for as long as they shall pay the rent."[8]

Most information about the Jews of Bucharest at the end of the seventeenth century undoubtedly dates to the reign of Constantin Brâncoveanu (1688-1714). Thus the Treasury Register of 1694-1701 indicates the exact amount cashed from the "Jewish guild," which included the Jews of Bucharest, representing their contribution to the annual tax and other levies owed to the exchequer.[9] As historian Constantin C. Giurescu puts it:

> "Just like the Armenians and the Bulgarians, under Brâncoveanu's rule the Jews of Bucharest were organized in a guild, which paid a fixed tax to the Treasury. [...] They used to dwell in the South-Eastern part of the city, in the Jigniţa quarter, where their synagogue was located. We also know the name of a doctor, 'Avram the Jew,' who cared for Brâncoveanu along with other, Christian physicians."[10]

After Brâncoveanu was deposed, the Jews' situation worsened. We read of the efforts by Ştefan Cantacuzino (1714-1715) to gain popularity and make people forget his role in the assassination of his predecessor in the letters of Anton Maria del Chiaro, Brâncoveanu's Italian secretary. We thus know that besides prohibiting the tax on livestock and exempting the clergy from any taxation, the prince "had the Jewish synagogue pulled down, even though it was situated in a remote place, and gave strict orders that the Jews no longer be allowed to gather for prayers."[11] We have no idea when the synagogue had been built, but we know that at the time it housed a *hevra kaddisha* (religious association) and an alms box.[12]

Despite these hardships, Jewish immigration to the Romanian Principalities visibly increased in the early eighteenth century. Thus, as of 1700, many Jewish merchants

listă România, Centrul de documentare, 1988) (henceforth abbreviated Spielmann, *IMER*), 226.

[7] M. A. Halevy, *Comunităţile evreilor din Iaşi şi Bucureşti până la 1821* [The Jewish Communities of Iaşi and Bucharest until 1821] (Bucureşti: Institutul de Istorie Evreo-Română, 1931).

[8] Spielmann, *IMER*, 226.

[9] Ibid., 3.

[10] Giurescu, *Istoria Bucureştilor din cele mai vechi timpuri*, 271. On page 358, Giurescu refers to the quarter as "Popescu."

[11] Spielmann, *IMER*, 22-23.

[12] Dr. Iosif Camil, "Un istoric. Comunitatea evreilor din Bucureşti, dela înfiinţare şi până azi" [A History. The Jewish Community of Bucharest, from its Establishment until Today], *Almanahul evreesc* 5704 (1943-1944): 206.

and creditors decided to settle in Wallachia for commercial purposes. They were regularly mentioned among the categories of traders targeted by the various taxation acts issued by the rulers of the time, clearly showing that Jews were already a settled population. Moreover, their increasingly intensive and active participation in the local social and economic life generated specific forms of self-administration, necessary both for communal life and to ensure their relations with the authorities. Organized in "guilds" from the time of Brâncoveanu's rule, the Jews enjoyed a status of internal autonomy, regulated by charters and privileges, which gave them the right to settle in exchange for various dues to the exchequer.[13] (We cannot, therefore, speak of privileges granted to Jewish trade, but rather of an acknowledgement of its profitability for the treasury).

Not only did the number of Jewish merchants increase, but also the variety of their merchandise. Moreover, if at first trade was the only activity they were permitted to practice, at this point references to Jewish craftsmen start to emerge: glass blowers, jewellers, silversmiths, etc. Their life in Bucharest is described by the same Antonio Maria del Chiaro in an account of 1717-1718:

> "as for people of other religions than the Romanian and Roman Catholic, there are many Jewish families. Their life is quite hard: they sell brandy and other stuff for a living. Besides Romanian, they speak German and Polish. They are only allowed to wear black or dark clothing, and they cannot wear yellow or red footwear, only black."[14]

After Brâncoveanu, rulers such as Nicolae (1715-1716 and 1719-1730) and Constantin Mavrocordat (1731-1733, 1735-1741, 1744-1748, 1756-1758 and 1761-1763) recognized the important role the Jews played in the emergence of internal markets, in the local trade flow and its connection to the international economy, as well as in the development of certain crafts and professions; these princes in their turn granted Jewish communities autonomy, rights and protection, and employed Jewish doctors and counsellors at their Courts.

We also have information about the Jews' economic condition at the time: a 1724 sale deed from Bucharest mentions the house of "Sora the Jewess" as a landmark in the Greek Church quarter, on the street leading to the princely court, whilst a document issued by the St. George Church in 1728 indicates that one of the church's shops had been previously kept by Leul the Jew.[15] Constantin C. Giurescu tells us that "on 1st June 1743, 'Josef the glass-blower, son of Daniil the Jew,' and his wife, 'Istera' (Esther), rented from Ban Manolache Lambrino and his wife, Lady Bălaşa, a piece of land near 'the lower gate of the Princely Court,' for 8 talers a year, to build a house on."[16] A document issued by

---

[13] Spielmann, *IMER*, Introductory study, XXXI. Spielmann mentions that the fiscal regime of the foreigners in Wallachia was still far more advantageous than in Moldavia because, unlike the Moldavian guilds, which were included in the overall taxpayer category, the Wallachian guilds were directly accountable to the Prince's Pantry.

[14] Ibid., 32.

[15] Ibid., 45, 59.

[16] Giurescu, *Istoria Bucureştilor din cele mai vechi timpuri*, 271.

the prince Grigore Ghica II in 1749 confirms that the house was built; he granted the Metropolitan of Wallachia several pieces of land together with the shops on them, among them the house of Josef, the Jewish glass-blower, whose "shack stands on Lady Bălaşa Brâncoveanu's grounds" (today Calea Moşilor).[17] The presence in 1749 of Jewish merchants on what was to later become Calea Moşilor is confirmed by yet another document issued that year, whereby Hristea Băcanul rented three shops near Zerda the Jewess.[18] Indeed, the importance of Jewish tradesmen at the time is underlined by a firman wherein Sultan Mahmud I ordered the elimination of both Jewish and Christian traders from the markets in the Danubian Principalities, as they competed with the Ottoman merchants.[19] A second firman issued by Sultan Mustafa III in 1764, reiterating the order, implicitly demonstrates the ineffectiveness of the first.[20]

As for the internal organization of Jewish society, it appears that following Ştefan Cantacuzino's 1714 demolition of the synagogue in the Jigniţa (or Popescu) quarter, Celibi Bally obtained the prince's permission to reorganize the communities, temples and Jewish settlements in Bucharest.[21] Thus, in 1730 the Spanish community underwent a definitive restructuring and gained official recognition.[22] The first Jewish school for boys and girls in the capital also seems to date from 1730.[23] (School was, in fact, a cardinal institution of the Jewish community: various documents of the time indicate the existence of Talmud-Torah schools in the synagogues, which taught in Hebrew and were maintained through mandatory financial contributions from the Jewish craftsmen's guilds).[24]

More and more Jewish merchants are mentioned in Bucharest and not just anywhere, but in the very heart of the town. We thus know that in 1762, the Jewish merchant Solomon rented rooms in the Şerban Vodă Inn, the best business spot of the city, while in 1764 a certain "Sorica the Jewess" lived in the Săpunari quarter. Ten years later we find Iancu the Jew on a "barren piece of land" belonging to the Metropolitan, while in 1777 two other Jews, Marco and Haim, are mentioned in the Old St. George quarter.[25] In 1782 a certain "Hîrşu the Jew" kept a shop on the main street.[26] In the shops of these merchants one could find tobacco, cotton, iron, rice, ropes and string, copperware, boots, salt, hardware and household items, but also jewellery. The few of them who owned properties (houses and/or shops) also bought and sold real estate.[27] In the late eighteenth and early

---

[17] Spielmann, *IMER*, 173.
[18] Lya Benjamin, Mihai Spielmann, Sergiu Stanciu, eds., *IMER*, vol. II/2 (Bucureşti: Hasefer, 1990) (henceforth abbreviated Benjamin, Spielmann, Stanciu, *IMER*), 534-535.
[19] Spielmann, *IMER*, 175-176.
[20] Benjamin, Spielmann, Stanciu, *IMER*, 54-55.
[21] Giurescu, *Istoria Bucureştilor din cele mai vechi timpuri*, 358.
[22] I. G. Cohen in the speech he gave at the Sephardic Community's bicentennial in 1930, cited by Spielmann in *IMER*, 23, note 4.
[23] Spielmann, *IMER*, 23, note 4.
[24] Benjamin, Spielmann, Stanciu, *IMER*, Introductory Study, LV.
[25] Ibid., 180.
[26] Giurescu, *Istoria Bucureştilor din cele mai vechi timpuri*, 271.
[27] Benjamin, Spielmann, Stanciu, *IMER*, Introductory study, LVIII.

nineteenth centuries the main field in which Bucharest Jews were active was the alcohol industry, including retail. This is proven by the many brandy distilleries built on locations provided by the exchequer which are mentioned in the various deeds of the time. Other trades included drapery and crafts, working with textiles (tailors, haberdashers, and cap-makers), leather (shoemakers, bookbinders), glassware (glaziers and glass-blowers), metal-work (tinsmiths) and food (bakers, cheese makers). Many Jews were craftsmen and merchants at the same time. The tax exemptions granted by the various rulers to Jewish goldsmiths and silversmiths are proof of their status in this epoch. Very few Jews were moneylenders; the important creditors were still in Constantinople. A whole series of random trades (hawkers, pedlars, carters, innkeepers, but also interpreters, doctors, etc.), completes the image of the Jewish contribution to Bucharest's economic life.[28]

The number of Jewish inhabitants of the capital continued to increase, as a result of both natural growth and immigration. During the Russian occupation between 1769 and 1774, the Bucharest community practically doubled.[29] Although not very accurate on the length of the Jewish presence in Bucharest, Franz Joseph Sulzer's notes of 1781 indicate that in those days most Wallachian Jews lived in the capital, where they had at least two synagogues.[30] Their number increased during 1782-1798, when after the opening of the Russian and Austrian consulates in Bucharest in 1782 and the French consulate in 1796-1798, more and more Jews from these lands (particularly from Bukovina and the Ukraine) started migrating to the Wallachian capital, where they were given the status of "foreign subjects," as they continued to be regarded as subjects of the country from which they had come.[31]

The Austrian consul Ignac Stephan Raicevici also described the trades practiced by Jews in the Danubian Principalities in his notes of 1782-1788, where he remarked that commerce and all small basic industries were entirely in the hands of foreigners, Galician Jews included, and that because there were so many Jews in Wallachia, they had gained permission to have synagogues in many places.[32]

As for the rulers' attitude toward the Jews, documents of the time reveal that some, like Constantin Mavrocordat (1731-1733, 1735-1741, 1744-1748, 1756-1758), continued to borrow money from the Jewish lenders in Constantinople. Others did their best to make the life of Jewish merchants as difficult as possible, such as Nicolae Caragea (1782-1783), who on 15th January 1783 forbade both the Jews and the Armenians to open their shops during the Orthodox feasts. In 1785, at the request of the townspeople, Mihai

---

[28] Paul Cernovodeanu, "Regimul evreilor sub fanarioţi (1711-1821)" [The Jews' Condition under the Phanariote Princes], in *Evreii în societatea şi conştiinţa istorică românească* [The Jews in Romanian Society and Historical Conscience] (Bucureşti: CSIER, 2003), 69.
[29] M. A. Halevy, "Comunitatea din Bucureşti în epoca fanarioţilor (1716-1821)" [The Community of Bucharest under the Phanariote Rule], *Sinai* III (1931): 99-100.
[30] Benjamin, Spielmann, Stanciu, *IMER*, 237-238.
[31] Gheorghe Parusi, *Cronologia Bucureştilor, 20 septembrie 1459 - 3 decembrie 1989* [Chronology of Bucharest, September 20, 1459 - December 3, 1989] (Bucureşti: Compania, 2007), 116.
[32] Benjamin, Spielmann, Stanciu, *IMER*, 250.

Şuţu (1783-1786, 1791-1793) ordered that the distillery next to the old princely court, kept by a Jew and a Christian (in other words, a Romanian-Jewish joint venture producing brandy on a spot rented from the priests of the princely churches!) be shut down because it represented a fire hazard to the neighbouring area.[33]

In his turn, Nicolae Mavrogheni allowed the Jews of Bucharest to rebuild their synagogue in the Popescu quarter in January 1787. In 1793 Alexandru Moruzi (1793-1796, 1799-1801) decided to set up a jewellers' guild, and appointed Eliazar "jeweller basha" or guild-master, because "he fully possesses the science and knowledge of this craft," and gave him a free hand in organizing the guild.[34] It is interesting to note that Eliazar can also be found, together with 50 other Jewish merchants, on the list of Austrian subjects doing business in Bucharest in 1804.[35]

In a decree of November 1793 Moruzi solved a conflict between the inhabitants of the Răsvan quarter and the Jews, by demolishing the synagogue the latter had erected in the Nicolescu Inn (for reasons of commercial competition); to prove his good intentions he then ordered the police in January 1794 to protect the Jewish guild against any sort of vexations. The ruler's care for Jewish rights can also be seen in the order he gave in July 1794 for the punishment of a certain Petre Croitorul, who had attempted to Christianize a Jewish child against his will. The culprit was sentenced to "one hundred strokes of the bastinado" and "exile across the border to Moldavia."[36]

From a document issued by the same Moruzi we know that there was a glass blower by the name of Moses in Bucharest in 1794, which produced glassware for the Princely Court. Preoccupied with the regulation of the crafts, Moruzi also dealt, among other things, with the activity of the Jewish moneylenders present on the Wallachian market: in May 1796 he issued a princely decree establishing the manner in which they were to operate.[37]

It is interesting to note that when Prince Constantin Hangerli (1797-1799) decided that "guest houses" should be built for the official travellers, particularly Turks, who came to the Wallachian capital on business and whom the locals had so far been obliged to host in their own homes, the princely decree issued to this effect in February 1798 mentioned that each guild should provide a lodging, while "the Jews and the Armenian together must give one." We know that two Jews were serving the princely court in 1798: a bookbinder, "Serşu the Jew," and a haberdasher, "Isaac the Jew," because in October Hangerli exempted each of them from taxes for his services and professional skill.[38] During the same year, the Jews in the Schitu Măgureanu quarter built a wooden syna-

---

[33] Ibid., 44, 250, 258-259, 261, 309-310, 281-282.
[34] Ibid., 389.
[35] N. Iorga, *Istoria Bucureştilor* [History of Bucharest] (Bucureşti, 1939), 206.
[36] Benjamin, Spielmann, Stanciu, *IMER*, 404, 426.
[37] Ibid., 410, 434-435.
[38] Ibid., 445, 458.

gogue (which would burn in the fire of 1813).[39] Moreover, a document of February 1800 mentions a "Jewish silversmith," Haim, who gave authorities details about the fate of liturgical items stolen a month before from the church in the Popa Petre quarter (because the thieves had been unwise enough to try and place the objects with him for sale). Also from 1800 comes the first mention of the procedure and formulation of the oath that the Jews of Wallachia were bound to take in the courts of law.[40]

The nineteenth century began with an outbreak of anti-Semitism (April and May 1801). Details can be found in the report of Michael Merkelius, the Austrian consul in Bucharest, to his superior in Vienna of 8th April; it seems that an Austrian Jew was accused of murdering a Christian on the first day of Easter. Under the deep conviction that Jews used Christian blood in their religious rituals, the local gentry launched violent attacks against the Jews. Prince Alexandru Constantin Moruzi had to intervene (during his second reign, 1799-1801) in order to restore order. The ruler's position toward the events is confirmed by his reaction to the document of 13th April wherein the police chief, Caragea, informed him of the petition filed by two Jewish merchants plundered by locals during the anti-Semitic turmoil of 8th April: Moruzi ordered the immediate punishment of the culprits. When Gheorghe Condorogiul, a "vagabond" who had also been involved in the initial unrest, started a renewed blood libel, instigating the population to attack Jews with weapons and bats, the prince put him in prison under "the sentence without end."[41]

Constantin Alexandru Ipsilanti (1802-1807) showed a similar attitude toward the Jewish population of Bucharest: in 1804, he addressed a letter to Metropolitan Dositei Filitti of Wallachia, in which he tasked him to explain to the people, and particularly the priests, that the allegations that Jews killed Christians in order to use their blood in religious rituals were untrue. The prince concluded that this was a mere calumny invented by "worthless, stupid men who wish to obtain unjust gains."[42]

As for the economic situation of the Jews at the beginning of the nineteenth century, we know from an 1802 report of the administrator of the princely court, Iancu Suţul, to the ruler, Mihail Constantin Suţu (1801-1802), that the Bucharest Jewish "guild" requested princely approval to increase the special tax on ritual slaughtering that provided the Jewish community with income to cover the wages of the *chacham*, the teacher, and all the other expenses incurred by community life, and the ruler granted his approval. The continuity of Jewish trade in the Sf. Vineri quarter is confirmed by a document of 1804 which mentions that Simon, son of Leib the draper, rented two shops from the Sf. Vineri Monastery for seven years; the source clarifies the lessee's obligations to the owner and is signed in Hebrew characters.[43]

---

[39] Parusi, *Cronologia Bucureştilor*, 137.
[40] Benjamin, Spielmann, Stanciu, *IMER*, 464-466, 467-468.
[41] Lya Benjamin, Ladislau Gyemant, eds., *IMER*, vol. III/1 (Bucureşti: Hasefer, 1999) (henceforth abbreviated Benjamin, Gyemant, *IMER*, vol. III/1), 285, 287.
[42] Ibid., 307.
[43] Ibid., 291, 308.

Additional proof of the presence of Jewish trade in the heart of the capital can be found in an 1816 document issued by Prince Caragea, which confirms the purchase deed of a certain Leibu, who had acquired a piece of land in the Sf. Vineri quarter by auction, with the approval of the Merchants' Guild, on condition that he would not build a synagogue, school or Jewish butchery on the premises, so that "Leibu the Jew would own the place and the buildings on it in good peace."[44] Interestingly enough, another "Leibu the Jew" (or perhaps the same) appears in a contract with the administrator of the Sf. Vineri church in 1835, whereby Leibu rented a piece of land in the Sf. Vineri quarter, on condition that he paid the priests and the church five lei per year and would not build a synagogue, Jewish school or butcher's shop on the premises.[45]

Information on Jewish life under Caragea's reign is available not only from documents of the time, but also from a book, *Lettres sur la Valachie*, published in Paris in 1821 by François Recordon, the ruler's Swiss secretary. Recordon tells us that about five or six thousand Jews lived in Wallachia at the time, mostly in and around Bucharest, Craiova and Ploieşti, where they could easily capitalize on their commercial skills and craftsmanship; they enjoyed general freedom in the practice of their religion, but had to face the usual insults from ordinary men, especially in the towns where intolerant inhabitants took pride in persecuting Jews. Recordon notes however that, although submitted to public disgrace and deprived of certain advantages that others enjoyed, the Jews of Bucharest were generally good spouses and parents, family men who looked for peace inside their homes and helped their coreligionists in need, who did not beg and lived in strict observance of the religious precepts.[46]

At about the same time, the Jewish "guild" became a "company." According to the register of crafts and ethnic companies and their debts for the last quarter of 1820, in which we also find the names and occupations of the members of the Jewish company of Bucharest, there were 127 craftsmen, grouped in 32 fiscal units. Each unit paid 14 talers and 48 coins per year, which amounted to a total of 460 talers and 96 coins.[47] Constantin C. Giurescu counts the 127 names as family heads, which leads to a total number of approximately 635 people (although as Moses Schwartzfeld notes, the company did not include all community members but only the craftsmen, making it impossible for us to determine the exact size of the Jewish population). The list comprises moneylenders, jewellers, silversmiths, a draper called Moses Bavaniste (probably Benvenisti), a "meat chopper," a "Jewish chancellor," distillers, tinsmiths, shoemakers, tailors, pedlars, haberdashers, hawkers, a supplier of seals, a chibouk lighter/filler, etc., giving a view of the Jewish contribution to Bucharest's economic life.[48] Iorga even provides the names of four

---

[44] Ibid., 395-396.

[45] Lya Benjamin, Ladislau Gyemant, eds., *IMER*, vol. III/2 (Bucureşti: Hasefer, 1999) (henceforth abbreviated Benjamin, Gyemant, *IMER*, vol. III/2), 88.

[46] François Recordon, *Lettres sur la Valachie* (Paris: Lecointe et Durey, 1821), 76-79.

[47] Benjamin, Gyemant, *IMER*, vol. III/1, 462.

[48] Giurescu, *Istoria Bucureştilor din cele mai vechi timpuri*, 272.

Jewish merchants registered two years before, in 1818: Abraham de Lion, Isaac Elias Kohen, Moses Zisu and Ephraim Nahmias. He additionally relates that Jewish tinsmiths worked in the Metropolitan's courtyard "making tin cannon balls filled with glass, pebbles and nails, for the four Romanian cannons taken from Cotroceni after Tudor (Vladimirescu)'s departure."[49]

In the meantime Jewish economic life continued to diversify. An unusual craft was recorded in 1835, when the Austrian subject Iancu Friedman offered to produce gunpowder for Prince Alexandru Ghica. The ruler resolved that the Department of Internal Affairs should "pay attention to the petition's contents"[50] (probably both literally and metaphorically).

The Jewish contribution to the development of Bucharest's industrial and commercial life is noted by Constantin C. Giurescu among others, who mentions that

> "it was also favoured by the chain of banks which emerged at the time, making credit much more accessible and safer. Bankers, and smaller banks, had been around from the first half of the nineteenth century. We may mention Solomon Halfon, who had a ciphered letter addressed to him on 17th September 1830 by the tax collector Ştefan Hagi-Moscu, whose disastrous bankruptcy in 1838, after some of his promissory notes had been denied in Vienna, hit many inhabitants of Bucharest, who had entrusted him not only with their savings, but also with their daughters' dowries, their minor children's money, and in some cases their entire fortune. Then there was Manoah Hillel, whose shop burnt in the 1847 fire and who bequeathed his massive fortune to the University of Bucharest for scholarships and awards. These bankers lent money but at high interest; they dealt with foreign banks, issuing promissory notes to them and honouring theirs."[51]

Just how important Hillel Manoah's activity really was (and Solomon Halfon's for that matter) becomes clear from many documents of the time, which reveal that, unlike in previous instances when rulers borrowed money from Jewish moneylenders, this time the state itself took loans. Thus besides the document issued by Grigorie IV Ghica in 1827, which exempted the moneylender Hillel Manoah and his brother Israel from any taxes to the Treasury and granted them various privileges as a reward for their service to the reign,[52] we also have the list of loans to the state Treasury in 1836, which shows that between January and August, Manoah lent the state 61,690 gold coins and 1,950,085 lei.[53] A document issued by the War Ministry in 1837 informs us that Manoah furthermore supplied the army. A year later, we find him rewarded once again for his services to the Treasury, this time by Alexandru Dimitrie Ghica. Even during Gheorghe Bibescu's reign (1842-1848), the state benefited from Manoah's financial help, as proven by the 1843 Treasury report to the prince on the deal struck with Manoah; the moneylender would bring in small silver coins of five and three kreuzers to the value of 10,000 gold coins, needed for

[49] Iorga, *Istoria Bucureştilor*, 207, 240.
[50] Benjamin, Gyemant, *IMER*, vol. III/2, 89.
[51] Giurescu, *Istoria Bucureştilor din cele mai vechi timpuri*, 168-169.
[52] Benjamin, Gyemant, *IMER*, vol. III/1, 548.
[53] Benjamin, Gyemant, *IMER*, vol. III/2, 131. The list also includes Solomon Halfon, with 2,860 gold coins and 90,090 lei.

a normal currency flow in Wallachia.[54]

Jewish life in Bucharest at the time is described in an 1841 letter of Dr. Iuliu Barasch, who had just been granted the right to issue prescriptions and was later appointed doctor of Dolj County by a princely decree of Gheorghe Bibescu in 1845. We read here that there were few Jews in the city, "perhaps about 2,000-2,500 souls altogether," made up of "two heterogeneous elements:"

> "Polish Jews who have managed to preserve their national costume, as everywhere else, except for a few minor changes. Most of them are professionals, but they are still barely educated; few of them are rich, if any [and] the so-called French or Spanish Jews, who have adopted Wallachian costume and speak among themselves in a Spanish-Castilian dialect, which is of course more or less corrupted. They can only communicate with the Christians and the Polish Jews in Romanian. […] Interest in intellectual issues and particularly in the progress of Judaism is, unfortunately, still a sort of *terra incognita* here [...] nobody has ever heard of a Jewish newspaper in these parts. [...] The Christian public's attitude to the Jews is quite bearable. As far as the material side goes, Jews fare quite well here; they don't pay any kind of taxes and are entirely free to practice all kinds of professions and industries."[55]

The first Jewish professional guild, the Bucharest Jewish tailors' guild, was founded in 1847. Designed to help investigate and solve problems arising between its members or between the tailors and their clients, the guild set down its rules and members' obligations.[56]

Jewish economic life continued to expand. Thus in 1848 an entrepreneur, Solomon Rosenthal, informed the capital's police that he had set up a carriage service which ran from Bucharest to Prince Gheorghe Bibescu's Băneasa estate.[57] Also in 1848 Jacob Marmorosch founded what was to become, over the next hundred years, one of Romania's most important and powerful banks: the Marmorosch Blank Bank.[58]

Jews contributed not only to the country's economy but also to political developments. In the Provisional Government's decree of 14th July 1848 for the appointment of the city council, we find Hillel B. Manoah among the proposed members. His name also appears among the signatories of the minutes of the assembly of Wallachian notables on 10th/22nd August 1848 who expressed confidence in Suleiman Pasha's speech and acknowledged the Regency that replaced the Provisional Government.[59] Davicion Bally, editor of *Pruncul Român* [The Romanian Infant], together with his wife, also contributed a sum of money to the 1848 Revolution. In the same newspaper, Bernhard Joseph Popper launched

---

[54] Ibid., 147, 174, 300-301.
[55] Ibid., 260, 261-262, 383.
[56] Ibid., 452-454.
[57] Ibid., 479.
[58] The Marmorosch Blank Bank operated between 1848 and 1951. Other Jewish banks included Berkovitz Bank, 1922-1945, Bernstein Leo S.A.R., Bucharest, 1947-1948, Friedman, Iuster & Comp Bank S.A.R., Bucharest, 1933-1940, Haim et Comp. Bank S.I.N.C., 1931-1947, Levy Bank S.A.R., 1944-1949, S. Mayer and Sons Bank, 1937-1948 (see www.arhivelenationale.ro/images/custom/ image/Pdf-uri/DJANuri/DMBAN_fonduri_si_co lectii_date_in_cercetare.pdf, accessed August 30, 2011).
[59] Benjamin, Gyemant, *IMER*, vol. III/2, 491-492, 497.

an appeal to the Jewish population of Bucharest to support the Revolution. Ordinary people, too, took part in the common effort, according to their means: when the authorities compiled a list of members of the National Guard, set up during the 1848 Revolution, the names included Ianche the skinner, Ghenhăr the tailor, Fredel, leader of the foreign Jews, Vais or Vasile the baptized, Iancu the Jew, Haim the tailor, Moisi the Jew and Freiţ the tailor. All these despite the fact that the revolutionary government had further complicated community life by abolishing the special tax for the community's expenses.[60]

When Alexandru Ioan Cuza leased the right to found the Bank of Romania to a group of English, French and Austrian bankers by an 1865 princely decree, as a public company with an initial capital of 25 million lei (operational in 1866 as a branch of the Imperial Ottoman Bank of Constantinople, and later as the Bank of Romania Ltd), among the founders was Jacob Löbel, Jacob Marmorosch's brother-in-law and an important philanthropist who together with his wife Carolina sponsored many charities.[61]

Although the 1848 Revolution failed to bring their emancipation, Jews continued to settle in Bucharest and contribute to the city's development. After the unification of Moldova and Wallachia and the creation of the Romanian state, there were large waves of immigration and by the turn of the century their number had reached 43,000, compared to 3,600 in 1860. Besides the usual trades, due to legal constraints on land ownership, settlement and certain professions, and as a result of the Haskalah movement (the Jewish Enlightenment) and of the Jewish conviction that education is the only asset one can easily carry around if forced to migrate, many Bucharest Jews went to universities in Romania and abroad and became doctors, architects, musicians, writers, scientists. They built synagogues and schools for their children but also canteens, hospitals (Elias, Caritas, etc.) and theatres (Jignita, Barascheum, etc.) open to everyone. Notwithstanding the political upheavals of the late nineteenth and early twentieth centuries, they served in the army during Romania's Wars of Independence (1877) and Unification (1918), although they were not its citizens (Romanian Jews were only naturalized as late as 1923, and stripped of their citizenship barely 15 years later). Persecuted by the anti-Jewish legislation of the late 30's and early 40's, but fortunately not deported, despite the plan to do so, their number reached 150,000 in 1942.

After the war, the Jewish population of the capital stabilized. During the communist regime, Jews were relegated to the category of "other minorities" and were literally sold for various amounts of varying currencies to foreign countries (primarily to the State of Israel, under several secret deals, but by default many of those who left for the USA, Germany, Argentina [preferred particularly by the Sephardim] and other countries had to buy their way out too).[62] Their number dropped drastically during the two main waves of *alyiah* in the 50s and 60s.

---

[60] Ibid., 503-505, 505-506, 509, 511.
[61] Parusi, *Cronologia Bucureştilor*, 293.
[62] More details in Radu Ioanid's book *The Ransom of the Jews* (Chicago: Ivan Dee, 2005).

Some statistical data

Unfortunately, there are no accurate statistics on the number of Jews in Wallachia and Bucharest during the sixteenth to eighteenth centuries. Only in the nineteenth century did various sources start to advance concrete figures. Thereafter information about the size of the Jewish presence in Bucharest at the time can be found in the works of both foreign travellers and local authors. Dionisie Fotino, for instance, thought that about 1,500 families of "Jews and foreigners" lived in Bucharest in 1815."[63] A counsellor of the Danish Legation in Bucharest, Clausewitz, mentioned in his writings that in 1824 the capital counted about 80-90,000 inhabitants, including 6,000 Jews and 4,000 Germans.[64] Anatol Demidov, Matilda Bonaparte's ex-husband, described Bucharest in 1837 as having 436,000 ordinary inhabitants, 3,598 boyars with their 5,757 servants, 256 clerics and 137 monks with their 1,058 servants, 2,583 Jews and 1,795 Jewish foreign subjects, residing in altogether 10,074 houses, including three printing houses.[65] Demidov is also our source for the two hospitals in the city: Pantelimon and Dr. Mayer's.[66]

Two Scottish travellers passing through Bucharest in 1839, Andrew Bonar and Robert McCheyne, missionaries of the Committee for the Conversion of the Jews, related in their diary that they were given three figures for the number of Jews in the city: 2,800 (advanced by the British Consul, Colquhoun), 5,000 and 7,000 (with the second as the most probable). They also mention seven synagogues belonging to the Polish Jews and a beautiful one belonging to the Spanish Jews, who were richer and more influential in the community.[67] More accurate figures can be found in a table prepared by George Florescu and published by Nicolae Iorga in his book *Istoria Bucureştilor*, showing 5,166 Jews out of a total population of 58,791 inhabitants.[68]

The Serbian traveller Vuici also arrived in Bucharest in 1839 and gives the overall figure of 80,000 inhabitants (without including the clerics), of which 2,500 were Jews, less than half the number mentioned by Clausewitz and very close to that advanced by the British Consul. Vuici mentioned only two synagogues, besides 130 Orthodox churches and one each for the Catholic, Lutheran, Calvin and Armenian congregations.[69]

From the following year, 1840, we have an interesting parallel drawn by the French traveller Vaillant, who records that Bucharest had 60,000 inhabitants at the time, of which 4,800 Jews (8%) with five synagogues, while Iaşi had 26,203 inhabitants, of which 12,740 Jews (almost 50%) with only two synagogues.[70] In his 1848 work on

---

[63] See http://www.romanianjewish.org/en/mosteniri_ale_culturii_iudaice_03_11_19.html, accessed June 30, 2013.

[64] Nicolae Iorga, *Istoria românilor prin călători* [History of the Romanians Through the Eyes of Travellers], vol. III (Bucureşti : Editura Casei Şcoalelor, 1929), 140.

[65] Iorga, *Istoria Bucureştilor*, 257.

[66] Ibid., 258.

[67] Giurescu, *Istoria Bucureştilor din cele mai vechi timpuri,* 272.

[68] Iorga, *Istoria Bucureştilor*, 251.

[69] Iorga, *Istoria românilor prin călători*, 158.

[70] Ibid., 240.

Moldova and Wallachia, Neugebauer confirmed five synagogues in Bucharest.[71] In 1857-1858, the German traveller Richard Kunisch estimated that the city had about 120,000 inhabitants who frequented 140 Orthodox, Catholic and Lutheran churches and Jewish synagogues.[72] Dimitrie Papazoglu mentioned that by 1871, the capital's population had reached 150,000, including the ethnic minorities: Greeks, Bulgarians, Serbs, French, Austrians, Germans, Hungarians, Italians, Russians, Armenians, Turks, Poles, Lipovans and "many Jews, as well as Gypsies."[73] In 1879 the French painter Edouard Marbeau wrote in the Paris paper *Le Correspondent* that Bucharest was a genuine Babylon, where besides the majority Romanians one could find minority Greeks, Albanians, Germans, Armenians, Serbs, Russians, Gypsies, Hungarians and Spanish or Polish Jews, who "mingled everywhere."[74] In 1904 Frédéric Damé estimated the number of Bucharest Jews at about 50,000, out of a total population of 290,740.[75]

For statistics from the beginning of the nineteenth century, the catagraphy[76] drafted by the Russian occupation troops in 1810-1811 shows that the total population of the capital numbered 24,041 people, of which 862 Jews of both sexes, settled particularly in the Colţea, St. George and Stelea quarters. With one exception, they were all tenants. Most had household servants; only the house owner had a Gypsy slave. The vast majority were Austrian subjects, but there were also German, French, Russian and even Turkish subjects among them.[77]

Twenty years later, the census of 1831 found a total number of 58,794 inhabitants in Bucharest; counting the floating population, the figure actually reached 70,000. Among them there were 2,583 Jews and 1,795 foreign subjects, without mention of their ethnicity. The census also counted the number of prayer houses and found only one synagogue.[78]

The Bucharest catagraphy of 1838 not only indicates the Jewish inhabitants by quarters, but also their name, age, address, profession, legal status (native or foreign subject), and even whether they were vaccinated or not. Here, Jews represented 5% of the total population of 63,204 inhabitants. The data shows that most were natives.[79] The 27th June 1840 report of the Internal Affairs Minister on the centralized data of the catagraphy

---

[71] Giurescu, *Istoria Bucureştilor din cele mai vechi timpuri*, 272.
[72] Lelia Zamani, *Negustori, negustoraşi şi negustoreli în vechiul Bucureşti* [Merchants, Tradesmen and Trade Deals in Old Bucharest] (Bucureşti: Vremea, 2009), 14.
[73] Dimitrie Pappasoglu, *Istoria fondării oraşului Bucureşti, Istoria începutului oraşului Bucureşti, Călăuza sau Conducătorul Bucureştiului* [History of the Establishment of Bucharest City. History of the Beginnings of Bucharest City. The Guide or Pilot to Bucharest] (Bucureşti: Fundaţia Culturală Gheorghe Marin Speteanu, 2000), 253.
[74] George Costescu, *Bucureştii Vechiului Regat* [Bucharest of the Old Kingdom] (Bucureşti: Universul, 1944), 112.
[75] Giurescu, *Istoria Bucureştilor din cele mai vechi timpuri*, 272.
[76] For the meaning of "catagraphy" see http://www.revistadestatistica.ro/Articole/2010/A6en _10_2010.pdf, accessed June 30, 2013.
[77] Cernovodeanu, "Regimul evreilor sub fanarioţi (1711-1821)," 68.
[78] Benjamin, Gyemant, *IMER*, vol. III/2, 31.
[79] Ibid., 185-221.

concluded there were 3,656 Jewish families in the capital.[80]

The first census using scientific means and methods, which was carried out in 1860, provided the first truly relevant information on the Jewish population of Bucharest. We thus learn that 121,734 people lived in the capital at the time, of which 3,600 (2.9%) were Jews. After the unification of the Romanian Principalities (1859) and the establishment of the monarchy (1866), massive emigration began. By 1878 the percentage of Jews among the city's population had reached 11.67% (20,749 out of a total of 177,648), by 1889 it increased to 12.95% (23,887 out of 184,488), in 1894 it stood at 13.46% (31,251 out of 232,009), and in 1899 it reached 15.34% (43,274 out of 282,071). Thereafter it decreased to 12.91% (44,084 out of 341,321) in 1912 and to 11.80% (76,480 out of 643,430) in 1930. Thus from 1878 to 1899 the Jewish population doubled, while from 1900 to 1912 it remained more or less constant (due among other reasons to the migration caused by economic conditions at the time). During World War I there was even a deficit of 981 people, while during World War II the number of Bucharest Jews, which officially reached 98,048 (32,802 households), in reality rose to 150,000 (1942) due to the arrival of refugees from the front lines.[81]

Of these huge numbers, after the massive emigration of the 50s and 60s, when close to 400,000 Jews moved to Israel, only around 5,000 remained in 1975, with 2 temples and 14 synagogues.[82] Barely two years later in 1977 were only 3,000 Jews left, and 13 synagogues.[83] Today there are fewer than 3,000 people and 6 synagogues standing, of which only two are in service, two serve as museums, one as a storehouse and one as a gym. This is all that is left of a 500-year history.

---

[80] Ibid., 240.

[81] *The Jewish Community of Bucharest* (Bucharest: The Federation of the Jewish Communities in Romania, 2007), 9.

[82] Parusi, *Cronologia Bucureştilor*, 722, 737.

[83] Ibid., 742.

FROM GENERATION TO GENERATION: DEMOGRAPHIC REPRODUCTION IN RURAL SZEKLERLAND, FROM THE SECOND HALF OF THE NINETEENTH CENTURY AND TO THE FIRST HALF OF THE TWENTIETH CENTURY

LEVENTE PAKOT

Introduction

Reproduction of a population is the outcome of a complex process (demographic, biological, historical, social-economic etc.). Due to the complexity of this process, the particular areas often serve as a meeting point for the different fields of science. Family historians approach population reproduction studying how wealth and land is passed from generation to generation. In these analyses, the relationship among subsequent generations living on the same land is surveyed. In quantitative population history the experiments mixing historical demography and genetics are highlighted. In order to trace the process by which the population of a parish reproduce themselves from one generation to the next French historical demographers Alain Bideau and Guy Brunet and their Canadian colleagues applied the notion of "effective" child, term used in population genetics.[1] According to these researchers the individuals whose descendants survived in the focused area play a very significant role in the population reproduction. An individual is considered as "effective child" if he or she grew up to adulthood, got married and had children within the framework of the local community. The notion of "effective child" comprises multiple demographic parameters. It summarizes the result of complex interaction of different factors: fertility of parental generation, infant and child mortality, inheritance, nuptiality and migration.

Alain Bideau and his colleagues provide a relatively plain schema of analyzing population reproduction (Fig. 1). The most important element of their schema is the first – the founding – generation. The criterion for defining the founding generation is concluding marriage within a well defined period. Children and grandchildren of the first generation represent the second and third generations, respectively. Assessing the number of children realizing demographic reproduction and grouping by parental generation require the processing of demographic events covering at least three generations.

This paper has been prepared by incorporating the above approach. We want to trace the process by which the populations of two Transylvanian parishes, Szentegyházasfalva (Vlăhiţa) and Kápolnásfalva (Căpâlniţa) reproduce themselves from one generation to the next in the period between second half of the 19th century and first half of the 20th cen-

---

[1] Alain Bideau and Guy Brunet, "Stay or Leave? Individual Choise and Family Logic: The Destinations of Children Born in the Valserine Valley (French Jura) in the Eighteenth and Nineteenth Centuries," *The History of the Family: An International Quarterly* 1, 2 (n.d.): 159-168; Alain Bideau et al., "La reproduction de la population aux XVIIe et XIXe siècles. Exemples Français et Québécois," *Annales de Démographie Historique* (1995): 137-148.

tury. For this reason we study the "effective" progeny of couples to determine how many of them produce children (heirs) who continue to live in these villages.

The communities under study

Szentegyházasfalva (Vlăhiţa) and Kápolnásfalva (Căpâlniţa) are neighbouring settlements. They are located along the southern skirts of Harghita Mountains, in the eastern part of Inner Transylvania, present-day Romania, at about 860 metres above sea level (see Fig. 2). The villages lay on the frontier, far from the economic centres of Transylvania. Their total population reached 4,000 in the 1900s. The majority of their inhabitants belonged to the Roman Catholic Church. Due to their geographical proximity (2 km) and the joint privileges received from the Princes of Transylvania, the history of the two villages was closely interlocked: they formed one parish until 1838 and one administrative unit until 1876.[2]

Fig. 1: Schema of analysis of the relation between generations.

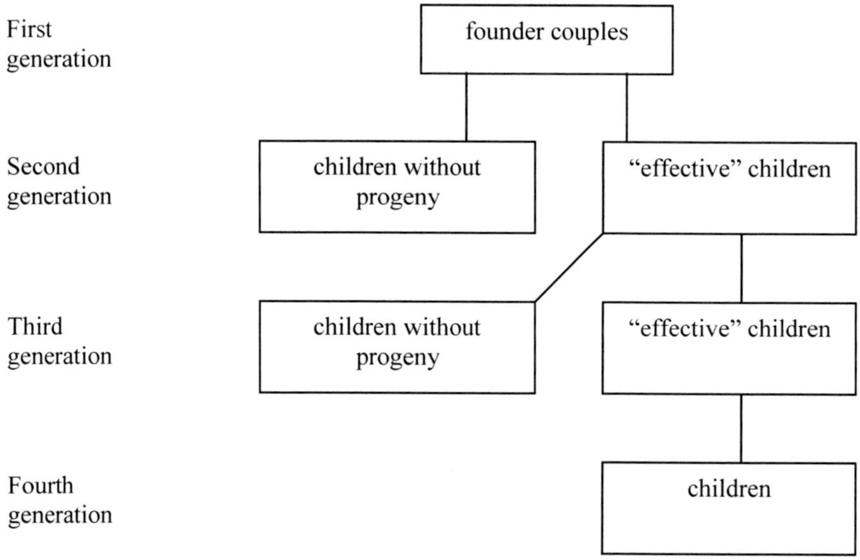

Source: Bideau and Brunet, "Stay or Leave," 140.

[2] For a history of the privileges of the communities, see Gusztáv Mihály Hermann, "Az Udvarhelyszéki Havasalja kiváltságos települései: a két Oláhfalu és Zetelaka" [The Privilegious Settlements in Havasalja, Udvarhelyszék District], in *Emlékkönyv Imreh István nyolcvanadik születésnapjára* [István Imreh Memorial Volume in Honour of His 80th Birthday], ed. András Kiss, Gyöngy Kovács Kiss, and Ferenc Pozsony (Kolozsvár: Erdélyi Múzeum Egyesület, 1999), 138-198. For a detailed account of public administration changes and the process of losing the privileges in the 1870s, see Judit Pál, *Városfejlődés a Székelyföldön 1750-1914* [Urbanization in Szeklerland 1750-1914] (Csíkszereda: Pro-Print, 2003).

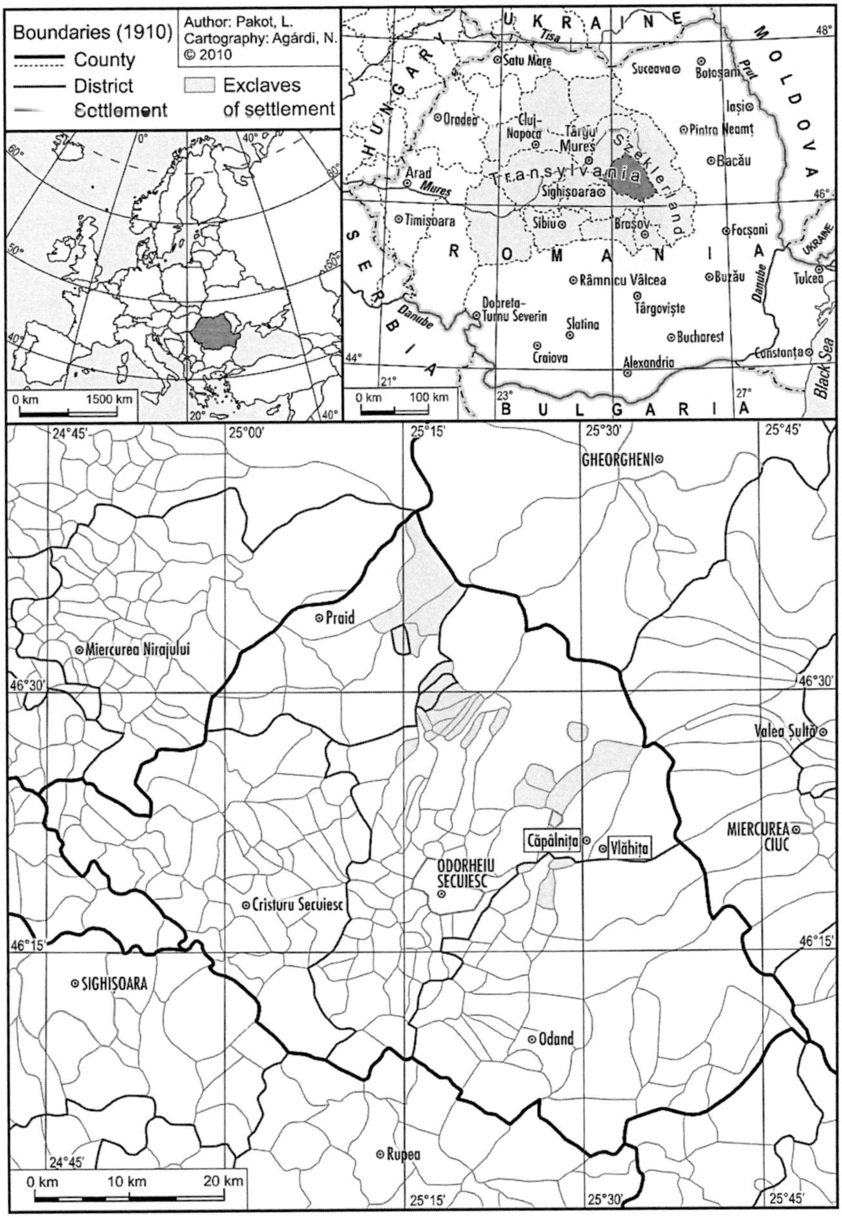

Fig. 2: The area under study

The discovery of iron ore sites close to the villages and the opening of mines were important events in the 19th century history of the two settlements. An industrial plant, Szentkeresztbánya was founded a few kilometres away from the villages in the 1850s, which provided the opportunity for the locals to secure some extra income. Due to contemporary financial and infrastructural conditions, mining remained a small-scale enterprise.

The majority of villagers were smallholders, and their living was provided by lumbering and woodwork in the communally owned woods and extensive animal husbandry (Table 1). Timbering and woodwork was carried out within a cottage industrial framework that required the close cooperation of related families. The number of water-driven sawmills operated by siblings or close relatives reached 100 according to the cadastre of 1909.[3] The economic development of Inner Transylvania raised the demand for woodenware. Timber used in construction and agriculture was transported in carriages by male family members towards the agriculturally more developed and more urbanised Southern Transylvanian regions.

A process of impoverishment due to growing population and fragmentation of landholdings started already at the end of the 19th century and covered the interwar period. According to Table 2 the proportion of smallholders – day-labourers with landholding below 5 cads. acres had become three times higher in 1941 than in 1910, while the landholding "middle class" almost disappeared.

An increase of population size and young age structure characterized these populations (Table 3). According to decennial census data population increase reached 55 percent between 1850 and 1941. Census data and the parish registers data on population movement shows that the main source of the population growth laid in the natural increase. Mortality reduced the value of natural growth, but migration has proven to be an affective brake of population growth also.

Data and methods

We reconstructed the demographic behaviour of the examined settlements from parish register data. An electronic database was compiled from 19th and 20th century parish registers. Based on the principles of the family reconstitution method set by Louis Henry and Michel Fleury,[4] and making use of available computerised database management facilities, we were able to reconstitute the most important demographic events of families and individuals. We divided the family sheets in our study into different categories as defined by Fleury and Henry.[5] But we used only the family sheets where the exact date of a couple's marriage was available.

We distinguish between generations. The first generation of the study is the couples

---

[3] Lajos Sándor, "Fűrészek, malmok, ványolók jegyzéke az 1909-es kataszteri telekkönyv és telekkönyvi rajzok alapján" [Saws, Mills and Fullers According to the Cadastre of 1909], in *Népélet a Kis-Homoród mentén* [Village Life in Kis-Homoród Region], ed. József Kardalus (Szentegyháza, 1998), 112-116; István Molnár, "Adatok a Hargita népi erdőgazdálkodásához" [Data on Sylviculture in Harghita County], in *A Székelykeresztúri Múzeum Emlékkönyve* [Memorial Volume of the Cristuru-Secuiesc Museum], ed. István Molnár and Nicolae Bucur (Csíkszereda, 1974), 307-325.

[4] Louis Henry and Alain Blum, *Techniques d'analyse en démographie historique*, 3rd ed. (Paris: INED, 1988).

[5] Michel Fleury and Louis Henry, *Nouveau Manuel de Dépouillement et d'exploitation de l'état civil ancien* (Paris: INED, 1965).

marrying between 1838 and 1855. The second generation and third is the children and grandchildren of the founding generation. We attempt to trace the life course outcomes of the second and third generations in order to know to what extent the descendants of particular families contributed – by marriage and child bearing in the local community – to the birth of the subsequent generation. Moreover, by focusing on the parents of those realizing reproduction, we investigate that what ratio this latter group represents among couples belonging to parental generation.

Following the method presented by Alain Bideau and Guy Brunet[6] we identified five different groups of children: 1) Type A: Children known to have died before their fifteenth birthday; 2) Type B: Children known to have died after their fifteenth birthday, but for whom it is not known whether they were married; 3) Type C: Children who left the parishes, and whose age at the date of departure is not known, and neither is their destination; 4) Type D: Children who married in the parishes, but who did not produce any children of their own who stayed in the parishes; and 5) Type E: Children who married and produced at least one child of their own who stayed in the parishes ("effective" children).

The second generation

The first generation of the study is the couples marrying between January 1, 1838 and December 31, 1854. A total of 383 first marriages were concluded in this period. Date of the end of the marriage (generally the date of death of the first spouse to die) was available in 91% of marriages, which shows that the majority of couples lived in the studied settlements after their marriages.

1,797 children were born within the marriage of the founding generation. The descendants can be related to 310 couples, which is 81% of the reconstructed marriages. In 13% of marriages no child was born and the remaining 6% left the settlements. The latter supposedly continued their lives elsewhere upon getting married. Considering fertile couples, the average is 5,8 children for one couple.

Table 4 presents the life course outcomes of children of founding couples. According to data, 40% of the children born in the second half of the 19th century contributed to the next generation. Statistical distribution of children belonging to groups A, B, C and D highlights an important issue. The high ratio of type A refers to severe infant and child mortality. 42% of the children died before reaching 15 years of age. Further characteristic feature of the second generation is outmigration. 8-9% of the children born here left the settlement before the date of their marriage. This value is considered as low in international comparison.[7] It seems that the second generation in the second half of the

[6] Bideau and Brunet, "Stay or Leave," 162.

[7] In the Valserine Valley in France, 36% of the descendants of the married cohort of 1760-1774 left the settlement (Ibid., 163). This ratio was one third in Jussy in Switzerland (Alfred Perrenoud, "Mobilité et reproduction à l'échelle d'une communauté rurale," in *Mesurer et Comprendre. Mélanges Offerts à Jacques Dupâquier* (Paris: P.U.F., 1993), 449-461).

19th century had a possibility to establish a family in a village. We may suppose this may be due to the relative abundance of the land, the high mortality in adulthood (ex. cholera epidemic in 1873) which created the opportunity for children in marriageable ages to establish locally etc.

Table 4 demonstrates population reproduction from children aspect. However, the average values of children by family may hide the differences deriving from the different situation of families. Henceforward our question is, what was the ratio of parents of children realizing demographic reproduction among the founding couples.

Table 5 demonstrates the distribution of founding families by number of all births and number of "effective" children. This distribution is rather uneven. 310 (81%) out of 383 couples had children in the parishes. However, due to the high infant and child mortality and the migration of survived children, ratio of couples with "effective" children has been decreased. According to our results, 71 couples managed to raise 1, 50 couples 2, 60 couples 3 and 74 couples 4 or more "effective" children. The 74 couples of the two parishes producing at least 4 effective children gave birth to 375 children, that is, 52% of descendants can be related to them. 19% couples provided the 52% of "effective" children.

The third generation

Family reconstruction data made the experience of the third generation available. Members of the second generation concluded 667 marriages. 13% of them were childless marriages. A total of 3,679 children were born, therefore there was an average 6.3 children to a fertile couple.

Life course outcome of children born in the fertile marriages of the second generation is included in Table 6. The most important tendency here is the decrease in numbers of effective children. While 40% of parental generation concluded marriage and had children in any of the two settlements, only 25% of the second generation did the same. Decrease in number of effective children can be related with two factors. One the one hand, infant and child mortality increased among the members of the third generation: 10% increase of mortality among children between age 0-15. On the other hand, migration increased by 7% among children compared to their parents.

The results of the distribution of couples by number of births and number of "effective" children are very similar to that of the first generation (Table 7). Again, the role in the production of the next generation is unevenly distributed. There was a small group of couples in this generation that contributed to the birth of the next generation in a great extent. However, an alignment process may be observed. Number of families with 4 or more effective children dropped from 19% to 8% compared to the first generation. Furthermore, "successful" descendants of this latter group provided 28% of the total effective children, whereas this figure is 52% regarding the older generation.

The study of sibships

Raising higher number of effective children is obviously in correlation with the stability and fertility of the marriage. Moreover, it is worth raising the question whether the differentiated infant and child mortality or the migration is the core reason for the differences in effective children in stable marriages with many children.

To answer the above question, we have examined the sibling groups of 4 and 7 among the second and third generation. Table 8 and Table 9 include their life course outcome. Based on the results, differences among sibling groups are mostly due to infant and child mortality. Here, outmigration plays less significant role than infant and child mortality. In general, the more children survived until adulthood, the more chance they had for successful reproduction. This correlation chiefly characterizes the descendants of the first generation. As for the members of the second generation, migration played a significant role in families without "effective" children or in families with only 1 or 2 "effective" children. However, its impact was less plausible than the effect of infant and child mortality. In families where at least three children realized reproduction, migration was of no importance.

Conclusion

In this paper we analyzed the process of demographic reproduction of two parishes in Transylvania in the period from the second part of the 19th century to the first part of the 20th century. By introducing the term of "effective" children – children contributing to the next generation within the framework of the local community –, population reproduction was highlighted from a specific aspect. Using the method applied by French and Canadian historical demographers and geneticist we studied to what extent the descendants of particular families contributed – by marriage and child bearing in the local community – to the birth of the subsequent generation. Moreover, by focusing on the parents of those realizing reproduction, we investigated that what ratio this latter group represented among couples belonging to parent generation.

Our results emphasize the demographic continuity and stability of the two settlements. Majority of those surviving infant and child mortality managed to establish family and bear children in the local community. Descendants of the generation establishing family in the 1840's and 1850's were less impacted by epidemics causing infant mortality. Descendants of the second generation were, however, influenced by increased infant and child mortality and increased outmigration. Nevertheless, majority of descendants of this generation remained in the settlement where they had been born. It seems that business opportunities of families did not impede their children to establish family in the two villages. Phenomenon observed in Western Europe – local marriage and reproduction on the one hand and permanent celibacy and migration on the other hand – at this time we did not observe here. However, from another aspect, it can be stated that the high infant mortality rate helped "solving" the competition between siblings.

Our focus on parental generation modified the above result chiefly by highlighting the inequalities of family reproduction. The main characteristic feature of population reproduction from one generation to the next is that the majority of subsequent generations establishing family and bearing children was brought up by a relatively small portion of the parental generation. Moreover, the analysis reflected on the fact that the most differentiating factor of reproduction was the infant and child mortality. Therefore, reproduction success of parent generations was due to different impact of the infant and child mortality. The results also showed that the role of out-migration was minor in contrast with the findings of French and Canadian studies, but the role played by out-migration became more and more important over time.

Our analysis is still a preliminary analysis. There is a need for more comparative micro analysis in order to understand the population processes in nineteenth and twentieth century Transylvania.

LIST OF ABBREVIATIONS

Census 1857: *Erdély 1857. évi népszámlálása* [The Census 1857 in Transylvania] (Budapest: KSH, 1992).

Census 1881: *A Magyar Korona Országaiban az 1881. év elején végrehajtott népszámlálás eredményei némely hasznos házi állatok kimutatásával együtt* [The Results of the Census 1881 in Hungarian Kingdom] (Budapest, 1882).

Census 1900: *A Magyar Korona Országainak 1900. évi népszámlálása.* II. *A népesség foglalkozása községenkint* [The Results of the Census 1900 in Hungarian Kingdom. II. Occupational Distribution of the Population by Settlements] (Budapest, 1904).

Census 1910 – Manuscript tables: *Népszámlálási feldolgozási táblák. 1910. évi népszámlálás. Foglalkozási adatok községenként* [Manuscript Tables of Census 1910. Occupational Distribution of the Population by Settlements], National Archives of Hungary, Budapest, XXXII-23-h, 883.

Census 1910 – The results: *A Magyar Szent Korona Országainak 1910. évi népszámlálása.* II. *A népesség foglalkozása és a nagyipari vállalatok községenkint* [The Results of the Census 1910. II. Occupational Distribution of the Population and Industrial Firms by Settlements] (Budapest, 1913).

Census 1941: *Népszámlálási feldolgozási táblák. 1941. évi népszámlálás. Foglalkozási adatok községenként* [Manuscript Tables of Census 1941. Occupational Distribution of the Population by Settlements], National Archives of Hungary, Budapest, XXXII-23-h, 486.

National Archives of Romania, branch Harghita, F 47: Arhivele Naţionale ale României. Direcţia Judeţeană Harghita, Miercurea Ciuc, Fund 47: *Colecţia registrelor de stare civilă*, 81, 82, 83, 84, 85, 728, 729, 730, 731.

Roman Catholic Parish Archive, Căpâlniţa: Kápolnásfalva Római Katolikus Egyházközség Levéltára, Fund *Roman Catholic parish registers 1776-1941*, vol. I-V.

Roman Catholic Parish Archive, Vlăhiţa: Szentegyházasfalvi Római Katolikus Plébánia Levéltára, Fund *Roman Catholic parish registers 1776-1941*, vol. II-X.

Varga, *Erdély statisztikája*: Varga, Árpád E., *Erdély etnikai és felekezeti statisztikája.* I. *Kovászna, Hargita és Maros megye. Népszámlálási adatok 1850-1992 között* [Ethnic and Denominational Statistics of Transylvania: Covasna, Harghita and Mureş Counties. Data of Censuses 1850-1992] (Csíkszereda: Pro-Print, 1998).

Table 1: Distribution of bread-winners by broad occupational groups in the two parishes, 1857-1941.

	Vlăhiţa					Căpâlniţa				
	1857	1880	1900	1910	1941	1857	1880	1900	1910	1941
Agriculture	75.7	86.1	78.1	82.7	76.0	91.1	93.6	93.6	88.0	93.8
Mining	0.0	0.1	0.0	0.0	14.6	0.0	0.0	0.0	0.1	0.0
Industry	5.7	2.4	5.7	5.5	3.5	0.7	1.6	3.6	5.7	2.8
Commerce	0.0	0.4	1.3	1.8	0.8	0.0	0.2	0.1	0.8	1.0
Trafic	0.0	0.0	0.6	0.2	0.1	0.0	0.0	0.4	0.3	0.1
Civil service, lib. prof.	1.5	0.4	1.6	1.2	2.0	1.0	0.3	0.1	1.2	1.1
Soldiers	0.0	0.0	0.0	0.4	0.6	0.0	0.0	0.0	0.1	0.0
Day-labourers	17.1	6.9	10.7	4.8	0.0	7.2	4.0	1.1	2.0	0.0
Domestics	0.0	3.8	1.6	1.4	1.6	0.0	0.3	1.0	0.4	1.0
Others	0.0	0.0	0.6	2.1	0.9	0.0	0.0	0.1	1.3	0.2
N	263	1320	1032	1038	1417	304	985	732	719	922

Sources: Censuses 1857, 1881, 1900, 1910 – The Results, 1941.

Table 2: Distribution of bread winners in agriculture in 1910 and 1941.

	Vlăhiţa		Căpâlniţa	
	1910	1941	1910	1941
Landowners, 100–200 cad. acres	0.0	0.0	0.3	0.0
Landowners, 50–100 cad. acres	0.0	0.0	0.3	0.0
Smallholders, 20–50 cad. acres	17.3	0.9	14.2	0.7
Smallholders, 10–20 cad. acres	35.9	8.7	31.3	12.7
Smallholders – day-labourers, 5–10 cad. acres	22.1	20.5	26.3	32.4
Smallholders – day-labourers 1–5 cad. acres	13.2	45.9	12.2	40.7
Smallholders – day-labourers <1 cad. acres	0.0	4.8	0.2	6.9
Office holders, farm hands	5.4	1.5	1.9	1.3
Labourers	6.0	17.8	13.3	5.5
N	846	1071	632	861

Sources: Censuses 1910 – Manuscript tables, 1941.

Table 3: Natural movement and estimated balance of migration by decade, 1850-1941.

Period	Births	Deaths	Natural increase		Intercensal increase		Migration	
			number	yearly average	number	yearly average	number	yearly average
1850-1856	978	870	108	15	51	7	-57	-8
1857-1869	2119	1266	853	66	462	36	-391	-30
1870-1879	2092	1663	429	43	111	11	-318	-32
1880-1889	2145	1899	246	25	121	12	-125	-13
1890-1899	2014	1343	671	67	249	25	-422	-42
1900-1909	1980	1340	640	64	168	17	-472	-47
1910-1919	1708	1296	412	41	114	11	-298	-30
1920-1929	2064	1296	768	77	377	38	-391	-39
1930-1941	2271	1363	908	76	994	90	86	8
1850-1941	17371	12336	5035	55	2647	29	-2388	26

Sources: Varga, *Erdély statisztikája*; National Archives of Romania, branch Harghita, F 47: 81-85, 728-731; Roman Catholic Parish registers of Căpâlniţa, vol. I-V; Roman Catholic Parish registers of Vlăhiţa, vol. II-X.

Table 4: Life-course characteristics of the second generation.

Life-course characteristics	Boys		Girls		Children	
	N	%	N	%	N	%
A: Died <15 years	389	42.5	357	40.5	746	41.5
B: Died >15 years	45	4.9	35	4.0	80	4.5
C: Outmigrated	80	8.7	75	8.5	155	8.6
D: Married, without progeny	47	5.1	43	4.9	90	5.0
E: "Effective" children	355	38.8	371	42.1	726	40.4
A+B+C+D+E	916	100.0	881	100.0	1797	100.0

Sources: Roman Catholic Parish registers of Căpâlniţa, vol. I-V; Roman Catholic Parish registers of Vlăhiţa, vol. II-X.

Table 5: Distribution of couples in the first generation by number of children and number of "effective" children.

Number of births	Number of „effective" children										Total
	0	1	2	3	4	5	6	7	8	9	
0	73										73
1	18	12									30
2	12	4	5								21
3	8	10	7	2							27
4	8	14	8	9	1						40
5	2	4	8	10	3						27
6	2	6	6	9	2	5					30
7	1	10	9	13	6	7	1				47
8	2	7	4	5	2		4		1		25
9	2	2		6	4	6	4				24
10		2		3	4	4	1	4			18
11			2	1	2	3	5				13
12			1	2	1						4
13						1	1	1			3
14							1				1
Total	128	71	50	60	25	26	17	5	1	0	383

Sources: Roman Catholic Parish registers of Căpâlniţa, vol. I-V; Roman Catholic Parish registers of Vlăhiţa, vol. II-X.

Table 6: Life-course characteristics of the third generation.

Life-course characteristics	Boys		Girls		Children	
	N	%	N	%	N	%
A: Died <15 years	1013	52.9	884	50.1	1897	51.6
B: Died >15 years	113	5.9	54	3.1	167	4.5
C: Outmigrated	229	12.0	250	14.2	479	13.0
D: Married, without progeny	124	6.5	96	5.4	220	6.0
E: "Effective" children	437	22.8	479	27.2	916	24.9
A+B+C+D+E	1916	100.0	1763	100.0	3679	100.0

Sources: Roman Catholic Parish registers of Căpâlniţa, vol. I-V; Roman Catholic Parish registers of Vlăhiţa, vol. II-X.

Table 7: Distribution of couples in the second generation by number of children and number of "effective" children

Number of births	Number of "effective" children 0	1	2	3	4	5	6	7	8	9	Total
0	87										87
1	42	7									49
2	22	9	5								36
3	30	15	10	3							58
4	10	22	3	5	1						41
5	11	17	15	6							49
6	17	12	15	8	1	2					55
7	16	15	20	17	4	2					74
8	7	13	15	3	7	2	1				48
9	4	15	22	12	8	3					64
10	3	7	10	15	6	1		1			43
11	2	7	6	11	4	5	1				36
12	1	4	5	3	2	1	1		1		18
13		1	2	1		2					6
14				1							1
15											0
16				1							1
17				1							1
Total	252	144	128	87	33	18	3	1	1	0	667

Sources: Roman Catholic Parish registers of Căpâlnița, vol. I-V; Roman Catholic Parish registers of Vlăhița, vol. II-X.

Table 8: Destination of children in sibship of four and seven children by number of "effective" children. First generation.

Life-course characteristics	Number of "effective" children 0	1	2	3	4	Total	Number of "effective" children 0	1	2	3	4	5	6	7	Total
Died <15 years	19	25	11	8	0	63	5	51	29	33	15	8	0	0	141
Died >15 years	1	5	2	0	0	8	0	3	5	6	1	1	0	0	16
Celibate	9	6	2	0	0	17	1	3	9	6	1	4	1	0	25
Emigrated	3	6	1	1	0	11	1	3	2	7	1	1	0	0	15
„Effective"	0	14	16	27	1	58	0	10	18	39	24	35	6	0	132
Total children	32	56	32	36	1	157	7	70	63	91	42	49	7	0	329
Total sibships	8	14	8	9	1	40	1	10	9	13	6	7	1	0	47

Sources: Roman Catholic Parish registers of Căpâlnița, vol. I-V; Roman Catholic Parish registers of Vlăhița, vol. II-X.

Table 9: Destination of children in sibship of four and seven children by number of "effective" children. Second generation.

Life-course characteristics	Number of "effective" children						Number of "effective" children								
	0	1	2	3	4	Total	0	1	2	3	4	5	6	7	Total
Died <15 y.	28	41	5	4	0	78	69	50	79	43	11	2	0	0	254
Died >15 y.	0	5	0	0	0	5	10	8	5	5	0	1	0	0	29
Celibate	7	12	1	1	0	21	27	26	14	12	1	1	0	0	81
Emigrated	5	8	0	0	0	13	6	6	2	8	0	0	0	0	22
"Effective"	0	22	6	15	1	44	0	15	40	51	16	10	0	0	132
Total children	40	88	12	20	1	161	112	105	140	119	28	14	0	0	518
Total sibships	10	22	3	5	1	41	16	15	20	17	4	2	0	0	74

Sources: Roman Catholic Parish registers of Căpâlnița, vol. I-V;
Roman Catholic Parish registers of Vlăhița, vol. II-X.

Expressions of Ethnic Identity and Affiliation in the Donation Practices of Macedo-Vlachs Living in the Hungarian Kingdom

Márta Nagy

Macedo-Vlachs first appeared in Hungary following the Turkish invasion of the country in the 16th century and they kept arriving there in the centuries to come. They appeared in Transylvania as early as around 1500,[1] while in Debrecen[2] and Jászság[3] in the course of the 17th century. According to contemporary censuses,[4] which also include the merchants' place of origin, they would arrive from Thessaly, Northern Epirus, predominantly from the towns of Siatista, Kozani, Kastoria and Moschopolis.

Macedo-Vlachs started to settle in Hungary *en masse* in the 18th century. It was at that time that the centre of the "Greek" Diaspora, formerly in Venice and then in Vienna, was transposed to Pest.[5] Contemporary colloquial language and a large portion of official documents (censuses) call Macedo-Vlachs "Greeks" because that was the *lingua franca* of Balkan trade.

Macedo-Vlach-Greek ethnic groups consisted of merchants engaged in re-export trade:[6] they transported their Eastern goods (spices, leather, expensive drapery, dried fruits, etc.)[7] across the country. They did not settle permanently in the Hungarian Kingdom, but in several locations – mostly in places important from a commercial perspective, such as Tokaj, Miskolc, Gyöngyös and Kecskemét – they established business-premises. Neither their economic activity, nor their numbers could be insignificant or negligible in the country, judging by the fact that a National Inspectorate headed by the palatine was established specifically for the inspection of "Greek merchants who took up their abode on this and the other side of the River Tisza" in 1665.[8]

Within a short time, "Greek" merchants in Hungary made great profit because they were entitled to an almost 100% duty concession. Following the Treaty of Požare-

---

[1] Füves Ödön, "A magyarországi görög telepesek a legújabbkori görög történelmi irodalomban" [Greek Settlers in Hungary in the Greek Historiography of the Contemporary Era], *Antik tanulmányok* 10 (1963): 66.

[2] Zoltai Lajos, *Debrecen százados küzdelme a görög kereskedőkkel* [Age-Long Struggle: The City of Debrecen contra Greek Merchants] (Debrecen: A Debreceni Tisza István Tudományos Társaság I. Osztálya, 1935), 3.

[3] Nagy Márta, *Görögök a Jászkunságban* [Greeks in Jászkunság] (Karcag: Győrffy István Nagykun Múzeum, 1988), 4.

[4] There were three nationwide censuses of "Greek" merchants, in 1754, 1769 and 1779 (Hungarian National Archives, Archives of the Royal Council of Governor C 42, fasc. Misc. 8, N° 2).

[5] Füves Ödön, "A görög kereskedők bevándorlása Pestre" [The Immigration of Greek Merchants to Pest], *Antik Tanulmányok* 22 (1975): 118-119.

[6] Füves, "A magyarországi görög telepesek," 67.

[7] Eckhart Ferenc, "Kereskedelmünk közvetítői a XVIII. században" [Mediators of Our Commerce in the 18th Century], *Századok* 52 (1918): 369.

[8] Tagányi Károly, *Országos felügyelőség a görög kereskedők fölött* [Hungarian National Inspectorate over Greek Merchants], *Magyar Gazdaságtörténeti Szemle* (1895): 79.

vac, signed by the Hapsburg and Ottoman Empires in 1718, the merchants of one had to pay only a duty of 3% on goods imported into the other, whether shipped by land or water, and vice versa.[9] This customs tariff provided significant advantages for the Macedo-Vlachs, who were Turkish subjects, in comparison with domestic merchants, who were obliged to pay a duty of 33%. Macedo-Vlach-Greek communities formed trading companies to facilitate their commerce. The companies gave loans to their members in temporary financial difficulties and also operated as quasi lower courts.[10]

The merchants took their profits home to their families on the Balkans. Their connections with the old mother country were still stable and undisturbed at that time. Many of them operated a joint venture, which means that one partner sold goods in a shop in Hungary, while the other took care of procuring them in the old motherland.

At that time Macedo-Vlachs could only rent shops, slaughterhouses, inns or pubs,[11] or the lands necessary for stock-farming, since the purchase of real estates legally became possible for them only following a decree Leopold II issued in 1790. By that time they had broadened their activities to involve money-lending. Thus, for example, they introduced the bill of exchange into contemporary Hungarian commerce and played a significant role in starting early capitalism in the country.

Macedo-Vlach-Greeks took up permanent settlement in the Hungarian Kingdom after the Oath of Allegiance in 1774.[12] The Empress Maria Theresia ordered them to take it so as to prevent any further outflow of "Greek" capital. The Oath of Allegiance obliged Macedo-Vlachs to resign from their status as Turkish subjects. That equalled losing their earlier duty concession and their chances of accumulating more wealth of any significance. Therefore, many of them chose to resettle in their native lands in the Balkans, while those bound to Hungary either by business or family ties decided to take the Oath of Allegiance and become subjects of the Hapsburg Empire.

The progressive assimilation of Macedo-Vlachs and Greeks started here, since their previously strong ties with the mother country were severed and those who had a Hungarian spouse were encouraged to melt entirely into their Hungarian environment. The Imperial Court of Vienna strove to accelerate this process by conferring titles of nobility upon them.[13]

---

[9] As opposed to this, domestic merchants had to pay a duty of 30%. Eckhart, "Kereskedelmünk közvetítői," 357.

[10] Nagy Márta, *Görög egyházművészeti emlékek Magyarországon / Μνημεία της εκκλησιαστικής τέχνης των Ελλήνων στην Ουγγαρία* [Relics of Greek Religious Art in Hungary] (Budapest: Görög Országos Önkormányzat, 1996), 12.

[11] Nagy, *Görögök a Jászkunságban*, 8.

[12] Nagy Márta, "Căi de asimilare în arta bisericească a diasporei greceşti din Ungaria" [Ways of Assimilation in the Religious Art of the Greek Diaspora in Hungary], in *Dilema Europei Centrale: convieţuire sau coexistenţă* [Central European Dilemma: living together or coexistence], ed. Elena Rodica Colta (Arad: Complexul Muzeal Arad, 2004) [Colecţia Minorităţi 6], 319.

[13] For instance, the titles of baron and count were conferred on the Sina and Nákosz families, respectively, while the Derras, Grabovszkys, Vrányis, etc., were ennobled. Papp Izabella, "Görög nemes családok Magyarországon a XVIII-XIX. században" [Greek Noble Families in Hungary in the 18th and 19th Centuries], *Posztbizánci Közlemények* 5 (2002): 20-36.

From the beginning of the 19th century Macedo-Vlach families with significant fortunes and titles of nobility (for example the families Sina and Nákosz) gave up commerce and chose more convenient walks of life: they invested money into real estate and land – they bought and leased them – or engaged in banking transactions.[14] Consequently, the earlier role of Macedo-Vlach-Greek merchants in Hungarian commerce was gradually taken up by the Jewry.[15]

After this overview of the appearance and economic activities of the Macedo-Vlachs in Hungary, just like their relations with government institutions, it is time to scrutinise the ethnic, religious and cultural environment they had to face in their self-chosen new mother country.

The Orthodox Macedo-Vlachs[16] from the Balkans found themselves in a majority Hungarian and Western Christian environment in their new homeland. It significantly differed from their own culture not only in its religion and language, but also in its customs – for instance, funeral ceremonies[17] – it's dressing and eating habits.

However, Macedo-Vlachs did not meet only Hungarians within the bounds of the Hungarian Kingdom. They also encountered other Orthodox ethnic groups from the Balkans, which had been living in the country for quite a while: Ruthenians, Vlahs, Serbs and even Orthodox Bulgarians, who started to immigrate into Hungary at the end of the 19th century.[18] Together with the Macedo-Vlachs a few Greeks also arrived in the country, for instance from the vicinity of Adrianople. These were the ethnic components of the Orthodox minority or Diaspora in the Hungarian Kingdom. Due to their common Balkan origins and their shared Orthodox faith Macedo-Vlachs mostly affiliated with these ethnic groups in their new homeland.

Macedo-Vlachs – those with large fortunes and moderate wealth equally – made large donations readily; they primarily supported community culture, sciences and education. Who exactly profited from their charity?

---

[14] For example, György Sina was the trustee of István Széchenyi's private means and a financial supporter of his economic projects, including the construction of the Chain Bridge. Kerényi Eszter, *Az arany ember, A gödöllői kastély görög ura: Sina György és fia, Sina Simon* [The Man with the Golden Touch, The Greek Master of the Gödöllő Castle: György Sina and his Son, Simon Sina] (Gödöllő: Gödöllői Városi Múzeum, 2003), 17-21.

[15] Papp Izabella, *Görög kereskedők a Jászkunságban: Kétszáz év dokumentumaiból* [Greek Merchants in Jászkunság: From the Documents of Two Hundred Years] (Szolnok: Jász-Nagykun-Szolnok Megyei Levéltár, 2004), 21.

[16] Macedo-Vlachs are the descendants of a mixed ethnic group involving the indigenous people of the Balkans (Thracians, Illyrians) and their ancient Roman conquerors. In the Hungarian Kingdom in contemporary documents they call themselves Macedo-Vlachs, thus indicating both their ethnic identity and their motherland. Nagy Márta, *Ohridi Szent Naum magyarországi kultusza* [The Cult of Saint Nahum of Ohrid in Hungary] (Budapest: Balassi Kiadó, Debrecen: Debreceni Egyetemi Kiadó, 2012), 28.

[17] Orthodox ethnic groups carried their dead to the church and then the grave in an open coffin. This custom, which was alien from the majority Catholic environment, was banned by the Royal Council of Governor in 1811. Füves Ödön, "A nyitott koporsóval való temetés megtiltása 1811-ben" [The 1811 Ban on Funeral Ceremonies with Open Coffins], *Orvostörténeti Közlemények* 42 (1967): 246.

[18] Ács Zoltán, *Nemzetiségek a történelmi Magyarországon* [Ethnic Minorities in Pre-Trianon Hungary] (Budapest: Kossuth Kiadó, 1996), 54-62.

A member of the immeasurably wealthy Sina Dynasty,[19] Baron Simon Sina, contributed to the building of the Hungarian Academy of Sciences. Not only so, but with the largest donation of all. In appreciation of this he was elected to sit on the Governing Board of the Academy. He also supported the Hungarian National Theatre – he even donated money to its pension fund – just like the equipment of the Hungarian National Museum's numismatic collection. He also financed some Hungarian painters (Miklós Izsó, Miklós Barabás) so that their devotion to creative work should be undisturbed.[20]

Apart from Baron Sina, other members of the Macedo-Vlach community also supported the building of the Hungarian Academy of Sciences – among them the Macedo-Vlach-Greek Parish of Pest, as it reads in contemporary literary magazine *Hölgyfutár*: "The Greek Parish of Pest donated two thousand Forints for the Academy."[21]

In 1809 a member of the extremely wealthy Nákosz family,[22] Sándor, contributed to the establishment of the Royal Hungarian Ludovica Military Academy a significant donation of ten thousand Forints.

János Szappanos, a citizen of Karcag, was one of the less wealthy members of the Macedo-Vlach-Greek community. Notwithstanding this, according to the testimony of his will of 12 April, 1816, his native town and the Hungarian King were the first in line for him when it came to donating money: "I hereby leave 100 id est a hundred to the local Noble Town, bequeath 50 id est fifty to His Majesty the King." It is equally clear from the will, however, that the testator left the largest sum, "2,000 id est two thousand" to "the non-united Greek Church of Karcag."[23]

Macedo-Vlachs were emotionally bound to their new, Hungarian homeland. It is clearly shown by the educational aims declared as of 1 January, 1809, in a document of the school maintained by the Macedo-Vlach-Greek community of Pest: "The task of Greek schools is to educate useful citizens for the good of His Majesty and the Kingdom." In addition, "to teach them subjects in the Old and New Greek languages the knowledge of which is indispensable both in issues of faith and morality and in matters of commerce and civil life."[24]

The donations given to the new mother country testify to the donators' intention to become its citizens and to melt into the majority environment, which – despite the ethnic and religious differences – might not have been so very alien for them. At the same time, they strove to preserve their ethnic identity along with their loyalty to their new homeland, which surfaced in the cultivation of their faith of old and of the Greek lan-

[19] The Sina family originally came from Moschopolis. Kerényi, *Az arany ember*, 8.
[20] Ibid., 30-31.
[21] *Hölgyfutár* [Ladie's Courier], July 31, 1960, 726.
[22] Szabó Krisztina, *A Nákosz család története* [The History of the Nákosz Family] (Budapest: Szépművészeti Múzeum Alapítvány az emberi értékekért, 2005), 19.
[23] Papp, *Görög kereskedők*, 296.
[24] Füves Ödön, "A pesti görög-román iskolák" [The Greco-Roman Schools of Pest], *Magyar pedagógia* (1971): 138.

guage. This endeavour is clearly illustrated by the above examples of the merchant, who gives in charity both to the King of Hungary and the Greek Orthodox Church of Karcag, and of the Macedo-Vlach-Greek community of Pest, which, in maintaining a school, aims both to educate useful citizens for Hungary and to teach Greek.

How is it possible that the Macedo-Vlachs of Pest, in their endeavour to preserve their ethnic identity, devoted money to the teaching of Old and New Greek and not of Vlach? The most perplexing aspect of this question resides in the fact that while New Greek was indispensable in making a livelihood, in commerce, Old Greek was a dead language even at the time.

Vlachs were an ethnic group of a "duplex consciousness and language" since in the course of the preceding centuries they had been thoroughly Hellenised culturally in their Macedonian old mother country. Thus, for example, their university, opened in 1774, bore the name of Greek Academy (Hellenikon Frôntisterion). Similarly, their books were published either in Greek or in Aromanian, which also uses the Greek alphabet, and they regarded Greek as their second mother tongue.[25] Therefore, paradoxically, their use of Greek is an expression of their affiliation to their own Vlach old mother country.

The above-mentioned Simon Sina contributed significantly to the financing of not only the Hungarian, but also the Greek Academy of Sciences.[26] His father, György Sina, supported the establishment of the National Observatory of Athens. Simon Sina even served for years as the Greek King Otto's envoy to Austria, Bavaria and Prussia, which he took up as a charity job.[27] All this clearly suggests that Macedo-Vlachs regarded not only their old homeland in Macedonia but also Greece as their mother countries, which is expressed in their donations to the latter.

It follows from the Macedo-Vlachs' affiliation with Greek culture and language that in their new mother country they were most ready to cast in their lot with Greek immigrants. For instance, the community in Pest maintained a hospital for the poor[28] and two Greco-Roman schools together with the Greeks from 1794 and 1796, respectively.[29]

At the same time, Macedo-Vlach donation practices also reflect an endeavour to preserve a Vlach identity as separate from Greek. Thus, although the Greek-Macedo-Vlach Parish of Pest had been running educational institutions since 1796 which went under the name of "Greco-Roman Schools of Pest,"[30] Macedo-Vlachs still established a

---

[25] Max Demeter Peyfuss, *Die Druckerei von Moschopolis, 1731-1769: Buchdruck und Heiligenverehrung im Erzbistum Achrida* (Wien: Böhlau, 1996).

[26] Kerényi, *Az arany ember*, 34.

[27] Ibid., 6, 32.

[28] The hospital worked, by all probability, from 1794 until 1931. Füves Ödön, "A pesti görög-román szegényápolda" [The Greco-Roman Charity Hospital of Pest], *Orvostörténeti közlemények* 50 (1969): 133-135.

[29] Füves Ödön, "Görög tanítóképző pesten 1812-1820 között" [The Greek Teacher Training-School in Pest, 1812-1820], *Antik Tanulmányok* 16 (1969): 91.

[30] "Σχολεια των ελληνικων και άπλοελληνικων μαθηματων της εν Πεστα συνδραμουσης Κοινοτητος της ανατολικης εκκλησιας της Κοιμησεως της υπεραγιας Θεοθοκου των Γραικων και Βλαχων και Γραικων της Μακεδονιας" [The schools teaching in ancient and modern Greek, which belong to the Greeks and Vlachs

separate Vlach school on 25 July, 1808.[31]

The following case clearly shows that Macedo-Vlach merchants demonstrated their ethnic identity not only in the face of their Greek brethren. The Orthodox Parish of Ráckeve consisted of a mixed community of Serbs and Macedo-Vlachs. In 1771 the wall-paintings in one of the chapels of its church were commissioned by T. Gianotisz, the parish churchwarden of Vlach origins.[32] The inscriptions of the mural paintings are in Greek – as opposed to the other inscriptions in the church, which are all in Church Slavonic. The use of Greek is also the expression of the Macedo-Vlachs' affiliation with their old motherland here. This is reinforced by the dedication of the chapel to St. John the Baptist, which evokes the St. John the Baptist Monastery in Moschopolis, a significant religious and cultural centre of their old mother country in Macedonia. This donation expresses – beyond the affiliation with the old motherland – a striving to preserve a separate Vlach identity even in the face of the Serbs. Serbs represented the most populous ethnic group within the Orthodox Diaspora in the Hungarian Kingdom. Because of their shared faith and Balkan origins, the Serbs posed the greatest threat of assimilation for the Macedo-Vlachs in the country.

The example of Nahum Bodza (born in 1784, in Balassagyarmat) is rather different. As a well-to-do citizen, at the beginning of the 19th century he started a fund for the Serbs of Pest-Buda and Szentendre both to help traders and craftsmen in launching their business and to assist the education of medical students.[33] Nahum Bodza's donation allows for the conclusion that this merchant of Macedo-Vlach origins actually became a member of the Serbian community of Pest.

Between 1790 and 1828 the office of the Bishop of the Buda Diocese of the Sebian Orthodox Church was fulfilled by Dimitrios Papaiannousis (Δημήτριος Παπαγιαννούσης), a Macedo-Vlach born in Kozani. Previously a monk at the Vatopedi Monastery of Mount Athos, then tutor to the Wallachian Prince's children in Bucharest, then Bishop of Belgrade and Metropolitan to the whole of Serbia, he became the Bishop of the Buda Diocese under the name of Dionisziosz Popović. As such, he personally covered the costs of the translation of religious books from Greek into Serbian for his Serbian parishioners.[34] Meanwhile, he also supported his Macedo-Vlach brethren: most churches of the Macedo-Vlach-Greek communities in Hungary were built during his bishopric, at

coming from Macedonia, and to the Greek Christian parishes of the Vlachs and the Greeks in Pest, which are named after the Dormition of Our Lady and which have given in charity for this purpose]. Füves, "A pesti görög-román iskolák," 135.

[31] Ibid., 136.

[32] Nagy Márta, *Ortodox falképek Magyarországon* [Orthodox Mural Paintings in Hungary] (Budapest: Dunakönyv Kiadó, 1994), 38.

[33] *Матица Српска 1826-1926* [Matitsa Srpska 1826-1926] (Нови Сад: Матице Српске, 1927), 501-503, and Vujicsics Sztoján, *Szerbek Pest-Budán* [Serbs in Pest-Buda] (Budapest: Fővárosi Önkormányzat Főpolgármesteri Hivatala és a Szerb Önkormányzat, 1997), 47-48.

[34] Павел_Римскій, *Животописаніе Діонусіа отъ Поповића* [The Life of Dionisziosz Popović] (Pest: Летописъ Матице Српске, 1857), and Margalits Ede, *Szerb történelmi repetórium* [A Repertory of Serbian History] (Budapest: Magyar Tudományos Akadémia, 1918), 193-194.

the end of the 18th and beginning of the 19th centuries.[35] His career and activities clearly exemplify the survival, even in the Late Meta-Byzantine Period, of some aspects of the phenomenon so fittingly termed "Byzantine Commonwealth" by Dimitri Obolensky[36] with reference to the Byzantine Empire.

Donation practices in Hungary also offer examples for the integration of Macedo-Vlachs into the Romanian community living here. They were clearly drawn together by the similarity of their languages. Thus, for instance, Manó Gozsdu (1802-1870), a man of Macedo-Vlach origins living in Pest, started a fund for Romanians in Hungary.[37]

The Macedo-Vlachs of Hungary transferred donations to their old homeland form their new, self-chosen one. That is, they took care of the institutions of their Vlach mother country even from a distance, which is a major evidence for the preservation of their Vlach identity. Especially Kozani owes much to its citizens resettling in the Hungarian Kingdom. Vlachs in Hungary gave in charity to its churches,[38] and they even maintained a school there, which makes its appearance in the history of Kozani as the "school of the companies" in the middle of 18th century.[39] E. R. Popović – a teacher in the Greek schools of Timişoara, Pest, Vienna, Zemun, Bucharest and Jassy, editor and writer – bequeathed his library, a collection of several hundred volumes and valuable manuscripts, to his hometown, Kozani. On the legacy of Pál Haris an agricultural school under the name of "Hariseon" was established in the town.[40]

The donations of Macedo-Vlachs in Hungary also reflect their pride in their Vlach origins. In the inscriptions commemorating their patronage they regularly had their hometown, their place of origin mentioned.

For example, Naum Bikerasz of Miskolc had the place of his origin identified in the inscription of the engraving he had commissioned from the famous Macedo-Vlach etcher Hristofor Zefar in 1743:

> "This icon of our Holy Father Naum the Thaumaturge [...] was printed [...] at the costs of the most worthy and most beneficent Kyrios Nahum, son of Saul Bikeras from Moschopolis."[41]

On the altar of the Macedo-Vlachs' church in Gyöngyös, which is made of the

---

[35] Nagy, *Görögök a Jászkunságban*, 23-24.

[36] Dimitri Obolensky, *A bizánci nemzetközösség, Kelet-Európa, 500-1453* [The Byzantine Commonwealth, Eastern Europe, 500-1453] (Budapest: Bizantinológiai Intézeti Alapítvány, 1999).

[37] Sasvári László, "Görögajkú ortodoxia Magyarországon a XVI-XX. században" [Greek-Speaking Orthodox Religion in Hungary], *Magyar Egyháztörténeti Vázlatok* (1994): 146.

[38] Füves, "A magyarországi görög telepesek," 68.

[39] Horváth Endre, *Az újgörögök* [Modern Greeks] (Budapest: Magyar Szemle Társaság, 1943), 57.

[40] Ibid., 57-64.

[41] See the entire inscription: "Η ΠΑΡΟΥΣΑ ΈΙΚΩΝ ΆΥΤΗ ΜΕΤΑ ΤΟΝ ΠΕΡΙΞ ΘΑΥΜΑΤΩΝ ΤΟΥ ΌΣΙΟΥ ΠΑΤΡΟΣ ΉΜΩΝ ΝΑΟΥΜ ΤΟΥ ΘΑΟΥΜΑΤΟΥΡΓΟΥ. ΣΥΝ ΔΡΟΜΗ ΤΟΥ ΠΑΝΟΣΙΟΤΑΤΟΥ ΆΡΧΙΜΑΝΔΡΙΤΟΥ ΚΥΡΙΟΥ ΚΩΝΣΤΑΝΤΙΝΟΥ ΔΑΠΑΝΗ ΔΕ ΤΟΥ ΈΠΤΙΜΟΤΑΤΟΥ ΚΑΙ ΧΡΗΣΗΜΟΤΑΤΟΥ ΚΥΡΙΟΥ, ΝΑΟΥΜ ΤΟΥ ΣΑΟΥΛ ΜΠΗΚΕΡΑ ΕΚ ΜΟΣΚΟΠΟΛΕΩΣ. ΆΦΙΕΡΩΘΗ ΠΑΡ ΆΥΤΟΥ ΈΙΣ ΤΟ ΜΟΝΑΣΤΗΡΙΟΝ ΤΟΥ ΆΓΙΟΥ ΝΑΟΥΜ ΑΨΜΓ /έπιστασια χριστ: ζεφαρ.)." The engraving is published in Nagy, *Ohridi Szent Naum*, Cat. 3.

famous "red marble" of Piszke and was erected in 1811, a Greek inscription announces that the costs of its construction were covered by Messrs. Thomasz and Theokharisz Janpasz from Kastoria.[42]

Similarly, Jorgosz Koisszióriu, who financed the gilding of the Virgin's throne in the Orthodox Church of Miskolc, found it important to have his birth-place, Moschopolis mentioned in the inscription:

> "The present throne, complete with its gilding, was commissioned by Mr. Koisszióriu of Moschopolis [...]. Miskolc, April 1807."[43]

Macedo-Vlachs living in a foreign land had a very strong sense of belonging together. This is suggested, for instance, by Maria Kirovics's will of 17 August, 1787: this woman from Jászberény bequeathed money not only to her own parish church in Gyöngyös, but also to other Macedo-Vlach-Greek churches in Pest and Kecskemét.[44] Other wills also reveal a similar tendency.[45] Let alone the above-mentioned Bishop Dionisziosz Popović of the Serbian Church, this native of Kozani, whose Serbian office did not restrain him at all from encouraging the construction of Macedo-Vlach churches in Hungary.

In the course of history the majority of Vlachs left their motherland, they were dispersed in Europe and did not form a nation – that would have required living together in the first place. In their habits of thought, however, several components of national consciousness feature.[46] It is clearly illustrated by the examples above, which demonstrate their strong attachment to their old Macedonian homeland and their sense of belonging together because of their common place of origin.

In sum, in the Hungarian Kingdom the donation practices of the Orthodox Macedo-Vlach ethnicity from the Balkans shed light on the fairly complex affiliations and relations connecting them in their new homeland with both the Western Christian majority culture so alien for them and the other minority Balkan cultures of their brethren, which may have been less so. They had versatile connections. On the one hand, they tried to assimilate into the majority Hungarian environment, which was a question of life and death for them at the beginning, and later a key to a social upward mobility on a par with their economic power. Due to the lack of nationhood, this assimilation did not pose diffi-

---

[42] See the inscription of the altar: "ΤΟ ΤΕΡΟΝ ΤΟΥΤΟ ΘΥΣΙΑΣΤΗΡΙΟΝ /ΚΑΤΕΣΚΥΑΣΤΗ ΔΑΠΑΝΗ/ ΤΩΝ Κ/ΥΡΙ/ΩΝ ΘΟΜΑ ΚΑΙ ΘΕΟΧΑΡΕΩΣ /ΤΑΝΠΑ ΕΚ ΠΟΛΕΩΣ ΚΑΣΤΟΡΙΑΣ ΕΙΣ /ΜΝΗΜΟΣΥΝΩΝ ΆΙΩΝΙΟΝ ΑΥΤΩΝΤΕ ΚΑΙ /ΤΩΝ ΑΥΤΩΝ ΓΟΝΕΩΝ. ΤΗΑ ΙΑΝΟΥΑΡΙΟΥ Α(?)811."

[43] Kárpáti László, "Az ortodox templom ikonjai és liturgikus tárgyai" [The Icons and Liturgical Objects of the Orthodox Church], in *A miskolci orthodox templom és sírkertje* [The Miskolc Orthodox Church and graveyard], ed. Dobrossy István (Miskolc: Borsod-Abaúj-Zemplén Megyei Levéltár, 2002), 69.

[44] The will is published in Papp, *Görög kereskedők*, 289.

[45] Papp, *Görög kereskedők*, 287-333.

[46] Elements of national consciousness involve the awareness of coming from the same place, a unified national economy and a national language (which is both a formative power of community and a specific feature of nationhood). Joó Rudolf, *Nemzeti és nemzetiségi önrendelkezés, önkormányzat, egyenjogúság* [National and Ethnic Autonomy, Self-Government and Equality] (Budapest: Kossuth 1984), 13-15.

culties for them. On the other hand, their "duplex consciousness and language" also led to open-mindedness, which made their integration easier.

They were naturally affiliated to their native Macedonian lands. Paradoxically, their Vlach identity gained expression not only in their donations to their birthplace, but also in their strong attachment to Greek language and culture, since they were a fundamentally Hellenised ethnic group. However, they also aimed to preserve their Vlach identity as separate from the Greek one. They acted similarly in the face of the Serbs, the most populous Orthodox ethnic group in Hungary.

In the donation practices of the Macedo-Vlachs in Hungary, the most important issue of Diaspora existence – the dilemma of national-ethnic self-preservation versus assimilation – surfaces just as conspicuously as in all the other aspects of Diaspora life. The issue of melting in is, however, rather complex in the case of the Macedo-Vlachs in Hungary, since they tried to assimilate not only to the majority national environment but also to their brethren leading a minority existence, on the one hand, and wished to preserve their ethnic identity as separate even from the latter's, on the other.

Patterns of Wealth Transmission in Eighteenth Century Sibiu

OANA VALENTINA SORESCU

„So spricht den Herr: Bestelle dein Haus,
denn du wirst sterben und nicht lebendig bleiben!"[1]

Introduction

The notion that one needed to prepare for a *good death* did not fade away with the Reformation, but rather underwent a transformation, which was also reflected in testamentary behaviour. Similarly to the Lutheran re-evaluation of the utility of religious art in a liturgical context, last wills and testaments gradually changed their function, from outlines of pious bequests to juridical instruments that aimed to ensure that the testator's family and friends were taken care of after death.

Although testamentary practice has been studied widely for the past several decades thanks to the efforts of the French school of historiography,[2] this issue has not drawn as much attention from Romanian historians and has been largely neglected in historical studies that focus on Transylvania during the eighteenth century.[3] The present paper aims firstly to draw attention to this gap, and secondly to discuss how testamentary practice evolved from a confessional perspective, focusing on a sample of eighteenth-century Lutheran wills from the archives of Sibiu/Hermannstadt.[4] Its contribution resides both in the attempt to apply and adapt methodology used in similar studies that have concentrated on German-language testaments from the Austrian part of the Habsburg Monarchy, and in its use of previously unstudied archival sources.

This research has however taken into consideration two facts: firstly, that the testators' confessional background cannot be regarded as a sufficient context or cause for a certain type of testamentary behaviour; secondly, that a host of other factors specific both to the eighteenth century and to this particular region – the city of Sibiu – have influenced this behaviour.

In order to assess the impact of these factors and their resulting behavioural norms, the study briefly discusses the main contextual frames that regulated the making of wills, from a religious, cultural and juridical perspective. The analysis itself focuses on the following elements: the formal characteristics of wills, the patterns of wealth division, the beneficiaries of wills, and the witnesses selected by testators.

---

[1] Is 38:1.

[2] François Lebrun, Michel Vovelle and Philippe Aries' seminal works have served as models for most of the relevant research in this field.

[3] Kinga S. Tüdős, *Erdélyi testamentumok.* Kötet 4. *Erdélyi nemesek és főemberek végrendeletei, 1661-1723* [Transylvanian Testaments, vol. 4, Transylvanian Nobles and Rulers' Wills, 1661-1723] (Marosvásárhely: Mentor, 2011) is the only collection of this type of sources than spans into the 18th century.

[4] Serviciul Județean Sibiu al Arhivelor Naționale [Sibiu County Department of the National Archives] (henceforth abbreviated SJSAN Sibiu), Fund *Magistrat-Testamente*.

Context

The formation of a Lutheran confessional identity in Transylvania was formally completed by the 1615 Mediaş Synod, when the fundamental doctrines of Lutheranism were adopted and the Saxon nation adhered to the Augustan Confession.[5] However, in practice, the process of confessionalisation was far from over. During the seventeenth century, crypto-Calvinist manifestations within formally Lutheran communities were gradually eliminated, while the tensions between the Catholic authorities in Vienna and the political representatives of the Saxons deepened.[6] While the effects of this process on the day-to-day life of the Transylvanian Saxons were wide-ranging, the internalization of Lutheran values did not "transform the Saxon cities into puritan communities."[7]

During the eighteenth century, the confessional divisions between the Austrian part of the Empire and the German-language communities in Transylvania were emphasized by fervent missionary activity from the former. In the case of Sibiu, both Jesuits and Franciscans received the right to settle within the city walls,[8] while Catholic preachers exhorted the Protestant inhabitants to renounce their faith, as they were all "verloren und verdammt," their sacraments "verwerftlicht" and all their Church services "null und nichtig."[9] Their efforts were fruitless, as the number of Catholics in Sibiu remained extremely limited throughout the eighteenth century.[10]

It was not just confessional adherence that influenced how the inhabitants of Sibiu envisaged the preparation for a *good death*. During the eighteenth century, certain aspects of Enlightenment thought materialized in a renewed preoccupation with philanthropy and charitable practices. For instance, an article in the *Siebenbürger Zeitung* mentioned the support given to the homeless and the poor in Sibiu by philanthropic persons and contrasted this practice with traditional Catholic piety:

> "Wahrheit, wohltätige Menschenfreunde, euer Mitleid hat eine schöne Richtung genommen, schöner und herrlicher als jener ihres, die Kirchen und Altäre bekleiden, um ihren Stolz zu zeigen und Gott einen Dienst zu erweisen."[11]

Philanthropy was thus regarded as ethically and socially superior to the traditional pious practices of Catholicism, which aimed to "clothe churches and altars," as expressions of pride and contrary to God's freely given grace. This passage underlines the fact that the behavioural norms of Lutheranism – the emphasis on service to one's neighbour – had

---

[5] Edit Szegedi, "Naşterea şi formarea identităţii confesionale luterane în Transilvania: între exigenţe teologice şi constrângeri politice" [The Birth and Formation of the Lutheran Confessional Identity in Transylvania: Between Theological Exigencies and Political Constraints], *Studia Universitatis Cibiniensis, Series Historica* 6 (2009): 131-133.

[6] Ibid., 136.

[7] Ibid., 139.

[8] Friedrich Teutsch, *Geschichte der evangelischen Kirche in Siebenbürgen*, Bd. II (Hermannstadt, 1922), 14-27. The Franciscans received this right in 1716 and the Jesuits in 1721.

[9] Ibid., 35.

[10] Ibid.

[11] *Aufklärung: Schriftum der Siebenbürger Sachsen und Banater Schwaben*, ed. Carl Göllner (Bukarest: Kriterion Verlag, 1974), 63-64.

not only been rather effectively internalized by the eighteenth century, but had also blended with the humanist impulses of the Enlightenment.

Both the formal aspects and the content of wills were to a certain degree regulated by the extant legislation regarding the transmission of wealth and the making of testamentary dispositions. Even before the Reformation, the Saxon University was preoccupied with keeping its patrimony in the right hands – those of the Saxon citizens – and passed several laws demonstrating this concern. For instance, in 1525 a decision of the University prohibited pious bequests to religious institutions "for the sake of the salvation of one's soul."[12]

The major legislative frame for testamentary practice was the 1583 code of laws entitled *Statuta Jurium Municipalium Saxonum in Transyvalnia*, based on Johann Honterus' collection of civil laws from 1544.[13] Several key points regarding the juridical form of wills and testamentary practice were outlined in the fifth chapter of the third book. For instance, only those who were of sound mind and clear comprehension could make wills.[14] These documents had to be signed by a minimum of two witnesses, with a precise date and location added. A testator could freely dispose of part of his or her fortune, but was obliged to leave two thirds (*Zweitheil*) to any direct heirs he or she might have. Male testators were free to dispose of one third of their *Zweitheil* (22% of a couple's entire wealth), while female testators could bequeath the same percentage from their *Drittheil* (11% of a couple's entire fortune) to anyone they so chose.[15]

A third piece of legislation that directly affected the making of wills, at least on a theoretical level, was a law passed by the Court of Vienna in September 1771, which stipulated that members of the clergy were prohibited from formally taking part in the drafting of wills, either as writers or as witnesses. The Habsburg authorities thus sought to limit the practice of leaving pious bequests by eliminating undue clerical influence on testators.[16] Austrian historians remain however sceptical of the effective impact of this law on testamentary practice, both in the Austrian parts of the Empire and in its other provinces.[17]

---

[12] The text of the decision reads as following: "Ein Beschluss der Sächsichen Universität, daß fortan keiner in seinem Testament sein Hab und Gut an Kloster oder Kirchen ‚für das Wohl oder die Erlösung seiner Seele' hinterlassen darf, es sei denn, seine Erben haben das Recht, die Erbschaft zu einem nach einer ‚würdiger' Preis zurückzukaufen. Hat der Verstorben kein lebendigen Verwandten oder Erben, haben die Bürger das Recht, Hab und Gut unter den gleichen Bedingung zu kaufen." *Das Privatrecht der Siebenbuerger Deutschen (Sachsen) im systematische Grundrisse*, ed. Friedrich Schuler von Libloy (Sibiu, 1848), 346.

[13] SJSAN, Collection of Manuscripts, I, No. 237: Matthias Fronius, *Statuta Jurium Municipalium Saxonum in Transylvaniae*, 1583 (henceforth abbreviated Fronius, *Statuta Jurium*).

[14] *An der Testierenden personen werden zur Zeit und Stunde des Bescheids nicht des Leibs Kräfte und Stärcke sonder rechter Verstand und das sie bey gutter Vernunfft sey erfordert*. Fronius, *Statuta Jurium*, fol. 152.

[15] Ibid., fol. 154r-v.

[16] Ordinance from 4.9.1771 (*Verordnungen* 5), Nr. 38, quoted in Michael Pammer, *Glaubensabfall und wahre Andacht: Barockreligiosität, Reformkatholizismus und Laizismus in Öberosterreich 1700-1820* (Wien: Verlag für Geschichte und Politik, 1994), 264.

[17] Pammer, *Glaubensabfall*, 264-266.

Analysis

The present article is based on an analysis of 20% of extant Transylvanian Saxon wills from the city of Sibiu, ranging from 1721 to 1800. Less than 4% of these wills were either written by the testator himself or were verbally delivered in front of witnesses who later committed them to paper.[18]

In several cases the writer of the will – someone other than the testator – is mentioned by name at the end of the document, along with the witnesses. Sometimes the writer also receives a small bequest (between one thaler and one gulden). The *Statuta jurium municipalium* placed great emphasis on the accuracy of testamentary dispositions, which had to reflect the testator's wishes as well as conform to the common juridical norms that gave it value as an official document. The dangers that arose from allowing persons who did not have specialized training to draft the will are for instance evident in the testament of Matthias Theil from 1744. The testator bequeathed his wife one third of his wealth, while also leaving her all goods that fell under the category of *Weiberschmuck*.[19] When the representatives of the *Theilamt* opened the document upon the death of the testator, there was a certain confusion regarding this bequest, explained thus:

> „Diesen Terminum: Weiberschmuck explicieren beyde Testaments Zeugen daß dadurch nicht Gold und Silber auch Edelstein, sondern Bett Wäsche und Weiber Kleidung von verstorbene verschenkt werden... und die Testaments Zeugen haben keinen besten Terminum bewust."[20]

Although the generic term *Weiberschmuck* was commonly used to designate feminine jewellery, in this case the testator had referred to a variety of household goods and to his wife's clothing. The representatives of *Theilamt* deemed it necessary to clarify this provision by requesting additional information from the witnesses, who justified their use of the term *Weiberschmuck* by explaining that they had been unaware of any better expression.

Not all of the wills analyzed met the minimum standards for juridical validity. Before 1751 nearly half of these documents were unsigned by the testator. This proportion gradually declined from sometime in the 1760s, with the number of testators who added their signature to wills rising significantly during the last two decades.[21] There was no considerable gender disparity from this perspective, as roughly 44% of female testators signed their wills, compared to 40% of male testators.[22]

---

[18] I have elected to use the masculine form throughout my study, only particularizing in regards to the gender of the testator when there was a considerable gender gap that warranted a differentiated analysis.

[19] SJSAN, Fund *Magistrat-Testamente*, Folder T 27, Will No. 8/1744.

[20] Ibid., fol. 15v.

[21] This should not however be taken as a direct indication of an increase in the level of overall literacy. The ability to sign one's name legibly at the end of a document did not necessarily entail the ability to read and/or write.

[22] The 4% difference may however indicate that female testators wanted to ensure to a greater degree that their final dispositions would be valid and respected after their death.

Analysis of wills also yields other information regarding the majority of testators, such as gender and marital status.[23] Women's wills represent roughly 35% of all testaments from 1721 to 1800, while mutual wills – whereby a married couple made reciprocal bequests – make up 4% of cases.

A high percentage (62%) of testators of both genders were married at the time of drafting the will, a status that was either explicitly stated or can be gleaned from the content of the testament and from how the testators' fortune was divided.

Less information can be gathered in regards to the testators' social and professional status. Around 79% of the wills analyzed do not mention any kind of profession, while 18% of testators were members of guilds and 3% worked in the administration. Compared to Austrian territory, where only 28.4% of wills kept silent about the testator's socio-professional status, it seems that the majority of testators from Sibiu did not regard the inclusion of this variable as necessary.[24]

The division of the estate itself followed certain patterns, which evolved during the period in question. Firstly, wealth could be categorized broadly into several elements: the percentage of the overall fortune (either the *Zweitheil* or the *Drittheil*), real estate, movable goods, jewellery, and money. As these five categories appear most frequently through-out the sources, their frequency has been analyzed in the first figure of this paper (Fig. 1).

The percentage of the overall fortune figures in 40% to 48% of the cases analyzed from 1761 to 1800, reaching its lowest value in 1731-1740 when it only appears in 20% of the testaments. The frequency of bequests containing real estate varies from 17% of cases in 1751-1760 to 5% in 1741-1750. Overall, these two categories constituted a significant part of bequests in the second half of the century, ranging from 50% to 60% in this period.

Movable goods (or *bewegliche Gütter)* varied greatly throughout the century, and exhibited no apparent connection to other types of bequests. This category reached its peak in 1721-1730 (33%), appearing with a frequency of only 5% from 1741 to 1750. Sometimes bequests were more detailed, and explicitly mentioned and described which objects were left and to whom. Several sub-categories of mobile goods stand out from a quantitative perspective: household items (cutlery, kitchen items made from precious metals, etc.), clothes (especially winter clothes, made from leather or embroidered items), as well as farm animals.

Jewellery features in 10% of the wills from the fourth decade of the century, and is mentioned relatively constantly until 1781, when its frequency decreases from 9% to

---

[23] Unfortunately, both the age and the level of education of the testator are very rarely mentioned in testaments. The former can sometimes be deduced indirectly from other information – i.e. the testator's profession, etc.

[24] Pammer, *Glaubensabfall*, 38.

1%. It is interesting to note that there was no considerable gender disparity in bequests of jewellery, as 44% male testators included this type of bequest in their wills.

Bequests in money (*Baargeld)* appear most frequently (37%) in the fourth decade, the same period when bequests in jewellery peaked. However, money was mentioned almost constantly, generally varying between 32% and 25%.

If we consider all these categories from a qualitative perspective, it may be stated that most testators preferred to leave either a percentage of their fortune or a sum of money to heirs and other beneficiaries. One reason for the preference for bequests in money is that it was easier to calculate and extract a certain sum from the overall fortune before the partitioning of a testator's estate.[25]

A second issue that appears when analyzing patterns of wealth transmission is the type of beneficiary of certain legacies or bequests (Fig. 2). The composition of testators' families was an important variable in the process of wealth division and transmission. For instance, married persons could leave a part of their fortune to their spouses, while those who had direct heirs – children or grandchildren – were inclined to include them as beneficiaries. As in the Austrian territories of the Habsburg Monarchy, information regarding the testators' marital status is generally reliable.[26] However, wills do not offer sufficient information on the overall structure of the family, as they do not always mention all direct heirs. Likewise, although in many cases it is explicitly mentioned that a couple has no direct heirs, as a justification for bequests to other categories of beneficiaries, in the majority of situations this status can only be gleaned indirectly. Furthermore, Austrian historians have remarked that married testators tended to include both spouses and direct heirs as beneficiaries, although the number of children had a negative impact on a spouse's inheritance.[27]

In the case of Sibiu, spouses were most frequently mentioned as beneficiaries between 1741 and 1760 (37%). This frequency never drops lower than 28% (1731-1740). If these results are correlated with the frequency of bequests to direct heirs, we observe that the latter category have a lesser chance of being included as beneficiaries in wills, even though by law they received two-thirds of the overall fortune at their parents' death. The frequency of bequests to direct heirs varies from 37% in the last decade of the century and 15.5% between 1741 and 1750. During the fourth decade, with the lowest frequency of bequests towards direct heirs, spouses are mentioned most frequently as beneficiaries (37%).

---

[25] These sums cannot however be used as indicators of a testator's overall wealth, as they vary widely. Some testators mention sums of 1300 Gulden while others bequeath only 2 Gulden to their witnesses. A more adequate image of economic status can be gleaned from inventories of the deceased's estate, which were made shortly after the testator's death by the officials of the *Theilamt*.

[26] Michael Pammer, "Death and the Transfer of Wealth: Bequest Patterns and Cultural Change in the Eighteenth Century," *Journal of Social History* 33, 4 (2000): 923.

[27] Ibid.

A third category of recipients comprised relatives – generally brothers, sisters, nephews and nieces, etc. This group is named with varying frequency, between 22.75% in the final decade and 0% from 1731 to 1750. The selection of this type of recipients depended heavily on the existence of members of the other two categories: thus, in the period from 1731 to 1750, when no mention of other relatives was made, spouses and direct heirs reached an overall level of 52.5% to 64%.

Testators could also choose to leave bequests to friends and neighbours. This situation was most frequent in the case of widowed persons who had no direct heirs. The frequency of bequests to this category varies from 4% (1721-1730) to 22.5% (1781-1790).

Finally, witnesses also appear as beneficiaries in a relatively standardized clause, through which the testator sought to repay their efforts. The practice of including witnesses as beneficiaries appears most frequently during the first three decades analyzed (18%, 25% and 32% of cases respectively) and slowly decreased from the mid-century, from 10% in 1751 to less than 2% in the final decade. It is interesting to note that bequests to witnesses appear most frequently between 1741 and 1750 (37%), when direct heirs and friends are only mentioned in 30.5% of cases, and relatives do not appear at all. It may thus be stated that witnesses had a greater financial incentive to testify to the validity and accuracy of a testator's last wishes when other categories of beneficiaries who could have fulfilled this role were lacking. By including witnesses as recipients of symbolic sums, testators sought to ensure that their last wishes were precisely adhered to.

The Saxons' relatively significant tendency to include spouses as beneficiaries of part of the overall fortune, even when direct heirs were also mentioned, may be seen as an indirect indication of their social status. It may be assumed that the majority of testaments included in this sample were part of an upper middle class, a social and economic category that distinguished itself from the Austrian nobility in how it transmitted its wealth. This nobility did not manifest such a high level of trust in their spouse's willingness to provide for heirs after the testators' passing, and preferred to divide their fortunes between the remaining direct heirs.[28]

Furthermore, the relatively prevalence of relatives, friends and witnesses as beneficiaries in testaments (40% for the entire period), compared to the percentage of widowed testators (36%) may indicate that these documents were not simply regarded as a means of sealing the traditional pattern of wealth transmission in accordance with the laws of succession. Persons outside the immediate family also had significant chances of receiving legacies or inheritances from testators: friends were mentioned for instance in 12% of the wills examined. This may be taken as a sign of the importance of social networks of friendship among the Transylvanian Saxons in Sibiu.

---

[28] Ibid., 917.

An extremely significant aspect in the study of testamentary practices is the inclusion of so-called pious and charitable clauses. Initially, these types of clauses were the primary reason to make wills, which outlined in detail the measures to be taken for the salvation of a testator's soul after his passing. In the case of Sibiu, only 10% of testaments in the sample contain pious bequests. All wills which leave a sum of money either for church services or for the betterment of certain religious foundations can be ascribed with certainty to Catholic testators. For the entire period, only 15% of the wills in the sample contain charitable clauses. The rate of both pious and charitable clauses was considerably higher in the case of widowed testators, occurring in 64% and 75% of cases respectively.

From 1771 to 1780, after the passing of the Imperial Ordinance prohibiting formal clerical participation in the making of wills, I have encountered three separate cases in which Catholic testators ask members of the clergy to serve as witnesses.[29] Although these cases are not necessarily statistically relevant, it is interesting to note that not only do the same two witnesses appear in each case – Johannes Rietz and Johann Georg, designated as a *Geisther* – but that all three testators left pious bequests to the local Franciscan monastery. Such a coincidence may indicate that the Catholic clergy did indeed exert some degree of influence on testamentary behaviour in the case of Catholic testators.

Overall, members of the clergy (both Catholic and Lutheran) appear as witnesses in 11% of the wills. This percentage is especially high in the last three decades of the century, when the rate of formal clerical participation rises to 14%. Thus it seems that the inhabitants of Sibiu remained relatively unaffected by the legislation passed in Vienna. Moreover, the tendencies in testamentary behaviour during this period appeared to directly contradict this legislation.

Conclusions

Comparison with Catholic wills from the Austrian territories of the Habsburg Monarchy has proved useful in many respects. Firstly, as has been pointed out, Lutheran testators from eighteenth-century Sibiu were seemingly less concerned about the formal characteristics of their testaments – the number of witnesses, the addition of their signature, etc. – and insisted on their identity as 'citizens of Hermannstadt' rather than on their social and professional status. Female testators were inclined to adhere more strictly to the rules and regulation of testamentary practice, an aspect that also occurs in the last wills of noble women from Austria during the same period. However, women in Sibiu also understood their right to dispose freely of a percentage of their wealth, and many chose to make use of wills as juridical instruments.

The information that can be extracted from these documents about the testators' education, age, and profession is relatively limited. One should however avoid extrapolations from the profession of witnesses: the testator's profession only coincides with that

[29] SJSAN, Fund *Magistrat-Testamente*, Folder G8, Will No. 2; Idem, Will No. 29; Idem, Will No. 30.

of his witnesses in a very limited number of cases. This may indicate that friendship networks were more important in selecting witnesses than common membership in guilds.

A surprising result was the relatively low occurrence of charitable bequests in Lutheran wills – less than 15% for the entire period. The situation is strikingly different from that encountered in Austria during the same century, where the majority of wills contained charitable as well as pious clauses. As has been briefly pointed out, Lutheranism emphasized the need to replace pious bequests with charitable ones, and, in general, the necessity to prioritize the needs of one's family and neighbours over those of religious institutions. Caring for one's spouse and direct heirs thus took precedence over the inclusion of charitable clauses benefiting those who had been treated unkindly by fate: the poor, the homeless and orphans. Although the humanist impulses of the Enlightenment praised charitable behaviour and regarded it as a contribution to the well-being of one's community, it seems that the Transylvanian Saxons adhered to a more traditionalist viewpoint in this respect. Charitable clauses that would have left either spouses or direct heirs in a financially unstable situation after the testator's passing would not have been acceptable from a confessional standpoint.

It may thus be stated that the core values of Lutheranism – caring for one's neighbour, the disappearance of pious bequests, and the importance of family and social ties in the community of believers – had been internalized at the level of testamentary behaviour by the eighteenth century. Furthermore, based on the sources that have been analyzed it is difficult to assert that a 'laicization' or 'professionalization' of will-making occurred during the eighteenth century in Sibiu. Religious rhetoric, devoid of any Catholic overtones (appeals to saintly intercession, to the Virgin Mary, to God as a judge, to one's sins, etc.) still featured frequently even during the last decades of the century, and members of the clergy played a significant part in the drafting of wills.

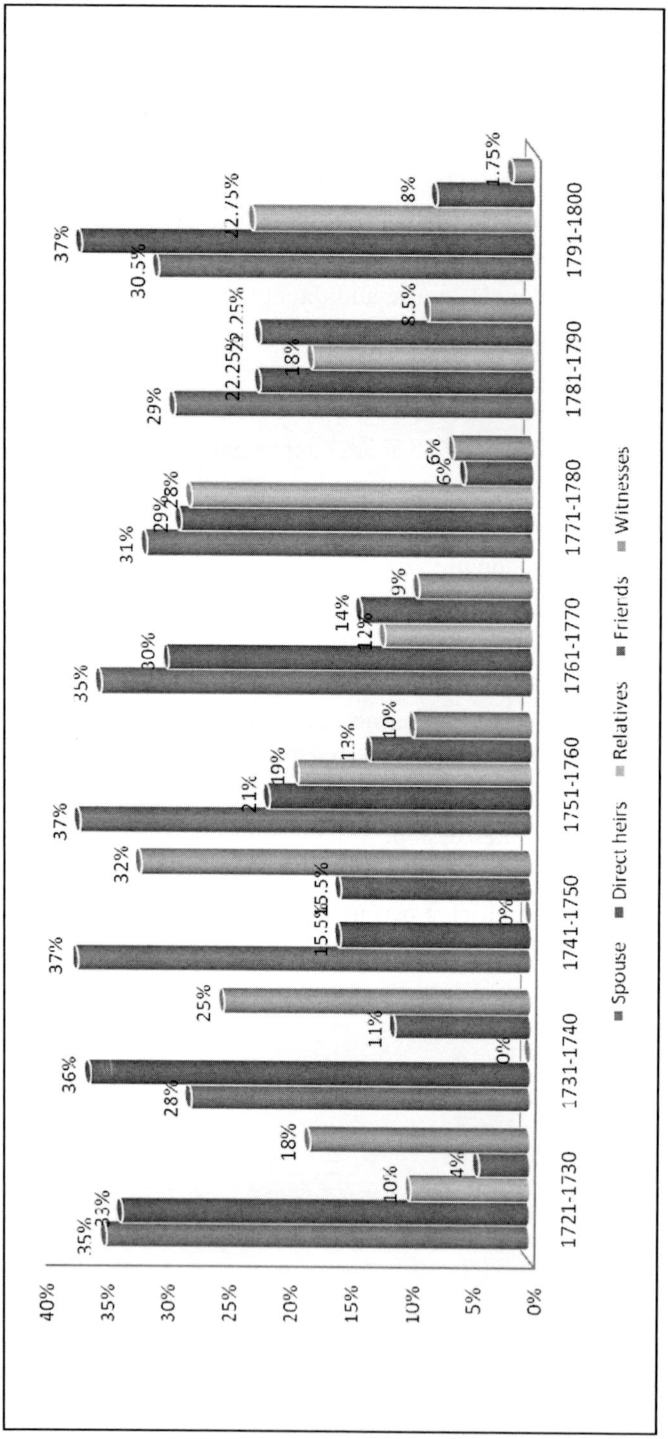

Fig. 1. Division and transmission of wealth according to categories of goods, 1721-1800

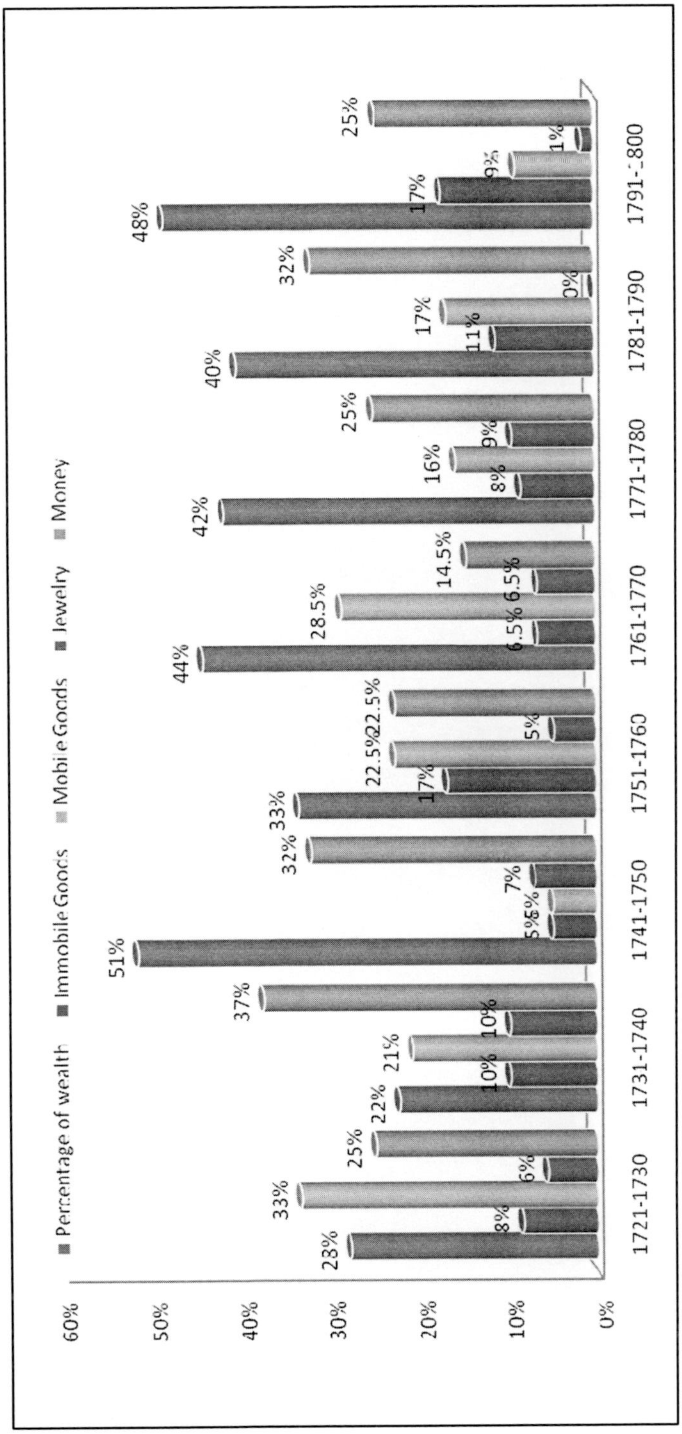

Fig. 2. Wealth distribution according to categories of beneficiaries, 1721-1800

BOOKS AND CONFESSIONAL IDENTITY: The Library of the Uniate Bishop Ioan Giurgiu Pataki

GRETA-MONICA MIRON

In the present study,[1] I intend to outline the bookish universe of the Uniate bishop Ioan Giurgiu Pataki as evinced by his library, which was started during the first three decades of the eighteenth century and was the very first Uniate ecclesiastical library that we know of. The sources I will use are two inventories: the first is an unpublished inventory which dates back to 1731 and recorded the assets of the Uniate diocese of Făgăraş after Bishop Pataki's death,[2] while the second was compiled in 1747, detailing the books that remained in the episcopal residence after the departure of bishop Ioan Inochentie Micu.[3]

This is a private-public library, founded at the time when the bishop was carrying out his studies, enriched during his episcopate and forming the core collection of the Episcopal library. With its approximately 200 volumes,[4] it was modest by comparison with the libraries of other members of the Catholic high clergy in Western Europe or the libraries of scholars in the Romanian Lands.[5] Nonetheless, the library was impressive for the Romanian Uniate priests at the beginning of the eighteenth century, whose precarious material status and whose ignorance – in the absence of a diocesan seminary – had kept

---

[1] I would like to thank Silvia Marin Barutcieff for the assistance she has provided me in the documentary work and Sever Oancea for his suggestions on reading the book collection inventory.

[2] Magyar Orszagos Levéltár [National Archives of Hungary] (henceforth abbreviated MOL), Fund *Erdélyi Fiscalis Levéltár 1527-1870*, fascicle 9, reel 32439, f. 83r, 90-92, 123r.

[3] Biblioteca Academiei Române, Filiala Cluj-Napoca [Romanian Academy Library – Cluj-Napoca Branch] (henceforth abbreviated B.A.R.F.C.N.), *Ms. Lat. 550*; the inventory was published by Magdalena Tampa, "Din începuturile Bibliotecii de la Blaj. Despre inventarul manuscris din 14 iunie 1747" [From the Beginnings of the Blaj Library. On the Manuscript Inventory of 14 June 1747], *Biblioteca şi cercetarea* III (1979): 126-145.

[4] In the inventory of 1731, the books are registered with call numbers, often either after a part of the title (without mentioning the author) or after the author's name (sometimes without mentioning the book's title). Rarely were both the book title and the author recorded. Hence, the difficulty in identifying them. Moreover, the author of the inventory did not go to the trouble of rendering the titles in other languages than Latin or Italian, which means that the volumes in Romanian, Greek or Hungarian appear simply as *Liber Wallachicus*, *Liber Graecus*, *Liber Hungaricus*. Naturally, there are differences between this inventory and the one in 1747, part of the books may have been lost or lent. The inventory of 1747 includes, besides the printed books, the lecture notes from the period of Pataki's philosophy and theology studies, Vasilica Eugenia Cristea, "Neam, tradiţie şi cultură la începutul secolului XVIII în Transilvania" [Ethnicity, Tradition and Culture at the Beginning of the Eighteenth Century in Transylvania] (PhD Diss., Institutul de Istorie "George Bariţ" Cluj-Napoca, 2012), 50-53.

[5] For instance, the libraries of certain Parisian abbots and capitular canons, who were rich and well-educated, many of them holding PhD titles from the Sorbonne, "the elite of an elite," as Christianne Thomassery calls them, for whom books were familiar objects, reached, on average, 1.500 books throughout the century, Christianne Thomassery, "Livres et culture cléricale à Paris au XVIIIe siècle : quarante bibliothèques d'ecclésiastiques parisiens," *Revue française d'histoire du livre* 6 (1973): 281-300. The library of a contemporary of bishop Pataki's, Constantin Cantacuzino from Wallachia, comprised approximately 400 volumes, Corneliu Dima-Drăgan, *Biblioteca unui umanist român. Constantin Cantacuzino Stolnicul* [The Library of a Romanian Humanist. Constantin Cantacuzino, the Stolnic] (Bucureşti: Comitetul de Stat pentru Cultură şi Artă, 1967), 109-278.

them away from books. However, the owner of the library was a distinguished personality in Romanian society: bishop Ioan Giurgiu Pataki had received his training at the Jesuit College from Cluj, at Pazmaneum College in Vienna and at Collegium Germanicum-Hungaricum in Rome, had a doctorate in Theology, and was a missionary Catholic priest in Transylvania between 1711 and 1713 and a Uniate bishop between 1715 and 1727.[6] I have therefore wondered what this bookish universe might have been like, since it belonged to a bishop who acquired his formal training in the Catholic schools, who was ordained priest in the Latin rite, and then switched to the Greek rite, who pastured a prevalently rural world of priests and believers, which was ignorant in matters of faith and rather attached to the Eastern rite and the external aspects of faith.

In terms of its structure, the library was overwhelmingly theological; it was a library of the Counter-Reformation, reflecting the intense activity in the field of religious scholarship, especially of patrology and conciliar studies, in the aftermath of Trent.[7] What are to be found in this library are several of the major clusters around which the libraries of the European Catholic clergy had crystallized since the mid-seventeenth century.[8] Next to the Bible and the Roman Catechism, there were added comments, discourses of the Church Fathers on the Holy Scripture, works of moral theology and homiletics necessary for religious practice.

The theological literature from the episcopal library is diverse as regards the authors, genres and purposes. It included works of reference written by Catholic European theologians, ranging from medieval authors like John Duns Scotus and Peter Lombard, who's *Sententiae* were considered the standard manual of introduction to systematic theology used in the medieval universities starting from the thirteenth century. Remarkable is the presence of St. Thomas Aquinas' work,[9] in tune with the evolutions on a European level, his *Summa Theologica* being considered the foundation of the entire theological culture in the seventeenth century. This was a work commonly encountered in the ecclesiastical libraries.[10] The author was also well appreciated in the circles of the Uniate

---

[6] For Pataki's educational background and activity, see Cristea, "Neam, tradiţie şi cultură," 10-84; Iacob Mârza, "Biserică, politică şi cultură la Ioan Giurgiu Patachi (1681-1727)" [Church, politics and Culture at the Ioan Giurgiu Patachi (1681-1727)], *Annales Universitatis Apulensis* 11/II (2007): 48-65; Radu Nedici, "Avatarurile unei cariere ecleziastice. Ioan Pataki, de la misionar apostolic latin la episcop unit de rit grec" [The avatars of an ecclesiastical career. Ioan Pataki, from Latin Apostolic missionary to Greek rite Uniate bishop], *Annales Universitatis Apulensis. Series Historica* 15, I (2011): 181-194.

[7] Henri-Jean Martin, *Livre, pouvoirs et société a Paris au XVIIe siècle. 1598-1701*, vol. 1 (Genève: Droz, 1998), 12.

[8] Roger Chartier, *Lecturi şi cititori în Franţa Vechiului Regim* [Readings and Readers in France during the Ancien Régime] (Bucureşti: Meridiane, 1997), 188.

[9] It is recorded only in the inventory from 1731, under the title *Theologia Divi Tomae*, MOL, *Erdélyi Fiscalis Levéltár 1527-1870*, fascicle 9, reel 32439, f. 91r.

[10] His *Summa theologica* was found in most of the libraries belonging to the French clergy. During the second half of the seventeenth century, in the Diocese of Reims, among others, it was the most commonly encountered book in the libraries of the parish priests, Dominique Julia, David Rice McKee, "Les confrères de Jean Meslier. Culture et spiritualité du clergé champenois au XVIIIe siècle," *Revue d'histoire de l'Eglise de France* 69 (1982): 75.

clergy throughout the eighteenth century. This is attested by the fact that in 1766 the Uniate bishop Atanasie Rednic chose to represent Thomas Aquinas iconographically in an image designed to explain the significance of the union with the Church of Rome.[11] Aquinas was represented among the Catholic saints next to St. Bonaventure, who is present in the Patakian library with a work dedicated to the novitiate.[12] Thomistic theology, reinterpreted, was also present in the bishop's library through the voluminous work *Theologia Scholastica* (13 volumes, Einsiedeln, 1687) of the Benedictine Reding, who was professor of Theology at the University of Salzburg.

An important segment of the theological section in the Patakian library is the polemical literature of controversy between the Catholics and the Protestants. This literature was useful to the Uniate bishop in positioning his own church in relation to the other churches from the Principality, in his discussions with members of the Catholic and Protestant ecclesiastical and secular elite. Thus, the library hosts two of the most impor-tant controversists of the Counter-Reformation, Robert Bellarmin with his *De Controversiis* and Martin Beccanus, a Jesuit theologian renowned in the German-speaking space. While it is true that the proportion of Catholic literature was overwhelming, the collection also included critical Protestant theological literature, represented by Zacharias Ursinus, professor at the University of Heidelberg, who was close to Philip Melanchthon, the main author and interpreter of the Heidelberg Catechism. Ursinus gathered his catechetical lectures in a theological textbook that became widespread in the seventeenth century among Protestants, especially among the Dutch.[13]

However, what distinguishes, in my opinion, this library from other Catholic libraries of the time is the presence of works devoted to the relations between the Catholic and the Orthodox Churches. This literature was most useful to Pataki both as a missionary priest and, later, as a Uniate bishop. The authors Pataki was interested in came from the eastern space but had acquired their training in the west, in Catholic schools, and were well acquainted with Greek theological literature, which they interpreted from a Catholic perspective. Therefore, it is no coincidence that the best represented author is Peter Arcudius, a native of the Greek island of Corfu, trained at the Greek College of St. Athanasius in Rome.[14] Sent by Pope Gregory XIV to the Polish-Lithuanian kingdom to preach eccle-

---

[11] Greta-Monica Miron, Maria Crăciun, "Tipografia de la Blaj şi comunicarea religioasă în societatea transilvăneană a secolului al XVIII-lea" [The Blaj Printing Press and Religious Communication in the Transylvanian Society of the Eighteenth Century], in *Istoria culturii. Cultura istoriei* [The History of Culture. The Culture of History], ed. Ionuţ Costea et al. (Cluj-Napoca: Argonaut, 2010), 116-151.

[12] Bonaventura, *Praestantissima opuscula pro religiosarum familiarum novitiis pie, sancteque imbuendis videlicet: Speculum disciplinae ad novitios. De institutione novitiorum. Regula novitiorum.*

[13] Charles D. Gunnoe jr., "Ursinus (Beer) Zacharias," in *The New Westminster Dictionary of Church History: the Early, Medieval and Reformation Eras*, vol. 1, ed. Robert Benedetto et al. (Louisville: Westminster John Knox Press, 2008), 658.

[14] He received his PhD in Theology and Philosophy from the Greek College, before an illustrious audience that included Cesare Baronius and Robert Bellarmin, Adrian Fortescue, *The Uniate Eastern Churches* (New Jersey: Gorgias Press, 2001), 154-155; *The Biographical dictionary of the Society for the Diffusion of Useful Knowledge*, vol. 3, part. 1 (London: Longman, Brown, Green, and Longmans, 1843), 312, http://www.ebooksread.com/authors-eng/society-for-the-diffusion-of-useful-knowledge-gre/the-biographical-dictionary.

siastical union with the Church of Rome, Arcudius was one of the artisans of the union from Brest (1596). He also contributed to the establishment of a Catholic seminary in Vilna, where he taught until 1603. His missionary activity fuelled his writing works of controversy, distinguishing himself as a polemicist, a translator of the classical authors and a good connoisseur of the Holy Fathers. The episcopal library includes his most important work, *Libri VII de concordia Ecclesiae Occidentalis et Orientalis in septem sacramentorum administratione* (Paris, 1619), in which he provided a full account of the Oriental Church's sacramental doctrine, described the rite of administering the sacraments and submitted the real or apparent deviations from the teachings of the Church Fathers to severe censorship.[15] The library also has two books on the Purgatory and the procession of the Holy Spirit,[16] as well as *Opuscula Aurea Theologica* (1630), a collection of the best works on the procession of the Holy Spirit, which he translated, edited and interpreted.[17] The works of Arcudius offered the readers the views of Eastern authors on two of the four Florentine points accepted by the Romanians through their union with the Church of Rome.

For acquiring knowledge of certain Greek theologians, the bishop could also resort to the work of another Greek author educated in Rome, Leo Allatios (1586-1669).[18] A passionate antiquarian, Allatios moved in the Italian humanist circles, entering in contact with Jacques Goar, Jean Morin and Gabriel Naudé, but also in those of the scientists and physicians of the time, thanks to his medical training. His interest in the relations between the Catholic and the Orthodox Churches was attested by both his activity in the Basilian Academy, founded by Cardinal Barberini in 1631, in order to reconcile the two churches, and by his writing. The theme of the relations between the Catholic and the Orthodox Churches was topical given that, against the background of the controversy with the Protestants, the papacy was interested in the union with the Orthodox Church. While not hosting his most famous works on this topic,[19] the library does include the first one devoted to this theme, *De aetate et interstitiis in collatione ordinum etiam apud Graecos servandis* (Rome, 1638), written for his patron, the bishop turned cardinal, Lelio Biscia, who appointed him custodian of his library and considered him his personal theologian.

---

[15] *The Biographycal Dictionnary*, 312-313; Fortescue, *The Uniate Eastern Churches*, 154.

[16] The inventory of 1747 recorded *De Spiritus Sanctus et Purgatorio in duobus tomis*. These must have been two of his works dedicated to this problem: *De Purgatorio igne* (Rome, 1637) or *Utrum detur Purgatorium et an illud sit per ignem* (Rome, 1622) and *Opuscula de processione Spiritus Sancti* (Rome, 1630).

[17] *Opuscula aurea theologica quorundam clariss. virorum posteriorum Graecorum [...] circa processionem Spiritus Sancti* (Rome, 1630). Among the authors included in the collection, there were: Ioannes Vecci, the Patriarch of Constantinople, Cardinal Visarion, Demetrii Cydonis, and Maximi Planudis.

[18] Allatios studied at the Greek College of St. Athanasius in Rome. He was Professor of Greek at the same college and a librarian in the Vatican Library. For Allatios' life, see Karen Hartnup, *On the Beliefs of the Greeks': Leo Allatios and Popular Orthodoxy* (Leiden: Brill, 2004), 53-80.

[19] These were the works *De consensione* and *De opinationibus*. In the former, he showed the similarities between the Orthodox and the Catholic doctrines and presented the historical relationship between the two Churches, citing exhaustively from Byzantine texts, and considering that there had essentially been no schism between East and West and that the true Orthodox were in communion with the Catholic Church. In the latter work, he made a comparison between Orthodox and Catholic popular beliefs and practices, ibid., 61, 73.

Pataki was also interested in *Graecia orthodoxa* (Rome, 2 volumes, 1652-1659), a collection of Greek authors who were favourable to Rome,[20] a work of reference therefore, which provided him with the opinions of the Eastern part in relation to Rome. Allatios addressed this relationship from an integrative historical perspective, attempting to show that the Orthodox were in fact misguided Catholics.[21] Allatios also served the interests of the papacy through *Confutatio Fabulae de Ioanna Papissa ex monumentis Graecis* (Rome, 1640), a work that may also be found in the episcopal library. Written at the request of Pope Urban VIII, who was concerned about the Orthodox and the Protestants ridiculing the fable, the book was a defense of the papacy, based on Greek authors, in which Allatios demonstrated that the legend had no historical foundation.[22]

Pataki was also interested in the contemporary authors' perspective on Catholic-Orthodox relations. As such, he acquired works by Kristóf Peichich (1666-1730), the representative of the Bulgarian Catholic intelligentsia, who had studied at the Urban College of the Propagation of the Faith. A missionary in Transylvania and Wallachia for a few years starting in 1698, he returned to the area in 1709, serving as a parish priest and a canon in Transylvania, Hungary, Wallachia and Croatia.[23] He was thus a contemporary of the Uniate bishop, also formed as a missionary, a connoisseur of the Central-Eastern space. Peichich's writings are a mirror of the experience he accumulated, their stated purpose being practical. Of his four works, the episcopal library hosted two: *Speculum veritatis* (Venice, 1725), a work belonging to the genre of the theology of controversy, in which he advocated the reunification of the Catholic and the Orthodox Churches, and *Mahometanus dogmatice et catehetice in lege Christi*, a sort of catechism for the Catholic missionaries active among the Muslims. His works reflect the expansion of post-Tridentine Catholicism into Eastern Europe and the policy adopted by the Habsburg Empire towards the religious integration of its subjects.[24]

Along with a literature which expressed the integrative vision of the Catholic Church in relation to the Orthodox Church, significant for the interest in acquiring knowledge of the other was also the Catholic exegesis of the Eastern rite and liturgy. The bishop's library included reference works in the field. One was the *Euchologion* of Jacques Goar, a theologian born in Paris, who studied Greek and was sent to the Orient by his superiors to learn about the Greeks' sources and theology. He was then an apos-

---

[20] In the library there is only one volume of the work. Among the authors Allatios edited were Veccus, Cartophilax of the Great Church of Constantinople, a staunch opponent of the Latins at first, who then became their friend and zealous defender; George Metochita, a deacon of the Great Church of Constantinople; Constantine Meliteniota, the author of a treatise on the union of the Greek and Latin Churches and of one on the procession of the Holy Spirit.
[21] Hartnup, *On the Beliefs of the Greeks',* 64-69.
[22] Ibid., 73.
[23] Iva Manova, "Historico-Philosophical Studies on Krastyo Peykich of Chiprovtsi (1666-1730): An Overview of the Literature and Some Critical Remarks," *Philosophia. E-Journal of Philosophy and Culture* (February 12, 2013).
[24] Ibid.

tolic missionary resident at Chios, who used the time he spent on the Greek island to establish relations with the Orthodox scholars and to study the conflicting issues between the teachings of the Catholics and of the Orthodox. His *Euchologion sive rituale Graecorum* (Paris, 1667) became a classic work on the Greek liturgy, significant through its erudite comments and the references to the original texts.[25] The Catholic erudition in Oriental scholarship was also illustrated by Eusèbe Renaudot, a French theologian and Orientalist who spent a good part of his life at the Court of Louis XIV and was a close acquaintance of Colbert's. He was a scholar who learned Arabic, Coptic and Syrian with a view to studying the churches in the Orient, a book enthusiast, the owner of a library of 8-9,000 volumes. He is present in the bishop's library with *Liturgiarum Orientalium Collectio* (Paris, 2 vols., 1715-1716), considered the most comprehensive collection to date of Oriental liturgies for the use of the Copts, the Jacobites, the Melkites and the Nestorians. The book is, however, also illustrative of the debates in the Catholic Church from that time, as well as for the disputes between the Catholics and the Protestants. Thus, Renaudot addressed in this work a key aspect of his theological writings, namely the continuity of the church's faith on the issue of the sacraments, which was at the core of the disputes between the Catholics and the Protestants. On the other hand, being one of the most prominent supporters of Jacques Bossuet in the controversies with Richard Simon and François Fénelon, he defended in this work Bossuet's Jansenist ideas.[26] The presence of the book in the episcopal library, next to a text by Bossuet himself,[27] illustrates thus the contacts of the Uniate ecclesiastical elite with the Jansenist ideas, from the first decades of the eighteenth century.[28]

The disputes within the Catholic Church at that time are also evinced by the works of moral theology found in Pataki's library. Those of Baldassare Francolini on penance[29] introduced Pataki to the debates between the rigorists and the probabilists. Pataki was familiar with Francolini's opinions from the time when he was a student in Rome, where he had attended his moral theology courses. A highly regarded and prominent professor at the Roman College in Rome, Francolini was an influential opponent of moral and disciplinarian rigorism. His probabilism was criticized by the rigorist Cardinal Giovanni Casimiro Denhoff in an instruction on penance from 1696. The critique reflects the tensions reached at the end of the seventeenth century between the probabilists and

[25] "Jacques Goar," in *The Catholic Encyclopedia*, accessed 12 February 2013, http://www.newadvent.org/cathen/06606c.htm.
[26] Nicholas Aloysius Weber, "Eusebius Renaudot," *The Catholic Encyclopedia*, accessed 3 March 2013, http://en.wikisource.org/wiki/Catholic_Encyclopedia_%281913%29/Eusebius_ Renaudot.
[27] Bossuet's text is included in *Opusculum bipartitum historiam Veteris Testamenti usque ad Jesum Christum methodo nova & ita facile chronologice propositam [...]*. The first edition appeared in 1707. An edition was also published at Tirnavia in 1732.
[28] For the penetration of Jansenist ideas into the Romanian cultural milieus, see Pompiliu Teodor, *Interferențe iluministe europene* [European Enlightenment Interferences] (Cluj-Napoca; Dacia, 1984), 86-88.
[29] The works in question are: *De dolore ad Sacramentum poenitentiae rite suscipiendum necessario: libri duo* (Roma, 1706) şi *De disciplina poenitentiae Libri III* (Roma, 1708).

the rigorists in the Society of Jesus, the movement towards anti-laxist positions undertaken by the leadership of the Jesuit Order.[30]

Along with this literature illustrating Pataki's interest in the contemporary movement of opinions within the Catholic Church, the best represented field in the library was the legal domain, the volumes of (canon and civil) law having a considerable proportion among the ecclesiastical books in the Episcopal library. The large number of books on law is a specificity of this library, which may be explained by the condition of the Uniate Church, which was at the beginning of its existence. As such, the compendia of canon law, the synodal constitutions and the conciliar documents were useful to the Uniate bishop for the identitarian and institutional definition of his church in relation to the Catholic Church with which it had become united. In the library we may find works that were widely read and disseminated in the entire Catholic Europe throughout the seventeenth and the eighteenth centuries,[31] true best-sellers of the genre. In effect, the spreading in Europe of a *quasi*-uniform canonical literature was facilitated by the fact that over the course of the twelfth-seventeenth centuries, the professors used the same *libri legales* in teaching law and the university curricula were the same throughout Europe.[32] Among the most widespread compendia of canon law present in the bishop's library is that written by the Salzburg professor Ludwig Engel, a renowned Benedictine canonist. His *Collegium Universi Iuris Canonici* was printed in 15 editions between 1693 and 1770, being appreciated for its brevity, clarity and well-founded information.[33] Pataki also acquired the work *Ius Canonicum Universum* of the Franciscan monk Anaklet Reiffenstuel, a professor at Freising. Often consulted by bishops and capitular canons, his works of ecclesiastical law (as well as those of theology) were published in thousands of copies in Germany, Italy, France and Spain.[34] The successful genre of commentaries was illustrated in the Episcopal library by the work written by Emmanuel Gonzalez Tellez, a professor of Law at the University of Salamanca. His commentary on the decrees of Gregory IX (a legal book that was well known in the thirteenth century) was considered the last comprehensive, massive canonical treatise that enjoyed wide circulation (first ed. Lyon, in

[30] Abigail Firey, ed., *A New History of Penance* (Leiden: Brill, 2008), 370. For the assertion of probabilism and the rigorist assault, see also Jean Delumeau, *Mărturisirea şi iertarea. Dificultăţile confesiunii. Secolele XIII-XVIII* [Confession and Forgiveness. The Difficulties of Confession. The Thirteenth-Eighteenth Centuries] (Iaşi: Polirom, 1998), 113-137.

[31] Most of the books of law in the episcopal library appeared (in first editions) during the second half of the seventeenth century, only a few (4) in the mid-sixteenth century and in the first decades of the seventeenth century.

[32] Kenneth Pennigton, "Sovereignty and Rights in Medieval and Early Modern Jurisprudence: Law and Norms without a State. Emmanuel Gonzalez Tellez," in *Rethinking the State in the Age of Globalisation: Catholic Thought and Contemporary Political Theory,* ed. Heinz-Gerhard Justenhoven, James Turner (Münster: LIT Verlag, 2003), 117-141, accessed 14 January 2013, http://classes.maxwell.syr.edu/his381/ GonzalezTellez2.html.

[33] A. van Hove, "Ludwig Engel," in *The Catholic Encyclopedia,* accessed July 22, 2013, http://www. newadvent.org/cathen/05429a.htm.

[34] Bayerische StaatsBibliothek, Digitale Bibliothek, accessed 8 February 2103, http://personen.digitale sammlungen.de/pnd/bsb00000282_00074-00.html?pos=1&suche=pn.

1673, it was reprinted in Vienna, Lyon and Frankfurt).[35] The commentaries of Henric Zoesius, a Doctor at Law and Rector of the University of Louvain, which were, for a while, official manuals in Austria, are also held in the library.

Important for their normative role as works of reference were the documentary works, the collections of papal decrees and conciliar documents, above all the decrees of the Council of Trent, which obviously could not be absent from the Episcopal library. As regards the conciliar history, the bishop had two works by Jean Cabassut, professor of Canon Law at Avignon, who was considered an authority in the field. One of them was *Notitia conciliorum Sanctae Ecclesiae* (Lyon, 1668), which he enlarged at the behest of Cardinal Grimaldi and published under the title *Notitia ecclesiastica historiarum, conciliorum et canonum invicem collatorum* (Lyon, 1680). Often revised and enlarged, it represented, for a while, under the title *Cabassutius*, an authority for the history of councils.[36] Besides this literature that was illustrative for the directions of evolution of the Catholic Church, other works that were useful, in terms of their comparative potential, were those referring to the situation in the area, the decrees of the diocesan synods from Esztergom and those of the Ruthenian provincial synods.

The interest in the local peculiarities is even more poignantly illustrated by civil law, dominated by corpora containing the legislation of the Kingdom of Hungary. They reveal the practical character of the episcopal library. The Uniate bishop needed such reference works because he had assumed the role of a representative and advocate of the Uniate clergy and parishioners.

The pragmatic character of the library is also highlighted by the homiletic literature, sermons, ascetic literature, and the literature serving pastoral needs. Bishop Pataki kept books of sermons close by, consulting them frequently, as attested by the fact that they dominated the small library in his bedroom. He kept on hand the Sunday and holidays sermons *Concionum Sylva Nova*,[37] by the Jesuit Matthias Faber, a parish priest at Neumarkt, professor at the University of Ingolstadt and then at the University of Tirnavia, as well as the funeral sermons and speeches *Centuria funebris* dedicated to parish-priests by Thomas Höfflich.[38] The author of ascetic literature he preferred was François Nepveau, the author of *Calendarium veritatis*, a Latin translation of the French original *Pensées et réflexions chrétiennes pour tous les jours de l'année* (4 vol., Paris, 1695). It was a work used in the Jesuit College from Vienna, with a wide circulation, as evidenced by its numerous editions (18 in French, the last one in 1850, and 11 in other languages).[39]

---

[35] Pennigton, "Sovereignty and Rights."

[36] *The Catholic Encyclopedia*, accessed 13 April 2013, http://catholicism.academic.ru/ 15794/Jean_Cabassut.

[37] *Concionum Sylva nova, seu Auctuarium. Cui accedunt Conciones Funebres, Nuptiales, et Strenales, posthumae* (Coloniae, 4to, tomus primus, 1695).

[38] He was a Doctor in Theology, a priest in Würzburg and principal of the St. Kilian nobiliary seminary, accessed 13 April 2013, http://www.ebookdb.org/reading/GC731D31G 66B24G32C33G660/Centuria-Funebris-In-Scenam-Vitae-Humanae-Cujus-Prologvs-Et-Epilo gvs-Mors-Actor.

[39] *The Catholic Encyclopedia*, entry compiled by Edward F. Garesché, accessed 15 March 2013, http://en.wikisource.org/wiki/Catholic_Encyclopedia_%281913%29/Francis_Nepveu; *Dictionnaire de bibliographie*

The best represented author in the homiletics section was Paolo Segneri, the Elder (1624-1694), the author of sermons and moralizing literature intended to contribute to the formation of Christian intellectuals. The presence in the library of his volumes *Quaresimale*, *Panegirici sacri*, *Il penitente instruito*, *Il cristiano instruito* and *Speculum non Fallax* indicates a predilection for this author, which is not surprising given the success he enjoyed in the area.[40]A famous preacher of his time, Segneri returned, for stylistic and linguistic models, to the ancients and the humanists, to Cicero and Boccaccio; the father of the church who was his guide was St. John Chrysostom and his favourite theologian was St. Thomas Aquinas.[41] Most of his sermons were mission, offensive sermons, which sought to change the lifestyles and moral behaviour of his readership.[42] Segneri remained a reference author for the Romanian Uniate ecclesiastical elite in the second half of the eighteenth century. The Enlightenment scholar Petru Maior translated and adapted some of the sermons included in *Quaresimale* and used Segneri as a source of inspiration for his own sermons.[43]

If, like most of the clerical libraries of the time, Pataki's library was dominated by theology, being, therefore, conservative, it nonetheless did not lack other domains like history, literature, science and arts. History books represented the bishop's second reading pole, with approximately 7% of the overall number of books, the fact that they were more expensive than theology books partly accounting for their more meager presence in the library. What distinguishes this library is the proportion of history books and the historiographical genres represented therein. For example, in the libraries of the Parisian clergy from the years 1706-1740, history books represented 32.5% of all the books, coming close to those of theology (38%); predominant was ecclesiastical history, while ancient history and the auxiliary sciences were best represented in the field of profane history.[44] Profane history prevailed in Pataki's library, as illustrated by memoirs and travelogues, in particular by regional history, or the history of influential military and political personalities in the area,[45] the history of Habsburg emperors and the Kingdom of Hungary. The bishop had an interest in recent history, especially in the events during the reign of Charles VI. History served therefore the hierarch's desire to be in touch with the latest political and military developments in the area. This interest is illustrated by the work of

---

catholique, part three, *Encyclopédie théologique* (Paris, 1856), 534.

[40] In Hungary, for instance, he was known not only among the high clergy but also among the monks and the parish priests, Orsolya Száraz, "Paolo Segneri (1624-1694) e la sua ricezione in Ungheria" (PhD Diss., University of Debrecen, 2010), accessed 13 February 2013, http://ganymedes.lib.unideb.hu.

[41] James Ford, Preface to *Twelve sermons from the Quaresimale* (London: Josepf Masters, 1857), IX-X.

[42] Jean Delumeau, *Păcatul și frica. Culpabilitatea în Occident secolele XIII-XVIII* [Sin and Fear. The Emergence of a Western Guilt Culture. 13th-18th Centuries], vol. II (Iași: Polirom, 1998), 192. Of Paolo Segneri the Elder's 53 mission sermons, 39 (73%) had admonishing or Dolorist overtones, ibid., 188.

[43] Laura Stanciu, *Iluminism central-european. Școala Ardeleană (1700-1825)* [Central-European Enlightenment. The Transylvanian School (1700-1825)] (Cluj-Napoca: Mega, 2010), 163.

[44] Thomassery, "Livres et culture cléricale," 287.

[45] We may find in the library the war memoirs of Prince Raimundo Montecuccoli, a general in the Austrian army.

Willibald Krieger on the imperial campaigns of the years 1716-1717 and the notes on the delegation that Charles VI sent to Constantinople after the Peace of Passarowitz, in 1719.[46] The latter belonged to Cornelius van den Driesch, a Jesuit from Köln who distinguished himself at the time through his oratorical and literary talent, and were written from the perspective of a participant in the events, since the author accompanied the delegation as the secretary and "historiographus" of its leader, Damian Hugo von Virmondt. The historical background of contemporary developments was provided by an anniversary history of the Roman-German emperors, *Triumphus Novem Saeculorum Imperii Romano-Germanici*, a triumphalist history with a biographical content, beginning with Charlemagne and the year 800 and going to the year 1700 (or 1725).[47]

Local history was also a subject of interest for the bishop, as proved by the volumes on Hungarian history included in the library, useful for understanding the history of the state in which the Romanians lived and the policy adopted by the Hungarian royalty towards its subjects. Chronicles and histories of the Kingdom of Hungary, in Latin and Hungarian, enriched the history domain of the library.[48] Local history was illustrated by a Transylvanian humanist author, István Szamosközy (Stephan Zamosius in the Latinizing form, 1570-1612), with a work on inscriptions in Dacia, illustrating the taste of the time for antiquarianism (*Analecta lapidum vetustorum, et nonnullarum in Dacia antiquitatum*, Padova, 1593).[49] Humanist historiography is also present through the work of architectural history *Regola delli cinque ordini d'architettura* by the Italian Giacomo Barozzi,

[46] The work is entitled *Historia Magnae legationis Caesareae quam fortunatissimus Caroli VI. Auspiciis augustum Imperantis post biennalis Belli confectionem suscepit illustrissimus et excellentissimus S. R. I. comes Damianus Hugo Virmondtius Maximi Caesaris primus nuper ad Possa-Rovicium caduceator, eiusdemquem agnus postea ad portam orator, autore Gerardo Cornelio Drieschio, Excellentissimo legato ab Epistolis, et Historia* (Vienna, 1721).

[47] Listed in the inventory of 1731 as *Triumphus novem saeculorum cum Thesib(?)* (no. 71) and in the one from 1747 as *Triumphus Novem Saeculorum Imperii Romano-Germanici,* because the full title is missing, it could be one of the two works beginning with the same title. Namely, "Triumphus novem saeculorum Imperii romano-germanici, Leopoldo Magno" (Vienna, 1700), the dissertation of Joseph Julio ab Hörmann, defended in 1700 at the Faculty of Philosophy of the University of Vienna or the work *Triumphus novem saeculorum Imperii romano-germanici Carolo Magno* based on the previous one, of the Jesuit Professor Antonio Bömer, who was "praeses" at the defense of the dissertation in 1700. The latter is an anniversary work, which celebrates Charles VI of Austria, whose reign is seen as the crowning of ten ages in which kings and emperors succeeded to the throne, beginning with Charlemagne. Each age comprises short biographies of the rulers, followed by the *memorabilia imperii*, Peter M. Daly, Richard Dimler, eds., *Corpum Librorum Emblematum. The Jesuit Series: Part One*, A-D (McGill-Queen's University Press, 1997), 63-65.

[48] Among the history works, we have identified *De Sacrae Coronae Regni Hungariae* of the Lutheran noble Pétér Révai (1568-1622). Other titles suggesting works on the history of Hungary are *Magna Hungaria* and Grateleni, *Chronica Hungariae* (which I have not identified). Another two works are wrongly listed among Bishop Pataki's books, given that they appeared only after his death. These are the works of the Jesuit professor from Tirnavia, Samuel Timon, *Epitome chronologica rerum Hungaricarum* (Casovia, 1734) and *Imago Hungariae* (this is the title in the inventory). The latter book may be *Imago antiquae Hungariae: repraesentans terra, adventus et res gestas gentis hunnicae* (Cassovia, 1733) or *Imago novae Hungariae, repraesentans regna, provincias, Banatus et comitatus ditionis hungaricae Historico gene restrictim perscripta* (Cassovia, 1734). It must have belonged to the library of Pataki's successor, bishop Inochentie Micu-Klein.

[49] For the significance of the presence of this book in the episcopal library, see also Ioan Chindriş, *Cultură şi societate în contextul Şcolii Ardelene* [Culture and Society in the Context of the Transylvanian School] (Cluj-Napoca: Cartimpex, 2001), 233.

known as Da Vignola.[50] The author, an artist who worked with Michelangelo, designed, among other things, Chiesa del Gesù in Rome, the mother-church of the Jesuit Order, which became a model for seventeenth-century Baroque church facades. His work was widely published and disseminated in the centuries following its publication. It was also to the humanist circles that the author of the sole ecclesiastical history work in the episcopal library belonged: written in the genre of biographies cultivated at that time, illustrating that this was *Vitae Pontificium* by Bartolomeo Platina (Sacchi).

The library also hosts a work of world history, useful for integrating local history within a broader historiographical horizon, that of the Jesuit Antonio Foresti, *Del Mappamondo Storico* (4 vols, Parma, 1690-1694). With a traditional outlook on history, written from the perspective of sacred history, meant to show God's intervention in human affairs, the glory of God on earth, the work enjoyed great success in Europe. The appetite of the public at that time for such a history was proved by its being translated into German and its being reedited, in a version augmented by other authors, in seven volumes (Venice, 1715-1716).[51] History books, therefore, were meant to entertain, inform, and provide examples. Some books were new, appearing in the first three decades of the eighteenth century and the acquisitions were in tune with the printing production of history books, which gradually increased in the first half of the century.[52]

In addition to these two major poles of reading, theology and history, the bishop's bookish universe also comprised other domains: above all, books of grammar, rhetoric and Aristotelian philosophy, which reflected the formative methods and ideals of the Jesuit colleges. The art of persuasion was the core of Jesuit education, and its target was "eloquentia perfecta," which was supposed to form a way of life, to help students' combine virtue with letters so as to acquire true Christian wisdom.[53] The bishop's library included the grammar of the Jesuit Manuel Alvarez (*Principia seu rudimenta grammatices ex Institutionibus Emmanuelis Alvarez)* and one of the most widespread rhetorical manuals in Jesuit schools, *De arta retorica* by the Spanish Jesuit Cipriano Suarez.[54] These textbooks were used in teaching at the gymnasium in Blaj in the second half of the century.[55] The Aristotelian philosophy taught in Jesuit colleges, according to *Ratio Studiorum*, was

[50] Pataki's library includes a translation into German.

[51] Edoardo Tortarolo, "Italian Historical Writing, 1680-1800," in *The Oxford History of Historical Writing: 1400-1800*, vol. 3, ed. José Rabasa et al. (Oxford: Oxford University Press, 2012), 373. The public success of the book is signalled at the local level by its presence in the library of a political man and scholar from Wallachia, trained at the University of Padua, Constantin Cantacuzino, who was a contemporary of Bishop Pataki's, Dima Drăgan, *Biblioteca unui umanist*, 21, 114.

[52] For the history books published in the printing press of the University of Tirnavia, see Erika Jurikova, "Signification of Latin Book Production of Academic Press of University of Trnava for Development of Science in the Territory of Today's Slovakia," in *Acta Conventus neo-Latini Upsaliensis*, ed. Alejandro Coroleu et al. (Leiden: Brill, 2012), 518.

[53] Gabriel Codina, "The 'Modus Parisiensis'," in *The Jesuit Ratio Studiorum of 1599: 400th Anniversary Perspectives*, ed. Vincent J. Duminuco (Fordham: Fordham University Press, 2000), 40.

[54] Cristea, "Neam, tradiţie şi cultură," 38.

[55] Stanciu, *Iluminism central-european*, 55.

also found in the Episcopal library: *Triennium Philosophicum* (2 vols, 1674) by Andreas Semery. The book comprises the three-year course of logic, physics and metaphysics taught by the author at the Collegium Romanum between 1668 and 1674. His lectures were based explicitly on the works of Aristotle *De anima*, *De Coelo*, *De Generatione et corruptione*, their theme being one that preoccupied the Jesuit philosophers of the seventeenth century, namely, what is possible or impossible.[56]

In conclusion, it can be said that the library illustrated the formative itineraries of Bishop Pataki (it included the books of his professors or of those who, at a certain point, taught at the education institutions he had attended) and the need for information he experienced as a Catholic missionary priest and as a bishop. This was a traditional library, considering the large proportion of theology works and of works published in Latin.[57] It largely represents a library of textbooks, mostly Jesuit, which may be explained by the widely spread type of such genre in that period,[58] and because of the practical needs in the diocese – for instruction, for establishing a book fund for the envisaged schools.

In its overwhelming proportion containing books by professors who belonged to the Orders of the Catholic Church (Jesuits, Franciscans, Dominicans, Cistercians, Oratorians), the library familiarizes the reader with the ideas of the Counter-Reformation, with a militant, polemical Catholicism. The large number of works of canon law illustrates the functionality of this library for a bishop who had to organize a diocese that was at the outset of its existence. Such literature could help the bishop in defining the identity of the Uniate Church in relation to the Catholic Church. Though small in number, the works referring to the relations between the Orthodox and the Catholic Churches, or to the rite and liturgy of the Eastern Church illustrate the bishop's interest in the Eastern dimension of the church he pastored.

The library reveals that through his intellectual magnitude, the Uniate bishop distinguished and distanced himself from his clergy, who were prevalently illiterate, and came closer to the educated high Catholic clergy from Transylvania. However, having his clergy in mind, he also gave the library a didactic purpose. Through its manuals, the renowned books that circulated in the Catholic world and were tested in colleges and universities, the library provided an important book fund for the formation of the future priests or for the documentation of the Uniate ecclesiastical elite, which was still forming in the first decades of the eighteenth century.

---

[56] John P. Doyle, "Wrestling with a Wraith. André Semery S.J. (1630-1717) on Aristotle's Goat-Stag and Knowing the Unknowable," in *The Impact of Aristotelianism on Modern Philosophy*, ed. Ricardo Pozzo [Studies in Philosophy and the History of Philosophy 39] (The Catholic University of America Press, 2004), 89-91. For the analysis of Semery's philosophy included in the lectures published then in *Triennium*, see ibid., 91-112.

[57] For instance, of the 178 books recorded in the inventories of 1731, 117 were in Latin (65.73%).

[58] See, in this sense, the considerations for the French space of Alison Forrestal, *Fathers, Pastors and Kings. Visions of Episcopacy in Seventeenth Century France* (Manchester: Manchester University Press, 2004), 13.

Bücher als Thermometer der gesellschaftlichen und wirtschaftlichen Veränderungen (16.-18. Jh.)*

Attila Verók

Da die Vererbung des allgemeinen Wissens und des kulturellen Erbes in Europa seit der Antike vorwiegend in schriftlicher Form geschieht, lohnt es sich in den meisten Fällen, die verschiedenen wissenschaftlichen Diskussionsthemen auch von der Seite der Buch-, Bibliotheks- und Lesegeschichte zu untersuchen. Diese Behauptung gilt auch für die im Rahmen des Tagungsbandes fokussierten Forschungsthemen wie Wirtschaft, Gesellschaft, Landschaft, Bevölkerung und Konsum. Je näher die bezügliche Epoche zu unserer Zeit liegt, desto mehr und relevanter kann man sich zu den betroffenen Fragen mit Hilfe der Bücher äußern.

Als Forschungsobjekt dient in dieser Studie die Buchkultur der deutschsprachigen Bevölkerung Siebenbürgens in der frühen Neuzeit. Auf Grund ihrer Bücherverzeichnisse und rekonstruierten Büchersammlungen versuche ich einige mögliche neue Aspekte zu den genannten Problemfeldern aufzuwerfen. Die modernen geistigen Strömungen vermittelnden Bücher können nämlich als zuverlässiges Thermometer der gesellschaftlichen und wirtschaftlichen Veränderungen jeder Zeit betrachtet werden. Im Fall der Siebenbürger Sachsen sind die buchgeschichtlichen Quellen bis 1750 in großem Maße erschlossen und warten auf eine gezielte Analyse bzw. Auswertung.[1]

An dieser Stelle gebe ich dem Themenkreis eine mögliche Annäherung, wo ich vor allem die Bücher mit Bezug auf die Umwelt, Wirtschaft, Landschaft und Landwirtschaft bzw. – aus dem Grunde meiner persönlichen Neigung zu Weinbau und Weinkunde

---

* Die Erstellung dieser Studie wurde im Rahmen des EU-Projekts TÁMOP-4.2.2.C-11/1/KONV-2012-0008 *IKT a tudás és tanulás világában – humán teljesítménytechnológiai (Human Performance Technology) kutatások és képzésfejlesztés* [Infokommunikationstechnologien in der Welt des Wissens und des Lernens – Human Performance Technology-Forschungen und Bildungsentwicklung]. Das Projekt wurde von der Europäischen Union finanziert und dem Europäischen Sozialfund cofinanziert.

[1] Sämtliche, vor 2003 bekannten buchgeschichtlichen Quellen der Sachsen Siebenbürgens liegen schon in Form eines Katalogs vor: *Lesestoffe der Siebenbürger Sachsen (1575-1750)* I-II. Herausgegeben von István Monok, Péter Ötvös, Attila Verók; Redaktion István Monok, Attila Verók; einleitende Studie von Attila Verók; übersetzt von Péter Ötvös, Attila Verók; Register von Attila Verók (Budapest: Országos Széchényi Könyvtár, 2004) [Adattár XVI–XVIII. századi szellemi mozgalmaink történetéhez = Materialien zur Geschichte der Geistesströmungen des 16.-18. Jahrhunderts in Ungarn; 16/4.1-4.2 – Erdélyi könyvesházak = Bibliotheken in Siebenbürgen; IV/1-2] (im weiteren Adattár 16/4). In den letzten zehn Jahren setzten sich die Forschungen vor und kamen neue Angaben bzw. Bücherlisten aus der genannten Zeitspanne ans Tageslicht. Sie wurden an verschiedenen Stellen veröffentlicht. Hier nenne ich nur einen Aufsatz, in dem es um den wichtigsten siebenbürgisch-sächsischen buchgeschichtlichen Fund der letzten Jahrzehnten geht: Attila Verók, „A gyógyítás szolgálatában a Barcaságtól Frankóniáig. Paul Francisci orvosi könyvtárának jegyzéke a 18. század elejéről" [Im Dienst der Heilkunde von Burzenland bis Franken. Verzeichnis der Medizinbibliothek Paul Franciscis vom Anfang des 18. Jahrhunderts], *Kaleidoscope. Művelődés-, tudomány- és orvostörténeti folyóirat*, online kiadvány [Kaleidoscope. Zeitschrift für Kultur-, Wissenschafts- und Medizingeschichte, online Ausgabe] 3, 5 (2012): 307-320, http://www.kaleidoscopehistory.hu/index.php?subpage=cikk&cikkid=119.

– Bücher mit Weinbaukenntnissen hervorhebe – mit der Anmerkung, dass auch die anderen Kategorien wie Kenntnisse zu Bevölkerung, Gesellschaft und Konsum in den siebenbürgisch-sächsischen Büchersammlungen präsent sind. Zu allen genannten Gattungen werden ausschließlich einige Beispiele erwähnt, damit im Text die Fußnoten nicht überquellen. Die Einzel- und Feinheiten können anhand der unten aufgelisteten Quellenausgaben einfach kontrolliert und wesentlich ergänzt werden. Hier biete ich dem Leser nur eine Kostprobe an. Was wichtig wäre, im Kreis der Historiker aller Art bekannt zu geben, dass es im allgemeinen lohnen würde, auch die buchgeschichtlichen Quellen zum Prozeß der Geschichtsforschung hinzuziehen. Sie können nämlich den unterschiedlichen Themen neue interessante Daten und Fakten sichern, im idealen Fall auch bei der Erkennung neuer Zusammenhänge Hilfe leisten oder neue mögliche Interpretationswege zeigen. Dies könnte auch in den Disziplinen Gesellschafts- und Wirtschaftsgeschichte der Fall sein, aber die von den Buchforschern erschlossenen Angaben sollten die Fachleute der oben genannten Wissenschaftsgebiete sinnvoll anwenden. Wir, Buchforscher haben vor, neuartige, bis jetzt gar nicht bekannten, grundlegenden Daten aus den von den Historikern nicht benutzten Quellen ans Tageslicht zu bringen und weiteren Forschungszwecken zur Verfügung zu stellen.[2]

Im Folgenden beschäftige ich mich mit unterschiedlichen Quellentypen, die einem bei der Untersuchung des im Titel angegebenen Themas etwas Konkretes und Nützliches vermitteln können. Es handelt sich hier erstens um die in den Nachlassinventaren der verstorbenen Bürger aufbewahrten Bücherverzeichnisse, die die Mehrheit der buchgeschichtlichen Quellen ausmachen, zweitens um die in weiten Kreisen benutzten, aber kaum erhalten gebliebenen Kalender, drittens um die alten Bücher, die uns heute noch sowohl in Privat- als auch in Institutionssammlungen zur Verfügung stehen und die sichersten Kenntnisse zur persönlichen Benutzung der Drucke dank der Einträge geben.

Massenquellen: die Bücherverzeichnisse

In den siebenbürgisch-sächsischen Bücherverzeichnissen befinden sich Titel-aufnahmen zahlreicher Drucke, die allgemeine Kenntnisse zu den oben genannten Segmenten des alltäglichen Lebens enthalten. Sie sind beispielsweise wie folgt: *Haustaffel*[3] mit nützlichen Ratschlägen, *Libri de re rustica*,[4] *Temperatur Büchl*[5] oder *Büchlein*[6] oder das merk-

[2] Aus diesem Grund habe ich beispielsweise die folgende Studie zur weiteren Anwendung im Bereich historische Forschung bewusst und gezielt veröffentlicht: Attila Verók, „Die erste historische Fachbibliothek im Donau-Karpatenraum? Martin Schmeizel und seine Büchersammlung", *Zeitschrift für Siebenbürgische Landeskunde* 35, 2 (2012): 134-149.

[3] Vgl. z.B. Adattár 16/4, 15. – Die Titelangabe ist zu allgemein, kann also nicht identifiziert werden.

[4] Vgl. z.B. ebenda, 28-29. – Die Titelangabe ist zu allgemein, kann also nicht identifiziert werden, obwohl wahrscheinlich ist, dass in den meisten Fällen das mehrmals herausgegebene Werk von Lucius Iunius Columella ist.

[5] Vgl. z.B. ebenda, 49. – Die Titelangabe ist zu allgemein, kann also das Werk nicht identifiziert werden.

[6] Vgl. z.B. ebenda, 77. – Die Titelangabe ist zu allgemein, kann also das Werk nicht identifiziert werden.

würdige Werk *Meteorologia* von Johann Garcerus.[7] In den Inventaren tauchen Bücher unter den Titeln *Distilierbuch*,[8] *Thierbuch*,[9] *Bericht von der Erdbebung*, *Ursprung und Bedeutung* von Jacob Schnitzler[10] bzw. verschiedene Handbücher und Lexika, die gleichfalls relevante Wissenswerte im Thema hätten beinhalten können. Nützliche Kenntnisse für die Landwirtschaft konnten die sächsischen Ackerbauern auch aus der landwirtschaftlichen Beschreibung unter dem Titel *Ein Buch vom Feldtbau* bekommen.[11] Die Fragen der Aufgaben im Haushalt und um das Haus werden in den Drucken wie *Oeconomia oder Haußbuch* praktisch behandelt.[12] Mit ganz konkreten Vorschlägen und Lösungen rückten die Autoren der so genannten *Haußhaltungsbücher* heraus,[13] die Probleme des alltäglichen Lebens durch ihre nützlichen Ratschläge zu mildern versuchten. Neben den im ganzen Europa allgemein benutzten Dokumenten von ähnlicher Thematik findet man auch ein Werk, das sich ausgesprochen an die siebenbürgischen Verhältnisse anpasst: *Sächsisches hand und haus Wirtschafts buch.*[14] Das Werk vermittelt dem Niveau der Zeit entsprechende Kenntnisse in Bezug auf jedes Segment des Lebens – selbstverständlich mit Topoi, Gemeinplätzen und sogar als zeitwidrig geltenden Informationen gewürzt, aber trotzdem auf verwendbare Art. Eine gleiche Funktion erfüllte zum Beispiel auch das *Cronstadtische Handbuch.*[15] Es hat aber neben den praktischen Anmerkungen auch die theoretischen Kenntnisse enthalten.

Am Ende der Aufzählung von Werken mit Wirtschafts- und Landschaftsthemen möchte ich einen Druck hervorheben, der das spezielle Interesse der Sachsen für den Weinbau glänzend beweist. Der Verfasser der Arbeit mit dem Titel *Kurtze Beschreibung und Unterrichte des Wein-baues* heißt Johann Paul Knoll, der im Untertitel seines 1711 in Dresden herausgegebenen Buches viel verspricht:

> „Allen, so mit dergleichen zu thun, besitzen, ümgehen, sich gebrauchen und erhalten, zu einem sonderbahren Nutzen; Nebst einem Offenhertzigen Wein-Artzt, Oder: Allerhand bewährten Mitteln, wie der Wein von der Kelter an sorgfältig zu warten, beständig gut zu erhalten [...]; Allen Haus-Wirthen mitgetheilet und mit einer Baumschule vermehret."[16]

Drucke mit gesellschaftlichem Inhalt (Politik, Bevölkerung, Tradition und Lebensweise anderer Völker usw.) tauchen öfters in den Titellisten der Bücherverzeichnisse auf. Eine kleine Auswahl kann überzeugend zeigen, dass das siebenbürgisch-sächsische Bürgertum sich auch für diese Wissensgebiete interessierte und viele Personen beschäftigten sich außer der Amtsbeamten mit gesellschaftlichen Fragen. In den Listen kommen

[7] Vgl. z.B. ebenda, 448. – In diesem Fall geht es um die Ausgabe des Jahres 1568 aus Wittenberg.
[8] Vgl. z.B. ebenda, 180. – Die Titelangabe ist zu allgemein, kann also das Werk nicht identifiziert werden.
[9] Vgl. z.B. ebenda, 544. – Die Titelangabe ist zu allgemein, kann also das Werk nicht identifiziert werden.
[10] Vgl. z.B. ebenda, 807. – Das genannte Exemplar erschien 1681 in Hermannstadt.
[11] Vgl. z.B. ebenda, 125. – Die Titelangabe ist zu allgemein, kann also nicht identifiziert werden.
[12] Vgl. z.B. ebenda, 49. – Die Titelangabe ist zu allgemein, kann also nicht identifiziert werden.
[13] Vgl. z.B. ebenda, 111. – Der Autor des erwähnten Exemplars heißt Nicolaus Herrmann.
[14] Vgl. ebenda, 519.
[15] Vgl. z.B. ebenda, 271. – Der Titel lautet anderswo: *Kronstädter Handbuch*. Nähere Angaben stehen der Identifizierung zur Zeit leider nicht zur Verfügung.
[16] Vgl. Adattár 16/4, 514.

Bücher wie folgt vor: *Der Politische wander mann*,[17] *Hierarchia Politica* von Georg Albrecht,[18] *Teutscher Fürsten-Staat* des Ludwig von Seckendorff,[19] die zahlreichen einschlägigen Werke von Johann Hübner,[20] die verschiedenen *Regentenbücher* oder *Regenten-Spiegel*,[21] Kommentare zum Beispiel über *Das Magnificat*[22] oder Völkerbeschreibungen beispielsweise über die Belgier, Türken, Franzosen, Araber und andere Ethnien der damals entdeckten geographischen Gebiete.[23] Die Reihe könnte fast ins Unendliche fortgeführt werden, weil die Palette dieser Gattungen so weitverzweigt ist. Es hat keinen Sinn, weitere Beispiele zu nennen, die Tatsache der Existenz von Büchern solcher Art ist auch daraus zu entnehmen.

Aus dem oben skizzierten kleinen Panorama ist ersichtlich, dass die sächsiche Bevölkerung Siebenbürgens – selbst wenn nicht auf dem höchsten Niveau der Wissenschaftlichkeit – mit den grundlegenden Wissenselementen der Wirtschaft, Landwirtschaft, darunter auch denen des Weinbaus, ferner mit den allgemeinen europäischen gesellschaftlichen Verhältnissen der Zeit im Klaren waren und aus den auf Grund zeitgenössischer Drucke erworbenen Kenntnissen vermutlich auch im Alltagsleben Nutzen ziehen bzw. eine teilweise durch Bücher vermittelte Weltanschauung formen konnte. Ich möchte aber jeden in Verbindung mit den vorgestellten Dokumenten zur Vorsicht ermahnen. In den anhand der Bücherverzeichnisse sich herauskristallisierenden sächsischen Lesestoffen in der frühen Neuzeit tauchen die Kenntnisse für Wirtschaft, Landschaft, Landwirtschaft (speziell Weinbau) und Gesellschaft auf den Blättern der Inventare nur in beschränktem Maße im Vergleich zu den theologischen und erbauungsliterarischen Werke auf. Obwohl die genannten, praktisches (land)wirtschaftliches Wissen enthaltenden Drucke für Hauswirtinnen im Kreis der damaligen Bevölkerung populär sein konnten, sind von diesen Büchern für heute kaum etwas erhalten geblieben. Der Grund dafür kann vielleicht in Erscheinung des durch die häufige Benutzung verursachten „Zerlesens" gesucht werden. Das aus kleinen Handbüchern und Taschenbüchern zu erhaltende Kenntnisse verbreitete praktische Wissen kann angenommen werden, ist aber heutzutage kaum nachzuweisen.

Eine Sache soll noch in Verbindung mit den Bücherverzeichnissen geklärt werden. Die wortkargen Titelaufnahmen machen die Identifizierung der Bücher in vielen Fällen unmöglich, also kann sein, dass die thematischen Größenordnungen sich damals anders gestalteten, als wir es heute beurteilen können. Und ob der geistige Inhalt der Bücher durch die Bevölkerung wirklich rezipiert worden war, ist immer eine Frage. Über die Wirkung der geistigen Strömungen kann man sich erst nach dem wirklichen

[17] Vgl. z.B. ebenda, 146.
[18] Vgl. z.B. ebenda, 109.
[19] Ebenda.
[20] Vgl. z.B. ebenda, 127.
[21] Vgl. z.B. ebenda, 56 oder 796.
[22] Vgl. z.B. ebenda, 211.
[23] Vgl. z.B. ebenda, 220.

Auffinden der Bücher sachlich äußern. Die handschriftlichen Einträge und andere Zeichen der Benutzung helfen uns dabei.

Eine beliebte Gattung: die Kalender

Im Fall der Kalender muss man mit einem ähnlichen Phänomen rechnen, als es vorher schon erwähnt wurde. Wenn man so etwas überhaupt sagen darf, dann waren die jährlich erschienenen Kalender der Abnutzung umso mehr ausgesetzt als ihre dickeren „Druckkamaraden". Die nur für eine zeitweilige Existenz verurteilte Kalender wurden nämlich in jedes Jahr herausgeschmissen, verbrannt oder als Verpackungsmaterial gebraucht, also überlebten sie die Jahrhunderte sehr selten. Man kennt deswegen so wenig von diesen Büchergattungen, obwohl es wohl bekannt ist, dass sie in der frühen Neuzeit massenweise benutzt worden sind. Ihre jährliche Veröffentlichung ist daher zur sicheren Einnahmequelle der Drucker geworden.

Die zweiteilige Struktur der Kalender formte sich verhältnismäßig früh: der eigentliche Kalenderteil und der aus der Wahrsagung, den allgemeinen belehrenden und unterhaltsamen Lesestoffen bestehende Teil. An den Kalenderteil wurden oft auch Kalendergedichte angehängt, die die wichtigsten Wissenswerten für die zu verrichtenden (land)wirtschaftlichen Arbeiten, sogar ab und zu Ratschläge für Gesundheit und Ernährung zusammenfassten. Diese Informationen wurden durch Wettervorhersagen ergänzt bzw. da wurde angegeben, für welche Arbeitstätigkeiten die einzelnen Tage geeignet waren. Dank dessen stößt man öfter auf wirtschaftliche und landwirtschaftliche kurze Erörterungen und einige Male speziell auch auf Anmerkungen mit Bezug auf Weinbau und Weinkunde. Kriege als gesellschaftliche Ereignisse kamen auch manchmal auf den Blättern zu Erwähnung.

Die Kalender zählten zu den billigsten Druckprodukten, die vorwiegend auf Land- und Wochenmärkten verkauft wurden. Da sie oft als ausschließliche Lesestoffe des Stadtbürgers, des Kleinadeligen und des gelernteren Bauern galten, spielten sie in der Verbreitung der (land)wirtschaftlichen – und gesellschaftlichen – Kenntnisse eine besonders große Rolle, dadurch, dass sie beispielsweise auch Ratschläge für landwirtschaftliche Tätigkeiten, Epidemien, Geburt, Hygiene, Ernährung und Heilung bekannt gaben. Unter den nützlichen Notizen tauchen manchmal auch Textstellen auf, in denen es um die schädlichen oder heilsamen Wirkungen des Weines auf den menschlichen Organismus geht.

Von den ungarländischen Kalendern wurde schon viel und von vielen geschrieben, demgegenüber beschäftigte sich die ungarische Forschung mit den siebenbürgisch-sächsischen Kalendern sehr wenig. Die deutschsprachige Bevölkerung Siebenbürgens nutzte vor allem Kalender, die in den Druckereien zu Hermannstadt und Kronstadt herausgegeben wurden. Da die Druckleistung beider Städte dank der rumänischen Forschung ziemlich gründlich dokumentiert ist, steht uns ein zuverlässiges Gesamtbild über die einst hergestellten Kalendern zur Verfügung.[24] Ohne auf die Einzelheiten einzugehen, möchte

---

[24] Im Fall von Hermannstadt sind wir in günstiger Lage, weil uns der Katalog der in der Stadt gedruckten

ich einige Beispiele herausgreifen, die überzeugend bestätigen, was oben in Verbindung mit Umwelt, Wirtschaft, Landwirtschaft, Weinbau und gesellschaftsbezogenen Kenntnissen gesagt wurden.

In dem 1644 in Hermannstadt herausgegebenen *Tag-Büchel, new vnd alt Allmanach* konnte man zum Beispiel *Von Fruchtbarkeit des Getreydes*, *Vom Weinwachs*, *Von bequeme Bestellung der Gartenfrüchte* bzw. *Von Krieg und Unfried* lesen.[25] Ebenso im Neuen und Alten Allmanach wurde 1675 *Vom Kriegs-Wesen*, *Von Seuchen und Krankheiten*, *Von den Feld-Früchten* geschrieben und dazu gehörte noch eine *Chronica Unterschiedlicher Historien so in Ungern und Siebenbürgen geschehen.*[26] Vom Anfang an standen die Zeitpunkte und Orte der Jahresmärkte in Siebenbürgen auf den Kalenderblättern, was sehr wichtig für das richtige Funktionieren des wirtschaftlichen Lebens des Landes war. Seit dem ersten Drittel des 18. Jahrhunderts berichteten die Kalender auch über die Ordnung der ungarischen und siebenbürgischen Posten.[27] Im Neuen und Alten Calender aus dem Jahre 1732 erfuhr man von einem *Kurtzen Bericht Unterschiedlicher merckwürdiger Begebenheiten welche Theils 1730 Theils 1731 durch die Zeitungen bekant gemacht worden*, was bedeutet, dass die wirtschaftlichen und gesellschaftlichen Neuheiten der vorherigen Jahre gesammelt und für das gemeine Volk weitererzählt wurde.[28] Ab diesem Zeitpunkt ist diese Methode in den siebenbürgischen Kalendern allgemein geworden. Der 1771 ebenfalls in der sächsischen Hauptstadt gedruckte und in zwei Varianten erschienene *Neuer Verbesserter und Alter Calender* kündete *Neu vermehrte und verbesserte Bauern-Practica* im voraus.[29] Gleiche Sachen findet man auch in der Ausgabe aus dem Jahre 1774.[30] Einen interessanten Beitrag enthält der 1801 bei Martin Hochmeister in Hermannstadt gedruckte *Siebenbürgischer neuer und alter Volkskalender*, der eine kleine Volksliedsammlung unter anderen aus den bei den landwirtschaftlichen Arbeiten oder bei der Weinlese zu singenden Liedern veröffentlicht.[31] Auch in den öfters vorkommenden, von der täglichen Heilung (meist vom Aderlass) handelnden Teilen erscheinen gelegentlich neben anderen natürlichen Heilmitteln auch die Trauben und der Wein als verbindliche Zubehöre der volkstümlichen Heilmethoden. (Die Kronstädter Kalender verfügten über einen ähnlichen Charakter und eine gleiche Thematik, deshalb wird hier durch wei-

---

Kalender zur Verfügung steht (vgl. Mircea Avram, *Calendarele sibiene în limba germană (Secolele XVII-XX)* [Die Deutsche Kalender von Hermannstadt (17.-20. Jh.)] (Sibiu: Biblioteca „Astra", 1979) (im weiteren Avram, *Calendarele*]. Zu Kronstadt nenne ich den Katalog von Julius Gross, *Kronstädter Drucke 1535–1886. Ein Beitrag zur Kulturgeschichte Kronstadts* (Kronstadt: Druck von Joh. Gött & Sohn Heinr., 1886). Nützliche Angaben kann man auch dem Katalog *Tipărituri româneşti 1539-1750 existente la Braşov. Catalog* [Rumänische bestehende Drucke in Braşov 1539-1750. Katalog] (Braşov: Biblioteca Judeţeană Braşov, 1980) entnehmen.

[25] Avram, *Calendarele*, 24 [Nr. 7] und *Régi magyarországi nyomtatványok* [Alte ungarländische Drucke] *1636-1655* (Budapest: Akadémiai Kiadó, 2000), 369-370 [Nr. 2078].

[26] Avram, *Calendarele*, 28 [Nr. 18].

[27] Vgl. ebenda, 37 [Nr. 38] und von hier stets weiter in der ganzen Epoche.

[28] Ebenda, 39 [Nr. 43].

[29] Ebenda, 56-57 [Nr. 76-77].

[30] Ebenda, 58 [Nr. 80].

[31] Ebenda, 77 [Nr. 119].

tere Auflistung die Anzahl der Beispiele nicht erhöht. Wer sich im Thema besser vertiefen will, kann die in der Fußnote Nr. 25 angegebenen Grundlagenkataloge noch eingehender untersuchen.)

Obwohl die genannten kurzen Texte in manchen Fällen gar nicht auf dem Laufenden waren, sondern altmodische und/oder unzuverlässige Kenntnisse vermittelten, beeinflussten das geistige Horizont der siebenbürgisch-sächsischen Bürgertums in puncto Wirtschaft und Gesellschaft in großem Maße, weil sie im Gegensatz zu anderen Druckprodukten der Zeit überall präsent und benutzt waren. Es ist schade, dass gerade diese kulturgeschichtlichen Quellen nur in so kleiner Zahl überliefert wurden, was die Forschung und Auswertung dieser einstigen Massenwaren ziemlich erschwert.

Rekonstruierte Lesestoffe heutzutage

Man hat Glück, weil eine große Menge Bücher aus den Privatbüchersammlungen der sächsischen Bürger heute noch zugänglich sind. Sie befinden sich vorwiegend in großen Institutionsbibliotheken wie zum Beispiel in der Bibliothek des Brukenthalmuseums[32] oder des Teutsch-Hauses in Hermannstadt, in der Bibliothek der Honterusgemeinde oder des Staatsarchivs zu Kronstadt,[33] in der Bibliothek des Gymnasiums zu Mediasch bzw. in anderen kleineren Sammlungen, die heute noch in Verwaltung der Evangelischen Kirche oder des rumänischen Staates liegen. Sie befinden sich sehr verstreut und bedürften mindestens eine virtuelle Vereinigung einiger Kataloge oder einer Datenbank.

Wie gesagt, diese großen Sammlungen kamen in großem Maße aus kleinen Bibliotheken von Privatbürgern zustande. Einer organisierten und nur auf die betroffene

[32] Zur Geschichte, Gestaltung und Zusammensetzung des Bibliothekbestandes siehe u.a. Friedrich Müller, „Die Incunabeln der Hermannstädter "Kapellenbibliothek"", *Archiv des Vereins für Siebenbürgische Landeskunde* 14 (1877): 293-358, 489-543; Friedrich Teutsch, „Geschichte des ev. Gymnasiums A. B. in Hermannstadt", *Archiv des Vereins für Siebenbürgische Landeskunde* 17 (1882): 1-132, hier 40-41 und 76-77; Carl sen. Albrich, *Geschichte des ev. Gymnasiums A. B. in Hermannstadt*. Programm des evangel. Gymnasiums A. B. und der damit verbundenen Realschule, sowie der evangel. Elementarschule A. B. zu Hermannstadt für das Schuljahr 1895/96, 1896, 12-13, 146-148; *Katalog des Baron Brukenthalischen Museums in Hermannstadt*, Bde 1-3 (Hermannstadt, 1896-1900); Attila Verók, *„a nagyszebeni evangélikus kollégium könyvtára"* szócikk [Stichwort „Bibliothek des Hermannstädter evangelischen Kollegiums"], in *Magyar művelődéstörténeti lexikon VIII. Középkor és kora újkor. Műhely – Paleográfia* [Lexikon für Kulturgeschichte Ungarns. Bd. VIII. Mittelalter und frühe Neuzeit. Atelier – Paläographie], Hg. Kőszeghy Péter, Tamás Zsuzsanna (Budapest: Balassi, 2008), 101 (mit weiterführender Literatur).

[33] Der stattliche Bestand der Kronstädter evangelischen Gymnasialbibliothek wurde während und nach dem Zweiten Weltkrieg zwischen der Bibliothek der Honterusgemeinde, d.h. der deutschen evangelischen Kirche (Schwarze Kirche) und dem Staatsarchiv zu Kronstadt geteilt. Mehr zum Prozess siehe Thomas Şindilariu, „Kriegsverluste, Wiederaufbau und Enteignung. Zur Archivgeschichte der Honterusgemeinde in Kronstadt ab 1944", *Zeitschrift für Siebenbürgische Landeskunde* 28, 1 (2005): 40-56. Zur Geschichte, Gestaltung und Zusammensetzung des einheitlichen Bibliothekbestandes siehe u.a. Julius Gross, *Katalog der von der Kronstädter Gymnasialbibliothek bei der 400jährigen Luther-Feier in Kronstadt ausgestellten Druckwerke aus dem Reformationszeitalter* (Kronstadt, 1883); Ders., „Zur ältesten Geschichte der Kronstädter Gymnasialbibliothek", *Archiv des Vereins für Siebenbürgische Landeskunde* 22 (1887): 591-708; Attila Verók, *„a brassói evangélikus kollégium könyvtára"* szócikk [Stichwort „Bibliothek des Kronstädter evangelischen Kollegiums"], in *Magyar művelődéstörténeti lexikon I. Középkor és kora újkor. Aachen – Bylica* [Lexikon für Kulturgeschichte Ungarns. Bd. I. Mittelalter und frühe Neuzeit. Aachen – Bylica], Hg. Kőszeghy Péter, Tamás Zsuzsanna (Budapest: Balassi, 2003), 443 (mit weiterführender Literatur).

Institutionsbibliothek spezialisierten Bücheranschaffungstätigkeit im 16.-18. Jahrhundert kann man sehr selten auf die Spur kommen. Der organisierte Buchhandel wurde erst in der ersten Hälfte des 19. Jahrhunderts in Siebenbürgen ausgebaut. Das bedeutet, dass die untersuchten Bücher zuerst von Privatpersonen oder Personengruppen (*et amicorum*-Gruppen) und erst danach von der breiteren, lesefähigen Bevölkerung benutzt wurden, als die Drucke in den Bibliotheksbestände einzelner Institutionen gerieten. Die in den Drucken enthaltenden Kenntnisse beeinflussten also in der ersten Runde das geistige Horizont des Privatmenschen und in der zweiten Runde die Weltanschauung einer breiteren Gesellschaftsgruppe – selbstverständlich vermittelt von Privatpersonen, die die Texte gelesen haben. In den öffentlichen oder teilweise öffentlichen Bibliotheken waren nämlich die Bücher für mehr Leute zugänglich als in den Privatsammlungen.

Da ich seit vielen Jahren in historischen Bücherbeständen in Kronstadt Rekonstruktionen durchführe, formuliere meine Erfahrungen und Eindrücke auf Grund der Sammlung der Kronstädter Gymnasialbibliothek – in der Hoffnung, dass die Behauptungen allgemein auch für die anderen siebenbürgisch-sächsischen Institutionsbibliotheken gelten. Sie stellte die zweitgrößte und zweitbedeutendste Büchersammlung des Donau-Karpatenraumes nach der *Bibliotheca Corviniana* des Königs Matthias I. (1458-1490) bis zum dritten Drittel des 18. Jahrhunderts dar. Daraus folgt, dass sie wesentlich mehr thematisch passende Drucke in Besitz hatte, als man bei den bürgerlichen Bücherverzeichnissen registrieren konnte. Die Bibliothek hatte nämlich einen humanistisch geprägten Sammelbereich und einen universellen Charakter, also waren mindestens die Grundlagenwerke der einzelnen Wissenschaftsgebiete da vorhanden und für die Leser zugänglich.

Ohne Aufzählung der zahlreichen Bücher – hier könnten nämlich Hunderte von Titeln angegeben werden – kann festgestellt werden, dass alle möglichen Drucke zu den untersuchten Themen in den heute noch zur Verfügung stehenden und rekonstruierbaren Teilen des Bestandes zu finden sind. Viele enthalten auch handschriftliche Einträge, Unterzeichnungen, Hervorhebungen usw., was überzeugend beweist, dass die Bücher von den Lesern aktiv benutzt worden waren. Und wenn sie schon gelesen wurden, kann angenommen werden, dass die beinhalteten Kenntnisse einen Einfluss auf die alltägliche wirtschaftliche, landwirtschaftliche und gesellschaftliche Tätigkeit der einzelnen Menschen ausübten. Die Bücher haben also ihre Funktion erfüllt. Das kann man sich ohne Weiteres vorstellen, wenn man sich die Wirtschafts- und Gesellschaftsgeschichte der Siebenbürger Sachsen in der frühen Neuzeit genauer anschaut. Da sie eine bestimmende schriftliche Kultur hatten, kann behauptet werden, dass – neben der immer schwächer werdenden oralisch-mündlichen Traditionsüberlieferung, dem sog. Wissenstransfer – die gedruckten Texte bei der Vermittlung der allgemeinen und Fachkenntnisse eine immer bedeutendere Rolle gespielt haben. Ohne die Wichtigkeit des Schrifttums hätten die Sachsen vermutlich keine so gut funktionierende Gesellschafts- und Wirtschaftsordnung ausbauen können, wie sie es getan haben. Das in Drucken vermittelte Wissen trug dem florierenden wirtschaftlichen und gesellschaftlichen Leben der Deutschen Siebenbürgens im 16.-18. Jahrhundert zweifelsohne stark bei.[34]

Fazit

Als Zusammenfassung möchte ich die Aufmerksamkeit wieder auf die Wichtigkeit der buch- und lesegeschichtlichen Quellen richten. Auch aus den oben Gesagten stellt es sich heraus, dass auch die Historie vieler Disziplinen (in unserem Fall die Kultur-, Mentalitäts-, Gesellschafts-, Wirtschafts-, Landwirtschafts-, Medizin- und Ernährungsgeschichte) durch nützliche Angaben und Zusammenhänge ergänzt werden können, wenn diese Quellen bei der Interpretation benutzt werden. Da dieses Phänomen heute ziemlich sporadisch in der ungarischen und rumänischen wissenschaftlichen Praxis wahrgenommen werden kann, lohnt es sich bestimmt, auf allen fachlichen Formen diese Möglichkeit populärer und allgemein bekannter zu machen. Eine ähnliche Veranlassung regte mich an, aus den Dokumenten der Siebenbürger Sachsen des 16.-18. Jahrhunderts einige hervorzuheben. Aus der Auswahl geht hoffentlich hervor, dass meine obige Feststellung besteht, und die buchgeschichtlichen Angaben als nutzbare und zuverlässige Quellen für die Forscher der einzelnen historischen Wissenschaftszweige und -gebiete betrachtet werden können. Die alten Drucke dienen in den meisten Fällen als ausgezeichnetes Thermometer der gesellschaftlichen, wirtschaftlichen und kulturellen Veränderungen einzelner Geschichtsepochen. Eine tiefere Analyse hätte die Aufgabe, die temporäre Frische und den nachweisbaren Einfluss der Drucke zu untersuchen. Das sollten aber die Wirtschafts- und Gesellschaftswissenschaftler mit ihren Mitteln herausfinden. Die Buchforscher haben ihre Aufgaben durch den Hinweis auf eine neue Gruppe möglicher Quellen, die in die Forschung einbezogen werden könnten, erfüllt. Was sich aus den buchgeschichtlichen Quellen abzeichnet, ergänzt sehr gut die Kenntnisse, die uns auf Grund anderer archivalischer, historischer Dokumente zur Verfügung stehen. Daher scheint es nützlich zu sein, auch die buch- und lesegeschichtlichen Angaben bei allerlei historischen Forschungen und Untersuchungen mindestens bezüglich der frühen Neuzeit in Betracht und Erwägung zu ziehen.

---

[34] Zur Unterstützung dieser Behauptung siehe die neueste Zusammenfassung im Thema: Michael Kroner, *Geschichte der Siebenbürger Sachsen*, Bde I-II (Nürnberg: Verlag Haus der Heimat Nürnberg, 2007-2008) [Schriftenreihe Geschichte der Siebenbürger Sachsen und ihrer wirtschaftlich-kulturellen Leistungen] (mit reichhaltiger weiterführender Literatur).

FAITH AND CHARITY.
Aspects Concerning the Material Situation of the Higher Greek-Catholic Clergy in the Second Half of the Nineteenth Century and the Early Twentieth Century

ION CÂRJA

Throughout its over two millennia of existence, the Church owned material assets, decided what was licit or illicit in the administration and use thereof, and laid down and assumed a series of decrees and practices related to the material aspects of human existence. Whether in medieval or in modern times, the Church was – in Catholic, Protestant or Orthodox Europe – a structure holding substantial economic powers, alongside the aristocracy and the central power in the state. The "wealth" of the Church has very often been a source of controversy, determining the laity to adopt critical standpoints towards it, especially during the modern period and in contemporary and recent history. At moments of crisis, rupture, or simply being unable to find viable solutions for the revival of their badly-faring economies, the European societies did not hesitate to sacrifice ecclesiastical assets, in the name of the nation and for its salvation, emblematic example in this respect being the French Revolution, which, in the fall of 1789, nationalized the properties of the Catholic Church in the Hexagon, in an attempt to restore the economy, whose plummeting fall seemed unstoppable. Until the reforms undertaken by the modern state, which created a neutral public space, taking over – gradually or abruptly – a number of functions from the ecclesiastical institution, especially matrimony and education, the Church had owned an important material patrimony.

Far from attempting to achieve a complete reconstruction of this picture, in this article we aim to raise a few questions and to sketch possible answers regarding the accumulation of material goods by the higher clergy and the elites of the Greek-Catholic Church during the second half of the nineteenth and the early twentieth century, and the purposes they were destined for. The level of the elites, comprising bishops and canons, lends itself more easily to the investigation we have in mind, because information about the assets owned by this restricted category of ecclesiastical personnel is more consistent and more readily available, even though the primary sources may be unequal in terms of their value and relevance.

The agenda of the bishops and canons of the Romanian Greek-Catholic Church and their program of ecclesiastical administration included economic objectives, connected with activities entailed by church administration, pastoral care, catechesis and education. Among the best known in this respect was Metropolitan Ioan Vancea, who deployed, in all probability, the most efficient ecclesiastical administration program in the Romanian Greek-Catholic Church up until World War I.[1] Besides its merits on the ad-

[1] See, on this theme: Ion Cârja, *Biserică şi societate în Transilvania în perioada păstoririi mitropolitului Ioan*

ministrative level, Ioan Vancea proved to be a very thrifty and efficient manager of his personal income and the Church revenues, a quality that was matched by his willingness to support, quite often from his own funds, the various efforts of the communities he pastored or to intervene for redressing situations that were economically critical. What is interesting, from this point of view, is the canonical visitation he made, accompanied by other members of the central metropolitan administration, in the period 1873-1876, in several territorial subunits of the Archdiocese of Alba Iulia and Făgăraş: the Archdeaconries of Alba Iulia and Târgu-Mureş and the Vicariate Forane of Făgăraş. Personally travelling to all these places, the metropolitan very often made his magnanimity felt, offering money to redress the numerous deficiencies noticed in the field, such as: the repair work to be done on churches, the complete inventory of the objects of worship, the purchase of books and vestments, the purchase of teaching materials for the denominational schools, the completion of the teachers' salaries.[2] The primary sources are unanimous in highlighting the generosity with which this bishop specifically addressed the immediate material needs of his Church and projected commitments that necessitated sustained, long-term financial effort.

In the period under study, the bishops' initiatives represented the first aspect of the economic dimension that church life inevitably entailed. Even a bishop with a shorter pastorate, as was Ioan Olteanu, who headed the Diocese of Lugoj in the periods 1870-1873 and 1873-1877, distinguished himself through such initiatives, among which we should mention the renovation of the episcopal residence from Beiuş.[3] What suggests the importance of economic issues in the daily ecclesiastical life of the Romanian Greek Catholics is the justification advanced by the Bishop of Gherla, Ioan Szabó, referring to his lack of interest in the canonical visitations to the diocese: the bishop stated that the people he shepherded in his parishes were so poor that he could not demand that they should bear the costs of his presence in their midst.[4]

Also of interest is the existence of a non-homogeneous and non-uniform economic endowment or material power in the component structures of the Romanian Greek-Catholic Metropolitan Province, founded by Pope Pius IX in 1853. Thus, the poorest diocese was, in all likelihood, the Greek-Catholic Diocese of Lugoj, a young diocese, with a

---

Vancea (1869-1892) [Church and Society in Transylvania during the Pastorate of Metropolitan Ioan Vancea (1869-1892)] (Cluj-Napoca: Presa Universitară Clujeană, 2007).

[2] For the documents attesting this canonical visitation, see Serviciul Judeţean Alba al Arhivelor Naţionale [Alba County Directorate of the National Archives], Fund *Mitropolia Română Unită Blaj. Cabinetul Mitropolitului*, file no. 957/1873-1876, passim.

[3] For a brief biographical overview of Bishop Ioan Olteanu, see *Şematismul Veneratului Cler al Arhidiecesei Metropolitane Greco-Catolice Române de Alba-Iulia şi Făgăraş pre Anul Domnului 1900 de la Sfânta Unire 200* [The Schematism of the Venerable Clergy in the Romanian Greek-Catholic Metropolitan Archdiocese of Alba-Iulia and Făgăraş in the Year of Our Lord 1900, 200 since the Holy Union] (Blaj: Tipografia Seminarului Arhidiecezan, 1900), 57.

[4] *Episcopul Ioan Szabó şi Sfântul Scaun. Corespondenţă (1874-1910)* [Bishop Ioan Szabó and the Holy See. Correspondence (1874-1910)], ed. Ion Cârja and Daniel Sularea (Cluj-Napoca: Presa Universitară Clujeană, 2007), 97.

missionary status, in the midst of the Banatian Orthodoxy, founded in the same year – 1853; by contrast, the Diocese of Oradea Mare had much more substantial revenue sources. Thus, according to data offered by correspondence of Augustin Lauran, the future canon and capitular provost, in 1873 the Diocese of Oradea had an area of 36 square leagues, which brought an annual income estimated at 30,000-60,000 florins, while the annual income that the Diocese of Lugoj could bring the bishop did not exceed even the sum of 9,000 florins.[5] In these circumstances, it is likely that some of the bishops, more attentive to the material aspects of their career, chose to transfer themselves to the diocese from Bihor, Olteanu and, later, Demetriu Radu embarking on the same course.

The material goods accumulated throughout the lives and careers of the higher Greek-Catholic clergy are synthetically mentioned in their wills, an excellent historical source that lends itself to investigations from various perspectives. Besides references to spiritual aspects, pertaining to their individual thoughts about the "great passage" (considerations regarding the human condition and the ephemeral and fragile nature of life on earth, details about the funeral procedure, services and charity acts to be made afterwards for the redemption of the testators' souls), the content of the wills lists the properties owned by the testator at the time of drafting the document and the destination they must be given after their owner's death. Usually, the bishops' wills were published in the press, shortly after their demise, which is how we know about Metropolitans Alexandru Sterca Şuluţiu's and Ioan Vancea's wills, while Victor Mihályi of Apşa never left, as far as we know, written testamentary instructions. In other cases, such as that of Vasile Hossu, the Bishop of Lugoj (1903-1912), who then transferred to Gherla (1916), the materials published in the press at the time of his death and funeral made references to his wealth and the destination he had given to certain amounts of money. As regards the canons, one of the most extensive and suggestive testaments was that of Ioan Boroş (1850-1937), who became an honorary bishop in 1922.

As a general observation, it can be said that issues of a material, economic nature form the largest part of the actual content of the wills. Testaments represent personal identity documents of the utmost interest, with self-perception elements that are difficult to find in other sources, except, perhaps, in memories and diaries. On the other hand, for a person who held the rank of bishop, his will is the last act of ecclesiastical administration, to the extent that the provisions of this instrument do not concern the purely private sphere, but also that of the institution, of the Church he pastored. Having so far been used in international historiography, and even in the Romanian historiography over the last two decades,[6] as sources for less conventional approaches, such as the history of attitudes to-

---

[5] See the letter Augustin Lauran sent to the Prefect of the Congregation de Propaganda Fide (22 August 1873), in original at the Archivio della Congregazione per le Chiese Orientali (Vatican), Fund *Scritture riferite nei congressi. Romeni 1865-1875*, box no. 1, ff. 469r-470r.

[6] Of the recent Romanian researches that have successfully used testaments as a source, mention should be made of: *Caiete de Antropologie Istorică* III 1-2 (5-6) (2004), thematic issue: *Oamenii şi moartea în societatea românească* [People and Death in the Romanian Society]; Mihaela Grancea, *Reprezentări ale*

wards death, the testaments of ecclesiastical dignitaries contain rather significant economic information, which has been little valorised so far in works of ecclesiastical history. We therefore wish to dwell, in what follows, on several wills left by members of the higher Greek-Catholic clergy in the nineteenth century, out of the belief that they are not unimportant for reconstituting the economic dimension of their existence.

Thus, the testament of the first Bishop of the Romanian Greek-Catholic province of Alba Iulia and Făgăraş, Alexandru Sterca Şuluţiu (1851-1867), presents extensively elements related to the material goods, without neglecting from the disclosure of his last wishes either his intellectual concerns (the works remaining in manuscript form) or his spiritual considerations in relation to the supreme moment of death. This testament was written on 23 October 1866, one year before the metropolitan's death, and contains 14 paragraphs, as published in the pages of *Gazeta de Transilvania* in September 1867. The document opens with remarks on the material goods, "my movable and immovable possessions," their condition and destination. On his installation at first as Bishop of Făgăraş, in 1851, Şuluţiu had found the episcopal domain and assets from Blaj "in a ruined and wretched state," relentless efforts being made to operate the necessary "meliorations and repairs." At the beginning of his pastorate, the material basis in Blaj did not ensure even his minimum subsistence, "not even my daily bread." In time, through wise management, the material endowment of Blaj progressed significantly, the testator says, the episcopal chattels becoming "ten times better than when I found and received them." The financial efforts to this end entailed the metropolitan's contracting loans from various sources. In this respect, Şuluţiu confesses in his will that he strove to repay the borrowed money, 21,000 florins, to the Erarium and about 8,000 florins to the Chapter and "other private" lenders. This was possible with great sacrifices, the testator claims, using an expression that he later reiterated: "with my huge patience and forbearance." The manner in which he managed his property was suggestively correlated with a certain conduct, characterized in particular by a modest and austere life, and by the way in which he assumed the episcopal rank:

> "This rather strict parsimony and husbandry of mine, forgoing what would have been vital to support my episcopal high rank, character and office, for had I not done so, I would have been one of those many who love the pump and throwing dinners and brilliant servants and boasting the full splendour and lust the modern world expects of a bishop, I would have squandered it all and, after my death, I would have left the clergy nothing but high and many debts."[7]

The purchase of the Şpring domain actually represented a particular gesture, in line with Metropolitan Şuluţiu's material acquisitions during his arch-pastorate. This ac-

---

morţii în Transilvania secolelor XVI-XX [Representations of Death in Transylvania during the 14th-20th Centuries] (Cluj-Napoca: Casa Cărţii de Ştiinţă, 2005); Marius Rotar, *Moartea în Transilvania în secolul al XIX-lea* [Death in Transylvania in the 19th Century], I-II (Cluj-Napoca: Editura Accent, 2006-2007).

7 "Testamentul în Domnul repausatului Arhiep. şi Metropolit Conte Alexandru Sterca Şuluţiu" [The Testament of Archbishop and Metropolitan Count Alexandru Sterca Şuluţiu, the Faithful Departed], *Gazeta Transilvaniei*, 10 September, 1867, 281-282.

quisition cost Şuluţiu one hundred thousand florins in urbarial bonds and was then established as an archdiocesan foundation, provided with operating bylaws – the "foundational points" of 23 April 1861.

In addition to the foundation he established for the benefit of the clergy, in his will Şuluţiu bequeathed certain assets to his relatives: furniture, garments, grain, wine, plum brandy, three carts with the incumbent equipment. Next, the metropolitan specified, in the fifth paragraph of his will, that of the entire fortune mentioned in the preceding paragraphs, what should first be individualized was an "episcopal fund," worth 2,000 florins. On his installation in office, Şuluţiu said he had not received "even a Kreuzer" from that fund, but now he had the opportunity to leave his successor a legacy of assets worth 2,000 florins, consisting of furniture, hay, straw, grain, wine and so on. After the separation of this episcopal fund from the total assets left after Şuluţiu's death, his will stipulated the remainder should be sold and divided into 12 equal parts, to be distributed to his relatives. The testament further stated, in an explicit manner, how this part of the property should be nominally split among his relatives. The relatives to whom he had bequeathed financial aid in his will, in particular the young men who were carrying out their studies, would have to display "exemplary moral conduct." After his death, his private papers and correspondence would be given to his nephews, Dionisie and Iosif Sterca Şuluţiu.[8]

In addition to the material assets and their recipients, Alexandru Sterca Şuluţiu's will contains an "intellectual" section, referring to the works he left in manuscript form, which are interesting in terms of retrieving his horizon of study, the subjects that preoccupied him and on which he had pondered throughout time. In the tenth paragraph, his will lists seven works of canon law, of ecclesiastical discipline and church history, "still unrevised and not definitively transcribed so far," to which are added "poetic works, woeful lyrics in their final draft, and in their vast majority written in ink," while the last paragraph, the ninth, refers to "a serious examination of the past and the future awaiting the Romanian nation, from the vantage point of its religion." The bishop's writing concerns show his priority interest in key issues for the identitarian expression of the Romanian Greek-Catholic Church: the priests' marriage according to the practice of the Eastern Church, the pope's prerogatives, ecclesiastical discipline in matrimonial matters, the 1855 Concordat between the Habsburg Empire and the Holy See, the conferences of the Romanian Greek-Catholic bishops held in Vienna in 1856, etc.[9]

From an economic perspective, Alexandru Sterca Şuluţiu's testament reveals a specific dimension of the entire Greek-Catholic elite during the period examined here, the accumulation of assets that would serve as a basis for foundation, charity and philanthropy activities, for the benefit of the Church, in other words, his embarking on a much

[8] Ibid., see the continuation in *Gazeta Transilvaniei*, 13 September, 1867, 285-286.

[9] Ibid.; a part of the manuscripts left by Metropolitan Şuluţiu have recently seen the light of print in the work: Alexandru Sterca Şuluţiu, *Scrieri teologice* [Theological Works], ed. Ioana Mihaela Bonda (Cluj-Napoca: Presa Universitară Clujeană, 2010).

needed modernization process, as regards the material side of ecclesiastical life. The archdiocesan clergy were the main beneficiaries of the estate Metropolitan Şuluţiu left when he passed away, followed, at a considerable distance, by his relatives, which suggests the fact that he had maintained his family relations over the course of his career and manifested a certain willingness to show his solidarity within the structure of his family of origin.

Ioan Vancea of Buteasa, Bishop of Gherla (1865-1869) and Metropolitan of Blaj (1869-1892), remained in the consciousness of the Romanian Greek-Catholic Church as one of the greatest Maecenas in the entire historical existence of Romanian Greek Catholicism. His will, dated 22 October 1887, begins by specifying that the metropolitan's wealth largely consisted of the foundation he had established (the "Vănceana Foundation"), endowed with statutes. The rest of his property, which included coins of precious metal, different types of bonds, or the price of the house that Vancea owned in Oradea – all these assets would be pooled together with the money obtained from other assets, which the testament lists testament with accuracy: precious metal objects, vases, table utensils, garments, furniture from the metropolitan residence, icons and portraits, livestock and carts with the incumbent equipment, grains, alcohol, etc.

If after the evaluation of these goods, it was found that the testator had no debts, steps would be taken to distribute the money to various beneficiaries, thus: 400 florins for the benefit of the poor in Blaj, after the metropolitan's death, the funeral expenses and the fees for the curing physician would be paid, and 2,500 florins would be given to the "Fundus Instructus" of the metropolitan domain. When those provisions were complied with, the remaining assets would represent "the remainder or my free legacy," the part of the metropolitan's inheritance destined, by will, to go to his relatives. The amounts of money provided to his relatives, in this part of his bequest, were significant, after all, for the material endowment of a high church representative of that time: thus, to George Vancea, the bishop's nephew and the administrator of the metropolitan domain, he left the sum of 8,000 florins; to the three sons of another nephew, Iosif Vancea, a former priest in Mănărade – 3,000 florins; to each of his nephews from his home village of Văşad – 1,000 florins; while to other relatives from Oradea, in Bihor County, and from Blaj he left various amounts (400, 600, 1,000, 4,000 florins). His documents and correspondence would be handed over to the diocesan archives, while his personal and family correspondence would be entrusted to his nephews George and Iosif Vancea. What would be left of the free bequest would come into the possession of the foundation the metropolitan had established. The Chapter was in charge of the execution of the will – two canons, together with the archdiocesan attorney, for whom money was provided as emolument.[10]

As mentioned in the will, the bulk of Metropolitan Vancea's legacy was the foundation he had created and endowed with statutes, the "foundational points," where he

[10] *Unirea*, 13 August, 1892, 262-263.

had initially deposited 32,000 florins, and later added another 36,000, the capital reaching shortly, thanks to the interest accumulated, 70,000 florins. Together with the Archdiocesan Consistory, the metropolitan decided to invest this capital by purchasing a domain, the noble estate of Miklós Macskásy from Sân-Miclăuş and Căpâlna, located in the County of Târnava Mică, not far from Blaj. This was a 700-acre land, with outbuildings and appurtenances, a four-stone mill on the Târnava Mică, a royal right for pub keeping and holding country fairs, which he purchased at an auction for the sum of 62,731 florins and 69 Kreuzers. To the purchase price were added various expenses, including transcription into the Land Register, repair works and so on, which raised the total cost at 80,000 florins. Registered under the metropolitan's name, he donated it as a foundation, called the "Vănceana Foundation," under the special title of the "Archdiocesan House," its current management being entrusted to the Archdiocesan Chapter, with the supervision of the Consistory. The statute stipulated that the beneficiaries of the foundation would be the secondary- and primary school teachers from the schools in Blaj, the young pupils and students from the archdiocese, to whom were allocated amounts of 100, 150, 200 and 300 florins, not forgetting the children who chose to learn various crafts, to whom were destined sums between 25 and 60 florins annually. All these stipends would be awarded on a competitive basis, to be duly advertised.[11] The statutes of Vancea's Foundation reveal once again the bishop's solidarity with his family, his willingness to help his relatives, which was also expressed in his testament; paragraph 12 of the "foundational points" laid down the rule that preferential access to the stipends provided by the Foundation would be given to the metropolitan's nephews, while outside these degrees of kinship, access to financial aid would be made freely, without other restrictions.[12]

In addition to the testament, the articles published in the press in 1892 are likely to complete Metropolitan Ioan Vancea's image as a good "manager" of the property belonging to the Church and of his own assets. Shortly after the death of the high priest, the newspaper *Unirea* published a synthesis entitled "Ioan Vancea's Activity as Archbishop and Metropolitan,"[13] which presents the relevant achievements of his arch-pastorate, and last but not least his charitable and eleemosynary initiatives. Thus, in 1873, when the Archdiocesan School Fund was established at the Archdiocesan School Congress, with the mixed participation of the laity and the clergy, Metropolitan Vancea had donated 6,000 florins. In 1885, a new wing was added to the seminary building, to accommodate the theology students, an investment which cost 18,000 florins. In 1889, at the Third Archdiocesan Synod, the Assistance Fund for Priests was created and Vancea donated 5,000 florins to it. Education was a favourite domain for Ioan Vancea's charitable actions, so he intervened to have the teachers' salaries at the schools in Blaj rise from 500 florins

[11] *Unirea*, 20 August, 1892, 270-271.
[12] *Unirea*, 27 August, 1892, 278.
[13] *Unirea*, 6 August, 1892, 250-252. The article was compiled, according to the author's own confession, with information taken from the work: *Metropolitul Dr. Ioan Vancea de Buteasa. Schiță biografică* [Metropolitan Dr. Ioan Vancea de Buteasa. A Biographical Sketch] (Blaj, 1890), written by Augustin Bunea.

annually to amounts ranging from 700 to 1,000 florins, to which were added various housing benefits for the married teachers. He established the fund for the retirement of teachers and their wives, to which he also contributed, in 1889, with the sum of 3,000 florins.[14]

Ioan Vancea Blaj helped endow the schools from Blaj with the necessary material infrastructure. He donated, from his own revenues, 2,000 florins for purchasing "the gym and physical fitness equipment," for enriching the museum of natural sciences and that of philology, as well as for opening two new rooms in the gymnasium building. In 1891, he built a "pompous" gym hall, on which the sum of 10,000 florins was spent from the Basilian Monks' Fund. The foremost edifice founded by Metropolitan Ioan Vancea, benefiting the education establishments in Blaj, was a new building for the Gymnasium, opened in 1884, erected exclusively with financial resources provided by the metropolitan, totalling 36,000 florins. During his pastorate, the elementary school for girls in Blaj was transformed into a secondary school with eight grades. The former boarding school for boys was expanded, with a view to turning it into a boarding school for girls, and it was endowed with a chapel. The building of a new boarding school for boys began, incurring expenses of 42,000 florins; it was unfinished at the time of Ioan Vancea's death. The metropolitan contributed 10,000 florins from his own funds to raise a new building for the *preparandia* [a pedagogical institute] and the normal schools in Blaj, to which were added approximately 7,000 florins from the Basilian Fund. The hierarch established two foundations to help the teachers in Făgăraş and Aiud. During his pastorate, 300 new school buildings were erected for the denominational elementary schools in villages and people's schools were organized in 195 communes, where, prior to 1869, there had been no school or the school teacher's salary had not been systematized under the state law. During the 23 years of his arch-pastorate, Ioan Vancea was directly involved in the construction of 100 new churches and about 200 rectories.[15] The mere enumeration of the projects he materialized, with the incumbent financial costs, reveals – despite the unavoidably encomiastic style in which they are written – that Vancea's administration was extremely competent and managed to achieve a material base suitable for religious life and denominational education in the Archdiocese of Alba Iulia and Făgăraş. Through this financial and investment effort, Vancea clearly upheld the modernization of church and school life, bringing, in this respect, his Church in tune with the spirit of the time.

About the last Metropolitan of the Romanian Greek-Catholic Church during the period of Austro-Hungarian dualism, Victor Mihályi of Apşa, the information on the economic aspects of his pastorate is scarcer, in the current state of research. He passed away without leaving, in all likelihood, any testamentary dispositions. His pastorate, as Bishop of Lugoj (1875-1895) and, respectively, as Metropolitan of Blaj (1895-1918), was not at all irrelevant from the perspective we have in mind, in the sense that the bishop whose

[14] Ibid.
[15] Ibid.

roots lay in Maramureş was just as sensitive as his predecessors to the needs of the Church and the denominational education. Victor Mihályi fit into the specific pattern of Greek-Catholic bishops from those times, marked by magnanimity and generosity, and keen on making investments for the Church and denominational education, even though it is obvious that from this point of view, he did not rise to the level of his predecessor, Ioan Vancea. Thus, as a bishop in the Banatian diocese, Mihályi established a foundation for the Romanian Greek-Catholic boarding school in Lugoj and provided that, after his death, the amount of 5,250 florins should be paid to that foundation.[16] He left a foundation worth over 182,000 crowns for the maintenance and embellishment of the cathedral in Blaj. He contributed sums of money to meeting some punctual needs, as, for example, in 1916, when he "granted our Greek-Catholic chapel in Braşov a complete set of sacred vessels, namely: a chalice, a paten, a star, a teaspoon and a lance, artistically wrought in gold, worth 420 cr[owns]."[17]

As shown in the lines published by *Unirea* after his death, Victor Mihályi annually allotted between 20,000 and 24,000 crowns to charitable purposes. Before moving the metropolitan administration to Oradea, at the order of the Hungarian government in the period 1916-1917, he had distributed 70,000 crowns to various charities. He was particularly open to charity acts, for the benefit of the poor students in Blaj, whom he repeatedly endowed with clothing, and of other impoverished people in the city hosting the metropolitan see, whom he helped with firewood, lumber, and grain. He founded the Romanian Greek-Catholic Orphanage in Blaj, which he continued to watch over; thus, he gave the orphans whose parents had been killed on the battle front securities worth 20,000 crowns.[18]

The funeral speech delivered at Mihályi's burial by Canon Vasile Suciu, the future metropolitan, outlines a picture inevitably marked by the panegyric nature of such a context, from which we can, nonetheless, retain some of the high priest's traits of conduct, important for his perspective on the material aspects of ecclesiastical life. "He was modest and simple in all, in victuals and in garments, and he lived an immaculate life," Suciu said. He also claimed that Mihályi had manifested exemplary rigor in managing the material assets:

> "He kept a detailed account of his revenues and expenses. He would even write down the *fillér* and had inventories for the most insignificant of things. He was scrupulous lest he should cause damage to anyone. He made the effort and raised the needed economic buildings, took over estates and built a new bridge over the Târnava Mare, all of which cost him tens of thousands of crowns. He did all of this from his own, leaving nothing to burden his successor with. He multiplied the wealth of the Metropolitan See, all at his own expense."[19]

---

[16] *Unirea*, 26 January, 1918, 1-2.
[17] *Unirea*, 22 January, 1916, 4.
[18] *Unirea*, 26 January, 1918, 1-2.
[19] Ibid., 2.

As regards Vasile Hossu, Bishop of Lugoj (1903-1912) and then of Gherla (1912-1916), the sources note his interest in charitable and eleemosynary activities, even if the information is, this time, more parsimonious. According to a *sui generis* activity report, which he submitted and published in *Unirea* at the end of the period of his pastorate in Lugoj, Bishop Hossu initiated the resumption of monastic life at the Monastery of Prislop, with government aid worth 10,000 crowns, 2,000 crowns being donated by the Bishop of Oradea, Demetriu Radu, and 4,000 crowns representing his own contribution. Through his perseverance, new churches were built in 23 communes from the Banatian diocese and another 28 were refurbished. For the construction and repair of churches and parish houses, he obtained 200,000 crowns from the government. Hossu created funds and foundations in the Diocese of Lugoj, thus: the Chapter's Reserve Fund, the Fund for the Holy Mass, the Diocesan Library Fund, the Diocesan Chancery Fund, the Diocesan Cultural Fund, and the Diocesan Subsidiary Fund. The bishop's contribution, through these foundations, to increasing the overall material wellbeing of the Banatian diocese amounted, according to his own assessment, to 120,000 crowns. Transferring himself to the helm of the Diocese of Gherla, Hossu left "a pompous Seminary, a *preparandia* for girls, and the foundations for a superior school for little girls."[20]

At the end of these case studies, we would like to mention the example of Ioan Boroş (1850-1937), a canon and provost in the same Diocese of Lugoj, who was elevated to the dignity of honorary bishop in 1922. The material accumulations he managed to carry out were downright remarkable, as shown in his testamentary provisions; thus, his will, dated 31 October 1931, was divided into three parts, the first of these presenting the real estate property, the houses and land Boroş owned in Lugoj and in Carei. The second part lists the "chattels" – the stocks and the amount of money he had deposited in various banks. This wealth deposited in banks is astounding, given its substantial amount and the large number of banks he had money in, as mentioned here, as well as the precision and accuracy with which the sums are presented. He had "stocks" at "Albina" Bank in Sibiu (77,500 lei), at the "Creditul Bănăţean" in Lugoj (48,750 lei), at "Grănicerul" in Dobra (4,000 lei), at "Banca Maramureşană" (500 lei), at "Banca Caraş-Severineană" in Lugoj (4,000 lei), at "Bihoreana" (1,000 lei), at "Banater Bank-Verein" (4,000 lei), at "Temesvarer Bank"/ Bank of Timişoara (1,500 lei), at the "Forestiera" Enterprise in Cluj (1,000 lei), at "Jaradek Költsön" (1,250 lei), at "Korona Jaradek Költsön" (1,000 crowns), "Pesti Hazai Nyeremény Költsön" (100 crowns), "Magyar Jelzatog Hitelbank" (100 crowns); he had deposits at: "Creditul Bănăţean" (255,501 lei), "Liberalitatea" (275,706 lei), the Cemetery Chapel (182,329 lei), the County Asylum (7,658 lei), the Fund for Widows and Orphans (20,174 lei), the Agricultural Bank in Lugoj (59,907 lei), "Schwäbischer C. Bank" (29,447 lei), "Albina" (18,430 lei) etc.; promissory loans at: Antoniu and Emilia Emborya Petrău (150,000 lei), Ioan Enescu (Lugoj, 10,000 lei), Mihai Bagiu (Satu Mic

[20] *Unirea*, 25 January, 1916, 3.

3,000 lei). Ioan Boroş had a life insurance at the company "Allgemeine Beamter Verein" in Vienna. In the third part, the document presents the gold and silver objects owned by the testator, and further lists the actual testamentary provisions, in the order of the recipients: family members, public church foundations, persons from the ecclesiastical milieus, individuals and families in various degrees of kinship with the testator. We should once again specify that he had the qualities of a good administrator, with openness towards the modern banking and financial instruments, coupled with generosity, a charitable and eleemosynary spirit, human solidarity, in full agreement with the precepts of Christian morality.[21]

The second half of the nineteenth century was a period in which the modernization process manifested itself at an ever wider scale in Europe, its effects inevitably having repercussions for Transylvania.[22] Against this background of general modernization, the Romanians from the Danubian Monarchy experienced a phenomenon of emancipation, not least economically; moreover, economic emancipation was endorsed and encouraged by the Romanians' leaders, as a compensatory alternative to their lack of perspectives on the political-national level, after the conclusion of the dualist pact.

This upward economic development had a positive impact upon the Romanians' ecclesiastical elites, as the bishops and the canons reached a level of prosperity that allowed them to launch initiatives on the charitable and eleemosynary level. What the sources present as the Greek-Catholic, in our case, clergy's wealth or material assets represented, in fact, two distinct aspects of the same problem: the property of the church (real estates, buildings, foundations, etc.) and the individual accumulation of wealth belonging to the people at the top of the ecclesiastical hierarchy, metropolitans, bishops, canons, derived from their wage income, bank deposits, inheritances, family inheritances or sales-purchases. From case to case, their interest in and ability to thrive economically placed some of them in possession of obvious material prosperity, which was also evidenced by the amount of money with which they supported investment and charitable activities, and which they mentioned in their wills. From Alexandru Sterca Şuluţiu to Victor Mihályi, the Greek-Catholic Archdiocese of Blaj became quite a remarkable landowner, accumulating, over the course of seven decades, material assets supporting a con-

[21] See the testament *in extenso* in: Ioan Boroş, *Memorialistica* [Memoirs], ed. Valeriu Leu, Nicolae Bocşan, Ion Cârja, Costin Feneşan, Cristian Sabău (Cluj-Napoca: Presa Universitară Clujeană, 2012), 297-308. On Ioan Boroş, see also: Gheorghe Naghi, "Corespondenţa lui Ioan Boroş cu George Bariţ (1879-1883)" [The Correspondence between Ioan Boroş and George Bariţ (1879-1883)], *Anuarul Institutului de Istorie "George Bariţ" din Cluj-Napoca* XLII (2003): 121-139; Sergiu Soica, "Activitatea Bisericii Greco-Catolice din Banat în perioada 1920-1945" [The Activity of the Greek-Catholic Church in the Banat in the Period 1920-1945], *Studia Universitatis Babeş-Bolyai. Theologia Graeco-Catholica Varadiensis* LV, 2 (2010): 167-174.

[22] See, on this theme: Iosif Marin Balog, Rudolf Gräf, Ioan Lumperdean, eds., *Relaţia rural-urban: Ipostaze ale tradiţiei şi modernizării* [The Rural-Urban Relationship: Aspects of Tradition and Modernization] (Cluj-Napoca: Presa Universitară Clujeană, 2010); Nagy Róbert, *Capitalul – forţă a transformării. Rolul capitalului german în industrializarea Transilvaniei (1880-1918)* [The Capital – Force of Transformation. The Role of German Capital in the Industrialization of Transylvania (1880-1918)] (Cluj-Napoca: Presa Universitară Clujeană, 2011).

tinually expanding network of funds and foundations, financial supporting the churches, the schools, the clergy, the teachers, as well as the pupils and the students, together with underprivileged people experiencing poverty. The clerical elite members were among the first Romanians who knew how to use the opportunities brought about by modernity: loans, banks, insurance companies. The metropolitans, bishops and canons accumulated material assets both for the ecclesiastical institution and for their "private safe box," they purchased houses and estates for themselves and for the Church, they established foundations and helped increase the existing capital.

The relationship between the higher clergy's material assets and their social-charitable and philanthropic work appears in some sources, especially in the church press, the picture not being devoid of encomiastic excesses and hyperboles, even though their willingness and openness to the efficient administration of both their personal property and that of the Church were real, as were their deeds of good for the benefit of those less favoured by fate. Beyond the higher clergy's personal propensity to charitable activities, one can speak of an institutionalization of charity in the period under consideration here, in the sense that the constitutional organization of the Greek-Catholic Church, through the three Provincial Synods, of 1872, 1882 and 1900, had laid the foundations for coherent and systematic practices in this domain. As the Church and its episcopate became stronger economically, in the auspicious context of modernization from the second half of the nineteenth century, its charitable activity and social work expanded and diversified.

Materielle Tradition und Innovation in der Sepulkralplastik des 15. und 16. Jahrhunderts von Sibiu/Hermannstadt und Nürnberg

Marco Bogade

Der komparatistische Ansatz, der den Ausführungen in diesem Beitrag zugrunde liegt, ist geleitet von der Grundthese eines sich parallel oder infolge des Ausbaus der wirtschaftlichen Beziehungen zwischen dem Heiligen Römischen Reich und dem Königreich Ungarn, respektive zwischen Nürnberg und Hermannstadt, etablierenden Kunst- oder Kulturtransfers im späten Mittelalter und in der frühen Neuzeit. Diese Überlegungen sind natürlich keineswegs neu. Die Grabplatten und Epitaphien in der Ferula der Hermannstädter Stadtpfarrkirche stehen in der (Kunst-) Historiografie des 20. Jahrhunderts in engem Zusammenhang mit der Sepulkralkunst im Nürnberger Patriziat. Die Idee des Kunsttransfers von West nach Ost des in Sebeş/Mühlbach geborenen Stadtpfarrers und Kunsthistorikers Viktor Roth, der bereits 1906 vermutete, „dass auch die beiden Hermannstädter Erzgrabplatten [Peter Hallers und Michael Lutschs] von Meistern hergestellt worden sind, die sich nur vorübergehend im Sachsenlande aufgehalten haben und dasselbe nach Ausführung ihrer Aufträge wieder verlassen haben“,[1] greift der Kunsthistorikers Wilhelm Pinder 1934 deutlich wertend wieder auf, wenn er von der Siebenbürgischen Kunst des Mittelalters ganz verallgemeinernd als „ostdeutsche Kolonialkunst“[2] spricht. Sind die bisher angeführten Beispiele der Verortung der Siebenbürgischen Kunst im ostmitteleuropäischen bzw. südosteuropäischen Kunst- und Kulturnetzwerk eher generalisierend, so ist der spezifische Nürnberger Bezug der Hermannstädter Grabplatte namentlich Peter Hallers – die Grabplatte für Michael Lutsch stammt aus der ersten Hälfte des 17. Jahrhunderts und soll daher von der Betrachtung ausgenommen werden – für Ioan Albu in seinem Band zu den Inschriften der Stadt Hermannstadt von 2002 plausibel.[3] Albu bezieht sich hierbei auf die Arbeit von Anamaria Haldner[4] von 1980, die über die Nürnberger Provenienz der Hallerschen Grabplatte hinaus den Namen der dort in der ersten Hälfte des 16. Jahrhunderts ansässigen Werkstatt des Rotschmieds Peter Vischer in die kunsthistorische Diskussion des Kunst- und Kulturtransfers in den Raum stellt, ohne jedoch näher auf dessen Vermittlungswege oder Akteure einzugehen.

Der Verweis auf die Nürnberger Werkstatt ist natürlich insofern evident und plausibel, wenn man sich das Material der Grabplatte Peter Hallers – die Bronze – vor Augen führt, die mit Ausnahme des etwa zehn Jahre später gegossenen Epitaphs für den

---

[1] Victor Roth, *Geschichte der deutschen Plastik in Siebenbürgen* (Straßburg, 1906), 132.
[2] Zitiert nach: Victor Roth, *Die deutsche Kunst in Siebenbürgen* (Berlin, 1934), VII.
[3] Ioan Albu, *Inschriften der Stadt Hermannstadt aus dem Mittelalter und der Frühen Neuzeit* (Heidelberg, 2002) [Quellen zur Geschichte der Stadt Hermannstadt 3], 62f.
[4] Anamaria Haldner, „Eine Nürnberger Plastik in Hermannstadt“, *Forschungen zur Volks- und Landeskunde* 23, 2 (1980): 123-124, 124.

Bürgermeister Georg Hecht d. J.[5] in Hermannstadt im Betrachtungszeitraum singulär bleibt. In der Sepulkralkultur des Nürnberger Patriziats hat das Material, ebenso wie bei den von der Vischer-Werkstatt stark beeinflussten Grabdenkmälern des Bamberger Domkapitels in der Nagelkapelle des Bamberger Doms eine Tradition.[6]

Die folgenden Ausführungen intendieren eine kurze Typologie der materiellen Zeugnisse der bürgerlichen Nürnberger und Hermannstädter Sepulkralkultur des späten 15. und 16. Jahrhunderts und gehen einigen zentralen Aspekten bei der Frage nach Tradition und Innovation in diesen beiden Städten nach. Diese komparatistische Betrachtung liegt, wie bereits erwähnt, in den engen wirtschaftlichen Verbindungen von Nürnberg und Hermannstadt begründet: Im alten Königreich Ungarn setzt die kaufmännische Tätigkeit der Nürnberger Haller mit Ruprecht (II.) Haller, Sohn von Ruprecht (I.) Haller aus Ziegelstein bei Nürnberg ein. Der Studie Andreas Kubinyis von 1963-1964 zufolge konnte dieser bereits in den 1480er Jahren als erfolgreicher Händler in Buda/Ofen sowie in Siebenbürgen nachgewiesen werden.[7] Die soziale Etablierung vor Ort zeigt sich „vorbildlich“ vor allem in der Figur des Hermannstädter Bürgermeisters und Sachsengrafen Peter Haller, der im Jahre 1500 als Sohn von Ruprecht II. Haller und der Anna Münzer in Buda/Ofen geboren wurde. Der (wirtschaftliche) Erfolg der Familie fand ihren Niederschlag in der Wappen- und Namensmehrung, die im Jahre 1528 von Karl V. verliehen wurde.

Die grundlegende Motivation nicht nur, aber eben auch für bürgerliche Kunststiftungen des Mittelalters und der frühen Neuzeit im Allgemeinen und für Stiftungen im Kontext der Sepulkralkultur im Besonderen bewegt sich im Spannungsfeld zwischen Repräsentation – Selbstdarstellung und Selbst-inszenierung – auf der einen Seite und der Memoria auf der anderen Seite, die Caroline Horch in ihrer 2011 erschienenen Monografie sehr treffend zur „anthropologische Grundkonstante“[8] erklärt hat. Das dem Bedürfnis nach Totengedenken und Totenerinnern entspringende und sich in der materiellen Kultur manifestierende Memorialbild, zu dem Otto Gerhard Oexle – aus ikonografischer und typologischer Sicht vielleicht etwas unbefriedigend – jedes Bildwerk rechnet, das der Memoria dient,[9] sei, nach Hans Belting, jedes Privatporträt, im Unterschied zum Stifter- und Amtsbildnis, und „[…] war in erster Linie stets für die Ausstattung des Grabmonuments […] bestimmt.“[10]

---

[5] Vgl. Samuel Möckesch, *Die Pfarrkirche der Augsb. Conf. Verwandten zu Hermannstadt* (Hermannstadt, 1855), § 87 und Albu, *Inschriften*, Nr. 82 und Abb. 39.

[6] Vgl. dazu die umfassende Studie von Sven Hauschke, *Die Grabdenkmäler der Nürnberger Vischer-Werkstatt (1453-1544)* (Petersberg, 2006).

[7] Vgl. Andreas Kubinyi, „Die Nürnberger Haller in Ofen“, *Mitteilungen des Vereins für Geschichte der Stadt Nürnberg* 51 (1963-64): 80-128.

[8] Caroline Horch, *Der Memorialgedanke und das Spektrum seiner Funktionen in der Bildenden Kunst des Mittelalters* (Königstein i. T., 2001), 20.

[9] Vgl. Horch, ebenda, 11.

[10] Zitiert nach ebenda, 11.

Die Memoria führte bereits in der römischen Antike zu einem vielschichtigen Totenkult, der auch seinen spezifischen Niederschlag in der materiellen Kultur respektive in künstlerischen Stiftungen fand. Und trotz aller Verallgemeinerung, die der Fokus auf die Funktionalität von Memorialbildern mit sich bringt, lässt sich schon bei römischen Zeugnissen der Sepulkralkultur ein „memoriales" Hauptelement feststellen, das in der europäischen Kunst- und Kulturgeschichte eine Tradition in vielen Facetten bildet: die Einbettung des Verstorbenen in einen genealogischen Kontext durch die Verbildlichung nicht nur von ihm selbst, sondern ebenfalls von bereits verstorbenen Familienmitgliedern. Diese der römischen sozialen Elite vorbehaltene Inszenierung konnte von einer Auflistung der Verdienste des Memorierten mit Hilfe von *tituli* ergänzt werden. Die Namensnennung als zweites zentrales erinnerndes Element ist, wenngleich funktional mit den römischen Konsulardiptychen verwandt, offenbar in seinen unterschiedlichen und umfassenden Ausprägungen im Wesentlichen eine Zutat des frühen Christentums und des frühen Mittelalters, folgt man den Ausführungen von Caroline Horch.[11]

Diese verkürzende Darstellung der Überlieferungsgeschichte wird in vielerlei Hinsicht der Komplexität und der Vielfalt der materiellen Zeugnisse der Sepulkralkultur naturgemäß nicht gerecht. Die beiden denkmalimmanenten und in die Bildsprache transferierten „memorialen" Bedeutungsinhalte sind, wenngleich typologisch und ikonographisch anders umgesetzt, auch in den spezifischen Grabdenkmälern des späten Mittelalters und der frühen Neuzeit in Nürnberg und Sibiu/Hermannstadt anzutreffen.

Unter den Nürnberger Denkmälern zeigt die Grabplatte der Anna Groß aus Sandstein im Germanischen Nationalmuseum in Nürnberg,[12] die ursprünglich aus dem Franziskanerkloster in Nürnberg stammt und etwa gegen 1300 angefertigt worden ist, ein ganzfiguriges Relief der Verstorbenen in Frontalansicht mit gefalteten Händen. Das nicht nur in Nürnberg weit verbreite umlaufende Schriftband nennt ihren familiären Stand (*UXOR MAGNI H[ENRICI]*) – das Wappen zur Linken Ihre Kopfes ist eine spätere Ergänzung – und ihr Sterbejahr 1294. Dieses wird im Jahre 1356 bei der Deckplatte des Tischgrabs von Konrad Groß,[13] möglicherweise dem Sohn oder Stiefsohn von Anna Groß, bereits in Bronze ausgeführt (Abb. 1).

Nur noch in Resten erhalten, zeigt es die Evangelistensymbole in Vierpassformen in den Ecken und zeichnet den Verstorbenen offensichtlich als Gründer (*fundator*) des Nürnberger Heilig-Geist-Spitals, dem Aufstellungsort des Grabmals, aus. Ob sich auf der später erneuerten Marmorgrabplatte, in Ergänzung zum Hochrelief des Verstorbenen im unteren Bereich des Grabmals, ursprünglich auch eine figürliche Darstellung, respektive

---

[11] Vgl. ebenda, v.a. 21f und 29ff.

[12] Nürnberg, Germanisches Nationalmuseum, Gd. 13. Vgl. dazu Heinz Stafski, *Die Mittelalterlichen Bildwerke*, Bd. 1. *Die Bilderwerke aus Stein, Holz, Ton und Elfenbein bis um 1450* (Nürnberg, 1965) [Kataloge des Germanischen Nationalmuseums Nürnberg], Nr. 20.

[13] Vgl. Tilmann Breuer, Friedrich Oswald, Friedrich Piel u.a., *Franken. Die Regierungsbezirke Oberfranken, Mittelfranken und Unterfranken*, 2., durchgesehen und ergänzte Auflage (München, Berlin, 1999) [Georg Dehio Handbuch der Deutschen Kunstdenkmäler. Bayern I: Franken], 763.

eine Gravur befunden hat, ist nicht bekannt. Typologisch ganz ähnlich wird der im Jahre 1296 verstorbene Patrizier Konrad von Neumarkt inszeniert, auf dessen Grabplatte[14] aus der Zeit um 1360, die wohl ebenfalls Teil eines Tischgrabs war, dieser mittels eines umlaufenden Schriftbands aus Bronze als *fundator huius clavstri*, also als Stifter des Katharinenklosters in Nürnberg, genannt wird (Abb. 4). Der einfach gespaltete Wappenschild zu seinen Füßen mit dem steigenden Löwen und dem Fisch im Bild, zeichnet ihn als Mitglied der Nürnberger Patrizierfamilie Muffel aus. Die Grabplatte, die vermutlich den oberen Teil eines Tischgrabs bildete, ist ihrerseits verwandt mit der von Herdegen Valzner (†1423)[15] im Nürnberger Heiliggeistspital, bei der die Inschrift des nur noch in Resten erhaltenen Bronzeschriftbands dem Verstorbenen die letzte Ruhe wünscht (*cui fidelis anima requiescat in pace*). Herdegen Valzner war ursprünglich in Prag ansässig, wo er Ratsherr war und zur Zeit König Wenzels IV. die Verwaltung der königlichen Kupferbergwerke in Kuttenberg/ Kutná Hora innehatte. Vermutlich noch vor dem Jahr 1400 migrierte er nach Nürnberg, wo er in den inneren Rat der Stadt aufstieg, als Bankier bzw. Geldgeber für Wenzel, Ruprecht III. und Sigismund fungierte sowie Pfleger des Heiliggeistspitals wurden.[16] In Anbetracht seiner einflussreichen Aktivitäten im böhmischen Montanwesen mag es vielleicht auch nicht verwundern, dass das heraldische Element seines Grabdenkmals, im Unterschied zu den vorher genannten, auch hier in Bronze ausgeführt und in den später stark überarbeiteten Stein eingelegt worden ist. Es zeigt zueinander schräggestellte Allianzwappen mit dem Wappenschild der Valzner (mit einer schräglinks gestellten Bank im Bild) rechts und der Waldstromer (mit den beiden gekreuzt aufgestellten Streugabeln) links.

Die Synthese von heraldischen und epigrafischen Elementen, die in der Sepulkralkunst Nürnbergs in Bronze ausgeführt wurden, setzt sich um das Jahr 1436 im Volckamer-Grabmal[17] fort, das sich in der St. Lorenz-Kirche befindet (Abb. 5). Betrachtet man den heutigen Bestand an den materiell spezifischen Sepulkraldenkmälern in der Nürnberger Kirche St. Lorenz, muss man sich vor Augen führen, dass – der Überlieferung Johann Wolfgang Hilperts zufolge – im Jahre 1812 insgesamt über 40 Bronzeepitaphien aus dem Kirchenraum entfernt und das Metall in der Folge veräußert und eingeschmolzen worden ist.[18] Der Volckamer-Grabstein ist von dieser „Säuberung“ als einziger verschont geblieben. Ebenfalls nur fragmentarisch erhalten, zeigt er ein an drei Seiten umlaufendes Schriftband u.a. mit den Hinweisen auf den Tod von Andreas Volckamer im Jahre 1436 als aktuellsten Eintrag und den seiner Gemahlin Margarethe Volckamer, geborene Haller, zwei Jahre zuvor. Offenbar war die Platte nicht für figürlichen Schmuck konzipiert, da an zentraler Stelle das schräggestellte geteilte Volckamer-

---

[14] Nürnberg, Germanisches Nationalmuseum, Gd. 46. Vgl. Stafski, *Bildwerke*, Nr. 44.
[15] Vgl. Breuer u.a., *Franken*, 763.
[16] Vgl. Michael Diefenbacher, „Valzner, Herdegen“, in Michael Diefenbacher, Rudolf Endres (Hg.), *Stadtlexikon Nürnberg*, 2. verb. Auflage (Nürnberg, 2000), 1128f.
[17] Vgl. Breuer u.a., *Franken*, 712.
[18] Vgl. dazu Christian Schmidt, *St. Lorenz und die Familie v. Haller* (Nürnberg, 2005), 14f.

Wappen in Bronze erscheint, das im unteren Bereich die Lilie, im oberen Bereich ein halbes Rad mit drei Speichen im Bild zeigt, das sich als Element der Helmzier wiederholt. Die beiden Medaillons in den unteren Ecken des Schriftbands illustrieren die Wappenallianz der Volckamer links und der Haller rechts.

In diesem Zusammenhang sein nur kurz darauf hingewiesen, dass Andreas Volckamer und Margarethe Haller als Stifterfiguren mit Stifterwappen jeweils auf den Innen- und Außenseiten der Predellaflügel des Deocarus-Altars von St. Lorenz (1436-1437) in Erscheinung treten.

Das heraldische und in Teilen auch memoriale Pendant zum Volckamer-Grabstein ist der Totenschild von Andreas Volckamer, der als Teil eines Konvoluts von Totenschilden der Patrizierfamilie an der nördlichen Mittelschiffwand von St. Lorenz bis heute angebracht ist. Der Todestag des Verstorbenen wird in dem umlaufenden Schriftband genannt; die heraldischen Elemente sind auch hier das schräggestellte Volckamer-Wappen mit Helm und Helmzier, das von dem kleinen Beischild der Margarethe Haller ergänzt wird.

Die Kirche St. Lorenz als zentraler Ort nicht nur der Repräsentation sondern auch der Memoria für die ansässigen Patrizierfamilien präsentiert bis heute sehr anschaulich das memoriale Medium des Totenschildes, dessen heraldische Natur offensichtlich ist und das sich in überaus großer Zahl von verschiedenen Patrizierfamilien aus dem späten Mittelalter und der frühen Neuzeit erhalten hat. Hervorzuheben ist dabei eine Reihe von Schilden der Schlüsselfelder und Nützel vom 16.-18. Jahrhundert, der Löffelholz und Deichsler vom 15.-18. Jahrhundert, der Imhoff vom 16.-18. Jahrhundert, der Stromer aus dem 15.-18. Jahrhundert oder der Rieter aus dem 15. und 16. Jahrhundert. Die Totenschilde können dabei als „Tafelbild" gemalt oder reliefiert sein; der Wappenschild (üblicherweise mit Helm und Helmzier) sowie Um- und Inschriften bzw. eine ergänzende Inschriftentafel sind seine Hauptelemente. Die memoriale Inszenierung ist und war jedoch nicht nur auf St. Lorenz beschränkt, sondern ist in dieser Form etwa auch in St. Sebald, in St. Ägidien (für die Patrizierfamilie Teztel) oder auch für die Spitalkirche Heilig-Kreuz in Nürnberg tradiert, in dem bis zum zweiten Weltkrieg die meisten der zahlreichen Hallerschen Familienstiftungen und Zeugnisse der Memoria untergebracht waren.[19]

Das Material Bronze, das im Rahmen der Nürnberger Sepulkralkultur für die St. Lorenz-Kirche weitgehend verloren gegangen ist, hat sich – wenngleich kleinformatig – bei den Epitaphien mit der spezifischen Synthese von Epigramm und heraldischen Elementen in großer Zahl auf den Nürnberger „Pestfriedhöfen" Rochus und Johannis erhalten, die ab 1518 aufgrund eines Verbots des Stadtrats, Bestattungen weiterhin im Umfeld der Pfarrkirchen durchzuführen, entstanden sind. Diese waren anfangs nur für das städtische Patriziat bestimmt, schnell jedoch für alle anderen Bürger freigegeben worden.

[19] Vgl. dazu Helmut Freiherr Haller von Hallerstein, Ernst Eichhorn, *Das Pilgrimspital zum Heiligen Kreuz. Geschichte und Kunstdenkmäler* (Nürnberg, 1969) [Nürnberger Forschungen 12].

Die Sepulkraldenkmäler zeigten unfigürliche, einfache Inschriftentafeln in rechteckiger Form, die von Wappen bzw. einer Wappenallianz ergänzt werden konnten.[20] Auch in Hinblick auf die familiären Verbindungen von Nürnberger und Hermannstädter Bürgern sein in diesem Zusammenhang exemplarisch und nicht singulär auf das frühe Bronzeepitaph für Barbara Haller[21] von 1523 verwiesen, das in einer dreizeiligen rechteckigen Tafel die Verstorbene mit Familienstand (Gemahlin von Jobst III. Haller) und Sterbedatum nennt. Eine dazugehörige Wappenallianz der Teztel und Haller war wohl noch bis ins 18. Jahrhundert überliefert. Wesentlich aufwändiger gestaltet ist das auch wiederum nicht singuläre Bronzeepitaph für Ulrich Haller aus dem Jahre 1555, das den bereits 1532 Verstorbenen und seine Gemahlin Katharina Haller (ihre Sterbedaten sind nicht mehr eingetragen worden), geborene Tucher, in einer zehnzeiligen Inschriftentafel nennt.[22] Zu dieser Tafel gehört die Haller-Tuchersche Wappenallianz in einer Dreipassform darüber (Abb. 2). Ein ergänzender Helm mit Helmzier und Oberwappen wird vermutet.

Das wortwörtlich zentrale Element der Reliefierung der Grabplatte Peter Hallers in der Ferula der Hermannstädter Stadtpfarrkirche ist die Wappenallianz, die im Unterschied etwa zum Volckamer-Grab in Nürnberg dreifach ausgebildet ist, wobei das seit 1528 gebesserte Haller-Wappen die beiden von Margaretha Schirmer, Peter Hallers erste Gemahlin, und Katharina Kemény, seine zweite Gemahlin, dominiert. Die Umschrift nennt sein Amt (*THESAVRARIVS AC CONSILIARIVS REGIS*) und sein Sterbejahr 1569 (Abb. 6). Das anfangs genannte memoriale Hauptelement von Grabdenkmälern, die Einbettung des Verstorbenen in einen genealogischen Kontext, geht im Vergleich zu den gezeigten Nürnberger Beispielen über die Verbildlichung von ehelichen Verbindungen in Form von Wappenschilden und Wappenallianzen hinaus. Einem „genealogischen Netzwerk“ gleich, erscheinen zusätzlich zur Wappenallianz Haller-Schirmer und Haller-Kemény in den vier Medaillons heraldische Allianzen mit Hallerschen Ahnenwappen von rechts oben nach links unten der Nürnberger Tucher (mit geteiltem Schild und einer Schrägrechts-Teilung oben sowie dem Mohrenkopf unten), der Nürnberger Rieter (mit der Melusine) und zwei nicht eindeutigen Wappen mit zwei Scheiben im Bild einerseits und mit einer aus einer Rose wachsenden Lilie andererseits.[23]

Abschließend sei noch auf ein Sepulkraldenkmal hingewiesen, das bei der Diskussion von Aspekten des spezifischen Kunst- und Kulturtransfers von Nürnberg und Sibiu/Hermannstadt als vermittelndes Objekt in Betracht gezogen werden kann und sollte. Gemeint ist der Grabstein für Bartholomäus II. Haller von 1551, der sich in der Bartho-

---

[20] Vgl. Otto Glossner, *Der St.-Johannisfriedhof zu Nürnberg*, 4. Aufl. (München, Berlin, 1991) [Große Baudenkmäler 216], 6.
[21] Vgl. Peter Zahn, *Die Inschriften der Friedhöfe St. Johannis, St. Rochus und Wöhrd zu Nürnberg* (München, 1972) [Die Deutschen Inschriften 13], Nr. 142.
[22] Vgl. ebenda, Nr. 807.
[23] Vgl. Marco Bogade, „Peter Haller von Hallerstein – ein unbekanntes Bildnis in Nürnberg“, *Zeitschrift für Siebenbürgische Landeskunde* 35 (2012), 1-7.

lomäuskirche in Frankfurt am Main befindet und als Epitaph, das sich ursprünglich auf dem Nürnberger Johannisfriedhof befand, sein Gegenstück[24] im Hallerschloss in Großgründlach bei Nürnberg hat. Das von einer Umschrift gerahmte, fast lebensgroße figurale Steinrelief präsentiert den Verstorbenen gerüstet und von jeweils drei Ahnenwappen flankiert. Interessant ist hierbei, dass die steinerne Grabplatte von einem Bronzeepitaph[25] in Form eines von einem Lorbeerkranz eingefassten Wappenschildes ergänzt wurde, das neben dem Hallerwappen das Beiwappen seiner Gemahlin Anna Memminger zeigt. Dass das Frankfurter Denkmalensemble in seiner materiellen Zusammenstellung nicht singulär auf die Patrizierfamilie Haller von Hallerstein beschränkt war, belegt etwa die Grabplatte für Christoph Kress von Kressenstein (†1535)[26] in der Kirche St. Georg in Nürnberg-Kraftshof mit einem Relief, das den Verstorbenen fast lebensgroß als Ritters inszeniert, der von Wappenschilden flankiert und von einer Inschriftentafel überfangen wird (Abb. 7). Zum Steinepitaph an der Wand gehört ein zweiteiliges, heute in den Boden eingelassenes Bronzeepitaph, das neben einer Inschriftentafel aus einem von einem Lorbeerkranz eingefassten Vierpass mit Wappenschilden besteht (Abb. 3).

Kann die bronzene Grabplatte Peter Hallers demnach als monumentales, heraldisches und epigrafisches Epitaph Nürnberger Typs interpretiert werden? Und ist, wenn man in Peter Hallers Grabgedicht liest *ME DEVS HIS CLEMES FOELICITER AVXIT IN ORIS,* der gütige Gott stand mir glücklich in dieser fernen Gegenden bei, die Verwendung der Bronze möglicherweise nicht nur eine repräsentierende, sondern vielleicht auch eine „sentimentale" Reminiszenz an seinen familiären Ursprung in Nürnberg?

[24] Vgl. Freiherr Haller von Hallerstein, Eichhorn, *Pilgrimspital*, 190-192.
[25] Frankfurt am Main, Historisches Museum. Inv. Nr. X17414.
[26] Vgl. Breuer u.a., *Franken*, 537.

ABBILDUNGEN

Abb. 1: Detail des Tischgrabs von Konrad Groß (†1356).

Abb. 2: Zweiteiliges Bronzeepitaph für Ulrich Haller (†1555).

Abb. 3: Zweiteiliges Bronzeepitaph für Christoph Kress von Kressenstein (†1535).

Abb. 4: Grabplatte des Konrad von Neumarkt (†1296). Um 1360.

Abb. 5: Grabplatte des Konrad von Neumarkt (†1296). Um 1360.

Abb. 6: Grabplatte von Peter Haller (†1569).

Abb. 7: Grabplatte des Christoph Kress von Kressenstein (†1535).

Pilgrimage Art in Eighteenth Century Transylvania: Icons, Woodcuts and Engravings

Anna Tüskés

The purpose of my paper is the analysis of the engravings representing the Roman Catholic pilgrimage sites in Transylvania dating from the 18th century. These sources constitute an exceptionally versatile group regarding their genre, forms of appearance and potential for use, ranging from front covers through book illustrations and thesis pages to so called devotional pictures and prayer cards. The iconographic analysis is justified by the fact that close to one third of the source material has so far been unknown to researchers covering the topic.

There are thirteen pilgrimage sites from the 17th and 18th centuries known in the region: Csíksomlyó / Şumuleu Ciuc, Gyulafehérvár / Alba Iulia, Kolozsmonostor / Cluj-Mănăştur, Kolozsvár / Cluj, Máriaradna / Radna, Mikola / Nicula, Nagykároly / Carei, Nagyszeben / Sibiu, Szászsebes / Sebeş, Temesvár / Timişoara and Tusnád / Tuşnad Sat. The mapping of religions shows a close relation to the density of pilgrimage sites: most pilgrimage sites can be found in the areas that remained mostly Catholic, or were quickly converted back to Catholicism.[1] It mostly occurs in these locations also that there are two pilgrimage sites within one city, either at the same time or consecutively, namely in Alba Iulia and Cluj.

In Transylvania, three pilgrimage sites became established before 1600 that also remained visited during the Baroque era. (1) The first was the Franciscan monastery church built by János Hunyadi in Şumuleu Ciuc; (2) the second Cluj-Mănăştur, which was a medieval pilgrimage site for Mary, but the icon of the Virgin was later destroyed; (3) and the third the basilica in Sebeş, where the sculpture of the Virgin was already revered in the Middle Ages as well, and when the Protestants occupied the church in the 16th century, the sculpture was not profanised. Therefore, Catholic pilgrimages did not stop arriving here during the era of the occupation. The establishment of the rest of the pilgrimage sites, besides Şumuleu Ciuc that was constantly being visited, falls to the three decades following 1690, when the evolution of pilgrimage sites was the most intense. (4) The (*Hodegitria*) picture of Mary in the St John Capistran chapel near to the Alba Iulia Cathedral was brought by Catholic Bulgarians, who fled from the Bulgarian Ciprovac to Transylvania. Pilgrims had already revered the picture in Ciprovac where it wept. In Alba Iulia it became a pilgrimage destination as of 1712. (5) In the Trinitarian Church in Alba Iulia the picture of the *Maria gravida* was revered. (6) In Cluj, there was a Loretto chapel beside the Franciscan church. (7) In the Holy Trinity Jesuit church in Cluj, pilgrims re-

[1] Gábor Tüskés, *Búcsújárás a barokk kori Magyarországon* [Pilgrimages of the Baroque Period in Hungary] (Budapest, 1993), 13-24.

vered the Hodegetria picture that wept in Nicula in 1699. (8) The Mount Carmel Virgin – *Episkepsis* image of the Franciscan church in Radna was placed on the altar in 1668. In 1695, the Turks occupied Lippa / Lipova and the chapel was set on fire, but the picture remained fully intact. Following the Turkish rule, István Novoslich, a Franciscan monk cleared the chapel and its surroundings in 1722; the pilgrimage church was built in 1767 and the image was placed on its main altar. They began to revere the picture following 1709, when it protected Arad from the pest. (9) Nicula: in the Assumption Cloister Church next to the St Nicholas Abbey on the grape hill, the weeping picture of Mary is revered. (10) At the border of Carei, the Holy Trinity Chapel had been completed by 1703.[2] (11) The Cross of the Trinitarian Church in Sibiu that was taken to Vienna.[3] (12) In the Jesuit church in Timişoara, the picture of Mary was revered. It was crowned in 1716 and named *Maria Serena*. It is only the (13) St Anne Chapel by the side of St Anne's Lake, close to Tuşnad Sat, that was built in the second part of the 18th century.

The cult objects central to pilgrimage sites are overwhelmingly images and sculptures of the Virgin Mary, and they belong to different iconographic types.[4] The most common is the Hodegetria type, but there are regular instances of the Lady of Mount Carmel or the Woman Clothed in the Sun. Amongst saints it is only St Anne who has a pilgrimage site. Amongst types from foreign countries, the Hodegetria of Alba Iulia came from Bulgarian territory. Amongst depictions coming from abroad, in the case of the one in Radna, specific data is available about who brought and purchased the object that later became a cult object: György Virchnossa, an elderly Bosnian man bought the picture from an Italian trader and he gave it to the chapel in Radna. The types that were created locally gave way to further copies.

The number of icons originating in Transylvania is considerably larger than of those coming from abroad. However, we rarely have trustworthy information regarding their exact location and time of origin. Most of the cult objects were created during the Baroque era, but in one instance the representation of Mary dates from the Middle Ages: in Şumuleu Ciuc, the sculpture central to the cult is medieval. In the case of some cult objects originating in Transylvania, information covers who, from where and under what circumstances carried the object from its place of origin to the location that later became the place of cult. The intermediary can be a person of the Church (Franciscans, Bulgarian Observant Franciscans, Trinitarians, and Jesuits) or a lay person having patronage over the given area. Count Zsigmond Kornis, who later became the gubernator of Transylva-

---

[2] Gábor Éble, *A nagykárolyi Szentháromság-kápolna története* [History of the Holy Trinity Chapel in Carei] (Budapest: 1910).

[3] Zsolt Kovács, "Effigies ad similitudinem. A bécsi trinitáriusok kalászos feszületének erdélyi másolatai" [Effigies ad Similitudinem. Copies of the Crucifix with the Ears of the Viennese Trinitarians in Transylvania], in *Stílusok, művek, mesterek. Erdély művészete 1690-1848 között. Tanulmányok B. Nagy Margit emléké-re* [Styles, Works, Artists. The Art of Transylvania between 1690-1848. Studies in Memory of B. Nagy Margit], ed. János Orbán (Kolozsvár, 2011), 295-313.

[4] Gábor Tüskés and Éva Knapp, *Népi vallásosság Magyarországon a 17-18. században* [Vernacular Religiousness in 17th and 18th Century Hungary] (Budapest, 2001), 27-42.

nia, played a decisive role in achieving that the Mary icon in Cluj and Sebeş reached a cult location. The Trinity Chapel in Carei was erected by Count Sándor Károlyi to commemorate the peace treaty of Karlowitz / Sremski Karlovci in 1699. He made orders about the celebration separately in 1718, and the Károlyi family did their pilgrimage alongside common people.

In the genesis legends and the motifs occurring in them the social aspect of the cult is expressed. Regarding content, these can be (1) historic motifs, for example the motifs of the Turks, Protestants or the Pest epidemic, or (2) motifs that travelled across locations – most regularly the following: the weeping of the image, and the preservation of the objects in times of destruction.

The sources have strong ties to the European tradition of the engravings regarding their historical context, the persons who engraved the cult objects, and the motifs behind why they were preserved along the centuries. Most of the representations were prepared in Hungary or by foreign masters who were commissioned from Hungary. Some of the images were preserved owing to various European public and private collections (such as the ones in Budapest, Milan and Nürnberg). The sources also give valuable insight into the visual culture of the various ethnic groups, religious communities and social classes.

The most important iconographic property of the engraving depictions is that they represent the icon or the sculpture that the religious cult centres on. They occasionally also present the narrower or broader context of the theme, or more rarely miracles or historical events linked to the icon. The iconography or label obviously shows that the creation, spreading and usage of the engraving is strongly linked with the given pilgrimage site.

Overview of Research History

The origins of scientific interest about pilgrimage sites in Transylvania are connected with the various genres of engravings. The beginnings go back to the first half of the 19th century. In 1836, Elek Jordánszky, the prebend of Esztergom published a book about the icons of Mary in Hungary, titled 'A Short Description of the Icons of the Blessed Virgin Mary in Hungary and its Adjacent Parts'. This book also published a one-page engraving illustration of the Şumuleu Ciuc, Cluj and Radna sculptures and icons.[5]

More recent research starting from the 1980s has analysed the historical, ethnographic, literary and art historical aspects of icons and objects represented in engravings. The authoritative studies regarding Baroque era pilgrimages, history of cults and vernacular religiousness have been done by Sándor Bálint, Gábor Barna, Margit B. Nagy, Ana and Daniel Dumitran, Géza Galavics, Enikő Hegedűs, Éva Knapp, Zsolt Kovács, Ferenc

[5] Elek Jordánszky, *Magyar országban 's az ahoz tartozó részekben lévő Bóldogságos Szűz Mária kegyelem' képeinek rövid leirása* (Pozsony / Bratislava, 1836), 97-99, 132-140; Gábor Tüskés and Éva Knapp, Utószó, in the reprint: Elek Jordánszky, *Magyar országban 's az ahoz tartozó részekben lévő Bóldogságos Szűz Mária kegyelem' képeinek rövid leirása* (Budapest, 1988), 3-49.

Mihály, Nicolae Sabău, Zoltán Szilárdfy and Gábor Tüskés.[6] The exhibitions and their respective catalogues presenting the veneration of Mary in Transylvania (in 2010, in Odorheiu Secuiesc) and the analysis of the icon in Cluj and Nicula (2011, Alba Iulia) brought significant new results into the research.

I mostly analyse the engravings of the 18th century, but I also present the notoriety and prevalence of the icon in the Trinitarian church of Alba Iulia through the four engravings representing the preceding image in Prague. Furthermore, I will present two sheets from the 19th century in the case of the Radna icon, to illustrate how types of representations have traditionally been transmitted throughout the centuries. In the course of my work I found some engravings that were previously unknown. New items of previously known engravings have also surfaced in new functions and different conditions. In my research I present the masters of engravings from Transylvanian pilgrimage sites, the main types of representation and the different forms of usage. In the course of my current research I have mostly reached new conclusions in the analysis of the engravings representing the icon in Cluj and Radna.

Engravers[7]

Observing the technique, the majority of images are copper engravings[8] and there are only a few woodcuts (Fig. 1-4).[9] In determining the masters, signatures are very helpful: more than half of the engravings are signed. Most of the masters we know by name are represented by one sheet each, and it is a rare occurrence that one master has engraved the

---

[6] Margit B. Nagy, "Adalékok a mikolai Mária-ikon történetéhez" [Addenda to the History of the Icon in Mikola], in Margit B. Nagy, *Stílusok, művek, mesterek* [Styles, Works, Artists] (Bukarest, 1977), 24-31; Éva Knapp, "Barokk kori mirákulumos könyvek magyarországi búcsújáróhelyekről" [Miracle Books of the Baroque Period from Shrines in Hungary] (PhD dissertation, Budapest, 1984); Zoltán Szilárdfy, Gábor Tüskés and Éva Knapp, *Barokk kori kisgrafikai ábrázolások magyarországi búcsújáróhelyekről* [Devotional Pictures of the Baroque Period from Shrines in Hungary] (Budapest, 1987); Sándor Bálint and Gábor Barna, *Búcsújáró magyarok. A magyarországi búcsújárás története és néprajza* [Hungarian Pilgrims. History and Ethnography of the Pilgrimages in Hungary] (Budapest, 1994); Ferenc Mihály, ed., *Mária-tisztelet Erdélyben. Mária-ábrázolások az erdélyi templomokban* [Cult of Mary in Transylvania. Representations of Mary in Transylvanian Churches] (Székelyudvarhely, 2010); Ana Dumitran, Enikő Hegedűs and Vasile Rus, ed., *Fecioarele înlăcrimate ale Transilvaniei. Preliminarii la o istorie ilustrată a toleranței religioase* [Lachrymose Virgins of Transylvania. Preliminaries to an Illustrated History of Religious Tolerance] (Alba Iulia, 2011).

[7] Catalogue of the woodcuts and copper engravings: Szilárdfy, Tüskés and Knapp, *Barokk kori kisgrafikai*; Dumitran, Hegedűs and Rus, *Fecioarele înlăcrimate*.

[8] Copper engraving illustration in the middle of the 1st page of *Pius affectus ad B. V. Mariam […]* bound after *Officium Rakocianum* (Claudiopoli: 1737): Széchényi National Library, 628.095; Roman Catholic Deanery, Târgu-Mureş; Muzeul Carpaților Răsăriteni, Sfântu Gheorghe.

[9] Some woodcuts: 1. Woodcut in the middle of the title page (48 x 40 mm): Mihail Manuil Olsavszky, *Elementa puerilis institutionis in lingua latina* (Claudiopoli: Typis Academ. Soc. Jesu per Andream Feij, 1746). University Library, Budapest, Fc 4901. Reprint (Nyíregyháza: IMI Print, 1999); 2. Signed woodcut on the verso of the title page: *Doctrina christiana […]*. In Monasterio Sanctissimae Triadis typis edita Balasfalvae. Per Michaele Betskereki. Anno 1757. University Library, Budapest, I 8r 102/2.coll. This woodcut illustrates also other books: *Ceaslov* (Blaj, 1766). National Museum of Union, Alba Iulia, CVR 660. See Dumitran, Hegedűs and Rus, *Fecioarele înlăcrimate*, 84-85; 3. Woodcut on prayer card (75 x 52 mm): Szebenben Nyomtt. Hochmeister Márton betüivel Tsász. Kir. Priv. Typog. és Bibliopola által. [Printed in Sibiu with the Types of Márton Hochmeister, Imperial and Royal Privilege Printer and Bookseller]. 1779. In the collection of Béla Szabó.

same topic using either the same or different iconography and in a significantly different size. Such cases are (1-2) the two copper engravings of Philipp Binder (at around 1770) with the icon in Cluj in itself and with a pilgrim and two copper engravings at around 1770 about the icon in Radna with views of the church and the monastery underneath it, (3) furthermore, two copper engravings of Johann Frank von Langgrafen at around 1700. Finally, the engravings made in the Remondini workshop are about the icon in Radna in itself, or surrounded by scenes of miraculous healings, and with the image of pilgrims arriving at the church.

In some cases it also occurs that one copper engraving is utilised in more functions or books. (1) Thus, for example, one of the copper engravings depicting the icon of Cluj was copied and became a cover for the book of Alfonsus Rodericus 'Practicing Christian Good Deeds and Perfection' translated by András Illyés, and published in Trnava in 1688.[10] The copper engraving was bound in the book at least ten years after it was published. The other copy is an independent devotional picture owned by the Historical Picture Gallery of the Hungarian National Museum.[11] (2) Another example is the copper engraving of Johann Heinrich Martin, which illustrates the book *Wahre und ausführliche Beschreibung des Ursprungs des [...] zu Clausenburg [...] vorgestellten Gnaden-Bilds [...]* published in 1735 in Cluj and in the undated book titled *Solatium solatiorum maximum* in Trnava.[12] (3) A third representation of the icon of Cluj features as illustration in two different books published in Cluj in 1735 and 1738.[13] (4) The copper engraving depicting the icon in Cluj by Joseph and Andreas Schmutzer Viennese engravers survives as cover of a book published in Trnava in 1736 and also as an individual prayer sheet. (5) The engraving of Philipp Binder representing the icon of Radna first appeared in the book *Wunder-scheinender Wald-schatten* in Buda in the press of Leopold Francis Landerer in 1769, and later in the same press it was used for the book of Stanislaus Losgott titled *Varia pietatis exercitia omnibus Christi fidelibus accommodata*, also as cover, two years later.[14]

The earliest currently known engraving representation of the sculpture in Şumuleu Ciuc was made by the Viennese engraver Franz Leopold Schmit(t)ner (1703-1761) in the mid-18th century in the form of a devotional picture. It survived in the heritage of

---

[10] University Library, Budapest, RMK I 316; Széchényi National Library, I. 1370/1.

[11] Hungarian National Museum, Historical Picture Gallery, inv. no. 1942/20.

[12] *Wahre und ausführliche Beschreibung des Ursprungs des [...] zu Clausenburg [...] vorgestellten Gnaden-Bilds [...]* (Clausenburg: Acad. S. J. Sim. Thadaeus Weichenberg, 1735). University Library, Budapest, Ac 4950. Bound before the 1st numbered page; *Solatium solatiorum maximum* (Tyrnavia, s.a.). Batthyaneum Library, Alba Iulia, I_2 VII.41.

[13] *Wahre und ausführliche Beschreibung*, bound at the end of the book; *Imago seu speculum [...]* (Claudiopoli, 1738), 6/b. Országos Széchényi Könyvtár, 308.955.

[14] 123 x 71 mm. [Stanislaus Losgott,] *Varia pietatis exercitia omnibus Christi fidelibus accommodata* (Budae: typis Leopoldi Francisci Landerer, 1769). University Library, Budapest, 08326; Széchényi National Library, 288.981; *Wunder-scheinender Wald-schatten [...]* (Ofen: Landerer, 1771). Széchényi National Library, 319358. Knapp, "Barokk kori mirákulumos könyvek," 100; Szilárdfy, Tüskés and Knapp, *Barokk kori kisgrafikai*, 190.

Sándor Bálint and is today in the inventory of the Ferenc Móra Museum in Szeged (Fig. 5). Schmitner completed several commissions coming from Hungary, mostly depicting Biblical scenes and scenes from the lives of Saints. This artist has also made copper engravings of the Mary pregnant icon of the Trinitarian Church in Alba Iulia.[15] While in the case of the former, he only depicted the icon, in the case of the latter he also composed the view of a city in the image. The question arises whether Schmitner was familiar with the engraving of Joseph and Andreas Schmuzers from 1739 and / or the representations of the preceding image of the icon in Prague. These were also prevalent in Hungary, as proven by three devotional pictures and a book illustration (Fig. 6-7).[16] The icon was revered in the Assumption of Mary medieval church in Prague. Its engraving appears in the book *Scala Jacob* published in Bratislava in 1748. The book contains various prayers appropriate for different times of the day and for different religious holidays. It has several illustrations including the representation of three Hungarian pilgrimage sites (Máriapócs, Sasvár, and Homokkomárom). Schmitner's composition is different from the illustration of the book and the devotional pictures in the sense that behind Mary there is a building on a rock, rather than the view of a city.

The copper engraving of Sebastian Zeller depicting the icon of Cluj survived as an individual sheet in the image collection of Count Ferenc Széchényi. Zeller worked in Bratislava in the latter half of the 18th century and engraved portraits, maps and city views.[17] In the above mentioned book *Scala Jacob*, there are several images by Zeller that were unknown to György Rózsa. For example the Crucifixion (following the composition of the Italian painter Francesco Trevisiani, Rome, San Silvestro in Capite, cappella del crocifissio); or the martyrdom of St John of Nepomuk.

From among Hungarian masters, Johann Philip Binder who was born in Bratislava but worked in Buda (1735/36-1811)[18] represented the icon of Cluj in two different copper engravings: the one created around 1770 shows the icon by itself, the other presents it together with the pilgrims praying to the icon. It is interesting about the latter that we can see the votive offerings that prove the miraculous healings hung up on the frame of the composition, such as clutches and objects of pledge shaping arms and legs.

Binder also made two engravings about the icon in Radna in two different compositions and sizes. In the cover depiction mentioned earlier, the icon appears on clouds under a canopy held up by angels. Under the icon is the distant view of the church and the Franciscan monastery with arriving ill pilgrims, and a stag among the trees. Around the

---

[15] Zsolt Kovács, "A gyulafehérvári trinitárius templom és rendház egykori berendezése" [The Interior Decoration and Furnishing of the Former Trinitarian Church and Monastery of Alba Iulia], in *Liber discipulorum. Tanulmányok Kovács András 65. születésnapjára* [Essays in Honour of András Kovács on His 65th Birthday], ed. Zsolt Kovács, Emese Sarkadi Nagy and Attila Weisz (Kolozsvár, 2011), 202, 204, fig. 1-2.

[16] Three devotional pictures in the collection of Ebenhöch, Pannonhalma. Book illustration: *Scala Jacob, per quam ascenditur ad coelum, sive liber precum piarum ex variis authoribus collectus* (Pozsony, 1748), 61. Collection of Zoltán Éder.

[17] György Rózsa, *Grafikatörténeti tanulmányok* [Essays in History of Graphics] (Budapest, 1998), 25-27.

[18] Ibid., 61-62.

canopy there are four Latin quotes: *Monstra te esse matrem* means "Show thyself to be a Mother;" *Duc eum ad Mariam* means "Carry him to Mary;" *Egem aspicite matrem* means "Look we need a mother;" *Ecce matrem vestram* means "Behold your mother." The first is a line from the Vespers hymn to Mary *Ave Maris Stella* ("Hail Star of the Sea"). As for thc other three I didn't find the source. The composition of the other engraving is a lot simpler: there is no canopy held by angels, the icon and the pilgrimage church appear in two separate frames and the pilgrims and the stag do not show up. The depiction was used as a cover by Mátyás József Heimerl (?-1784), the first printer of Timişoara[19] in the publication 'Light Grove Hill' in 1773, but its devotional picture copy is also known.

	University Library RMK I 400/a:1	**University Library RMK I 400/a:2**	**Széchényi Library RMK I 1640**
Coat of arms of István Altorjai Apor	Flyleaf	-	Before dedication
Holy Trinity	Before 1st numbered page	-	Before 1st numbered page
Crucifixion	Between pp. 60-61	-	Between pp. 60-61
Icon of Máriapócs	Between pp. 142-143	-	Between pp. 142-143
Icon of Győr	-	Between pp. 190-191	Between pp. 190-191
Eucharist	Between pp. 248-249	Between pp. 248-249	Between pp. 248-249
Jesus the good shepherd	Between pp. 334-335	-	Between pp. 334-335
Emblem of the Jesuits	Between pp. 374-375	-	Between pp. 374-375
Icon of Cluj	Between pp. 382-383	-	Between pp. 382-383
Allegory of *Regnum Marianum* with the coats of arms of Hungary and Transylvania, together with the icons in Máriapócs and Cluj	Between pp. 400-401	-	Flyleaf
St. Joseph	Between pp. 408-409	Between pp. 408-409	Between pp. 400-401

Among the 18th century engravers, the Viennese copper engraver making covers and allegorical scenes, the above mentioned Johann Frank von Langgraffen created the allegorical scene where the icons of Máriapócs and Cluj appear together. One copy of this print can be found in Péter Pázmány's 'Prayer Book' published in Trnava in 1701, in a

[19] István Berkeszi, *A temesvári könyvnyomdászat és hírlapirodalom története* [History of the Book Printing and Newspaper Literature in Timişoara] (Temesvár, 1900).

copy located in the University Library of Budapest, bound as illustration between pages 400 and 401. The other copy appears bound following the introduction in the *Magna Hungarorum Domina* published in Cluj in 1738.[20] It is insightful to compare three copies of the 1701 edition of Péter Pázmány's 'Prayer Book' from the perspective of publishers using the engraving illustrations. The three copies compared in this study are held in the Széchényi National Library and the University Library Budapest.

From comparing the different copies of the book it is clear that Langgraffen made a series of illustrations consisting of many items, but not the whole series were bound in the individual copies. In the copies that I know the number of copper engraved illustrations ranges between 4 and 10. The themes of illustrations have variety: Holy Trinity, Crucifixion, the icons in Máriapócs, Cluj and Gyor, the Eucharist, Jesus the good shepherd, St. Joseph and so on. The illustrations in this varied iconography partly match the chapters of Pázmány's 'Prayer Book' that they were bound in front of. For example, the copper engraving representing Joseph is just before the chapter about Joseph. There are small differences in the position of a few illustrations.

The Remondini press in Bassano, which was in business for two centuries, published four devotional pictures representing the icon of Radna. The composition of the devotional pictures is varied: the devotional picture from around 1730 depicts miraculous events around the icon in 14 scenes. The two devotional pictures that can be dated at around 1770 only show the icon, one being a simple rectangle, the other in a Baroque-style frame. The fourth devotional picture from around 1780 depicts miraculous events around the icon in seven scenes and there is the distant view of the pilgrimage site below the icon, with the pilgrims arriving in a procession.

We do not know the engraver of the two 19th century sheets representing the icon in Radna, but we know their publisher. The bookbinder and publisher of Bratislava, Alajos Bucsánszky (1802-1883)[21] published a devotional picture with Hungarian, Latin and German text (Fig. 8)[22] in a style close to the artwork of the Viennese engraver lady, Dorneck. It is worth observing from this aspect the double tiers of the halo of the child Jesus, a feature that can be traced back to a devotional picture reproduced from a copper engraving at around 1800. Márton Bagó, a publisher from Buda (?-1873), who published a number of Greek Catholic weekly papers for the Rusyns living in Hungary, released four brochures containing songs to praise the Lord in 1848. The covers of these are decorated by the woodcut of the icon in Radna (Fig. 9).[23]

---

[20] Engraving bound after the introduction (182 x 132 mm): *Magna Hungarorum Domina [...]* (Claudiopoli: Acad. S.J., 1738). University Library, Budapest, Gb 2705.

[21] Gábor Kovács I., "Bucsánszky Alajos útja a kalendárium- és ponyva-tömegtermeléshez" [Alajos Bucsánszky's Way to the Calendar and Trash Mass Production], *Magyar Könyvszemle* 101, 1 (1985): 1-17.

[22] Hungarian National Museum, Historical Picture Gallery, inv. no. T744.

[23] *Négy szép istenes énekek* [Four Beautyful Godly Songs] (Buda, 1848). University Library, Budapest, Hd 2765/27.

From surveying the engravers whose name is known, it can be concluded that more than half of the 18th-19th century engravings of Transylvanian holy sculptures and icons were made by well known masters from Hungary and abroad. Research has enriched the activities of these engravers with some new engravings that have been unknown so far, for example in the case of Sebastian Zeller. In several cases the preceding pictures can be defined as well. In the case of a signed copper engraving I did not find data about the work or personal details of the artist, Joseph Ender. In the case of another representation, the fact that the copy was worn out made it impossible for me to distinguish and recognize the signature. It can also be concluded that the signed engravings constitute the highest quality pieces of the material, and their secondary use and the repeated versions of engraving them prove the long continuity of their history.

Iconography

During the iconographic analysis, I have arranged the engravings based on their main motifs. This grouping also makes it possible to observe the changes or consistency of the iconography across various periods. Based on the above, the engravings can be placed in seven categories: (1) most of the engravings depict the revered object itself, with or without explanatory notes. (2-3) In some cases each, the object appears together with the buildings of the pilgrimage site, with or without the pilgrims. (4) In a few cases, the object can be seen with the buildings of the pilgrimage site, surrounded by pilgrims and scenes of miraculous events. (5) In further cases we can see the object as part of another composition; in one case (6) the icon is surrounded by pilgrims, and in one case (7) it appears surrounded by signs of miracles.

We can make important observations about one devotional picture based on the icon in Radna, made in the Remondini workshop. The coloured copper engraving dated from around 1780 follows an engraving from 1750; the North Italian artist follows his preceding picture with small differences and simplifications regarding both the icon and the depiction of the miraculous events and the pilgrimage site from a distance. The print of Binder around 1773 could also have followed the engraving from 1750, if only distantly, as its preceding image. While he leaves the miraculous events from around the icon, the pilgrimage church and the trees around the monastery, the motif of the fenced garden to the left and the divisions made in the garden all point towards this theory.

The revered object is shown as part of another composition in the copper engraving of Binder which appears as the first of the series of twelve illustrations of the miracle book published in Buda in 1763, presenting the history of the pilgrimage site of Radna.[24] Binder depicts the Italian trader selling the icon to the elderly Bosnian man, György Virchnossa which was later placed on the altar in the chapel of Radna.

---

[24] Éva Knapp and Gábor Tüskés, "Barokk kori mirákulumos könyvek illusztráció-sorozatai" [Illustration Series of Miracle Books in Baroque Period], *Magyar Könyvszemle* 112, 1 (1996): 30-32; Éva Knapp and Gábor Tüskés, *Populáris grafika a 17-18. században* [Vernacular Graphics in the 17-18th Centuries] (Budapest, 2004), 131-153.

A copper engraving made in 1830 shows the icon in a manner different from all previous depictions (Fig. 10-11).[25] The unknown master, who was possibly not very highly trained in Arts, depicted three events of Miklós Dániel's life and he added some explanatory text. The three events are as follows: 1. On 2nd August, 1825, Miklós Dániel was on his way home to his estate called Keresztménes[26] in Arad County, following his investigations in several counties on behalf of the Hungarian Royal Treasury. On the mountains he got into a sudden downpour where all his horses drowned. However, he escaped miraculously after one hour of drowning – just when his brother called Antal found out about the danger from the carter travelling ahead, pleaded to the Virgin Mary of Radna and his prayer was heard. 2. On 19th March, 1829 he was robbed in Pest and accused by the authorities. However, thanks to Divine Providence the burglars and most of his wealth were found. 3. He was sentenced to death in Pest despite his innocence on 3rd September 1830. Because of the upcoming coronation of Ferdinand V to King of Hungary, (Bratislava, 28th September 1830) he asked for mercy, resolving that he would build a chapel in the location of the event recounted first. The engraving was probably commissioned by one member of the aristocratic family of Dániel of Szamosújvár, perhaps his brother Antal, to place emphasis on his plea for mercy for his family member. From our perspective, the depiction of the first event is interesting. In the foreground, we can discover carts and animals floating in the flow of the water on the road as a result of the downpour. In the distance, on the peak of the mountain, there is the figure of Antal kneeling in prayer to the icon of Mariaradna. The engraver did not entirely succeed in evoking the icon of Radna, the Madonna does not resemble the icon of Radna at all.

Usage of the engravings

As we have seen earlier, the engravings representing religious objects fulfilled various functions. The pictures were used in publications, mostly as covers or front pages, more rarely as internal illustrations. The one page depictions belong in a separate group. These can fill the entire first page of leaflets, devotional pictures, thesis pages, prayer sheets or company pages. Alternatively they can be in the middle of pages surrounded by longer text.

The prevalence and users of engravings can be traced based on the function, quality and inscription language of the prints. In the first half of the 18th century the engravings are predominantly in Latin but a prayer sheet in German has also survived from this era; in the second half of the 18th century it was also Latin inscriptions that remained in the biggest quantities, but a Hungarian language inscription is also known. The first half of the 19th century is dominated by Hungarian and German inscriptions. The high quality book illustrations, one page thesis sheets and other prints presenting a more complex iconography were made for the nobility, while woodcuts, devotional pictures showing the icon only and prayer sheets were certainly made to serve the devotional needs of wider groups in the first place.

---

[25] 23,5 x 26,5 cm. Hungarian National Museum, Historical Picture Gallery, inv. no. 1833 II.

[26] Minişel, Arad county.

Copper engravings were sometimes coloured, such as the big size leaf representing the icon of Cluj owned by the Historical Picture Gallery of the Hungarian National Museum, Budapest (Fig. 12).[27] Engravings could have been printed not only on paper but also on coloured silk.

The usage of images can be illustrated by one of the copper engraving depictions of the icon of Cluj.[28] It is the copper engraving of Joseph Ernst Mansfeld,[29] embellished by cover and watercolour painting as a colouring, as well as with textile patches and metal threads (the so-called "nun work").[30] Klára Csilléry bought the item in 1968 in Budapest (in the pawnshop BÁV) and it is now held in the Religious Art Collection of the Hungarian Museum of Ethnography. We see a similar nun work on a copper engraving of the altar of Radna in the exhibition "Icons from Transylvania. Romanian Art – European Heritage" (Fig. 13).[31]

One engraving of the icon of Radna, a big woodcut copy from around 1800 is a good example of the engravings that were pressed and distributed in large quantities, to be purchased cheap at the pilgrimage site.[32] This sheet has so far, to my knowledge, has been unknown and it is currently in a private collection.

To conclude, it can be said that among icons of Mary in Transylvania the most varied iconography is seen in the depictions of the Cluj and Radna icons in engravings. The gradual shallowing and emptying out of the iconography can be traced well, as the images became more and more popular. This is further proven by the change in the language of inscriptions over time as well.

Further research is needed in the case of three Mary-sanctuaries: (1) what happenned with the Mary sculpture of Sebeş which was first brought to Kóród / Coroi and than in the Jesuit church of Cluj by Zsigmond Kornis, (2) where is actually the *Maria gravida* icon of Alba Iulia and (3) what happenned with the Mary icon of the Jesuit church of Sibiu. Regarding the second question, Zsolt Kovács tried to investigate in his

---

[27] Hungarian National Museum, Historical Picture Gallery, inv. no. T 9287.

[28] Ana Dumitran, "Icoana ca intermediar al miracolului şi expresie a identităţii confesionale. Studiu de caz: Beatissima Virgo Claudiopolitana" [Icon as Intermediary of Miracle and Expression of Confessional Identity. Case Study: Miraculosa Beatissimae Virginis Maria Claudiopolitana], in *Identitate confesională şi toleranţă religioasă în secolele XVIII-XXI* [Religious Identity and Confessional Tolerance in the 18th-21st Centuries], ed. Daniel Dumitran and Botond Gudor (Alba Iulia, 2011), 74, note 28, fig. 4.

[29] Other copy of the copper engraving with colouring in the Ecclesiastical Art Museum of Marosvásárhely / Târgu-Mureş: Kisanna Barabás, "A marosvásárhelyi Egyházművészeti Múzeum magánáhitatra serkentő 18. századi szentképei" [The 18th Century Devotional Pictures of the Marosvásárhely Ecclesiastical Art Museum], in *Stílusok, művek, mesterek*, ed. János Orbán, 320, fig. 7.

[30] On nun works see: Éva Knapp and Gábor Tüskés, "Feldíszített katakomba szent ereklyék Magyarországon" [Decorated Relics of Catacomb Saints in Hungary], in *Devóció és dekoráció. 18. és 19. századi kolostormunkák Magyarországon* [Devotion and Decoration. 18th and 19th Century Convent Work in Hungary], ed. László Lengyel (Eger, 1987), 25-44, 118-121.

[31] Alba Iulia, Apor Palace, 25 April - 15 Mai 2013. Organized by Ana Dumitran. Inv. Ar. 657. An other copy of the engraving was published: Gábor Barna, "A fogadalmi tárgyak kutatásáról" [On the Research of Votive Objects], in *"Mária megsegített" Fogadalmi tárgyak Máriaradnán* ["Virgin Mary helped." Votive Objects in Radna], vol. I, ed. Gábor Barna (Szeged, 2002), 17.

[32] 365 x 295 mm.

study about the former furnishing of the Trinitarian Church in Alba Iulia whether there was a remaining icon.[33] However, he did not succeed to find a trace in Katona / Cătina as there was no icon in the inventory of the parish church. Until a few years ago there was a big and fairly good quality painting of the Mary pregnant in the church of a neighbouring village, Mócs / Mociu. The researcher reckons it might be just that. Unfortunately a few years ago when the church was handed over to local Greek Catholics, the priest sold this altar picture – thus in the lack of good photographs this theory is difficult to prove. It would be worth going to Mócs in case the locals have photographs of the painting.

The third case is even more difficult: there is currently only one 18th century copper engraving known about the Sibiu icon in the Germanisches Nationalmuseum in Nürnberg.[34] This represents Mary sailing on the house of Loretto, with the child Jesus in her arms. Inscription at the bottom of the page: *Marianische Gnadenbilt von der Gutten Hoffnung genandt in der Kürchen Soc. Jesu zu Hörmanstadt in Sinnbürgen*. On the script ribbons around Madonna's figure and around the Holy Spirit hovering above her head, it reads: *Salve Regina Mater Misericordiae Vita Dulcedo et Spes nostra salve* (Hail, holy Queen, Mother of Mercy, our life, our sweetness and our hope.) *Jesum Benedictum Fructum Ventris tui nobis post hoc exilium ostende.* (After this our exile, show unto us the blessed fruit of thy womb, Jesus.) So lines 1-2 and 8-9 of the Salve Regina Marian Psalm. From the mouths of the four puttos hovering around Mary's figure, words are coming as well: *O clemens, O pia, O dulcis Virgo Ma[ria]* (O clement, O loving, O sweet Virgin Mary.) – which is line 11 of the psalm.

---

[33] Kovács, "A gyulafehérvári trinitárius templom," 214, note 95.
[34] Szilárdfy, Tüskés and Knapp, *Barokk kori kisgrafikai*, Cat. no. 335.

ILLUSTRATIONS

ELEMENTA
PUERILIS INSTITUTIONIS
IN LINGVA LATINA.

Claudiopoli Typis Academ. Soc. JESU
per Andream Feij Annô 1746.

Fig. 1: Mihail Manuil Olsavszky, *Elementa puerilis institutionis [...]*, Claudiopoli, 1746.

Fig. 2: *Ceaslov*, Blaj, 1766.

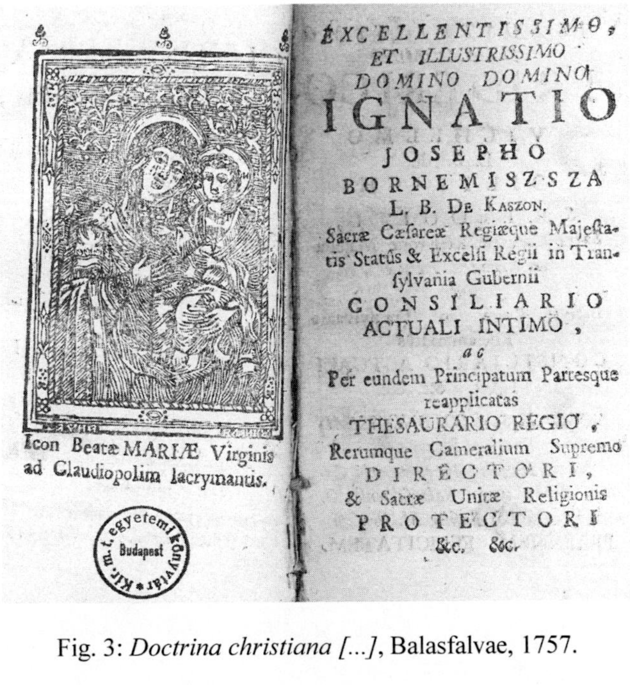
Icon Beatæ MARIÆ Virginis
ad Claudiopolim lacrymantis.

EXCELLENTISSIMO,
ET ILLUSTRISSIMO
DOMINO DOMINO
IGNATIO
JOSEPHO
BORNEMISZSZA
L. B. DE KASZON,
Sacræ Cæsareæ Regiæque Majestatis Status & Excelsi Regii in Transylvania Gubernii
CONSILIARIO
ACTUALI INTIMO,
ac
Per eundem Principatum Partesque reapplicatas
THESAURARIO REGIO,
Rerumque Cameralium Supremo
DIRECTORI,
& Sacræ Unitæ Religionis
PROTECTORI
&c. &c.

Fig. 3: *Doctrina christiana [...]*, Balasfalvae, 1757.

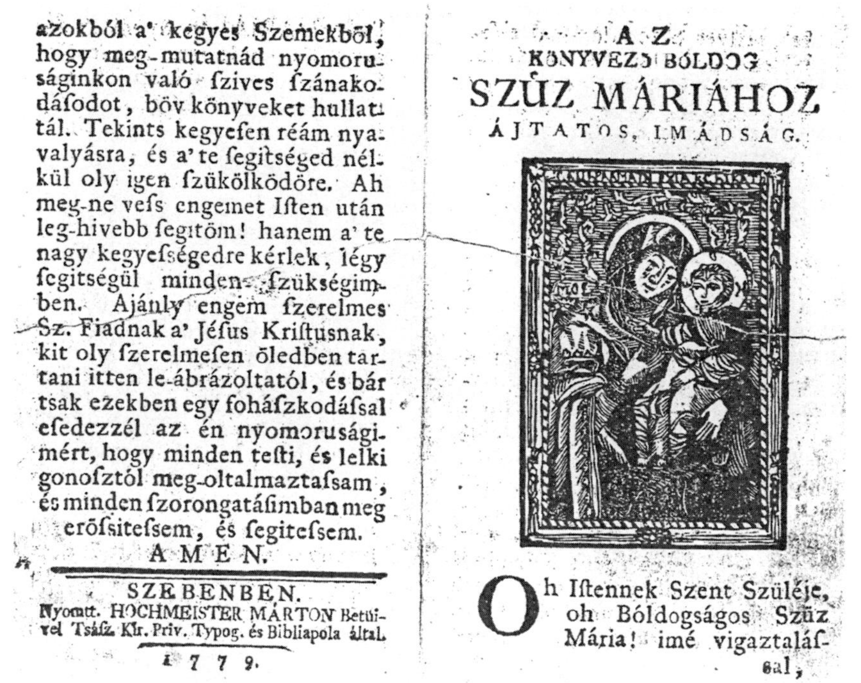
azokból a' kegyes Szemekből, hogy meg-mutatnád nyomoruságinkon való szives szánakodásodot, böv könyveket hullatál. Tekints kegyesen réám nyavalyásra, és a' te segitséged nélkül oly igen szükölködöre. Ah meg-ne vess engemet Isten után leg-hivebb segitöm! hanem a' te nagy kegyességedre kérlek, légy segitségül minden szükségimben. Ajánly engem szerelmes Sz. Fiadnak a' Jésus Kristusnak, kit oly szerelmesen öledben tartani itten le-ábrázoltatól, és bár tsak ezekben egy fohászkodással esedezzél az én nyomoruságimért, hogy minden testi, és lelki gonosztól meg-oltalmaztassam, és minden szorongatásimban meg erösitessem, és segitessem.

A M E N.

SZEBENBEN.
Nyomt. HOCHMEISTER MÁRTON Betüivel Tsász. Kir. Priv. Typog. és Bibliapola által.
1 7 7 9.

A Z
KÖNYVEZŐ BÓLDOG
SZŰZ MÁRIÁHOZ
ÁJTATOS, IMÁDSÁG.

Oh Istennek Szent Szüléje, oh Bóldogságos Szűz Mária! imé vigaztalással,

Fig. 4: Icon of Cluj on a prayer card.

Fig. 5: Fr. L. Schmit(t)ner, Madonna sculpture of Şumuleu Ciuc.

Ad DEUM & Sanctos. 61

rigidum, devium cor meum: & fac, ut DEUM suum verè amet. Da mihi amorem, ut exurat in me multitudinem peccatorum meorum, & accendat; ut tibi in holocaustum nunc & in hora mortis meæ, & in æternum ardeam, Amen.

CULTUS
MAGNÆ MATRIS
Semperque
IMMACULATÆ VIRGINIS
MARIÆ.

AVe Maria gratiâ plena, Dominus tecum; tua gratia sit mecum. Benedicta tu in mulieribus: & benedicta sit sancta Anna Mater tua, ex qua sinè peccato, & macula processisti. Ave sanctissima Maria, Mater DEI, Regina cœli, Porta paradisi, Domina mundi, pura,

Fig. 6: Icon from the Assumption of Mary church, Prague.

Fig. 7: Icon from the Assumption of Mary church, Prague.

Fig. 8: Icon of Radna on a prayer card.

NÉGY SZÉP ISTENES

ÉNEKEK.

1. Szent Emerencz fényessége, 's a' t.
2. Gábriel angyal küldetett atya Istentől,
3. Üdvözlégy egeknek gyöngy kisasszonya.
4. Jaj ha kinját tekintem a' fán függőnek.

Budán,
nyomatott Bagó M. betűivel 1848.

Fig. 9: Icon of Radna.

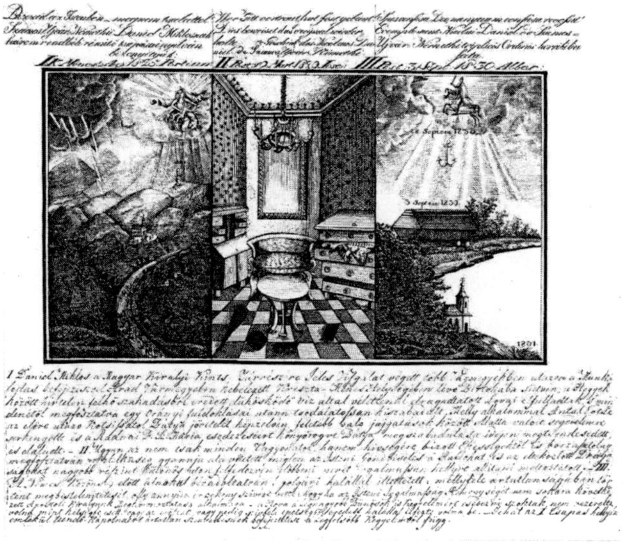

Fig. 10: Unknown artist:
Three events of Miklós Dániel's life.

Fig. 11: Detail.

Fig. 12: Joseph Ernst Mansfeld, Icon of Cluj.

Fig. 13: Unknown artist, Altar of Radna.

DU BERCEAU A LA TOMBE.
Les âges de la vie dans l'iconographie roumaine des XVIIIe-XIXe siècles et l'influence des modèles étrangers

CRISTINA BOGDAN

Cette étude se propose de présenter la manière dont les Roumains d'antan percevaient les étapes de la vie humaine, à travers deux thèmes iconographiques apparentés – la *Roue de la Vie* et les *Degrés des âges* – mais qui ont puisé à des sources d'inspiration différentes. Les artistes ont choisi le dessin, la miniature, la gravure ou la peinture murale pour tracer les images de la trajectoire humaine du berceau à la tombe et pour comprendre les classes d'âge qui font d'un individu un enfant, un adulte ou un vieillard.

Le problème des étapes que l'homme traverse le long de sa vie et les caractéristiques qui leur sont associées ont préoccupé les philosophes, les médecins ou les hommes de lettres dès l'Antiquité, vu que l'âge est, d'une part, le signe indiscutable de la condition mortelle de l'homme et la preuve certaine de sa périssabilité et, d'autre part, l'élément à même de rapprocher l'être humain (avec le rythme de son devenir) des rythmes cosmiques[1].

En fonction de l'auteur en question, les âges de la vie s'inscrivent d'habitude dans un modèle avec 3, 4, 6, 7 ou 12 étapes, mais une chose s'impose constamment : l'idée que l'homme doit se conduire conformément à son âge, afin de ne pas perturber l'ordre du monde dont il fait partie. En d'autres termes, chaque étape de l'existence représente une sorte de seuil de la croissance ou de la décroissance, avec des attitudes, des conduites et un *modus vivendi* très précis.

Dans un ouvrage dédié à la perception des âges dans la pensée médiévale occidentale (*The Ages of Man: A Study in Medieval Writing and Thought*), J. A. Burrow situe les trois théories fondamentales sur les âges de la vie en fonction de la catégorie à laquelle appartiennent leurs promoteurs : les biologistes (3 âges), les physiologistes (4 âges) et les astrologues (7 âges). Le schéma triadique – *augmentum, status, decrementum* – est présenté dans la *Rhétorique* d'Aristote, et repris par Dante dans *Il Convivio*. La variante saisonnière se revendique de Pythagore, étant reprise dans les ouvrages de Diogène Laërce ou d'Ovide (les *Métamorphoses*) et, plus tard, dans les textes du médecin arabe Avicenne ou d'Albert le Grand (*De aetate*). Pour ce qui est de la distribution en 7 âges, d'après le modèle des 7 planètes connues dans le monde antique, elle appartient à Ptolémée, et ne s'est imposée qu'au XIIe siècle dans l'imaginaire occidental.

À chacune de ces représentations d'un *cursus aetatis* peuvent être associées des explications de nature symbolique. Les âges de la vie peuvent être enfermés dans une vi-

---

[1] Éric Deschavanne et Pierre-Henri Tavoillot, *Philosophie des âges de la vie. Pourquoi grandir ? Pourquoi vieillir ?* (Paris : Bernard Grasset, 2007), 100.

sion ternaire, d'après l'image de la Sainte Trinité ou suivant le schéma tripartite du temps – *passé*, *présent*, *avenir* ; ils peuvent prendre 4 visages, comme les 4 vêtements successifs de l'année (les saisons) ; ils peuvent être disposés dans 6 étapes, comme les 6 jarres des noces de Cana, où Jésus Christ a transformé l'eau en vin (Saint Augustin) ; ils peuvent être mis en relation avec les 7 planètes[2] (connus dans le monde antique) ou les 7 Sacrements de l'Église, tout comme ils peuvent rappeler les 12 mois de l'année, les 12 signes du zodiaque, les 12 apôtres ou les 12 portes du Jérusalem céleste[3].

Mais au-delà de ce fondement théorique des escaliers qui montent vers l'âge de la maturité et puis descendent vers le gouffre de la mort[4], ce qui nous intéresse dans l'étude présente est la manière dans laquelle les Roumains d'antan se sont représenté, visuellement, le passage par la vie, les associations qu'ils ont faites entre les différents âges et leurs traits spécifiques, ainsi que les modèles que les artistes ont suivis, du monde post-Byzantin ou de l'univers occidental.

Dans l'espace balkanique, la succession des étapes de l'existence a été transposée dans l'image de la *Roue de la Vie*, le plus souvent selon les prescriptions systématisées dans le chapitre *Comment on représente le temps mensonger de cette vie* du manuel de peinture de Denys de Fourna. La Roue des âges de la vie est le troisième d'une série de cercles qui retracent le devenir tout d'abord au niveau du macrocosme – le cercle des saisons et des signes du zodiaque – et, ensuite, au niveau du microcosme – l'ascension et la déchéance de l'homme.

L'iconographie roumaine du thème est elliptique, les maîtres du pinceau n'ayant gardé de la série de cercles que celui des âges de la vie qu'ils réduisent, d'habitude, à trois. « Les seuils » de l'évolution et de l'involution de l'homme sont concentrés ainsi : l'enfant ou l'adolescent, l'homme mûr et le vieillard cèdent successivement leur place à l'autre, tout le long du parcours circulaire qui prend fin dans la gueule béante du dragon.

On retrouve cette séquence picturale dans la décoration de plusieurs édifices du culte d'une certaine aire géographique du pays, parlant de la manière dont les artisans itinérants étaient influencés non seulement par le texte des guides de peinture, mais surtout par les images vues dans d'autres églises. Dans quelques villages de la zone de Sibiu (Răşinari, Fântânele[5], Tălmăcel, Ocna Sibiului), par exemple, la scène a été peinte dans la décoration intérieure ou extérieure des édifices religieux.

---

[2] *Puerulus* (jusqu'à 7 ans) – la Lune ; *Puer* (7-14 ans) – Mercure ; *Adolescens* (14-21 ans) – Vénus ; *Iuvenis* (21-35 ans) – le Soleil ; *Vir* (35-49 ans) – Mars ; *Senior* (50-65 ans) – Jupiter ; *Senex* (jusqu'à la mort) – Saturne.

[3] Axel Kahn et Yvan Brohard, *Les âges de la vie. Mythes, Arts, Sciences* (Paris : la Martinière, 2012), 137-140.

[4] Il existe en ce sens une bibliographie fondamentale (surtout pour ce qui est de la perception des âges au Moyen Âge) : S. Shahar, *Growing Old in the Middle Ages* (Londres, 1977); E. Sears, *The Ages of Man : Medieval Interpretation of the Life Cycle* (Princeton, 1986); M. Goodlich, *From Birth to Old Age. The Human Life Cycle in Medieval Thought (1250-1350)* (Lanham, 1989); J. A. Burrow, *The Ages of Man: A Study in Medieval Writing and Thought* (Oxford : Clarendon Press, 1988).

[5] Aujourd'hui la représentation de la Roue de la Vie n'existe plus.

À l'église de Răşinari, Grigore Ranite, peintre d'église, a représenté (en 1761), sur la face sud de la tour clocher, les sept âges de la vie, en y ajoutant un détail destiné « à christianiser » bel et bien la scène. Dans un coin de l'image il a figuré Jésus Christ sur un nuage, la croix à la main droite. La vie, avec toutes ses étapes, n'est plus donc coordonnée par cette instance d'origine païenne qui échappe à tout contrôle – la *Fortune* –, comme il arrivait d'habitude dans l'art occidental, dès le Moyen Age[6]. Le peintre d'église de Răşinari propose ainsi un message chrétien : l'existence n'est pas à la merci du hasard capricieux, mais apparaît régie par les lois de la Providence Divine. Le phénomène avait déjà été saisi par Didron dans le périmètre de l'iconographie religieuse athonite, qui avait transformé un motif circulaire archaïque, issu du coffre des symboles du paganisme, « en une roue sanctifiée par le christianisme, qui a fait du destin aveugle une providence éclairée ».

La scène du narthex de l'église « Cuvioasa Paraschiva » [Sainte Paraskévi la Pieuse] de Tălmăcel, peinte en 1780 par Panteleimon, nous dévoile une Roue de la Vie beaucoup plus simplifiée, ne gardant que 3 étapes fondamentales de la vie humaine. L'enfant (ou l'adolescent) habillé d'un vêtement long, vert, les bras attachés à la roue, semble monter avec confiance, son pied gauche vivement élevé, tandis que le vieil homme, vêtu de rouge, glisse sans aucune chance de retour vers la gueule béante du monstre Léviathan (une image rappelant les scènes du Jugement Dernier). Symétriquement placé entre les deux, au-dessus la roue, habillé d'un vêtement censé attester par les couleurs (rouge et vert) sa position médiane entre les âges opposés, de l'enfance et de la vieillesse, l'homme mûr a un air imposant, renforcé par la posture des bras et la présence du chapeau, et confirmé encore par le texte de l'inscription.

Les légendes qui accompagnent les images nous indiquent le statut des personnages de la manière suivante : au-dessus du jeune en ascension : *C'est le moment de vivre* ; au-dessus de l'homme mûr en haut de la roue : *Superbe, celui qui me ressemblera* et au-dessus de celui qui glisse vers la bouche de l'enfer : *Oh, j'ai été quelqu'un et voilà maintenant où j'en suis*.

Un modèle compositionnel similaire, d'une certaine façon, apparaît sur la porte d'entrée de l'église « Naşterea Sfântului Ioan Botezătorul » [La Nativité de Saint Jean Baptiste] d'Ocna Sibiului (peinte dans la première moitié du XIXe siècle), où les trois personnages sont accompagnés par les inscriptions : *Je veux hériter* ; *J'hérite* ; *J'ai hérité.* La roue apparaît inscrite dans un ovale rouge foncé, inscrit, à son tour, dans un demi-cercle comme une chaîne de nuages blancs. D'un côté et de l'autre côté de ces trois contours circulaires, là où dans ce genre de scènes apparaissaient deux anges qui tiraient les ficelles de la roue, il y a ici deux personnages sommairement habillés d'un vêtement de feuilles vertes (autour de la taille et des cuisses), représentant Adam et Ève. L'homme mûr au-dessus de la roue, appartenant à une couche sociale riche, à juger selon ses vête-

[6] Pour les différences entre la Roue de Fortune et la Roue de la Vie, voir Cristina Bogdan, « Sous le signe de *Chronos* ou de *Fortuna*. Les avatars d'un motif iconographique – *la roue de la vie* – dans l'espace roumain et bulgare (XVIIe-XIXe siècles) », *Revue des Études Sud-Est Européennes* XLVIII, 1-4 (2010) : 91-108.

ments, indique l'arbre portant des pommes rouges autour duquel le serpent enroulé offre à Ève le fruit interdit. De cette façon, le trajet circulaire de l'homme vers la mort et la silhouette terne du vieil homme qui glisse implacablement vers la gueule béante du monstre Léviathan acquièrent sens et justification, car la mort est la conséquence[7] du péché d'Adam et Ève, présents dans cette scène. L'image s'éloigne ainsi des prescriptions du guide de peinture, prouvant le désir d'innovation du peintre anonyme.

Dans la plupart des fresques des églises roumaines (tout comme dans celles bulgares ou grecques), ce sont deux anges qui « tirent les ficelles » de la vie (conformément aux indications de Denys de Fourna), symbolisant le passage continuel entre la dimension diurne et celle nocturne :

> « Faites, du côté droit et du côté gauche de la roue, deux anges, ayant chacun au-dessus de leur tête la moitié des saisons, et tournant la roue avec des cordes. Au-dessus de l'ange qui est à droite, écrivez : < le Jour > ; au-dessus de celui de gauche < la Nuit > […] »[8]

Un cas intéressant dans l'espace de Transylvanie est celui de la similarité visuelle entre une gravure (signée par Prixner sc. Pest.) représentant la Roue de la Vie dans le *Calendrier* pour 100 ans imprimé à Buda en 1814[9], la peinture sur bois exécutée par Ioan Eliazar (Lazăr Toacaci) de Piroșa (Valea Chioarului) en 1833 à l'église « Sfinții Arhangheli Mihail și Gavril » [Saints Archanges] de Răstoci (département de Sălaj) et la miniature de Picu Pătruț de *Stihos adecă viers*, de 1844[10]. Il est très possible que le peintre Ioan Eliazar ait connu la gravure de Prixner et s'en soit inspiré[11]. Pour ce qui est de Picu Pătruț, qui avait sûrement eu l'occasion de voir la Roue de la vie dans la décoration extérieure de l'église de Rășinari, il choisit de poursuivre dans sa miniature non pas le modèle offert par le guide de peinture ou par Grigore Ranite (le peintre d'église de Rășinari), mais le modèle plus laïque du *Calendrier* de Buda. La Roue de la vie n'apparaît plus ici contrôlée par les deux anges, mais par une incarnation de *Chronos*, portant sur sa tête un sablier. Les inscriptions des trois images (du *Calendrier*, de la peinture de l'église de Răstoci et de la miniature de Picu Pătruț) confirment l'emprunt de l'information d'un support à l'autre. Au-dessus de la scène apparaît le titre *L'inconstante roue du monde et ses dangereuses vagues*, et à côté des trois moments de la vie on peut lire, à l'intérieur de la roue, les légendes suivantes : *Je veux hériter, J'hérite, J'ai hérité.* Près de la roue est représentée une tombe, au-dessus de laquelle est écrit, en caractères

[7] « Voilà pourquoi, de même que par un seul homme le péché est entré dans le monde et par le péché la mort, et qu'ainsi la mort a atteint tous les hommes : d'ailleurs tous ont péché… », cf. *Romains* 5 : 12, *La Bible*, Traduction Œcuménique (Les Éditions du Cerf et Société Biblique Française, 1988).

[8] Denys, moine de Fourna, *Guide de la peinture*, trad. P. Durand, *Manuel d'iconographie chrétienne grecque et latine* (Paris : Imprimerie Royale, 1845), 410.

[9] Anca Elisabeta Tatay, *Tradiție și inovație în tehnica și arta ilustrației cărții românești tipărite la Buda (1780-1830)* [Tradition et innovation dans la technique et l'art de l'illustration du livre roumain imprimé à Buda (1780-1830)] (Alba Iulia : Altip, 2010), 48-54; 150-151.

[10] *Picu Pătruț. Miniaturi și poezie* [Picu Pătruț. Miniatures et poésie], éd. Octavian O. Ghibu (București : Întreprinderea poligrafică « Arta Grafică », 1985), 164 et fig. 112.

[11] Tatay, *Tradiție și inovație*, 54.

cyrilliques, *De la poussière je suis et à la poussière je suis retourné*, comme un rappel des mots du texte de la messe des morts.

Les similarités compositionnelles sont évidentes, avec la mention que dans la miniature de Picu Pătruţ on ne retrouve pas la partie consacrée, dans les deux autres images, à l'eau et au bateau (beaucoup simplifiée dans la peinture de Răstoci, par rapport à la gravure de Prixner). Quant aux personnages de la roue, il faut remarquer qu'ils ne présentent pas de différences réelles d'âge à l'exception de la variante proposée par Ioan Eliazar ; dans les autres, le personnage apparaît dans tous les séquences sous les traits d'un jeune homme.

Par rapport aux images, commentées antérieurement, des églises de Mărginimea Sibiului, dans ces trois scènes, l'Enfer (suggéré par la bouche béante du monstre Léviathan) est absent, tandis que l'idée du passage dans le monde d'au-delà est suggérée par l'inclusion dans le schéma compositionnel de certains symboles manifestement funéraires : la tombe avec épitaphe, la croix du tombeau, la faux, le serpent (comme signe de la tentation par laquelle la mort est entrée dans le monde).

Dans d'autres zones du pays, où nous avons pu identifier cette scène (dans le département de Maramureş[12], d'Argeş[13] ou de Vâlcea[14]), outre la bouche béante du Léviathan, la Mort est elle aussi représentée, afin de respecter ainsi, par juxtaposition, ce que le guide de Denys de Fourna prescrivait :

> « Puis, au-dessous de lui, faites un tombeau, dans lequel est un grand dragon, ayant dans la gueule un homme à la renverse et dont on ne voit plus que la moitié. Près de là, dans un

[12] Aux églises de Lăpuş (« Adormirea Maicii Domnului » [La Dormition de la Vierge]) et Dobricu Lăpuşului (« Sfinţii Arhangheli » et « Intrarea Maicii Domnului în Biserică » [Présentation de la Vierge au Temple]), que nous présenterons plus en détail ci-dessous.

[13] À l'église de « Sfânta Treime » [La Sainte Trinité] du monastère de Valea, peinte en 1797 par Radu, Constantin, Şerban, Stroe (conformément à l'inscription sur l'un des piliers du porche), dans le registre supérieur de la face sud on déchiffre encore, vaguement, la roue et un reste très pâle du personnage qui tombe. L'édifice du culte « Sfinţii Arhangheli Mihail şi Gavril » de Schitu Matei (la commune de Ciofrângeni), peint en 1857 par le peintre Dumitru (signé sur la face nord de l'église) préserve une bonne conservation de la scène de la Roue, près de la confrontation entre le jeune Prince et la Mort, sur la face sud dans le registre inférieur, accompagnée par les inscriptions suivantes : « *La vie de l'homme est comme une roue qui tourne, jusqu'à un certain moment, puis le pécheur descend dans la tombe* ». À côté du jeune homme en ascension, il y a le texte : « *Maintenant, si je vivais* ». Au-dessus du personnage couronné, on lit l'inscription : « *L'homme imposant qui va se montrer devant moi* », et à côté du vieil homme tombant dans la gueule du dragon : « *Oh, j'ai été quelqu'un et voilà maintenant où j'en suis* ». Dans la même commune (Ciofrângeni), à l'église dédiée aux « Saints Archanges » aussi, du petit village de Duculeşti, dans la décoration du mur ouest du porche (faite en 1872, et refaite en 1998 par le peintre Constantin Ciubuc) on voit une variante de la Roue de la vie qui pourrait avoir apparue sous l'influence de celle de Schitu Matei (malheureusement, nous ne savons pas comme la scène était avant le renouvellement de la décoration, la variante actuelle étant une variante moderne, stylisée, qui présente 4 étapes de l'existence).

[14] À Vâlcea, la scène pouvait être vue, dans le passé, à l'église de « Saint Nicolas » de Dozeşti, peinte en 1828 par le prêtre Vasile Dozescu et à l'église des « Saints Voïvodes » de Păuşa (Călimăneşti), décorée en 1857. Malheureusement, aucune de ces représentations n'existe plus, mais celle de Dozeşti a été dessinée par Maria Golescu dans un de ses cahiers d'études, préservé dans les collections de l'Institut de l'Histoire de l'Art « G. Oprescu» de Bucarest ; elle l'a aussi décrite en détail dans l'article « La Roue du monde », *Revista Istorică Română* IV (1934). Des détails sur l'image perdue de Păuşa peuvent être lus dans l'article de Victor Brătulescu, « Comunicări » [Communication], *Buletinul Comisiunii Monumentelor Istorice* XXVI, fasc. 76 (1933), 91.

tombeau est la Mort, armée d'une grande faux. Elle l'enfonce dans le cou du vieillard qu'elle s'efforce de tirer en bas. »[15].

Dans l'espace roumain, la Mort n'est pas proprement incluse dans la scène (à deux exceptions, à Dozeşti, dans le département de Vâlcea – disparue aujourd'hui[16] – et à Bârza en Olt, une représentation tardive), comme il arrive, par exemple, dans les églises de certains monastères de Bulgarie (Troyan – « L'Assomption de la Vierge » – et Preobrajenski – « La Transfiguration »[17]), peintes par le fameux peintre d'églises Zakharie Hristovitch de Samokov (1810-1853)[18]. Elle apparaît dans la proximité immédiate de la Roue de la Vie, soit dans la confrontation avec le Jeune Prince (comme à Schitu Matei, département d'Argeş), soit comme un personnage indépendant, dans une composition plus ample à caractère eschatologique (à Dobricu Lăpuşului, en Maramureş).

La juxtaposition des séquences visuelles est interprétée par Andrei Paleolog comme une intention non dissimulée d'en indiquer l'ordre de lecture:

> « Si à Schitu Matei, la Roue de la Vie rejoint seulement le dialogue entre < la Mort > et < Le jeune Prince >, à Dozeşti, la fable < Le Vieil homme et la Mort > est accompagnée par < Samson terrassant le lion >, < la Grue >, < la Roue de la Vie > et < la terrible Mort > à cheval. De telles associations, nullement fortuites, nous confortent dans l'idée que la peinture extérieure des monuments de Valachie propose un vaste programme invitant à philosopher moins sur le thème de la précarité de l'existence, que sur celui de la valeur de la vie et de l'espoir. »[19]

Parfois, au même artiste peuvent être attribuées plusieurs séquences picturales avec la *Roue de la vie*, présentes dans les édifices qu'il a décorés. C'est le cas de Radu Munteanu d'Ungureni, un peintre qui a exercé son activité durant la période 1767-1800 en Ţara Lăpuşului, Maramureş et sur Valea Someşului[20]. Les églises de « Sfinţii Arhangheli » et « Intrarea Maicii Domnului în Biserică » [La Présentation de la Vierge au Temple] de Dobricu Lăpuşului (département de Maramureş), peintes probablement entre 1798 et 1800, ont inclus dans la décoration du narthex, sur la face ouest, une image de ce

---

[15] Denys, moine de Fourna, *Guide*, 410.

[16] Golescu, « La Roue », 299 : « À Dozeşti, la scène (...) est réduite à une simple roue tournée par un personnage grossièrement dessiné, et coloré en vert, qui a remplacé les deux anges et qui reste debout, sous la roue. À la gauche du spectateur il y a un autre personnage qui monte ; au-dessus de la roue, un troisième est assis, portant une couronne sur sa tête, c'est l'homme mûr ; à la droite, un quatrième, le vieil homme, s'écroule dans la tombe ouverte. À côté, on voit la bouche du dragon d'où la Mort sort à un cheval rouge, la faux à la main. »

[17] Voir pour détails concernant les deux monastères, *Bulgarian Monasteries*, éd. Stefan Stamov (Sofia, 2004), 81-103 ; Ivan Gaberov et Plamen Pavlov, *Orthodox bulgarian monasteries* (Veliko Tarnovo : Gaberoff, 2004).

[18] Bogdan, « Sous le signe de *Chronos* ou de *Fortuna* », 95-96.

[19] Andrei Paleolog, *Pictura exterioară din Ţara Românească (sec. XVIII-XIX)* [La Peinture extérieure de la Valachie (XVIIIe-XIXe siècles)] (Bucarest : Meridiane, 1984), 58-59.

[20] Ecaterina Cincheza-Buculei, « Câteva date noi despre meşterii bisericilor de lemn din Maramureş, secolul al XVIII-lea (Ţara Lăpuşului) » [Quelques données nouvelles sur les artisans des églises en bois de Maramureş au XVIIIe siècle (La région de Lăpuş)], *Studii și Cercetări de Istoria Artei. Seria Artă Plastică* 27 (1980) : 28-36; Marius Porumb, *Dicționar de pictură veche românească din Transilvania (sec. XIII-XVIII)* [Dictionnaire de peinture roumaine prémoderne de Transylvanie (XIIIe-XVIIIe siècles)] (București : Editura Academiei, 1998), 248-252.

genre. La scène dans le cas de l'église des Saints Archanges est mieux préservée ; nous pouvons ainsi découper 8 âges, inscrits sur les rayons de la roue (15, 25, 30, 40, 50, 60, 70, 80). Il est intéressant d'observer comment l'artiste marque le passage par les étapes de la vie, en créant un parallélisme entre les âges par l'intermédiaire des couleurs des vêtements dont les personnages sont habillés, ou par le jeu de la présence / absence du chapeau. À 15 ans, l'adolescent, les cheveux longs et tête nue, est habillé de bleu ; à 25 ans, le jeune homme imberbe, portant un chapeau, est habillé de vert ; à 30 ans, l'homme est représenté portant des habits rouges ; haut sur la roue, à 40 ans, l'homme à l'âge complet, portant une couronne sur sa tête, est habillé de vêtements des 3 couleurs – bleu, rouge et vert – de la partie ascendante, qui vont se retrouver sur le côté descendant aussi (rouge pour l'homme de 50 ans, vert pour l'homme de 60 ans et bleu pour celui de 70 ans). Les âges d'un côté et de l'autre du cercle sont drapés donc de vêtements de la même couleur : bleu pour 15 et 70 ans ; vert pour 25 et 60 ; rouge pour 30 et 50. Quant au vieil homme (de 80 ans) qui glisse vers le gouffre de l'Enfer, situé au pôle opposé par rapport à l'homme à l'apogée de sa vie (40 ans), celui-ci est figuré nu, la moustache, la barbe et les cheveux blancs, ses bras tendus vers le monde où il s'écroule. On peut encore déchiffrer quelques unes des légendes : à 25 ans – *le monde est délectation* ; à 40 – *qui peut se comparer à moi ?* ; à 50 – *oh, monde, je me dirige vers la mort* ; à 60 – *oh, monde, comme je me suis trompé* ; à 70 – *fatigue et douleur* ; à 80 – *hélas, pauvre moi !*

La scène de l'autre édifice religieux de bois de Dobricu Lăpuşului (« Intrarea Maicii Domnului în Biserică », dont la peinture a été signée dans le registre du Paradis, sur la face est du narthex, très près du plancher – « Munteanu Radu le peintre ») est aujourd'hui difficile à déchiffrer, à cause de la couche de peinture qui a été superposée, au milieu du XIXe siècle, sur la composition initiale[21]. De la vieille Roue, couverte avec des fragments censés évoquer l'Enfer, ont été conservés le contour (deux courbes rouges, et l'espace au milieu coloré de jaune) et la partie supérieure, où se trouve le personnage à l'apogée de sa vie (40 ans, dans ce cas). Dans la partie gauche de l'image, il semble que nous pouvons encore discerner l'un des personnages de la Roue, vêtu de vert, mais vu l'état précaire de conservation de la scène, on n'a pas plus d'informations.

Nous recevons plus de détails dans la décoration de l'édifice du culte de « Adormirea Maicii Domnului » [La Dormition] de Lăpuş (département de Maramureş), sur la face ouest du narthex, près du Paradis et de l'Enfer (des découpages de la scène plus ample du Dernier Jugement). La Roue de la vie a ici 8 rayons, chacun marqué avec un chiffre et accompagné d'une figure humaine. Il est intéressant de voir qu'à la différence de toutes les autres images de l'espace roumain, où l'ascension des âges est faite de la gauche à la droite, ici le développement est inverse, à la droite de l'image se trouvant l'enfant qui monte sur la roue, et à la gauche le vieux, qui se prépare à descendre dans

[21] Cincheza-Buculei, « Câteva date noi », 32, note 19 : « Dans la même place s'est signé le peintre du XIXe siècle, 1857, qui a intervenu sur la peinture de Radu Munteanu dans le narthex, et a repeint l'abside de l'autel, nous léguant une décoration dépourvue de valeur : 'Moşuţ Vasilie' ».

l'au-delà. Les similarités compositionnelles, ainsi que les ressemblances entre les textes des inscriptions adjacentes nous légitiment à supposer une influence exercée par cette image sur Radu Munteanu, d'autant plus que nous avons des informations précises que le peintre avait connu la peinture de Lăpuş avant le moment de la décoration des édifices de Dobricu Lăpuşului (approximativement 1798-1800), vu que l'on lui avait commandé une icône avec la Sainte Trinité pour cette église-là (La Dormition de Lăpuş) en 1767[22].

Dans le cas des monuments du culte de l'espace roumain où l'on la rencontre (à la différence de ceux de l'espace bulgare, par exemple), la Roue de la vie est représentée comme une roue à rayons, employée pour les chariots des paysans ; elle n'apparaît pas comme une image abstraite, un cercle ou une succession de cercles concentriques, ayant le soleil au centre[23] (comme c'est la cas à l'église de « La Nativité de la Vierge » d' Arbanassi) ou comme une femme habillée de vêtements riches, tenant une coupe (comme aux églises des monastères de Troyan et Preobrajenski).

Dans l'espace roumain (à la différence de Bulgarie), la scène apparaît le plus souvent beaucoup simplifiée par rapport aux détails donnés par les guides de peinture, renonçant aux cercles qui figurent le devenir au niveau du macrocosme (l'alternance des signes zodiacaux et des saisons), l'accent étant mis sur la succession des âges de l'homme. Une explication possible de cette option nous est suggérée à la fin de l'article de Maria Golescu de 1934, dédié à ce motif iconographique :

> « La valeur décorative de cette composition, ainsi que sa signification parénétique, ont contribué à sa transmission le long des siècles ; la raison pour laquelle on ne la rencontre plus souvent pourrait être, pensons-nous, le fait qu'elle demande, vue l'exécution minutieuse et la richesse de détails, un temps trop long, étant difficile à rendre dans les fresques, dont la technique consiste justement d'une exécution aussi rapide que possible. Cette même raison clarifierait aussi la tendance constante à simplifier la représentation. »[24].

Une variante de ce motif iconographique se retrouve aussi dans un autre contexte que celui de la peinture des monuments religieux, dans la décoration d'une pierre tombale de l'église de « Sfinţii Apostoli Petru şi Pavel » [Les Saints Apôtres Pierre et Paul] (Bărboi) de Iaşi, construite entre 1841 et 1844 (à la place d'un édifice plus ancien, datant du XVIIe siècle) par l'architecte grec Andrei Caridis. La transcription de l'inscription funéraire, ainsi que la description de la scène[25] sculptée en pierre ont été faites par Maria Golescu

---

[22] Dana Tarnavski Schuster, « Biserici de lemn din Ţara Lăpuşului » [Églises en bois de Ţara Lăpuşului], *Buletinul Monumentelor Istorice* [Bulletin des Monuments Historiques] XLII (1973) : 48 : « Cette sainte icône a été payée par Budea Vasalie d'Ungureni et a été faite par Radu Munteanu le peintre d'Ungureni ».

[23] Cristina Bogdan, « Les représentations de la Mort dans les scènes avec la *Roue de la Vie* dans la peinture roumaine et bulgare (XVIIIe-XIXe siècles) », *Actes du XIVème Congrès International d'Études sur les Danses macabres et l'Art macabre en général*, tome I (Chartres, 2012), 68.

[24] Golescu, « La Roue ».

[25] Maria Golescu, « 'Lumea aceasta deşartă şi amăgitoare' : o piatră de mormânt din biserica Bărboi de la Iaşi » [« Ce monde vain et illusoire » : une pierre tombale de l'église Bărboi de Iaşi], *Cronica Numismatică şi Arheologică* 109 (1938), 2-3 : « Une ligne sépare l'inscription de la représentation du fameux « monde vain et illusoire ». De l'essieu à manchon partent huit rayons vers le centre de la roue, dans laquelle s'inscrivent deux carrés qui se croisent. Les rayons se continuent à l'extérieur de la roue par des consoles supportant des ornements floraux sur lesquels, à la gauche du spectateur, montent, l'un après l'autre, l'enfant, l'adolescent et

dans un article paru dans *Cronica Numismatică și Arheologică* de 1938. L'hypothèse de la chercheuse, que nous partageons, est que l'auteur de cette œuvre en marbre (censée couvrir la tombe d'aga Filaret Athanasios, décédé en 1850) serait l'architecte de l'édifice, Andrei Caridis, qui a fait aussi en 1841 une icône sculptée pour le même édifice du culte. L'artiste grec aurait pu connaître ce motif iconographique dans son espace d'origine, étant donné que la scène était présente en Grèce et dans quelques uns des monastères du Mont Athos.

Les âges de la vie ont été représentés non seulement sur une structure circulaire (comme dans les exemples antérieurs), mais rangés aussi sur une échelle double, un motif « né dans l'estampe dès le XVe siècle et lié à la *Roue de Fortune* »[26], qui ne se généralisa dans l'art occidental qu'au XVIIe siècle. Les *Degrés des âges* sont répartis sur les volées ascendante et descendante d'une échelle, le palier central correspondant généralement à l'âge de cinquante ans. Cette scène, fréquemment retrouvée dans l'imagerie populaire occidentale à partir du XVIIe et jusqu'à la fin du XIXe siècle, est assez peu figurée dans l'espace roumain. Elle apparaît notamment dans une composition incluse dans le cahier de modèles de Radu Zugravu (Radu le Peintre), sous l'influence d'un prototype occidental.

On sait que les sources employées par ce peintre pour ses dessins et croquis sont très différentes, des modèles de tradition byzantine et post-byzantine aux sources occidentales, comme les gravures en bois et en métal, ou les illustrations des livres de l'art occidental des XVIe-XVIIIe siècles. Certaines des gravures d'Albrecht Dürer[27], par exemple, lui étaient sans aucun doute familières et l'ont influencé. Un nombre d'images sont empruntées à l'art occidental, d'après la manière dont elles sont rendues : à la page 113^{r} du manuscrit 4602 B.A.R., nous rencontrons une variante occidentale de représentation de Saint Christophe portant l'enfant Jésus sur son épaule. Une source occidentale a dû être aussi le point de départ d'une scène que Teodora Voinescu intitule, vaguement, *Composition allégorique liée à la Mort*, et qui est en fait une illustration du thème connu comme *Degrés des Âges*. Nous ne savons pas exactement quelle a été la source de Radu Zugravu, mais il est certain que son dessin s'approche de point de vue compositionnel de

---

le jeune homme, représentés de profile. À côté du rayon du sommet de la roue, l'homme mûr est figuré assis, le sceptre à la main, en position frontale. À partir de lui, les consoles renversées écroulent l'homme qui vieillit, le vieux et, finalement, le vieillard dans la gueule béante du dragon, sous le rayon au milieu de la partie inférieure. D'un côté et de l'autre du dragon, deux anges, le Jour et la Nuit, tirent les ficelles de la roue pour la tourner. Au-dessus, le soleil et la lune représentent l'année et le mois. Dans les quatre coins de l'image sont représentés des têtes d'enfant soufflant : les symboles des vents. (...) Sur le cartouche se trouvant à la base de la pierre sous le dragon, on voit un squelette allongé. Sur les côtés, sur les deux premiers cartouches, un peu plus longs, on lit l'inscription grecque : 'Pardonnez-moi, passants' ; puis, dans deux cartouches plus petits, on voit un ange agenouillé soufflant dans la trompette et, dans quelques cartouches plus longs, de nouveau, l'inscription avec le même sens, et dans la partie supérieure de la pierre, la représentation du pélican déchirant sa poitrine pour ressusciter avec son sang les petits tués par le serpent qui ne se voit pas. ».

[26] Frédéric Maguet, « Les objets qui représentent le temps : les Degrés des âges », *Les temps de la vie* (*Les Dossiers du Musée National des Arts et Traditions Populaires*) 4 (1995) : 15.

[27] À la page 17^{v} du manuscrit 5307 B.A.R., il y a un modèle d'après la *Lutte des anges* de l'*Apocalypse* illustrée par Albrecht Dürer.

l'une des premières gravures sur les âges de la vie que nous devons à Christophoro Bertelli (graveur et vendeur italien d'estampes, qui a fait son métier à Modène, dans la deuxième moitié du XVIe siècle). Il a créé deux gravures (afin de figurer de manière distincte les âges de la vie de l'homme et de la femme) qui pourraient être considérées prototypes[28] pour les nombreuses gravures et estampes populaires de plus tard.

Neuf étapes de la vie de l'homme sont réparties sur une échelle à 4 échelons ascendants (incluant les âges de 1 à 30 ans) et à 4 échelons descendants (pour les âges de 50 à 80 ans), à l'intersection des deux côtés opposés se trouvant l'homme mûr (40 ans). Les âges sont symbolisés par l'intermédiaire des animaux, placés dans les niches au-dessous de chaque échelon de l'échelle : un goret, un agneau, une chèvre, un bœuf, un lion, un renard, un loup, un chien et un âne.

Les détails de la composition de Bertelli[29] se retrouvent aussi dans le modèle proposé par Radu Zugravu, avec de petites modifications dans le contour des personnages (par exemple, le squelette à la faux qui se trouve dans l'arche à la base de l'échelle apparaît dans la variante roumaine sans ailes, à la différence de l'image de l'artiste italien, ou d'une représentation (influencée probablement par l'estampe de Bertelli) datant de la deuxième moitié du XVIe siècle (environ 1550-1575) sur une assiette, présente dans la collection du Musée National d'Art de Nürnberg.

Les animaux-signe de l'âge sont placés dans la même succession dans le dessin de Radu Zugravu (avec leurs noms inscrits au-dessus), tandis que les échelons destinés aux personnages arrivés à une certaine étape de leur existence sont marqués de lettres (i, k, l, m, n, h, r), et les personnages en bas (l'enfant assis dans une sorte de trotteur en bois et le vieux assis sur la plaque funéraire de son tombeau ouvert) sont accompagnés par la même lettre – p – comme pour accentuer la symétrie des positions occupées au début et à la fin de la vie.[30]

Bien que le cahier de Radu Zugravu ait circulé dans les milieux artistiques de l'époque, étant reconnu aussi d'après le nom du dernier propriétaire et continuateur de cet art au XIXe siècle, Avram de Târgoviște[31], l'allégorie des âges de la vie n'est pas devenue un thème d'intérêt pour nos peintres ou graveurs de plus tard. Dans la peinture murale, nous rencontrons d'autres représentations de la Roue de la vie (vers la fin du XIXe siècle[32]), mais le thème des Degrés des âges n'était pas spécifique à ce milieu de repré-

---

[28] Edouard de Keyser, « Le thème des degrés des âges dans l'estampe et l'imagerie populaire », *Bulletin de la Société Archéologique, Historique et Artistique. Le Vieux Papier pour l'étude de la vie et des mœurs d'autrefois*, fasc. 261 (1976) : 494.

[29] *Ibid.* : « Dans une arche ménagée sous l'escalier se voit la Mort aiguisant sa faux, tandis qu'un ange conduit un élu vers la gauche et qu'à droite, un démon armé d'une fourche tire par la jambe un réprouvé. De côté se voient, à gauche, l'ange accompagnant l'élu et, à droite, le démon entraînant le damné. Le coin supérieur gauche de la gravure est réservé à la représentation du Christ dans une nuée accueillant les élus, tandis qu'à droite se voit l'enfer avec Satan entouré de démons ».

[30] Teodora Voinescu, *Radu Zugravu* (București : Meridiane, 1978), 47.

[31] *Ibid.*, 29.

[32] À l'église de « Sfântul Nicolae » [Saint Nicolas] de Bârza, département d'Olt, fondée en 1856, refaite en 1869, la scène intitulée *La Vie passagère du monde illusoire* s'approche le plus (dans l'espace roumain) des

sentation, et la gravure populaire sur bois, qui se répand dans l'espace transylvain, ne l'embrasse point. Apparu lors de la deuxième moitié du XVIIe siècle, et développé vers la fin du siècle suivant (comme nous indique la fondation d'une guilde de maîtres graveurs en bois à Gherla en 1777, au but d'établir certaines normes dans l'exercice de ce métier[33]), l'art de la gravure populaire est principalement intéressé par les thèmes religieux[34], car le résultat final du travail des artistes (comme ceux de Nicula, Gherla ou Hăşdate), est censé accomplir les mêmes fonctions que la beaucoup plus coûteuse icône sur verre ou sur bois.

Empruntée à l'Europe occidentale, l'image pouvait être vue assez souvent en Transylvanie à la fin du XIXe siècle et au début du XXe, dans les maisons des familles hongroises, appartenant aux couches sociales moyennes, comme nous démontrent les quelques gravures (accompagnées de textes en Hongrois) que nous avons réussi à identifier jusqu'au présent, dans la collection du Musée Ethnographique de Transylvanie à Cluj, ou dans des collections privées. La source de l'une de ces images figurant les âges de la femme (provenue d'une maison du village d'Imper, le département de Harghita) est une chromolithographie de l'école française de la fin du XIXe siècle (environ 1880), qui avait bénéficié d'une large diffusion au niveau européen[35] ; une preuve en ce sens est la présence des textes, qui sont écrits, selon le marché de vente des gravures, en français, allemand ou hongrois.

Les 9 échelons de la montée et de la descente féminine sont accompagnés de brèves descriptions, censées suggérer la spécificité d'un intervalle temporel. La petite fille au ballon et à la palette est présentée par la légende : *À dix ans, l'enfant joue heureux, dans la joie de son innocence* ; la jeune fille, son amoureux agenouillé devant elle, est

---

indications du guide de Denys de Fourna, ayant au centre l'image du *monde vain et illusoire* (en tant qu'un homme couronné) et conservant les deux séquences concentriques, la succession des saisons et des signes zodiacaux. Le passage de l'homme à travers les âges est accompagné par des textes suggestifs : **Petit enfant de 7 ans** (*Quand est-ce que le temps passera pour que j'aille au royaume de haut ?*) ; **Enfant de 14 ans** (*Oh, année, passe plus vite, pour que j'aille plus vite là-haut !*) ; **Jeune homme de 21 ans** (*Voilà que je suis près de la chaise*) ; **Jeune homme de 28 ans** (*Quel homme est plus haut que moi et qui pourrait me dépasser ?*) ; **Homme de 48 ans** (*Année, je me demande, ma jeunesse est-elle passée ?*) ; [indéchiffrable] **56 ans** (*Oh, comme tu me trompes, monde perfide !*); **Vieil homme de 75 ans** (*Hélas, hélas, oh, mort, qui peut t'échapper ?*). Dans la partie inférieure de la scène est représentée la Mort à la faux orientée vers la tête du vieil homme à demi avalé par le dragon (*L'enfer dévore-tout*). Les paroles du vieux renferment tout le désespoir du damné, sans possibilité d'évasion (*Hélas, qui me délivrera de l'enfer qui dévore tout ?*). La scène a été probablement repeinte au XXe siècle, vu que l'église a souffert des réparations en 1931 et 1943, et les textes des inscriptions sont écrits à caractères latins (non pas cyrilliques, comme c'était la coutume le siècle précédent).

[33] I. Cristache-Panait, « O breaslă a xilografilor din Transilvania » [Une guilde des graveurs en bois en Transylvanie], *Revista Muzeelor* 13 (1967) : 221-222; Marius Porumb, « Breasla pictorilor români fondată la Gherla » [Guilde des peintres roumains fondée à Gherla], in *Un veac de pictură românească din Transilvania. Secolul XVIII* [Un siècle de peinture roumaine en Transylvanie. Le XVIIIe siècle] (Bucureşti: Meridiane, 2003), 79-83.

[34] Marika Kiss-Grigorescu, Cuvânt înainte [Avant propos], *Xilogravura populară din Transilvania în sec. XVIII-XIX* [Gravure en bois populaire en Transylvanie aux XVIIIe-XIXe siècles] (Bucureşti: Arta Grafică, 1970).

[35] Nous avons identifié des exemplaires de ce genre dans divers musées ethnographiques de l'espace européen, comme par exemple le *Musée de la vie populaire* (néerl. *Museum voor Volkskunde*, ou depuis 2000, *Huis van Alijn*) de Gand (Belgique).

définie par les mots : *À 20 ans, dans la fleur de l'âge, elle garde son amour dans la cellule de son cœur* ; la femme, tenant l'enfant dans ses bras, son mari à côté d'elle, l'entourant protecteur de son bras, est figurée avec l'étiquette : *À l'âge de 30 ans, les joies maternes lui procurent tout le temps les bonheurs les plus grands* ; avec ses enfants adolescents agenouillés devant elle pour recevoir sa bénédiction, la femme est dans la position de projeter dans ses descendants l'image d'une étape dépassée (*À 40 ans, les enfants lui rappellent avec joie qu'elle a eu leurs âges aussi*). Au sommet de l'échelle, à l'apogée de la vie, elle jouit d'une nouvelle posture : *À 50 ans, en retrouvant sa tranquillité, son petit-fils la rend si heureuse !* Sur le côté descendant de l'échelle de la vie, les inscriptions adjacentes rappellent plus ou moins explicitement la proximité du dénouement : *À l'âge de 60 ans, le chemin (de la vie) mène déjà en bas. Le crépuscule de la vie s'approche à pas lents ; À l'âge de 70 ans, l'arrière petit-fils est une raison de joie pour la vieille grand-mère ; À l'âge de 80 ans, complètement affaiblie, elle s'appuie épuisée sur son petit-fils dévoué ; À l'âge de 90 ans, toute blanche, elle est prête, tout le temps, pour le dernier voyage.* Symétriquement, sous l'échelle, en deux médaillons situés d'un côté et de l'autre de la séquence centrale (présentant la scène de la création d'Ève, conformément à la *Genèse* chrétienne) sont représentés, chacun accompagné par un ange, le moment de l'apparition dans le monde (*L'âge de la petite enfance. Pour toute sa vie, les anges sont les gardiens de la petite enfant)* et du départ (*Si elle vient déjà d'avoir cent ans, de Dieu elle demande grâce, priant sans cesse*).

De cette façon, la stratification des âges (essentielle dans les époques passées) est codifiée à plusieurs niveaux, par le recours à certaines occupations, attitudes et comportements spécifiques à une période de l'existence, ainsi que par les textes-étiquette, qui accompagnent les personnages.

Curieusement, on n'a plus aujourd'hui que la chromolithographie avec les âges de la femme (une raison en pourrait être aussi le fait qu'elle appartenait à une femme, fille de meunier, née en 1910 environ, à Imper), bien que le modèle français offrît aussi une variante similaire, complémentaire, pour les âges de l'homme. Nous n'excluons pas la possibilité qu'elle soit perdue. De la même communauté (le village d'Imper, commune de Plăieşii de Jos, département de Harghita) provient aussi la chromolithographie encadrée (no. d'inventaire A 589) et exposée dans une maison de Harghita, replacée dans le Parc ethnographique national « Romulus Vuia » de Cluj. Il s'agit toujours des âges de la femme, dans une disposition similaire (9 étapes échelonnées sur les deux côtés de l'échelle, et la nouveau-née et la vielle femme au seuil de la mort dans les médaillons au-dessous de l'échelle ; entre les deux s'interpose, cette fois-ci, à la place de la scène de la création d'Ève, une image domestique, ayant comme protagonistes une mère qui file au rouet et une fille qui berce un bébé). Cette variante manifestement plus populaire que celle analysée plus haut (les vêtements des personnages nous l'indiquent) a circulé dans d'autres zones de Transylvanie aussi, ce qui fait qu'un exemplaire détérioré se trouve dans la collection – datant de 1912 – du Musée ethnographique privé de Geleji Kiralyne

Anna, du village de Rimetea, département d'Alba. Cet exemplaire (datable de 1900 environ) a aussi un équivalent pour les âges de l'homme, conservé dans la même collection privée de Rimetea[36].

Les gravures qui présentent les âges de la vie (répandues en Europe occidentale, mais aussi en Russie[37] aux XVIIIe-XIXe siècles) sortent de la sphère de l'art académique, afin de rejoindre celle de l'imagerie populaire, et perdent graduellement leur dimension religieuse, afin de renforcer leur coloration sociale. Facile à saisir, leur message devient explicite, accentuant les valeurs spécifiques associées au masculin et au féminin (lorsque les gravures ne figurent plus des couples, mais traitent des âges de l'être humain conformément à la ségrégation de genre) : la réussite sociale de l'homme d'une part, l'accomplissement en famille (par la maternité) de la femme, de l'autre.

Le succès durable de ce type de représentation, confirmé par le nombre impressionnant d'éditions imprimées[38] et par la perpétuation de certains schémas compositionnels, nous autorise à affirmer qu'en Occident le thème a été l'un des plus connus et des plus appréciés par le grand public, les gens préférant une telle image dans leur maison, comme un miroir des transformations que le temps entraîne, mais aussi comme un mémento des joies et des difficultés de chaque étape existentielle.

La beauté des images réside dans leur caractère paradoxal : d'un côté, nous avons affaire à une segmentation de la vie en cycles ou seuils qui délimitent (le plus fréquemment) chaque dix ans, de l'autre côté la scène réunit dans un espace de la simultanéité des moments appartenant à une chronologie de l'individu, d'une succession donc. De cette façon, l'image réussit un artifice – saisi et subtilement nommé par Frédéric Maguet (« elle propose une projection synchronique d'un phénomène diachronique »[39]) – et offre au spectateur la possibilité de voir tout un *cursus aetatis*, avec les attentes, les modifications, les évolutions et les involutions de chaque étape.

Alain Charraud[40] a proposé une analyse structurale de l'image, en fonction du décodage de ses 2 axes (*horizontal* et *vertical*) et des 4 zones qui pourraient être séparées (l'échelle, la partie gauche et la partie droite sous l'échelle, l'aire du demi-cercle placé à la base des échelons et le plan éloigné). Sur l'axe horizontal nous surprenons la vie avec ses moments essentiels, autour desquels les rituels de passages (la naissance et la mort) sont mis en scène, tandis que sur l'axe vertical nous est racontée l'histoire de l'intégration de l'homme dans la société, la manière dont il traverse les âges, en accumulant des expériences (au niveau affectif, mais social aussi), laissant derrière soi les gestes, les attitudes

[36] Ces représentations nous ont été signalées par M. le Professeur des Universités Dr. Daniel Dumitran et Mme Dr. Ana Dumitran, qui les ont rencontrées lors de leurs recherches de terrain là-bas.
[37] Voir Pierre-Louis Duchartre, *L'imagerie populaire russe et les livrets gravés : 1629-1885* (Paris : Gründ, 1961).
[38] de Keyser, « Le thème », 500.
[39] Maguet, « Les objets », 16.
[40] Alain Charraud, « Analyse de la représentation des âges de la vie humaine dans les estampes populaires du XIXe siècle », *Ethnologie française* 1 (1971).

et les comportements des étapes parcourues et fermées[41]. Le côté gauche (« l'âge de puérilité ») et le côté droit (« l'âge d'imbécillité et d'enfance ») sont associés à l'état naturel de l'homme, en opposition avec l'échelle qui quantifie son devenir en plan social. La zone au-dessous de l'arche est régulièrement destinée à des scènes qui relèvent d'un autre temps que le temps ordinairement connu (La Genèse, le Dernier Jugement, la séparation des espaces posthumes – la Paradis et l'Enfer), tandis que l'arrière-plan « délimite une quatrième zone, celle des phénomènes cosmiques, qui souligne plus particulièrement le côté cyclique et permanent de la nature : les arbres aux différentes saisons, le ciel, les astres »[42].

Les deux thèmes antérieurement analysés dans l'espace roumain, et particulièrement dans celui transylvain (*la Roue de la Vie* et *les Degrés des âges*), bien qu'ils illustrent le même motif de l'itinéraire de l'homme à travers les âges, renferment quelques différences majeures, du **support** de représentation (la Roue de la Vie apparaît surtout dans la peinture murale[43], tandis que les Degrés des âges n'apparaissent que dans les gravures, les lithographies ou les dessins), aux **sources** d'inspiration (post-byzantines pour la Roue de la Vie, occidentales pour les Degrés des âges) ou à la **lecture/réception** que l'on pratique (La Roue de la vie, par l'inclusion dans le programme iconographique d'un édifice du culte, à côté d'autres scènes à caractère religieux ou moralisateur, impose une réflexion dans l'esprit chrétien, tandis que les Degrés des âges, par l'accent mis sur la dimension sociale du devenir humain et le positionnement du tableau dans l'espace privé de la maison, invite à une méditation à caractère laïque, sur la signification du passage par différents échelons à niveau social et familial, et sur la nécessité d'assumer des rôles spécifiques). Le point d'intersection de ces deux visions – religieuse et laïque – est la constatation du passage vers l'inévitable dénouement, mais aussi la reproduction d'attitudes adéquates correspondant à des périodes bien délimitées de l'existence.

Symbole suggestif de la naissance et du changement, de l'évolution et de l'involution, la Roue de la Vie est en soi un rappel de la cyclicité du parcours humain, caractérisé par des hauts et des bas avant de plonger dans la mort. Parfois, le motif de la roue est sublimé sur les façades des monuments roumains (surtout valaques) en celui de l'horloge solaire[44], qui égrène, à son tour, les heures de la vie, régie par la même successi-

[41] Maguet, « Les objets », 17 : « L'axe verticale mesure, de bas en haut, l'intégration dans la société, l'implication de l'homme dans les affaires communes en même temps que son ascension sociale ; cet axe culmine au sommet du pont, à la cinquantaine ».

[42] Alain Charraud, *apud* Maguet, « Les objets », 18.

[43] Nous la rencontrons aussi dans des gravures (telle celle du Calendrier de Buda) ou dans des miniatures (comme celle crée par Picu Pătruț ou celle du manuscrit d'*Albina* (*Floarea Darurilor*) [L'Abeille, (la Fleur des Dons)], copié par Sava Popovici de Rășinari, voir Gabriel Ștrempel, *Copiști de manuscrise românești până la 1800* [Copistes de manuscrits roumains jusqu'à 1800], vol. I (București, 1959), *apud* Paleolog, *Pictura*, 86.

[44] Paleolog, *Pictura*, 60 : « À Cioroiu – Gura Oltețului (Olt), l'horloge solaire – horloge astronomique – compte les instants de l'éternité cosmique. En fin, l'horloge solaire mesure la durée de la lumière qui baigne la nature, peinte sur la façade de l'église de Iernaticu-Bărbătești (Vâlcea). Les horloges solaires mesurent en heures la lumière, mais aussi la vie qui passe. Elles comptent le temps et, par cet implacable comptage, elles

on perpétuelle de la lumière et des ténèbres.

La brièveté de l'existence terrestre, ainsi que l'impossibilité de connaître l'heure dernière engendre l'idée de la préparation continuelle pour le moment de la séparation de l'âme et du corps. Le message proposé, à l'aube de la modernité, par les peintres d'église roumains, qui ont estimé nécessaire d'inclure la Roue de la Vie dans les programmes iconographiques des monuments qu'ils ont décorés, est à la fois un avertissement et un *praeparatio mortis*. Le statut de « miroir » vers la mentalité, attribué aux images récurrentes à un moment donné, se voit ainsi confirmé. La suggestion de Laurent Gervereau, conformément à laquelle l'image n'existe que dans un contexte, car elle n'est pas atemporelle, mais représente le produit d'une interaction[45], acquiert tout son sens si l'on interprète attentivement les rapports établis entre l'iconographie des églises roumaines peintes aux XVIIIe et XIXe siècles et la mentalité des communautés rurales au milieu desquelles (et souvent aux frais desquelles) s'élevaient lesdits lieux de culte.

---

vous remettent en mémoire et vous indiquent la perspective du passage dans l'au-delà ».

[45] L. Gervereau, « Tuons les images », in *Derrière les images*, dir. M. O. Gonseth, J. Hainard, R. Kaehr (Neuchâtel : Musée d'ethnographie, 1998), 125.

ILLUSTRATIONS

Fig. 1: *La vie insensée du monde trompeur*, fresque extérieure de l'église du monastère de la « La Transfiguration » (Preobrajenski, Bulgarie), peinte en 1849 par Zakharie Hristovitch de Samokov.

Fig. 2: L'homme à 30 ans, haut sur la roue, monastère de la « La Transfiguration » (Preobrajenski, Bulgarie) (détail).

Fig. 3: Fresque extérieure de l'église du monastère de « L'Assomption de la Vierge » de Troyan (Bulgarie), peinte en 1847-1848 par Zakharie Hristovitch de Samokov.

Fig. 4: L'église des « Saints Archanges » de Răstoci, département de Sălaj, peinte en 1833 par Ioan Eliazar (Lazăr Tocaci) de Piroşa.

Fig. 5: L'église des « Saints Archanges » de Dobricu Lăpuşului, département de Maramureş, peinte probablement entre 1798 et 1800.

Fig. 6: *La Roue de la vie* dans la décoration extérieure de l'église de « Saint Nicolas » de Dozești, peinte en 1828 par le prêtre Vasile Dozescu.

Fig. 7: *La Vie passagère du monde illusoire*, l'église de « Saint Nicolas » de Bârza, département d'Olt, fresque de la deuxième moitié du XIXe siècle.

Fig. 8: *Les Âges de la femme*, Imper, département de Harghita.

Fig. 9: *Les Âges de la femme*, Imper, département de Harghita.

MASTER AND DISCIPLE: FAMILY TRADITION, PROFESSIONAL SOLIDARITY AND ARTISTIC INNOVATION. Romanian Painters Either Side of the Carpathians and the Depictions of Saint Christopher (1730-1850)

SILVIA MARIN-BARUTCIEFF

Between 1730 and 1850 the visual representation of Saint Christopher, well-known in fourteenth-century Roman Catholic churches in Transylvania, was disseminated with increasing frequency in the territories of Wallachia and Transylvania. Interest in the topic was directly proportional with the transformations in the Orthodox iconographic programme south and north of the Carpathians, especially after 1750; these changes involve greater freedom of expression for painters in relation to their Byzantine models, and an increase in the number of western sources which these same artists used as inspiration in their personal creations. Starting from these observations, the present paper aims to identify possible trajectories for the circulation of Saint Christopher's image, the possible agents of this process of dissemination, and the family and professional relationships between those who accorded the saint a significant place in church painting.

The notes in the present text are based on the personal archives of the author, who in the period 2000-2013 visited about 1,500 churches in present-day Romania. In this iconographic corpus, over 170 visual representations of Saint Christopher were identified, almost all of them in parishes that are now Orthodox. In what follows we discuss only churches in Wallachia and Transylvania painted by artists known to have been apprenticed or guided by a senior colleague, and only in terms of their depiction of St Christopher.

Changes in the iconographic programme south of the Carpathian

The period between 1730 and 1850, particularly from 1790, is characterized by cultural fertility in Romanian religious iconography. Popular sensitivity, expressed more and more clearly after 1750, would peak in the next century. Concentrated in what Răzvan Theodorescu calls *folk art*, it cohabits without major conflicts with the art of the Brâncoveanu court and its descendents.[1] The social changes of the eighteenth century lead to the appearance of cultural elements that relate late mediaeval Romanian culture to the modern period. The founders of churches were no longer exclusively princes and high boyars, but came from other social categories as well (more and more varied ones), which thrived in the urban environment (townsmen, merchants, artisans) or in the country (bailiffs, rich peasants). Muntenia and Oltenia built churches frantically; where there were no

[1] Răzvan Teodorescu, *Civilizaţia românilor între medieval şi modern: Orizontul imaginii (1550-1800)* [Romanians' Civilization between Medieval and Modern: The Horizon of Image (1550-1800)] (Bucureşti: Meridiane, 1987), vol. 2, 196.

wealthy persons, the village community decided to raise its own church and each member of the rural community contributed somehow, as the inscriptions above the entrance doors, with long lists of names, demonstrate. The collective memory also records foundations by *haiduci* (soldiers), like the church at Dealul Cornii, commune of Lădeşti-Vâlcea, which according to local tradition was built at the expense of the *haiduc* Dragu, in 1789, or the church at Nemoiu, built in 1832 by the *haiduc* Coman.[2]

The topics that saturate the sacred imaginary at that period underline, once again, the popular nature of this culture. The ascendancy of orality over writing, the rich folkloric elements, and the interference between the two levels have already been outlined in studies from the inter-war to the present day.[3]

In the first issue of the magazine *Boabe de grâu* from January 1933, Maria Golescu called attention to some topics that beguiled the rural community of the eighteenth and nineteenth centuries, and which still decorate church walls. Around 1800 the painters from local schools find it appropriate to add some episodes of popular origin to the scenes prescribed by the *hermeneia*, including events from village life or narrative sequences enjoying a wide circulation in the collective imaginary. Thus, besides the *Christ Cycle*, the *Marian Cycle*, saints etc., a curious eye could discern, especially in the nineteenth century, hunting scenes, dancing bears and their leaders [*ursari*] playing different instruments, village round dances, motifs from the *Physiologus*, the parable of the unicorn from *Barlaam and Josaphat*, the Wheel of Life and representations of Death in surprising forms.[4]

Who, then, were these painters and how much freedom did they enjoy? Who supervised their works? What manuals guided them through the iconographic labyrinth? The answers to these questions take shape from the manuscripts owned by the artisans, at some point, as well from documentary data on their activity. The transformations at the stylistic and iconographic levels are the result of changes in the second half of the eight-

---

[2] Local tradition speaks about them today as outlaws (*haiduci)*, romantic figures preserved in the collective memory as persons practicing brigandage in the area, giving to the poor the money taken from the rich, using these pecuniary resources to build churches as well. We have not found by now many pieces of information as far as they are concerned. They might also be soldiers in the service of bailiffs. Concerning the cultural status of the 19th century outlaw as a brigand, see Mihaela Grancea, "Haiducul şi tâlharul – o dilemă culturală? Schiţă de imagologie istorică şi literatură comparată" [The Outlaw and the Brigand – A Cultural Dilemma? Draft of Historical Imagology and Comparative Literature], in *Romantism şi modernitate. Atitudini, reevaluări, polemici* [Romanticism and Modernity. Attitudes, Reassessments, Polemics], ed. Andi Mihalache, Alexandru Istrate (Iaşi: Editura Universităţii "Al. Ioan Cuza," 2009), 507-546.

[3] As far as the popular culture and its themes are concerned, we mention Maria Golescu's studies and, later, Cătălina Velculescu's and Mihai Moraru's ones. The expressivity of iconography in rural churches, many times ignored, represented an object of research for several generations of authors, from Victor Brătulescu to N. V. Drăghiceanu and A. Sacerdoţeanu, from Radu Creţeanu, Teodora Voinescu, Andrei Pănoiu, Ioana Cristache-Panait, Andrei Paleolog to Cristina Bogdan and Ana Dumitran.

[4] For the different faces of Death, as it appears in the national area, see Cristina Dobre-Bogdan, *Imago Mortis în cultura română veche (sec. XVII-XIX)* [Imago Mortis in Ancient Romanian Culture (17th-19th Centuries)] (Bucureşti: Editura Universităţii din Bucureşti, 2002). For the role and circulation of popular books in the Romanian Principalities, see Radu Creţeanu, "L'influence des livres populaires sur les beaux-arts en Valachie aux XVIIIe et XIXe siècles," *Synthesis* III (1976): 101-120.

eenth century. In Wallachia, church painters acquired the right to free professional association.[5] A 1765 charter of Prince Alexandru Ipsilanti mentions the right to organize into a guild, which would result in the emergence of schools of mural painting.[6] In the late eighteenth and early nineteenth century, the new category of artisans counted more and more members, most in the villages. Their manner of life influenced the style of their painting, which here and there lacks canonical rigour in favour of (sometimes involuntary) expressiveness. Themes, motifs and symbols from legends and engravings populate the artists' imaginary. These artists meditated upon them and added novel elements according to their personal sensitivity. Simultaneously, pattern books started to spread, which the painters copied from their fellows or passed down from one generation to the other within the same family; this is a significant, sometimes redundant, source for mural decoration.[7]

From the eighteenth century Dionysius of Fourna's manual of iconography passed through the painters' hands,[8] translated into Romanian by the painter Mihai from Târgovişte, who probably bequeathed it to his son, also a painter.[9] Radu the painter, a well-known artist of the post-Brâncoveanu period, owned a pattern book around 1750 in which we find non-local drawings and engravings, including a drawing of Christopher in the western variant.[10] In the next century, chancellor Răducan of Oltenia copied a painting manual, dated 15th August 1815, and a quarter-century later, the hieromonk Gherontie copied out the *Iconografia, arta de a zugrăvi templele şi icoanele bisericeşti* [Iconography, the Art of painting Churches and Icons] at Hurezi, a manuscript edited in 1891 by Bishop Ghenadie of Râmnic. These works represent the dowry of the church and icon painters. The popular character of the *hermeneias* was underlined in the early twentieth century by Vasile Grecu, who stated that they "appeared out of the practical needs of the church painters' workshops" and not from dogmatic constraints.[11]

---

[5] The issue concerns the Orthodox communities of Transylvania too, as long as they select their artists in view of the criterion of notoriousness gained at the edifices south the Carpathians.
[6] Radu Creţeanu, "Zugravii din Teiuş" [The Painters of Teiuş], *Magazin istoric* IV, 12/45 (1970): 14.
[7] Dobre-Bogdan, *Imago Mortis*, 80.
[8] A monk and a painter, Dionysius of Fourna wrote the book between 1728 and 1733. Cf. Anastasia Tourta, "Moştenirea bizantină în pictură după căderea Constantinopolului" [Byzantine Heritage in Painting after the Fall of Constantinople], in *De la Întruparea Cuvântului la Îndumnezeirea Omului. Icoane bizantine şi postbizantine din Grecia* [From the Incarnation of the Word to the Deification of Man. Byzantine and Post-Byzantine Icons of Greece], ed. Konstantinos Sp. Staikos, catalogue of the exhibition at Romania's National Art Museum, 6 October 2008 - 15 January 2009, Rom. transl. by Ilie Frăcea (Bucureşti: National Art Museum, and the Cultural Greek Foundation, 2008), XXIX.
[9] Ştefan Meteş, *Din istoria artei religioase române* [Elements of Romanian Religious Art], vol. I. *Zugravii bisericilor române* [Painters of Romanian Churches], in *Anuarul Comisiunii Monumentelor Istorice pentru Transilvania* (1926-1928 [1929]): 21.
[10] See Romanian Academy Library, Romanian manuscripts no. 4602, f. 113r, in Teodora Voinescu, *Radu Zugravu* (Bucureşti: Meridiane, 1978).
[11] Vasile Grecu, *Carte de pictură bisericească bizantină. Introducere şi ediţie critică a versiunilor româneşti după redacţiunea lui Dionisie din Furna, tradusă la 1805 de arhimandritul Macarie, cît şi după alte redacţiuni mai vechi, traduceri anonime* [Byzantine Church Painting Book. Introduction and Critical Edition

Sponsors are interested in the artisans' abilities to finish the work. The documents of the time record contracts in which the painter commits to meet the deadline agreed upon, to use quality paints, but also to paint the scenes the founder asked for in the interior church decoration.[12] Such a contract is signed on 19th July 1826 between the *clucer* [lord steward] Costache Vlădăianu and the painter hired to decorate the church of Saints Nicholas and Spyridon at Craiova. To win his client's trust, the painter notes in detail the themes that he agrees to include in the mural ensemble.[13] The sponsors' concern was well-founded, as not all of those who called themselves painters were gifted, and the intentions proclaimed do not always match the results obtained. In the period covered by the present paper, from 1730 to 1850, we can find very good painters, skilled draughtsmen familiar with the tradition in whose tutelage the new generations grow, but we also find, especially around 1800, artisans with a limited artistic education.

In order to avoid the destruction of mural painting by shoddy workers, the Church tried to control the phenomenon, as attested by a document issued in 1781 by Bishop Filaret of Râmnic, requiring painters to submit to testing at the diocese before starting their activity.[14] As the number of churches and painters was continually increasing, the authorities were frequently overwhelmed by the situation. Churches often eluded ecclesiastic vigilance; as we go farther from the time when the only founders were the princes and boyars, and especially as we go farther from town, painters took more and more liberties

---

of the Romanian Versions after Dionysius of Fourna's Edition, Translated in 1805 by Archimandrite Macarie, As Well As after Other Older Editions, Anonymous Translations] (Cernăuţi, 1936), 33.

[12] Meteş, *Din istoria artei*, 75. For the artistic activity of the painters in Moldavia, see Emil Diaconescu, "Contracte de zugravi de biserici" [Contracts of Church Painters], *Studii şi cercetări de istoria artei. Seria Artă plastică* 14, 1 (1967): 95-129.

[13] "I entrust my document to the honourable tax-collector Costache Vlădoianu so it could be known that he hired me to paint their church here, dedicated to St. Nicolas and St. Spyridon, from the beginning to the end, as shown below:

The alter should be painted on white, the high vault, with angels and the sacrifice of Abraham from the Bible on the sides; upward, repairs should be made, and the evangelists should be painted on white background; lower, the great martyrs should be on white too, with their crowns gilded with gold and the ornaments of their clothes gilded with gold and silver. As for the iconostasis, I will make it… <stained text> frightened and I will gild everything with gold and silver, as well as the twelve great feasts included in the iconostasis and the other saints, these will all be gilded with gold and silver. The narthex will also be painted in white, with Mother of God Platitera up on the ceiling and the four liturgical fathers and lower, the Life-Giving Spring, the Tent of Salvation and other two feasts of the Mother of God, whichever they would choose, and lower the blessed founders of the church and in the pulpit in white; and I will gild with gold Manoil's crown, and paint the front iconostasis with sufficient gold and make girdles with painted flowers all around the church outside.

The above mentioned painting is my commitment by this document, to do on my expenses, with my food and my painters and labourers, for quality work, as fine as one can find nowhere else, due to both the paints and gold and the skill. And he is supposed to offer the timber to make the scaffolding that is thick poles, ropes and a servant to take care of our necessities. And the price was decided to 1,700 thalers, that is one thousands and seven hundreds; and we have received at the beginning … <blank> thalers, that is … <blank> lei, and the rest of it will come in portions, as the work will advance. And to make it safer, I wrote the document myself and signed." Cf. Nicolae Stoicescu, "Cum se zugrăveau bisericile în secolul al XVIII-lea şi în prima jumătate a secolului al XIX-lea" [How Churches Were Painted in the 18th Century and the Early 19th Century], *Mitropolia Olteniei* XIX, 5-6 (1967): 421-422.

[14] Meteş, *Din istoria artei*, 73.

with the iconographic programme. The painting is more narrative, the apocryphal elements are more numerous and, on the whole, there is more appetite for the sensational. Painting extends to the outside, where the artists give vent either to their own imagination or to the imagination aroused by the collection of parables and stories assimilated in the original environment. Of course, the avoidance of schematism is, generally, commendable, differentiating religious foundations one from another, although in some cases to the detriment of artistic quality. Let us however mention the most remarkable cases, where originality of perspective meets artistic skill; let us look at instances where skilled and conscientious painters deviated from the canon.

On both sides of the Carpathians: the circulation of Saint Christopher's image

From the altar to the church façade, painters disclosed their identity, moving their signatures from inside to outside the churches as we approach modernity. In the mid-eighteenth century there were several centres of mural and icon painting in Oltenia and Muntenia, at Râmnicu Vâlcea, Craiova, Piteşti, Buzău and Bucharest, with active and mobile members willing to prove their artistic skills and piety, working not only in the important towns but also in less accessible places. Preserved epigraphic testimony to their efforts give us their names:

> "Grigorie, Ioan, his son, 1760;" "Gavrilă the painter from Craiova, 1809;" "in the days of the emperor Alexandru Pavlovici of all Russia, with the blessing of our most holy bishop Nectarie of Râmnic, in 1812, September 20th, by dean Gheorghe the painter;" "Matei the painter, Raicu the painter, Bratu Dumitru. And the work was ended in June 30th, 1825;"[15] "priest Vasilie the painter (1828);" "decorating and painting it, as it can be seen, in August 1837. Priest Mathii, by pain(t)ers, Gheorghie, Ioan and Nicolae [of L]ăpuşata;" "1843, August 14th, painters Gheorghe Bănică, Grigorie, Ioan, Nicolae."[16]

This will never be a complete image, as some of the inscriptions were destroyed or became illegible over time. On the basis of what has been preserved, we can however reconstruct church painters' activity south of the Carpathians. We are relatively well-informed about the activity of the most important artists and school leaders, Constantinos the Greek and Pârvu Mutu, painters to the Cantacuzino boyars and Prince Constantin Brâncoveanu, who both played a major role in the early circulation of St Christopher typology.[17] Given the period – the seventeenth and early eighteenth centuries – their spon-

---

[15] Maria Golescu, "Biserica din Budeşti" [The Church of Budeşti], *Arhivele Olteniei* XVIII, 101-103 (January-June 1939): 92.

[16] For the last two inscriptions, see *Inscripţii medievale şi din epoca modernă a României. Judeţul istoric Vâlcea (sec. XIV - 1848)* [Medieval and Modern Inscriptions in Romania. The Historical County of Vâlcea (14th century - 1848)], ed. Constantin Bălan (Bucureşti: Editura Academiei Române, 2005), 607 and 638.

[17] For the two painters, see C. Bobulescu's studies, "Zugravii. Pârvu Mutul, Constantinos grecul (1682-1735) şi Nifon Udrescu, stareţul mănăstirii Secului (1657-1765), cu autobiografia lui Ghenadie Pârvulescu arhimandritul (22 octombrie 1805-6 - 6 septembrie 1873)" [The Painters. Pârvu Mutul, Constantinos Grecul (1682-1735) and Nifon Udrescu, the Prior of the Monastery of Secu (1657-1765), with an Autobiography of Ghenadie Pârvulescu the Archimandrite (22 October 1805-6 - 6 September 1873), *Arhiva Românească* V (1940); Victor Brătulescu, "Inscripţii şi însemnări din biserici" [Inscriptions and Notes in Churches], *Mitropolia Olteniei* XIV, 10-12 (October-December 1962): 700; Victor Brătulescu, "Dascălii de zugravi Ioan

sors were the princes and high boyars, who in almost all cases wanted an image of Saint Christopher carrying the Christ-child in the churched they founded.

In the latter eighteenth century, the situation would change. The number of painters circulating the theme increased, exploding in the next century, when the depiction of Saint Christopher, once highly unusual, is now overwhelmingly frequent in iconographic programmes, in the sub-Carpathian area in particular. Of all the types of illustration of this saint, modernity seems to prefer the animal-headed image, occurring at the same time as painting shifts towards the exterior, where scenes with apocryphal or secular content appear. The echoes of the legend of a handsome young man who renounced his beauty, asking God to replace his human appearance with an animal one, impressed rural communities so much that zoomorphism became the most popular feature of this image, with consequences for his visibility in church. We will try to follow below the trajectory of these representations on both sides of the Carpathians, to see what are the results of choosing one type or another, and to what extent we can speak about relationships between these artists.

Where the large church of the Polovragi monastery had this type of representation at the beginning of the century, Grigorie Ranite and his younger brother Gheorghe Ranite preserved it in the area, using it in 1734[18] in the church founded by Imperial Counsellor Matei Glogoveanu.[19] We can see here a foundation commensurate with the important function the Romanian boyar held in the Austrian state, of which Oltenia was at the time part. There two monuments, Polovragi and Glogova, are related through the two brothers, who might have been familiar with that version of St Christopher due to their father, Hranite, one of the most gifted artists of the Hurezi school, who worked on painting the Polovragi monastery in 1703.[20] He must have been a significant teacher not only to his sons, but also to other artists.[21] Later, at the hospital church of Polovragi, painters named

---

şi Mincu de la Râmnic şi Argeş" [Painter Apprentices Ioan and Mincu from Râmnic and Argeş], *Mitropolia Olteniei*, 11 (November-December 1963): 860-861; Teodora Voinescu, *Pârvu Mutu Zugravu* (Bucureşti: Meridiane, 1968).

[18] The painting is signed by several painters: Dimiu, Vasile, Grigorie, Ştefan, Gheorghe, Şerban and Stan.

[19] The church is built in 1730, a time when Oltenia was part of the Habsburg Empire (1718-1739). Matei Glogoveanu appears in 1719 in the list of the highest class boyars in Mehedinţi. He will assert himself in politics, due to his philo-Austrian father-in-law, Staico Bengescu, and the church of Glogova is started in the year when Matei becomes imperial counsellor, i.e. 1731, short before he dies. The Austrian report records him as one of the honourable boyars of Oltenia, a speaker of his native language exclusively, as the documents show: "[…] Sie beede den Matheum Glogovenul der Ob Er Schon wie fast alle Bojaren keiner audern als seine Muttersprache Kündig, die reputation habe ein ehrlicher Mann zu sein [...]." Eudoxiu de Hurmuzaki, *Documente privitoare la istoria românilor* [Documents regarding Romanian History], vol. VI, 1700-1750, apud Octav-George Lecca, *Familiile boiereşti româneşti. Istorie şi genealogie (după izvoare autentice)* [Romanian Boyar Families. History and Genealogy (According to Authentic Sources)], ed. Alexandru Condeescu (Bucureşti: Libra & Muzeul Literaturii Române, w. y.), 311. The painting will be done with financial help from the widower Stanca Glogoveanu, first in 1732, then in 1764. Cf. Radu Creţeanu, "Biserica din Glogova" [The Church of Glogova], *Mitropolia Olteniei* 6-7 (1956): 361.

[20] We refer to the monastery of Polovragi, situated today in the county of Gorj.

[21] For the edifice where brothers Ranite worked in 1734, see Creţeanu, "Biserica din Glogova," 356. For the life and activity of Grigore Ranite, see also Marius Porumb, "Grigore Ranite – un pictor craiovean peregrin în

Gheorghe and Ioan paint the first lamb-headed Saint Christopher on present Romanian territory and also preserved the earlier type of the saint carrying the Christ-child. We assume that this Gheorghe was the son of Hranite, who had painted the first zoomorphic image in the area at the skete of Păpuşa. This Gheorghe was recorded between 1740 and 1742 at the Serbian churches of Szentendre, Estergom and Ráckeve.[22] Gheorghe's brother, Grigore, repeated the model from Polovragi in the nave of the church at Răşinari, introducing thus the zoomorphic Saint Christopher in Transylvania.[23] The saint's iconography thus proves to be a family story, generating art tradition in both sub-Carpathian Oltenia and Transylvania.

In the same area of Oltenia, Anghel the deacon joined other painters at the church of Padina (1813), built the year before with the financial support of the archpriest Dobre and his wife Ioana.[24] This version of the lamb-headed young man would be borrowed and represented on the walls of the church in his own village, Dozeşti. The famous Vâlcea family of several generations of artists from Dozeşti[25] would show consistent interest in the uncommon variant of the saint; a proof is the late painting in the church at Turceşti-Lespedea, made, according to the inscription, by Ion Dozescu, in 1878. Matei from Craiova was the main artist at Budeşti Vâlcea (1825), helped by his brother Raicu; twelve years later he was paid to work at Crainici, Mehedinţi, assisted by Constantin and Fotache from Craiova.[26] In both monuments, Christopher, this time with the head of a lamb, joins the gallery of saints in the apse of the nave. A continuator of the school of Matei Zugravu, Gheorghe Bănică paints the church of Obeni, Vâlcea in 1843, opting for the mild zoomorphic version.[27]

Besides painting manuals, further sources of inspiration for painters were the ico-

---

Transilvania" [Grigore Ranite – a Painter from Craiova in Pilgrimage to Transylvania], in *Artă românească, artă europeană. Centenar Virgil Vătăşianu* [Romanian art, European art. Virgil Vătăşianu Centenary], ed. Marius Porumb, Aurel Chiriac (Oradea: Muzeul Ţării Crişurilor, 2002), 173-180; Ana Dumitran, "Un zugrav de elită: Grigore Ranite" [An Elite Painter: Grigore Ranite], *Annales Universitatis Apulensis. Series Historica* 14, I (2010): 83-98.

[22] In all of the cases, he worked with another painter from Banat, Nedelcu Popovici. See Dorina Sabina Pârvulescu, *Pictura românească din Banat. Secolul al XVIII-lea* [Romanian Painting in Banat. The 18th Century] (Timişoara: Editura Graphite, 2006), 35-36. At Ráckeve, Gheorghe Ranite and Nedelcu Popovici are the authors of the painting on the Royal doors. Cf. Vojislav Matić, *The Serbian Ráckeve Orthodox Monastery* (Budapest: Platoneum, 2009), 36.

[23] For the physiognomic morphology of Saint Christopher, see "L'art de fuir le canon. Une classification morphologique des représentations de Saint Christophe en Roumanie," in *Actes du XIVème Congrès International d'Études sur les Danses macabres et l'art macabre en général*, ed. Cristina Bogdan, Silvia Marin-Barutcieff (Bucureşti: Editura Universităţii din Bucureşti, 2010), 211-229.

[24] The list with the names of painters was copied in the volume edited by Bălan, *Inscripţii*, 753.

[25] We can find references to them in several researchers of sacred iconography in Oltenia; see Andrei Pănoiu, *Pictura votivă din nordul Olteniei* [Votive Painting in North Oltenia] (Bucureşti: Meridiane, 1968), 15, 18-19; Andrei Paleolog, *Pictura exterioară din Ţara Românească (secolele XVIII-XIX)* [Exterior Painting in Walachia (18th-19th Centuries)] (Bucureşti: Meridiane, 1984), 28.

[26] Matei, the son of Ilie from Craiova, is recorded in the capital of Oltenia, as an inhabitant of the Sfântul Spiridon suburb. Mentioned, for the first time, at the church of Zorleşti, in 1813. Cf. Andrei Pănoiu, "Matei zugravul – un premergător al picturii moderne româneşti" [Matei the Painter – a Forerunner of Romanian Modern Painting], *Revista Muzeelor* 4, 1 (1967): 71.

[27] Pănoiu, *Pictura votivă*, 23.

nographic programmes in the area where they lived or worked. In four villages that now make up the commune of Uda, Argeş, the zoomorphic character seems to have been copied from one church to another. First painted in 1807 at Şetrari by Anghel, who signed the work in the prothesis,[28] it was used two decades later by Nicolae at Cotu, then in 1830 at Ciorâca; in 1831 at Branişte, the name of the painter is Ioan.[29] Near the village of Branişte, in the southern area neighbouring the counties of Argeş and Olt, along the rivers Cotmeana and Vedea, the legend of the lamb-headed saint proved extremely popular, and the number of representations is significant (Hârseşti,[30] Urlueni,[31] Floru, Ciureşti, Optaşi-Măgura).

The skills of some of these artists were appreciated by their colleagues from Transylvania and the Banat, who often invited them to come to work there. The Romanians' denominational identity in the Habsburg Empire and their problematic political status until the reforms of Emperor Joseph II entitled them to look for models south of the Carpathians among celebrated artists. From this standpoint, towns such as Vâlcea, Craiova and Piteşti were the main centres attracting the attention of the Transylvanian communities.

The journeys of one of the most important painters in both Oltenia and Transylvania, Grigore Ranite, prove that gifted artists circulated long distances for professional reasons.[32] Trained by his father, Grigore was, together with Gheorghe, a major disseminator of the Brâncoveanu iconographic programme beyond the frontiers of Wallachia. After contracts with the monastery of Tismana and the church of Vădenii Gorjului (both in 1732), he was called to the Saint Nicholas Church in Şcheii Braşovului (1738), an important artistic centre for Romanians from both provinces in the eighteenth century due to its strategic geographical position.[33] In 1741 and 1742 the two Ranite brothers worked in the Banat and, as we have seen, in the Serbian Orthodox churches of Hungary.[34] In the 1750s they returned to their native Oltenia, where Grigore decorated the chapel of the diocesan

---

[28] Victor Brătulescu, "Meşteri zugravi, constructori şi ctitori de pe Vedea şi Cotmeana, regiunea Argeş" [Painters, Builders and Founders at Vedea and Cotmeana, the region of Argeş], *Glasul Bisericii* XXI, 5-6 (1962): 515-518 and 559; Brătulescu, "Dascălii de zugravi Ioan şi Mincu de la Râmnic şi Argeş" [The Painters' Teachers Ioan and Mincu from Râmnic and Argeş], *Mitropolia Olteniei* 11-12 (1963): 869. Radu Creţeanu mentions the activity of this painter in the area of Piteşti-Costeşti between 1787 and 1810, see "Zugravii din Vâlcea" [The Painters from Vâlcea], 89.

[29] The repainting from the beginning of the 21st century affected the representation of Saint Christopher as well, see *infra*.

[30] Repainting in the 20th century.

[31] The representation in the nave of the church of "Adormirea Maicii Domnului" [Dormition of the Mother of God] in Urlueni, commune of Lereni, disappeared, after the repainting done at the end of the 20th century. (Piece of information offered by priest Sandu Munteanu during the research made on 29 September 2007.) The painting of the church had been made by Vlaicu from Câmpulung and Niţu Dascălu from Piteşti. See Paleolog, *Pictura exterioară*, 96.

[32] Vasile Drăguţ, *Dicţionar enciclopedic de artă medievală românească* [Encyclopaedic Dictionary of Romanian Medieval Art] (Bucureşti: Vremea, 2000), 360; Marius Porumb, *Dicţionar de pictură românească veche din Transilvania. Sec. XIII-XVIII* [Dictionary of Old Romanian Art in Transylvania. 13th - 18th Century] (Bucureşti: Editura Academiei Române, 1998), 317; Marius Porumb, *Un veac de pictură românească din Transilvania. Secolul al XVIII-lea* [A Century of Romanian Painting in Transylvania. 18th Century] (Bucureşti: Meridiane, 2003), 55.

[33] Drăguţ, *Dicţionar*, 360.

[34] Porumb, "Grigore Ranite – un pictor craiovean peregrin," 176.

church of Râmnic (1753) and the skete of Crasna (1757-1759), assisted for the latter by his son Ioan.[35] In 1760 and 1761, the same Grigore painted the church of Cuvioasa Paraschiva in Răşinari, again with his son.[36] This was a significant moment in the evolution of mural painting in the whole intra-Carpathian area, as Grigorie would consolidate his relationships with the village in several ways, first and foremost by training the painters Iacov and Stan from Răşinari,[37] as well as the painters working in the Banat, Vasile Diaconul and Şerban Popovici.[38] Grigore Ranite also stood sponsor at the marriage of Iacov, son of Man from Răşinari, in 1754 at the monastery of Sărăcineşti in Oltenia, further demonstrating his standing in Răşinari.[39]

Simon Oprovici from Craiova signed his name to the wooden church of Saint John the Evangelist at Apoldu de Jos on 10th August 1772,[40] a year after painting the church at Poiana Sibiului.[41] Pantelimon, who worked on the frescoes at Tălmăcel, Zărneşti and Sâmbăta de Jos, was also from Wallachia, whence he brought his sources of inspiration.[42]

In 1770, Simeon from Piteşti, together with his former apprentice Nicolae, painted the church of the Holy Archangels at Ghelari. It is known that the priest of Argeş had settled as a parish priest at Silvaşu de Sus around 1760.[43] Between 1759 when the monastery of Prislop was painted and 1789, Simeon was very active as a painter and an icon painter, being recorded in his village of adoption (1765-1797), as well as at Cinciş (1776), Zolt (1777), Nucşoara (1779), Subcetate (1783), Baru (1785), Sânpetru (approx. 1785), Densuş (1789).[44]

Even when painters were from Transylvania, many of them were the disciples of painters from Muntenia and Oltenia who were settled, temporarily or permanently, beyond the mountains. In other instances, artists went to learn in Râmnic, a centre of cultural effervescence at the time, to Curtea de Argeş or to the villages and hamlets in the south, where they painted religious edifices together with famous masters.[45]

The geographical positioning of Ţara Făgăraşului and of Ţara Bârsei next to Wallachia and the intense trade relations between the regions favoured cultural exchange,

---

[35] It seems that this is the first mention of the collaboration between father and son. Ioan will be afterwards known as father Ioan Grigorovici. See ibid., 177.
[36] Porumb, *Un veac de pictură*, 58.
[37] Ana Dumitran, Elena Cucui, "Sfânta Troiţă într-un trup în opera zugravilor de la Feisa" [Holy Trinity in One Body in the work of the painters at Feisa], *Nemus* II-III, 3-6 (2007-2008): 139-154.
[38] Pârvulescu, *Pictura românească din Banat*, 49; Eadem, *Pictura bisericilor ortodoxe din Banat între secolul al XVII-lea şi deceniul al treilea al secolului al XIX-lea* [Painting of Orthodox Churches in Banat between 17th Century and Third Decade of 19th Century] (Timişoara: Editura Excelsior Art, 2003), 170-171; Porumb, *Dicţionar*, 449; Dumitran, "Un zugrav de elită," 85.
[39] Dumitran, Cucui, "Sfânta Troiţă într-un trup," 141.
[40] Meteş, *Din istoria artei*, 120; Ana Dumitran, Elena-Daniela Cucui, *Simon Bălgrădeanul* (Alba Iulia: Altip, 2009), 7.
[41] Dumitran, Cucui, *Simon Bălgrădeanul*, 7.
[42] Porumb, *Dicţionar*, 280.
[43] Porumb, *Un veac de pictură*, 68.
[44] Ibid., 68.
[45] This is the case of Stan and Iacov from Răşinari who, in 1761, worked at Curtea de Argeş. See Porumb, *Dicţionar*, 23.

resulting in commissions from one side of the Carpathians to the other, but also in the establishment of schools of painters educated in the spirit of Brâncoveanu and post-Brâncoveanu style art. One such was Father Ionaşcu, from the village of Iaşi in Făgărăş, who painted the murals at Avrig and Sâmbăta de Sus.[46] A note from 1737 on a manuscript with the lives of the saints shows that Ionaşcu was also a bookbinder.[47] Maybe the painter discovered different hagiographic themes in the pages of the manuscripts, themes which he might have transmitted to his apprentices from Sâmbăta de Sus. One student of the monastery painting school was Teodor, who in 1791 painted the church of Mărgineni, where an interesting Saint Christopher has been preserved to this day,[48] together with a colleague named Gaftanail.[49] This Teodor passed on his art to his son Sava, who signs the painting at the church of Saint Nicholas at Calbor in 1813, and at the porch of the church at Sâmbăta de Jos in 1814.[50] Both iconographic ensembles include images of Christopher. Another family, the Grecu, with three generations of artists working in Făgăraş and the valley of the Hârtibaci, also contributed to spreading the animal imagery. Thus it is found in the church at Sărata, painted around 1810 by Nicolae and Alexandru Grecu, brothers from Săsăuş, the first generation, then at Ţichindeal in 1818, painted by a younger Nicolae from the second generation, and three years later at Voivodenii Mici, painted by the same young Nicolae and Gheorghe from Săsăuş.[51] Unfortunately, two of these were re-painted in the last two decades. We can still notice, however, that the prototype is the dog-headed saint with his head turned in each case to the viewer's left, a sign of stylistic relation. At Sărata, the wall painting presents the hybrid variant of the dog-headed saint bearing the Christ-child, already known in the region in the villages of Ţara Făgăraşului and Ţara Bârsei, the closest being Mărgineni.[52]

---

[46] Ioana Cristache-Panait, "Rolul zugravilor de la sud de Carpaţi în dezvoltarea picturii româneşti din Transilvania (secolul al XVIII-lea - prima jumătate a secolului al XIX-lea)" [The Role of Painters South the Carpathians in the Development of Romanian Painting in Transylvania (18th Century - Early 19th Century)], *Studii şi Cercetări de Istoria Artei*, series *Artă Plastică* 31 (1984): 74.
[47] Ibid.
[48] Ibid., 75.
[49] Marius Porumb states that a few decades ago, in the narthex there was still an inscription preserved, recording the painter Gaftnail. See *Dicţionar*, 236.
[50] Ibid.
[51] For the artistic contribution of the Grecu family, see Meteş, "Zugravii bisericilor române," 120-122; Valeriu Literat, "Două biserici din Ţara Oltului" [Two Churches in Ţara Oltului], in Idem, *Biserici vechi româneşti din Ţara Oltului* [Old Romanian Churches in Ţara Oltului], ed. Nicolae Sabău (Cluj-Napoca: Dacia, 1996), 228-241; Idem, "Biserici din Ţara Oltului şi «de pe Ardeal» zugrăvite de o familie de pictori" [Churches in Ţara Oltului and in Transylvania Painted by a Family of Painters], *Anuarul Comisiunii Monumentelor Istorice pentru Transilvania* (1932-1938): 3-54; I. Fulea, "Biserici monumente istorice pictate de familia Grecu" [Historical Monument Churches Painted by the Grecu Family], in *Arhiepiscopia Sibiului – pagini de istorie* [The Archiepiscopate of Sibiu – History Pages] (Sibiu, 1981), 211-226; Maria Zintz, "Pictura murală din sudul Transilvaniei în secolele XVIII-XIX. O familie de zugravi din sudul Transilvaniei: familia de zugravi Grecu" [Mural Painting in South Transylvania in the 18th -19th Centuries. A Family of Church Painters in South Transylvania: The Grecu Family], *Crisia* 16 (1986): 455-475; Silvia Marin-Barutcieff, "Picturing the Difference. Image of the Jew in Several Orthodox Churches of Southern Transylvania (Part One. Elements of Jewish Costume)," *Studia Hebraica* 9-10 (2009-2010): 430-446.
[52] Representations of the hybrid type are present at Sânpetru (1784), Mărgineni (1791), Prejmer (1791),

The painters from Ţara Făgăraşului are later seen in central Transylvania, in Mureş, Alba or Hunedoara. In the villages of Mureş, for instance, many wooden churches were painted by artists from the areas of Mărginime, Ţara Oltului or even Oltenia and Muntenia.[53] Vasile Drăguţ stated that the circulation of artists led to the "stylistic unification of painting north and south the Carpathians,"[54] but we consider this an iconographic and less a stylistic unity, visible in the case of at least some topics, such as the iconography here discussed.

We cannot ignore the contribution of painters from the artistic centre of Feisa, established by Iacov from Răşinari.[55] His son Gheorghe carried on his profession and artistic gift, painting both icons and murals after 1763.[56] He introduced the image of Saint Christopher at Sartăş in 1780, painting together with Toader Ciungariu, as we learn from the inscription at the entrance. The animal representation reached the area less than a decade after that at Răşinari, in the painting in Geogel village by Gheorghe Tobias, where the saint is lamb-headed, as in the church from Mărginimea Sibiului.[57] Some important names in Central and North Transylvania are Father Nicolae from Feisa, another son of Iacov, Vasile Ban, apprentice to Nicolae,[58] Porfirie Şarlea, and Ştefan and Matei Şarlea, the last four also kinsmen.[59] Porfirie Şarlea, a son of Vasile Ban, a name that certifies the artistic tradition of his family,[60] painted the lamb-headed Saint Christopher in the church

---

Braşov-Dârste (1833). The most ancient ones, probably dating from post-1780, are the evidence of either familiarization with a Greek visual source, or a correct identification of the referent by the painting and of the superposition of the two literary versions, the eastern hagiographic and the western ones, the latter hypothesis being the less probable.

[53] Ionaşcu, originating from Făgărăş, painted the iconostasis of the church of Iernut; here too, in 1740, David from Curtea de Argeş, before settling to Bihor, painted icons; Marcu from Vlaşca painted, in 1751, the church of Sântandrei, a place where he settled down. Iacov from Răşinari decorates in 1787 the nave of the edifice from Cuştelnic. See also Vasile Drăguţ, "Bisericile de lemn de pe Mureş, Arieş şi Târnave în lumina mesajului lor istoric şi artistic" [Wooden Churches on the Rivers of Mureş, Arieş and Târnave in the Light of Their Historical and Artistic Message], in Ioana Cristache-Panait, *Biserici de lemn, monumente istorice din Episcopia Alba Iuliei, mărturii de continuitate şi creaţie românească* [Wooden Churches, Historical Monuments of the Episcopate of Alba Iulia, Testimonies of Romanian Continuity and Creation] (Alba Iulia: Editura Episcopiei Ortodoxe a Alba Iuliei, 1987), 24.

[54] Drăguţ, *Dicţionar*, 24.

[55] For the activity and the representatives of the School of Feisa, see Cristache-Panait, "Rolul zugravilor," 83-84; Eadem, *Biserici de lemn*; Porumb, *Dicţionar*, 125; Idem, *Un veac de pictură*, 46-47.

[56] For his activity, see Ana Dumitran, "Pictura românească în judeţul Alba până la mijlocul secolului al XIX-lea. Demersuri pentru o bază de date" [Romanian Painting in the County of Alba by Mid-Nineteenth Century. Steps for a Data Basis], *Patrimonium Apulense. Anuar de arheologie, istorie, cultură, etnografie, muzeologie, conservare, restaurare* XII (2012): 47-50.

[57] We do not know yet where Gheorghe Tobias borrows it from, which might have been his sources. The mural painting from 1770 was paid, according to the inscription, by the "founders Buta Ioan and Magdalină, David Crăciun and Barbara. Painter Tovie father Gheorghie," see Dumitran, "Pictura românească în judeţul Alba," 205.

[58] Ana Dumitran, Elena-Daniela Cucui, "Zugravul Porfirie Şarlea din Feisa. Profilul iconarului" [Painter Porfirie Şarlea from Feisa. Profile of the Icon Maker], *Nemus* IV, 7-8 (2009): 219.

[59] Dumitran, "Pictura românească în judeţul Alba," 50-51.

[60] The vertical kin relationship is between Porfirie Şarlea and Vasile Ban. The former was the illegitimate son of the latter and of Rafila Şarlea that is why he will have the mother's last name. His father will however take care of the son's artistic instruction. Between Ştefan and Matei Şarlea, the previous researches show a horizontal kin relation, the two being brothers, while their father is not yet known. See Dumitran, "Pictura

at Cuci on the southern side of the nave, and at Deag on the north wall.[61]

At least some of these painters' apprentices used the animal-headed Saint Christopher, spreading his image from one church to another. Thus Toader Popovici, apprentice to Iacov from Răşinari, used the motif at the church of Comori and afterwards at Lăpuşna.[62] An artist named Toader is recorded by tradition at Mura Mică as having painted the walls of the village church;[63] probably he is the same person who painted the church at Lăpuşna. At Mura Mică, Saint Christopher finds a place near the door again, in an eschatological partnership with Death, preparing his rake and scythe to reap the souls.[64] Therefore, the theme enjoys quite a free circulation in the area, most of the time using the dog-headed form, like it appears at Urisiu de Jos or at Maioreşti.[65]

Another painter working in central and northern Transylvania in the same period, Ştenţel Condrat, used Saint Christopher in the churches of Năsal [66] and Culpiu.[67] Nicolae Bădău from Lupşa, icon and wall painter, started to decorate churches too; his works in the early nineteenth century in Ţinutul Hălmagiului disseminated the image that he had surely encountered in Valea Arieşului.[68] He seems to have been the apprentice of Toader Ciungariu, who worked with Gheorghe from Răşinari at Sartăş, where there is a Saint Christopher as we have seen. Nicolae Bădău used Saint Christopher at Troaş in 1813, but in a "tamed," anthropomorphic variant.[69] Represented in a cartouche as a bust, he occupies the southern surface of the western wall of the nave. It is possible that Bădău opted for the cartouche due to the small painting surface, where a window was cut. In approximately the same period, Bădău was called to Juliţa to decorate the wooden church of the neighbouring village (1813 again).[70] Placed this time in the narthex, at the western ex-

românească în judeţul Alba," 51-52; Dumitran, Cucui, "Zugravul Porfirie Şarlea," 219-221.

[61] In the village of Deag there are two wooden churches. In the present study we are referring to the one dedicated to the Saint Archangels.

[62] The church was built in 1779 in the village of Comori and brought in 1935 in Lăpuşna. Cf. Cristache-Panait, *Biserici de lemn*, 229.

[63] Ibid., 224.

[64] For the eschatological values of the theme, see Silvia Marin-Barutcieff, "Accompagner Saint Christophe, le protecteur contre « la male mort ». Des thèmes eschatologiques dans l'iconographie occidentale et roumaine," in *Dying and Death in 18th-21st Century Europe*, ed. Marius Rotar, Victor Roşu, Helen Frisby (Cluj-Napoca: Accent, 2009), 247-260.

[65] Of the 7 representations of Saint Christopher identified on the current territory of the county of Mureş, the one at Mura Mică is the only lamb-headed one, the other six illustrating the canine version.

[66] Cf. the inscription above the entrance door, which resisted the unfortunate repainting of the edifice.

[67] Ioana Cristache-Panait attributes this to him, by stylistic analogy with the monument from Sărmaşu, see *Bisericile de lemn*, 180.

[68] See the representations from Geogel (1770) and Sartăş (1780).

[69] In July 2006, the last figure of the year was not integrally readable any more, unless in its upper part, where a curve might correspond to figures 2 or 3. Coriolan Petreanu indicates the year 1813, in accordance with a piece of information provided by the priest of the village in the third decade of the 20th century. See Coriolan Petreanu, *Bisericile de lemn din Arad* [Wooden Churches from Arad] (Sibiu, 1927), 7. Ioana Cristache Panait also proposes 1813 as the painting date, cf. Ioana Cristache-Panait, "Prezenţa zugravului Nicolae de la Lupşa Mare în pictura bisericilor de lemn de pe Valea Mureşului de Jos" [The Presence of Painter Nicolae from Lupşa Mare in the Painting of the Wooden Churches from Valea Mureşului de Jos], *Mitropolia Banatului* XXVII, 1-3 (1977): 158.

[70] For his biography, see Dumitran, "Pictura românească în judeţul Alba," 66-67.

tremity of the north wall, a dog-headed Saint Christopher is the first martyr in the row. Ten years later, at Şteia in the valley of Crişul Alb, the saint is on the southern wall near the entrance door; here Bădău explores the visual versions of the saint, opting for a double representation as soldier and as Christ-bearer. The latter version was painted in 1829 in the village of Stânceşti, by Moise Borşoş from Abrud, an apprentice of another famous painter with a long career, Simion Silaghi, Borşoş painted the church at Birtin, Hunedoara, in the same year together with Simion's son, also Simion.[71] A decade earlier, Borşoş probably painted the church at Almaş-Sălişte, showing Saint Christopher as Christ-bearer.[72]

Although Maramureş is not part of the Transylvanian perimeter, we also examine here the artistic achievements of that area as far as these relate to the Saint Christopher theme. Of the examples identified so far, some were circulated by two painters working in the region. One of these, Radu Munteanu from the village of Ungureni in Ţara Lăpuşului, is recorded in 1767, when he painted an icon at Lăpuş.[73] In the 1770s Munteanu wandered from one church to the other in the historical Maramureş, neighbouring his home region. In 1780 he painted the interior of the church at Deseşti, a village in Valea Marei, together with Gheorghe.[74] The elongated silhouette of a giant Saint Christopher can be seen in the lower segment of the north wall of the nave. The saint has a beard, as in late mediaeval representations which were the basis of dissemination of the Christ-bearer type in the Greek world. But at Deseşti we find a new type, as the child is absent from the giant's shoulder. In his left hand, Christopher holds the cross of martyrdom, and in the right a large sword. Radu Munteanu's manner is post-Byzantine, rustic and decorative.[75] At the end of the century he returned to his native region, where he painted two churches for the Greek Catholic communities of the village of Dobricu Lăpuşului, attributed on the basis of stylistic analogies with the murals at Deseşti and dated to the last three years of the century.[76] Interestingly, the two Christophers are not similar. At the church of the Holy Archangels, he has either a lamb's or a dog's head (it is difficult to discern which) and the same characteristic features as in Deseşti, a cross and a sword, elements that can be rec-

---

71 The inscription attesting the paternity of the decorations is still preserved.

72 The attribution of paternity in the case of the wall painting at Almaş-Sălişte was made on the basis of stylistic analogies. For the relations between the artists Silaghi and Moise Borşoş, see Ana Dumitran, "Pictorul Simion Silaghi-Sălăgeanu. În căutarea identităţii" [Painter Simion Silaghi-Sălăgeanu. Looking for His Identity], *Annales Universitatis Apulensis. Series Historica* 16, I (2012): 209-210; Dumitran, "Pictura românească în judeţul Alba," 67.

73 Anca Pop-Bratu, *Pictura murală maramureşeană. Meşteri zugravi şi interferenţe stilistice* [Wall Painting in Maramureş. Painters and Stylistic Interferences] (Bucureşti: Meridiane, 1982), 42.

74 Porumb, "Biserici de lemn din Ţara Maramureşului" [Wooden Churches in Ţara Maramureşului], in *Monumente istorice şi de artă religioasă din Arhiepiscopia Vadului, Feleacului şi Clujului* [Historical and Religious Art Monuments in the Archiepiscopate of Vad, Feleac and Cluj] (Cluj-Napoca: Arhiepiscopia Ortodoxă Română a Vadului, Feleacului şi Clujului, 1982), 106; Pop-Bratu, *Pictura murală*, 43.

75 Pop-Bratu, *Pictura murală*, 42.

76 Bogdana Tarnavschi, "Biserici de lemn din Ţara Lăpuşului şi din Ţara Chioarului" [Wooden Churches from Ţara Lăpuşului and Ţara Chioarului], in *Monumente istorice şi de artă religioasă* [Historical and Religious Art Monuments], 147-148; Porumb, *Dicţionar*, 111-112.

ognized in the painting from Wallachia as well, where they are usually included in the equipment of the soldier-saints. At the church of the Presentation of Mary, on the other hand, the martyr is depicted as conventionally human, but only the upper part of the body can be made out today. A decade after these works by Munteanu, one of his apprentices included Christopher when painting the church at Libotin, opting for the mild version with the lamb's head.[77] The church had been built in 1671 and brought to Libotin for a Greek Catholic parish. The painting dates from 1811, the year of the transfer between the two villages, and the iconographic programme demonstrates (as does Saint Christopher) that artists made no distinction between Orthodox and Greek Catholic churches, using their gift wherever they were called, regardless of the denomination.

Another painter familiar with Saint Christopher's theme, a representative of late Baroque stylistics in Maramureş, signed the painting at Corneşti in the Valea Cosăului in 1806, noting in the inscription "[…] and I have painted here, the humble painter Toader Hodor from Vişeu de Mijloc."[78] Hodor chose the dog-headed version of Saint Christopher, his head turned to the viewer's right, in the red dress specific to martyrs, holding in his left hand the rod that burst into leaf at Antioch, his place of baptism according to Eastern hagiography. That Hodor is aware of the hagiographic text is proven by the second image we have, in the church of Bârsana, where the artist elaborated a whole iconographic programme in the Baroque manner. The work on Valea Izei was not his alone; Hodor benefited from the help of another artist, Ioan Plohod from Dragomireşti. Iconic images were abandoned in favour of narrative scenes such as the martyrdom of Saint Christopher. The executioner, in Austrian military dress and wearing a tricorne on his head, prepares to behead the martyr. It is obvious that the religious discourse is contaminated with political ideology, with the martyr representing the in-group of underprivileged Romanians. The visual construction lets us understand the stereotypes of persecution: the victim is deprived of power, destroyed in his body, but at the same time spiritually above the sacrificer. The visual relationship between the depictions at Corneşti and Bârsana is beyond doubt. In the latter case, Christopher's figure is no longer clear but can be recognised without difficulty by comparing the two; the martyr wears a red shirt girded with a brown belt and leans on a rod.

These artists, their disciples who followed them in their peregrinations, and other anonymous persons travelling from one side of the Carpathians to the other enthusiastically disseminated the theme of Saint Christopher in the eighteenth and nineteenth centuries.

---

77 An attribution made by analogy with the church from the neighbour village, Rogoz, where Radu Munteanu signed the painting. Bogdana Tarnavschi, "Biserici de lemn," 142.

78 Porumb, "Biserici de lemn din Ţara Maramureşului," 117.

ILLUSTRATIONS

Fig. 1A: Polovragi Monastery, painted by Hranite et al., 1703.

Fig. 1B: Church of Glogova, painted by Grigorie Ranite and Gheorghe Ranite, sons of Hranite, 1734.

Fig. 2A: Polovragi Monastery, Hospital Church, painted by Gheorghe Ranite and Ioan, 1738.

Fig. 2B: Polovragi Monastery, Hospital Church, painted by Gheorghe Ranite and Ioan, 1738.

Fig. 3A: Church of Budeşti, painted by Matei from Craiova and Raicu, 1825.

Fig. 3B: Church of Crainici, painted by Matei from Craiova, Constantin and Fotache, 1837.

Fig. 4A: Church of Calbor, painted by Sava, son of Teodor, 1813.

Fig. 4B: Church of Sâmbăta de Jos, painted by Sava, son of Teodor, 1814.

Fig. 5A: Church of Almaş-Sălişte, painted by Moise Borşoş, disciple of Simion Silaghi, 1819.

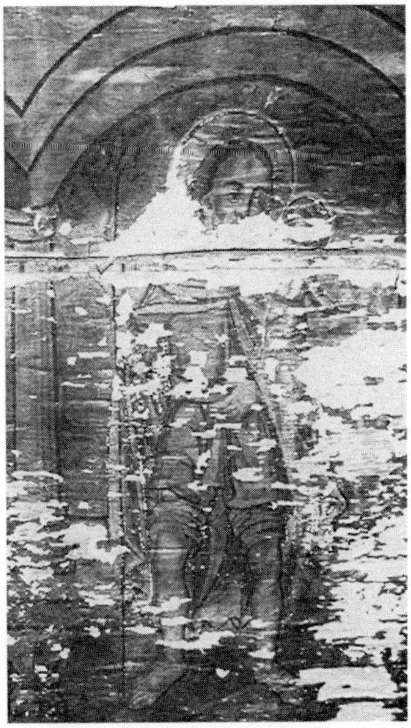

Fig. 5B: Church of Stânceşti, painted by Moise Borşoş, disciple of Simion Silaghi, 1829.

Fig. 6A: Church of Deseşti, painted by Radu Munteanu, 1780.

Fig. 6B: Church I of Dobricu Lăpuşului, painted by Radu Munteanu, about 1798-1800.

"*THAT HE MAY BE THE DONOR AND BE REMEMBERED IN THE HOLY LITURGY*"
Donations of Artwork to Romanian Churches in Transylvania Down to the Mid-Nineteenth Century

ANA DUMITRAN

Insofar as Christianity is above ethnic or state affiliations as a religion, there should be no difference in how places of worship are maintained and cared for. Nevertheless the political history of the Romanians has given rise to forms of behaviour which, while not radically different from one side of the Carpathians to the other, have taken their own particular forms. South and East of the mountains, the Romanian states developed from the fourteenth century onwards, while in Transylvania the Romanian population was at a crossroads of the Catholic and Orthodox worlds, exposed for centuries on end to the pressures of proselytism and to other influences far more powerful than those faced by their co-religionists in Wallachia and Moldavia.

One result of this state of affairs is that while the oldest Romanian Orthodox churches were built in Transylvania, in the absence of a central ecclesiastical authority able to impose its own architectural standards in line with the canon of Byzantine style, these were inspired by the Western models at hand, at first Romanesque and later Gothic. The result was a synthetic style which also served to illustrate the degree to which Romanians, especially the nobility, adapted to the demands of the Hungarian state into which they were required to integrate.

This same wish to be in step with the times can also be seen in efforts to adorn churches once they were built. However, the recruitment of painters and craftsman to carry out the earliest mural works seems to have been a confused and doubtful process, given that there were even fewer suitable painters for the job than there were master builders. Thus they were trained in an era and a region where artistic cross-currents played their part in blurring ethnic and confessional boundaries, and their work shows marked signs of adapting to different demands from different clients. Differences in doctrine met linguistic differences, so that Slavonic inscriptions are found alongside the figures of Hungarian saints, paintings in the Byzantine style adorn Catholic churches, and themes from the Catholic repertoire are found painted on the walls of Orthodox churches. The Romanian patrons' openness to Western artistic tastes especially enabled such an admixture was, as did a lack of instruction in the teachings of their own church, the dual confession of many families and the limited number of professional artists at work, with the same painters carrying out commissions on Catholic sites and then on Orthodox ones.

These were the defining features of a society predominantly made up of bondsmen and ministered by a church without political support, and such initial conditions explain why doctrinal particulars were secondary to the visual message, with the prime concern being that the pictures be painted to last and accompany successive generation in their prayers. In turn, the long life of paintings depended on the quality of the materials and techniques that the artists used, which must have contributed substantially to the cost of their work. However, only those of high social standing and with an income to match could pay such considerable sums, which explains why the first paintings in Transylvania for Romanian clients adorned churches under the patronage of noble families, who had the resources to build these in stone.

The oldest such painting that we know of dates to 1313-1314, and is the earliest layer of the fresco at the stone chapel built by the gentry of Streisângeorgiu, itself the oldest mediaeval church in Romania, built in the early decades of the twelfth century. The evidence of this fresco shows us that by that time, it was already conventional practice to record the names of donors and their desire to see their sins forgiven, as well as the painter's own name.[1] This is a sign of advanced artistic development, as Vasile Drăguț correctly argued in his study,[2] though the only other surviving evidence for such practice, the painting of 1311 at Sântămăria Orlea,[3] was however carried out a time when the church was most probably Catholic and, by implication, not a Romanian house of worship.[4]

We no longer have any way of knowing how many Romanian places of worship may have been painted in the thirteenth to fifteenth centuries, even for the stone-built churches: but all the painted churches known today were open to the parish at large, although in every case where inscriptions preserve the names of donors they belonged to the social elites: indeed the presence of these inscriptions, and the miniscule dimensions of these houses of worship, leave room for the opinion that these were private chapels. Noble patronage was motivated by the hope of "aid and succour on the dreadful day of

---

[1] "In the year 6 thousand 8 hundred and 20 and 2, I began this church with the help of Saint George and the Mother of God and all the saints, for the sake of the *knez* Balea (Balotă?) and the forgiveness of his sins, and for the sake of the priest Naneș and the forgiveness of his sins. Teofil the Painter" (apud Marius Porumb, *Dicționar de pictură veche românească din Transilvania. Sec. XIII-XVIII* [Dictionary of Early Romanian Painting in Transylvania, Thirteenth to Eighteenth Century] (București: Editura Academiei Române, 1998), 388; this is the main source for all artworks mentioned in this article where no other references are given).

[2] Vasile Drăguț, "Streisîngeorgiu. Observații preliminare privind picturile murale" [Streisîngeorgiu. Preliminary Remarks on the Wall Paintings], *Revista Muzeelor și Monumentelor*, series *Monumente Istorice și de Artă* 1 (1978): 42. Another concrete example might perhaps have been furnished by the vestiges of painting at the first stone church at Peșteana, known to have been in use in the 11th-13th centuries. This fragmentary painting was discovered in 1925-1926, when the ruin which housed it was incorporated into the second church, dated to the 13th century, to create the current church. The fragment is now once again covered over, but is considered the oldest known mediaeval Transylvanian painting (Ileana Burnichioiu, "Biserici parohiale și capele din comitatele Alba și Hunedoara (1200-1550)" [Parish Churches and Chapels in the Counties of Alba and Hunedoara, 1200-1550] (PhD diss., București: Universitatea Națională de Arte, 2009), 301, note 221).

[3] Of the three layers identified, the first has been dated to 1311, with the others datable to the 14th and 15th centuries prior to 1484. Their extent and exact overlap have not yet been established (apud Burnichioiu, "Biserici parohiale și capele," 308-309, 311-312).

[4] The initial Catholic affiliation is supported by the Latin inscription of 1311, by the prominence of the consecration crosses in the paintings and by records that the tithe was paid to the Papacy in 1315 and 1332-1335, as well as by the late date – 1447 – at which the estate became the property of the noble family of Cândea from Râu de Mori.

Christ's Judgement"[5] and was decisive for the churches; it is most visible in the era of the autonomous Principality of Transylvania (sixteenth to seventeenth centuries) when the elite continued to use the old houses of worship even though they may have changed denomination and converted to Calvinism. Thus they used the old churches alongside parishioners who had stayed Orthodox, and the churches became bi-confessional.

We may develop the theme of noble patronage a little here. As we have seen, patronage provided not just that the churches be built but also that they are furnished with all that was needed for worship, including paintings; we must also note a relationship between the size of noble domains and the existence or density of church buildings.[6] In other words, a house of worship could only be founded where the lord of the domain gave his support, so that it is obvious why Orthodox churches are most frequently found where the Romanian social elite was most compact. This is why the regions of Hațeg-Hunedoara, Zarand, Maramureș and Făgăraș are not just the most studied and best-known examples, but are also the territories that offer the clearest picture of the development of Romanian church architecture in Transylvania. Not only do these regions offer the oldest examples of church-building, but here we also find the greatest concentration of such buildings. Churches multiplied with the division of domains when large families gave up joint rule of their lands and moved on to individual ownership. This inevitably leads to the question of how could Orthodox churches be built on royal domain, or on the domains of Catholic nobility, of the Saxon population or especially of the Bishop and chapter of Alba Iulia? The answer is as predictable as it is painful; in these instances we must assume not only confessional impediments but also a lack of funds, given that the serf population was generally in a precarious economic situation. An optimistic answer would be that wooden churches could be built, perishable structures which did not carry the same prestige as stone-built churches and have left no traces. We must also bear in mind that even the old stone churches mostly go unmentioned in documentary sources, right down to the eighteenth century.[7] Only because the buildings themselves survived do we know today that they were painted at all. Although any such churches have disappeared, along with the art that may have been on their walls and any information about who funded the painting work, we may expect at least some surviving examples of panel painting: but even these turn out to be very late, with the oldest icon, a donation by the nobleman Luca of Urisiu and his family, dated no earlier than 1539.

On the one hand, we are thus forced to conclude that there were few churches. Furthermore, in many cases these were built considerably earlier than the painting work

[5] Inscription of 1443 on the church at Densuș, founded by the Mușina family; Ecaterina Cincheza-Buculei, "Din nou despre pictura bisericii Sf. Nicolae din Densuș" [Further Remarks on the Paintings in the Church of St Nicholas at Densuș], *Ars Transsilvaniae* XIX (2009): 93. A similar phrase is found in the inscription at Ribița (Porumb, *Dicționar*, 333). Though the phrasing differs, in the inscription of 1313-1314 at Streisângeorgiu the purport is the same as in that of 1408 (Ibid., 390).
[6] Burnichioiu, "Biserici parohiale și capele," passim.
[7] Ibid., passim.

itself was carried out, which may mean not only that such work cost considerable sums for which several generations had to save, but also that these costs were seen as the exclusive concern of elite groups, even though the whole parish benefited. We see the same phenomenon in Strei and Streisângeorgiu, where in both cases the stone churches were built by local nobility and the founders' descendants then took charge of the painting work, but where the graveyards had developed even around earlier, wooden buildings to show that these were parish churches.[8] We also have some idea of the costs involved even in building a stone church of modest size, an *ecclesia lapidea simplex*, from the facts recorded in a document of 1418, where the parish church of Folt was estimated to be worth 10 marks.[9] This cannot have been a particularly large sum, but all the same the parishioners who used this as their house of worship did not contribute to building costs: rather the church was under the patronage of a local noble family and was bequeathed in wills just like any other item of their property. Thus it seems that to build and paint a church were seen as prerogatives of the nobility, so that where there was no local elite to take on these tasks, often enough this meant there would be no place of worship.

On the other hand, the scarcity of stone churches and consequent scarcity of painted churches also casts doubt on the possibility that wooden churches of the era might have been adorned with wall-paintings. Information on wooden churches in the mediaeval era is very scarce indeed, but one piece of evidence that supports such a claim is the reference to a wooden church of the Romanians at Fărcădin (*capella wolachalem lignea*), valued at 5 marks together with its graveyard in 1538 – the equivalent of just 30 florins, or a horse and cart.[10] We do not know whether this low sum reflected the considerable age and ramshackle state of the church, or whether it was the true value, in which case it must have been a very small building. The recorded cost nevertheless illustrates either the poverty of the parishioners, if they paid for the building, or the inclination which the lords of the domain felt to provide for the spiritual needs of their subjects, if they paid. In either case, this value cannot also have included the costs of painting, which all on its own would have come to more than the sum mentioned.

After such modest beginnings, from the latter sixteenth century Romanian church painting in Transylvania would suffer from both the inevitable ravages of time and the strictures imposed by Protestantism. Though the new creed would not lead to iconoclasm as such, it nevertheless made investment in the adornment of churches much harder, by channelling the financial resources of possible donors towards donations of books, missals and liturgical items. In any case, when the Orthodox rite Romanians from Transylvania were finalising their union with Rome at the end of the seventeenth century that created the Greek Catholic Church, there were two characteristic features of the region's

[8] Ibid., 319-327.
[9] Ibid., 353.
[10] Adrian Andrei Rusu, *Ctitori și biserici din Țara Hațegului până la 1700* [Donors and Churches in the Haţeg Region Down to 1700] (Satu Mare: Editura Muzeului Sătmărean, 1997), 203.

Romanian churches, as contrasting as they are complementary. While on the one hand the presence of an iconostasis (*altaria sanctorum*) decorated with images of the Virgin Mary is commended in churches,[11] on the other hand there are penalties prescribed for priests and parishes who do not make the effort to have icons of Jesus, the Virgin Mary and Saint Nicholas in their churches, at the very least.[12] The first feature can be illustrated by the splendid iconostasis of the wooden church at Lupşa, of which twenty-one pieces have survived, while we can reconstruct the second feature through an inscription of 1741 on an icon at Benesat, recording circumstances which cannot have differed greatly from those of the seventeenth century:

> "Let it be known that this Meţ Pascu and his son Meţ Dateu and his brother Meţ Ioan made this church on the meadows, and seeing that the church has neither censers nor banners nor icons nor candlesticks, it is most bare of all those things that are needful [...]."

Though the elements which made up the positive side of such a state of affairs have disappeared over time – more due to the renovations of the eighteenth to twentieth centuries than because of Protestant pressure! – the inscription is useful for the light it sheds on how much of the negative may be explained by simple poverty, or even indifference.

From the very little surviving evidence, we may observe that donations of artwork to churches remained the preserve of the social and economic elite. These were primarily the local elites but also included some high-ranking figures in Wallachia and Moldavia, who chose such endowments as a way to mark their ties, whatever these may have been, on Transylvanian soil. The best-known case is undoubtedly the church of Saint Nicholas at Şcheii Braşovului, with its inscription of 1598 describing the church as a foundation by the voivodes of the Principalities:

> "This church was built at the Godly instigation of some Christian lovers of Christ, by the gift and mercy of the Orthodox princes of Moldavia and Wallachia [...] After this, in the year 7092, the year of Christ 1584, the Orthodox prince Io Petru Voievod Cercel, seeing that this church had grown old *and was not painted*, caught fire with Godly zeal and adorned it with all the icons of God and of the saints, and built the chapel and the porch with six pillars. After this, in the year 7103, the Orthodox prince Io Aron Voievod, following the example of the good old lords, painted the chapel and the porch with the images of God and of the saints and made the porch. And from this time forth, whoever God shall choose to be the prince should have mercy and give alms all the more."

This is as clear a statement as we could wish for that the appearance and even the very existence of a house of worship were the responsibility of princes, offering them ways to display the exalted rank to which they had been raised. Like the Byzantine em-

---

[11] Andreas Freyberger, *Relatare istorică despre unirea Bisericii româneşti cu Biserica Romei făcută în anul 1701 şi despre cele ce au urmat în problema unirii până în noiembrie 1702 / Historica* relatio *unionis Walachicae cum Romana Ecclesia*, Romanian version and introduction by Ioan Chindriş (Cluj-Napoca: Clusium, 1996), 36-37.

[12] Item 24 of the Synod of Union, 14th September 1700: Nicolaus Nilles, *Symbolae ad illustrandam historiam Ecclesiae Orientalis in terris coronae S. Stephani*, vol. I (Innsbruck, 1885), 254.

perors, the "good old lords," they were obliged to care for the state of the churches, and their zeal for this task was a guarantee that their reign would be blessed by God and that future generations would remember and pray for them.

Some similar impulse must have given rise to the fresco of which tiny fragments have been found in the ruins of the Metropolitan's palace at Alba Iulia. When the voivode Michael the Brave built a church near the walls of the mediaeval citadel in 1597, this cannot have been his only contribution to the adornment of the palace complex. Likewise, we know that the church built at Turnu Roşu in 1653 was built "on foundations [by] the Christian prince of Wallachia, Io Mateiu Băsăraba Voievod [...] and at His Majesty's expense" and we may suppose that his donations paid for more than just the stonemasons' work. This was also the case of the church of Saint Nicholas at Făgăraş, where again the inscription records only that it was "raised from its foundations and built [in 1697] at the sole cost" of the voivode Constantin Brâncoveanu, who also paid for the sumptuous painted iconostasis by Preda, dated 1698-1699, even if there is no inscription mentioning him by name: the fact that the painter was sent from the princely court is itself the guarantee that Brâncoveanu paid for his work. The same Preda also painted the walls of the church together with his sons in 1721, although this work was paid by another, unknown donor, since by this time the voivode had died.

At lower ranks of the social hierarchy we find a similar gesture at Teiuş, where the nobleman Petru Raţ and his wife, the *generosa domina* Zamfira, from the family of the Wallachian voivode Mircea Ciobanu, paid for the painting work in the Romanian church, where the votive image even today attests their donation. Although even the Romanian nobility found it hard to raise the funds for large-scale works, the community of Aromanian merchants increasingly lent their support and paid for the church of Saint Nicholas in Hunedoara to be painted in 1654, as well as for the magnificent iconostasis in the church at Bungard (Sibiu region) several decades later.

Most often though the adornment of Romanian churches in the era of the Principality was restricted to donations of single icons, which in this period too were the only painted images in the wooden churches. Indeed when the iconostasis itself was fully complete, wall-painting would be superfluous; we have already mentioned one example of such a complete iconostasis at the wooden church at Lupşa, donated by the otherwise unknown Dumitru and Rosanda, whose names are mentioned on the icon of the *Deisis*. There cannot have been many such complete pieces, however, in the sixteenth and seventeenth centuries, since ordinarily only a few single pieces survive from the accumulated donations of the years.[13] The most famous example is the image of the Virgin and Child,

---

[13] At Budeşti-Josani, Budeşti-Susani, Dezmir, Nadăş, Păniceni, Ţelna, Urisiu (1539), Agârbiciu (1555), Bica (1563), Susenii Bârgăului (1646), Hunedoara (1654), Ciolt (1671), Ilişua (1673), Săliştea Sibiului (1674), Nicula (1681), Lujerdiu, Şcheii Braşovului (1688), Deda (1690), Dragomireşti (1697), Dobrin and Sânbenedic. The triptych held by the Brukenthal Museum in Sibiu is of unknown provenance, as is the small icon of Jesus from somewhere in Northern Transylvania, currently held by the Greek Catholic church at Ponorel (Alba county). Cf. Porumb, *Dicţionar*, passim; Nicolae Iorga, *Scrisori şi inscripţii ardelene şi*

painted by Luca of Iclod and presented to the church at Nicula by the nobleman Ioan Cupşa in 1681; it is well-known for having wept miraculous tears on 15th February 1699, which explains why the icon has survived. No details of its donation are noted on the icon itself, being recorded instead in the inquest into the miracle.[14] Thus this piece may be seen as typical for all those objects for which we know neither donors nor painter, which have always outnumbered those for which one or both sets of names are known.

A very similar case is the icon of the Virgin Mary painted by Luca of Iclod in 1673 for the church at Ilişua, at the request of "the servant of God, Matei, and his wife Aniţa and their children Griga, Ştefan, Ioana," a family of serfs known in the village by the name of Stanciu; we learn all this from witness testimony concerning the icon's miraculous tears, wept on 26th February 1729.[15] Another witness states that the icon "belonged to the Sztancs family," who commissioned it when the church was built.

Several similar suggestions of ownership have been found; the royal icon in the wooden church at Reghin bears an inscription stating that "This holy icon belongs to Gheorghie the Greek. The year being 1748, Toader the painter," an icon at Orăşti is inscribed "This icon belongs to Onea Ispas, Ioniţă. 1772. The year being 1772, Fe(bruary) the 25th day,"[16] an icon painted in the late eighteenth or early nineteenth century records that "this belongs to Ion Stăniasă and his wife Nuţa,"[17] an icon from the same period in the so-called church of the serfs in Letca bears an inscription that it belongs to "the priest Onisiea and his wife Marie,"[18] and an icon painted in 1810 for the wooden church at Pianu de Sus records that "This icon belongs to Ion Mărincaş and his wife Mărie, that it may be their memorial."[19]

We know more about the altar icon "of Cătina Muscăcească," which "belonged to Gligoraş" but which the painter-priest Ursu Broină "sold for seven *mărieş* [an old coin] and kept the money."[20]

---

maramureşene [Documents and Inscriptions from Transylvania and Maramureş], vol. II (Bucureşti, 1906), 54; Alexandru Efremov, *Icoane româneşti* [Romanian Icons] (Bucureşti: Editura Meridiane, 2003), 121-133; Florin Dobrei, *Biserici ortodoxe hunedorene* [Orthodox Churches of Hunedoara County] (Reşiţa: Editura Eftimie Murgu, 2011), 67.

14 Cf. Ana Dumitran, Enikő Hegedűs, Vasile Rus, *Fecioarele înlăcrimate ale Transilvaniei. Preliminarii la o istorie ilustrată a toleranţei religioase* [Weeping Virgins of Transylvania. Preliminary Remarks Towards a Pictorial History of Religious Tolerance] (Alba Iulia: Editura Altip, 2011), 379.

15 Ibid., 386, 392-393.

16 Ana Dumitran, "Pictura românească în judeţul Alba până la mijlocul secolului al XIX-lea. Demersuri pentru o bază de date" [Romanian Painting in the County of Alba to the Mid-Nineteenth Century. Some Steps Towards a Database], *Patrimonium Apulense* XII (2012): 252.

17 Collection of the Municipal Museum at Sebeş.

18 Iorga, *Scrisori şi inscripţii*, 123.

19 Collection of the Orthodox Archbishopric of Alba Iulia, inv. nr. 5.

20 Silvia Marin-Barutcieff, "Între Arhanghelul Mihail şi tatăl pământesc: o declaraţie de loialitate şi ataşament faţă de împăratul Iosif al II-lea în pictura religioasă din Transilvania" [Between the Archangel Michael and the Earthly Father; A Declaration of Loyalty and Allegiance to the Emperor Joseph II in Transylvanian Religious Painting], *Apulum*, series *Historia & Patrimonium* XLVIII (2011): 28; cf. also Silvia Marin-Barutcieff, "Aproapele de departe, străinul de aproape. Între Iosif al II-lea ca *pater familias* şi maghiari ca alteritate nocturnă. Teme iconografice într-o biserică transilvană din secolul al XVIII-lea" [Foreign

Although this evidence is terse in the extreme and widely dispersed both chronologically and geographically, it nevertheless suggests that icons were only ever held in houses of worship, in other words that we would look for them in vain in Romanian private homes – at least until the sudden boom in the popularity of glass-painting. This was even the case when the initial intent was otherwise, proven by the inscription on an icon from Honțișor:

> "This icon was painted by Costandin son of Ursan and bought by Mnera On *to stand in his house*, in the year of Christ 1774, the month of March."

This icon too ended up in a church, in obedience to what seems to have been an iron law. Thus to present an icon to a church was not just an act of charity but also a way to show piety, since the icon's intrinsic sacred character made it unsuited to the domestic realm.

The complete absence of panel paintings in the thirteenth and fourteenth centuries deserves some attention, as does the apparent total replacement of wall paintings by icons from the sixteenth century onwards. Certainly, it is hard to credit that the artists who worked on wall-paintings – either surviving or lost to time – did not also paint portable artworks, but whatever the case may have been, icons were not needed in stone-built churches with painted iconostases. Icons would have been displayed in wooden churches, where the walls were presumably not painted, and both icons and churches vanished in the course of renovations over successive centuries. At least some icons might have been imported, as we see in the case of sixteenth-century pieces ordinarily attributed to itinerant Moldavian artists or directly to workshops attached to the great monasteries of Northern Moldavia; there is little evidence of local, Transylvanian workshops producing icons in the sixteenth and seventeenth centuries. Throughout this period, commissions were given either to itinerant painters or artists summoned specifically to carry out larger works, such as the painting at Lupșa and Hunedoara, or were placed with scattered workshops, particularly that of Luca of Iclod. These workshops could not develop to any great extent while the only commissions came from village social elites, at a time when Protestant distrust of images would lead, if not to actual iconoclasm, then at least to an attitude that considered the visual message of icons as secondary compared to the written message of books. An example here is the panelled roof of the wooden church at Lupșa, already mentioned many times, which was painted in the Renaissance style in 1694 by two Unitarians from Colțești; it would be interesting to know whether the patrons who commissioned this work saw it more as a means to assure the salvation of their souls, or as an act of civic responsibility expressing their care for the parish. Whatever the case may be, the association of this typically domestic decorative element and the imposing traditional iconostasis placed there several decades earlier is unusual.

While only a few examples of wall-painting and some isolated icons have been

Neighbours and the Stranger Next Door. Between Joseph II as *pater familias* and the Hungarians as Night-Time Otherness. Iconographic Themes in an Eighteenth Century Transylvanian Church], *Annales Universitatis Apulensis*, series *Historica* 15, II (2011): 219.

preserved from the centuries discussed so far, the eighteenth century proves to be an extremely rich source of evidence, even if only by comparison with the scant remains of earlier ages – since for this century too, only a bare fraction of what was created has survived. Evidently more was created than during previous centuries, and thus more has survived if only for simple quantitative reasons. We must therefore take care to keep a sense of perspective, since otherwise the greater number of inscriptions on artworks might lead us to assume some far more radical shift in custom and mentality than was actually the case.

For example, although a few mediaeval stone churches are assumed or known to have been built at the behest of local noble families, or by the gift of a voivode from Wallachia or Moldavia (whatever his known or unknown motives), we know nothing at all about events when a wooden church was built: who took the initiative, how did the parish take part, what was recorded in the donors' inscription, who consecrated the building? The census (*conscriptiones*) of the earlier eighteenth century restricted themselves merely to noting the existence of places of worship, but when canonical visitations were carried out in 1761 to gather information to help the Greek Catholic church recover buildings which had been taken over by the Orthodox, the results yield evidence for no more than vague speculations on these questions. It is quite remarkable how little interest the visitations showed in icons and wall paintings, while chalices, censers, books, vestments, altar cloths and bells were all mentioned.[21] This being the case, the evidentiary value of inscriptions from the eighteenth and nineteenth centuries grows substantially, although even these offer only a partial view of the reality.

Let us begin with the older monuments, where we may establish that in some cases, throughout all the repairs and rebuilding they underwent, there was a concern to perpetuate the memory of earlier donors, even if the information given in the newly-painted inscriptions is hardly ever conclusive as to how these donors contributed to the adornment of the churches. The commonest source of evidence for such involvement remains the votive image, which usually undergoes only light retouching while the church itself is entirely repainted or even painted for the first time.

One of the earliest examples is the stone church of Saint George at Lupșa, which we learn was built in 1421

> "by a boyar named Stănislav. And then in the year 1750, the holy altar was painted at the expense of a Christian here in Lupșa named Olia Ion, who gave 18 florins so that it may be his eternal memorial."

This inscription refers only to the painting of the altar; indeed it is hard to believe that 18 florins would have been enough for all of the painting work, which reaches impressive

[21] Greta Monica Miron, „... *poruncește, scoale-te, du-te, propoveduește ...*" *Biserica greco-catolică din Transilvania. Cler și enoriași (1697-1782)* ["... Obey, Arise, Go Forth and Preach ..." The Greek Catholic Church in Transylvania. Clergy and Parishioners (1697-1782)] (Cluj-Napoca: Presa Universitară Clujeană, 2004), 354-368; the altar cloths, specifically, were the antimensions.

proportions. Nevertheless, the greater part of the nave walls is covered with work datable to the mid-eighteenth century, beneath which an older painting is visible where the plaster has come away, datable to the fifteenth century.[22] Yet an impenetrable silence shrouds these earlier layers of the fresco.

The same is also true at Prislop, where the stone church is known to have been built in 1564 by the "generous and Christian *lady* Zamfira, daughter of the generous *lord* Io Moisi Voievod Basarab of Bucharest"[23] – it cannot be the case that it was only painted for the first time in 1759, "by the charity and at the expense of these following: Varlaam Ieromonah Toplița(n), my disciple Mihail and Sil(ivestru?) the hieromonk, the priest's sons Balint and Teodosie [...] and Metodie the monk and Nichita the monk also in the monastery." Rather the phrase "it was painted as it is seen" should be taken in its strict sense, to mean that this painting looked different from older painting work, hidden from view by the new images until the repair work of 1910.

We encounter a similar situation in Zlatna, where an inscription of 1744 expands upon an earlier inscription of 1696 and offers a fairly detailed picture of the history of the church of the Dormition of the Virgin, also yielding information on the successive layers of painting:

> "[In the year 1424 … this holy church was built], at first with a porch to the middle of the wall, at [the sole expense] of the lord [S]tănislav Hraboru and his lady Anca, and for that work it is shown above that the costs were fifteen hundred florins, and when they died, it remained unfinished. Then in the year 1696, the lords Dobra Anghel and Iacov Ioanăş took up the work and the arches of the porch and the tower were built at these lords' expense, and the cost was … hundreds. In the year 1744 in August, the 15th day, the lord Roşca Ion died and left the church two hundred and 50 florins that it may be painted, so that he may be a donor and remembered in the holy liturgy. This holy church was painted in the days of the Empress Maria Theresa […] when [Ioan I]nochientie of Sad was bishop. He who toiled and watched over and founded this work [of] the building of the altar and the painting of the church was the priest Ivan, and also his son the priest Pătru [...]."

We may observe that all initiatives can be attributed to prominent members of local social and economic elites, laymen, at whose expense the works were carried out. Only for the last stages of the work do the priests also contribute, describing themselves as toiling at, watching over and founding the work and thereby arrogating to themselves the initiative, organisation and at least part of the costs. The same thing very likely happened in 1424 and 1696, since the officiating priest would almost inevitably be involved when a house of worship was to be built or rebuilt. Nevertheless, in the known cases their names are

---

22 Marius Porumb, *Pictura românească din Transilvania*, vol. I *(sec XIV-XVII)* [Romanian Painting in Transylvania, vol. 1, 14th-17th Centuries] (Cluj-Napoca: Editura Dacia, 1981), 32.

23 A statement which has shown to be inaccurate in itself, since the church seems to date from the fourteenth century (G. Balș, "Despre biserica Prislopului" [On the Church of Prislop], *Buletinul Comisiunii Monumentelor Istorice* XXIV, 69 (July-Sept. 1931): 97-100). The tradition that it was founded by Saint Nicodim of Tismana must have been known to the authors of the 1759 inscription, since it was written down very shortly afterwards in 1762, probably by one of these, in the rhymed chronicle "The Lament of the Holy Monastery of Silvaș."

mentioned only at Streisângeorgiu, Ribița, Baica, Hunedoara, Letca[24] and Săliștea Sibiului.[25] In contrast, in the eighteenth century almost all inscriptions mention the names of the serving priests at the time of building, renovation or adornment. Does this indicate closer clerical involvement in caring for the good order and functioning of churches, or does it merely reflect our better knowledge of the state of affairs thanks to the preservation of more inscriptions?

It may be that the answer to both questions is yes, since the ecclesiastical authorities were clearly involved in fund-raising to repair the old buildings at least in the case of Streisângeorgiu, where one of the inscriptions of 1743 allows us to identify Zaharia Cioca, the archdeacon of Hunedoara, as a donor, who paid to have the figures of the donors of 1408 repainted, while in 1724 we find the archdeacon Dumitru of Alba Iulia in a similar role in Geoagiu de Sus.

Churchmen of the rank of archdeacon (*protopop*) made even greater contributions as donors in cases where a church had previously been unpainted. The best-preserved example today is the church at Daia Română, where

> "the high-born archdeacon Avram paid for the painting of the altar and for the iconostasis and for the icon of the Most Blessed Virgin, together with his wife Ioana; and the painters were Ștefan and Constantin" and
> "The honourable and high-born archdeacon Avram paid for the painting of the holy church, together with the honourable and high-born archdeacon Petru, and it was painted in the year of Christ 1745."

As a sign of his gratitude for the wages paid, the painter Constantin himself offered a royal icon of the Deisis as a donation. Another well-known case is that of Nicolae Pop, episcopal vicar and archdeacon at Biia, who showed great zeal in urging parishes to rebuild and adorn the churches under his jurisdiction. Like his fellow priests at Daia and Hunedoara he was the scion of a noble family, and in 1744 he set an example to his subordinate priests by paying for the church of the village where he had been born to be rebuilt and painted.[26]

The royal icons of the now-vanished wooden church at Iclandu Mare were donated by the archdeacon Gavril, who was unable to pay for them all at once and thus commissioned them by instalments in 1745 and 1753. The venerable wooden church at Lupu was renovated and painted by the efforts of the archdeacon Maniu of Broșteni, who also paid for the church at Broșteni to be built and equipped with all that was necessary for divine service, including icons and possibly wall-painting.[27] In 1750 the archdeacon Ladislau of Colun renovated the church of the village where he had been born, *propriis suis expensis [...] cum omnibus internis picturis et imaginibus.*[28]

---

[24] Iorga, *Scrisori și inscripții*, 123 (church of the bonded serfs).
[25] Porumb, *Dicționar*, 349 (vanished church).
[26] Miron, *Biserica greco-catolică din Transilvania*, 327.
[27] Ibid., 330.
[28] Ibid., 340.

Although we have no concrete evidence on costs and payment for painting work in the churches at Mănărade and Sibiu (the Orthodox church at Maieri), in each case the money was most likely provided by the same patron who had paid for the churches to be built; the former is generally reckoned to have been founded by the Greek Catholic bishop Petru Pavel Aaron, while the latter was built by the efforts of the Orthodox bishop Gherasim Adamovici using funds left by his predecessor, bishop Ghedeon Nichitici. While waiting for the cathedral at Blaj to be built, Bishop Inochentie Micu had the chapel of the castle where he had taken up his episcopal residence repaired and restored, and commissioned an iconostasis, specifying that the work must match that on donations from voivodes of the neighbouring Principalities to the churches at Hurez and Cozia.[29]

It is more difficult to quantify the amounts donated by priests, since the formularies of the day do not use exact terms, although records relate that almost all work to adorn churches happened at the prompting and direction of priests. It is clear that the most costly work was mural painting, with the sum needed to paint the whole church generally being contributed by several donors. Some were certainly priests, as was the case in 1753 at Rieni and Pogăceaua, and in 1811 at Libotin. Certainly, the priest was only able to pay for part of the work and generally preferred to pay for the altar paintings, as happened in 1769 at Berbești and Mogoș-Cojocani, in the late eighteenth century at Selişte and in 1812 at Voievodenii Mari, or to pay for the iconostasis and related work as we see at Sărata (county of Bistrița-Năsăud) and Bucium-Izbita. The situation must have been much the same at the now vanished wooden church of Sânpetru de Câmpie, where I believe that the painting work of 1752 must have been for the altar alone, while the second round of work in 1780 saw the rest of the church painted (rather than any part being repainted). This was also probably the case when the family of Șerbu the priest paid for the church of Saint Paraschiva in Rășinari to be painted in 1758 and 1761, when "the priest Adam Lupia and his wife Maria" paid for decoration of the chapel of the church tower at Topârcea, when "the priest Constantin and the donor priest Iacov and the priest Grigore" paid for the upper part of the iconostasis in a monastery church in Valea Mărului in 1751, and when "the priest's wife and the priest, that is Pica Paladie and Botiş Grigorie" paid for the iconostasis in the church at Valea Stejarului in 1809 "to be an eternal memorial." Perhaps we need not take absolutely literally Petru Maior's claim that the priest Constantin of Jabenița, "took heart, and for all his poverty, built a little church with much effort and painted it very beautifully."[30] Nevertheless, though we may not know all the details, our ignorance in no way lessens the value of his deeds, since Maior's reference is the only mention of this otherwise unknown moment in history. We have only seven references to cases where the priest is the only named donor for painting work. Four of these are from the eighteenth century and concern Ocna Sibiului (though only if we accept that the term

[29] For the terms of the contract, cf. Porumb, *Dicționar*, 402.
[30] Ibid., 196.

ispravnic may be understood as donor)[31] and the churches of Velț, Sâncel and Veștem, for which there is only indirect evidence from the visitations of 1761.[32] The other three references are from the following century: an inscription on the south wall of the apse of the wooden church at Totoreni records that "This holy altar was made at the expense of Father Popovici Mihai, parish priest in Totoreni in the year 1818 June," while an inscription on the prothesis niche of the stone church at Viștea de Jos records that "The priest Ioan Șandru donated that this holy altar may be painted as an eternal memorial. Panteleimon the painter, 1819," and an inscription on the narthex of the stone church at Cristian (Brașov county) records that "the priest Stoica Popovici bore all expense for the church at Cărstian to be painted. 1821 Oct. 24," though this claim is neatly contradicted by the votive image which shows his wife Bucura alongside the priest. Other portraits which may perhaps show the donors who paid for painting work are those of "the priest Vasilie of this parish" in the church of Bicaz from the late eighteenth century, of the priest Ioan Cocanovici of Pâclișa, in 1807[33] and of the priest Aron Oprea of Almașu Mare-Suseni, in 1835. An unambiguous case is that of the archdeacon Maniu, portrayed as donor for the church at Broșteni and the painting work, who was painted along with several members of his family in 1743.[34]

Similarly scarce are inscriptions recording cases where priest and parish together raised the sums needed for painting work. We encounter such situations at Șebiș (1764), Deal (1789), Lunca Mureșului (1810), Ponor (1809, 1823) and Răstolița (1812). The remaining inscriptions which refer to painting in churches fall into five categories: those which record that the work was paid for from church funds;[35] those which record that the political authorities paid for the work;[36] those which name several donors with or without

---

[31] "fiind ispravnic popa Ioan ot Vizocnă la acest lucru" (ibid., 194, 272).

[32] Miron, *Biserica greco-catolică din Transilvania*, 326, 330.

[33] Ioana Rustoiu, Dănilă Vaida, *Cronica parohiei Pâclișa (1901-1944)* [Chronicle of the Parish of Pâclișa, 1901-1944] (Alba Iulia: Editura Altip, 2008), 107.

[34] *Șematismul veneratului cler al archidiecesei metropolitane greco-catolice române de Alba Iulia și Făgăraș pre anul Domnului 1900* [Clerical Directory of the Greek Catholic Romanian See of Alba Iulia and Făgăraș for the Year of Our Lord 1900] (Blaj, 1900), 190.

[35] Feisa (1751), Rădești, the monastery at Strâmba Fizeșului, Sartăș (1780), Valea Lungă-Hunedoara, Tău (iconostasis, 1822-1829), Mirăslău (iconostasis).

[36] The paintings in the Greek Catholic cathedral at Blaj were paid for by the state Treasury in 1749 once the Imperial Court assumed patronage over the church: Augustin Bunea, *Din istoria românilor. Episcopul Ioan Inocențiu Klein* [An Episode of Romanian History. Bishop Ioan Inocențiu Klein] (Blaj, 1900), 25. There is a reference to such "royal and imperial" charity at Zăbrani, in 1772 (Porumb, *Dicționar*, 457). The now-vanished wooden church at Bucuresci was built and probably painted at the expense of the "Inspector of the domain of Deva" in 1809: Ioana Cristache-Panait, *Arhitectura de lemn din județul Hunedoara* [Wooden Architecture in the County of Hunedoara] (București: Editura ARC 2000, 2000), 75. Similarly in the nineteenth century, the county authorities gave money for painting work in the churches at Copand (1856) and Sânbenedic (church of the Archangels, 1861), although the church of the Archangels at Șpălnaca was painted in 1858 "from the village coffer": Ioana Cristache-Panait, *Biserici de lemn monumente istorice din Episcopia Alba Iuliei, mărturii de continuitate și creație românească* [Historical Wooden Churches of the See of Alba Iulia as Evidence of Romanian Continuity and Creative Spirit] (Alba Iulia: Editura Episcopiei Ortodoxe Române a Alba Iuliei, 1987), 75.

specifying the contribution of each;[37] those which name only the priests and churchwardens, and perhaps the rulers and leading churchmen at the time of painting;[38] and those which more or less directly state that the whole parish was involved in paying for the work.[39]

Care was clearly taken to record names, whether these be the names of those who donated the money, those who administered the donations, or simply those who happened to be reigning at the time the painting work was carried out: this evident care makes it all the more puzzling that we have so many cases where the names are missing. In many cases, the painters themselves signed and dated works, some of considerable size and extent needing significant funds which must have been accumulated over time from a great many donors. It may be that it was precisely the scale of the donations that led to the decision not to record all participants in an inscription – perhaps helped along by disagreements during the course of the work itself.

There are traces of such conflicts in the case of Sânpaul, painted in 1789, where the inscription records not just the usual information (including the mention that the whole village gave money) but also a comment by the painter with a clear undertone of injured pride:

> "And it was painted by myself, the humble painter Dimitrie Ispas *and I bear nobody any ill will for anything*, but rather wish them health and long life and the forgiveness of their sins in this world [and] the eternal life to come, amen."

Even more stinging are the words of the donors to the church at Benesat, captured in 1741 in the form of a testament on the back of an icon as an indirect record that this too was part of their donation:

> "They did not put this writing into the holy church from pride or for praise, but rather so that our sons shall have no quarrel over the state of the church, so that when we are gone they may praise the Father and the Son and the Holy Ghost. So let nobody say that we have acted from pride, but rather to make a memorial for our forefathers and to our sons and for all our kin. Amen."

The lack of an inscription thus proves that most often, wisdom prevailed over disagreements, so that no mention survived for future generations. In other instances, we may consider donation by the whole community to be implied, or that the individual donors themselves wished that their names not be mentioned, choosing instead some other

---

[37] Most often the names of donors are simply listed and the work is dated by the names of the emperor, bishop and other persons of the time, or the names are accompanied by the comment that the work is to be a memorial to them and their families. We gave at least 61 such cases for the eighteenth century and may add at least a further 21 for the nineteenth century.

[38] At least 40 cases dated to the 18th-19th centuries.

[39] The most commonly used formulas are "at the sole expense of the village" (at least 10 cases, 18th century), "at the expense of the commune and village"(one case, 18th century), "all those who have borne [the costs]" (one case, 18th century), "the expense of the people" either in part or in whole (32 cases, 19th century), at the cost of "the Orthodox Christians" or other non-specific phrases, appended to the names of individual donors (11 cases, 18th-19th centuries).

form of memorial such as triptychs or diptychs, which have not come down to us. To give some idea of the extent of such silence, from a number of around 230 cases of various types mentioned so far from the eighteenth and nineteenth centuries alone, in around 50 churches the paintings bear only the names of the artists. I have not considered here those churches for which we have no information at all about the wall-paintings, iconostases and attendant work, firstly because most often the state of preservation does not allow us to conclude that there never was any inscription and secondly because the survey that we can manage is already very fragmentary, with the greater part of the churches and their painting being lost today. The percentage difference is certainly significant even if we cannot reconstruct exact figures here; the more closely we look at these ritual items, the clearer the importance of their "memorial" function for the donors at least, especially in the case of painted works – of which the icons were by far the most significant, since the believer who knelt before them or kissed them thereby gained direct access to the divine.

The holy aura of icons was thus more tangible than that of wall-painting, meaning that those who could afford to donate icons to churches gained additional merit thereby; and it is likewise true that being smaller, and thus less costly, icons allowed considerably more donors to give up some of their property in the hope of that "good answer at the time of Christ's dreadful judgement" asked for them in the liturgy. This hope is most often expressed in formulas of expiation such as "that they may have an eternal memorial" or "that this may be the alms given by themselves and by all their kin." Listing all such inscriptions recorded in the bibliography used here, we have 314 inscriptions on icons, 23 on the painted doors of the iconostasis, 13 on various crosses, 6 on candlesticks, 5 on banners, 4 on tetrapod tables, 3 on oblation tables and 2 on gates; there were also one each on a door, a liturgical veil, an antimension, an epitaph, a pyx and a ciborium. The total number is significantly in excess of inscriptions on wall-paintings, regardless of detailed or lack thereof, and thus exceeds even further the number of mural inscriptions recording the names of donors, individually or collectively. We should bear in mind that these numbers are the lower limits of available data, and moreover, represent a bare minimum for the historical state of affairs. We cannot even begin to estimate actual numbers for historical times, but we know that our understanding is severely limited not least by lack of knowledge about how other surviving painted ritual objects may have been paid for. Even so, the numbers offer sufficient insight into the importance donors attached to their gifts, which were not just a – certainly sincere – expression of piety but also a display of socio-economic status and, not least, a way to secure an honoured seat in church. The question of who took which pew was a delicate problem, perhaps the truest expression of how hierarchies were constructed in each parish.[40]

[40] A telling example is found in the protocol of the wooden church at Cojocna in 1797, recording "all the aid that has been given to the holy church, and who gave it" to establish seating in the pews: Nicolae Sabău, "Informații privind construirea bisericii de lemn din Cojocna, jud. Cluj (1794-1796)" [Some Notes on the Building of the Wooden Church at Cojocna, County Cluj, 1794-1796], *Anuarul Institutului de Istorie și*

For the most part, we do not know the prices paid for such donations, but their greater or lesser value is reflected in the quality of the materials and in the workmanship of the execution, and it is true today that these qualities increase in direct proportion with age. More exactly, the older an icon, the more artistically and materially valuable, and we may assume that the monetary cost was greater than that of more recent pieces, no longer painted with "good colours,"[41] in which the paints soon lost their lustre, the thin layer of tempera could not withstand the tools and flaked away, spoiling the image, and where the gold originally applied all across the icon to make the whole work glow was often replaced with various substitutes; in such late works, even the basic material of wood gave way to glass, much more fragile but also much cheaper. All these details would have been discussed in the initial consultation between painter and client; clients could duly choose between "fine works which remain as they are made" but which were concomitantly costly, and "ordinary work which does not last long and turns black" but which often proved more tempting as the only affordable option, costing only half as much.[42]

In the eighteenth century, only three churches were able to afford the very best quality adornment and employ the finest artists, these being the precursor churches of the Greek Catholic cathedral. These were the church of Maieri II in Alba Iulia, where Iosif of Hurez was commissioned to paint the iconostasis in 1716-1717, the church built by Constantin Brâncoveanu at Făgăraş, where Preda had painted the iconostasis for the voivode of Wallachia in 1698-1699 and where he now returned to paint the walls together with his sons Preda and Teodosie, and the chapel of the episcopal palace, anticipating the church of the Holy Trinity in Blaj, where Inochentie Micu likewise commissioned one of Brâncoveanu's painters for the iconostasis. As for the rest, all the Romanian churches of Transylvania, even that at Şcheii Braşovului, were painted only as a result of their own parishioners' efforts or through gifts from representatives of the local elite.

The lower social standing of donors at the time is reflected in the artistic value of the paintings, and in the stylistic degeneration which make works of the time so markedly different from those of the Brâncoveneanu era and from earlier centuries in general. We may observe though that the wealthiest donors hired the services of the most gifted painters, in an age when the daily trade of these artists depended more and more on smaller orders and on work picked up more or less by chance as they travelled the country. Often enough we can establish that when an artist was at work in a parish, the neighbouring parishes also took the opportunity to commission new painting work. From the latter eight-

---

Arheologie Cluj-Napoca XXII (1979): 373-374.

[41] The expression is repeatedly used in a contract drawn up sometime between 1816-1819, and I believe that this emphasis is symptomatic of how often poor-quality paints were used by then: Nicolae Iorga, *Scrisori şi zapise de meşteri români* [Documents and Sources from Romanian Master Craftsmen] (Bucureşti, 1926), 62-64.

[42] Cf. the correspondence from February 1789 between the merchants Ioan Pană of Braşov and Hagi Constantin Pop of Sibiu, where the latter reveals his intention to pay for the royal icons for the church at "Groapă," almost built (Porumb, *Dicţionar*, 47).

eenth century onwards the growing number of workshops led clients to prefer artists near at hand. This undiscriminating tendency worked to the advantage of some artists who could thereby truly monopolise work in the area where they were well-known, and even assured work for future generations. The best artists continued to work in larger markets, at least while still young, but only one painter, Ștefan Tenețchi, was able to build a career which could be called international today, with works evenly spread between Romania, Serbia and Hungary.[43] The most talented of them all was the *celeberrimus pictor*, Efrem Micu, the only eighteenth-century church artist known to have had academic training, who painted the iconostasis of the church of Saint Barbara in Vienna; in Transylvania, however, he only worked as a portrait painter.[44]

In the first half of the nineteenth century, professional academically-trained painters began to appear in Romanian society, while traditional painting remained the preserve of rural workshops whose products increasingly became marked by lack of talent and by dull, almost mechanical, copying of models whose message had long ago been lost. This development would on the one hand lead to the almost total Westernisation of church painting in the latter nineteenth century, and on the other hand would show up the limits of craftsman art. In parallel, the whole parish would increasingly come to be involved in the upkeep of churches, including their painting, with individual donations lingering for a while in icons and other ritual objects. To what extent does this shift illuminate a growing sense of collective responsibility? Or was it simply that greater attention was paid to recording such collective donation in the inscriptions? To what extent does it indicate a falling-away in piety? Or does it merely reflect greater costs? The only thing that is certain is that all these aspects played some part, to a different extent in each case. There are plentiful examples to show that the common factor was, all too often, the destruction of older paintings to make way for work of middling quality at best. It would be well worth considering the extent to which these renovations were due to socio-economic advances and the consequent demographic boom, which required larger houses of worship, to the physical degradation of earlier paintings, or to mere changes in artistic taste which required that the older painting be replaced. Extensive further research is required for any such analysis.

---

43 Porumb, *Dicționar*, 413-417; Nagy Márta, "Stefan Tenecki and the products of his workshop in Hungary," *Зборник Матице Српске за ликовне уметности* (Novi Sad) 25 (1989): 85-93.

44 "Efrem Micu alias Klein von Munti Celeberrimus Pictor," in Marius Porumb, *Un veac de pictură românească din Transilvania. Secolul XVIII* [A Century Transylvanian Romanian Painting. Eighteenth Century] (București: Editura Meridiane, 2003), 74.

ILLUSTRATIONS

Fig. 1: *Mother of God with Child*, 1539; Urisiu de Jos (Mureș County).

"† МОЛИТВА РАБА БОЖЯ ПАНЬ ЛУКА ѾТ УРИСИУ И ПОДРУЖІЄ СВОС И ЧАДОМЬ ВЛѢТ ҂ЗМЗ МСЦЬ МАРТ ҃А ДНЬ"

(*inscription on the frame, on the lower side*)

Fig. 2: *Deesis*, Second half of the seventeenth century; Lupşa Monastery (Alba County).

"ПОМЕНИ ГОСПОДИ ДУМИТРУ РОСАНДА"

(*inscription on the middle of the icon*)

Fig. 3: Luca from Iclod, *Mother of God with Child*, 1673; Ilişua (Bistriţa-Năsăud County).

“РАБ БЖІЙ МАТѲЄ Й ЖЄНА ЄГО АННЙЦА Й ЧАДЙ ЄГО ГЛИГА ЩТЄФАН ІѠНА
СТВОРИ СЙЮ ИКОНУ Й ДАДЄЮ ДО ХРАМУ С. ІѠАНА У СЄЛѢ ЄЛИШЄО.
РОКУ БОЖОГО ҂АХОГ МЄСЄЦА ФЄВРУАРѦ”

(*inscription on the frame, on the lower side*)

Fig. 4: Ivan and Nistor from Răşinari, *Mother of God with Child*, 1720; Certege (Alba County).

"Această icoană au dat la Certeză Bustan Dumitru şi Drag Nicula, Gane Ioan, Adam Simion, Adam Ion, Petru ..., msţa septemvrie 13 zile. Şi am scris eu Popa Ivan Zugravu ot Răşinari şi Nistor Zugravul. 7229. 1720"

(*inscription on the frame, on the lower side*)

Fig. 5: Dormition Church, Zlatna; inscription on building of the church in 1424
and it's painting in 1696.

"[La ani 1424 ...] s-au zidit această sfântă biserică, dintâi cu tinda până la mijlocul zidului, cu toată cheltuiala dumnealui jupănului Stănislav Hraboru i jupuniţa ego Anca, şi păntru acest lucru cătă arată mai sus s-au aflat cheltuiala cincisprăzece sute de florinţi, şi murind, au rămas neisprăvită. Iar la ani 1696, atuncia s-au apucat jupănu Dobra Anghel şi jupănu Iacov Ioanăş şi o au zidit-o cu toată chieltuiala dumnealor, bolta tinzii şi turnul, şi s-au făcut cheltuiala [...]"

Fig. 6: Ivan and Nistor from Răşinari, votive painting (Constantin Brâncoveanu and the priest Ioan), 1723; Ocna Sibiului (Sibiu County)

"Constandin Basarab voivod Brancoveanul care a făcut bisearica aceasta, făcutu-s-a 1701, şi s-au zugrăvit leat 1723, şi fiind ispravnic popa Iion ot Vizocnă la acest lucru."

Fig. 7: Ivan and Nistor from Răşinari, votive painting, 1724; Geoagiu de Sus (Alba County)

"[Dum]itru protopop ot Carlova, titoru bisearicii.
Rucopiseţi Popa Ivan zugrav i Nistor. 1724, mes. mai, 5 zile."

Fig. 8: Iacov from Răşinari, *Mother of God with Child*, 1747; Şilea (Alba County)

"ПОМЕНИ ГОСПОДИ ІАКѠВ ЗУГРАФ И МАРИА ЕГО. ҂АΨМS. 1746"

(*inscription on the right leg of the throne*)

Fig. 9: Ivan and Nistor from Răşinari, *Apostel Mathew*, 1758; Răşinari (Sibiu County)

"Această s[fântă] (icoană au) plătit Bucur cel tinăr."

Fig. 10: Gheorghe Zugrav and Crăciun Zugrav, mural painting
in the church from Cojocani (Alba County), 1769.

"Acest sfânt oltariu s-au zugrăvit cu cheltuiala molitfii sale Popa Ilie ş-a preuteasii, făr de alte ceale cheltuiale, bani 30 de florinţi vonaş. Pomeni Gospodi ierei Popa Ilie, preuteasa Ioana, Niculae, Andreiu, ierei Ion, ierei Florea, Floare, Mariia, Vasilie, Mariia. Gheorghie Z[ugrav], Crăciun Z[ugrav]"

Fig. 11: Simion Silaghi, *The Descent of Christ into Hell*, 1775; Fodora (Sălaj County).

"Popa Vasilie şi soţu dumisale Anna. Această s[fântă] icoană au plătit robii lui Dumnezeu aceştea: Ciopeiu Gligoraş, Ci[opeiu] Savu, Todor, Ho... Danilă, Horoat Gavrilă, Sim Mihaiu. Zugrav Sălăgean Şimon. An D[o]m[nului] 1775, mesiţa ianoar 14."

(*inscription on the back of the icon*)

Fig. 12: Stan from Răşinari and Ioan Covaci, inscription referring to the painting of the church from Deal (Alba County), 1789.

"† Acest oltari au plătit popa Vasilie, popa Ioan, popa Dumitru, popa Petru, popa Achim, popa Ioan, Avram ... [Nicol]ae Bogdan, Toma Bogdan, Ion Avram, Ion Radu, Cozma Bădilă, Avram Bădilă, Toma Pătru, Ion Bodea, Savu Bodea, Dumitru Bodea ..., ...ihu, Nicolae Cioca, Marian Popa, Ion Radu, Mathei Cioca, Ilie Dancu, Gligor Roşca, Constandin Dancu, Ilie Nedelcu [?], Nicolae Stan, Pătru Aioanei [?], Ananie Bogdan, Bucur Bogdan, Savu Pătru, Vasilie Dancu, Vasilie Negrea, Vasile Budreală, Precup Cioca, Filip Fechetă, Cozma Stan, Toma Cioca, Ion Coman ...eo [?] Cioca, Bucur Şchiopu. Anul 1789.
Stan Popovici Zug[rav], Ianăş Covaci Zug[rav]"

Fig. 13: Simion Silaghi and Teodor Ciungar, inscription referring to the painting of the St. George church from Lupşa (Alba County), 1810.

"În zilele oblăduirii preaînălţatului împărat Franţiscu, vicarăş Nicolae Husovici, s-au zugrăvit acest s. oltariu şi fruntariu prin sârguinţa acestor aicea numiţi ctitori: ci[nstit] p[ărinte] protopop şi asesor de conzistoriu Ioan Nandra ... Elena, Şpan Ilie cu fiii dumisale Popa Ioan, Nicolae, Petru, soţu dum. Todora, popa Gavriil, şpan domnesc şi crâznic bisericii, soţu dumisale Ióna, fii[i] Dumitru, Luca Ion, Avram, Vasilie, Todor, Ion, Nicolae, Măcăeţ Todor, Bădău Simeon, Sârb Todor, Alb Todor ... Todor Şerban, Nicolae ... Vasile Dascăl, Pop Ion, Todor Şpan, Nandra Ion, Hente Ion, Todor Şpan, Pătru Măcăeţ, Simeon Bădău ... Popa Petru şi fiiul său, Popa Ioan protopop [?], cu cheltuiala a tot poporul, la ani Domnului 1810, cine cât a vrut."

Fig. 14: Dimitrie Dimitriu from Bucharest, royal icon on the iconostasis from Bucium-Izbita (Alba County), 1836

"† În zilile prealuminatului şi preaosfinţitului D[omn] D[omnul] Episcop E *[sic !]* Vasilie Moga şi fostul Ci[nstit] D[omn] Protopopu Iosif Ighian s-au făcut această tâmplă prin cheltuiala părint[elui] Gheorghie Suci, paroh neunit din Izbita, începându-se la anul 1835, maiu, in 17, şi deplinu s-au săvârşit în tăetură şi în zugrăvit la anul 1836, septemvrie în 26. S-au tăiat din lemn de Iosif Bârsan, săpătoriul din Răşinari, iar zugrăvirea de Dimitrie Mitrovici, român din Bucureşti, în Ţara Româneas[că], împreună cu Simon Silaghi zug[rav] din Abrud şi Anton Şimon din Cluj. Spre veş[nica] pom[enire]."

(*inscription on the back of the iconostasis*)

Fig. 15: Painter from Nicula, *Mother of God with Child*, glass icon, 1797; Bârsăuța (Sălaj County).

"Anul 1797. Bonda Nede au plătit această iconă."

(*inscription on the lower side of the icon*)

Fig. 16: Painter from Nicula, *The Nativity*, glass icon, 1821; Urisiu de Jos (Mureş County).

"Această sfântă icoană am cumpărat eu popa Aron din Urisiu de Jos şi cu preoteasa Paraschiva, leat 1821, pintru vecinica pomenire, noi şi fiilor noştri. Vasilie, Ana, fii[i] noşti."

(*inscription on the back of the icon*)

GREEK PATRONAGE OF THE ARTS IN LVIV IN THE SIXTEENTH AND SEVENTEENTH CENTURIES

WALDEMAR DELUGA

Greek emigrants settled in many cities and towns of the Polish-Lithuanian Commonwealth as a small but wealthy ethnic group of Orthodox citizens of the multinational state. The Greeks settled in new localities, and their spiritual leaders exerted an immense impact on the religious transformations of post-medieval Europe.[1] Following the fall of Constantinople, they appeared in Venice and contributed to the growth of the Polish-Lithuanian Commonwealth; they also emigrated to Eastern Europe via Moldavia and Wallachia, and followed the routes of Latin merchants to arrive in the cities of Central Europe. The migrations, typical of the Balkan nations, contributed to the emergence of the specific mentality of the region's inhabitants.[2] Greek merchants contributed to development of trade, especially in wine that was imported from Hungary and Moldavia, while Greek theologians took part in the interdenominational dialogue.[3]

In 1580, Duke Wasyl Ostrogski opened a school, called the Academy, in his estate, where students were instructed in theology as well as languages: Greek, Church Slavonic and Latin.[4] Patriarch Meletios Pigas of Alexandria sent Cyril Lucaris, later to become Patriarch of Constantinople, to the Polish-Lithuanian Commonwealth. At that time, a Greek named Dionisos Rallu, the metropolitan bishop of Kizikos and an ardent propagator of union of the Churches, arrived in Ostrog. As a descendant of the imperial Palaiologos family, his support for the union brought him to the Polish-Lithuanian Commonwealth, where the Duke made him archimandrite in Drohobuż. He was not the only Greek to arrive in Ostrog; Eustathius Nathanael from Crete became the tutor of the Duke's sons Aleksander and Konstanty. Emanuel Moschopulos also came to settle in the city. Duke Ostrogski held numerous talks on matters related to the Church union, also

---

[1] Cf. Jan Stradomski, *Spory o „wiarę grecką'' w dawnej Rzeczypospolitej* [Disputes About the Greek Faith in the Former Polish-Lithuanian Commonwealth] (Kraków, 2003); K. Kuczara, "Misja patriarchy jerozolimskiego Teofanesa III w obronie „wiary greckiej" w Rzeczpospolitej po unii brzeskiej" [The Mission of the Patriarch of Jerusalem Teofanes III in Defense "the Greek Faith" in the Polish-Lithuanian Commonwealth After the Union of Brest], in *Od Zborowa do NATO (1649-2009): Studia z dziejów stosunków polsko-ukraińskich od XVII do XXI wieku. Historia* [From Zborów to NATO (1649-2009): Studies in the History of Polish-Ukrainian Relations from the Seventeenth to the Twenty-First Century. History], ed. M. Franc, K. Pietkiewicz (Toruń: Wydawnictwo Adam Marszałek, 2009), 17-34; Idem, "Arsenios z Elassonu – Grek w służbie Cerkwi prawosławnej we Lwowie" [Arsenios of Elasson – One Greek in the Service of the Orthodox Church in Lviv], *Przegląd Historyczny* 101, 1 (2010): 89-99.

[2] P. M. Kitromilides, "Balkan Mentality: History, Legend, Immigration," *Nations and Nationalism*, 2 (1996): 163-191.

[3] N. Iorga, *Choses d'Orient de Roumanie* (Bucarest, 1924), 81.

[4] Cf. T. Kempa, *Książę Konstanty Wasyl Ostrogski (ok. 1524/25). Wojewoda kijowski i marszałek ziem wołyńskich* [Prince Constantine Vasil Ostrogski (c. 1524-1525). Governor and Speaker of the Lands of Kiev and Volyn] (Toruń, 1997).

with representatives of the apostolic nunciature in Cracow, which he visited accompanied by his sons Konstantyn and Janusz and by the Greek archimandrite Dionisos Rallu Palaiologos of the Drohobuż monastery.[5] The monk was probably familiar with the inner history of the talks, and he could have been the Duke's advisor on matters of the doctrine. During the negotiations, cooperation was agreed between the Ostrog College and the papal scholarly institutions in Rome. Ostrogski was particularly keen on cooperating with Greek scholars then living in Italy. Meletios Pigas, the Patriarch of Alexandria in the years 1592-1595, also corresponded voluminously with Duke Ostrogski and the stavropegic brotherhood in Lviv.

Rallu's suggestion of moving the Patriarchate to the Polish-Lithuanian Commonwealth was also seriously discussed. Ostrog was to become the seat of the Patriarchate, and archimandrite Palaiologos to be invited there as the first resident Patriarch. After Patriarch Jeremias II Tranos of Constantinople was dethroned for the second time and imprisoned on Rhodos by the Turks, the Roman diplomacy endeavoured to release the Patriarch and persuade him to settle in Poland. Eager to have the Patriarchate's seat moved, Antonio Possevino visited Lublin in August 1584 to meet Ostrogski, whom he presented with the papal gift of the Roman catechism in Greek (the so-called catechism of Trent). He also presented the view of the Secretary of State, Cardinal Tolomeo Galli di Como, who suggested Lviv or Vilnius as the seat of the Patriarchate, which would result in a universal union. However, Jeremias turned down the invitation. He resumed the throne in 1587 after vigorous lobbying by his associates. Yet he did visit the Polish-Lithuanian Commonwealth a year later to convene, with the King's consent and as the guest of Chancellor Jan Zamojski, a provincial synod that contributed to a revival of the church hierarchy. Next he travelled to Moscow, where he supported Boris Godunov's reforms, accepting the foundation of a new Patriarchate in the capital city of Northern Ruthenia and the raising of Metropolitan Job to the throne. He again visited the Polish-Lithuanian Commonwealth in 1589, confirming the reforms of Patriarch Joachim of Antiochia, an ardent propagator of the idea of independence of Orthodox brotherhoods.

The idea of moving the Patriarchate from Constantinople to the Polish-Lithuanian Commonwealth was revived early in the seventeenth century, when the Uniate metropolitan Józef Welamin Rutski, in his memorial to the papal nuncio Antonio Santa Croce, suggested that the rank of Patriarch be conferred upon Piotr Mohyła.

At the end of the sixteenth century, the Orthodox townsfolk of cities in the Polish-Lithuanian Commonwealth formed confraternities, organizations of parishioners subsequently approved by the Patriarch of Constantinople. Sometimes, their activity was met with opposition on part of the Orthodox bishops. To begin with, they were involved in charity and education; gradually, they evolved into an institutional power capable of opposing Catholic expansion in the Polish-Lithuanian Commonwealth. Patriarch Jeremias II

[5] Cf. J. Krajcar, "Konstantin Basil Ostrožkij and Rome in 1580-1584," *Orientalia Christiana Periodica* 35, 1 (1969): 200-202.

Tranos backed the confraternities, giving them the title of stavropegions and admitting them to the synods. A confraternity founded in Lviv grouped together numerous Greeks. The Patriarch of Constantinople failed to visit Lviv in 1589, as the city was stricken by plague at that time, but issued a decree approving the confraternity, school and printing house established by Patriarch Joachim of Antiochia. That year, he visited Krasnystaw, Tarnopol and Kamieniec.

The Orthodox inhabitants of Lviv played an important role in shaping the religious community, especially through the stavropegic confraternity grouping townsfolk representatives. The organization of parishioners establishing their own confraternity already became an important area of activity for ethnic Greek settlers at the end of the sixteenth century. The confraternity chose as its seat the Church of the Assumption, also called the Wallachian Church, an example of the harmonisation of Eastern and Western traditions, built in 1559 with the financial assistance of Moldavian hospodar Alexander Lăpuşneanu and his wife Ruxandra. Information about the ceremony and its consecration can be found in the hospodar's letters, sending money and instructions about the erection of the church.[6] A document of 1565 shows that he also funded the tower.[7]

In 1571, the church burnt down; its reconstruction was financed by the Mohyła family. Two letters were sent to King Sigismund III Vasa, one asking for a charter to the Ruthenians granting them privilege of erecting the church, and the other proposing that the king summon the Lviv town council to assist the builders.[8] From further letters it follows that the Moldavian Governor, Piotr himself, approached the king in person. The stavropegic confraternity of Vilnius also gave financial support; the stavropegion's archives included a 1591 contract for rebuilding the Assumption Church to designs by Paweł Rzymianin.[9] In that period, the tower founded by Constantine Korniakt was built; hence the structure's name, the Korniakt tower. In that period, Korniakt was already an influential member of the confraternity, which in 1597 appointed a second master Wojciech Kapinos, and a year later master Ambroży. In 1603, Filip Teodorowicz Malarz and Prokop Fedorowicz brought money for the rebuilding work, and in 1611 Konstanty Mohyła gave further funds to aid their completion.

The Assumption Church held an iconostas dated 1629-1638, which the Lviv historian of art Mieczysław Gębarowicz found at the Orthodox church in Grzybowice Wielkie; he discovered that the iconostas had been sold in 1767 through the offices of sculptor

---

[6] Archiwum Historyczne we Lwowie [Historical Archives in Lviv], Fund 29, op. I, nos. 24-26. Cf. *Jubilejnoe izdanie v pamiat' 300 letnago osnovanija Lvovskogo Stavropigijskogo Bratstva* [The Jubilee Edition in Honour of the Tercentenary Foundation of the Stauropigial Brotherhood in Lwów] (Lvov, 1886), nos. XIV-XVII; I. S. Swiencickij, *Opis Muzeja Stauropigijskago Instytuta vo Lvovie* [Description of the Museum of the Stauropigial Institute in Lwów] (Lvov: 1908), nos. 29-31, 36; I. Szaraniewicz, *Ruskie Muzeum Instytutu Stauropigialnego we Lwowie* [Ruthenian Museum of Stauropigial Institute in Lwów] (Lwów: 1937), 9.

[7] *Jubilejnoe izdanije*, nos. XVII, XIX; Swiencickij, *Opis Muzeja Stauropigijskago*, nos. 39, 40.

[8] Ibid., 9.

[9] W. Łoziński, *Sztuka lwowska XVI i XVII wieku. Architektura i rzeźba* [Art in Lwów in Sixteenth and Seventeenth Centuries. Architecture and Sculpture] (Lwów, 1901), 51.

Jan Starzewski.[10]

One of the best known Greeks in Lviv, whom Mieczysław Gębarowicz calls a magnate and patron, was Constantine Korniakt, born in 1520 in Rethymno, Crete. His brother Michael (†1563) spent the years 1545-1563 trading in Lviv.[11] A wealthy merchant, Constantine Korniakt, called Coreto de Candia in documents, previously resided in Constantinople and Wallachia, and for many years was a revenue officer for the Moldavian hospodar Alexander Lăpuşneanu. After the death of his elder brother Michael, Constantine inherited his estate and expanded it with money borrowed from another Cretan by birth, Jacob Basilikos, who was the despot of Moldavia for a short time. In 1566, King Sigismund Augustus granted him the privilege to import and sell wine in the Polish-Lithuanian Commonwealth, and in 1568 he received the privilege to distribute Crimean liquors from sultan Selim II.[12] He also imported cotton, honey, ox hide and furs. In 1571, when Korniakt was the wealthiest inhabitant of Lviv, the king raised him to the rank of nobility (coat of arms: Krzyż). In 1575 he married Anna Dzieduszycka (†1616), consenting to unfavourable financial conditions and promising no longer to pursue trade in person. Their sons Konstantyn, Aleksander and Michał studied in Padua. Their father purchased a number of estates in the Przemyśl and Lviv regions, including about 40 villages, the two small towns Hussaków and Kulików, and the crown lands of Szczerzecz near Lviv. In addition Constantine Korniakt became involved in the activities of the stavropegic confraternity, to which he had been admitted as early as 1569.[13] He funded the tower for the Orthodox Church of the Dormition in Lviv, and was among the founders of the Three Saints chapel. He built a house in the market square designed by Piotr Barbon, which was subsequently purchased by Jakub Sobieski and known as the "royal house" from 1674, when the latter's son Jan Sobieski was elected king. Constantine Korniakt died in 1603 and was buried in the Wallachian Church, as a generous benefactor.

A portrait from the church has been preserved, now kept in the collection of the Lviv Historical Museum. Mieczysław Gębarowicz shows that the portrait is actually a copy of the original sepulchral banner by an anonymous painter, probably commissioned by Korniakt's sons.[14] The original banner was most likely destroyed, hence the new version. According to the Stavropegion's expense ledger, a new damask banner was ordered. Later it was pasted on a wooden base, which changed its shapes and dimensions. Interestingly, the background damask was probably of Turkish origin, very similar to the one found in the Moldavian embroidery showing Jeremi Mohyła. The deceased man's pose is typical of presentations of the early seventeenth century, which confirms the thesis of an earlier prototype.

---

[10] M. Gębarowicz, *Portret XVI-XVII wieku we Lwowie* [Portrait of the Sixteenth and Seventeenth Century in Lwów] (Wrocław, Warszawa, Kraków, 1969), 83.

[11] I. Lylo, *Narysy z istoriji hrećkoj hromady Lvova XVI- XVII stolit'* [Notes on the History of the Greek Community in Lviv in Sixteenth and Seventeenth Centuries] (Lviv, 2002), 107.

[12] Ibid., 109.

[13] Ibid., 112.

[14] Gębarowicz, *Portret*, p. 25, il. 6-7.

The sepulchral banner likely served as the model for a further, full-length portrait of Korniakt, hands joined in prayer, by Łukasz Doliński. At the bottom is a Latin inscription copied – according to Gębarowicz – from the original banner.[15] The man's costume, a black fur-lined coat and traditional patterned dress differs from the prototype. However, with all those differences, the man's face is the same.

The sons of Constantine Korniakt became largely assimilated and converted to Catholicism, departing from their ancestors' religion.[16] Konstanty Franciszek Korniakt Junior settled on an estate near Przemyśl and married Elżbieta Ossolińska (†1646). One of his sons, Karol Franciszek (1612-1672) participated in the Polish campaigns and battles near Zbarazh and Berestechko. In 1657, he owned 11 villages in the Przemyśl region. In 1650, during the struggles for the Przemyśl lordship, he took sides with the Uniates as an ardent Greek Catholic. He fought in many wars; for example, he financed companies during Chmielnicki's insurrection and commanded his own company in the battle near Berestechko in 1651. This generosity made him popular with the nobility of Przemyśl. In 1664, Korniakt married Katarzyna Bełżecka, daughter of the Podole Governor Aleksander, who had three sons, Antoni Karol, Michał and Franciszek, and three daughters: Katarzyna, Franciszka and Jana.[17] He died in 1672 in Przemyśl.[18] His daughter inherited the town of Hussaków and went to live there with her husband Konstanty Krasicki. A portrait of Antoni Korniakt is now one of the oldest items in the Ossolineum collection in the Historical Museum in Lviv, to which it was added as early as 1828.[19] The portrait of a young man shows the son of Karol Franciszek Korniakt; it is dated about 1686 and considered to be the work of a good artist.

In 1582, a Greek merchant, Yanni Afendyk, arrived in Lviv and bought a house in Ruska Street.[20] In 1591, he was admitted to the stavropegic confraternity along his son Piotr. Yanni traded with Gdańsk. In 1678, King Jan III Sobieski granted a privilege to his wife Maria Afendyk, exempting her from taxation.[21] The collection of the Historical Museum in Lviv includes the epitaph of Maria Afendyk from 1700. The painting, coming from a Wallachian church and showing Crucifixion, is probably the work of a Latin artist, as the feet of Christ are nailed to the cross with a single nail. The epitaph was added in later: the Latin inscription on the plate was replaced with a Cyrillic one, and Greek initials were added on the cross. The deceased woman's full-length portrait was also added to the left: the artist has faithfully rendered the costume of Maria Afendyk, with a rosary in her hand.

[15] Ibid., p. 26, il. 8.
[16] Lylo, *Narysy z istoriji*, 114.
[17] *Polski Słownik Biograficzny* [Polish Biographical Dictionary], vol. 11 (Warszawa, 1968), 82.
[18] Lylo, *Narysy z istoriji*, 114-115.
[19] Gębarowicz, *Portret*, 80.
[20] Lylo, *Narysy z istoriji*, 104.
[21] Ibid.

The Langisz family settled in Lviv at the end of the fifteenth century. The merchant Marek Langisz purchased a house in the city. His elder son Bartosz frequently broke the law, while the other son Gabriel went to a fraternal school in Lviv, became an influential merchant in the city, trading with the East and Moscow, and took part in the activities of the stavropegic confraternity. His elder daughter Barbara married a nobleman of Greek origin Teodor Tomy, the son of Dawid Tomy (Tomkiewicz). A painting which is probably her portrait, from the stavropegic confraternity's collection, is kept at the Historical Museum in Lviv.[22] The portrait of Barbara Langisz, deceased in 1635, is considered to be one of the oldest coffin portraits.[23] As Gębarowicz argues, the artist skillfully portrayed the deceased, stressing her female beauty with jewels and the light refracted upon them. The next daughter, Maria was the wife of Mano Mazapeta; after his death, she married a Polish nobleman, B. Gosławski.[24] Gabriel Langisz initiated the construction of a monastery which his other two daughters Kandyda and Olimpiada were to join; however, he abandoned the plan after protests from the Jewish community as the planned convent was too close to the local synagogue.[25]

Mano Mazapeta was an influential patrician in the Greek Diaspora community of Lviv, where he settled in the mid-sixteenth century, residing in the house of his father-in-law Marek Langisz, where he owned a collection of Greek books. Mazapeta's coffin portrait is now kept in the Historical Museum in Lviv, as one of the oldest portraits of a member of the Greek Diaspora in the Polish-Lithuanian Common-wealth.[26]

Mazapeta's son Konstantyn, a member of the stavropegic confraternity, lived near the Church of the Assumption and ordered books for the stavropegic library. In 1649 he went to Warsaw and died there suddenly.[27] His only son Konstantyn (†1687) moved to Chernihiv for political reasons.

Krzysztof Mazaraki was another representative of the Greek Diaspora who came to Lviv early in the seventeenth century. In 1645 he was admitted to the stavropegic confraternity, of which also his son Iwan (†1667) was a member. The other son Iwan junior (†1690), represented the Orthodox community at the royal court in Warsaw. In 1678, he was among the envoys sent to Persia by King Jan III Sobieski.[28]

Jerzy (Georgios) Papara (†1701) came to Lviv in the early half of the seventeenth century.[29] He had been born in Ioannina in Epirus, and resided also in Moldavia. The 1658 deed of his ennoblement contains the information that he served in the Cossack

---

[22] Ibid., 117.

[23] H. Hotkevich, *Albom istorychnyh portretiv* [Album of the Historical Portraits] (Lviv, 1910), fig. 5.

[24] Lylo, *Narysy z istoriji*, 117.

[25] W. Łoziński, *Patrycjat i mieszczaństwo lwowskie w XVI i XVII wieku* [The Nobility and Bourgeoisie in the Sixteenth and Seventeenth Centuries in Lwów] (Lwów, 1892), 323.

[26] H. W. Jakushchenko, *Kataloh zbirki zhyvopysi Lwivskoho Istorychnoho Muzeju* [Catalogue of the Collection of Paintings from the Historical Museum in Lviv] (Lviv, 1987), 76.

[27] Łoziński, *Patrycjat*, 239.

[28] Lylo, *Narysy z istoriji*, 123.

[29] Łoziński, *Patrycjat*, 234.

army. In the king's diplomatic service, he participated in negotiations with the Cossacks. He owned estates in Biatycze, Kupiszwola and Zełdce. His was related to the later bishop of Suchava – Dosydeusz. His own brother Cyriak Papara, captain of horse and courtier of the Moldavian hospodar, was ennobled in 1676.[30]

One of the most important personages among the Greek Diaspora in Lviv was Hatzikiriakis Vourliotis. According to Russian archives, he settled in the city in 1667,[31] while Dory Papastratos believes that he only appeared there in 1674.[32] A rich entrepreneur, he conducted various kinds of business in the Polish-Lithuanian Commonwealth, but also ordered works of art. He was born about 1640 in Vourla near Ephesus and in 1680 visited St. Catherine's monastery on Mount Sinai.[33] He pursued business activities in many localities, Jerusalem, Constantinople, Chios, Bucharest and Moscow, imported goods including amber and furs and exported them across Poland and to Silesia.[34] From archival sources we know that he imported paper from Gdańsk to order of the stavropegic confraternity in Lviv and exported paper further afield, to such faraway places as the St. Catherine monastery on Mount Sinai.[35]

The monks of the Krekhiv monastery, Nikodem Zubrzycki and hegumen Dionizy Sinkiewicz, made a number of devotional graphic works for Hatzikyriakis. Particularly noteworthy is the view of Mount Sinai held at the French National Library in Paris, a large woodcut showing a symbolic presentation of the mountain, monastery and numerous scenes from the Old Testament. Hatzikiriakis presented many Orthodox dignitaries, including the Patriarch of Constantinople, with copies of the engraving. Several years after the first version, Zubrzycki prepared another variant of the composition ordered by Hatzikyriakis and designed for St. Catherine's monastery on Mount Sinai, differing from the previous one with many elements of the composition itself and with a detailed legend on the lower border. Just one copy survives till the present day; however, it is thought that this was made in the early eighteenth century. It is held in the collection of the University Library in Uppsala. The block ordered by St. Catherine's monastery (where it is still kept today) was in use for several decades, as demonstrated by small defects. Whilst in Lviv, Hatzikiriakis also commissioned other engravings related to Mount Sinai.[36]

Hatzikiriakis is also known as the donor for painting work for the Assumption Church in Lviv. The collection of the Stavropegic Confraternity Institute in Lviv once

---

[30] Lylo, *Narysy z istoriji*, 158.

[31] B. Fonkin, "Sinait Hatzikiriakis iz mestnosti Vurla. Neskolko dopolnienij k biografii" [Hatzikiriakis Sinait from the Town Vurla], in *Filevskie chtenija. K 300-letiju pamiatnika arhitektury XVII stoletija „Cerkov Pokrova v Filiah" (1690-1693)* [Fili's Reading. Tercentenary Monument of Architecture. Orthodox Church in Fili (1690-1693)] (Moskwa, 1993), 31.

[32] N. Papastratou, *O Sinaítis Hatzikyriakis ék Chóras Vourla. Grámmata-xulougrafíes 1688-1709* [Hatzikyriakis Sinaitis from the Village of Vourla. Letters-Woodcuts 1688-1709] (Athens, 1981), 13.

[33] Eadem, *Paper Icon. Greek orthodox religious Engraving 1665-1899*, vol. 2 (Athens, 1990), no. 382.

[34] Fonkin, "Sinait Hatzikiriakis," 32.

[35] Papastratou, *O Sinaítis*, 16.

[36] Papastratos, *Paper Icon*, nos. 397, 402, 403, 415.

included two paintings showing Jerusalem and Mount Athos, donated by the wealthy Greek.[37] One of them, showing the Holy City, was painted by Jan Malinowski in 1696 and is now kept at the National Art Gallery in Lviv. The painting consists of two parts: the upper part shows a panorama of the Holy City, the lower the map of the Holy Land, and the center contains a portrait of the founder and an inscription:

> "*Anno Domini 1696* [...] Keepsake from Mister Hadzia Kiriak the steward of Mount Sinai. *Joannes Malinowski pinxit.*"

The presentation of Jerusalem uses the graphic model frequently copied in book illustrations. The other painting, showing the monasteries on the peninsula Athos, is now kept at the division of the Lviv Painting Gallery in Olesko. Its composition also refers to graphic models.

In 1690 Hatzikiriakis sent money through Mikołaj Michalewicz to Jarosław to buy roofing for the local church. Hatzikiriakis spent almost thirty years in Lviv, and also travelled to Moscow, where an account of his stay in Russia contains numerous new pieces of information. He arrived in Moscow in 1697 with hierodeacon Seraphin. Late in his life, he settled in the Paudolopi (?) monastery on Chios and became a monk.[38]

In the mid-seventeenth century, diplomatic and religious contacts with Constantinople and other Eastern Churches continued. In 1644 Metropolitan Melecjusz of Ephesus, Exarch of Little Asia, came to the Polish-Lithuanian Commonwealth as a representative of the Eastern Patriarchate. On the basis of the rule of Patriarch Joachim of Antiochia, he founded confraternities at the Orthodox churches in Sambor and Drohobycz.[39] His writings of those days have survived.[40] The metropolitan probably visited Gdańsk, as his portrait has been preserved made by the Dutch engraver Willem Hondius after a drawing by Steven de Praet.[41] The inscription identifies the model's age: Meletius was sixty-eight in 1647.

Greek merchants settled in many cities of the Polish-Lithuanian Commonwealth, and also in Russia. Large groups lived in Kiev[42] and Nizhyn.[43] Also worth mentioning is the Greek community in Lublin, where the Greeks built their own Orthodox church in 1786, having acquired the consent of King Stanisław Poniatowski. The church was subordinate to the Patriarchate in Constantinople and was only taken over by Moscow during the partitions. In that same period, the Greeks also settled in Kalisz.

---

[37] Swiencickii, *Opis Muzeja Stauropigijskago*, p. 196, nos. 250-251.
[38] Papastratou, *O Sinaítis*, 33-35.
[39] Szaraniewicz, *Ruskie Muzeum*, 97.
[40] *Svodnaja halycko-ruska litopis* [Summary of Halych-Ruthenian Litopis] (Lvov, 1874), 300-301.
[41] W. Deluga, "„Orientalizujące" portret Willema Hondiusa" [Oriental Portrait of Willem Hondius], *Porta Aurea* 6 (1999): 174, il. 6.
[42] S. Mazarati, "Grieki Kieva (istorija i sowremennost')" [Greeks from Kiev, History and Contemporaneity], in *Zapysky Istoryko-Fiłolohichnoho Tovarystva Andrija Bilećkoho* [Notes of the Historical and Philological Society Andrij Bilecki] (Kyjiv, 1997), 67-81.
[43] H. Onishchenko, "Hreki w Nizhini: Ternawioty" [Greeks in Nizhin: Ternaviot's], in *Hrećkie Pravosłavja w Ukrajini* [Greek Orthodoxy in Ukraine] (Kyjiv, 2001), 117-122.

The discussed history of ethnic Greeks in the Polish-Lithuanian Commonwealth, who were particularly active in Lviv in the sixteenth and seventeenth centuries, demonstrates their extensive participation in the city's cultural life, as attested by the surviving relics. As a small ethnic group in Lviv, the Greeks greatly influenced transformations of the Orthodox culture. Their financial contribution to the building and endowment of local Orthodox churches was huge. Settled in Lviv and forced to compete fiercely with Armenians and Jews, they not only joined the nobility but even changed denomination, departing from their ancestral faith. Usually the second or third generation of Greek families became Roman Catholics, thereby assuming Polish customs.

ILLUSTRATIONS

Fig. 1: Dormition church, Lviv.

Fig. 2: Portrait of Greek Mano.

Fig. 3: Portrait of Greek Papara.

Fig. 4: Constantine Korniakt house, Lviv.

Fig. 5: Portrait of Constantine Korniakt, 1669, Lviv History Museum.

Fig. 6: Portrait of Constantine Korniakt, Lviv History Museum.

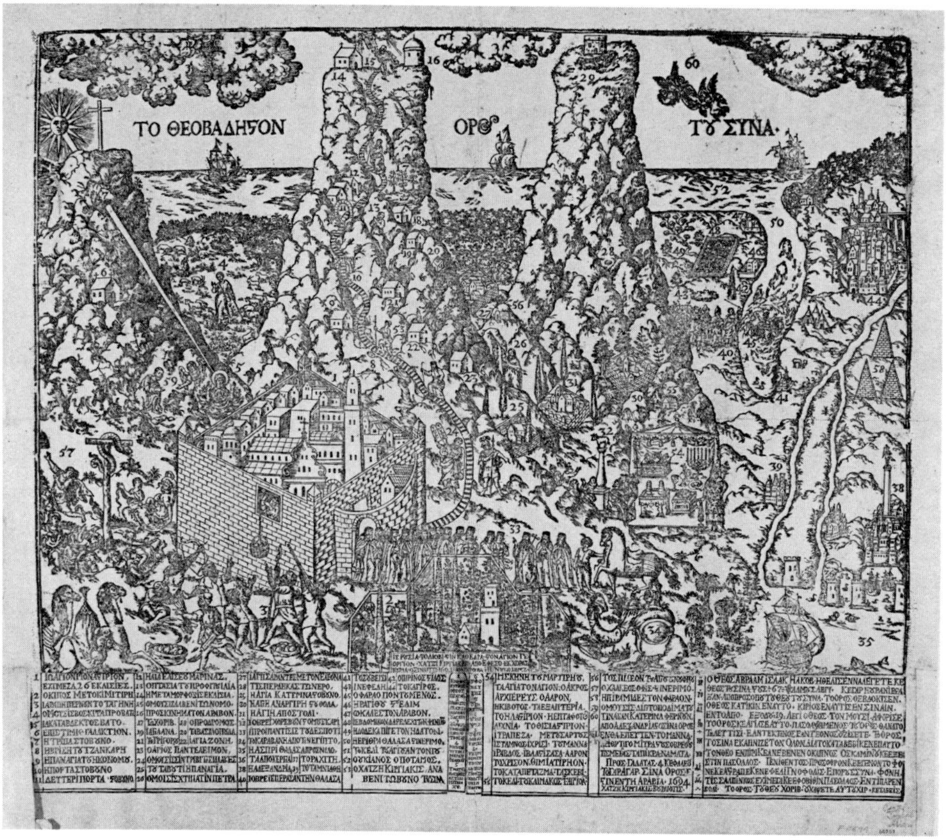

Fig. 7: View of Sinai by Nikodem Zubrzycki, woodcut.

Fig. 8: View of Jerusalem by Malinowski.

Fig. 9: View of Athos.

AFFLUENCE AND AUSTERITY.
Romanian Students from Transylvania and Their Life in the European Universities (1850-1919)

CORNEL SIGMIREAN

Starting in the nineteenth century, an increasing number of Romanians from Transylvania started to attend universities, polytechnic institutes, Grande Écoles, schools of fine arts, conservatoires and other institutions of higher education in Europe.[1] Their experience of the large university cities, with a different culture and civilisation, constituted a unique experience whereby characters were shaped and new lifestyles adopted, the Romanian elites taking a decisive step in embracing the values of modern society. Analysis of 3,250 Romanian students from Transylvania who attended European universities from 1867 to 1918 shows that 25.93% of them were born and raised in farming families.[2] As for geographic origin, most lived in the countryside, since at the beginning of the nineteenth century agriculture was the main livelihood of 85.9% of the Romanians. In 1880, only 82,200 Romanians lived in cities, representing only 3.4% of the total number of Romanians living in the historic regions of Hungary.[3] Thus their encounter with school and university was formative for many Romanian students. In modern society, education – as Eric Hosbawm has stated – opened the way to the upper and middle classes of society.[4] Through knowledge and education, lower-class youths sought to enter a new social category by means of their future professions, to gain access to culture and to higher status. Education represented the main means to social development, which was a general phenomenon in the nineteenth century, a time of extraordinary academic expansion.

Naturally, in the creation of modern society in Transylvania, many endogenous factors had a great influence, such as Austro-Hungarian state policy to reform and develop Central European society in accordance with the Western model. Nevertheless, as the historian Keith Hitchins has noted in the Romanian case, the intellectuals educated in the European universities had a special role in this process, acting as the main mediator between the rural areas whence they originated and urban cosmopolitan society, in which they attended university.

Thus 15,205 Romanian students attended the Greek Catholic and Orthodox theo-

---

[1] For the academic itineraries of the Romanian intellectuals in Transylvania see Cornel Sigmirean, *Istoria formării intelectualității românești din Transilvania și Banat în epoca modernă* [History of Formation of Romanian Intellectuality from Transylvania and Banat in the Modern Days] (Cluj-Napoca: Presa Universitară Clujeană, 2000); Lucian Năstasă, *Itinerarii spre lumea savantă. Tinerii din spațiul românesc la studii în străinătate (1864-1944)* [Itineraries to the Scholars World. Young Men from the Romanian Space Studying Abroad (1864-1944)] (Cluj-Napoca: Limes, 2006).

[2] Sigmirean, *Istoria formării intelectualității,* 219.

[3] Keith Hitchins, *România. 1866-1948* [Romania. 1866-1948] (Bucureşti: Humanitas, 1996), 225.

[4] Eric Hobsbawm, *Era imperiului. 1857-1914* [The Age of Imperialism 1857-1914] (Chişinău: Cartier, 2002), 226.

logical institutions in Transylvania and Central and Western Europe universities from 1801 to 1919.[5] From 1850 to 1919, there were 13,164 students enrolled, 1,693 of whom attended universities outside historic Hungary, in Austria, Germany, Italy, Belgium, France etc. In all, the academic geography of Romanian intellectuals encompasses 118 academies and universities in Europe.

The universities attended, the course of studies, the cultural milieus of student life, the trends in politics and philosophy that inspired the future professionals or politicians, are essential elements for reconstructing the history of intellectuals. But highlighting the day-to-day aspects can provide another way to reconstruct the phenomenon of academia. Integration into the life of university cities, the conditions of student life, sustenance, everyday life in a university city and the sacrifices made in order to attend school can represent key elements for a history of the education of intellectuals.

At first there was the excitement of the big city, finding a place to stay, the integration into the academic life of the city. In his memoirs, Petru Groza writes of his encounter with Budapest, where he arrived in 1903 with his colleague, Rudolf Opreanu, to attend law school:

> "As we arrived in Budapest, our main concern was, naturally, to find a room. And we started wandering the narrow and tortuous streets around the university, viewing several rooms for rent announced by plates affixed on gates, until we found one indicating 'twin room, separate entrance, 22 florins.' We will never forget this plate as it is deeply engraved into our memory on account of what followed next. Indeed, we went up the stairs, we saw the room, and happy that we found it, we paid the rent for one month, i.e. 22 florins. Afterwards, we went back to the railway station to take our luggage. But when we got back in the evening with our luggage, we realized that we had forgotten the name of the street. We lost our room and our money."[6]

Naïve, provincial and convinced that they had to live close to their studies, the two young men looked for another room, as close to the university as possible. And they found it on Képiró Street: "The next day we found out" – as Groza remembers – "that we were on a street that had a reputation in Budapest, where prostitution was legalized and institutionalized. And then, we continued our pursuit."

The adventures of Groza and his colleague Opreanu were not typical of all Romanian students. Most of them had older peers waiting for them at the railway station, or had been given precise instructions by their families. Axente Banciu, a professor and journalist in Brașov, writes in his memoirs about a more fortunate arrival in Budapest:

> "As I arrived at the railway station, after leaving my luggage I took out my notebook where I had written down the clear itinerary that my former teacher, Dr. Valer Braniște,

[5] Cornel Sigmirean, "Intelectualii români din Transilvania și universitățile din Europa (1801-1919)" [The Romanian Intellectuals from Transylvania and the Universities from Europe (1801-1919)], in *Universități, intelectuali și cultură în Transilvania secolului al XIX-lea* [Universities, Intellectuals and Culture in the Nineteenth Century's Transylvania] (Sibiu, Astra Museum, 2013), 33.

[6] Petru Groza, *Adio lumii vechi! Memorii* [Farewell to the Ancient World! Memories] (București: Compania, 2003), 52-53.

> had given me, and I started to walk down Kerepesi Street. From here, as indicated in the notebook, I turned onto Muzeum Körút from where, passing by the statue of Arany in front of the National Museum, I reached Kálvin Square, which I knew was close to the Danube, with Doczauer at the corner of Vámház Boulevard, where our people have lunch and where you find everything you need – as Professor Branişte told me – Romanian advisers, guides and friends. Without talking to any Hungarian, there I was, speaking again my language with my brothers."[7]

When he reached the restaurant, he noted that there were people talking Romanian at one table, and I. Baptist Boiu, the son of Zaharia Boiu, was playing the *Doina lui Lucaciu* [Lucaciu's Song)] on beer glasses after dinner. Those who left for Vienna set off for different adventures. Iuliu Moisil, who attended school from 1879 to 1884, writes about the events marking his departure for Vienna:

> "I and Solomon Haliţă left together, travelling by carriage from Beclean to Apahida, and then by train through Cluj, Oradea, Pesta and Vienna; our mentor was Sever Mureşianu. This was the first time we had travelled by train [...]. As we arrived in the 'Emperor's village' – as Romanians in Transylvania used to call the Austrian city – we started looking for a place to stay. There are rooms for rent everywhere, cheap and well-furnished and, most of all, clean. I and my brother-in-law immediately found a room for two, for 14 florins per month, not far from the city centre on Belvedere Street. As some friends had recommended, the next day we met the head of the Theresianum kitchen on Favoriten, an institute founded by Maria Theresa for noblemen' sons, which included both primary and secondary schools." [Titu Maiorescu also attended school here]. "Romanian students had the privilege of getting their food in this famous kitchen at low prices: lunch for two for 20 florins (without bread). Lunch consisted of four dishes: soup, boiled meat or vegetables, steak and dessert, in sufficient amounts, which sometimes substituted for dinner too."[8]

According to Iuliu Moisil life in Vienna was not expensive. A single room (cabinet) was 6-7 florins per month, and a twin 12-14 florins, including service and morning coffee.

> "One could have lunch in restaurants for about 34 kreuzers (soup 6 kr., boiled meat with two types of side dishes 24 kr., bread 2 kr., and tips 2 kr.; desert was 12 kr., but one could have half for 6 kr. Dinner – including steak and wine – was too expensive for the students, and we only afforded dinner on the occasion of the *România Jună* meetings or the New Year's Eve party and other events. In the evening, the students usually had sausages, bread and a bottle of *Abzugbier*, which was good and very cheap. The scholarships provided by the foundations which maintained most of the Romanian students amounted to approximately 200-400 florins per year. Monthly expenses amounted to 40 florins for maintenance plus other expenses: tuitions, books, clothes, transportation by train (50% discount). It was more difficult for the students who received only 200 florins per year. But in Vienna, they could have lunch at the *Volksküche* for approximately 12-14 kr. Here the food was very appetizing, but one had to serve one's own meal. Some students earned trust from the heads of the restaurants, so that they lunched on credit for years, and paid it off after they had ended their studies."

---

[7] Axente Banciu, *Vălul amintirilor* [The Veil of Memories], ed. Stelian Mândruţ and Adrian Andrei Rusu (Cluj-Napoca: Presa Universitară Clujeană, 1998), 177-178.

[8] Iuliu Moisil, *Viaţa studenţilor români din Viena în a doua jumătate a sutei a XIX-a. Amintiri* [Life of Romanian Students in Vienna of the Second Half of the 19th Century. Memories] (Năsăud, 1928), 370.

Alexandru Vaida Voevod, attending the Faculty of Medicine at the University of Vienna, did not experience the hardships which some Romanian students encountered there in the latter nineteenth century and the first two decades of the twentieth. He was born into a rich family, and when he started his studies in Vienna, his father found him a place to stay close to the university, in VIII Schlösselgasse, where all the institutes were located and where he lived together with his colleague Gustav Goldschmidt:

> "We paid 38 fl. per month each. And in return we received: for breakfast - a cup of coffee, milk and a croissant (or a baguette); for lunch – broth, boiled meat and sauce, potatoes cooked in butter, vegetables and dessert; for dinner, steak, potatoes, and salad; laundry, lighting (oil lamp) and heating was included. The food was very good and more than sufficient. From time to time Frau Munk served us salmon or carp from the Danube."[9]

In their search for a landlord, the students also resorted to improvisations and extreme solutions. Many Romanian students at the Royal University or the Technical University in Budapest, lacking financial means, lodged for a while at the Petru Maior Society. Every year, two to four students were accommodated in the rooms of the Society. As Alexandru Lupeanu-Melin remembered:

> "There were few Romanian students in Budapest [who] until they had had the chance to look for a place to stay with the Jews in Józsefváros district, did not sleep on the floor or the tables at Petru Maior, using as pillows the thick volumes of Hurmuzachi or the collections of the Vulcan Family. And what marvellous pillows they were! With a Romanian book under one's head, worried by the events of the day that had just ended, in an ocean of foreigners, one would had the feeling that Transylvania was not that far away, and that the unseen hand of mother was hidden in the yellowing pages."[10]

Among the students who lodged at the Petru Maior were George Bilașcu (a medical student, later university professor), G. Pop, A. Alexi, Simion Sfetozar, George Orzu, Ilie Precupaș (all at law school), Ioan Curiția, Nicolae Sulică (both philosophy), Isidor Pop (law school), Aurel Anderco (philosophy), Ioan Jantea (law school), Aurel Stan (technical studies), Anton Bălăcioiu (law school), and many others.[11]

In 1896, on the occasion of the quarter-centenary of the *România Jună* Society, a proposal was aired to set up an *Internat Academic* in Vienna to provide lodgings for Romanian students in the capital of the Austro-Hungarian Empire who were deprived of financial means.[12] Funds would be raised by donations and readers' fees, with individuals and institutions donating 1,000 florins or 2,000 lei. In 1906 the fund amounted to 13,743 crowns, insufficient to set up the *Internat*. In 1914 the Cuza villa in Vienna was being

---

[9] Alexandru Vaida Voevod, *Memorii* [Memories], vol. I, ed. Alexandru Șerban (Cluj-Napoca: Dacia, 1994), 64.

[10] Alexandru Lupeanu, "Ce era „Petru Maior" pe vremuri" [What "Petru Maior" Was Once], *Lumea universitară* 2-5, 1-55 (March 1922): 25.

[11] Petru Ilieșiu, *Raport general istoric despre activitatea Societății „Petru Maior" a Junimei Române din Budapesta, 12 June 1876* [General Historic Report on the Activity of "Petru Maior" Society of the Romanian Youth from Budapest, 12 June 1876] (Budapest, 1877), 9.

[12] Gheorghe Moisescu, "Centenarul societății academice-literare „România Jună" din Viena, 1871-1971" [Centenary of the Academic and Literary Society "România Jună" from Vienna 1871-1971], *Almanahul Parohiei Ortodoxe Române din Viena XI pe anul 1972*, 146.

auctioned, and suggested for purchase for the lodging-house project. The war started and the initiative was abandoned.

Studies, lectures, libraries and laboratories helped young Romanians ease themselves into academic life. At the beginning of each academic year were the famous "freshers' fairs." Both in Vienna and in Budapest, these festive events were organized in hotel halls and centrally-located restaurants; in 1899, the Romanian students in Vienna organized the event in the saloon of the Mitzka restaurant in the Schottengasse, which was spacious but insufficient given the large number of participants. In 1911, it was organised at the Johannishof restaurant, an opportunity for the students to bond, party and meet the members of the Romanian community in Vienna.

The balls organized by the Petru Maior Society in Budapest or by *România Jună* in Vienna were also important events in the lives of the students. The Petru Maior Society organized the first ball in 1869, which later became an annual event. The representatives of the student organizations in Vienna, Graz, and Cluj were all invited to such balls and soirées, as were Serb and Croat university colleagues, important Romanian politicians and members of the Romanian community in Budapest. The programme of such soirées included songs by the Petru Maior choir, classical recitals, and papers on literary or national history. In 1895, for example, the soirée was organized at the Vigadó (Reduta), where the pianist Alma de Dunca Şchiau performed. The programme included compositions by Ciprian Porumbescu, Liszt, P. Mascagui, Alexandru Mocioni (*Pensée fugitive*), Schubert and G. Dima.[13] In 1898, the soirée was organized under the patronage of Alexandru Mocioni de Foeni and the singers Valeria Pop, Ecaterina Mezei, Matilda Olteanu and Virginia Gall were also invited. The programme included works by I. Vidu, Carol R. Karos, Mendelssohn Bartholdy, et al. The *Annual Report* of the Petru Maior Society recorded that "many people from Budapest and from all over the world were present."[14] In 1912 a banquet was held in the grand hall of the Pester Lloyd hotel on the occasion of the Society's jubilee, at which fine food was served: asparagus soup, sturgeon with tartare sauce, beef and vegetables, royal pudding, green ewe's cheese, coffee, beer and white wine.

In Vienna, the first ball organized by the *România Jună* was held in 1872. Alexandru Vaida Voevod, a habitué of many of the society's events, stated that the Romanian ball was always thought to be one of the most glamorous in Vienna.[15] Sextil Puşcariu also remembered that the balls of the *România Jună* were always attended by an archduke representing the Imperial House.[16] Art-world personalities in Vienna were also present. Eduard Strauss, the famous composer, attended the soirées and balls and dedicated a polka to

[13] *Raportul Societăţii „Petru Maior" în anul 1895/96 şi 1896/97* [Report of "Petru Maior" Society for the Year 1895/96 and 1896/97] (Budapesta, 1897), 11.
[14] *Raportul Societăţii „Petru Maior" în anul 1897/98* [Report of "Petru Maior" Society for the Year 1897/98] (Budapesta, 1898), 15.
[15] Vaida Voevod, *Memorii*, vol. IV (Cluj-Napoca: Dacia, 1998), 36.
[16] I. Grămadă, *Societatea Academică Social-Culturală „România Jună" din Viena (1871-1911)* [Academic and Literary Society "Young Romania" from Vienna (1871-1971)] (Arad, 1912), 118.

the society, *Fleurs roumains*. Moreover, Ciprian Porumbescu dedicated the waltz *Florile dalbe* [Immaculate Flowers] to *România Jună*, subsequently known as *Camelli*, in memory of Theresa Kanitz, one of the hosts of the balls.[17] The 1896 quarter-centenary celebrations started with a "freshers' fair" at the Kaiserhof. On Saturday, the third day of the event, a banquet was organized, attended by 200 people, and the last day of the event ended with an Anna Hof dance, with an orchestra conducted by Johann Strauss.[18]

For the students in Vienna and Budapest, New Year's Eve, Easter and Christmas were always reasons to celebrate. At the New Year's Eve party in Vienna, which was an occasion of great delight and joy, the members of the Romanian community in Vienna and the officers of the Vienna garrison were present, together with the students:

> "The youths were dancing, the elders were enjoying their glasses of beer or wine, and at midnight, one of the members, usually the president of the *România Jună*, bid farewell to the year that had just ended, and saluted the new year to come. All would congratulate each other, and the party would restart more vividly, and would last until dawn on 1st January. The party was held in one of the most beautiful places in Vienna."[19]

In 1877 New Year's Eve was celebrated in Vienna with a marvellous soirée, with concerts and dancing in the saloon of the Metropol Hotel on Franz-Josefs-Kai, followed by a festive banquet at midnight.[20] In 1898 New Year's Eve was organized in the hall of the Goldene Birne restaurant, with concerts and dance, with the support of Dr. Johann Gänsbacher of the Vienna Conservatoire.

Living the *belle époque* to the fullest, students led a Bohemian lifestyle in the late nineteenth and early twentieth century. Learning in classes, libraries or laboratories mixed with life in the cafés and pubs of the city, where intrigue, gossip and student parties added flavour. "In almost every café there was a table with Romanian students," as Ion I. Lapedatu remembered from his period of study in the Hungarian capital.[21] The Romanian students in Budapest preferred to go to Doczauer, Dankoszky, Szikszai (Vámház-Körut and Kerepesi-út), Elked (Kecskeméti and Magyar-utca), and in the evening to the small Scholtz pub (Kigyó-utca), where there was a table with Romanians, and another one with Slovaks and Serbs.[22] It was preferred for its Dreher beer and *szafaláde* sausages. The more discerning diner could have *cvarghel* (a type of blue cheese). Most Romanian students in Budapest remembered the Micsek as their preferred café, where they were enchanted by the Western literary and art magazines available and the discussions about Sascha Schneider, Vereşceaghin and Böklin.[23] They would go more rarely to the Jäger-

---

[17] Ibid., 76.

[18] Sextil Puşcariu, *Călare pe două veacuri* [On the Horseback of Two Centuries] (Bucureşti, Editura pentru Literatură, 1968), 292.

[19] Moisil, *Viaţa studenţilor români*, 373.

[20] Moisescu, "Centenarul," 129.

[21] Ion I. Lapedatu, *Memorii şi amintiri* [Memoirs and Memories], ed. Ioan Opriş (Iaşi: Institutul European, 1998), 72.

[22] Banciu, *Vălul amintirilor*, 213.

[23] Mircea Popa, *Ilarie Chendi* (Bucureşti: Minerva, 1973), 33.

horn café (Vadászkörut), "where" – as Banciu recalls – "the youths did not dare to enter, as it was frequented by figures of rank. Father G. Bogoevici, the priest of the Romanian Orthodox Church in Budapest, Silviu Suciu, Ministry Councillor, G. Moldovan, clerk in the Ministry of Finance, Simion Popescu, post office head clerk, Dr. Vraciu and, not as often, Gheorghe Alexici, had their cappuccinos here."[24]

Fascinated by the Bohemian ambiance of café life, some students would continuously postpone their exams and graduation. Alexandru Vaida Voevod remembered some colleagues who continued their studies for ten to twelve years.[25] Passing through Budapest, Sextil Pușcariu met Florian Munteanu, a medical student who did not pass any of his exams but was consulted by fellow students when they were sick.[26] Even though he was not certified as a physician, his medical knowledge acquired through practice recommended him as a good practitioner; he died in Budapest without ever graduating. Many students prolonged their stay in the university cities for years without graduating. Lucian Blaga mentions a cousin, Simion Lașiță, who attended the University of Jena for six or seven years without passing a single exam.[27]

Entertainment and café life were not the happy lot of all Romanian students: for many of them, hardships and austerity were more dominant. In 1887 Alexandru Neagoe, student at the Faculty of Medicine of the University of Vienna, wrote in desperation to his protector, Ioan Micu Moldovan, a priest in Blaj, that he was "poorly dressed, ragged, almost barefoot, and have no hat etc. My family has forgotten about me. This is why I look like a Gipsy! Furthermore, I fell into bad company and took the wrong path! Nevertheless I thank my companions for giving me the opportunity to know the world and people!"[28] Another student, Teodor Bota, studying in Vienna, confessed to the same priest in Blaj:

> "I tend to believe that the whole world is against me, so that I die of starvation. For a month and a half now I have stopped living, I languish, I lead an awful life, I have sold all my clothes and linen; the shirt that I wear is all I have left."[29]

Alexandru German, student at the School of Medicine of the University of Budapest, wrote in desperation to Moldovan, asking him for help in obtaining a grant from the foundations in Blaj: "to sustain myself, I was obliged to give private tutoring and write every night for a miserable remuneration [...]. I am busy with lectures all day, I tutor in the evening, and I write all night long."[30]

Hundreds of letters and requests to the Romanian foundations prove the desperation that Romanian students felt on account of lack of money or difficulty in adapting to

---

[24] Banciu, *Vălul amintirilor*, 213.
[25] Vaida Voevod, *Memorii*, vol. IV, 37.
[26] Pușcariu, *Călare pe două veacuri*, 293.
[27] Lucian Blaga, *Hronicul și cântecul vârstelor* [The Chronicle and the Song of Ages], ed. Dorli Blaga (București: Humanitas, 2012), 27.
[28] Direcția Județeană Cluj a Arhivelor Naționale [The Cluj County Division of the National Archives], Fund *Ioan Micu Moldovan*, File 13,458, f. 2.
[29] Idem, File 9,689, f. 1.
[30] Idem, File 11,941, f. 2.

life in the cities of the Danube or in Germany. They often requested dispensations from the foundations supporting their tuitions in order to transfer to other university cities where life was "more bearable." However, even if academic life was a happy and untroubled experience for some, and for others it took a dramatic turn, the years of study shaped a new human and intellectual profile in the Romanian youth. Contact with European culture and civilization expedited the assimilation of modern social values, laying the groundwork for separation from traditional values and the adoption of a new, more Western lifestyle.

Between National Passion and Individual Interests. A Possible Interest-Group in Transylvania. 1867-1874*

Alexandru Onojescu

Romanian historiography on Transylvania after 1989, freed from the ideological limitations of Communism, started to focus on new areas of research, including social history and history of elites. Familiarity with Western historiographical literature has increased over time, resulting in greater openness. Prosopographical studies on various elite categories began to appear, analysing the Romanian clergy,[1] the financial[2] or commercial[3] elite, the military elite,[4] the political[5] and cultural[6] elite. Unfortunately, the historical analysis of Romanian elites from Transylvania stopped at this point, although much that was useful had been achieved despite the difficulty and scarcity of primary sources.

Naturally, the next step would be to study these elites from an associative perspective, building on a theory of interest groups and the power relations between them. There have been several attempts, which either unravelled in trying to develop a methodological framework or did not even attempt to do so.[7] Indeed, such a goal is complicated enough. It is very difficult to construct a methodological framework for the study of associations or interest-groups in Romanian society in Transylvania in the nineteenth century. First, such a topic requires an approach situated somewhere between history, sociology, political science, business studies, organizational analysis etc. Second, most studies on associations or interest-groups are concerned with the democratic system of contemporary America. Third, in spite of an impressive corpus of several hundred books and arti-

---

* This study was supported by CNCS-UEFSCDI, through the research project PN-II-PCE-2011-3-0040.

[1] Cornel Sigmirean, *Intelectualitatea ecleziastică: preoţii Blajului (1806-1948)* [The Ecclesiastical Intellectuals: the Priests from Blaj (1806-1948)] (Târgu-Mureş: Editura Universităţii "Petru Maior," 2007).

[2] Vasile Dobrescu, *Funcţii şi funcţionalităţi în sistemul de credit românesc din Transilvania până la primul război mondial: studiu de caz* [Functions and Functionalities in the Romanian Credit System from Transylvania until World War I. Case Study] (Tîrgu Mureş: Editura Universităţii "Petru Maior," 2006).

[3] Ruxandra Moaşa Nazare, *Sub semnul lui Hermes şi al lui Pallas: educaţie şi societate la negustorii ortodocşi din Braşov şi Sibiu la sfârşitul secolului al XVIII-lea şi începutul secolului al XIX-lea* [Under the Sign of Hermes and Pallas: Education and Society in Orthodox Merchants of Braşov and Sibiu in the Late Eighteenth Century and Early Nineteenth Century] (Bucureşti: Editura Academiei Române, 2010).

[4] Liviu Maior, *Românii în armata habsburgică: soldaţi şi ofiţeri uitaţi* [Romanians in the Hapsburg Army: Forgotten Soldiers and Officers] (Bucureşti: Editura Enciclopedică, 2004).

[5] Vlad Popovici, *Studies on the Romanian Political Elite from Transylvania and Hungary (1861-1918)* (Cluj-Napoca: Editura Mega, 2012).

[6] Lucian Nastasă, *Intelectualii şi promovarea socială: (pentru o morfologie a câmpului universitar)* [Intellectuals and Social Advancement: In Search of a Morphology of the Academic Field] (Cluj-Napoca: Limes, 2004); Andreea Oana Dăncilă, "Elite culturale româneşti în Transilvania în prima perioadă a secolului al XX-lea" [Romanian Cultural Elites from Transylvania in the First Half of the Twentieth Century] (PhD diss., "Babeş-Bolyai" University, Cluj-Napoca, 2012).

[7] Valentin Orga, "Grupul neoactivist de la Orăştie. Premise. Constituire. Activitate (1885-1914)" [The Neoactivist Group from Orăştie. Premises. Constitution. Activity (1885-1914)] (PhD diss., "Babeş-Bolyai" University, Cluj-Napoca, 2002); Vlad Popovici, *Tribunismul (1884-1905)* [Tribunism (1884-1905)] (Cluj-Napoca: Presa Universitară Clujeană, 2008), 255-272.

cles, no general theory has yet been developed that is universally accepted by various scholars.[8] As we shall see even for the case of the United States, there are at least three traditions of interest-group theories: pluralist, economic and exchange theory. Thus we must be cautious in using and adapting these theories for the Transylvanian case.

The purpose of this paper is to fill this gap partly, by analyzing a particular interest-group which was formed and active in Sibiu between 1867-1874. We can state definitively that we are dealing here with a group that included many socio-professional areas and had the professed ambition to enforce certain goals upon Romanian society in Transylvania; political passivism, economic associative ideas, utilitarianism, the establishment of a free national economy, and an invigoration of Romanian culture. After outlining the most important methodological and theoretical aspects, we will trace the origin of this group, how it took shape, the main actors and their interactions. We also hope to assess its decision-making process and its profile in the Transylvanian public sphere.

One aspect in our approach foregrounds power elite theory; according to C. Wright Mills, the power elite consists of "those political, economic, and military circles which as an intricate set of overlapping cliques share decisions having at least national consequences."[9] The whole idea revolves around a "triangle of power," which consists of executive politicians, corporate executives and the upper echelons of the military, who form an interlocking directorate.[10] Further, Mills believed that in the case of the post-war American political system a single elite occupied the "top command posts" and could take the "key decisions" regarding all aspects of society (governmental, military, financial, educational, cultural, social, etc.). Finally, the power elite consists of people who enjoy "money, power, and prestige."[11] They are of similar origin and education, have similar careers and lifestyle, all of which leads to their easy intermingling and a self-awareness of their own.[12]

Even so Mills did not see the power elite as being completely homogenous. He acknowledged the existence of factions and policy conflicts, and the possibility of opposing personal ambitions.[13] Still, internal discipline and communal interests were much stronger than any divisions. Moreover, Mills concurred with a pluralist view when he made a distinction between the power elite, the "middle levels of power" and the masses. He defined the middle level as "a great scatter of relatively equal balancing units" in the States, in pressure groups and within Congress. At times the power elite needed to take some of these competing units into account, even if Mills did not regard them as significant in the great scheme of power politics.[14] As Shirley Zimmerman puts it, interest

---

[8] David Knoke, "Associations and Interest Groups," *Annual Review of Sociology* 12 (1986): 2.
[9] C. Wright Mills, *The Power Elite* (New York : Oxford University Press, 1999), 18.
[10] Ibid., 8.
[11] Ibid., 9.
[12] C. Wright Mills, "The Structure of Power in American Society," *The British Journal of Sociology* 9, 1 (Mar., 1958): 34.
[13] Mills, *The Power Elite*, 283.
[14] "The Three Elites of C. Wright Mills," last modified June 19, 2013, http://www.mmisi.org/ pr/11_01/

groups have been an institutional feature of the American political system anyhow, since its beginnings. In favour of this argument, suffice it to point to the numerous committees and subcommittees that inhabit the US Congress.[15]

There is no general definition of interest groups accepted by all political science scholars. However, we will use two definitions for the purposes of this study. Interest groups are "vehicles through which the policy concerns and preferences of citizens can presumably be articulated in the policy process."[16] They are also "individuals with common goals that form organizations to further their common interests or values."[17]

As we can see, the main purpose of interest organizations is generally to act as mediators between the government and various sectors of the population. In the specific case of the Transylvanian passivists, their disavowal of the constitution of 1867 resulted in a unique phenomenon. The various interest groups on the Romanian political scene rather mediated the relationship between ordinary people and the main institutions, whether these were ecclesiastical (the two Archdioceses), political (the Romanian National Party of Transylvania), financial (the Albina bank) or cultural (the "Astra" cultural association). In the absence of a state of their own or recognition of their national rights, these institutions offered the Romanians public policies, functioning rather like a subgovernment which interceded between the general Romanian population and the Hungarian government in Pest. In other words the Romanian interest groups, especially the passivist group, had an indirect role in the political mediation between Romanians and the governing system. Only once did the passivist group have the chance to act directly: in 1872, at the special request of Lónyay Menyhért, prime minister of Hungary, who wanted to reach an agreement with them.[18]

One of the most important aspects of interest groups is the membership problem. Why do people join this kind of organization and remain members? A first answer comes from the pluralist theories of the 1950s, the most prominent being David Truman's "disturbance theory." In short, Truman argued that group formation has two important causes. First, societal change: as society progresses, it becomes more complex and interests multiply, becoming more diversified. A second aspect recognizes particular events (called "disturbances") which disrupt the regular flow of societal change.[19] Truman gave no exact definition of what he called disturbances, but for a more accurate description we can turn to other scholars such as Jeffey M. Berry: "any significant event or series of events,

---

norton.pdf.

[15] Shirley L. Zimmerman, "Interest group theory, and systems theory," in *Understanding family policy*, ed. Shirley L. Zimmerman (Thousand Oaks: Sage Publications, 1995), 145.

[16] James L. Franke and Douglas Dobson, "Interest Groups: The Problem of Representation," *The Western Political Quarterly* 38, 2 (Jun., 1985): 224.

[17] William C. Mitchell and Michael C. Munger, *American Journal of Political Science* 35, 2 (May, 1991): 515.

[18] "Acte prealabili şi memorandulu dela Blasiu 1872," *Transilvania*, February 15, 1875, 41-45.

[19] Anthony J. Nownes & Grant Neeley, "Public Interest Group, Entrepreneurship and Theories of Group Mobilization," *Political Research Quarterly* 49, 1 (Mar., 1996): 122.

other than leadership activity, which directly stimulates the formation of an interest group."[20] The pluralist view is essentially political, because it states that interest groups are political in nature.[21]

In the 1960s a new "exchange theory" gradually evolved through the work of Mancur Olson,[22] Rober H. Salisbury[23] and Terry M. Moe.[24] The Olsonian model of interest groups starts from an economic base. Individuals do not join groups because of disturbances and generally they do not associate when their interests are at risk. Departing from the pluralist idea, Olson believes that group goals are insufficient for members to join since political group goals are defined as collective goods, meaning that even if they do not participate, individuals will benefit from the actions of a certain interest group (the "free-rider" problem). In order for members to be attracted, groups must offer selective material benefits unavailable to free-riders.[25] This explanation mostly holds for large groups. In small groups, the free-rider problem can be surmounted by cooperative behaviour, whereby interests are more likely to find organized political expression.[26] Consequently they have better chances at the formative stage and have greater odds of survival. Two further questions remain to be answered. First, what are these selective benefits? Second, who is responsible for the exchange of these benefits?

Incentive systems were first conceptualized by Peter B. Clark and James Q. Wilson, who opted for a triadic system of incentives. Usually the most important and most tangible incentives are the material – "rewards that have a monetary value or can easily be translated into ones that have."[27] In economic interest groups these are usually sufficient. But there are times when the decision to join a group can easily be shaped by non-economic gains, which Clark and Wilson defined as "solidary" and "purposive" incentives.[28] David Knoke takes a similar approach, preferred to call them "affective incentives" and "normative appeals" even if the definition is the same.[29] Solidary incentives are intangible inducements that derive from friendship, status or social acceptance. Purposive incentives derive mostly from ideological, moral or religious beliefs, and are very close to the Olsonian concept of collective goods. Again, small groups tend to be privileged, be-

[20] Jeffrey M. Berry, "On the Origins of Interest Groups: A test of Two Theories," *Polity* 10, 3 (Spring, 1978), apud Nownes & Neeley, "Public Interest," 133.
[21] Zimmerman, "Interest group," 144.
[22] Mancur Olson, *The Logic of Collective Action: Public Goods and the Theory of Groups* (Harvard University Press: 1965).
[23] Rober H. Salisbury, "An Exchange Theory of Interest Groups," *Midwest Journal of Political Science* 13, 1 (Feb., 1969): 1-32.
[24] Terry M. Moe, "A Calculus of Group Membership," *American Journal of Political Science* 24, 4 (Nov., 1980): 593-632; Idem, "Toward a Broader View of Interest Groups," *The Journal of Politics* 43, 2 (May, 1981): 531-543.
[25] Nownes & Neeley, "Public Interest," 122-123.
[26] Moe, "Toward a Broader," 534.
[27] Peter B. Clark & James Q. Wilson, "Incentive Systems: A Theory of Organizations," *Administrative Science Quarterly* 6, 2 (Sep., 1961): 134.
[28] Ibid., 135.
[29] Knoke, "Associations and Interest," 10.

cause solidary and purposive incentives will more likely appear in small organizations.[30] A particular aspect is worth mentioning here; at some point in their argument Clark and Wilson talk of the "leadership function" which is to create, clarify and promulgate substantive goals, but also to maintain an organization's integrity by obtaining and distributing incentives.[31]

The leadership function is the main core in Salisbury's theory of interest groups, in which an exchange implies the existence of a manager (the "group entrepreneur") who is the engine of the enterprise, with an important role in its creation and maintenance.[32] In short, the exchange is a very simple process: typically the group entrepreneur offers a mix of incentives to members and states the group goals, while he receives higher status, better material compensation, power, prestige or personal accomplishment.[33]

A third paradigm in the formation of interest groups was advanced by Jack Walker in the 1990s. In short, building on exchange theory, Walker argues that the most important aspect in the formative stage of an association is to attract patronage rather than members. Furthermore, he strongly believes that interest organizations start to form at the instigation of a patron, who recruits the group entrepreneur and finances his efforts to attain policy goals.[34]

Our objective now is to analyze a specific interest group that gradually grew to become a power elite, dominating some of the most important institutions of Romanian society in Transylvania: the passivist group from Sibiu (1868-1874). We can assume with certainty that in this era we are dealing with a single elite, as Mills did for the post-war US. Professionalization would follow only in the late nineteenth and early twentieth century with the development of new institutions (political, cultural, educational and financial). Before that, it is clear enough that the same people inhabited the few political or cultural institutions (the Romanian National Committees of 1861 and 1863, the Transylvanian Diets of Sibiu 1863/64 and Cluj 1865, the "Astra" cultural association in 1861).[35] These institutions functioned under the strict supervision of Vienna and Pest, the two centres of power affecting the Romanians in Transylvania. We can also note the existence of some groups within the Romanian elite. Until 1865 the primary division was based on socio-professional categories with goals of their own: civil servants, the free professions and the ecclesiastical hierarchy.

After 1865, the gap was mostly ideological and two major groups evolved: activists and passivists. We can already see that Truman's idea of disturbances has a practical

[30] Moe, "Toward a Broader," 536-537.
[31] Clark & Wilson, "Incentive Systems," 134.
[32] Salisbury, "An Exchange Theory," 12.
[33] Ibid., 26-27.
[34] Nownes & Neeley, "Public Interest," 124, 129.
[35] Popovici, *Studies on*, 10-17; Alexandru Onojescu, "Politică şi strategii de grup la elita românească din Transilvania (1860-1869)" [Politics and Group Strategy pertaining the Romanian Elite from Transylvania (1860-1869)] (PhD diss., "Babeş-Bolyai" University, Cluj-Napoca, 2012).

application in the case of the passivist group from Sibiu. The creation of the dualist political system, the dissolution of Transylvania's self-government and its assimilation into Hungary acted as a powerful catalyst in its formative stage. The same can be said for the activist group. Both groups were centred in Sibiu even if they advocated two different political tactics. The activists wanted to lead a fight within the new constitutional establishment, by sending representatives to the Hungarian Parliament and holding positions in the administration and judiciary, despite their limited number. The passivists supported total abstinence from every electoral process until Transylvania's old provincial rights were reinstated. Thus the Romanian political scene in Transylvania saw a ceaseless war between these two factions. Realistically, the group with the best chances to influence the Romanian population was the one which could gather more members, strengthen its financial power and organize better, which was solidly coherent and had a strong leadership and access to decisional factors inside the community.[36]

In what follows we track the most important steps in the formation and activity of the passivist group from Sibiu (1867-1874), from its earlier stages of association to when it became an interest group. Here we will use Knoke's thesis that an association is "a formally organized named group, most of whose members – whether persons or organizations – are not financially recompensed for their participation." From the moment an association tends to influence government decisions, the members of the association start to act as an interest-group.[37]

The Cultural "Directorate"

The general assembly of "Astra" in Cluj (14th/26th-16th/28th August 1867) was a real turning point in the tense relations between the activists (led by Orthodox Archbishop Andrei Şaguna) and the passivists (led by Ioan Raţiu and George Bariţ) for two reasons. First, after an active public campaign to denigrate Şaguna, the passivists managed to obtain his dismissal as chairman of "Astra," and consequently to delegitimize his position as a national leader. Second, they succeeded in imposing a new leadership on this hitherto stagnant cultural association.

Various sources prove that events were specially organized to reach these two objectives. For instance, the organizer of the general assembly was the archpriest Ioan Pamfilie of Cluj, a well-known friend and business partner of passivists such as Visarion Roman or Ioan Raţiu. Likewise, the president of the assembly (in Şaguna's absence) was Iacob Bologa, an ex-civil servant who had strong passivist sentiments and was convinced that his dismissal as counsellor at the Transylvanian Supreme Court in Vienna was Şaguna's work. But the real masterminds were Ioan Raţiu and George Bariţ (*in absentia*) who instilled the idea that the leadership of the cultural association should be changed. After intense backroom negotiations, Raţiu and others promoted the candidacy of Vasile

[36] Zimmerman, "Interest group," 143-144.
[37] Knoke, "Associations and Interest," 2.

Ladislau Popp, a well-known Romanian civil servant and active supporter of passivism. As Raţiu desired, the election was nominal and public, and all who participated in the consultations voted accordingly. This voting procedure was not necessarily accepted under the bylaws of the cultural association.[38] Şaguna was not the only member thrown out of "Astra"'s leadership. Timotei Cipariu likewise lost the vice-presidency to Ioan Hannia, first Orthodox archpriest of Sibiu and Iacob Bologa's brother-in-law. Bariţ kept his office as first secretary and Ioan V. Russu, Greek Catholic archpriest of Sibiu, kept his post as second secretary. The rest of the leadership were persons who, one way or another, would be linked to the passivist group of Sibiu: Ioan Popescu, Paul Dunca de Sajo (a true political moderate), David Urs de Margine or Ilie Măcelariu. In order to assure their control of the association in coming years, some of these would occupy two positions in "Astra"'s Central Committee, thereby restricting the access of others.

"Astra" fits best in Clark and Wilson's category of solidary organizations.[39] Their true goal was prestige at the highest levels. In most cases such goals have to be uncontroversial and related with some kind of cause, rather than an issue. Thus in the case of the passivist group, the real goal had to be associated with a higher interest for the association, and not particularly with Andrei Şaguna's person – so that the official motive for his dismissal was the inability to launch "Astra"'s journal *Transilvania*, one of the association's main purposes, written in its founding statute.[40] Another important aspect worth mentioning is that the passivist group was at that time still in formation. Its true power and organizational capabilities would be shown only a year and a half later in attaining its main political goal, the victory of the passivist tactic.

The Political "Directorate"

The political "directorate" was by far the most important to passivists, their *raison d'être*. Their stated goal was to instil in the minds of the Romanian constituency a total abstinence from any sort of election and participation in administration, under the constitutional establishment of the dual monarchy.

Again, based on the political ideological map drawn by Raţiu and Bariţ, the Sibiu passivist group managed to annihilate all activist tendencies in Transylvania in approximately four years. The process had multiple stages: the conference of Miercurea (1869); the private conference in Turda (1870); the ad-hoc committee (1871); the activist conference in Sibiu (1872); the passivist conference in Alba Iulia (1872); and the reconcilement conference in Blaj (1872). Since space does not allow us to describe all phases, we offer here a case study of the conference of Miercurea and the formation of the Central Electoral Committee.

---

38 Keith Hitchins & Liviu Maior, *Corespondenţa lui Ioan Raţiu cu George Bariţ. 1861-1892* [The Correspondence of Ioan Raţiu with George Bariţ. 1861-1892] (Cluj-Napoca: Editura Dacia, 1970), 151-153.

39 Clark & Wilson, "Incentive Systems," 141-142.

40 *George Bariţ şi contemporanii săi* [George Bariţ and his Contemporaries], volume X, ed. Ştefan Pascu (Bucureşti: Editura Minerva, 1993), 81-82.

The conference of Miercurea (March 1869) was by far the most important for its organisation and fundamental outcomes. The passivist programme, drafted and accepted by a clear majority, was to be a landmark for every other important conference. It also marked the moment when the passivist group from Sibiu took permanent shape. As sources reveal, the initiative again came from Bariţ and Raţiu, this time through the tireless work of Visarion Roman, an entrepreneur and self-made man. The two took no active part in the organization of the conference, even if they were in close touch. After a series of local conferences held in Cluj, Dej, Turda, Răşinari/Sibiu, Miercurea, Abrud and Roşia came the initiative to summon a general conference with the sole purpose of choosing the political direction that Romanians should take on participation in the electoral process.

At first Ilie Măcelariu, a well respected ex-civil servant and ex-MP, was inclined to accept activism as a solution for the Romanian problem. Măcelariu was exactly what Roman, Bariţ and Raţiu needed as a front man to convene a general conference. Having built a reputation by defending the passivist program in the Hungarian Parliament, and regarded as a political underdog, he was also one of the few who still had good relations with Andrei Şaguna. Thus the group was strengthened when Măcelariu accepted a position as acquisitions inspector in the "Transilvania" Romanian-Saxon insurance institute, with an annual wage of 1200 fl. After he accepted the job and discussed matters with Visarion Roman and Iacob Bologa (at that time a member of the board of Transilvania), they had the idea of sending telegrams to Gavril Manu, Raţiu and Bariţ for feedback, in order to muster a general conference. After receiving positive feedback, the organizing committee was enlarged by Ioan Hannia, also a member of the board of Transilvania.[41]

This is not the place to expatiate on all aspects of the conference organization. We will merely state that the organisers' true goal was to assure a passivist majority in order to reach their ultimate goal: the imposition of passivist doctrine. Two aspects are fundamental. First, applying exchange theory, we can fully assess the impact of material selective incentives on Ilie Măcelariu. At first, his core political ideology was activism. Even if he had serious doubts about the effectiveness of passivism, he accepted the position as front man, and afterwards as president of the Central Electoral Committee of the newly-founded Romanian National Party of Transylvania. It is very clear that he joined the Transilvania insurance institute as a preamble to his later actions. Măcelariu became a true passivist, defending the policy in all his later public statements.

Second, it is very interesting to analyze the composition of the Central Electoral Committee. The twenty-five members of this Committee can be divided by confession and socio-professional status into several groups. The first group was the organizing

---

[41] Vasile Netea, *Noi contribuţii la cunoaşterea vieţii şi activităţii lui Visarion Roman. Corespondenţa sa cu George Bariţiu şi Iosif Hodoş* [New Contributions regarding the Life and Activity of Visarion Roman. His Correspondence with George Bariţiu and Iosif Hodoş] (Sibiu: Editura "Revistei Economice," 1942), 9-23; Bujor Surdu, "Corespondenţa dintre George Bariţ şi Visarion Roman (1867-1879)" [The Correspondence between George Bariţ and Visarion Roman (1867-1879)], *Anuarul Institutului de Istorie Cluj-Napoca* V (1962): 317-322.

committee: Iacob Bologa, Ioan Hannia, Visarion Roman and Ilie Măcelariu. They were the decisional core of the passivist group. All four were Orthodox and all had a good relationship with Andrei Şaguna, which deteriorated over time. Thus beyond ideological incentives, another perceptible connection between them was anti-Şagunism. The first two were brothers-in-law, married to the daughters of Petru Bădilă, archpriest of Miercurea. Miercurea was also the hometown of Măcelariu, where he was a well-known leader. One last noteworthy aspect is that at that time, all four occupied functions in the Transilvania insurance institute.

The next group represents the socio-professional category of entrepreneurs or traders: Ioan Axente Sever, Demetriu Iuga and Ioan G. Ioan, the first a well-known character from the 1848 Revolution who had strong economic ties with Ioan Pamfilie, Ioan Micu Moldovan, Ioan Raţiu, Nicolae Stoia (also a member of the CEC) and Visarion Roman. The latter two represented Braşov and were included on the Committee as a strategy to ensure the city's loyalty to passivism: the Braşov region was strongly disputed between activists and passivists.

Next follows the compact group of Greek Catholic clerics: Ioan Antonelli, Ioan V. Russu, Ioan Pamfilie, Simion Balint, Ioan Micu Moldovan and Ilie Vlassa. Most of them developed their ecclesiastic career in the radical national atmosphere of Blaj in the liberal period (1860-1865), having strong ties with Bariţ and Raţiu. Some also developed strong economic ties with other members of the CEC.

The last compact group had only Orthodox members: a cleric (Nicolae Popea), two former officials (Nicolae Găetan and Ioan Bran de Lemény), and two lawyers (Avram Tincu şi Ioan Nemeş). Their presence in a passivist Committee is remarkable to say the least. All were close to Şaguna, but one way or another they joined the CEC. For example, the two officials may have turned against Şaguna because he did not support them when they were dismissed; participation gave them a chance of revenge. As for the others, Moe's theory of solidary incentives derived from social pressure may also apply here. Failure to join could cost them (ostracism, loss of status) more than participation, even if they were not totally in agreement with passivism as a tactic.[42]

As a result we can clearly see that all kinds of incentives were available for members to join the CEC: kinship, friendship, professional relationships, economic ties, increased prestige and status, and ideological goals all combined to make it a coherent institution, its sole purpose to guide the Romanian constituency.

The Financial "Directorate"

As already mentioned, an important factor in the success of any interest group is its financial strength. We have already explained why the Romanian elite had to create their own institutions to provide themselves with status and financial security. Thus from 1868 we find some of the most prominent Romanian figures leading or working in various fi-

[42] Moe, "A Calculus," 617.

nancial institutions. The Transilvania insurance institute, a Romanian-Saxon joint venture, is one example; Iacob Bologa, Ioan Hannia and David Urs de Margine were members of the board. Likewise Visarion Roman and Ilie Măcelariu worked as acquisitions inspectors.

These board members and employees tried their best to assure a Romanian majority in both the board and share-owners, but failed to do so. They did not have the financial strength and had to deal with numerous vexations from their Saxon counterparts. Although Bologa and Hannia remained on the board until the statutes of the Albina were accepted by the government, Visarion Roman and Măcelariu left the enterprise earlier. This was the first phase of their attempt to procure a financial and insurance institute for themselves. In this case, just as later, the initiative came from Visarion Roman.

In this case we see once again how an economic enterprise is discussed in closed circles. In June 1869, Roman mentioned to Bariţ the existence of draft statutes of a purely Romanian financial institute. The second person who learned about the idea was Iacob Bologa, who read the draft at Roman's request and gave it personally to others designated by the author.[43] We can assume that these designated persons were members of the Founding Committee: Hannia, Bologa, Urs de Margine, Dunca de Sajo, Măcelariu and Visarion Roman. Suffice to say that five of them worked for Transilvania or were still members of its board. A few months later Alexandru Mocsonyi, Anton Mocsonyi and Timotei Cipariu were also included, the first two were to ensure that the Albina statutes would be approved by the Hungarian authorities. After the official approval came the share issue. Again a supervising committee was elected with Alexandru Mocsonyi as president, Dunca as vice-president, Hannia as treasurer and Roman as interim director.

Unfortunately, the share issue coincided with political disputes between activists and passivists about the ad-hoc committee.[44] As a result, important socio-economical groups from Braşov or Sibiu did not purchase shares in the foundation issue of the Albina bank. Instead, Romanians from the Banat proved extremely confident investors, substituting for the activists. Brokers from this area were also the most assiduous: Aurel Maniu from Lugoj and Simeon Mangiuca from Oraviţa amassed the largest number of shares (434 and 414 respectively). Next on the list was Ilie Măcelariu, who gathered just 160 subscriptions from the Sibiu area. Nicolae Filimon from Pecica-Română and Ştefan Antonescu from Bocşa-Montană, both in the Banat, also gathered over 100 subscriptions each (108 and 103 respectively). Thus, from a total of 3,000 shares needed, purchasers from the Banat subscribed 1059 shares (35.3%) through only four collectors.[45]

---

[43] On the history of "Albina" financial institute see: Mihai D. Drecin, *Banca "Albina" din Sibiu, instituţie naţională a românilor transilvăneni (1871-1918)* ["Albina" Bank from Sibiu. National Institution of the Romanians from Transylvania (1871-1918)] (Cluj-Napoca: Editura Dacia, 1982), 31-50; Bujor Surdu, *Visarion Roman (1833-1885)* (Cluj-Napoca: Presa Universitară Clujeană, 2008), 114-140.

[44] Dumitru Suciu, "Activitatea politică a lui Ilie Măcelariu după conferinţa de la Miercurea" [The Political Activity of Ilie Măcelariu after the Conference of Miercurea], *Studia Universitatis Babeş-Bolyai, Series Historia* 2 (1977): 49-51.

[45] Nicolae Petra-Petrescu, *Monografia institutului de credit şi economii „Albina". 1872-1897* [The Monograph of the Credit and Economy institute "Albina". 1872-1897] (Sibiu: Editura Institutului „Albina," 1897), 104-106.

After some difficulties the share issue ended with all shares accounted for. The next step was to convene the general assembly on 14th March 1872, to ensure that the bank could operate to normal legal standards. The general assembly also had to fill the five vacant posts on the board. Thus the members of the board were Alexandru Mocsonyi, Anton Mocsonyi, Paul Dunca, Iacob Bologa, Ioan Hannia, David Urs de Margine, Timotei Cipariu, Gregoriu Matei, Ilie Măcelariu, Archbishop Ioan Vancea, Dr. Aureliu Maniu and Ioan Popescu.

The first meeting of the new board was held on the same day. Alexandru Mocsonyi was elected chairman of the board, Bologa and Urs de Margine as vice-presidents. The next day Visarion Roman was appointed as managing director (still interim) and Măcelariu as board representative to the directorial council. A few months later, the directorial council was completed with the election of Iacob Bologa. Thereafter the passivist group from Sibiu, represented by Bologa, Roman and Măcelariu, coordinated the executive branch of the Albina. In a short while they also succeeded in gaining full control on the board.

At first the geographical origin of board members was balanced with three from the Banat, two from Blaj and seven from Sibiu. The bank statutes clearly stated that at least five members of the board had to reside in Sibiu. The first to resign their office were Vancea and Urs de Margine; the latter changed his mind and returned, welcomed back by his colleagues. He then resigned once and for all in September 1874, replaced as member and vice-president of the board by Ioan Meţianu, the Orthodox curate from Oradea-Mare. Another resignation, somewhat expected because of his age, was Timotei Cipariu. In his place the board recruited Vincenţiu Babeş, a representative from the Banat and the right hand of Alexandru Mocsonyi. At this point, before Alexandru Mocsonyi's resignation, membership ratio was four from the Banat, seven from Sibiu and one from Făgăraş; the last-mentioned member had to move to Sibiu once appointed attorney to the bank. Thus the ratio was 3:1 in favour of the Sibiu passivist group. Since it was difficult for members from the Banat to travel to Sibiu, the Sibiu residents made most of the decisions. There was a clear and obvious disproportion between the Banat share-holders' capital investment and their access to the decision-making process.

We believe that this was a very powerful motive for Alexandru Mocsonyi's resignation, as was the dissolution of the Banat credit unions. However the trigger came when the board decided to buy a house to turn into a bank office. Mocsonyi felt excluded from the decision, to which he would not agree.[46] His resignation led to the election of Iacob Bologa as chairman of the board, as a result of which the passivist group from Sibiu had total control of the bank.

---

[46] Serviciul Judeţean Sibiu al Arhivelor Naţionale [The Sibiu County Branch of National Archives], Fund *Banca "Albina,"* Minutes of the Administrative Board, files 101-122.

Conclusions

Having presented the formation and principal actions of the Sibiu passivist group from 1867-1874, we can finally come to some conclusions. First, the group behaved as a power elite for the entire geographical area of Transylvania and the major Romanian institutions: the "Astra" cultural society, the Romanian National Party of Transylvania and the Albina bank. Their domination would last until 1881, when other groups started to make their presence felt by questioning the passivists' authority.

Second, we have seen how some interest group theories suggest the importance of the leader in the formation and maintenance of groups. Moreover, some scholars suggest that the existence of patrons is also important. None were available for our group. We can speak of patronage only to the extent of a spiritual-ideological patronage: behind many passivist actions stood George Bariţ and his political ideas, but he never contributed financially to the formation of the group. Nor did our group have a recognized leader as Andrei Şaguna was for the Transylvanian activists, or Alexandru Mocsonyi for the Banat. Instead we can find a front man, delegated to fill the position of a "group entrepreneur": Ioan Hannia and Iacob Bologa for "Astra;" Ilie Măcelariu for the RNPT; and Visarion Roman for the Albina. Nevertheless decisions were taken by a closed circle (four to five maximum), giving the group an oligarchic character.[47] Such a feature is even more evident if we consider the secrecy around their goals.

A third feature of the passivist group was the existence of "large members" whose contribution could cause a change in objectives. Such members may remain in a group whether or not they approve the goals as long as selective incentives continue to be supplied, or they can leave, jeopardizing the organization.[48] For example, Paul Dunca de Sajo or David Urs de Margine were inclined to accept the activist ideology but supported the foundation of the Albina. Alexandru Mocsony was a similar case: his resignation from the board could have led to the break-up of the Albina.

Fourth, passivist success was due to both its decision-making coherence (being a small group), and the organization incoherence of the activists in Sibiu. In most cases, activism was advocated by members who held public offices or were MPs, few of them from the free professions. Only in 1872 were they able to take the lead in the national movement for a short time.

Finally, all initiatives taken by the passivist group from Sibiu nonetheless had a clear single goal: ensuring autonomy (cultural, political, economical) in relation with the Hungarian state. As such, beyond material and solidary interests, there was always a higher and ultimate purposive goal, political in nature, that marked all its actions.

---

[47] Knoke, "Associations and Interest," 11.

[48] Moe, "Towards a Broader," 535; Franke Dobson, "Interest Groups," 226.

Social Mobility in Transylvania at the End of the First World War

Valer Moga

Social mobility is an omnipresent phenomenon, its amplitude determined by the degree of modernisation in the society under examination. The Romanians of Transylvania in the 1910s were far from the upper limits of mobility, but formed a social group that underwent renewal and diversification at the time.

In order to avoid being overwhelmed by the immensity of a statistical evaluation of the whole social milieu, the author of the present study has chosen to examine a cohort of 1633 members.[1] These are the appointed and elected members of the Great National Assembly at Alba Iulia. We must emphasise here that this article is not directly concerned with the changes in Transylvania's political status when the province was incorporated into the Romanian state. Rather this simply provides the context within which a representative cohort was formed, largely made up of persons who had reached prominence through their own efforts in rural or urban communities, in cultural institutions, schools, universities, banks and other financial bodies, and the realm of politics.

The socio-professional structure of this cohort confirms what is already broadly known about Romanian society in Transylvania at the time. It reflects the persistence of traditional forms, but also the signs of progress and modernisation, both stratification and mobility. Thus the farmers and landowners still dominate to a striking degree, with 372 in the cohort as a whole, making up 22.78% of the total 1633. They are distributed fairly predictably along a spectrum that runs from the smallholders and "*econom*" farmers to the great landowners.[2] Not far behind the farmers come the 330 members of the clergy (20.20%). Next by proportion we find the schoolteachers at 154 members (9.43%) and professors at 78 members (4.77%). The great majority of these worked in the church schools system and thereby represent a further extension of the church's presence in the intellectual and cultural life of society. The 86 craftsmen (5.26% of total) are a group that combines traditional tendencies with those of modernisation, as we shall see in the study. There was a growing influence from the agents of social innovation in the form of the free professions; 190 lawyers (11.63%), 35 from the banking sector (2.14%), 31 doctors and pharmacists 31 (1.89%). Along with the groups that were present in smaller numbers,

---

[1] Valer Moga, "Introducere în cercetarea activității electorale din Transilvania, în noiembrie-decembrie 1918" [An Introduction to the Study of Electoral Trends in Transylvania, November-December 1918], *Annales Universitatis Apulensis. Series Historica* 16, I (2012): 253-264.

[2] The term was in common use in Transylvania in the late nineteenth century, but fell out of use in the first quarter of the twentieth century. It refers to farmers who were at the very top of the smallholder class or who could already be classed as mid-sized landowners. The defining characteristics were good husbandry, successful market orientation and a reliable income. We could also use the term *farmer* as a synonym for *econom*.

the salesmen, industrialists, engineers, journalists et al., they make up a whole which shatters the image of social homogeneity noted in the province in the not too recent past. There was also a non-negligible number of students at 49 (3% of total), heralding the social reconfigurations to come in the interwar decades.[3]

Constraints imposed by the nature of the sources and the chosen methodology require that we limit ourselves, in the present to study, to groups that form the base of society, the farmers and craftsmen, and to the most representative of the educated groups in the period under study, the clergy and lawyers.

Returning to the theme of *social mobility*, we expect to be able to find all forms of the phenomenon in Romanian society in Transylvania at the end of the First World War. Tracking the socio-professional changes in the rise or fall of individuals, we will establish the widespread presence of *vertical mobility* in both of its forms, both upward and downward, though it is true that the latter form is more rarely met with. A look at successive generations and the evaluation of the son's social position relative to that occupied by his father also offers an overview of *intergenerational mobility*. Such an approach requires that we specify that the present work is not a purely sociological study, but rather one in which sociology and its instruments serve as an historical auxiliary discipline. The analysis is not based on interviews with persons in direct contact with the researcher, which would be the only way to be able to fix all variables. Rather in the present case the members of the cohort are persons from the past, and certain variables may be missing from their biographies, such as ages, level of education and father's profession. Likewise, the analysis is always based on the profile of the son, whose biographical details cannot reveal the facts of his father's socio-professional status.

In this context, the actual content of the concept of *structural mobility* becomes very important. In the present case, vertical mobility is far more the result of structural changes, be these social, economic or, to repeat, political, than of personal qualities or of studying one or another subject.[4]

The group of farmers and landowners is particularly prone to display *social immobility*. We can consider this claim justified in terms of relative analysis, when for instance we compare farmers with members of the liberal professions – for example with

---

[3] The cohort described above was outlined on the basis of the data in the holdings *Documente, Marea Adunare Națională întrunită la Alba-Iulia în ziua de 1 Decembrie 1918*, tomurile I-VI [Documents of the Great National Assembly of Alba Iulia 1st December 1918], held at the National Unification Museum in Alba Iulia, and in numerous monographs, articles, newspapers and journals of the day. Some of these will be further cited in what follows.

[4] My use of the conceptual and methodological terms of social mobility is based on such works as Norman Goodman, *Introducere în sociologie* [Introduction to Sociology], transl. Ioana Rădulescu (București: Lider, 1992), 191-197; Anthony Giddens, *Sociologie* [Sociology], transl. Radu Săndulescu and Vivia Săndulescu (București: ALL, 2000), 289-296; Allan Johnson, *Dicționarul Blackwell de sociologie. Ghid de utilizare a limbajului sociologic* [The Blackwell Dictionary of Sociology. A Guide to the Use of Sociological Terms], transl. S. G. Drăgan and V. Russo (București: Humanitas, 2007), 219-220; *Dicționar de sociologie* [Dictionary of Sociology], ed. Gilles Ferréol (Iași: Polirom, 1998), 119-125; *Oxford. Dicționar de sociologie* [Oxford Dictionary of Sociology], ed. Gordon Marshall (București: Univers Enciclopedic, 2003), 372-376.

doctors or lawyers. It can also be seen to be justified in the aspect of intergenerational mobility. The hereditary nature of the profession is so pervasive that there are hardly any cases in which a farmer's father had any other status than that of farmer himself. Taken for itself, the group of Romanian farmers in Transylvania had already undergone the phases of modernisation and stratification.

Manifestations of mobility were more frequent at the upper end of the social scale. For instance the "farmer" Ioan Albu owned large estates in Ghilad in the county of Timiş, and from 1912 attended courses at the technical institute in Mittweida, Saxony. He bolstered his personal prestige and used the title of engineer from 1918, though he continued to live off his estates. In 1925 he was recorded along with associates, perhaps family members ("Albu Ioan & Co."), as the principal owner of 467 *iugăr* in the cadastral records.[5]

A similar case was to be found a long way off in the county of Sătmar; this was Nicolau Barbul, a landowner in Mocira.[6] From 1900 he attended the Royal Academy of Agriculture in Debrecen and the Royal Academy of Agriculture in Keszthely, Hungary. For all that, in 1918 he declared his occupation as landowner. He also used the term *arendator*, revealing that this was a large estate. However, having studied at the higher level and developed intellectual concerns, he moved on from the status of farmer, becoming involved in politics and journalism.[7]

Ioan Prescurea of Retişdorf in the county of Târnava Mare inherited his status as a great landowner from his father.[8] Ioan Prescurea senior, the notary for his community, sent his son to attend courses at the Faculty of Law and Political Science at the Royal Hungarian University in Budapest (1899-1900) and then at the corresponding faculty at the "Ferencz József" University in Cluj. After 1918 his experience in farming brought him the post of county adviser on agriculture for the counties of Târnava Mare and Odorhei. From 1924 onward we find him in the post of prefect of the county of Târnava Mare.

Although he is by no means the last who could be mentioned, we will conclude for now with Nicolae Vulcu of Iclandu Mare in the county of Turda-Arieş.[9] We do not

---

[5] National Unification Museum of Alba Iulia (henceforth abbreviated MNUAI), holdings *Documente, Marea Adunare Naţională întrunită la Alba-Iulia în ziua de 1 Decembrie 1918*, vol. III, 646; *Gazeta Oficială* 5 (Sibiu, 1919): 24; László Szögi, *Studenţi români din Transilvania la universităţile din Europa în secolele XVI-XX* [Romanian Students from Transylvania at the European Universities, Sixteenth to Twentieth Centuries], ed. Cornel Sigmirean (Târgu-Mureş: Editura Universităţii "Petru Maior," 2011), 216; *Anuarul „Socec" al României-Mari* [The Yearbook of Greater Romania], vol. II (Bucureşti: Socec & Co. SA, 1924-1925), 827.

[6] Today in the county of Maramureş.

[7] MNUAI, holdings *Documente*, tom III, 208-216; *Dicţionarul personalităţilor Unirii. 1918 – 85 de ani – 2003. Trimişii românilor transilvăneni la Marea Adunare Naţională de la Alba Iulia* [Dictionary of Unification Biography 1918 – 85th Anniversary – 2003. Romanian Transylvanian Delegates to the Great National Assembly of Alba Iulia], ed. Ioan I. Şerban and Nicolae Josan (Alba Iulia: Altip, 2003), 233; Cornel Sigmirean, *Istoria formării intelectualităţii româneşti din Transilvania şi Banat în epoca modernă* [The History of the Romanian Intelligentsia in Transylvania and the Banate in the Modern Age] (Cluj-Napoca: Presa Universitară Clujeană, 2000), 680.

[8] Retişdorf is today Retiş in the county of Sibiu.

[9] Today in the county of Mureş.

know whether he had undertaken higher study, but he embarked on life with substantial wealth put at his disposal by his father, Stan Vulcu of Sălişte, Sibiu, probably a prosperous sheep breeder. Married to Irina Moldovan, the daughter of the Greek Catholic archdeacon of Cătina, Nicolae Vulcu bought extensive agricultural properties around Iclandu Mare – Cătina after 1890, becoming one of the biggest landowners on the Transylvanian Plain. He also had political support in his rise. He was a member of the Romanian National Party and then of the National Peasant Party, becoming vice-president of the latter's regional branch in Mureş in 1936. After 1918 he settled in Târgu-Mureş and held important political posts: deputy to the lower house (1919-1920), senator in the upper house (1928-1931, 1932-1933) and member of the Mureş county council (1926-1930, 1937-1938).[10]

None of these four ever gave up the status of farmer. Although they do not strictly fit into the methodological criteria for upward social mobility, nevertheless we cannot speak of them in terms of social immobility either.

We also find the smallholders and middle-sized landowners transcending the limits of their status as farmers. The need for personal prestige, or the more practical need to find some other source of supplementary income, impelled peasants to take on additional occupations.

It is impressive that of the 372 farmers in the cohort under study here, nearly 50 served as mayor, both before and after the First World War. Stoiu Sârb for example, who was registered as the cadastral owner of 32 *iugăr* of farmland, was mayor of the community of Cuvin in the county of Arad uninterruptedly from 10th January 1905 to 10th September 1929.[11] Teodor Cornea, a peasant who had graduated from the secondary school, was mayor of the community of Meziad for twenty years under both Hungarian and Romanian rule.[12] After the war he also had political support and was a member of the National Liberal Party.[13] Other peasants served parliamentary terms after 1918, were elected to local or county councils, or appointed to the chambers of agriculture.

The spread of modern industries in the province offered many Transylvanians the chance to combine two or even three occupations to have the corresponding level of income. Such behaviour can especially be noted in regions where time between the tasks of farming could be devoted to mining work. A special case here is that of Toader Atanasiu from Sighiştel, Bihor. Having attended the Greek Catholic secondary school in Beiuş, he owned farmland and coal mines and was a member of the supervisory board of the Şo-

---

[10] MNUAI, *Documente*, tom III, 808-816; Traian Bosoancă, *Mureşenii şi Marea Unire* [Citizens of Târgu-Mureş and the Great Unification] (Târgu-Mureş: Ardealul, 2000), 246-250.

[11] MNUAI, *Documente*, tom II, 143-153; *1 Decembrie 1918. Mărturii ale participanţilor. Ioachim Crăciun: documente la un sfert de veac de la Marea Unire*, [Eyewitness Testimony. Ioachim Crăciun: Documents a Quarter-Century on from the Great Unification], vol. II, ed. Mircea Vaida-Voevod and Gelu Neamţu (Bucureşti: Editura Academiei Române, 2008), 257-258.

[12] County of Bihor.

[13] MNUAI, *Documente*, tom II, 223-233; *Dicţionarul personalităţilor Unirii*, 103; *1 Decembrie 1918. Mărturii ale participanţilor*, vol. I, 101-102.

imul bank of Vaşcău, regarded by his contemporaries as one of the "Romanian intellectuals that adorn Vaşcău," involved in every kind of Romanian political activity at the beginning of the twentieth century. In 1901 he was awarded a prize by the Beiuş branch of the "Astra" association for his achievements in orchard-planting.[14] We find such farmer-miners in Lupeni, Ghelari, Săcărâmb in the county of Hunedoara, or in Capnic in the county of Sătmar.[15]

The portrait of society offered above does not deny the existence of hereditary professions as a phenomenon, a characteristic feature of traditional societies: but it does destroy the image of a farming class utterly enclosed by the constraints of social immobility. Also in the social class of direct producers, the *craftsmen* offer an image that at first sight seems dominated by inherited jobs and by social immobility. This image is supported, among other things, by the craftsmen's membership in trade associations which conserved some of the features of the mediaeval guilds and contributed to the sedentarisation of the trades. Returning to intergenerational change, we find that in the group of 86 craftsmen in the cohort under study, those whose father's occupation is known were most often the sons either of craftsmen themselves or of farmers. Here the situation in the county of Hunedoara is relevant, where we find considerable incidence of inherited professions in Deva, Dobra and Haţeg. The very rare exceptions seem to exist only to prove the rule. This was the case with Silviu Bologa (1874-1960), whose father was an Orthodox priest and whose mother's father was a judge. I do not believe that we are dealing with a case of downward mobility here, since the rank of master wheelwright in Turda, owning his own workshop, gave him a social status at least equal to that of his parents.[16]

A more thorough analysis, however, yields data on a process of differentiation and even reveals forms of social mobility. In the first instance, there is a distribution dependent on place of residence. Some of these craftsmen who practised typically rural trades – carpenters, blacksmiths or potters – were tied to their native soil in much the same way as farmers were. They learned their trade in the family, and then passed it on to their own children. It is no accident that the adult education programmes launched by the "Astra" association, by craftsmen's unions and even by the national churches sought to break such immobility by offering young Romanians the chance, most often through stipends, to learn those trades that were considered "urban."[17] Their main aim was to in-

[14] MNUAI, *Documente*, tom II, 223-233; *Dicţionarul personalităţilor Unirii*, 100; *1 Decembrie 1918. Mărturii ale participanţilor*, vol. I, 361-363; Vasile Dobrescu, *Funcţii şi funcţionalităţi în sistemul de credit românesc din Transilvania până la Primul Război Mondial* [Public Offices and the Civil Service in Romanian Lending Associations in Transylvania up until the First World War] (Târgu-Mureş: Editura Universităţii "Petru Maior," 2006), 177, 270, 290; *Revista Economică* 27 (Sibiu, 1901): 279.

[15] Today Cavnic, county of Maramureş.

[16] MNUAI, *Documente*, tom I, 919; Daniela Comşa, Eugenia Glodariu and Maria M. Jude, *Clujenii şi Marea Unire* [Citizens of Cluj and the Great Unification] (Cluj-Napoca: Muzeul Naţional de Istorie a Transilvaniei, 1998), 87.

[17] At the diocesan and metropolitan levels the churches disbursed funds to secondary school pupils, university students and young men who wished to become apprentices.

crease Romanian presence in the economy and, by implication, in the population of Transylvania's towns. Even if this was merely the beginning of a process which often did not unfold as quickly as the promoters would wish, it grew steadily from the beginning of the twentieth century.

The "Astra" had a coherent plan with well-determined goals to promote the trades. One relevant source document here was published in 1911 and entitled "Aid to journeymen and apprentices" [1864-1902].[18] The list details 405 sums of money disbursed over almost four decades to almost as many Romanian journeymen and apprentices.[19] These were small sums, but the relevance of the text lies in what it reveals of how the association's leaders tried to direct the training of apprentices and journeymen.

What is certain is that the "Astra" programme appealed to the hopes of families, be these rural or urban, who wanted to learn specifically urban trades. One proof here is that 100 stipends – by far the most numerous category – were awarded to apprentices and journeymen learning to become shoemakers. Not that we should imagine that there were no cobblers in the countryside: but this type of footwear is far better suited to the paved streets of town. Under the heading of "carpenter" we most often find cabinet-makers and furniture carpenters – 26 cases – since construction carpenters were listed separately. Likewise, qualified tailors most often had their shops in urban settings.[20] There can be no doubt that the four *maşinişti* (mechanics) and one photographer in the list also practised in urban areas.

In this period, printers and typesetters were also treated as one of the skilled trades, reaching the rank of master printer after having served as apprentices and journeymen. Of all the instances at the time, we have not one case of a printer who attended much more than primary or sometimes secondary schooling; however, we do not rule out that some such cases may come to light. A tradesman could then go on to run his own print shop. Furthermore, the apprenticeship and journeyman work necessarily included a good knowledge of Romanian language and grammar. A typesetter would become a voracious and careful reader, *volens nolens*. Thus the historian very often finds persons who became printers in the early twentieth century and went on to become editors, journalists or booksellers. For example Petru Bariţiu, the nephew of George Bariţiu, declared his profession as printer in Cluj in 1911.[21] He had also founded his own printing house, the *Tipografia "Carmen,"* also in Cluj, as owner and manager in 1904. As was usual in those years, it was at the same time a publishing house. The same Petru Bariţiu was editor of the Cluj daily newspaper *Răvaşul* in 1905, founded two years earlier by Elie Dăianu.[22]

---

[18] "Ajutoare pentru sodali (calfe) şi învăţăcei de meserii," *Transilvania* 4 (1911): 375-383.

[19] Since names were very rarely repeated, there were very nearly as many beneficiaries as there were sums disbursed. The amounts varied from 20 to 100 de crowns per year. An apprentice or journeyman would primarily rely on family support, and only thereafter from stipends from various foundations.

[20] The "Astra" awarded 23 grants for apprentices and journeymen in this trade.

[21] *Transilvania* 4 (1911): 510; MNUAI, *Documente*, tom II, 611-615; Comşa, Glodariu and Jude, *Clujenii şi Marea Unire*, 47-49.

[22] *Răvaşul* 48 (1905): 1.

Răvaşul was printed in the "Carmen" print works.

A typical tradesman in this branch was Nicolae Bratu, born in 1881 in Răşinari, county of Sibiu, to a peasant family. In 1894 he began his apprenticeship at the printing house of the *Tribuna* newspaper in Sibiu, where he worked until 1903.

The training of skilled workers in these urban trades was an area where the economic revolution of the guilds resonated with the new, modern methods of professional development. The journeymen's years of wandering took young Romanians to important European cities, where they perfected their crafts working in the industry in question or attending trade schools and technical colleges.

After nine years of work, Nicolae Bratu must have already fulfilled his apprenticeship but nevertheless he too left on the "pilgrimage" to other countries. For six years he worked in important print shops in Berlin, Munich and Dresden, learning further secrets of the typographical art. In 1909 he returned to Sibiu and bought the print shop of Henric Meltzer, where the next year he began to publish the *Foaia Poporului*, the weekly journal of the "Astra." He prospered as a printer and by the 1930s was able to extend his business and found the *Tipografia "Carmen*" in Bucharest. The public prestige which this brought helped him into important public positions, among them the presidency of the Sibiu Chamber of Commerce and Industry, and terms in both the upper and the lower house of parliament.[23]

Another typical career which matches those shown above was that of Ioan Pescariu (1888-1963). The son of a peasant from Şura Mare in the county of Sibiu, he attended primary school in his home village and thereafter became an apprentice at the print works of the *Tribuna* newspaper in Sibiu (1902-1904) and in the print shop of the Archiepiscopal Seminary in Blaj, where he worked as a typesetter until 1910. He then settled in Budapest, where he worked in a bookshop and qualified in that trade also, so that later, in 1943, he declared his profession as bookseller.[24] At the same time he was the editor of the nationally-minded newspaper *Lupta*, which appeared in Budapest. After 1918 he settled in Turda, where he opened the first Romanian bookshop of the town, the "*Librăria Populară*." He also founded the *Turda* daily newspaper as owner-editor.[25]

In the final quarter of the nineteenth century printer's apprentices were not the most numerous group among the recipients of the "Astra" stipends, but they were far from being neglected. The association, based in Sibiu, granted funds to eleven young men who wanted to learn this particular trade. For four of these, the apprenticeship was a way to leave behind them their parents' peasant lifestyle and join the Romanian townsmen of Transylvania.[26]

---

[23] MNUAI, *Documente*, tom I, 207; *1 Decembrie 1918. Mărturii ale participanţilor*, vol. I, 63-64.

[24] *1 Decembrie 1918. Mărturii ale participanţilor*, vol. II, 210.

[25] Comşa, Glodariu and Jude, *Clujenii şi Marea Unire*, 119-120; MNUAI, fond *Documente*, tom I, 975.

[26] These four came from Gura Râului, Poplaca (Sibiu), Bran (Făgăraş) and Vâlcele (Trei Scaune). Cf. *Transilvania* 4 (1911): 378-382.

Another example of success was Ioan Petraşcu. Born in 1876 to a peasant family in Doştat, from the age of 14 to 19 years old he was an apprentice tailor. Joining the Hungarian army broadened his horizons, and upon his discharge he continued his professional training, working in Budapest and Prague. He also attended tailors' colleges in Vienna and Paris, and as an old man would proudly recall

> "[…] at 27 years old I settled down in Sibiu, in 1903, and there I opened my shop in the main street of town, right in among the foreign merchants, and I was the first Romanian to have my own tailor's shop in the centre of Sibiu."[27]

A similar though somewhat less spectacular case was that of Nicolae Oancea (1888-1958) of Dobra, who served his apprenticeship in Lugoj and then worked in the furrier's trade in Budapest, Berlin and Leipzig. After the end of the First World War he opened his own atelier in Deva.[28] Similarly, Vasile Urdea (1853-1928) became a furrier and skinner in Sighişoara, having learned the trade in Vienna.[29]

A rather more unusual but nonetheless important case was that of Iuliu Muja, born in 1878 to a peasant family in Copand in the county of Turda-Arieş.[30] After his apprenticeship he became a master hairdresser and barber, working in salons in Karlsbad, Prague, Budapest and Paris. By 1918 he already owned one of the most important salons in the centre of Cluj.[31]

As we may observe, these skilled tradesmen exemplify intergenerational upward mobility. However, at the level of their own profession most of these craftsmen and tradesman had a horizontal career trajectory, not much interested in leaving their livelihood behind to seek better status. There were a few such cases, but these were exceptional. The best collective example is that of the three leaders of the Romanian Section of the Social Democrat Party in Hungary, who in 1927 all became members of the Social Democrat Party in Romania; Ion Flueraş, a wheelwright in Sibiu, Iosif Jumanca, a printer in the same town, and Tiron Albani, a joiner in Craiova and then in Budapest. At least in their journalistic careers we may consider them autodidacts, since none of them attended any school beyond the primary level, and Albani did not even finish all classes at that level. Each one served terms in parliament after 1918, with Ion Flueraş being most significant as both politician and trade unionist; he sat in the lower house (1928-1930, 1931-1932) and in the upper (1939-1940), and was chairman of the trades union congress (1926-1939).[32]

---

[27] *1 Decembrie 1918. Mărturii ale participanţilor*, vol. II, 212-213.
[28] Victor Şuiaga, *Hunedorenii la Marea Unire. 1 Decembrie 1918* [Citizens of Hunedoara and the Great Unification. 1 December 1918] (Deva, 1993), 47.
[29] Bosoancă, *Mureşenii şi Marea Unire*, 244-245.
[30] Today Copăceni, county of Cluj.
[31] Comşa, Glodariu and Jude, *Clujenii şi Marea Unire*, 53.
[32] *1 Decembrie 1918. Mărturii ale participanţilor*, vol. I, 29-30, 129-130, 166; *Politics and Political Parties in Roumania* (London: International Reference Library Publishing Co., 1936), 446; Sorin Radu, *Ion Flueraş (1882-1953). Social-democraţie şi sindicalism* [Ion Flueraş (1882-1953). Social Democracy and Trade Unionism] (Bucureşti: Nemira, 2007), 352.

In the persons and groups under study here we find that social mobility was directly related to the level of schooling and of political and civic engagement.

The absolute numbers and the percentages presented above now bring us to discuss the educated classes, starting with the clergy, who were most numerous and the most influential due to their public role and the way they interwove themselves into the day-to-day life of society. A general look at the clergy as a group in any given period, as in our case in the last quarter of the nineteenth and the first half of the twentieth century, reveals the image of a veritable "Brownian motion" which may directly correspond to social mobility in the sociological sense, but cannot be ignored for all that. Very few priests, whether Orthodox or Greek Catholic, stayed in one parish from their ordination through to retirement. Most of them served in multiple posts during the course of their careers, and by implication also moved from place to place as the needs of the church or their own hopes for more lucrative and prestigious benefices required. The higher they aimed, the longer the climb on the clerical career ladder and the greater the variety of the posts that they held. To move from the post of chaplain to parish administrator (and in the Greek Catholic Church the post of priest-co-operator) and finally to parish priest might take several years and involve moving from one parish to another. A candidate wishing to become protopope might spend several years at the rank of administrator to another protopope, but not before proving himself by qualifying as a priest to a class I parish, a stage which required at least five years of service to the church or in school and convincing results at the parish level.[33]

In studying intergenerational mobility among the Greek Catholic clergy, we are particularly helped by a number of sources which help us to identify their father's profession.[34] We have thus been able to ascertain biographical data for 97 of the 157 clergy, which at 61.78% represents a firm basis for overall analysis.

For Orthodox clergy, the proportion is considerably smaller, at only 59 out of 173 or 34.1%. Nevertheless we will consider these figures, with all due caution, in order to have some basis for comparison. Despite our reservations, they provide enough data to assure us that our conclusions are not entirely wrong.

---

[33] Paul Brusanowski, *Reforma constituţională din Biserica Ortodoxă a Transilvaniei între 1850-1925* [Constitutional Reform in the Transylvanian Orthodox Church, 1850-1925] (Cluj-Napoca: Presa Universitară Clujeană, 2007), 262. The situation was not substantially different in the Greek Catholic church.

[34] *Şematismul veneratului cler al Archidiecesei Metropolitane Greco-Catolice Române de Alba-Iulia şi Făgăraş pre anul Domnului 1900 de la Sânta Unire 200* [Clerical Dictionary of the Greek Catholic Romanian Metropolitan Archdiocese of Alba-Iulia and Făgăraş, Year of Our Lord 1900, Year of the Holy Union 200] (Blaj: Tipografia Seminariului Archidiecesan, 1900), 673-782; Victor Bojor, *Canonicii Diecezei Gr[eco] Cat[olice] de Gherla acum: Cluj-Gherla 1875-1937* [The Canons of the Greek Catholic Diocese of Gherla Now: Cluj-Gherla 1875-1937] (Cluj: Imprimeria Fondului Cărţilor Funduare Cluj, 1937), 65-273; Cornel Sigmirean, *Intelectualitatea ecleziastică. Preoţii Blajului (1806-1948)* [The Church Intelligentsia. The Priest of Blaj (1806-1948)] (Târgu-Mureş: Editura Universităţii "Petru Maior," 2007), 417; Nicolae Comşa and Teodor Seiceanu, *Dascălii Blajului* [The Acolytes of Blaj] (Bucureşti: Demiurg, 1994), 237.

Father's profession	Priest	Farmer	Teacher	Notary	Cantor	Professor	Lawyer	Mayor	Salesman	Craftsman	Captain	**Total**
Greek Catholic	44	38	5	3	2	1	1	1	1	1	-	**97**
%	45.36	39.17	5.15	3.09	2.06	1.03	1.03	1.03	1.03	1.03	-	**100**
Orthodox	33	17	3	2	-	-	1	-	1	1	1	**59**
%	55.93	28.81	5.08	3.38	-	-	1.69	-	1.69	1.69	1.69	**100**

Table 1

For both of the churches, the tables show that the vocation of priest was largely hereditary. Broadly, this is as a sign of social immobility, reflecting a lag behind the process of general social modernisation. The phenomenon may perhaps be explained by the prestige that a priest enjoyed in traditional society, depending on his rank in the church hierarchy, quite aside from simple immobility. Those who belonged to such multi-generational priestly families spoke of the situation as the basis of their family's particular reputation. For instance, the writer Nicolae Breban was the last of the line of Alexandru Breban, the protopope of the district of Baia Mare and from 1931 canon of the Greek Catholic diocese in Maramureş; he describes his family as just one such typical case:

> "[...] my father told me that we had already had ten generations of priests in the family, and that this was why my *tătuca*, my grandfather, had forced his youngest son, Văsălica, despite all the inclinations that he had shown for theatre or for the law as professions, to become a priest, so that *the tradition should not be lost*."[35]

We read of Gheorghe Popovici, Orthodox protopope of the district of Lugoj 1887-1927, that "all of his forebears from the distant past were priests."[36] Such cases are by no means exceptional for either of the Romanian churches of Transylvania.

Where priests display intergenerational social mobility, their fathers are most often farmers, which is easily explained by the predominance of this class in Transylvanian society. Taken all in all, the scarcity of other professions in the table simply confirms our appraisal at the start of the study that the process of stratification in Transylvanian Romanian society was in the early stages.

Intragenerational mobility over the course of a career shows how a given individual's status changes over the course of his life. In the case of the clergy, this kind of

[35] Nicolae Breban, "Fragment din 'Sensul vieţii Memorii IV' (În curs de apariţie la Editura Polirom)," [Fragments from 'The Meaning of Life', Memoirs, IV (in press, Editura Polirom)], *Nord Literar* 6 (37) (2006), accessed 22nd July 2013, http://www2.nord-literar.ro/index.php?option =com_content&task=view&id = 517&Itemid=46.

[36] *1 Decembrie 1918. Mărturii ale participanţilor*, vol. II, 232.

mobility poses unusually tough methodological problems. In fact, scholars have almost exclusively concentrated on intergenerational mobility as a factor, while intragenerational mobility occupies a marginal position and is thus notably under-researched.[37]

In such a strongly hierarchical institution as the church, a member may traverse very few or very many ranks in the course of his career. A parish priest may have plenty of opportunity to become a protopope. In the Greek Catholic church, he may even be able to become a canon, or even to become head of chapter. If we look at the career of the Orthodox priest Elie Miron Cristea, we may see a truly remarkable rise; he was a hieromonk in 1903, Bishop of Caransebeş in 1910, Metropolitan of Romania in 1919, Patriarch of Romania in 1925. Despite all this, a trained sociologist might object that these were merely the stages of one single career and that we thus cannot speak of social mobility. We read in one specialist dictionary that "In a stratified system, the profession itself is the essential criterion for classification, to which we may assign various grades of power and prestige."[38] Granted, when we speak of Miron Cristea as regent (1927) or as chairman of the Council of Ministers (1938) we speak in other terms, but even in these roles he did not cease to be a priest and Patriarch.

Despite all these reservations, when looking for intragenerational mobility in the clergy we will consider only changes of profession – those who "dropped out," to use a modern expression. Similarly, we will note clergy's participation in initiatives outside the church, their membership of political parties and their exercise of important roles in local or central administration as factors that favour such mobility.

Before embarking on the analysis itself, we must return to the concept of *structural mobility*. In strictly sociological terms, such mobility is due to a general shift in the structure of society itself. In a given period the importance of any given profession may fall drastically, so that social actors leave that profession. In much the same way, economic development may lead to the appearance of new jobs and roles which have better status, and which become professional centres of gravity. Generally speaking, in such a context we speak more of group mobility than of the mobility of individuals. Thus we may see that we may also speak of structural mobility in Transylvania after the First World War. A particular political outlook and concept of the "unitary national state" would only be codified some years later in the Romanian Constitution, but even in 1919 it generated a massive demand for Romanian functionaries in all institutions at the local and county level. Likewise, the foundation of the "Dacia Superioară" University in Cluj and a whole network of Romanian-language secondary schools in the major towns created the urgent need for a large professional Romanian teaching class.

It is also notable that no more than 14 Romanian deputies were elected to the lower house in Budapest in the parliament of 1906-1910. To this number we may add the Romanian metropolitan bishops, who were members of the house of lords, the upper

---

[37] Johnson, *Dicţionarul Blackwell de sociologie*, 219.

[38] "Mobilitate socială (Mobilité sociale)," in Ferréol, ed., *Dicţionar de sociologie*, 119.

house of the Hungarian parliament. By contrast, in the first parliament of Greater Romania, elected in 1919, the National Romanian Party of Transylvania held 169 seats in the lower house and 76 in the senate.[39]

In what follows, we will see how the Orthodox and Greek Catholic clergy on the one hand, and the lawyers on the other hand, reacted to this challenge. One of the most far-reaching campaigns in this direction was organised by the Ruling Council through its Ministry of Religion and Public Education, as an intensive training course for Romanian-language teachers. The course was planned for 15th-19th September 1919 under the aegis of the "Dacia Superioară" University. We should also mention here that the hopeful applicants already had some training, either in seminary or teacher training college, and some experience in teaching. Overall there were 198 candidates for posts as secondary school teachers, of whom 96 were priests and 48 had graduated from seminary, making a total of 144 clergymen.[40] The available biographical data for members of our research cohort allow us to draw up the following statistical breakdown of intragenerational mobility among the clergy. Some of the variables give above may have greater values, with the figures in the table being derived from the extant sources. Nevertheless, as in the case of evaluating intergenerational mobility, there is enough data to assure us that our conclusions are not entirely wrong.

Clergy	Intragenerational mobility	Roles in local administration	Roles in central administration	Parliament, one term	Parliament, multiple terms	Member of one political party	Member of several political parties in succession	**Total**
Orthodox	12	11	3	15	17	28	5	**173**
%	6.93	6.35	1.73	8.67	9.82	16.18	2.89	**100**
Greek Catholic	6	18	4	15	13	30	3	**157**
%	3.82	11.46	2.54	9.55	8.28	19.1	1.91	**100**

Table 2

[39] Ioan Scurtu and Ion Bulei, *Democrația la români 1866-1938* [Romanian Democracy] (București: Humanitas, 1990), 98.
[40] *Gazeta Oficială* 28 (Sibiu, 1919): 292-297; 32 (1919): 330-335; Valer Moga, *„Astra" și societatea* [The "Astra" and Society] (Cluj-Napoca: Presa Universitară Clujeană, 2003), 84-85.

Membership of a political party, terms served in parliament or posts in local or central administration do not constitute forms of intragenerational mobility as such. They were included in the table all the same as factors tending to favour mobility, which furnish further information about the career of persons already engaged in social mobility.

In a conservative professional milieu such as the clergy, the lesser extent of intragenerational mobility is hardly surprising. Nevertheless we see that Orthodox priests were far more dynamic and adaptable, perhaps explained by the fact that in 1918 Transylvania united with a state that was overwhelmingly Orthodox.

The priests we have in mind here did not leave holy orders but chose to pursue careers which were not directly linked with the church. As has already been shown, most of them chose the teaching profession.

The first example to look at is that of Ioan Lupaş (1880-1967). In 1918 he was Orthodox parish priest and protopope in Sălişte, despite having studied well beyond his training at the seminary and teacher training college in Sibiu (1905-1908); he had attended courses at the Faculties of Letters and Philosophy in Budapest and Berlin and on 29th May 1905 received his doctoral degree from the Royal Hungarian University in Budapest.[41] He was deported to Sopron county in 1916 and then imprisoned for three months in Budapest in 1917 for political reasons, and forced to give up his teaching post at the Sibiu seminary and college, restricting himself to his priestly duties. He was a corresponding member of the Romanian Academy from 11th June 1914, and was elected a full member on 30th May 1916.[42] When Transylvania united with Romania, all academic and political paths were open to him once more. He became professor of modern Romanian history at the Faculty of Literature and Philosophy at the "Dacia Superioară" University in Cluj (1919-1946). Alongside Alexandru Lapedatu, he was founder and director of the Institute for National History in Cluj (1920-1945), and wrote some significant works of history. Having a particular interest in public life and politics, he was also a member of the Romanian National Party. In 1926, he followed the example of Octavian Goga and Vasile Goldiş and joined a party from the Old Kingdom, the People's Party of General Alexandru Averescu, feeling that as an Orthodox priest this was his natural political home. He much admired the radical national sentiments of the politician-poet Goga, and followed him into the National Agrarian Party (1932-1935) and then into the National Christian Party (1935-1938), becoming chairman of the local Sibiu party branch for the latter. He was elected to the lower house three times (1919-1920, 1922-1926, 1926-1927) and served as Minister for Health and Social Welfare (1926-1927) and as Minister for Religion and the Arts (1937-1938).[43]

---

[41] Sigmirean, *Istoria formării intelectualităţii*, 435, 713.
[42] Dorina N. Rusu, *Istoria Academiei Române. Repere cronologice* [A History of the Romanian Academy. Chronologies] (Bucureşti: Editura Academiei Române, 1992), 137, 141.
[43] *Politics and Political Parties in Roumania*, 457-458.

This distinguished academic and political career came to a halt under the Communist regime. Ioan Lupaş was arrested and imprisoned at Aiud (1948-1950). Once released, he was arrested once again on the night of 5th/6th May 1950 when so many Romanian public figures were rounded up. After another five years in prison at Sighet, his health was too poor for him to resume life as a researcher.[44]

The Ruling Council's policy on staffing the schools of Transylvania allowed other priests from the region to become secondary teachers in the new state school system, if they wished to take a temporary or definitive break from their church career. Not far behind this group in numerical terms were the priests who took up careers in public administration, which offered attractive salaries.

Nicodim Cristea (1889-1970) was an Orthodox chaplain in Cluj in 1918. After attending the seminary and teacher training college in Sibiu, he also took degrees from the Royal Academy of Law in Bratislava (1910-1912) and from the Faculty of Law and Political Science at the University in Budapest, where he received a doctorate in law on 19th June 1915.[45]

In the first years after the war, a priest, teacher, professor or lawyer did not always willingly renounce his first choice of work to take up an administrative career. These professional men also heeded the calls of the Ruling Council, which faced an acute lack of Romanian-speaking civil servants. Thus we find Nicodim Cristea leaving his parish in Cluj, where indeed he was only a chaplain, to become sub-prefect in the district of Hida, in Cojocna county.[46] He did not stay in post long, since in 1923 he was elected mayor of Zalău, and in 1926 the new prime minister Alexandru Averescu appointed him prefect of the county of Sălaj. We should also mention here that after a brief period in the People's Party, Nicodim Cristea joined the National Peasant Party. The fall of Averescu's government after just one year on 3rd June 1927 also meant the end of Nicodim Cristea's career as prefect. He then returned to Cluj, where he practised as a lawyer for 13 years. After Northern Transylvania was awarded to Hungary in 1940, Cristea, like many other voting members of the Alba Iulia National Assembly of 1918, became a refugee. He settled in Bucharest, where his status as an ordained priest and his knowledge of the law brought him a post as legal adviser to the Patriarch of Romania.[47]

Zenovie Pâclişanu (1886-1957) never strayed far from the altar in his search for a

---

[44] Claudiu Secaşiu, "Noaptea demnitarilor. Contribuţii privind distrugerea elitei politice Româneşti" [The Night of the Dignitaries. Towards a Study of the Destruction of the Romanian Political Elite], in *Anul 1948 – instituţionalizarea comunismului. Comunicări prezentate la Simpozionul de la Sighetu Marmaţiei (19-21 iunie 1998)* [1948 – The Institutionalisation of Communism. Papers Presented at the Sighetu Marmaţiei Symposium (19th-21st June 1998)], ed. Romulus Rusan (Bucureşti: Academia Civică, 1998), 908; Mircea Păcurariu, *Cărturari sibieni de altădată* [Sibiu Booksellers of Yesteryear] (Cluj-Napoca: Dacia, 2002), 370-376.

[45] Sigmirean, *Istoria formării intelectualităţii*, 518, 613; *Noi. Organul studenţimii române* 5 (Cluj, 1913): 66-68, 70.

[46] Today in the county of Sălaj.

[47] *Cultura Poporului* 111 (Cluj, 1925): 2; I. D. Petru, "Militanţi pentru libertatea şi unitatea poporului român: Dr. Nicodim Cristea (1889-1970)" [Activists for the Liberty and Unity of the Romanian People: Dr. Nicodim Cristea (1889-1970)], *Telegraful Român* 27-28 (1981): 1.

professionally and socially rewarding career; we may call him an example of career mobility by choice. After a glittering academic record studying theology in Blaj and Budapest, and a doctorate from the Vienna *Augustineum*,[48] he served for a while as priest in Blaj and then became a professor and first director of the central archiepiscopal library. Shortly thereafter his career took him to Bucharest for some time. The leaders of the Greek Catholic church had realised that although they now counted as one of the lesser religious groupings in Greater Romania, one way to compensate for this drawback was to be sure that they always had good men in various government posts. Zenovie Pâclişanu was inspector general for Catholic, Reformed and non-Christian denominations in the Ministry of Religion and Arts (1920-1923), director general in the same ministry (1923-1944) and a cultural adviser in the Ministry of Foreign Affairs (1944-1947). Alongside all of these posts, and despite moving from city to city, he also found time to make a name for himself as a church historian. From 5th June 1919 he was a corresponding member of the Romanian Academy.

When the Greek Catholic Metropolitan of Blaj appointed him vicar-general for Wallachia and Moldavia, a clandestine office, he drew the attention of the Communist authorities and secret police and was repeatedly arrested, sentenced, and tortured; he died in prison on 31st October 1957.[49]

When Transylvania was ceded from Hungary to Romania in 1918, this created significant opportunities for structural mobility for the relatively large and well-trained group of Romanian lawyers in the province. They were of all ages, some of them not even 30 years old and some over 70. Nevertheless, among the 190 lawyers belonging to the cohort under study here, the leading group were in their early middle age, born between 1880 and 1889. Although they had not been among the founding generation of the new wave of activism at the beginning of the century, they grew to political awareness in this neo-activist period and took on its tempo. We find their names among the organisers of the great political rallies for universal suffrage in 1911.[50]

Some of them had begun their studies, surely for financial reasons, at the Royal Academy of Law in Oradea or at the Lutheran law school in Sibiu. Most however graduated from the Faculty of Law and Political Science in Budapest or its equivalent in Cluj, which could award doctorates. Though some of this group took their doctorates in politi-

---

48 Theological Faculty of the Archdiocese of Blaj, Royal Hungarian University of Budapest. Faculty of Theology (1906-1910), University of Vienna. Faculty of Theology (1910-1911), "Augustineum" Vienna (1912-1914); cf. Sigmirean, *Istoria formării intelectualităţii*, 351, 698; Idem, *Preoţii Blajului*, 226; Szögi, *Studenţi români*, 111, 132.

49 Rusu, *Istoria Academiei Române*, 153; Claudiu Secaşiu, "Istoricul Zenovie Pâclişanu în închisorile comuniste (1949-1953, 1957)" [The Historian Zenovie Pâclişanu in Communist Prisons (1949-1953, 1957)], *Buletinul cercurilor ştiinţifice studenţeşti* 5 (Alba Iulia, 1999): 221-234; Iacob Mârza, "Etape şi momente din viaţa, activitatea şi opera istorică a lui Zenovie Pâclişanu" [Life, Work and Historical Writings of Zenovie Pâclişanu], in Zenovie Pâclişanu, *Relatio Rumenorum e terris coronae Sancti Stephani ad Reformationem saec[ulis] XVI et XVII*, ed. Andreea Mârza and Iacob Mârza (Sibiu: Techno Media, 2010), 10-20.

50 *Românul* 22 (1911): 1; 115 (1911): 1; 166 (1911): 4; *Tribuna* 190 (1911): 6; 228 (1911): 5.

cal science, the faculties did not necessarily prepare them for political careers as such: nevertheless they acquired here the skills which would serve them later in their administrative careers in the Romanian state.

Looked at through the lens of intergenerational mobility, the group of lawyers' shows very different features and leads to different conclusions from those found in the case of the Romanian clergy. Here we are no longer dealing with a predominantly inherited profession which would be a sign of social immobility. Of the 149 members of this group whose father's profession is known, shown in the table below, very few lawyers were themselves the sons of lawyers; instead their fathers were most commonly farmers.

At this point it is useful to recall the problems which the British sociologist Anthony Giddens identifies in the study of social mobility. Giddens points out that it may not always be justified to assume that movement from a blue-collar to a white-collar occupation necessarily means upward mobility, since well-qualified blue-collar workers may well be better off financially than the average white-collar worker.[51]

This is true even though mobility can be classed as upward or downward by applying various criteria such as profession, prestige and power.[52] However, when we seek to define social status within a hierarchy, we cannot afford to overlook income and wealth, which are not much discussed but fundamentally form the basis for power and wealth. Adapting Giddens' remarks to apply them to Transylvanian society at the turn of the twentieth century, we are faced with the problem of whether mobility from the status of farmer to that of lawyer can always be seen as upward mobility. Our analysis shows that the fathers of lawyers were predominantly farmers, for reasons which have already been discussed. Of the 35 persons in this sub-cohort, 11 are mentioned in the sources as "great landowners" or in similar terms.[53] Evidently their sons surpassed their fathers in terms of professional prestige and access to power, but they remained dependent on the family estates which they stood to inherit one day. Indeed at this time and place, ownership of more or less extensive tracts of farmland was characteristic for other social groups as well such as professors, doctors or officer, who may have had no evident connection with farming as a livelihood.

The great number of priests who encouraged their sons to become lawyers shows us that the age of hereditary clergy was drawing to a close. Likewise, we may talk of intergenerational mobility when the sons of priests became doctors, engineers or teachers.

Alongside such high-status fathers, the table also shows that there were some lawyers who were born to far more modest households headed by teachers, notaries or even in one instance a labourer, who nevertheless supported their sons through their costly legal studies. Here we should bear in mind that the father's profession as declared to a census-taker may perhaps conceal other sources of income which go unmentioned.

---

[51] Giddens, *Sociologie*, 295.

[52] Ferréol, ed., *Dicţionar de sociologie*, 119; Johnson, *Dicţionarul Blackwell de sociologie*, 219.

[53] Sigmirean, *Istoria formării intelectualităţii*, 378, 467, 471, 479, 640, 661.

We should also consider that various foundations, the churches, banks and other institutions awarded stipends so that deserving pupils could go on to tertiary education.

Father's profession	Farmer	Greek Catholic priest	Orthodox priest	Lawyer	Teacher	Judge	Notary	Professor	Civil servant	Tradesman	Doctor	Major	Businessman	Labourer	**Total**
	35	32	23	16	11	7	7	6	6	2	1	1	1	1	**149**
%	23.48	21.47	15.43	10.73	7.38	4.69	4.69	4.02	4.02	1.34	0.67	0.67	0.67	0.67	**100**

Table 3

Given that the law is a liberal profession, lawyers had plentiful opportunity for horizontal mobility over the course of their career. Here there is to say the least an element of contrast with, for instance, the Orthodox clergy, where of a total 173 persons only 12 (or 6.93%) showed signs of intragenerational mobility; almost one third of lawyers followed such a trajectory, at 64 of 190 individuals or 33. 68%.

Such mobility was widely divergent and included career highs and lows in the inter-war decades, so that to have at least a modest starting point we will begin at the lowest level, with instances where lawyers gave up their profession to become notaries public.

Such a wish most likely reflects the wish to attain a certain level of comfort and security away from the hurly-burly of the courtroom. When Transylvania switched statehood in 1918-1920, this opened up a great many positions as notaries public to Romanian lawyers, who had only had limited chances before the war. In search of a viable client base, lawyers who became notaries did not necessarily always move home to live in a larger town, although we have identified 22 cases so far in which they did just that. Sometimes they chose retirement, as did Ioan Suciu, who had worked as a lawyer and been involved in politics for half a century in Arad and in Cluj and from 1930 chose the peace and quiet of a notary's office in Chişineu Criş.[54]

In terms of socio-professional mobility, the most important initiative that affected Romanian lawyers in Transylvania was the campaign to involve them in the judicial system in the province, from 1919 onwards. Official records from 1918 show that there were 1750 magistrates and 1383 clerks of court in the judiciary. The Hungarian incumbents no

[54] *1 Decembrie 1918. Mărturii ale participanţilor*, vol. I, 350.

longer exercised their offices once they refused to swear loyalty to the Romanian state, as required by an order in council of 19th February 1919 signed by Aurel Lazăr, the provincial government's Minister of Justice. Some magistrates from the Old Kingdom offered to help, motivated by national sentiment, but this fell on deaf ears in the main Ministry of Justice in Bucharest.[55] In such a situation, the only available pool of trained talent were the Romanian lawyers, who generally also held diplomas qualifying them to serve as magistrates.

We should not imagine however that there was a throng of Romanian lawyers who were impatient to move one rung up the career ladder by taking up the posts left vacant by Hungarian magistrates unwilling to take the oath and use Romanian as the language of justice. In most cases, the magistrates' salaries could hardly compete with the income of a law practise. At least in the cases of the courts and tribunals subordinate to the appeal courts in Cluj and Târgu-Mureş, nominations were made without consulting those concerned. As a result, many lawyers did not accept the positions and the Ministry of Justice had to fall back on other candidates.[56]

Some of those who nevertheless did change career paths were nominated to important posts in the judiciary right from the start. Such was the case of Andrei Ille, a lawyer in Tinca in the county of Bihor. On 29th January 1920 he was appointed section president of the court of appeal in Oradea and a decade later was made presiding judge over the whole court.[57] Other notable careers were launched by the same recruitment policy. Simeon Cheţian, a simple country lawyer in Agnita, became president of the tribunal in Dumbrăveni in March 1919, though only for a few months. In October 1919 he was president of the tribunal in Oradea, and in October 1924 counsel at the court of appeal in the same city. On 12th July 1933 he was appointed counsel to the supreme court, and his case was by no means unique.[58]

Just as with Table 2, so too in this case the exercise of roles in the local or central administration and terms served in parliament do not directly conform to the profile of mobility. These were temporary posts, after which the holder would then return to the practise of law. Nevertheless they have been tabulated and quantified here since they are decisive elements of the individual biographies, and they complete the general professional framework for the phenomenon of mobility. There were also cases however where posts in national politics became permanent, radically changing the status of those who held them. Iuliu Maniu for instance, the chairman of the Romanian National Party and the National Peasant Party and prime minister, was never out of parliament and never returned to Blaj where he had been a lawyer for the Greek Catholic Archdiocese. He became a professional politician. From 1919 Caius Brediceanu was under-secretary of state, mini-

---

[55] *Gazeta Oficială* 11 (1919): 111-114.
[56] Ioan P. Papp, "Instaurarea justiţiei româneşti în Ardeal" [The Establishment of the Romanian Judiciary in Transylvania], *Transilvania* 76 (1945): 7, 10-11.
[57] *1 Decembrie 1918. Mărturii ale participanţilor*, vol. II, 150-151.
[58] Ibid., 61-62.

ster, and Romania's ambassador in capitals on many continents, in short a career politician and diplomat.[59] His early days as a lawyer practising in Lugoj remained a mere memory.

Lawyers	Intragenerational mobility	Posts in local administration	Posts in central administration	Parliament, one term	Parliament, multiple terms	Member of a single political party	Member of multiple political parties in succession	**Total**
Absolute numbers	64	66	16	33	45	60	19	**190**
%	33.68	34.73	8.42	17.36	23.68	31.57	10	**100**

Table 4

The establishment of Romanian tertiary education in Transylvania opened up further paths to promotion for the Romanian lawyers in the small towns. Perhaps the most representative example is that of Romul Boilă. A lawyer in Târnăveni in 1906, by 1st October 1919 he was already professor of constitutional law at the Faculty of Law in Cluj. He was dean of the faculty three times (1923-1924, 1929-1930, 1932-1935).[60] Alongside him we may also mention Victor Onişor and Petru Poruţiu, both formerly lawyers in Bistriţa, Valer Moldovan, a lawyer in Turda and Cassiu Maniu, a lawyer in Şimleu Silvaniei, merely from the cohort under study. All these became professors either of law or of political science at the "Dacia Superioară" University in Cluj.

The purpose of an analysis of social mobility is to determine the degree of modernisation in a society, as a measure of the equality of opportunity that an individual or group enjoys if they wish to move from a lower socio-professional status to a higher one. This being so, we must draw some conclusions from the present study. As has become evident in writing up this article, the study is merely a beginning and is by nature partial and selective. Nevertheless it offers a fairly comprehensive image of how social mobility manifested in its various forms. If we look at farmers and craftsmen from the perspective of the parental generation, the imagine is one of immobility. If we shift our perspective to the generation of the sons, we are surprised by the extent of intergenerational mobility

[59] Lucian Predescu, *Enciclopedia Cugetarea* [The Encyclopedia of Cogitation] (Bucureşti: Cugetarea - Georgescu Delafras, [1940]), 129; *1 Decembrie 1918. Mărturii ale participanţilor*, vol. I, 65-67.

[60] *Politics and Political Parties in Roumania*, 411; Traian Bosoancă, "Din viaţa şi activitatea lui dr. Romul Boilă" [Life and Work of Dr. Romul Boilă], *Acta Musei Porolissensis* 23, 1 (2000): 243-256; 25 (2003): 621-634.

which seems to be an organic process, with no evident connection to political developments. More important in its scale and its effects on Transylvanian society and its ethnic groups is the structural mobility, implicitly an intragenerational phenomenon, produced by the geo-political shifts of the post-war years. For some this meant upward mobility, but for others it meant dislocation. Whole groups of the social elite heeded the call to abandon their old professions and occupations, either temporarily or definitively, to staff the institutions of a province that had set out in a new direction in the history of states.

THE GERMAN SECRET SERVICES IN ROMANIA: "KRIEGSORGANISATION RUMÄNIEN"/ "ABWEHRSTELLE RUMÄNIEN" AND INTELLIGENCE COOPERATION BETWEEN ROMANIA AND GERMANY OVER THE DEFENCE OF THE ROMANIAN OIL-FIELDS, 1939-1944

OTTMAR TRAŞCĂ, DENNIS DELETANT

In the field of historical research in Germany, Romania and other states, an examination of the activity of intelligence services has been a theme of constant interest. Despite this fact, literature regarding the presence of the German intelligence services in Romania, as well as on the collaboration in the realm of intelligence in the period 1939-1945, is thin and weak from the factual and interpretative point of view. Although in German historiography the military intelligence service – OKW/Amt Ausland Abwehr – and, in particular, its head in the years 1935-1944, Admiral Wilhelm Canaris, have been the subject of special attention from historians, yet study of the intelligence structures – the residences – of the Abwehr established on the territory of the Third Reich or in neutral, allied or occupied states, the so-called "Abwehrstelle" or "Kriegsorganisation" seems to have been overlooked to date by historians. As regards the operations of "Kriegsorganisation Rumänien" and "Abwehrstelle Rumänien," and the intelligence collaboration between Romania and the Third Reich, the specialist literature offers some spasmodic information for the years 1939-1940, more precisely that regarding the cooperation between the Abwehr residence in Romania – "Kriegsorganisation Rumänien" and the Army Secret Service ("Serviciul Secret al Armatei Române"), headed at the time by Mihail Moruzov, with a view to protecting the oil-fields and the export of Romanian oil products for the German war machine from the sabotage actions planned by the British and French secret services.[1] On the other hand, German studies on the subject provide very little information on the context in which the "Kriegsorganisation Rumänien" – the name of the Abwehr residencies in neutral or allied states – became "Abwehrstelle Rumänien" – the designation of the Abwehr residences in the states controlled or occupied by the Reich – and the cooperation between this German intelligence service in the period October 1940 - August 1944 with the Romanian Intelligence Service ("Serviciul Special de Informaţii Român"), led by Eugen Cristescu.[2]

---

[1] See in this regard Walter Hagen (Wilhelm Höttl), *Die geheime Front. Organisation, Personen und Aktionen des deutschen Geheimdienstes* (Linz, Wien: Nibelungen Verlag, 1950), 284-285; Paul Leverkuehn, *Der geheime Nachrichtendienste der deutschen Wehrmacht im Kriege* (Frankfurt am Main: Bernard & Graefe Verlag für Wehrwesen, 1957), 106-111; Helmuth Spaeter, *Die Brandenburger – eine deutsche Kommandotruppe – zbV 800* (München: Verlagsagentur Walther Angerer, 1978), 93-122; Oskar Reile, *Der Deutsche Geheimdienst im Zweiten Weltkrieg. Ostfront. Die Abwehr im Kampf mit den Geheimdiensten im Osten* (Lizenzausgabe, Augsburg: Weltbild Verlag, 1990), 319-322; Werner Brockdorff, *Geheimkommandos des Zweiten Weltkrieges* (Lizenzausgabe, Augsburg: Weltbild Verlag, 1993), 81-93.

[2] Serviciul Secret al Armatei Române became the Serviciul Special de Informaţii Român (SSI) on 15 November 1940.

The activity of the German secret services in Romania during the Second World War has been covered both by Romanian historians both during the period of Communist rule as well as after its collapse in December 1989. Unfortunately, the works which appeared before 1989 suffered the influence of a double censorship exerted by the Communist regime, that of content and interpretation. In fact, the few works published before 1989 and in the years immediately following the events of 1989 were authored by former *Securitate* officers, Horia Brestoiu who benefited from uninhibited access at the time to papers from the Romanian intelligence services during the Second World War. The collapse of the Communist regime in December 1989, followed by the gradual introduction into the public domain of documents hitherto held in the fettered archives of the *Securitate*, provided the foundations for academic investigation of some of the subjects which had been superficially treated in the years 1945-1989, among them not surprisingly research into the presence and activity of the German intelligence services in Romania during World War II. Thus monographs, articles, and document collections were published after 1989 analysing certain aspects of Romanian-German intelligence cooperation during the Second World War, including that between 1937 and 1944 of the "Serviciul Secret al Armatei Române"/ "Serviciul Special de Informaţii" (SSI), headed successively by Mihail Moruzov and Eugen Cristescu, and the OKW/Amt Ausland/Abwehr, a cooperation administered by the "Kriegsorganisation Rumänien" (1939-1940) and the "Abwehrstelle Rumänien" (1940-1944). In spite of the existence of what appears at first sight to be a significant amount of specialist literature – and here we have in mind outstanding studies on the heads of the SSI, Mihail Moruzov (1924-1940) and Eugen Cristescu (1940-1944) – studies by such scholars as Cristian Troncotă, Florin Pintilie and Alin Spânu,[3] the cooperation between the SSI and "Kriegsorganisation Rumänien"/ "Abwehrstelle Rumänien" receives summary treatment. This is due primarily to the absence in these works of archival sources and literature in German, both of which are indispensable to the study of this subject. Moreover, Romanian-German intelligence cooperation during the Second World War relies in Romanian historiography principally the memoirs of Eugen Cristescu with regard to the structure and activity of the SSI, recorded during his imprisonment in Communist jails (1946-1950), and less on archival sources, thereby placing a question mark on the veracity of certain information and interpretations. In this regard we feel it suffices to adduce in support of our contention the fact that the majority of Romanian historians who have tackled the subject of the German intelligence services in Romania between

---

[3] Cristian Troncotă, *Eugen Cristescu. Asul serviciilor secrete româneşti* [Eugen Cristescu. The Ace of the Romanian Secret Services] (Bucureşti: Roza Vânturilor, 1994); Idem, *Mihail Moruzov şi Serviciul Secret de Informaţii al Armatei Române* [Mihail Moruzov and the Secret Service of the Romanian Army] (Bucureşti: Editura Evenimentului Românesc, 1997); Florin Pintilie, *Serviciul Special de Informaţii din România (1939-1947)* [Special Intelligence Service from Romania (1939-1947)], vol. I-II (Bucureşti: Editura Academiei Naţionale de Informaţii, 2003); Alin Spânu, *Istoria serviciilor de informaţii/contrainformaţii româneşti în perioada 1919-1945* [The History of the Romanian Secret Services between 1919-1945] (Iaşi: Casa Editorială Demiurg, 2010).

1939-1944 use as a reference point Eugen Cristescu's claim that during the war no less than eleven German intelligence services were operating legally or secretly in Romania.[4] In fact, during the war only the two rival German services, OKW/Amt Ausland Abwehr, represented by "Kriegsorganisation Rumänien" / "Abwehrstelle Rumänien," and "Amt VI (SD-Ausland)" of the RSHA (Reichssicherheitshauptamt – The Reich Central Security Office) were active in Romania,[5] all the other intelligence bodies mentioned by Cristescu being in fact constituent parts of the two services mentioned above. Consequently, despite the existence at first sight of a substantial number of studies which have tackled more or less the cooperation between the Romanian and German intelligence services, we can state that at the moment there is nothing in Romanian and German historiography on the subject which is academically rigorous. This present study proposes to use archival evidence from Romania, Germany and Austria, as well as relevant secondary literature, to describe the creation and work of the Abwehr residence in Romania between 1939 and 1944, as well as the Romanian and German measures taken to protect the Ploieşti oilfields against the sabotage efforts of the British and French secret services.

Although Romania and Germany were for much of the interwar period in opposite political camps, the policy of gradual *rapprochement* towards the Third Reich practised by the Romanian government after the dismissal of Nicolae Titulescu as Foreign Minister[6] was followed by a similar development in relations between the intelligence services of the two states. Romanian and German archival documents disclose that fact that the year 1937 represented the beginning of intelligence contact between the Army Secret Service under Mihail Moruzov and the German Military Intelligence – OKW/Amt Ausland Abwehr, directed since 1935 by Admiral Wilhelm Canaris. Thus, on the orders of Moruzov, Major Constantin Gheorghe Ionescu-Micandru travelled to Berlin in the period 12-24 February 1937 in order to establish an initial unofficial contact with the Abwehr. Later, in June 1939, after a break of more than two years, cooperation between the two secret services was resumed and extended, the principal objective in the period before the outbreak of the war being an exchange of information regarding the military po-

[4] Troncotă, *Eugen Cristescu*, 90, 210-214.

[5] For the structure, personnel and attributions of Amt VI (SD-Ausland) of the RSHA see especially Institut für Zeitgeschichte München, ZS (Zeugenschriftum) 291-Walter Schellenberg ; ZS 429-Wilhelm Höttl; ZS 1579-Wilhelm Waneck; Michael Wildt, *Generation des Unbedingten. Das Führerkorps des Reichssicherheitshauptamtes* (Hamburg: Hamburger Edition, 2003), 391ff; Reinhard R. Doerries, *Hitler's Last Chief of Foreign Intelligence. Allied Interrogations of Walter Schellenberg* (New York, London: Routledge, 2003), passim; Idem, *Hitler's Intelligence Chief Walter Schellenberg. The Man Who Kept Germany's Secrets* (New York: Enigma Books, 2009), 41ff.

[6] For the development of relations between Romania and Germany in the period following Titulescu's dismissal see Andreas Hillgruber, *Hitler, Regele Carol şi Mareşalul Antonescu. Relaţiile germano-române. 1938-1944* [Hitler, King Charles and Marshall Antonescu. Romanian-German Relations. 1938-1944] (Bucureşti: Humanitas, 1994), 43ff; Ioan Chiper, *România şi Germania nazistă. Relaţiile româno-germane între comandamente politice şi interese economice (ianuarie 1933-martie 1938)* [Romania and Nazi Germany. The Romanian-German Relations between Political Rules and Economic Interests. January 1933-March 1938] (Bucureşti: Elion, 2000), 201ff; Rebecca Haynes, *Politica României faţă de Germania între 1936 şi 1940* [Romanian Policy towards Germany between 1936-1940] (Iaşi: Polirom, 2003), 25ff.

tential of the Soviet Union and the activity of the Comintern and of the Soviet secret services in Romania, the Balkans and Germany.[7] Romanian-German intelligence cooperation intensified after the outbreak of war with the two services, alongside the exchange of information regarding the Soviet Union, being obliged to adopt and apply measures for the protection of the Ploieşti oil-fields and the delivery of oil to Germany.

As was to be expected, the outbreak of hostilities on 1 September 1939 with the German attack on Poland highlighted the diametrically-opposed interests of the belligerant camps regarding Romanian oil, the country's most important export becoming the object of a veritable economic war between Germany and the Western Allies. In order to deprive the Reich of the fuel necessary for the Wehrmacht, the governments of Britain and France decided in the early months of the war the implementation of a strategy for:

1. The immediate acquisition of the entire stockpile of oil in Romania and the signing of binding contracts for the following six months' production;
2. The blocking of land and maritime routes to Germany;
3. The destruction of the Ploieşti oil-fields.

The strategy of the western allies was favoured by the fact that Britain in particular controlled important, well-established oil companies in Romania which held a dominant position in the Romanian oil industry. Using these companies Britain and France bought oil on the open market by paying a higher price. Furthermore, these Western-controlled companies concluded contracts with their parent companies in London under which the surplus amounts of their own production would be exported to Britain and France. The economic offensive launched by the Western Allies in Romania in the period September-October 1939 had a double impact, leading to an increase in prices and, through the growth in the amount purchased, to a decrease in oil exports to Germany.[8]

---

[7] For contacts between the two services in the period 1937-1939 see Arhiva Consiliului Naţional pentru Studierea Arhivelor Securităţii [Archive of the National Council for Study of Security Archives] (henceforth abbreviated CNSAS), Fund *Informativ*, no. 209906 (Constantin Gheorghe Ionescu-Micandru), f. 93-101. The memoir signed by Constantin Gheorghe Ionescu-Micandru dated 08.06.1946 referring to his activity at the head of Section III "G" of the SSI; Arhivele Naţionale ale României. Direcţia Arhivele Naţionale Istorice Centrale [Central Historical National Archives Direction of the National Archives of Romania], Fund *Preşedinţia Consiliului de Miniştri-Serviciul Special de Informaţii* (henceforth abbreviated ANIC, Fund *PCM-SSI*), no. 24/1937, f. 26-34. Report of Major Constantin Gheorghe Ionescu-Micandru on his journey to Berlin in the period 12-24.02.1937; f. 52-71. Report of Major Constantin Gheorghe Ionescu-Micandru on his mission to Berlin (26.10-03.11.1939); f. 72-92. Cooperation with the Abwehr. The discussions in Bucharest with Major Erich Pruck, head of the Eastern Front Agency of the Abwehr 22-25.11.1939; see also Troncotă, *Mihail Moruzov*, 75ff; doc. no. 22: 276-284; doc. no. 32: 321-327; doc. no. 47: 343-349; doc. no. 48: 353-368; doc. no. 49: 369-272; doc. no. 52: 374-379; Pintilie, *Serviciul Special de Informaţii*, vol. I, 214ff; Lionede Ochea, *Serviciul Special de Informaţii al României în perioada celui de-al doilea război mondial. Studii şi articole* [Special Intelligence Service of Romania during the Second World War. Studies and Articles] (Alexandria: Tipoalex, 2010), 85ff.

[8] See Maurice Pearton, *Oil and the Romanian State* (Oxford: Clarendon Press, 1971), 244-251; Philippe Marguerat, *Le III-e Reich et le pétrole roumain, 1938-1940. Contribution à l'étude de la pénétration économique allemande dans les Balkans à la veille et au début de la Seconde Guerre mondiale* (Genève, Leiden: Sijthoff, 1977), 169-175; David Britton Funderburk, *Politica Marii Britanii faţă de România (1938-1940)* [Great Britain Policy towards Romania (1938-1940)] (Bucureşti: Editura Ştiinţifică şi Enciclopedică, 1983), 156-157;

Faced with an Anglo-French economic strategy which threatened its supplies of Romanian oil, Germany reacted immediately by applying diplomatic pressure on Bucharest to safeguard oil deliveries to the Reich. In this economic conflict the Reich also achieved success, concluding economic agreements with Romania on 29 September and 21 December 1939. Under the agreement initialled on 29 September Romania undertook to export cereals and oil to the Reich in quantities, as great as its transport capabilities would allow, receiving in turn war material of Polish origin,[9] while the Romanian-German economic agreement of 21 December 1939 stipulated an increase in the exchange rate in favour of the Reichsmark and the "political" undertaking of the Romanian government to guarantee under any conditions the export of 130,000 tons of oil to the Reich.[10]

Parallel to the economic offensive, the British and French governments planned the destruction of the oil-fields. To this end, on 11-12 September 1939 the French ambassador Adrien Thierry and the British minister Reginald Hoare agreed in principle with Prime Minister Armand Călinescu to destroy the fields in the event of German or Soviet aggression against Romania, with the sabotage plans to be drawn up as quickly as possible. The two diplomats offered the help of British and French specialists, and a guarantee of 200,000 pounds sterling for the launch of preliminary operations. The Romanian premier rejected, however, the Allies' offer and underlined the fact that the destruction of the oil-fields would be planned and carried out exclusively by Romanian experts.[11]

The Romanians' refusal to accept the Anglo-French plans for destruction of the oil-fields was driven by what had happened in this context after the First World War and the complex international situation at the time. Although in 1916 Romania had applied a sabotage plan of its oil-fields as demanded by the Allies, involving the destructions of 1677 wells, 26 refineries, storage tanks, factories, and 827,000 tons of oil, after the war the Allies procrastinated for many years under different pretexts in honouring their undertaking to give compensation for the damage caused.[12] This led Bucharest to adopt a much more reserved attitude in 1939-1940 towards proposals by the Western Allies to destroy the oil-fields. Furthermore, the Romanian government was forced to take account of the

---

Gheorghe Buzatu, *O istorie a petrolului românesc* [A History of the Romanian Oil] (Iaşi: Casa Editorială Demiurg, 2009²), 353-356.

[9] Politisches Archiv des Auswärtigen Amtes Berlin (henceforth abbreviated PAAAB), R 29696, *Büro des Staatssekretärs, Rumänien*, Band 1, 1. November 1938-31. Januar 1940, E 82818-82819. Telegramm Nr. 673 der deutschen Gesandtschaft in Bukarest vom 29.09.1939, gez. Carl Clodius, Wilhelm Fabricius; *Akten zur deutschen auswärtigen Politik* (henceforth abbreviated *ADAP*), Serie D. *1937-1945*, Band VIII. *Die Kriegsjahre*, Erster Band., *4. September 1939 bis 18 März 1940* (Baden-Baden, Frankfurt am Main, 1961), doc. no. 166: 134-135.

[10] PAAAB, R 29696, E 82968-82969. Telegramm Nr. 1036 der deutschen Gesandtschaft in Bukarest vom 19.12.1939, gez. Carl Clodius, Wilhelm Fabricius; *ADAP*, Serie D, Band VIII, doc. no. 678: 726-727.

[11] Arhivele Ministerului Afacerilor Externe [Archives of the Ministry of Foreign Affairs] (henceforth abbreviated AMAE), Fund 71/*Anglia*, vol. 40, f. 369-374. Note on the discussions between Prime Minister Armand Călinescu with the French ambassador, Adrien Thierry, and the Minister Plenipotentiary of Britain in Bucharest, Reginald Hoare, on 11-12.09.1939; Buzatu, *O istorie a petrolului românesc*, 359-360.

[12] See Buzatu, *O istorie a petrolului românesc*, 364-366.

international situation arising from the conclusion of the Nazi-Soviet Pact and the outbreak of the Second World War as Romanian diplomats attempted to avoid involvement at any cost in actions of a hostile nature against the Third Reich.

Even if the Romanian authorities carried out in due time the military and technical preparations for the destruction of the oil-fields in the event of German or Soviet aggression,[13] they gradually abandoned plans to sabotage the oil-wells. For the Romanian government such an extreme measure represented the ultimate rationale, one to be applied only if Germany (with or without the support of Hungary) or the Soviet Union unleashed military operations against Romania and all of the country's means of armed resistance were exhausted. On the other hand, for the Western Allies, the destruction of the oil-fields represented one element in an ambitious plan to block the supply of oil and raw materials from South-Eastern Europe to Germany. In order to interrupt the supply of oil to Germany, the British and French intelligence services drew up several plans of systematic sabotage of the oil-fields and of the transport links to Germany in order to avoid a repetition of the situation in 1917 when the German authorities were able to restore to a large degree oil production interrupted by the destruction in 1916.

Therefore, in the second half of September 1939, the French engineer Léon Wenger, the former director of the "Petrofina" oil company, was sent to Bucharest with instructions to study the possibility of destroying the oil-wells, refineries, and storage tanks, and to obtain the agreement of the Romanian authorities in this regard. The plan drawn up by Wenger on 1 October 1939 had two variants:

> 1. "A plan of rapid destruction" which entailed the destruction in 24 hours of all the refineries, pumping stations, reserve stocks (approximately 80% of production capacity) and possibly of some deposits, which would have led to the halting of oil production for a period of at least six months;
> 2. "A methodical programme," which required between 10 and 30 days and would have affected about 90% of production capacity and which would have ensured at the same time the destruction of the means of transport.[14]

The need to destroy the oil-fields and to block means of transport of oil to the Reich, especially those on the Danube, was underlined by ambassador Adrien Thierry in a report addressed to the Quai d'Orsay on 28 September 1939.

> "In my opinion," wrote the French diplomat, "we have a decisive interest in building without delay a dam across the Danube so that the river traffic between Romania and Germany is completely interrupted. It seems that after a period of flux which is due to

---

[13] Grigore Gafencu, *Preliminarii la războiul din răsărit* [Preliminaries to the Eastern War] (Bucureşti: Globus, 1996), 281.

[14] See Léon Wenger, "Rapport sur la Destruction de l'Industrie Pétrolière" (CNSAS, Fund *Penal* 10644, vol. 12, f. 263-268); also Auswärtiges Amt 1939/1941 No. 6, *The Secret Documents of the French General Staff* (Berlin: Deutscher Verlag, 1941), doc. no. 9: 36-38; *Acestea erau garanţiile anglo-franceze. Planurile de distrugeri ale aliaţilor în regiunea petroliferă română şi pe Dunăre* [These were Anglo-French Guarantees. Plans of Allied Destruction in Romanian Oil Region and on the Danube] (Bucureşti: Institutul Grafic "Arta," 1940), doc. no. 30: 5-7; Léon Wenger, *55 ans de pétrole 1904-1959. Souvenirs de Léon Wenger* (Paris: Fabre, 1968), 195-196; Buzatu, *O istorie a petrolului românesc*, 367-368.

changes brought about by the war, traffic is about to become more intense than ever. I am informed that the Germans, in particular, intend to send a part of their Rhine fleet up the Danube in order to make good the shortage of vessels which is evident at present in the Romanian sector of the Danube. [...] There is no doubt that interruption of navigation on the Danube would be an advantage for us at least equal to the destruction of the sources of oil, since it would paralyse at the same time all the transports of oil and cereals. These transports represent over 80% of the total Romanian exports to the Reich. The operation could be carried out in a fairly simple manner and I am in a position to have all the necessary means for its execution."[15]

The plans made by the British and French intelligence services for destroying the oil-fields and for blocking the Danube did not remain a secret from Berlin. This led OKW/Amt Ausland Abwehr to adopt measures to thwart the Allies' intentions. These measures entailed in essence the establishment in Romania in August 1939 of an Abwehr residence designated "Kriegsorganisation Rumänien" and the deepening of cooperation with the Secret Service led by Moruzov with a view to setting up a Romanian-German intelligence body designed to protect Romanian oil production and combat any attempts at sabotage.

At the outbreak of the Second World War OKW/Amt Ausland Abwehr headed by Vice-Admiral Wilhelm Canaris had the following structure at its core:

1. Abteilung Z (Personal und Finanzverwaltung) – the central department under Major-General Hans Oster, charged with administration and personnel;

2. Abteilung Ausland – the foreign department commanded by Commander Leopold Bürkner, whose tasks included monitoring of the foreign press, relations with the armies of other states, colonial matters, the organization of the military attachés in conjunction with the Foreign Ministry;

3. Abteilung Abwehr I (Geheimer Meldedienst) – headed by Colonel Hans Piekenbrock and tasked with the gathering of military intelligence abroad;

4. Abteilung Abwehr II (Sabotage und Sonderaufgaben) – under the command of Colonel Erwin von Lahousen, responsible for planning and carrying out special operations;

5. Abteilung Abwehr III (Spionageabwehr und Gegenspionage) – led by Colonel Franz Eccard von Bentivegni, charged with counter-intelligence and combating the activity of enemy intelligence bodies.[16]

---

[15] *Acestea erau garanțiile anglo-franceze*, doc. no. 31: 9.

[16] See Bundesarchiv-Militärarchiv Freiburg im Breisgau (henceforth abbreviated BMF), MSG (Militärische Sammlung)/13454. Bericht des Generalmajors Erwin von Lahousen "Geheimorganisation Canaris." Organisation des Amtes Ausland/Abwehr (1938/1939-1943); Der Bundesbeauftragte für die Unterlagen des Staatssicherheitsdienstes der ehemaligen Deutschen Demokratischen Republik Berlin (henceforth abbreviated BStU), MfS HA IX/11 FW 470 Akte 1, fol. 5. Struktur des OKW-Spionage und Sabotageamtes "Abwehr/Ausland" 1943; *Das Amt Ausland-Abwehr im Oberkommando der Wehrmacht. Eine Dokumentation* [Materialien aus dem Bundesarchiv, Heft 16], bearbeitet von Norbert Müller unter Mitwirkung von Helma Kaden, Gerlinde Grahn, Brün Meyer, Tilman Koops (Koblenz: Bundesarchiv, 2007), 480. Anlage 2: Aufbau und Gliederung des Amtes Ausland/Abwehr im OKW (Stand: 30.09.1938); 482-497. Anlage 4: Stellenbesetzung des Amtes Ausland/Abwehr im OKW (Stand: März/August 1943).

Apart from these departments OKW/Amt Ausland Abwehr also comprised the Abwehr residences called "Abwehrstelle" (Ast) or "Kriegsorganisation" (KO). At the beginning of the Second World War the Abwehrstelle residences carried out their work exclusively on the territory of the Reich, each territorial district (Wehrkreis) having an Abwehrstelle. Later, with the extension of hostilities both in the West and in the East, new Abwehrstelle were created in the occupied territories in the years 1939-1941, in Poland, Belgium, France, Denmark, Norway, Yugoslavia, Greece and the Soviet.[17] As regards the Abwehr residences of the "Kriegsorganisation" (KO), these operated under diplomatic cover within the consulates, legations or embassies in neutral states or those allied with the Third Reich. In September 1939, there were "Kriegsorganisation" residences in Argentina, Denmark, Switzerland, Estonia, Finland, Greece, Italy, Yugoslavia, Latvia, Lithuania, Holland, Portugal, Romania, Sweden and Turkey. In the years 1940-1941, following the German occupation of some of the states mentioned above, the "Kriegsorganisation" residences in the occupied countries were replaced by "Abwehrstelle," but at the same time new "Kriegsorganisation" residences were created in Afghanistan, Iran, China and Hungary.[18] From the organizational point of view, the "Abwehrstelle" and "Kriegsorganisation" residences had a structure similar to that of the headquarters in Berlin, being led by officers appointed by the central command of OKW/Amt Ausland Abwehr. As regards the chain of command and the attributes of the two types of Abwehr residences there were certain differences since the "Abwehrstelle" were subordinated to Abwehr III (Gegenspionage, Spionageabwehr)-counter-espionage, while the "Kriegsorganisation" – which operated in neutral states or those allied with Germany – were subordinated to Abwehr I (Geheimer Meldedienst)-intelligence, the priority of these residences being the acquisition of military intelligence. In the case of "Kriegsorganisation," in the absence of a head named by the central command of the Abwehr, direction was provided by the German military attaché accredited to the respective state. Moreover, the head of the "Kriegsorganisation" had a dual subordination in relation to his superiors, being subordinated militarily to the OKW/Amt Ausland Abwehr, while as an officer under diplomatic

---

[17] Thus at the height of the Third Reich în 1942 the following Abwehrstelle existed: Königsberg (Wehrkreis I), Stettin (Wehrkreis II), Berlin (Wehrkreis III), Dresden (Wehrkreis IV), Stuttgart (Wehrkreis V), Münster (Wehrkreis VI), München (Wehrkreis VII), Breslau (Wehrkreis VIII), Kassel (Wehrkreis IX), Hamburg (Wehrkreis X), Hannover (Wehrkreis XI), Wiesbaden (Wehrkreis XII), Nürnberg (Wehrkreis XIII), Wien (Wehrkreis XVII), Salzburg (Wehrkreis XVIII), Danzig (Wehrkreis XX), Posen (Wehrkreis XXI), Kiel, Wilhelmshaven, Krakau, Ostland, Ukraine, Kopenhagen, Oslo, Den Haag, Brüssel, Paris, St. Germain, Angers, Bordeaux, Dijon, Bukarest, Athen, Saloniki, Belgrad, Prag. BMF, RW 5 – OKW/Amt Ausland/Abwehr – /689, fol. 140-142. Amt Ausland/Abwehr Z Nr. 220/2.42 geh. vom 05.02.1942 betreffend Maßnahmen zur Personalersparnis im OKW den ihm nachgeordneten Dienststellen (Abwehrstellen), gez. Generalmajor Hans Oster.

[18] BMF, MSG (Militärische Sammlung)/13454. Bericht des Generalmajors Erwin von Lahousen "Geheimorganisation Canaris." Organisation des Amtes Ausland/Abwehr (1938/1939-1943); PAAAB, R 101832, *Abwehr allgemeines*, Band 1, *31. Dezember 1940-31. Dezember 1942*, E 264246-264249. Amt Ausland/ Abwehr Nr. 3308/41 g.K. I H West vom 18.09.1941 betreffend Aufstellung der bei deutschen Missionen im Ausland eingebauten Abwehr – bzw. KO – Beauftragten und ihrer eingebauten Hilfskräfte, gez. Oberst Hans Piekenbrock.

cover he answered to the head of the German diplomatic mission.[19]

Since at the beginning of the Second World War Romania was a neutral state, the Abwehr residence in the country had until October 1940 the title “Kriegsorganisation Rumänien.” Although archival sources do not indicate the exact date of the setting-up of the residency, we believe that “Kriegsorganisation Rumänien” (KOR) began its work shortly after the signing of the Molotov-Ribbentrop Pact and before the outbreak of war, at a time when the opening of hostilities was predictable. The first documentary mention of the existence the Abwehr residence in Romania is offered by a telegram sent to the higher authorities in Berlin on 30 August 1939 referring to the military moves made by the Soviet Union on the frontier with Romania and Poland. The telegram is signed “K.O.R.” and countersigned by the German minister Wilhelm Fabricius.[20] The tasks and attributions of the “Kriegsorganisation” and of the residency head were laid down in “Richtlinien für Kriegsorganisationsleiter” (K.O.-Leiter) [Directives for the leaders of the Kriegsorganisation], drawn up by the OKW/Amt Ausland Abwehr on 31 august 1938. The principal task of the head of the “Kriegsorganisation” was the procurement of military intelligence through the residence, which included officers with diplomatic cover and those Abwehr agents working in the respective country (the so-called “Vertrauens-Leute,” abbreviated to “V-Leute”). The residence also had the role of recruiting new agents and of running the existing agents according to the orders and instructions received from the Centre, as well as the transmission to Berlin of the information received from the above. The “Kriegsorganisation” residence was formally forbidden to gather intelligence against the host country and was expected to operate principally against neighbouring countries, the head of the residency being at the same time obliged to keep the military attaché up to date with results.[21] “Kriegsorganisation Rumänien” operated until the beginning of October 1940 when, in the context of the accession to power of General Ion Antonescu, of the establishment of the German Military Mission and of Romania’s entry into the German sphere of influence, OKW/Amt Ausland Abwehr decided to transform the “Kriegsorganisation Rumänien” residence into “Abwehrstelle Rumänien.” Thus on the order of the High Command of the Wehrmacht (OKW) of 3 October 1940 “[…] the organs of the Abwehr of Amt Ausland which are already active in Romania are to be moved into the Abwehrstelle Rumänien” with headquarters in Bucharest.[22] Even if the

---

[19] BMF, MSG (Militärische Sammlung)/13454. Bericht des Generalmajors Erwin von Lahousen “Geheimorganisation Canaris.” Organisation des Amtes Ausland/Abwehr (1938/1939-1943); PAAAB, R 101832, E 264235-264240. Pol I M 3606 geheime Reichssache. Postchiffré vom 13.02.1942 betreffend “Dienstanweisung für die Zusammenarbeit der Angehörigen des Amts Ausland/Abwehr mit deutschen Missionen in Ausland.”

[20] PAAAB, R 102033, Pol I M Akten betreffend Agenten und Spionagewesen-Nachrichten, Band 1. 30.August-12 September 1939, Pol I M 4052 geheim. Telegramm Nr. 391 der deutschen Gesandtschaft in Bukarest vom 30.08.1939, gez. K.O.R., Wilhelm Fabricius.

[21] BMF, RW 49 – Abwehrstellen –/20. Amt Ausland/Abwehr Nr. 2783/8.38 Abw. I H Ost geh. vom 31.08.1938 betreffend “Richtlinien für Kriegsorganisationsleiter” (K.O.-Leiter), gez. Oberst Hans Piekenbrock.

[22] BMF, RH 31-I – Deutsche Heeresmission in Rumänien –/24 (a), fol. 57-61. OKW Nr. 1748/40 g.K. WFSt/Abt. L (II) betreffend Wehrmachtdienstellen beim Chef der Deutschen Wehrmacht-Mission in

"Abwehrstelle" residences functioned only in the Reich or in the occupied territories, Romania was the only state allied to Nazi Germany in which an "Abwehrstelle" operated, representing from this point of view an atypical case. During its existence (October 1940 - August 1944), "Abwehrstelle Rumänien" was to represent not only the principal German intelligence body in Romania, but also the only one recognized and officially accepted by the Romanian state.

Archival evidence allows us to identify the officers who led the two Abwehr residences in Romania in the years 1939-1944. Although we do not have details of the head of "Kriegsorganisation Rumänien" at the time it was set up, nevertheless, being in mind that in the absence of a commander appointed by the OKW/Amt Ausland Abwehr, the military attaché was the *de facto* chief of the residence, we can assume that in the period August - December 1939 that function was held by Colonel Carl Wahle, the German military attaché in Bucharest.[23] This assumption is also supported by the fact that contact between the Abwehr and the Romanian Secret Service in October and November 1939 was managed through Colonel Wahle,[24] until the latter's mission ended with the appointment of Major Dr Hans Wagner[25] at the head of "Kriegsorganisation Rumänien." In contrast to the majority of "Kriegsorganisation" residence heads who came from Abwehr I (Geheimer Meldedienst)-intelligence and were subordinated to this department, Major Dr Hans Wagner, an experienced counterintelligence officer of section III F specialized in combating secret enemy services abroad, was subordinated to Abwehr III (Gegenspionage, Spionageabwehr)-counterintelligence. His posting to Bucharest was the direct consequence of the order given by the OKW on 13 October 1939 setting up the so-called "Ölschutz Organisation Rumänien" [The Organization for the Protection of the Oil-Fields in Romania],[26] and Wagner was given the task by OKW/Amt Ausland Abwehr of creat-

---

Rumänien vom 03.10.1940, gez. Generalmajor Walter Warlimont.

[23] Carl Wahle (1892-1970), German career officer. Passed out from the Infantry Officers' School in Glogau (1912-1913). Commissioned as lieutenant (1913), fought in the First World War. Military attaché in Prague (13.06.1937-14.06.1938); military attaché in Bucharest (01.08.1938-15.10.1940); commander of 267 Infantry regiment (15.10.1940-01.01.1942); military commander of Hamburg (01.07.1942-16.11.1943); commander of 214 Infantry division (01.01-15.02.1944); commander of 719 Infantry division (15.02-01.08.1944); commander of 47 Infantry division (01.08-04.09.1944); prisoner of the Americans (04.09.1944-1947). Colonel (01.10.1938); Major-General (01.07.1942); Lieutenant-General (01.12.1943). BMF, Pers 6/2025-Generalleutnant Carl Wahle.

[24] Troncotă, *Mihail Moruzov*, doc. no. 48: 353-368; doc. no. 52: 374-379.

[25] Hans Wagner (1893-?), career officer and German civil servant. He joined the army with the rank of lieutenant in 1914, fought in the First World War and passed into the reserve on 22.07.1919. Doctor in law (1921); bank official (1921-1934). Reactivated on 01.03.1934, he was named an official in Abwehr III-counterespionage of the OKW/Amt Ausland/Abwehr; assigned to section III F – combating enemy secret services in both the east and the west, and in neutral states (from 03.10.1934); head of "Kriegsorganisation Rumänien" (10.12.1939-10.09.1940); chief of "Kriegsorganisation Schweden" (03.10.1940-09.05.1945). Major (01.10.1938); lieutenant-colonel (01.09.1941); colonel (01.04.1944). BMF, Pers 6/11504-Oberst Dr. Hans Wagner; PAAAB, R 101937, Pol I M, Akten betreffend Abwehr, Einbau Dr. Hans Wagner (04.09.1940-23.04.1942).

[26] Institut für Zeitgeschichte München, F 23-Tagebuch Erwin von Lahousen/Abwehr II 1939-1943, fol. 26. Note of 13.10.1940; Gert Buchheit, *Der deutsche Geheimdienst. Geschichte der militärischen Abwehr* (München: List Verlag, 1966), 249.

ing and directing this body in close collaboration with the Romanian authorities.[27] Wagner remained at the head of "Kriegsorganisation Rumänien" until 10 September 1940, being named at the beginning of the following month chief of "Kriegsorganisation Schweden," under the diplomatic cover of assistant to the German military attaché in Stockholm (with the cod-name "Hans Schneider").[28]

The transformation of the "Kriegsorganisation Rumänien" residence into "Abwehrstelle Rumänien" brought with it a reorientation of its intelligence tasks. Between October 1940 and August 1944 "Abwehrstelle Rumänien" was subordinated to Abwehr I (Geheimer Meldedienst), with stress being placed on the acquisition of military intelligence principally from the Soviet Union and the Middle East. In fact both officers who followed as heads of "Abwehrstelle Rumänien," Colonel Erich Rodler[29] (17.10.1940-30.04.1944) and Colonel Friedrich (Fritz) Sebastian Baur[30] (30.04-23.08.1944), were in-

---

[27] PAAAB, R 101925, Pol I M, Akten betreffend Abwehr, Einbau des Major Kurt von Rohrscheidt (18.12.1939-16.02.1942), E 320065-320067. Amt Ausland/Abwehr Nr. 46823/40 g. Abw. III (Wi/A) vom 29.04.1940 betreffend Dienstanweisung für den Verbindungs-Offizier Bukarest (V.O. Bukarest).

[28] PAAAB, R 101937, E 319831-319835. Amt Ausland/Abwehr Nr. 2841/40 g.K. Abw. III (F/A) vom 15.10.1940 betreffend Dienstanweisung für den V.O. Stockholm, gez. Oberst Franz Eccard von Bentivegni.

[29] Erich Rodler (1884-1948); Austrian career officer. Passed out from the Infantry officers' school in Prague (1899-1903) and the military academy in Wiener-Neustadt (1908-1912). He entered the Austro-Hungarian army with the rank of lieutenant (1903), was a General Staff officer (1911); intelligence officer (1913). During the First World War he served as an intelligence officer in the Austro-Hungarian army and passed into the reserve in 1920 with the rank of major. He was an official in the administration in the Tyrol (1933-1938), in which capacity he also gathered intelligence which served German interests to the detriment of Italy. Arrested by the SS in 1938, he was released at the request of OKW/Amt Ausland/Abwehr, which he joined in the same year. Commander of "Abwehr-Nebenstelle Innsbruck" (01.04.1938-18.06.1940), of "Abwehrstelle Salzburg" (19.06-16.10.1940), and of "Abwehrstelle Rumänien" (17.10.1940-30.04.1944). He retired on age grounds on 01.05.1944; and was placed in the reserve on 31.12.1944. Summoned 04.05.1947 to the headquarters of the Soviet command in Vienna, he was arrested by the Soviet occupation authority (SMERŞ). Deported to the Soviet Union, he was sentenced for espionage and ended his days in Soviet prisons on 20.02.1948. Major (01.11.1938); lieutenant-colonel (01.03.1940); colonel (01.03.1942). BMF, Pers 6/2513-Oberst Erich Rodler; *Österreichisches Biographisches Lexikon 1815-1950*, IX. Band. *Ráz-Sav* (Wien: Verlag der Österreichischen Akademie der Wissenschaften, 1988), 197.

[30] Friedrich Sebastian Baur (1895-1973), Austrian career officer. He passed out from the military academy in Wiener-Neustadt (1912-1914). He entered the Austro-Hungarian army with the rank of lieutenant (1914); served in the First World War as a pilot, serving on the Romanian front where he was seriously wounded in 1916 at the Oituz pass. Retired on 01.03.1919 with the rank of captain (26.11.1921). Called up again on 01.10.1938 to the OKW/Amt Ausland/Abwehr and assigned to Abteilung Abwehr I-Section I intelligence. Officer in "Abwehrstelle Wien" (01.10.1938-17.03.1939); transferred to Bucharest under diplomatic cover of assistant secretary, tasked with the passport service in the German legation (17.03.1939), but in reality he headed Section I intelligence of the "Kriegsorganisation Rumänien," the precursor of "Abwehrstelle Rumänien" (17.03.1939-17.10.1940); head Abwehr I-intelligence in "Abwehrstelle Rumänien" (17.10.1940-01.09.1942); seconded as officer to the General Staff "Don" under the command of Major-General Arthur Hauffe – attached to the "Mareşal Ion Antonescu" Army Group (01.09.1942-15.02.1943); he took part as a representative of "Abwehrstelle Wien" in the specialist courses for Abwehrstelle commanders (15.02-01.08.1943); head of Abwehr I of "Abwehrstelle Rumänien" (01.08.1944-23.08.1944); head of Abwehrstelle Rumänien (30.04-23.08.1944); served in the "Southern Ukraine" Army Group (23.08.1944-01.03.1945); commander of the 236 Grenadiers' Regiment (01.03-09.05.1945). At the end of the Second World War he settled in Linz where he died on 10.10.1973. Major (01.10.1938); lieutenant-colonel (01.10.1941); colonel (01.02.1944). Staatsarchiv Wien/Abteilung Archiv der Republik/05/DWM, *Personalakten Oberst Friedrich Sebastian Baur*; PAAAB, Deutsche Gesandtschaft Bukarest, Karton 2. *Personalakten Amtsrat Fritz Baur*; AMAE, Fund 14/*Reprezentanţi-Germania*, B 24- Fritz Baur/ adjunct chancellor.

telligence officers with a vast experience in the field, having served in the former Austro-Hungarian army and absorbed in 1938 into Abwehr I. Collaboration between the Abwehr residences in Romania and the SSI was managed through the Section for Foreign Relations (Section III "G") under the command of lieutenant-colonel Constantin Gheorghe Ionescu-Micandru (code-name "G. Iorgu").[31] The exchange of information between the two services was effected through written notes forwarded to Section III "G" by the liaison officer designated by "Kriegsorganisation Rumänien"/"Abwehrstelle Rumänien," lieutenant-colonel Hermann Stransky Ritter von Stranka und Greifenfels (code-name "Sandu")[32] – who had an excellent knowledge of Romania and the Romanian language – the notes being translated into Romanian and sent for resolution to the relevant sections in SSI, while the reply was translated into German and handed to the Abwehr liaison officer. The exchange of information was also carried out through meeting organized every month between the head of the Abwehr residence in Romania and the SSI Director, or on the occasion of the visits made to Bucharest by Admiral Wilhelm Canaris or by the heads of the three principal departments in the central OKW/Amt Ausland Abwehr. During these meetings there was a short exchange of opinions on the intelligence obtained by the two secret services, and especially on the measures taken to prevent sabotage in the oil-fields.[33]

---

[31] Constantin Gheorghe Ionescu-Micandru (1898-1950), Romanian career officer. Graduate of the infantry officers' military school (1916-1917). Joined the army as second-lieutenant (1917), served in the First World War. General Staff officer (01.11.1930-31.10.1931); head of the Second Department Intelligence of the Air Division (01.11.1931-01.04.1932); head of the Adjutant and Staff Bureau of the General Staff (01.04.1932-31.10.1936); head of the Eastern Front department of the Army Secret Service (01.11.1936-31.10.1939); head of the Foreign Relations Department, later Section III "G" of the SSI (01.11.1939-31.07.1944); technical consultant in the SSI (01.08-01.10.1944). A member of the National Resistance Movement, he was arrested by the Communist authorities in March 1946. Sentenced on 26.06.1948 to forced labour for life and 10 years loss of office for "war crimes;" he served his sentence in the prisons in Aiud and Jilava. He died in Jilava jail on 13.07.1950. Captain (10.05.1925); major (16.10.1935); lieutenant-colonel (08.06.1940). Arhivele Militare Române Piteşti [Romanian Military Archives Piteşti] (henceforth abbreviated AMR), Fund DCI/1972, no. 1170, f. 1-72; CNSAS, Fund *Informativ*, no. 209906 (Constantin Gheorghe Ionescu-Micandru), passim.

[32] Hermann Otto Vincenz Stransky Ritter von Stranka und Greifenfels (1896-?), forestry engineer and Austrian career officer. He obtained a degree in silviculture (1913-1920); volunteered to serve in the First World War, was demobilized as a lieutenant in the reserve. In July 1920 he settled in Romania where he worked for several forestry companies until 1932. In July 1920 he settled in Romania where he worked for several forestry companies until 1932: "Tişiţa" in Mărăşeşti (1920-1925), "Foresta Română" in Bucharest (1925-1926), "Bangra" in Lunca Bradului (1927-1932), and between 1932-1934 was involved in the timber trade. In 1934 he returned to Vienna, joined the Austrian Nazi Party and was forced to flee to Germany because of his political activity. He settled in Berlin where he became a civil service in the Reich Ministry of the Economy, delaying with the timber trade (1937-1939). He was called up on 15.01.1939 into Abwehr I; member of "Abwehrstelle Breslau" (01-05.09.1939, 23-25.09.1939); officer in the general staff of the German 8th Army (06-22.09.1939); group leader "Abwehrstelle Krakau" (26.09-11.12.1939); officer in Abwehr (11.12.1939-11.01.1940); liaison officer of "Kriegsorganisation Rumänien"/"Abwehrstelle Rumänien" to the Romanian Secret Service and then the SSI (12.01.1940-23.08.1944). Captured by the Soviets on the streets of Vienna in 1945, he remained a prisoner until 1955. Captain (01.05.1939); major (01.10.1940); lieutenant-colonel (01.09.1944). BMF, Pers 6/9059-Oberstleutnant Hermann von Stransky Ritter von Stranka und Greifenfels.

[33] CNSAS, Fund *Informativ*, no. 209906 (Constantin Gheorghe Ionescu-Micandru), f. 93-101. The memoir signed by Constantin Gheorghe Ionescu-Micandru dated 08.06.1946 referring to his activity at the head of Section III "G" of the SSI.

The protection of the oil-fields was indeed the main priority of the OKW/Amt Ausland Abwehr and its residences in Romania, at least in the period 1939-1940. Major Hans Wagner's orders stipulated in fact that his principal task was to protect "the interests of the German war economy in Romania," and the creation in cooperation with the Romanian authorities of an intelligence structure to protect the oil region (wells, pipes, refineries), the factories whose production was for Germany, the warehouses for cereals and other goods for export to the Reich, the oil storage tanks, the places for transhipping goods, the ports, and railway and river hubs on the Danube from acts of sabotage by the enemy secret services.[34] In addition to these aforementioned structures under the control of Abwehr III-counterespionage, on 14 December 1939 Canaris gave the order for the creation of a parallel body to ensure the security of the installations and storage facilities both within the oil region as well as in ports, and of communications, especially of the railways and on the Danube.[35] This organization, composed of officers, non-commissioned officers and carefully selected soldiers, belonging to the famous special unit OKW/Amt Ausland Abwehr, "Baulehrbataillon z.b.V. 800," which became on 1 June 1940 "Lehrregiment Brandenburg z.b.V 800," was coordinated by Abwehr II (Sabotage, Sonderaufgaben)-sabotage and special missions.

Thus at the end of December 1939 and the beginning of 1940, a detachment of twelve officers and men led by Captain Kurt Drögsler (a chemist with the code-name "Victor Luptar") was sent to the oil region of Ploieşti to act under various covers and Romanian code-names.[36] At the same time, the Romanian Secret Service set up in early January 1940 the so-called "Ploieşti" agency, headed initially (January-December 1940) by lieutenant Constantin I. Antonescu,[37] and later (December 1940-1942) by Major Gheorghe Filimon,[38] with the mission to cover the activity of the German agents and to prevent acts of sabotage in the entire oil region. Within the "Ploieşti" agency special supervisory teams were set up, formed from experienced agents of the Romanian Secret Service and placed under the command Gheorghe Untăreanu (code-named "Gheorghe Albu" or "B. Dănilă"), who served also as the assistant head of the "Ploieşti" agency and

---

[34] PAAAB, R 101925, E 320065-320067. Amt Ausland/Abwehr Nr. 46823/40 g. Abw. III (Wi/A) vom 29.04.1940 betreffend Dienstanweisung für den Verbindungs-Offizier Bukarest (V.O. Bukarest).

[35] Institut für Zeitgeschichte München, F 23-Tagebuch Erwin von Lahousen/Abwehr II 1939-1943, fol. 34. Note of 14.12.1940.

[36] CNSAS, Fund *Informativ*, no. 262170 (Virgil Atanasiu and others), vol. 2, f. 1-11. Note of the General Direction of the Securitate from 16.06.1951; Spaeter, *Die Brandenburger*, 98-101; Brockdorff, *Geheimkommandos*, 81-82.

[37] Constantin I. Antonescu (1894-1942), Romanian career officer. He entered the army as a second lieutenant in the reserve (1916) and fought in the First World War. Promoted to lieutenant on 01.05.1918, backdated to 01.09.1917. Head of the "Ploieşti" agency of the Romanian Secret Service (January-11.12.1940). Captain (15.10.1922); major (15.04.1933); lieutenant-colonel (25.10.1939). See ANIC, Fund *Preşedinţia Consiliului de Miniştri-Cabinet Civil Mihai Antonescu*, no. 106/1940, f. 3. Decision no. 5957 of 11.12.1940 of the director of SSI, signed Eugen Cristescu.

[38] Gheorghe I. Filimon (1902-?), Romanian career officer. Passed out of the military engineers' school (1920-1922). Joined the army with the rank of second lieutenant (1922). Head of the "Ploieşti" agency of the SSI (11.12.1940-1942). Lieutenant (01.04.1926); captain (01.01.1934); maior (31.10.1940); see also CNSAS, Fund *Informativ*, no. 25433 (Gheorghe Filimon), vol. 1-2, passim.

who worked closely with the members of the detachment of Kurt Drögsler.[39] Thus two joint Romanian-German teams were formed to protect the strategic assets mentioned above against sabotage.[40] The second detachment, placed under the command of Captain Heinrich Verbeek,[41] was given the mission of enduring the security of river traffic on the Danube against sabotage by the Allied secret services. Its members acted under different forms of cover (tourists, sportsmen, customs officers) with the tacit approval of the Romanian and Bulgarian authorities, on board vessels on the Danube or in the ports situated along the river.[42] Verbeek's detachment also received an important mission from Abwehr II. Being preoccupied by the danger of an Allied landing in Romania in order to occupy or sabotage the oil region, Abwehr II drew up in April 1940 sabotage plans against a possible Allied landing on the Romanian Black Sea coast. According to the plan (codenamed "Operation Sigmaringen"), Verbeek's detachment was to blow up the Cernavodă bridge and block the Sulina channel in order to delay the advance of the Allied forces towards the country's interior.[43]

The results of the security measures adopted in the oil region and of Romanian-German intelligence cooperation were not slow it appear. If in the months of November and December 1939 the number of acts of sabotage, fires and incidents considered to be sabotage was relatively high,[44] a fact which produced "a state of extreme irritation" at the level of the OKW and of the Reich government and which led Canaris to make a sudden visit to Bucharest between 10-12 December 1939,[45] after the adoption of the aforementioned measures and the transformation of the oil region into a militarized zone in January

---

[39] Kurt Drögsler (1898-?), Austrian chemist and officer. Before the war he worked in Vienna and was later enrolled in "Lehrregiment Brandenburg z.b.V 800" and sent to Ploieşti (1940-1942). Details of his subsequent military career are not known.

[40] CNSAS, Fund *Penal*, no. 12595 (Gheorghe Untăreanu and others), vol. 2, f. 284-295. Note from 01.02.1956; vol. 5, f. 88-92. Declaration of Gheorghe Untăreanu of 28.09.1954; f. 183-190. Undated declaration of Gheorghe Untăreanu; f. 223-226. Declaration of Gheorghe Untăreanu of 30.11.1950.

[41] Heinrich Verbeek (1895-?), German soldier. He volunteered in the First World War and was promoted to lieutenant in 1917. Passed into the reserve with this rank and was reactivated on 01.01.1939, being assigned to OKW/Amt Ausland Abwehr. Officer in "Abwehrstelle Wien" (01.09.1939-01.04.1940); officer in "Lehrregiment Brandenburg z.b.V 800," tasked with the command of the detachment for the protection of Danube river traffic (02.04.1940-10.06.1941); commander of an "Abwehrtrupp" on the eastern front (11.06.1941-31.07.1942); commander of "Abwehrtrupp 204" on the eastern front (01.08-06.12.1942); commander of the Abwehr school "Pestalozzischule" of the unit "Lehrregiment Kurfürst" (19.02.1943). Lieutenant-major in the reserve (01.06.1925); captain in the reserve (01.01.1940); major in the reserve (31.12.1943). BMF, Pers 6/194930-Major der Reserve zur Verwendung Heinrich Verbeek.

[42] BMF, Pers 6/194930-Major der Reserve zur Verwendung Heinrich Verbeek, no pagination. Beurteilung ohne Datum betreffend Hauptmann der Reserve zur Verwendung Heinrich Verbeek, gez. Major Wolfgang Abshagen; Buchheit, *Der deutsche Geheimdienst*, 249; Spaeter, *Die Brandenburger*, 111-122; Brockdorff, *Geheimkommandos*, 82.

[43] Institut für Zeitgeschichte München, F 23-Tagebuch Erwin von Lahousen/Abwehr II 1939-1943, fol. 60. Note of 19.04.1940; fol. 61. Note of 21.04.1940.

[44] PAAAB, R 29696, E 82940. Vermerk vom 05.12.1939, gez. Wilhelm Keppler; E 82942-82943. Telegramm Nr. 962 der deutschen Gesandtschaft in Bukarest vom 06.12.1939, gez. Carl Clodius, Wilhelm Fabricius; E 82946. Telegramm Nr. 971 der deutschen Gesandtschaft in Bukarest vom 06.12.1939, gez. Wilhelm Fabricius.

[45] Troncotă, *Mihail Moruzov*, doc. no. 59: 404-405; doc. no. 60: 405-411; Hillgruber, *Hitler, Regele Carol şi Mareşalul Antonescu*, 101.

1940,[46] the number of such incidents gradually fell. Although the British and French employees in the oil industry (amongst them, obviously secret agents of Allied intelligence services) were shocked to see the presence of the German and Romanian supervisory teams in the oil region, in stations, and in ports on the Danube, the drastic security measures did not discourage London and Paris from planning further acts of sabotage, quite the contrary. Thus at the beginning of December 1939 both the Abwehr and the Romanian Secret Service received information that the British were planning to blow up the Iron Gates on the Danube. The British plans were to deny oil supplies delivered by barge along the Danube and centred on blocking the points in the Kazan defile (Iron Gates), either by blockships or by detonating the cliffs on the Yugoslav side. They were to be supplemented by the pre-emptive chartering of all available river vessels and the creation of a shortage of pilots at the Iron Gates by offering them – through the Goeland Transport and Trading Company, set up in January 1940 by the British Government with William Harris-Burland as general manager, to concentrate under one management measures of economic warfare – extended paid holidays.[47] The plans to block the Danube by sinking barges had been drawn up by Section D of MI6 (British Intelligence) and Naval Intelligence in September 1939, and were to be coordinated by the Naval attaché in Bucharest, Captain Max Despard.

These plans were closely monitored by the Romanian Secret Service, through the services of an agent who had been infiltrated into the British group, Captain in the reserve Gogu Constantinescu, a former administrator for the "Unirea" oil company), and by the Abwehr, using the agents in Verbeek's detachment in the port of Giurgiu.[48] On the basis

[46] PAAAB, R 29696, E 82948. Telegramm Nr. 974 der deutschen Gesandtschaft in Bukarest vom 07.12.1939, gez. Carl Clodius, Wilhelm Fabricius; E 82959. Telegramm Nr. 984 der deutschen Gesandtschaft in Bukarest vom 09.12.1939, gez. Wilhelm Fabricius.

[47] Lieutenant-Colonel William Harris-Burland (1902-1985). After qualifying as a chartered accountant, Harris-Burland worked in Poland, Romania and Germany in the inter-war years. In 1939, he returned to Britain and offered his services to the War Office which recruited him into Military Intelligence Research (MI(R)) and sent him to Poland with a small party under the command of Colin Gubbins. Following the fall of Poland the party escaped to Romania where Harris-Burland was placed in charge of the Anglo-Danubian Shipping Company in Bucharest and given responsibility for chartering barges on the Danube to prevent them falling into German hands. He continued this activity as General Manager of the Goeland Transport and Trading Company, created specifically for this purpose in February 1940. After the entry of German troops into Romania Harris-Burland paid off the Goeland staff and in February 1941 joined the Special Operations Executive's (SOE – a British intelligence and sabotage agency) Belgrade office. He was captured with other members of the office, including Tom Masterson, George Taylor and Hugh Seton-Watson, by Italian forces while withdrawing to the Adriatic coast. Held at Ciancino in the Apennines, the group was exchanged for some Italian prisoners and returned to England via Spain in June 1941. Harris-Burland was then posted to Istanbul as head of the SOE office with responsibility for chartering Turkish shipping, partly to keep it out of German hands, and partly to divert materials useful to the Germans such as chrome ore. In September 1944, he was appointed to the British Military Mission to Romania in charge of transport. He was recalled to London in March 1946 to work on the reorganization of the German iron and steel industry and posted to Germany where he remained until 1953 when he returned to England and became Director of Accounts and Statistics in the British Transport Commission (Dennis Deletant's interview with William Harris-Burland, 10 August 1984.)

[48] CNSAS, Fund *Penal*, no. 12595 (Gheorghe Untăreanu and others), vol. 2, f. 284-295. Report of 01.02.1956; vol. 5, f. 23-39. Declaration of Gheorghe Untăreanu of 08.08.1951; Troncotă, *Mihail Moruzov*,

of the information obtained, Wilhelm Fabricius, the German minister in Bucharest, intervened alongside George Gafencu, the Romanian Foreign Minister on 4 April 1940, with a peremptory request that a convoy of British barges be inspected. At first the Romanian government refused the request but following a warning issued by Fabricius that the Germans would act unilaterally, the Romanian authorities authorized an inspection, discovering a large quantity of revolvers, tear-gas pistols, large guns and 400 cases of explosives on board the lighter "Termonde."[49] However, to avoid attracting reprisals from London, the Romanian government refused to treat the episode as a sabotage attempt, regarding it only as a question of smuggling. Consequently, the sailors and British secret agents on board the "Termonde" were not arrested but were expelled from the country, a decision which not unnaturally angered the Reich government.[50]

The thwarting of the British plan to interrupt navigation on the Danube, followed by the expulsion of a large number of agents from the oil region in the months from April to June, were considered by the Abwehr blows which brought the Allied espionage and sabotage network in Romania to its knees.[51] In spite of this, the results of Romanian-German intelligence cooperation in the first half of 1940 were put in question following the discovery by German troops on 19 June 1940 in the railway station at La Charité-sur-Loire of the entire archive of the Deuxième Bureau (Military intelligence) of the French General Staff. The captured documents, exploited for propaganda and published later by the German authorities,[52] showed clearly both the duplicity of the authoritarian regime of King Carol II in foreign affairs in the period 1939-1940, as well as the extent of the Allied spy and sabotage networks in the Ploieşti region. Berlin, therefore, put pressure in Bucharest to expel the British and French subjects who were still active in the oil industry

doc. no. 94: 491-496; Spaeter, *Die Brandenburger*, 111-117.

[49] PAAAB, R 100042, Pol I M, Akten betreffend Agenten und Spionagewesen – Nachrichten – Band 10, 21. März-10. April 1940. Pol I M 4820 g. Telegramm Nr. 447 der deutschen Gesandtschaft in Bukarest vom 04.04.1940, gez. Wilhelm Fabricius; Aufzeichnung vom 06.04.1940, gez. Bernd Otto Freiherr von der Heyden-Rynsch; Pol I M 4822 g. Telegramm Nr. 452 der deutschen Gesandtschaft in Bukarest vom 05.04.1940, gez. Wilhelm Fabricius; Telegramm Nr. 453 der deutschen Gesandtschaft in Bukarest vom 05.04.1940, gez. Wilhelm Fabricius; Pol I M 4885 g. Telegramm Nr. 464 der deutschen Gesandtschaft in Bukarest vom 06.04.1940, gez. Oberst Alfred Gerstenberg; Hillgruber, *Hitler, Regele Carol şi Mareşalul Antonescu*, 102; Troncotă, *Mihail Moruzov*, doc. no. 94: 491-496; Maurice Pearton, "British Policy towards Romania," in *Romania Observed*, ed. Dennis Deletant, Maurice Pearton (Bucharest: Editura Enciclopedică, 1998), 81-83.

[50] PAAAB, R 29697, *Büro des Staatssekretärs, Rumänien*, Band 2, *1. Februar-31. Juli 1940*, E 136831-136832. Telegramm Nr. 476 der deutschen Gesandtschaft in Bukarest vom 09.04.1940; E 136855-136856. Aufzeichnung vom 17.04.1940, gez. Ernst Woermann.

[51] PAAAB, R 100045, Pol I M, Akten betreffend Agenten und Spionagewesen – Nachrichten – Band 13, 15. Mai-17. Juni 1940. Pol I M 8398 g. Telegramm Nr. 894 der deutschen Gesandtschaft in Bukarest vom 12.06.1940, gez. Dir, Burg; Wilhelm Fabricius.

[52] See PAAAB, R 29112, Dienststelle Ribbentrop, Akten betreffend Documente "La Charité" Nr. 1-98, 1939-1940; Auswärtiges Amt 1939/1941 No. 6, Berlin, 1941; see also *Polnische Dokumente zur Vorgeschichte des Kriege*, erste folge (Berlin: Zentralverlag der NSDAP. Franz Eher Nachf., 1940), no. 36: 82-83. Despite its title 'Polish documents on the Early History of the War', the volume contains several of the secret documents of the French General Staff, captured by the Germans on 19 June 1940 at La Charité sur Loire, and translated for publication into German. Some of the captured documents were published by the Romanian authorities in autumn 1940 in a brochure entitled *Acestea erau garanţiile anglo-franceze*, passim.

since they were considered agents of the Allied intelligence services. Mihail Moruzov, who was placed in a delicate position after the discovery of the secret French documents, was forced to accede to the German request and to ask, in a note addressed on 1 July to the Second Bureau for Intelligence of the Romanian General Staff, for the expulsion of 30 British and French subjects suspected of "undertaking a secret mission to carry out possible acts of sabotage" in the oil region.[53] Since in the following period for various reasons the Romanian government dragged its feet over the measures requested by Mihail Moruzov, the German government decided to intervene abruptly and forcefully demanding the expulsion of the persons in question. On 24 June, the head of "Kriegsorganisation Rumänien," Major Hans Wagner, informed Moruzov that in order to "create a favourable atmosphere" for Romania in the high-level talks due to take place in Salzburg, it was necessary that "a. All the persons mentioned in the documents below be immediately expelled; b. Wide and urgent publicity to this be given in the press and radio."[54] In the light of the international situation and the nature of an ultimatum of the request, the Romanian side was forced to carry out the German demand and expelled at the end of June 32 British and 11 French subjects suspected or proven to have been involved in preparing acts of sabotage in the oil region.[55]

Even if Berlin delivered a major blow with this measure to the Allied intelligence services, the network of these agents in Romania was far from being completed erased. On the contrary, it remained active. On the basis of the evidence gathered by German agents on the spot, the Abwehr intervened again on 12 September with the Romanian Secret Service requesting the expulsion of 23 British subjects from the Ploieşti region.[56] The situation was to deteriorate even further for British intelligence after the advent to power of the National Legionary regime in the first half of September. Besides the drastic curb on the freedom of action and the continual supervision of the Abwehr and the SD, the British agents and subjects in Romania had to face what the British minister in Romania, Sir Reginald Hoare, characterized, not without reason, a "terrorist campaign" launched by the sinister legionary police.[57] As a result, the majority of the British subjects in the oil region was forced to leave Romania in the second half of September 1940. Furthermore, 7 British citizens accused of sabotage of German oil cars – some of them being indeed Special Operations Executive (SOE – a British intelligence and sabotage body) agents[58] –

---

[53] ANIC, Fund PCM-SSI, no. 24/1937, f. 311-316.

[54] Ibid., f. 330-331.

[55] PAAAB, R 27347, Handakten Hasso von Etzdorf, Abwehr: Länder (III), 1939-1940, E. 66067-66068. Abschrift vom 30.07.1940 betreffend die Zerschlagung des feindlichen Nachrichten- und Sabotagedienstes.

[56] PAAAB, R 27347, E 66069-66071. Schreiben der Abwehrabteilung III Nr. 711133/40 g Abw (Wi 5) vom 12.09.1940 betreffend Ausweisung von Ausländern aus Rumänien, gez. Oberst Franz Eccard von Bentivegni.

[57] Elisabeth Barker, *British Policy in South-East Europe in the Second World War* (London: Macmillan, 1976), 40; See also Ivor Porter, *Operaţiunea „Autonomous". În România pe vreme de război* [Operation Autonomous. With SOE in Wartime Romania] (Bucureşti: Humanitas, 1991), 82-83.

[58] Barker, *British Policy*, 40. Their names were Alfred Crawford Anderson, John Edward Treacy and his wife Esther, Reginald Young, Charles Brasier, Alexander Miller and Percy Clark. Anderson was arrested on 24 September, Mr and Mrs Treacy, Young and Brasier on the following day, Miller on 1 October, and Clark on 3

were arrested between 24 September and 3 October 1940 by the legionary police, being part – according to the reports sent to Berlin by the German legation in Bucharest – of a spy network led by the British military attaché Lieutenant-Colonel Geoffrey Macnab.[59] The arrests and interrogation were carried out by the legionary police together with SD and Gestapo representatives in Romania.[60] Those arrested were so abused that when the British diplomats found them in the custody of the legionary policee "not one of those held could stand on their feet."[61] From Ploieşti the arrested men and Mrs Treacy were taken to Bucharest and imprisoned, and were released only in October following strong diplomatic protests made by the British Minister, Sir Reginald Hoare, to General Ion Antonescu and after a certain amount of bribery of officials by Ion Popovici,[62] using SOE funds.[63] Immediately after their release they were sent to Istanbul where Treacy and Anderson were obliged to undergo medical treatment. By the beginning of October more than 400 British subjects, including workers and engineers, had been either expelled or forced to leave Romania,[64] which effectively put an end to SOE plans of sabotage in Romania.[65]

October (see the report on the arrests dated 23 October 1940 from Heydrich, head of the Sicherheitspolizei and the SD, to Ribbentrop, German Foreign Minister, PAAAB, R 100114, Inland II Geheim, Band 422, Berichte und Meldungen zur Lage in und über Rumänien, 1937-1940, D II 1203 g. Bericht des Chefs der Sicherheitspolizei und des SD B. Nr. 6056/40 g – IV A 2 – vom 23.10.1940 über die Aufdeckung einer englischen Sabotageorganisation im rumänischen Erdölgebiet von Ploeşti, gez. SS-Gruppenführer Reinhard Heydrich).

59 Lieutenant-Colonel Geoffrey Alex Colin Macnab (1899-1995), British military attaché to Romania, 1938-1940.

60 PAAAB, R 100773, Inland II Geheim, Band 93, Akten betreffend Rumänien: Tätigkeit des SD, der Abwehr, der Agenten und der Polizeiattachés 1940-1944, D II 858 g/40. Telegramm Nr. 1673 der deutschen Gesandtschaft in Bukarest vom 27.09.1940, gez. Kurt Geißler, Wilhelm Fabricius; D II 878 g/40. Telegramm Nr. 1690 der deutschen Gesandtschaft in Bukarest vom 01.10.1940, gez. Wilhelm Fabricius; R 27347, E 66081-66084. Abwehrabteilung Nr. 195/10.40 II/A Öl. Bisheriges Untersuchungsergebnis der Engländerverhaftungen.

61 Porter, *Operaţiunea „Autonomous,"* 83.

62 Ion Popovici was born in Bucharest on 20 May 1898 and was a chemical engineer by profession. He worked for the British-owned "Unirea Oil Company" and became a close friend of the director of the company Alfred George Gardyne de Chastelain (1906-74), who in early 1940 became head of SOE operations in Romania. Popovici was recruited into SOE and acted as a bagman for the agency in Romania until his arrest in August 1941; see AMR, Fund 5465. *Direcţia Justiţiei Militare*, no. 2218: 21. He is believed to have died in Bucharest in 1946.

63 The sum involved was £5000; see The National Archives, London, HS 5/830. On 7 January 1941, Hoare drew the attention of the Romanian Foreign Minister ad interim, general Ion Antonescu, to his previous notes to him of 9 October and 9 November 1940 in which he enquired as to whether those responsible for the ill-treatment of the British subjects had been identified and measures taken against them. Hoare informed him of the result of the enquiries made on behalf of the British legation which established that "the ringleader in brutality" was a Victor Enechescu (or Enăchescu) from Ploieşti. Another person involved was Gheorghe Cârciumaru who was "almost certainly connected with the Legionary Police at Ploieşti." Other legionaries thought to have been implicated in the maltreatment were a certain Gabriel Popescu, a Ianacescu, and a Professor Grigorescu (The National Archives, London, HS 5/830).

64 Valeriu Florin Dobrinescu, Ion Pătroiu, *Anglia şi România între anii 1939-1947* [Great Britain and Romania between 1939-1947] (Bucureşti: Editura Didactică şi Pedagogică, 1992), 96.

65 However, SOE's activities in pro-Allied propaganda in Romania continued until the arrest of Romanians agents in August 1941. Moreover, the operations of the British MI6 (Intelligence Service/SIS) network in

Although once the transformation of the "Kriegsorganisation Rumänien" residence into the "Abwehrstelle Rumänien" in October 1940 took place and the centre of gravity of the German intelligence effort in Romania moved towards the gathering of military intelligence from the Soviet Union and the Middle East, the defence of the Ploieşti oil region and of the rail and river links remained priorities for the Abwehr.[66] In its turn, the SSI continued to accord particular attention to the security of the oil region, creating under a decree-law of 16 September 1942 relating to sabotage in factories and storage facilities, on the German model[67] Section V Countersabotage led by Lieutenant-Colonel Alexandru Proca.[68] The country's area was divided into 7 regions for the section's purposes, the 4th region commanded by Captain Ungurelu Longin,[69] with its headquarters at Ploieşti, being responsible for the oil fields.[70] Although in the period 1940-1944 there were a few isolated accidents, fires and explosions which might have been put down to sabotage, the importance of these in the context of oil production and export to the Reich from Romania was minimal. In fact, the battle for "the black gold," waged by the Abwehr with the Allied intelligence agencies in the corridors of the secret front in Romania was won in 1940, which ensured the continued supply of fuel to the German war machine down to Romania's *volte-face* 23 August 1944. The Abwehr's victory would not have been possible, however, without the intelligence contribution of the SSI, one which was decisive in this regard. The destruction of the British and French sabotage networks in the oil fields removed any possibility that the export of Romanian oil to Germany might be interrupted. Foreseeing this defeat, the British diplomat Robin Hankey – head of chancery at the British legation in Bucharest – had noted in September 1940 that "for the future our hopes of stopping oil seem to rest almost entirely on air opera-

Romania remained undiscovered until June 1944: see Dennis Deletant, "Researching MI6 and Romania, 1940+49," *The Slavonic and East European Review* 89, 4 (October 2011): 662-689.

[66] Staatsarchiv Wien/Abteilung Kriegsarchiv, B 653 – Nachlass Erich Rodler, B 653:3 Oberst a. D. Erich Rodler "Rumänien im Schatten des Hakenkreuzes (Mit der Deutschen Heeresmission 1940-1944 in Rumänien)."

[67] *Monitorul Oficial*, I, 217, September 17, 1942. Decree-Law no. 687 of 16.09.1942 to combat the transmission of information and sabotage in public and private enterprises and warehouses.

[68] Alexandru Proca (1900-1945), Romanian career officer and chemistry graduate of the University of Iaşi. He passed out of the infantry school of officers in 1919 and was commissioned as second lieutenant in the same year. SSI officer (01.04.1935-11.09.1944); head of Section V Counter-sabotage SSI (09.1942-11.09.1944). Dismissed from the SSI, he was arrested by the Communist authorities in March 1945 and committed suicide while detained on 29.03.1945. Captain (01.10.1929); major (31.03.1938); lieutenant-colonel (18.07.1942). AMR, Fund *Memorii bătrâni*, letter P, no. 158, f. 1-61.

[69] Ungurelu Longin (1912- ?), Romanian career officer. Graduate of Bucharest Polytehnic and the infantry school of officers (1931-1933). Joined the army as a second lieutenant (1933); moved to the technical branch on 31.08.1941. Head of Region IV-Counter-sabotage Ploieşti (09.1942-23.08.1944). Passed into the reserve on 04.01.1947, arrested by the Communist authorities on 06.12.1949 and sentenced to 8 years in jail for "intense activity against the working class." Released in 1957. Lieutenant (24.01.1938); captain (01.11.1942). CNSAS, Fund *Penal*, no. 1782 (Ungurelu Longin şi alţii), vol. 5, f. 3-19. Declaration of 04.05.1951 of Ungurelu Longin.

[70] CNSAS, Fund *Penal*, no. 1782 (Ungurelu Longin şi alţii), vol. 2, f. 402-408. "Instrucţiuni cu privire la activitatea şi atribuţiile ofiţerului şef de regiune contrasabotaj;" f. 409-413. "Decizia Preşedinţiei Consiliului de Miniştri;" f. 414-428. "Instrucţiuni cu privire la activitatea delegaţilor însărcinaţi cu măsurile de prevenire a actelor de spionaj şi sabotaj în întreprinderi."

tions, supplemented by anything that can be done of a less regular character."[71] Indeed, Hankey's forecast proved correct since production and export to the Reich was only seriously interrupted by the Allied air-raids from April to August 1944.

---

[71] Barker, *British Policy*, 40.

Incomplete Modernization and State Socialism in East-Central Europe.
A Framework of Analysis of Post-Communist Local Political Elites

Roxana Marin

Introductory notes: Three types of state socialism and incomplete modernization

The region of Eastern and Central Europe has been historically imposed as a geo-political reality, a separate entity often contrasted to Western, civilized, advanced and democratically consolidated Europe. Conceptual clarification is required straight away: the present study employs the collocation "state socialism" when referring to the *ancien régime* before 1989 in the countries of East-Central Europe, preferred to similar, sometimes – though mistakenly – interchangeable terms such as "Communism," "totalitarianism," "authoritarianism" or "socialism." The usage "state socialism" here is motivated, first, by the general lack of clarity and accurate description in the afore-mentioned terms, and, second, by the particular accuracy it entails: "state socialism" – or for that matter "really existing socialism" – isolates the very essence of the regimes installed in 1947/8 in East-Central Europe, *i.e.* the outcome of Soviet imposition in the region of regimes conceived as socialist and designed to lead towards Communism, although eminently unable to realise the utopia of economically equal individuals A conceptual history for each of the afore-mentioned terms is beyond the immediate scope of the present paper; suffice to say that "totalitarianism" seems too strong a concept to describe the period after Khrushchev's secret speech of 1956, while "authoritarianism" appears too weak a notion to account for the initial period of Stalinist terror regimes in East-Central Europe.

Each Central and East European country that experienced regime change in 1989 displays its own peculiarities regarding the causes of the revolution and the manner in which it occurred. The pattern is undoubtedly similar – popular protests followed by negotiation between two opposing sides, ending in the overthrow of the Communist *nomenklatura* and its replacement by a new reformist elite –, but case studies or, at least, separate analysis of groups of countries can provide a more in-depth understanding of the Revolutions of 1989. The specificities of each Communist regime lie in what Ken Jowitt identified in *The New World Disorder* as the mixture of causes generated by "regime political culture," "elite political culture" and "community political culture" in each country facing radical change in 1989.[1]

Herbert Kitschelt et al. advance a way to analyze regime change in East-Central Europe by employing case studies of pairs of states with similar socio-political and economic features – hence highlighting the discrepancies in each case. They distinguish three

[1] Kenneth Jowitt, *The New World Disorder: The Leninist Extinction* (Berkeley, California & Los Angeles: University of California Press, 1992), 55-56.

types of Communist regime and hence three types of "post-modern revolutions" and transitions: "patrimonial" Communism, "national-accommodative" Communism and "bureaucratic-authoritarian" Communism.[2] The "patrimonial" Communist regimes of Romania and Bulgaria arose in the context of an economy strongly dominated by agriculture and a social composition clearly dominated by peasants; as a result, these societies were rural, featuring extensive personal rule (favoured by the small nepotistic ruling clique, but also by the Orthodox Church), predominantly vertical relations of personal dependency (*i.e.* patron-client relations) and favouritism in public affairs. Consequently, when the Communist parties seized power after 1945, they were small in size and insignificant in the political arena, primarily because they represented the interests of the almost absent working class. After acquiring power, the Communist leaders initiated intense industrialization to enlarge the working class and hence their popular support. Both the co-optation and the repression practiced by the regime generated a weak and inert opposition. Monolithism, rather than factionalism, of the party is the norm in this case.

The second type of Communist regime, the "national-accommodative," is specific to Poland and Hungary, where prior to 1945 industrialization had mostly achieved its goals, generating however a largely unorganized working class. Rural communities did survive here, but the towns sheltered independent–minded intellectuals in governmental positions; rational, bureaucratic procedures and impersonal legal relations were to be found in the governance of such states prior to the installation of state socialism, together with a certain degree of elite contestation. In Catholic Poland and Protestant Hungary the Communist parties were also small, but their role in the anti-fascist resistance during World War II and then in post-war reconstruction helped them to greater popular support. After they took power, they found themselves unable to institutionalize the regime fully, despite the existence and implementation of a repressive system: opposition mounted, helped primarily by the Catholic Church, independent of state authority but dependent on an external authority (*i.e.* Rome). The regimes were somewhat tolerant of dissident movements, which led to violent popular outbreaks that undoubtedly shook the Communist states' ability to preserve order and even, to some extent, their own existence (*e.g.* the Hungarian Revolution of 1956, the Poznan uprising of 1956, the Gdansk strike of 1970, the Solidarity strike of 1988, etc.). Allowing for domestic differences, the leaders of these "national-accommodative" regimes adopted policies that would somehow suggest a degree of national autonomy towards the "Soviet hegemony."

Finally, the "bureaucratic-authoritarian" Communist regimes in the German Democratic Republic and Czechoslovakia were instituted in countries that had experienced a significant democratic period prior to 1933/1938 and began modernization long before 1945. Both the GDR and Czechoslovakia were industrialized states with an extensive

---

[2] Herbert Kitschelt, Zdenka Mansfeldova, Radoslaw Markowski and Gábor Tóka, *Post-Communist Party Systems: Competition, Representation, and Inter-Party Cooperation* (Cambridge & New York: Cambridge University Press, 1999), 23-26.

working class that was largely organized and unionized. As a result the Communist parties were an important force on the political scene. The countries were urbanized; here informal relations were generally abandoned, in favour of impersonal procedures and legal-rational, bureaucratic governance. Once the Communist parties seized power in these states, they appealed to a significant mass of workers and constructed a highly organized and disciplined political apparatus. This is why any attempt at opposition to the regime was rapidly and violently repressed (the Prague Spring of 1968 or the revolt of 17th June 1953 in the GDR were singular episodes of violent opposition in these countries).

Three types of post-Communist local elites and the "Leninist legacy" as applied to three Municipal Councils

In a renowned contribution to the flourishing field of transitological studies after the *annus mirabilis* 1989, the American scholar Kenneth Jowitt ventured to analyze what he compellingly labels "the Leninist legacy," *i.e.* the set of institutional practices, societal customs, behavioural and attitudinal inclinations specific to the social climate imposed by the *ancien régime*, and subsequently inherited by the post-Communist socio-political arrangement. Having introduced the main features of the three types of Communist dictatorships identified by Kitschelt et al., the present paper attempts to exemplify the "Leninist legacy," the heritage of the regimes, in local political elites in three of the six countries briefly presented above; the cases are specifically chosen to represent three instances of the three types of "Communist dictatorships" in East-Central Europe in 1947/8-1989: Tecuci (in Romania) as the prototype of a legacy of "modernizing-nationalizing" state socialism; Česká Lípa (in the Czech Republic) as symptomatic of "bureaucratic-authoritarian" Communist dictatorship; and Oleśnica (in Poland) as the epitome for "national-accommodative" state socialism.

The three towns are quite similar in terms of population and economic activity, while the units of analysis for each were the members of the municipal or local councils. This paper aims to identify those main characteristics in "elite political culture" that were reproduced and perpetuated from the defunct regime to the post-Communist era, according to which kind of state socialism the elites had previously belonged to or experienced. Different views of Communist dictatorship yield different forms of "elite political culture" and different attitudes to the challenges of democracy. Directly corresponding to the three types of Communist dictatorship (national-accommodative, bureaucratic-authoritarian and modernizing-nationalizing"), this paper identifies three types of post-Communist elite at the local level: (a) "predominantly democratic," (b) "democratic elitist," and (c) "predominantly elitist." Starting from this premise, the present study looks at (1) the social biographies of local political elites in the three cases (particularly father's social status, and age), (2) the power networks and interactions of the local political elites, and (3) the values embraced by the three elite groups. Employing these tools and the case-studies provided by three small-to-medium communities and their elites, this study is inclined to conclude that there is a direct and immediate dependency between the form of state socialism in each of six Eastern or Central European countries and the outlook (i.e. activities, attitudes, behaviours) of post-Communist political elites, even at the local level. Significantly, some findings on the world-views of post-Communist local political elites are sometimes negatively constructed to oppose the previous regime's traditions and practices; these tendencies, frequently found among members of the present-day municipal councils in the selected countries, were also considered and likewise interpreted as indicating a conspicuous "legacy" of the Communist past.

The first variable considered is that of age, to make sense of the extent to which the selected council members were exposed to the previous period of state socialism. The age of local councillors in Tecuci varies from 33 to 72 years old. In Česká Lípa, the youngest municipal councillor is 27 years old, while the eldest is 67 years old. In Oleśnica, the youngest councillor is 32 years old, while the eldest is 66, the lowest among the three cases. The greater part of the local council in Tecuci is composed of persons 40-50 years old (30%) or 50-60 years old (25%). The average age of the local political elite in Tecuci is 52.4 years. For the municipal council of Česká Lípa, a stable majority (40%) are aged 50-59, as in Tecuci; the average age in the Czech case is 47.24 years, unsurprisingly lower than in Tecuci. Age distribution for the municipal council in Oleśnica is concentrated, as expected, around the 40-49 range (42.85%), with 28.58% aged 50-59 and 21.42% aged 60-66 group. The average age of the local political elite in Oleśnica is 51.35 years, closer to Tecuci but in-between the two other cases.

Age is instrumental in the selection and election of political elites, being a mark of maturity, seriousness, stability and constancy. Generally, older members of the political elite are seen as more professional and politically experienced, with a good reputation among the electorate of a rather small community – they are married, with children, have stable jobs and recognised careers. Moreover, mature, middle-aged individuals embrace view-points which are not too obsolete and remote (specific to the older political elite who lived and worked in the previous totalitarian regime), but not too superfluous and volatile (specific to the young political elite). To some extent, the middle-aged local political elite is realistic and pragmatic, free of both the idealism of the youngest and the traditionalism and conservatism of the oldest. Moreover, the age of the local political elite is crucial to the conjectures proposed by this paper, since almost three-quarters of council members scrutinized here underwent "primary" and "secondary" socialization during the last stages of state socialism: in 1989, at the collapse of the Communist regimes, they were in their twenties and thirties, hence completely socialized under state socialism, shaped and reshaped by the precepts and practices of the *ancien régime*. It is thus to be expected that these individuals would dominantly display features and attitudinal and behavioural traits inherited from state socialism.[3]

[3] For a comprehensive analysis on the primary and secondary socialization during state socialism, see James

a. How elitist is the local political elite in Tecuci, Česká Lípa and Oleśnica?

Following Eldersveld,[4] the present paper asks how "elitist" is the local political elite in Tecuci, Česká Lípa and Oleśnica? This refers not exclusively to the economic status of members of the local councils but also to their general perceptions of such democratic features as citizen participation, social mobility, economic equality, etc., and to congruence or divergence between their values and perceptions and those of the electorate they represent.

One major indicator analyzed here is the occupation of the councillors' fathers, in order to assess the degree of social mobility within the local political elite. Moreover, a local representative's social background can give a hint of his attitudes towards the poor sectors of the population, the socially disadvantaged, etc. In Tecuci, according to the answers which members of the local council gave to the questionnaire, the majority of them (78.94%) come from a lower- or working-class family. In such cases, their fathers had only a lower- to middle-school education (with only four or eight classes and an elementary education). In Česká Lípa, the council largely (68%) comprises individuals from lower- and working-class families, with a very slight difference from Tecuci. In Oleśnica, the majority of councillors (53.33%) have a middle-class background, with only 26.66% from a lower-class family. Hence a significant degree of social mobility exists among the current members of the three local councils, with 78.94% in Tecuci, 68% in Česká Lípa and 26.66% in Oleśnica coming from poor, less educated families. There is no case of downward social mobility among the local councillors, and only three cases (15.78%) for Tecuci, eight cases (32%) for Česká Lípa and eight cases (68%) for Oleśnica of social immobility. Using Boudon's[5] formula to calculate the rate of upward social mobility in the local political elite,

$$AM = \frac{\Sigma n_{ij} \times 100}{N}$$

$$AM = \frac{16 \times 100}{19} = 84.21 \text{ (for Tecuci)}, \quad AM = \frac{17 \times 100}{25} = 68 \text{ (for Česká Lípa), and}$$

$$AM = \frac{6 \times 100}{19} = 31.57 \text{ (for Oleśnica)},$$

we see that 84.21% of council members in Tecuci, 68% of council members in Česká Lípa, and only 31.57% of council members in Oleśnica are socially and occupationally above their fathers. The overwhelming proportion of upwardly mobile municipal council-

---

R. Millar and Sharon L. Wolchik, eds., *The Social Legacy of Communism* (Cambridge & New York: Cambridge University Press [Woodrow Wilson Center Series], 1994).

[4] Samuel Eldersveld, *Political Elites in Modern Societies. Empirical Research and Democratic Theory* (Ann Arbor: The University of Michigan Press, 1989).

[5] Raymond Boudon, ed., *Tratat de sociologie* [initially published in French as *Traité de sociologie* (Paris: PUF, 1992)] (București: Humanitas, 1997), 178.

lors is unsurprising in the context of the regime changes of 1989 and the subsequent gradual social developments, generally somewhere between "the last should be first" and "everyone gets ahead," a combination which in practice results in a veritable "some get ahead."[6] The lower level of upward mobility in the Polish case is in fact surprising, though not accidental considering the nature of state socialism in Poland which allowed increasing social mobility and the development of a middle-class (53.33%). Actually, especially in Romania, the high level of upward mobility among the local elites is due to the fact that the mass of the population was rural or proletarian under state socialism, generating a great wave of young individuals after 1989 who aspired to a better social and occupational status than their worker or peasant fathers. A slightly lower rate of upward mobility is found among members of the municipal council in Česká Lípa, also because of the initial social status of their families of origin: in socialist Czechoslovakia, especially in the period of the 1968 Prague Spring, a sort of middle-class petty bourgeoisie gradually started to develop against a background of political and socio-economic reforms, *détente* and apparent relaxation, hence breaking the social monopoly of the working class. A small fragment of the present political elite originates in these petty bourgeois families: in the case of Česká Lípa, the proportion is 28%.

b. Values embraced by the local political elite

Analysis of the opinions and attitudes adopted by the local political elite is paramount in describing this group. Certain values embraced by representatives of the local elite can be explained by their social background: for instance, those from lower-class families can be expected to favour economic equality. Other values are acquired in the process of socialization (i.e. education, episodes of primary socialization, etc.).[7] According to the local councillors' answers, the features most valued in a democracy are citizen participation (33.33% of councillors in Oleśnica, 35.29% in Tecuci and an overwhelming 59.09% in Česká Lípa), the avoidance of political conflict (35.29% of councillors in Tecuci and a comparable 33.33% in Oleśnica) and innovative, gradual, piecemeal change (29.41% of councillors in Tecuci, 16.66% in Oleśnica, 18.18% in Česká Lípa). Conflict avoidance is not a democratic priority for the councillors in Česká Lípa (9.09% of respondents), 13.63% of whom see economic equality as central, mainly due to the presence of a strong leftist side within the Council, including Social Democrats and Communists. In Oleśnica, 16.66% of responses prioritise economic equality and welfare, partly due to the profes-

[6] Tomaś Kolosi and Andraś Róna-Tas, "The Last Shall Be the First? The Social Consequences of the Transition from Socialism" (paper presented at the *Meeting of the ISA Research Committee 28 on Social Stratification*, Trento (Italy), May 14-16, 1992, in manuscript at the CEU Library).

[7] The present research evaluated the attitudes of the local political elite – i.e. of the members of the Local Council in Tecuci and of the Municipal Councils of Česká Lípa and Oleśnica, respectively – towards five values: four of them refer to the fundaments of the democratic construct and they were quantified by question no. 9 in the administered questionnaire: citizen participation; gradual, innovative change; the importance of the political conflict; economic equality. The attitudes towards state intervention in economy were quantified through attitudinal intensity scale (I strongly agree with – I agree with – I partially agree with – I disagree with – I strongly disagree with – Don't know/ don't answer).

sional status of the councillors (in small communities, teachers and former/current non-governmental activists are traditionally concerned with welfare and social security issues, while intrinsically they bear leftist views), but also to their age (many are retired older persons, politically socialized primarily under a Communist regime that put a marked emphasis on economic equality and on eliminating or attenuating differences in the standard of living among citizens – otherwise immanent in any social arrangement). More importantly in the case of Tecuci, none of the respondents saw economic equality as central to democracy; this attitude proves a clear break with the *ancien régime*'s practices of encouraging economic equality, at least at the rhetorical, declarative level. Moreover it shows that once an individual has acquired high social and occupational status, he/she tends strongly to reject economic equality in favour of the merit or competition which lifted him or her from the masses. Hence, a clear rejection of two values was observed among the local councillors: those of economic equality and political conflict. The majority of local councillors in Tecuci see the avoidance of political conflict as beneficial for democracy and for the general good. Unusual as it may appear, among members of the local council in Tecuci there is an irreducible contradiction between what Dahl labelled "political participation" and "political contestation,"[8] between "political liberty" (expressed in conflict) and "political equality" (expressed in participation).[9]

It might reasonably be hypothesized that, while economic equality as a fundamental policy might appear far-fetched, a certain degree of societal welfare is somehow inseparably associated with the democratic *desideratum*[10] as an indispensable prerequisite for democratic development; moreover, the two "new democracies" that registered the most significant and comprehensive achievements in democratic development, Poland and the Czech Republic, conspicuously learned this instrumental lesson properly and internalizated the value, translating it at the local level through a political elite who value economic equality and a concern for the citizens' welfare as a part of democracy, despite

---

[8] Robert Dahl, *Modern Political Analysis* (Englewood Cliffs, New Jersey: Prentice-Hall, 1984), 31.

[9] Joel Aberbach, Robert Putnam and Bert Rockman, *Bureaucrats and Politicians in Western Democracies* (Cambridge: Harvard University Press, 1981), 172-173.

[10] The relationship between economic welfare and democratic advance (a rather passive relation, influence-type one, since it is assumed that democracy develops and evolves at a certain level of economic standard for the citizens of the polity) is commonplace in the general study of democratic development and consolidation. Among the scholars that perceived economic welfare as *sine qua non* for the democratic drive, particularly in the "new democracies," see the renowned seminal work of Seymour Martin Lipset, "Some Social Requisites of Democracy: Economic Development and Political Legitimacy," *American Political Science Review* 53, 1 (March 1959): 69-105, but also Uk Heo and Alexander C. Tan, "Democracy and Economic Growth: A Causal Analysis," *Comparative Politics* 33, 4 (July 2001): 463-473; Adam Przeworski, "Democracy and Economic Development," in *The Evolution of Political Knowledge*, ed. Edward D. Mansfield and Richard Sisson, vol. II (Columbus, Ohio: Ohio State University Press, 2004), 300-338; Hristos Doucouliagos and Mehmet Ali Ulubasoglu, "Democracy and Economic Growth: A Meta-Analysis," *American Journal of Political Science* 52, 1 (January 2008): 61-83; John Gerring, Philip Bond, William T. Barndt and Carola Moreno, "Democracy and Economic Growth: A Historical Perspective," *World Politics* 57 (April 2005): 323-364; Alina Rocha Menocal, "Analyzing the Relationship between Democracy and Development: Defining Basic Concepts and Assessing Key Linkages" (paper prepared for *the Wilton Park Conference on Democracy and Development*, Steyning (West Sussex, UK), October 23-25, 2007), 1-17.

a Communist past that at least rhetorically put great emphasis on the (otherwise dangerous and quite unrealistic) idea of economic equality. Generally, the feature which local political elites in East-Central European countries most value for democracy is citizen participation, with an overall average of 42.57% of the total population studied; nevertheless, the consensus that the primacy of this value substantively defines "democracy" is definitely clearest in the council of Česká Lípa, resulting in a more "democratic" local elite in the Czech case.[11] The discussion of democracy's capacity to avoid conflict is largely open, since it is not clear to members of the three councils whether democracy should provide an arena for clashing interests, opinions, perspectives, policies and behaviours, or create the channels through which conflict is neutralized and institutionalized. In this sense, the most evident discrepancy is between the Czech case (where a mere 9.09% of respondents perceive conflict avoidance as paramount for democracy) and the quite similar proportions in the Romanian and Polish cases (a clearly more significant 35.29% and 33.33%, respectively, argue that conflict avoidance is of the utmost importance for any democratic system). As a result, one might commonsensical contend that the political leadership in Tecuci and Oleśnica display a consensual, "consociational" decisional style, focused on bargaining, compromise, dialogue and negotiation in decision-making, whereas the local political elite in Česká Lípa display a rather confrontational, conflicting decisional style, oriented towards debate and polemics in decision-making.

To sum up: using a classification based on acceptance of participation-conflict and economic equality-interventionism, the majority of local councillors in Tecuci fall into the categories of populists (accepting citizen participation but seeking to avoid political conflict) and statists/anti-egalitarians (partially accepting state intervention in the economy, but rejecting economic equality). The majority of councillors in Česká Lípa can be categorized as democrats (accepting both citizen participation and political conflict) and statists-egalitarians (clearly accepting state intervention in the economy and partially desiring economic equality). The council of Oleśnica is typical for democrats and statists/anti-egalitarianists, borrowing from both the Romanian and the Czech cases, yet again an in-between instance.

Concluding remarks

The present paper isolates one main explanatory variable to account for the differences among the three selected cases:[12] the different forms of "Leninist legacy" corresponding

[11] The "democratic" political elite is one of the four typologies constructed by Virgil Stoica, *Cine conduce Iașul?* [Who Governs Iași?] (Iași: Editura Fundației Axis, 2003), 203-206. The scholar distinguishes among four types of elites, by triangulated between the level of their acceptance/ rejection of citizen participation as a defining value of democracy and the degree of their acceptance/ rejection of political conflict within a democracy. The resulting types of political elites are: (1) "authoritarianists" (i.e. rejection of both citizen participation and political conflict), (2) "populists" (i.e. acceptance of citizen participation combined with rejection of political conflict), (3) "pluralists" (i.e. rejection of citizen participation associated with acceptance of political conflict), and (4) "democrats" (i.e. acceptance of both citizen participation and political conflict).

[12] The research considers, in fact, in its entirety, three independent variables accounting for differences in the two cases: (1) the legacy and the type of the former regime, (2) the level of administrative decentralization,

to the three types of state socialism elucidated above and informing "elite political culture"[13] and of "democratic elitism."[14] The term "elite political culture" means different things in the literature. Robert Putnam famously referred to some form of attitudinal and behavioural aggregates in the elite group, generally constant, hardly changeable, stable; the term accounts for "patterns of beliefs and attitudes (prevalent among members of the political elite) about the economic, political, social, cultural systems."[15] In applying the observations drawn from usage of these concepts, we can only wonder whether the three selected councils of the municipalities of Tecuci, Česká Lípa and Oleśnica have acquired a sense of group consciousness as an elite; such an "elite consciousness" conducive to "democratic elitism" at the local level is hard to operationalize and subsequently measure, but an attempt might employ such indicators as the degree of group cohesion and the acknowledgement of specific traits that a local councillor should possess. The presence of elite consciousness is a prerequisite if we are to speak of and comprehensively analyze the "elite political culture" developed under state socialism, and different in the national-accommodative, bureaucratic-authoritarian or patrimonial forms.

For the specific cases in this paper, there is surely a more profound sense of group solidarity (which respondents commonly refer to as "collegiality" and "team spirit") and cohesion among members of the local councils: they generally think alike, have the same priorities, embrace the same values, have a largely similar social and family background, they resemble each other, to some extent even in demographic terms (approximately the same age, religion, ethnicity). However, this is not sufficient: do they feel that they belong to the town's elite, to the upper strata of the community?

The various links and interactions of local political elites in formerly state socialist countries are compelling indicators of the "Leninist legacy," as the networks of power represent inherited contacts which the elite has preserved in the present social structure. Answers to the questionnaire show that members of the local council in Tecuci most frequently establish and develop contacts with business groups (19.51% of responses). In the case of Tecuci, the established networks of power are particularly significant, since relations between the two groups extend to family connections. Therefore, an insistence on personalized politics becomes more visible in the case of the Tecuci elite, where nepotist connections are still to be sporadically encountered. The problem arises exactly in such highly-localized relations among elites that tend to virtually monopolize the entire range of connections which local elite can establish and cultivate. The conspicuous predominance of local connections, created exclusively within the narrow confines of the town, de-

---

and, finally, (3) the "elite political culture." For the time being, this paper discusses briefly the last one.

[13] Elite political culture is "a set of informal adaptative (behavioural and attitudinal) postures that emerge as response to and consequence of a given elite's identity-forming experiences." Jowitt, *New World Disorder*, 51-52 and 54-56.

[14] John Higley and Heinrich Best, eds., *Democratic Elitism: New Theoretical and Comparative Perspectives* (Leiden, The Netherlands: BRILL, 2010).

[15] Robert D. Putnam, *The Beliefs of Politicians. Ideology, Conflict, and Democracy in Britain and Italy* (New Haven, Connecticut: Yale University Press, 1973).

monstrates the tight-knit character of the local political elite in Tecuci. On the other hand, since the political and the economic elite overlap in Tecuci, the elite's closest connections are with business entities and groups, which may frequently be developed beyond the immediate space of the town. Therefore, the same individuals are reluctant to create and sustain broader, looser relations in their capacity as political elite, though at the same time they often establish business connections outside the town in their capacity as economic elite. If C. Wright-Mills describes a famously inseparable and inextricable interconnection of political, economic and military elites in American society in the 50s,[16] Tecuci faces the reality of a virtual overlap between the political and economic local elites: the potentates of the town are at one and the same time the economic magnates and political leaders.

In Česká Lípa, the most common interactions are with reform and civic groups (25.39% of responses); the council is largely formed of individuals with extensive political experience in local officialdom, representing the middle class of the town, highly educated and financially independent.

It is important to note that the local elite of Oleśnica is as isolated as the other two groups in terms of power networks and interactions with elites at the national level. Overall, the members of the Oleśnica council are the most isolated in terms of power networks and elite interactions, with only 5.26% of councillors establishing contacts with other groups beyond their constituencies. The increased isolation of the Czech and Polish local political elites is partially explained through the more significant degree of decentralization: in both the Czech and the Polish cases, the local elite focuses primarily on immediate issues for their communities, linking their interests to groups within these communities, while contacts with elites beyond the town become increasingly sporadic. The Oleśnica political elite's most important community relations are with neighbourhood groups – 39.47% of responses – and, more significantly, with civic and reform groups – 21.05%. Comparison shows that elite relations with the neighbourhood are most frequent – and thus most important – in the Polish case. In Oleśnica, a significant number of councillors are professionals employed in civil society organizations, closely linked to the work of various NGOs, particularly in the field of education. Somewhat unusually, therefore, the members of the political elite are simultaneously members of the civil society sector. The local political elite in Oleśnica is characteristic for the "predominantly democratic"[17] type of "democratic elitism."

---

[16] Famously, C. Wright-Mills argues, in his *The Power Elite* that the political elite (the "political directorate") is tightly linked to the economical (the "corporate chief tenets") and military elites (the "war lords"). The connections go back to the childhood of the members of these elites; the members of these three groups shared the same familiar and educational backgrounds; established links since high-school or college and, since then, they preserved the same personal relations: they meet in rather informal than formal fashion, there are even psychological similarities between them (e.g. their behaviour is the same in contexts of crisis). See Charles Wright-Mills, *The Power Elite* (Paris: Maspero, 1969).

[17] In what follows, the paper distinguishes between three types of "democratic elitism": (1) "predominantly elitist," (2) "democratic elitist," and (3) "predominantly democratic," in the attempt to fit the three cases into comprehensive categories.

Surprisingly, the members of the local council in Tecuci do display a sense of prominence within the community, if not economically speaking (for those who are the leading entrepreneurs of the town), then at least where reputation is concerned; in a small community such as those analyzed here, the prestige attached to a well-regarded occupation (doctor, engineer and especially teacher) or to "great deeds" of community service (for those administering public spaces, for instance) is a particularly important mark of distinction, conducive to a sense of elitism. As a rule, a member of the council attributed with above-average socio-economic and educational status might identify as part of the political elite. The nature of the councillor's profession is equally important, with lawyers, white-collar workers and businessmen being the most frequent incumbents here; they are more apt for leading roles owing to their skills acquired in training and through experience. Incumbents are preferred to non-incumbents because "they already wear the mantle of the elected public official."[18] Guided by experience and with the weight of precedent to justify his or her actions, an incumbent is prone to crystallize "elite group awareness." Similarly, another attribute of political elites is that their local connections make them known and trusted throughout the constituency, increasing the chances that they will perceive themselves as distant from the mass. The local elite in Tecuci thus falls under the category of a "predominantly elitistic" group.

Conversely, the group consciousness of the council of Česká Lípa may be seen through the paradigm of "democratic elitism,"[19] *i.e.* the more or less natural reconciliation between the democratic *desideratum* of popular sovereignty and the elitist conception of actual rule by the few. The Česká Lípa elite particularly takes such an approach to the public, administrative affairs of the community: while well aware of their position in the power hierarchy of the town, the local elite here tend to confound themselves with the bulk of the population they represent, at least at a discursive level. Nevertheless, this attitude is conspicuously contradicted by the clear discrepancy in education between elite and electorate: the political elite of Česká Lípa are highly educated, with the large majority of councillors having post-graduate and even doctoral degrees. This provides exactly the distinctiveness and group consciousness of members of the Česká Lípa council, in contrast with the outlook of their constituency.

In the global study of "elite group consciousness" and "democratic elitism" *per se*, the communities of Tecuci, Česká Lípa and Oleśnica historically experienced a totalitarian past with a corresponding political culture at all three levels (regime, elite, community). Even more than two decades after the collapse of Communism, the legacy of the *ancien régime* remains. As already observed, the local political elite in Tecuci is rather statist/anti-egalitarian, which seems a paradox given the outlook of the defunct Communist regime: the image of the state as prominent in the socio-economic realm is preserved,

---

[18] David Butler, Howard R. Penniman and Austin Ranney, *Democracy at the Polls* (Washington, D.C.: American Enterprise Institute, 1981), 98.
[19] Higley and Best, eds., *Democratic Elitism*.

while economic equality is strongly rejected, exactly opposing the goals of the former leadership. In Czechoslovakia until 1989, the "theme" of the regime was the same, but the "variation" was not a modernizing-nationalizing,[20] patrimonial[21] dictatorship, as in Romania, but a bureaucratic-authoritarian,[22] welfare[23] Communist dictatorship. Conversely, in Česká Lípa in today's Czech Republic, the elites tend toward a "welfare state" approach in local policy, somehow acknowledging the social benefits of the former regime without nostalgia: this is probably why they fit into the category of statist-egalitarians, since a significant proportion are concerned with the social problems of the community they represent (especially unemployment) and still cherish economic equality as an indispensable value in democracy. The local councillors in Oleśnica incline towards the protectionist state, although paradoxically the Polish variant of state socialism, national-accommodative Communist dictatorship,[24] was the least restrictive in socio-economic and political terms and the most market-oriented. The statist-egalitarian perspective among the political elite in Oleśnica looks back to the more permissive type of Communist regime Poland experienced. All in all, the local elites examined here typify three countries which underwent widely-reported regime change in their recent history, marking a somewhat consistent process of "elite circulation" in the Czech and Polish cases, and a persistent "elite reproduction" in the Romanian case.[25]

The "voucher privatization"[26] of the early 90s has its repercussions in the world view of the local political elite in the Czech Republic today, since, as shown, middle-aged members of the council in Česká Lípa are inclined to favour statist stances and state intervention in economy. In the Romanian case probably the most obvious element inherited from the defunct regime and perpetuated at the local level is the political elite's perseverance in capturing leadership positions in other societal spheres as well, especially economic and social ones, less so in the cultural sphere. Not only do the local political elite in Tecuci monopolise economic activity, but they also lead the social life of the town

---

[20] Dragoș Petrescu, *Explaining the Romanian Revolution of 1989: Culture, Structure, and Contingency* (Bucharest: Editura Enciclopedică, 2010), 12, 47-48, 76, 113-118, 404.

[21] Kitschelt et al., *Post-Communist Party Systems*, 39.

[22] Ibid.; Juan L. Linz and Alfred C. Stepan, *Problems of Democratic Transition and Consolidation: Southern Europe, South America, and Post-Communist Europe* (Baltimore, Maryland: The Johns Hopkins University Press, 1996).

[23] Konrad H. Jarausch, "Care and Coercion: The GDR as Welfare Dictatorship," in *Dictatorship as Experience: Towards a Socio-Cultural History of the GDR*, ed. Konrad H. Jarausch, transl. by Eve Duffy (New York: Berghahn Books, 1999), 59-60.

[24] Kitschelt et al., *Post-Communist Party Systems*, 39.

[25] Iván Szelényi and Szonja Szelényi, "Circulation or Reproduction of Elites during the Postcommunist Transformation of Eastern Europe: Introduction," *Theory and Society* 24, 5, *Special Issue on Circulation vs. Reproduction of Elites during the Postcommunist Transformation of Eastern Europe* (October 1995): 615-638.

[26] Gil Eyal, "Anti-Politics and the Spirit of Capitalism: Dissidents, Monetarists, and the Czech Transition to Capitalism," *Theory and Society* 29, 1 (February 2000): 49-92 (50). See also the renowned Gil Eyal, Iván Szelényi and Eleanor Townsley, eds., *Making Capitalism Without Capitalists: The New Ruling Elites in Eastern Europe* (London: Verso, 1998).

through their positions in the hierarchy (as leading doctors, school principals, chairs of administrative committees, administrators of public space, etc.).

Moreover, surveying the councils in Tecuci, Česká Lípa to Oleśnica, we observe a monolithic elite, highly homogeneous in biography and demography, in their values, priorities and patterns of recruitment, cherishing party loyalty, political experience and collegiality (team spirit) especially, opposing a more heterogeneous elite group, demographically more diverse, with different values and cultural standards, with an intermediate case in Oleśnica, where a monolithic type of elite in terms of education, family background and occupational status is tempered by a constant concern with the problems of the immediate constituency and by meaningful involvement in civic and reform groups. Monolithism and the predominance of a "political model" might be reminiscent of elites under the former regime, while a "pragmatic model" and a fragmented elite group would correspond to a tradition of circulating elites and technocratic petty bourgeoisie during state socialism. Instead, nowadays the "pragmatic model" of "organizational and personal commitment," of efficiency and effective management, surpasses the importance of the "political model" of party and ideological loyalty: though the party affiliation and ideological affinities become crucial and even indispensable, they lose their importance in the face of localized community problems. Problem-solving, respect for the community, competence and the capacity to pinpoint development opportunities for the town take precedence when a group establishes itself as a local political elite. One may argue that the members of the three councils show signs of beginning to perceive themselves as a quite distinct group of notables within their respective communities. However, the "elitist exercise" is far from being a constant in the elite worldview in these three small communities, and the local elites have a rather "popular" view of leadership.

The variable of the "Leninist legacy"[27] of the Communist *ancien régime* appears central to the present analysis of differences between local elite groups, as significant characteristics of the local political elites in these cases are directly influenced by the worldview of defunct state socialism, preserved even in the post-Communist, transitional era. Particularly this legacy influences segments of the councillors' social biographies, the construction and design of power networks and elite interactions, the values embraced by the elite groups, etc. Yet the different cases of "Communist dictatorship" and their reverberations in the present local elite *milieu* are necessary but not sufficient to explain the complete landscape constructed and shaped by each local political elite in its own community, considering that a long series of post-Communist, transitional structural changes indiscriminately and indubitably marked these landscapes. In a nutshell, long-lasting traits of incomplete modernization[28] – proved by the dominance of informal networks and

[27] Kenneth Jowitt, "The Leninist Legacy," in *The Revolutions of 1989*, ed. Vladimir Tismăneanu (London: Routledge, 1999), 213-230.

[28] For an in-depth, path-breaking analysis of "incomplete modernization" in East-Central Europe, see the renowned Iván T. Berend, *History Derailed: Central and Eastern Europe in the Long Nineteenth Century*

interactions at the local elite level, by the rejection of political conflict, by the mixed views on gradual change, etc. – have been remodelled over almost half-a-century of state socialism, and afterwards translated in the outlook and behaviour of post-Communist elites in East-Central Europe. Notwithstanding these continuities, it is crucial to discern how the different forms of state socialism coped with the various limitations, incongruences and inconsistencies springing from the paradigm of incomplete modernization, and how they led afterwards to different types of post-Communist elites (even at the local level).

(Berkeley & Los Angeles, California: University of California Press, 2003), and idem, *Decades of Crisis: Central and Eastern Europe before World War II* (Berkeley & Los Angeles, California: University of California Press, 1998).

ANNEXES

1. The age of the members of the Local Council of Tecuci and of the Municipal Councils in Česká Lípa and Oleśnica

Age	**Number of members of the Municipal Council (expressed as a percentage from the total – 19, 25 and 19, respectively)**		
	Tecuci	**Česká Lípa**	**Oleśnica**
20-29	0%	8%	0%
30-39	5.26%	24%	7.14%
40-49	31.57%	16%	42.85%
50-59	36.84%	40%	28.57%
60-69	21.05%	12%	21.42%
70-79	5.26%	0%	0%
Over 80	0%	0%	0%

2. The social position of the fathers of the members of the Local Council of Tecuci and of the Municipal Councils in Česká Lípa and Oleśnica

Father's social status			
	Tecuci	**Česká Lípa**	**Oleśnica**
Lower class (with average or under-average studies)	78.94%	68%	26.66%
Middle class (with high-school or university studies)	15.78%	28%	53.33%
Upper class (with university studies)	5.26%	4%	20%

3. The interactions, contacts and the networks of power entertained by the members of the Local Council of Tecuci and of the Municipal Councils in Česká Lípa and Oleśnica (Q: To which of the following groups do you have the most numerous contacts and interactions?)

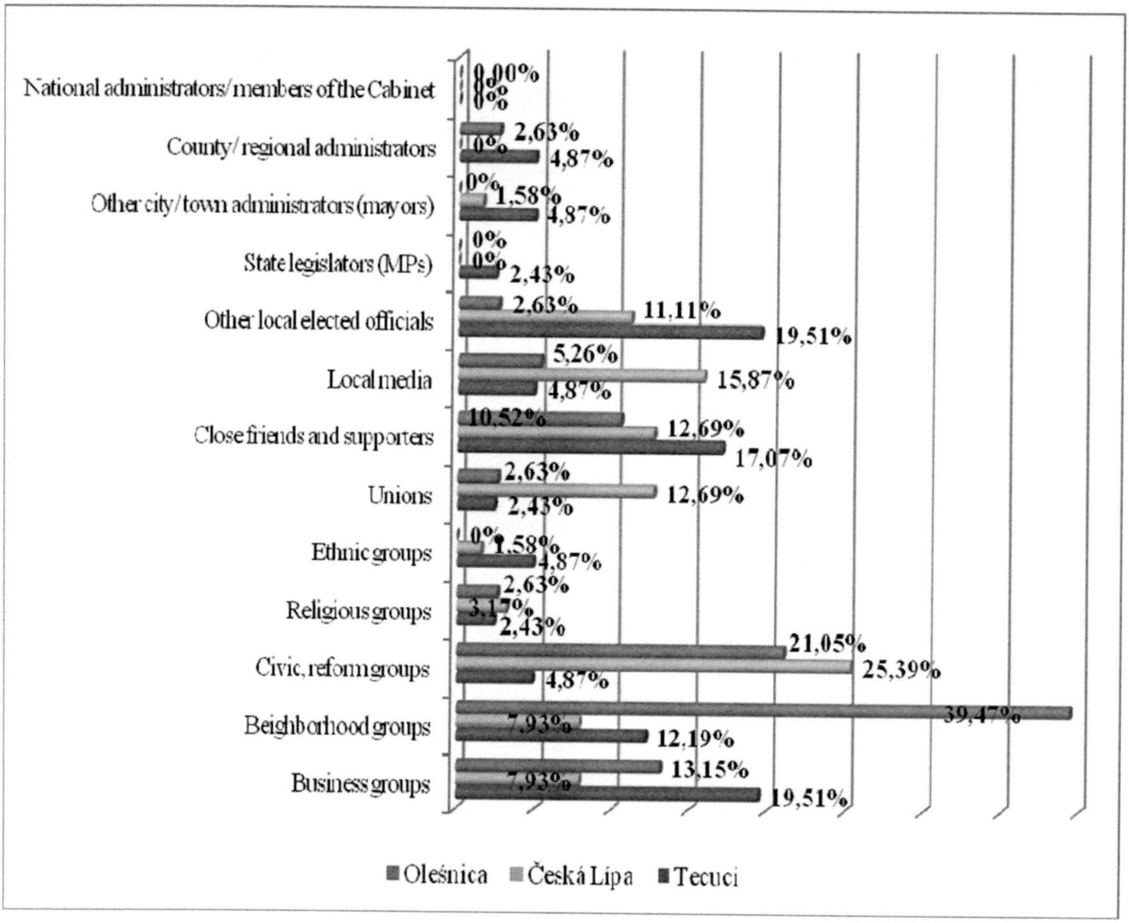

4. The values of the members of the Local Council of Tecuci and of the Municipal Councils in Česká Lípa and Oleśnica.

4.a. The most cherished aspect of a democratic arrangement

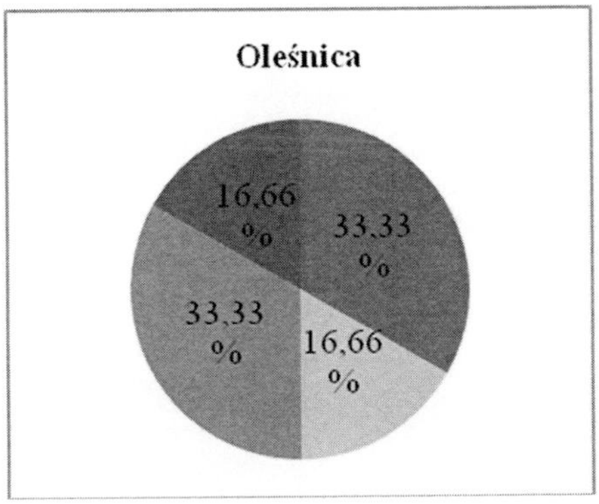

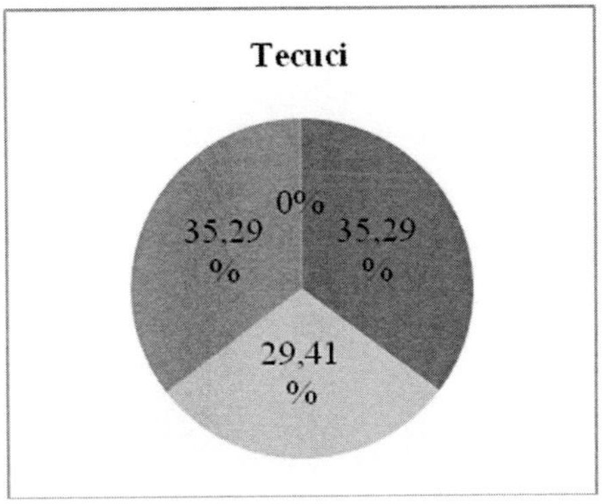

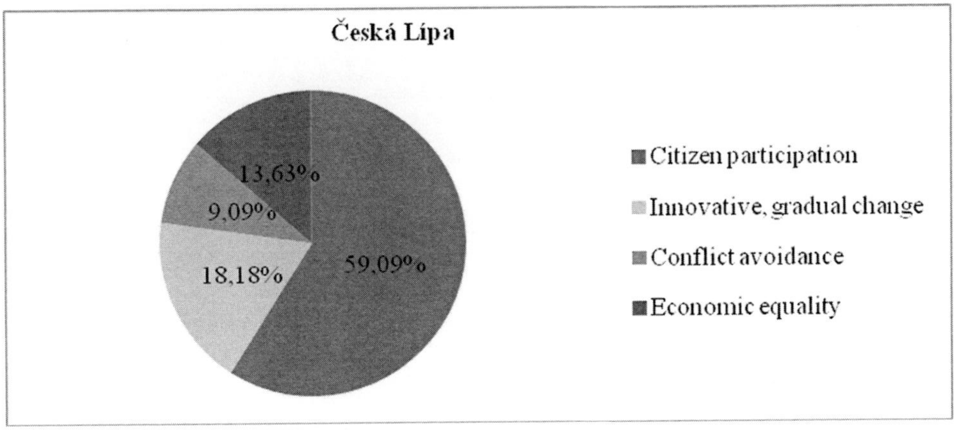

4.b. Types of post-communist local political elites according to value orientation

		State intervention in economy	
		Acceptance	Rejection
Economic equality	Acceptance	**Statists-egalitarianists** (*e.g.* Česká Lípa)	**Anti-statists-egalitarianists**
	Rejection	**Statists-anti-egalitarianists** (*e.g.* Tecuci, Oleśnica)	**Anti-statists-anti-egalitarianists**

		Political conflict	
		Acceptance	Avoidance
Citizen participation	Acceptance	**Democrats** (*e.g.* Česká, Lípa, Oleśnica)	**Populists** (*e.g.* Tecuci)
	Rejection	**Pluralists**	**Authoritarianists**

TERRITORIAL EXPANSION OF HIGHER EDUCATION IN COMMUNIST ROMANIA (1948-1989). An Outline of Patterns and Factors*

VLAD PAŞCA

Post-war higher education evolved toward general growth and specialization, in the context of socio-economic and political demands for continuous further training of individuals, for better research results and for innovation.[1] It is still a matter of debate whether in the Western world this phenomenon was shaped by the political-economic establishment or by the individual's pursuit of a better life, but in socialist countries higher education certainly served as one means to achieve the economic growth so keenly envisaged by Communist political rulers.

For this reason, higher education was subject to planning in European socialist societies. The planned economy needed to employ a suitable number of specialists; therefore student enrolment plans and course specializations had to be designed to comply with the claims of the regime, which aimed at full employment and the rational management of both material and human resources (as opposed to unemployment, speculation, and ultimately "chaos and misery").

In the case of Romania, the shift from an agricultural base to an industrial economy led to additional serious efforts conducted on educational grounds. The expansion of higher education was one such effort.[2] University cities increased from four before the war to thirteen in 1948, accompanied by an increase in the total number of students. Figures continued to rise throughout the period, reaching a height of nineteen centres of higher education and over 100,000 full-time students per year – four times the interwar numbers – during the 1970s. Later in the 1980s, enrolment dropped significantly and the network stagnated.

Higher education in Communist Romania was redesigned with the educational reform of 1948, which established a state-controlled educational system. Institutions bore

---

* Acknowledgements: This research has been carried on in the project PN-II-ID-PCE-2011-3-0476, *Economic Planning, Higher Education, and the Accumulation of Human Capital in Romania during Communism (1948-1989)*, supported by the Romanian National Research Council.

[1] Guy Neave, "Patterns," in *History of the University in Europe*, ed. Walter Rüegg (Cambridge: Cambridge University Press, 2011), 4: 31-65; UNESCO, *Statistical Yearbook* (Paris: UNESCO Publish., 1992), 3-239 and table 3.11.

[2] For an overview upon the Romanian higher education system during communism, see Jan Sadlak, *Higher Education in Romania, 1860-1990. Between Academic Mission, Economic Demands and Political Control* (Buffalo, NY: 1990), 23-64; Idem, "Planning of Higher Education in Countries with a Centrally Planned Socioeconomic System: Case Study of Poland and Romania" (PhD. diss., State University of New York, Buffalo, 1988); Bogdan Murgescu, *România şi Europa. Acumularea decalajelor economice (1500-2010)* [Romania and Europe. The Accumulation of Economic Disparities (1500-2010)] (Iași: Polirom, 2010), 384-391.

different names (universities, institutes, academies and conservatories) and delivered day courses (for full-time students) as well as evening classes and distance learning.[3] In terms of numbers, full-time students formed the actual majority, but in particular cases the other two categories of students could shift the balance.

From 1948 the reformed Ministry of Education (under various names) had the annual responsibility of planning both student admission quotas and the development of the institutional higher education network. The resultant plans had to be submitted to the State Planning Committee and other state agencies involved in the matter. The final say, however, belonged informally to the Communist leadership, namely the members of the Politburo and later on – after Nicolae Ceauşescu had built up his power – to the Secretary-General of the Romanian Communist Party (formerly the Romanian Workers Party).

In this study I address several questions related to the development of the institutional network of higher education, in order to outline its patterns and parameters, as well as possible outcomes. I was particularly curious about the reasons behind the placing of institutes, and about the agents/people involved in this decision-making process. I was interested in finding out whether any model was specifically employed or whether patterns just happened to emerge freely from the process. And if such a pattern of growth can be traced, was it structured horizontally (territorially) or vertically (relating to density)? Or both? And how far did the liberal (pre-Communist) legacy count in shaping the network? As for the dynamics of growth, was there a radical shift or a mellow increment? Did the expansion resemble the disintegration of powerful hubs, or was it rather a way to sustain the already congested larger centres?

I have tried to answer these issues by using statistical data and collecting information from the archival records of the former Romanian Communist Party, the Council of Ministries and the Ministry of Education.[4] Given that Party documents were mainly projections and that the statistical data revealed the facts, I had the chance to match the leadership's desire with the realities that resulted, thus assessing how Party and state worked together in this matter.

The evolution of higher education was permanently assessed in the Communist period and in consequence policy makers issued directives and guidelines – when necessary – which aimed at improving the system. These measures also affected the configuration of the higher education network, either radically or in a rather conservative manner. In 1948, there was an explosion of newly-founded centres of higher education in Braşov,

---

[3] In 1973, universities and academies had to comprise at least 4 departments/faculties each, whereas institutes could have at least two. Conservatories were oriented towards musical (in a more general extent – towards art) education (Arhivele Naţionale Istorice Centrale [The National Central Historical Archives], Bucureşti (henceforth abbreviated ANIC), Fund *C.C. al P.C.R., secţia Cancelarie* (henceforth abbreviated *CC – Cancelarie*), no. 84/1973, f. 67). However, names could be given in an arbitrary manner, thus partially ignoring the rules. In this article I will use a neutral term – institution of higher education.

[4] There were special fields – theological, military and police higher education – that I haven't taken into account, mainly because public data also didn't count them in and secrecy prevailed upon these three (therefore, there is a lack of information concerning these).

Craiova, Galați, Târgu-Mureș, Petroșani, Arad, Brad, Câmpulung Moldovenesc and Constanța. At the same time, institutes and departments were added in Bucharest, Cluj, Iași and Timișoara. Three years later, when the first five-year plan was to be implemented, an inter-ministry commission was set up to coordinate the development of the higher education system in close accordance with the plan's directives; after collecting suggestions, the Commission decided to merge the Institute of Mines in Brad with that in Timișoara.[5] In addition, more institutes and departments were created in established university cities. This allowed the twelve centres to grow, but smaller ones had to be sacrificed for the sake of improvement in higher education. A four-year educational plan in 1953 required that all forestry institutes be merged into a single site in Brașov/Stalin City.[6] This meant that there was no higher education in Câmpulung Moldovenesc after 1953. Likewise, the Fisheries Institute of Constanța went to the more powerful agro-naval centre of Galați.[7] Four years later the Agro-Veterinary Institute in Arad was closed.

During the remaining years of Gheorghe Gheorghiu-Dej's rule, the nine remaining centres (of the initial thirteen) entered another phase of consolidation, and the network only grew territorially in the early 1960s with the founding of three-years teacher training colleges to supply the rapidly growing public education system. These institutes were created in the towns of Bacău (1961), Baia Mare (1961), Pitești (1962), Oradea (1963), Suceava (1963), and the revived Constanța (1961).[8]

Later on, during the rule of Nicolae Ceaușescu after 1965, there was more improvement and less territorial expansion. Only four further centres were added – Ploiești (1967), Sibiu (1969), Hunedoara (1970) and Reșița (1971) – while significant institutional changes took place in the established system. Unified management was the goal in medium and small centres, so that institutes merged to become Universities – in Craiova (1966), Brașov (1971) and Galați (1974) – and Institutes of Higher Education – in Pitești, Bacău, Oradea, Constanța, Baia Mare, Sibiu and Suceava (mid 1970s). In 1976 branch technical colleges were established in industrial complexes in Arad, Bistrița and Miercurea-Ciuc, although they were not institutionally independent.[9] In geographical terms, the expansion of higher education came to an end in the mid-1970s, thus introducing a phase of stagnation and ultimately recession.

Founding a higher education institute was no easy task. One had to be sure that a suitable location, buildings for the campus, teaching staff and plenty of money were available, but more importantly – as the socialist system demanded – that its graduates were needed in Romanian society. Decision-makers discussed these issues when it came to founding a new institute, and usually several reasons were weighed at the same time.

---

[5] ANIC, Fund *Președinția Consiliului de Miniștri* (henceforth abbreviated *PCM*), no. 233/1951, f. 45.
[6] Idem, no. 676/1953, f. 8.
[7] Ibid., f. 6.
[8] Similar institutes had been established in 1959-1960 in the older centres (București, Cluj, Iași, Timișoara, Craiova, Brașov, Galați, Târgu-Mureș) (*CC - Cancelarie*, no. 39/1967, f. 149).
[9] *CC - Cancelarie*, no. 44/1976, f. 93.

The Party rulers discussed some of the locations proposed by the Ministry of Education (or other state agencies), made amendments or simply changed what they considered unsatisfactory.

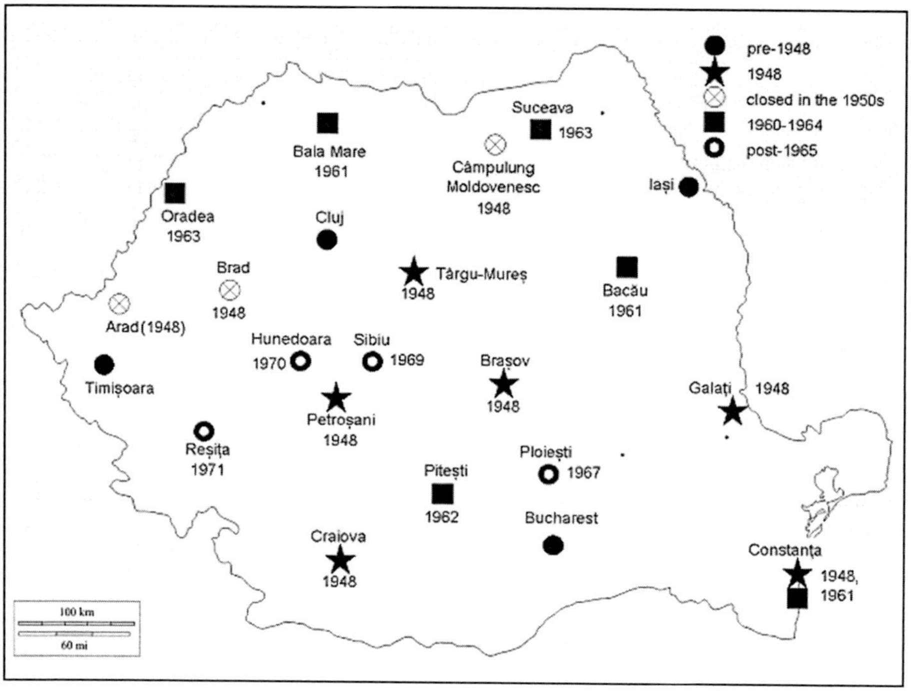

Map 1. Territorial distribution of the higher education network (with year of founding).

Typically the Ministry of Education proposed changes in the system, in close cooperation with the State Planning Committee. And since those in charge were members of the *nomenklatura*, their proposals aimed at the party leaders' consent; therefore not much debate was involved, or at least not on fundamental issues. However, Nicolae Ceauşescu repeatedly used his authority either to change a location and impose his personal view on a certain matter, or to order post-ponement and revision. All in all, the system seemed to be regulated by "objective" economic concerns, but at the same time there was a certain discretionary side to decisions.

Apart from the top-down political component, namely the sole desire of the rulers, I will enumerate the most important factors that could have influenced the dynamics of the higher education network.

1. *The socio-economic imperative.* As I suggested above, one of the particularities of the socialist planned economy was that it cared for higher education only as long as this was needed to provide highly qualified personnel, thus making educational investment effi-

cient for the development of the country in the context of the forced economic growth imposed by the Communist Party.[10]

2. *The foreign model – Soviet or Western?* In the early 1950s, when political leaders were keen to show their allegiance to Stalinist principles, the Soviet model suggested that similar specializations should tend to be concentrated in a single institute controlled by its corresponding branch ministry. There was the Naval Institute in Galați, the Electro-Technical Institute in Craiova, the Mechanical Institute in Brașov/Stalin City, the Coal Institute in Petroșani, or the Fishing Institute in Constanța. Moreover, the Soviet model was explicitly on show[11] and imitated, for instance in founding the short-lived Institute for Communal Management (Institutul de Gospodărie Comunală) in Bucharest (1951) after the model of the "K. D. Pamfilov" Academy in Moscow.[12]

The Western model or campus type attracted interest since the late 1960s, when it came to represent a possible solution to the problems of overcrowding and the scattering of resources. The Romanian Communist leadership suggested this model for future development. Nicolae Ceaușescu even expressed his regret that the Polytechnic Institute in Bucharest had not been built in the American manner some forty kilometres away from the city.[13] This remark had its effect almost immediately, with the founding of the National Platform for Physics at Măgurele, south of Bucharest, in 1974,[14] which included both educational and research facilities.[15]

3. *Hungarian minority rights.* When the Medical Institute in Târgu-Mureș (the capital of the Magyar Autonomous Region) had been founded in 1948, its mission was to train Hungarian-speaking doctors for settlements densely populated by Hungarians (especially within this region). There was also the Institute of Theatrical Art in the same city, which prepared aspiring Hungarian-speaking actors. However, the anti-Soviet uprising in Hungary in 1956 and acts of solidarity in Romania led to a gradual return to nationalist politics, and the minority factor soured as a result. Teaching in Hungarian had to make way for some teaching in Romanian, so that segregation tendencies could be liquidated and patriotic feeling consolidated.[16] The "Bolyai" University was merged into the "Victor Babeș" University in 1959 and courses taught in Romanian were introduced at the Medical Institute in Târgu-Mureș in 1962, clear signs that higher education taught in Hungarian could not develop any further. Likewise, one of the arguments for the revival of Arad (inhabited by a considerable Hungarian population) was that a pedagogical institute

---

[10] For a greater perspective, see Murgescu, *România și Europa*, 336-341, 384; Janos Kornai, *The Socialist System. The Political Economy of Communism* (Oxford: Clarendon Press, 1992), 203-218.
[11] See, for instance: *PCM*, no. 233/1951, f. 70.
[12] Idem, no. 179/1951.
[13] *CC - Cancelarie*, no. 137/1967, f. 50-51.
[14] Founding had been decided in 1971 (Idem, no. 105/1971, f. 69).
[15] "Istoric," University of Bucharest – Faculty of Physics, accessed May 28, 2013, http://www.fizica.unibuc.ro/Fizica/Prezentare/Istoric/Main.php.
[16] *CC - Cancelarie*, no. 18/1962, f. 52.

would be "a very important centre of Romanian culture."[17]

4. *Optimum placement.* Location could be conditioned by distance to other, similar centres and by the existence of other potential outlets nearby. For instance, Arad is not far from Timişoara and at a relatively short distance from Cluj. This situation offered it no chance for development, and although local authorities unsuccessfully tried to poach some of Timişoara's institutes, the Agro-Veterinary Institute was taken from Arad to its southern rival in the end (1957).[18] In the south, the technical trade colleges in Alexandria and Turnu Măgurele – requested by the local authorities – seemed too much to Ceauşescu, who stated in 1976 that Craiova and Bucharest were quite enough.[19] It seems that Alba Iulia influenced the development of its neighbour Sibiu's educational potential in 1976. And in the south-east, perhaps Galați achieved the status of a centre at the expense of its twin city Brăila.

5. *Availability of infrastructure and teaching staff.* The decision-makers and the planners tried to keep spending on higher education (which became tax-free in 1962) under control, especially by cutting investments and demanding that the existing infrastructure (lecture rooms, dormitories, catering halls, laboratories and libraries) be used at full capacity. Furthermore the number of teaching staff was never been plentiful, making higher education management a cautious quest for optimal solutions. If an institute moved to another city, some of its best lecturers had to move as well.

This factor certainly had a brake-effect on the explosive tendency of the network. Since the early 1950s, merging of the institutes was planned. As a result Brad, Arad and Câmpulung Moldovenesc were left without higher education institutes, and instead development went along with the consolidation of existing centres or infrastructure.
One of the most spectacular mergers was the National Institute of Chemistry. Since 1971, a plan designed by the Ministry of Education had specified that the chemistry departments at the Polytechnic and the University in Bucharest should come together into a National Institute of Chemistry,[20] but the change was actually put into practice only six years later,[21] leading to speculation that the dictator's wife Elena Ceauşescu – whom propaganda had turned into a famed chemist – had been personally involved in the affair.

6. *The principle of unity.* There was certainly one full-scale guideline influencing the shape and dynamic of the institutional network of higher education, which laid down that related educational and economic activity should stay together. Later, during Ceauşescu's regime, this principle of unity was subsumed under the formula of the "education-research-production complex" which held that higher education could be improved and

---

[17] Miron Constantinescu's words; Idem, no. 137/1967, f. 49.
[18] *PCM*, no. 85/1951, f. 1-2; Idem, no. 377/1957 (proposals by *Sfatul Popular Arad* / Arad's City Council).
[19] *CC - Cancelarie*, no. 44/1976, f. 38-38v.
[20] Idem, no. 105/1971, f. 69.
[21] Idem, no. 71/1977, f. 174.

transmitted most of all through interactive experience. To give only a few examples, this reason served as an argument to set up the Institute of Coal and Mines in Petroşani (located in the coal basin of the Jiu Valley), the Institute of Petroleum and Gas in Ploieşti (located in Prahova's oilfield), the Forestry Institute in Braşov (surrounded by wooded mountains), and the technical trades colleges spread throughout the country (Hunedoara, Reşiţa, Piteşti, Baia Mare etc.).

There were of course instances when such proposals were ignored. The case of the Light Industry Institute in Iaşi is representative. In 1957, when transfer was first discussed, Bucharest, Timişoara and southern Transylvanian cities had larger light industries and there was also concern that workers and specialists in light industry would not want to send their offspring hundreds of kilometres away to study the parents' specialization.[22] The politics of *status quo* proved stronger this time, as also in the late 1960s, when Ceauşescu rather rhetorically criticized the placement of agronomical institutes in cities and defended their relocation to the countryside, as "even the Bulgarians" did.[23]

7. *Cultural tradition and educational potential*. Non-technical higher education institutes were founded based on the cultural tradition of the host cities and on condition that they met educational demand, in terms of both social and territorial coverage. These factors counted especially in Sibiu's growth and in the consolidation of regional capitals.[24]

8. *The population factor*. A city that had potential both in terms of input of students and inclusion of graduates was most likely to host higher education institutes. Large cities eventually faced the issue of overcrowding, connected to the scarcity of infrastructure and other material resources. In the case of Bucharest, decision-makers tried to transfer as many institutes as possible outside the capital. Such significant exports were: the Institute of Mines (merged with the Institute of Coal in Petroşani), the forestry institutes (merged into the Forestry Institute in Braşov), the Light Industry Institute (to Iaşi), the Petroleum and Gas Institute (to Ploieşti), the Food Industry Institute (to Galaţi). In the late 1960s, Bucharest still concentrated over 40% of the student population. Moreover, there were fears that some institutes would return to the capital, possibly because of the growing base of prospective students, so that the Ministry of Education declared in 1966 that overcrowding of the capital must be avoided and decongestion policy followed.[25]

All of these considerations, including the political factor, combined in discussion on the founding or siting of an institute. Conversely, some reasons could counterbalance one another (for instance, consolidation against decongestion of centres, or consolidation of

---

[22] *PCM*, no. 164/1957, f. 2-13.
[23] *CC - Cancelarie*, no. 39/1967, f. 78.
[24] Until 1969, the existing Orthodox Theological Institute and the Military Academy didn't make Sibiu suitable for public enlistment. The city's "rich means of documentation and information," as the Ministry of Education put it (Idem, no. 87/1969, f. 86), made the philology and history department affordable.
[25] Idem, no. 39/1967, f. 114.

centres against development of education-production units).

As long as dialogue was possible, the intertwining of factors was affected by the bargaining process. The growing tendency towards accelerated expansion of higher education met permanent resistance at the same time, but the two tendencies were manifested by different actors. The usual "pushers" were the ministries – i.e. the economic establishment – or local authorities, and sometimes the Politburo – when touched by revolutionary enthusiasm. Those who worked with real figures and were responsible for the efficiency of the system – for instance the State Planning Committee, the Ministry of Finance, and the Ministry of Education – generally tried to mitigate the zeal of the others (whether this was ideologically based or otherwise). However, things did not depend on institutions as much as on the people involved.

Map 2. The dynamics of the higher education network. (Size = average total students/year, daily attendees). Initial state and changes were pointed out.

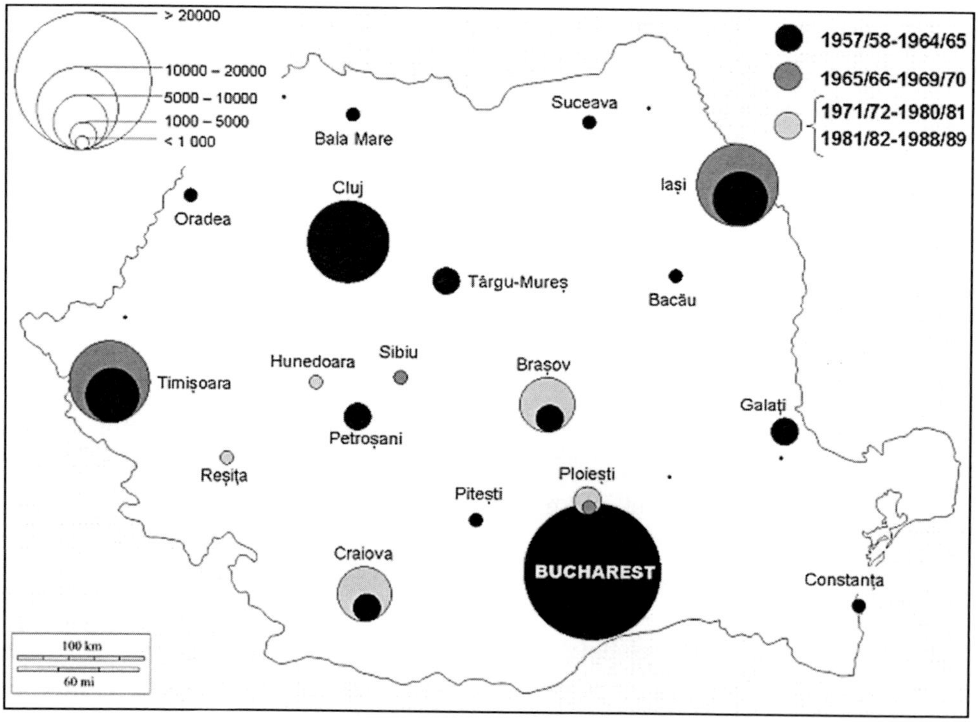

The subtle competition to found (or even close) higher education institutes took place across the whole hierarchical scale, from teaching staff and parents all way up to the Politburo/Executive Committee of the Communist Party. Seeking popularity, investment and graduates for their economy back home, local Communist leaders employed their personal connections and patrons, as well as their persuasive skills, to drive central leadership decisions in favour of their region. These actions could hardly be documented, since they were informal and to some extent secret, but there is proof that some transfers, mergers or siting decisions could be avoided. For instance, despite all the facts furnished by the Ministry of Education and the Council of Ministries, the transfer of the Light Industry Institute from Iaşi was successfully prevented by the intervention of the rector (1957).[26] At other times such initiatives could meet a curt answer, as when Nicolae Ceauşescu critically remarked in 1976:

> "We don't have to do it just because the County Committee asks. There are many County Committees that ask."[27]

Apart from the systemic or other challenges, there was also the issue of dealing with the "burden" of the past. It seems that the legacy of the institutional network in pre-Communist times was adopted and given a similar importance under Communism.

Table 1. Share of student enrolment (average total/year, daily attendees)

Location	**1938**	**1948**	**1951-1955**	**1956-1960**	**1961-1965**	**1966-1970**	**1971-1975**	**1976-1980**	**1981-1985**	**1986-1989**
Bucharest	67%	58%	57%	54%	47%	44%	43%	39%	36%	37%
Cluj	15%	17%	14%	16%	14%	14%	13%	13%	12%	11%
Iaşi	15%	9%	10%	12%	14%	15%	15%	15%	15%	15%
Timişoara	1%	7%	6%	6%	9%	9%	9%	10%	11%	11%
Braşov		3%	3%	3%	3%	3%	3%	4%	5%	4%
Craiova		1%	2%	2%	2%	3%	4%	5%	5%	5%
Galaţi		1%	1%	1%	2%	2%	2%	2%	3%	3%
TOTAL	100%	96%	93%	94%	91%	90%	89%	88%	87%	86%

Source: *Anuarul statistic al R.P.R./R.S.R./ României*. Computed data[28]

The university centres of Bucharest, Iaşi, Cluj and Timişoara had flourished as provincial capitals of culture and education (even national, in the case of Bucharest). Cluj and Timişoara had been added to Romania's higher education network after World War I by annexation of the Austro-Hungarian provinces of Transylvania and the Banat. During Communist rule, these four hubs maintained their prominence, together garnering at least 75% of the total number of students each year. Of course, beside cultural continuity there were particular arguments for their continued prominence, such as the efficient use of resources, availability of teaching staff and the general tendency of local authorities and notables to try to maintain their gains. There was also a matter of prestige and symbolic status that kept these four centres in the lead.

---

26 This case was filed in *PCM*, no. 164/1957, f. 1-14; *CC – Cancelarie*, no. 25/1957, f. 2.

27 *CC – Cancelarie*, no. 44/1976, f. 38-38v.

28 Ibid.

Nevertheless there were shifts in this most select group. Bucharest went through a relative decline owing to the decongestion policies and to faster growth in the rest of the system (for instance the increasing share of the medium-sized centres, Timişoara, Braşov, Craiova and Galaţi).

Fig. 1. Dynamics of enrolment in Cluj and Iaşi (daily-attending students)

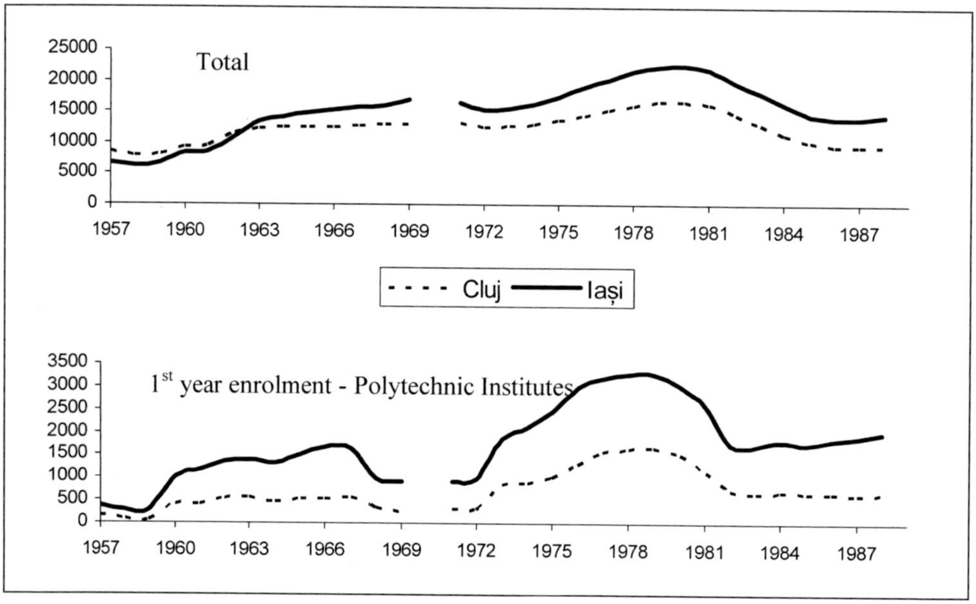

Source: The National Institute of Statistics[29]

Furthermore, Iaşi caught up with and overtook Cluj from 1963, with 50% more full-time students in the academic year 1988/1989.[30] This edge came mainly from the significant difference between the first-year enrolment at the Polytechnic and Agronomical Institutes in each city, while Cluj stayed steadily (although not far) ahead of Iaşi in enrolments to the University and Medical Institute. There is no information as yet about the leadership's decision that Iaşi should become the second most populous higher education centre; maybe future demographic research will shed a light on this phenomenon too.

As has been noted, the Communist period witnessed a general tendency towards association between industry and higher education on one hand and continued support for regional capitals on the other. During the 1950s facilities and technical institutes were subordinated to their representative economic branch ministry (as in the Soviet model),

[29] Computed data. See the figures in "Higher Education in Romania (1948-1989). Number of students by location."

[30] The numbers of inhabitants were close: 265,000 (Iaşi) to 262,000 (Cluj) in 1977, 344,000 (Iaşi) to 328,000 (Cluj) in 1992.

whereas in the 1960s the whole higher education system became subject to the Ministry of Education so that a more centralized form of organization emerged to manage a horizontally growing, poly-centric network. Following the rather revolutionary geographical expansion of 1948-1953, which corresponded to the Stalinist phase, the development of higher education network quickly led to mergers and an organizational restructuring of the institutes. In the early 1960s a new expansionist wave emerged (the teacher training colleges), still moderate, which covered some 5% of the system.

Shortly after Ceaușescu came to power, the Ministry of Education asserted that "the existing network of higher education institutes fulfils the requirements of economy and culture" and that in the future efforts "will be oriented towards consolidating the existing network" (1966).[31] After additional foundations (Ploiești, Hunedoara, Reșița, Sibiu), under the principle of "education-research-production," a general merger came about in the 1970s, following the criterion of location rather profile. For instance, short-term teacher training colleges and recently founded short-term technical trade colleges came together into so-called Institutes of Higher Education in the cities of Pitești, Bacău, Oradea, Baia Mare and Constanța. On the contrary, the National Institute of Chemistry and the National Platform for Physics assembled formerly scattered divisions and departments with similar profiles. Powerful hubs continued to maintain their dominance and gradually grew. In the mid-1980s, after the steep decline of enrolment due to austerity measures and economic stagnation, the network entered a phase of contraction and full-time students were no longer admitted in Pitești, Bacău, Oradea, Reșița, Hunedoara, Sibiu and Suceava.[32]

On the whole, the pre-Communist hubs prevailed throughout this period, and from a larger perspective this proves that the Romanian higher education network was highly inertial in the twentieth century. Apart from this, the dynamics of the network under Communism seem to have been highly dependent on the political-economic set of factors, even if various other factors also influenced their outcome and manifestation. The natural expansionist tendency was tightly controlled and eventually even some "pushers" had to advocate retrenchment, thus accepting the unpredictability of a system that claimed to be one of the most predictable.

---

[31] *CC – Cancelarie*, no. 39/1967, f. 114.

[32] In 1984, the sub-engineers institutes became subordinated to the Polytechnic Institutes in Bucureşti, Iaşi, Cluj and Timişoara (*CC – Cancelarie*, no. 30/1984, f. 100-101). However, these continued to host evening courses and periodical training.

SOURCES OF THE PICTURES

DANIEL DUMITRAN, **Die Landesbeschreibungen als Reformierungs-instrument: Fürstentum Siebenbürgens im letzten Jahrzehnt Maria Theresia's**

Fig. 1: "Josephinische Landesaufnahme" of the Grand Principality of Transylvania: *Comitatus Albensis* (http://ro.wikipedia.org/wiki/Fi%C8%99ier:Komitat_Wei%C3%9Fenburg_Gro%C3%9Ff%C3%BCrstentum_Siebenbuergen_1769-1773.jpg).

Fig. 2: "Josephinische Landesaufnahme" of the Grand Principality of Transylvania: *Carlsburg vel Fejérvár* (Section 170) (*Az első katonai felmérés Erdély és a Temesi Bánság*, DVD, Budapest, 2005).

Fig. 3: "Josephinische Landesaufnahme" of the Grand Principality of Transylvania, with the 280 Sections (Andor Borbély, Julia Nagy, „Magyarország I. katonai felvétele II. József korában," in *Az első katonai felmérés*, DVD, Tab. XVI).

Fig. 4: Map of the Grand Principality of Transylvania, with the first county division of Joseph II from 1784 (*Erdély története*, 2nd vol., *1606-tól 1830-ig* (Budapest: Akadémiai Kiadó, 1986), 1104, Map no. 48).

MARCO BOGADE, **Materielle Tradition und Innovation in der Sepulkralplastik des 15. und 16. Jahrhunderts von Sibiu/Hermannstadt und Nürnberg**

Fig. 1: Detail of the grave-stone of Konrad Groß (†1356). Nürnberg, Heilig-Geist-Spital. Photo: Marco Bogade.

Fig. 2: Two-piece bronze epitaph for Ulrich Haller (†1555). Nürnberg, Johannis-friedhof. Photo: Marco Bogade.

Fig. 3: Two-piece bronze epitaph for Christoph Kress von Kressenstein (†1535). Nürnberg-Kraftshof, St. Georg. Photo: Marco Bogade.

Fig. 4: Grave-stone of Conrad von Neumarkt (†1296). About 1360. Nürnberg, Germanisches Nationalmuseum, Gd. 46. Photo: Marco Bogade.

Fig. 5: Grave-stone of Conrad von Neumarkt (†1296). About 1360. Nürnberg, Germanisches Nationalmuseum, Gd. 46. Photo: Marco Bogade.

Fig. 6: Grave-stone of Peter Haller (†1569) in the Ferula of the Evangelical Parish Church in Hermannstadt/ Sibiu. Photo: Marco Bogade.

Fig. 7: Grave-stone of Christoph Kress von Kressenstein (†1535). Nürnberg-Kraftshof, St. Georg. Photo: Marco Bogade.

ANNA TÜSKÉS, **Pilgrimage Art in Eighteenth Century Transylvania: Icons, Woodcuts and Engravings**

Fig. 1: Mihail Manuil Olsavszky, *Elementa puerilis institutionis in lingua latina* (Claudiopoli: Typis Academ. Soc. Jesu per Andream Feij, 1746). Budapest, University Library, Fc 4901.

Fig. 2: *Ceaslov* (Blaj, 1766). Alba Iulia, National Museum of Union, CVR 660.

Fig. 3: *Doctrina christiana [...]*. In Monasterio Sanctissimae Triadis typis edita Balasfalvae. Per Michaele Betskereki. Anno 1757. University Library, Budapest, I 8r 102/2.coll.

Fig. 4: Icon of Cluj on a prayer card. In the collection of Béla Szabó.

Fig. 5: Fr. L. Schmit(t)ner, Madonna sculpture of Şumuleu Ciuc. Ferenc Móra Museum, Szeged.

Fig. 6: Icon from the Assumption of Mary church, Prague. *Scala Jacob, per quam ascenditur ad coelum, sive liber precum piarum ex variis authoribus collectus* (Pozsony, 1748).

Fig. 7: Icon from the Assumption of Mary church, Prague. Devotional pictures in the collection of Ebenhöch, Pannonhalma.

Fig. 8: Icon of Radna on a prayer card. Budapest, Hungarian National Museum, Historical Picture Gallery, inv. no. T744.

Fig. 9: Icon of Radna. Budapest, University Library, Hd 2765/27.

Fig. 10-11: Unknown artist: Three events of Miklós Dániel's life. Budapest, Hungarian National Museum, Historical Picture Gallery, inv. no. 1833 II.

Fig. 12: Joseph Ernst Mansfeld, Icon of Cluj. Budapest, Hungarian National Museum, Historical Picture Gallery, inv. no. T 9287.

Fig. 13: Unknown artist, Altar of Radna. On the exhibition "Icons from Transylvania. Romanian Art – European Heritage," Alba Iulia (National Museum of Union, Alba Iulia, Inv. Ar. 657).

CRISTINA BOGDAN, ***Du berceau à la tombe.* Les âges de la vie dans l'iconographie roumaine des XVIIIe-XIXe siècles et l'influence des modèles étrangers**

Fig. 6: *The Wheel of Life* in the outdoor decoration of the church of "Saint Nicolas" of Dozeşti, painted in 1828 by the priest Vasile Dozescu (representation no longer exists, but it was designed by Maria Golescu in one of her notebooks, preserved in the collections of the Institute of the History of Art "G. Oprescu" of Bucharest).

Fig. 8: *The Ages of Woman*, Imper, county of Harghita (private collection).

Fig. 9: *The Ages of Woman*, Imper, county of Harghita (Inventory No. A 589, from the collection of the National Ethnographic Park "Romulus Vuia" Cluj).

Fig. 1-5, 7: Photos by Cristina Bogdan.

SILVIA MARIN-BARUTCIEFF, **Master and Disciple: Family Tradition, Professional Solidarity and Artistic Innovation. Romanian Painters Either Side of the Carpathians and the Depictions of Saint Christopher (1730-1850)**

Fig. 1-6: Photos by Silvia Marin-Barutcieff.

ANA DUMITRAN, ***"That He May Be the Donor and Be Remembered in the Holy Liturgy"* Donations of Artwork to Romanian Churches in Transylvania Down to the**

Mid-Nineteenth Century

Fig. 1-14, 16: Photos by Ana Dumitran
Fig. 15: Photo in the archive of the Museum from Zalău.

WALDEMAR DELUGA, **Greek Patronage of the Arts in Lviv in the Sixteenth and Seventeenth Centuries**

Fig. 1-6: Photos by Waldemar Deluga.
Fig. 7: View of Sinai by Nikodem Zubrzycki, woodcut, Uppsala University.
Fig. 8: View of Jerusalem by Malinowski, Lviv National Gallery.
Fig. 9: View of Athos, Olesko castle.

VLAD PAŞCA, **Territorial Expansion of Higher Education in Communist Romania (1948-1989). An Outline of Patterns and Factors**

Map 1. Territorial distribution of the higher education network. Source of maps' outlines: http://d-maps.com/carte.php?num_car=25483&lang=en.
Map 2. The dynamics of the higher education network. Source: The National Institute of Statistics. See the figures in "Higher Education in Romania (1948-1989). Number of students by location," compiled by Vlad Paşca, http:// levantul.files.wordpress.com/2013/06/statistical _data_he_romania_1948-1989.pdf.

CONTRIBUTORS

MARCO BOGADE, Dr. phil., Federal Institute for Culture and History of the Germans in Eastern Europe at the University of Oldenburg

CRISTINA BOGDAN, PhD, University of Bucharest, Faculty of Letters

ION CÂRJA, PhD, "Babeş-Bolyai" University of Cluj-Napoca, Faculty of History and Philosophy

DENNIS DELETANT, Dr., Visiting Ion Raţiu Professor of Romanian Studies at Georgetown University, Washington, and Emeritus Professor of Romanian Studies at the School of Slavonic and East European Studies, University College, London

WALDEMAR DELUGA, Dr. hab., Cardinal "Stefan Wyszynski" University of Warsaw

MARIUS DIACONESCU, PhD, University of Bucharest, Faculty of History

DAVID DO PAÇO, PhD, European University Institute, Max Weber Programme, Florence

ANA DUMITRAN, PhD, "National Museum of Union", Alba Iulia

DANIEL DUMITRAN, PhD, "1 Decembrie 1918" University of Alba Iulia, Department of History, Archaeology, and Museology

MONIKA IMREGH, PhD, "Karoli Gáspár" University of the Reformed Church in Hungary, Budapest

KÁLMÁN ÁRPÁD KOVÁCS, PhD, "Pannonia" University of Veszprém, Department of Ethics and Cultural Anthropology

ROXANA MARIN, PhD Candidate, University of Bucharest

SILVIA MARIN-BARUTCIEFF, PhD, University of Bucharest, Faculty of Letters

GRETA-MONICA MIRON, PhD, "Babeş-Bolyai" University of Cluj-Napoca, Faculty of History and Philosophy

VALER MOGA, PhD, "1 Decembrie 1918" University of Alba Iulia, Department of History, Archaeology, and Museology

MÁRTA NAGY, Dr. hab., University of Debrecen

RADU NEDICI, PhD, University of Bucharest

EVA ONDRUŠOVÁ, Mgr., History Institute of Slovak Academy of Sciences, Bratislava

ALEXANDRU ONOJESCU, PhD, "Babeş-Bolyai" University of Cluj-Napoca

LEVENTE PAKOT, PhD, Demographic Research Institute, Budapest

MÁRIA PAKUCS-WILLCOKS, PhD, "Nicolae Iorga" Institute of History, Bucharest

VLAD PAŞCA, PhD Candidate, University of Bucharest

CORNEL SIGMIREAN, PhD, "Petru Maior" University of Târgu-Mureş, Department of History and International Relations

OANA VALENTINA SORESCU, MA, "Babeş-Bolyai" University of Cluj-Napoca

OTTMAR TRAŞCĂ, PhD, "George Bariţiu" History Institute of Cluj-Napoca

ANNA TÜSKÉS, PhD, Institute of Literary Studies, Research Centre for the Humanities of the Hungarian Academy of Sciences, Budapest

ATTILA VERÓK, PhD, "Eszterházy Károly" College, Eger, Department of Education and Science Technology
FELICIA WALDMAN, PhD, University of Bucharest, Faculty of Letters